Financial Aspects of the United States Pension System

A National Bureau
of Economic Research
Project Report

Financial Aspects of the United States Pension System

Edited by Zvi Bodie and John B. Shoven

The University of Chicago Press

Chicago and London

Zvi Bodie is associate professor of finance and economics at the School of Management, Boston University. John B. Shoven a professor of economics at Stanford University. Shoven is director and Bodie a codirector of the National Bureau of Economic Research project on the economics of the United States pension system.

This book was prepared with the support of National Science Foundation Grant no. DAR-8019616. However, any opinions, finding, conclusions, or recommendations herein are those of the authors and do not necessarily reflect the views of NSF.

The University of Chicago Press, Chicago 60637
The University of Chicago Press, Ltd., London

Library of Congress Cataloging in Publication Data
Main entry under title:

Fiancial aspects of the United States pension system.

(A National Bureau of Economic Research project report)
   Includes index.
   1. Old age pensions—United States—Addresses, essays, lectures.   2. Pension trusts—United States—Addresses, essays, lectures.   3. Old age pensions—United States—Finance—Addresses, essays, lectures.   I. Bodie, Zvi.
II. Shoven, J. (John)   III. Series: Project report (National Bureau of Economic Research)
HD7106.U5F535   1983   332.6′7254   83-9119
ISBN 0-226-06281-3

Relation of the Directors to the Work and Publications of the National Bureau of Economic Research

1. The object of the National Bureau of Economic Research is to ascertain and to present to the public important economic facts and their interpretation in a scientific and impartial manner. The Board of Directors is charged with the responsibility of ensuring that the work of the National Bureau is carried on in strict conformity with this object.

2. The President of the National Bureau shall submit to the Board of Directors, or to its Executive Committee, for their formal adoption all specific proposals for research to be instituted.

3. No research report shall be published by the National Bureau until the President has sent each member of the Board a notice that a manuscript is recommended for publication and that in the President's opinion it is suitable for publication in accordance with the principles of the National Bureau. Such notification will include an abstract or summary of the manuscript's content and a response form for use by those Directors who desire a copy of the manuscript for review. Each manuscript shall contain a summary drawing attention to the nature and treatment of the problem studied, the character of the data and their utilization in the report, and the main conclusions reached.

4. For each manuscript so submitted, a special committee of the Directors (including Directors Emeriti) shall be appointed by majority agreement of the President and Vice Presidents (or by the Executive Committee in case of inability to decide on the part of the President and Vice Presidents), consisting of three Directors selected as nearly as may be one from each general division of the Board. The names of the special manuscript committee shall be stated to each Director when notice of the proposed publication is submitted to him. It shall be the duty of each member of the special manuscript committee to read the manuscript. If each member of the manuscript committee signifies his approval within thirty days of the transmittal of the manuscript, the report may be published. If at the end of that period any member of the manuscript committee withholds his approval, the President shall then notify each member of the Board, requesting approval or disapproval of publication, and thirty days additional shall be granted for this purpose. The manuscript shall then not be published unless at least a majority of the entire Board who shall have voted on the proposal within the time fixed for the receipt of votes shall have approved.

5. No manuscript may be published, though approved by each member of the special manuscript committee, until forty-five days have elapsed from the transmittal of the report in manuscript form. The interval is allowed for the receipt of any memorandum of dissent or reservation, together with a brief statement of his reasons, that any member may wish to express; and such memorandum of dissent or reservation shall be published with the manuscript if he so desires. Publication does not, however, imply that each member of the Board has read the manuscript, or that either members of the Board in general or the special committee have passed on its validity in every detail.

6. Publications of the National Bureau issued for informational purposes concerning the work of the Bureau and its staff, or issued to inform the public of activities of Bureau staff, and volumes issued as a result of various conferences involving the National Bureau shall contain a specific disclaimer noting that such publication has not passed through the normal review procedures required in this resolution. The Executive Committee of the Board is charged with review of all such publications from time to time to ensure that they do not take on the character of formal research reports of the National Bureau, requiring formal Board approval.

7. Unless otherwise determined by the Board or exempted by the terms of paragraph 6, a copy of this resolution shall be printed in each National Bureau publication.

(Resolution adopted October 25, 1926, as revised through September 30, 1974)

Contents

Acknowledgments

This volume, consisting mostly of papers presented at a conference held at Amelia Island Plantation, Florida, 24–26 March 1982, is part of the National Bureau of Economic Research ongoing project on the Economics of the United States Pension System, which has been generously supported by the following organizations: American Telephone and Telegraph Company, the Boeing Company, E. I. du Pont de Nemours and Company, Exxon Corporation, Ford Motor Company, International Business Machines Corporation, the Lilly Endowment, the National Science Foundation, the Proctor and Gamble Fund, and the Sarah Scaife Foundation. We wish to express our gratitude to them for helping make this work possible.

The many people whose advice and assistance have contributed greatly to this volume include Martin Feldstein, who as president of the National Bureau launched the NBER pension project in 1980; National Bureau research associates Jeremy I. Bulow and Laurence J. Kotlikoff; and National Bureau staff members Altheia Chaballa, Kirsten Foss, Annie Zeumer, and Anna Uhlig.

Any opinions expressed in this volume are those of the respective authors and do not necessarily reflect the views of the National Bureau of Economic Research or any of the sponsoring organizations.

Introduction

Zvi Bodie and John B. Shoven

One of the greatest challenges facing the United States economy now and increasingly in the decades ahead is to provide retirement income security in an environment characterized by a rising ratio of retired to working age population and high and unpredictable rates of inflation. The institutions and mechanisms that are developed to meet this challenge will have an impact on almost every facet of our economy.

In the past three decades, the most salient developments in the United States system of retirement income provision have been a decline in the relative importance of family support and labor force participation of the aged and an increase in the role of social security and pension plans. Between 1950 and 1970 the percentage of the aged living with their children declined from 31% to 9%. Today fewer than 3% of elderly households receive income from their children, and these contributions represent less than 1% of the income of the elderly. Furthermore, between 1950 and 1980 the proportion of men aged 65 and over participating in the labor force fell from 40% to 20%.[1]

Difficulties in financing an extended retirement without major family support have been eased considerably by sizable increases in real social security retirement benefits. Between 1950 and 1980 the proportion of elderly households receiving such benefits rose from 20% to 90%, and the average level of real benefits tripled. These benefits now represent the major source of income for 54% of the aged. However, the continued provision of real social security benefits at levels stipulated under current

Zvi Bodie is associate professor of finance and economics at the School of Management, Boston University, and research associate, National Bureau of Economic Research. John B. Shoven is professor of economics at Stanford University and research associate, National Bureau of Economic Research.

Most of the facts and much of the discussion in the first two sections of this introduction are based on Kotlikoff and Smith (1983).

1

law is becoming a subject of debate as demographic changes have, according to many experts, placed the system in a long-term financial crisis. Changes in fertility rates are expected to lower the ratio of social security contributors to beneficiaries from the current value of 3.2 to 1.5 by the year 2040. Unless significant actions are taken or unless these projections are in error, social security tax rates have been projected by some to rise as high as 25% by the early part of the next century to meet projected benefits.

A number of experts, therefore, think that an increasing share of the burden of retirement income provision in the future will fall on employer-sponsored pension plans. Like social security, these pension plans have grown rapidly over the past three decades. Between 1950 and 1980 the percentage of elderly households receiving benefits from these plans grew from 10% to over 30%.

In addition to its impact on retirement income security, the growth of pension plans raises some important questions for labor and financial markets. For example, how will it affect labor mobility and the participation of older persons in the work force? What impact will it have on the size and allocation of the nation's stock of capital?

The National Bureau of Economic Research project on public and private pensions was established to explore issues such as these. A comprehensive program of study of the economic impacts of pensions was begun in 1980 and has so far generated numerous working papers and journal articles. Appendix A at the end of this introduction contains a complete list of them. In addition to these research papers, the National Bureau of Economic Research has published a fact book, *Pensions in the American Economy* by Laurence J. Kotlikoff and Daniel E. Smith, whose purpose is to provide a reference base of pension data that is accessible to a wide audience.

The present volume is the first in a series of three planned conference volumes, and it concentrates on the financial aspects of the pension system. The second volume will deal with the role and impact of pensions on the United States labor market, and the final one will deal with the special issues faced by public pension plans. Most of the chapters in this volume were originally presented as papers at a conference at Amelia Island Plantation, Florida, held March 24–26, 1982, and we have included the discussants' comments on each of these.

In this introduction, we intend to give the reader an overview of the issues discussed and the findings reported in these papers, making references to other selected NBER research papers published elsewhere. We group the papers and our discussion of them according to the following seven questions:

1. How financially sound is the private pension system in the United States?

2. What are the rights and obligations in a corporate defined-benefit pension plan?

3. What is the impact of taxes and the Employee Retirement Income Security Act of 1974 (ERISA) on corporate pension policy?

4. Is a firm's unfunded pension liability correctly reflected in the market value of its common stock?

5. What is the impact of inflation on the private pension system, and how desirable and feasible are alternative indexing schemes?

6. What is the role of a mandatory, pay-as-you-go public pension plan such as Social Security in a free market economy such as that of the United States?

7. What is the current financial status of the elderly, and how vulnerable are they to inflation?

How Financially Sound Is the United States Private Pension System?

In recent years there has been great public concern about the financial soundness of the United States retirement income system. Much of this attention has focused on the Social Security system, but some doubts have been raised regarding the financial soundness of corporate pensions as well. The question is whether United States corporations have sufficient assets in their pension plans to pay for the promised pension benefits.

To examine this issue, one must first distinguish between two basic pension types: defined benefit and defined contribution. A defined-contribution plan is one in which the sponsor's obligation is completed when it makes contributions to a retirement investment fund in trust for the employee. In many cases, workers have some choice as to the investment vehicle in which these funds are deposited, but the worker bears the entire risk of the performance of the investment portfolio. No explicit retirement annuity is promised during the accumulation period, and on reaching retirement age the worker receives the total amount accumulated in the form of a lump sum distribution or an annuity. Defined-contribution plans are always fully funded by definition.

The typical defined-benefit plan is a corporate promise to pay retirement benefits based on the retiree's number of years of employment and level of earnings during the immediate preretirement years. Although an employee generally forfeits any claim to benefits when he or she leaves the company after only a few years of employment, the benefits of an employee who stays with a firm for some minimum number of years become "vested." That is, the employee becomes entitled to benefits even if he or she subsequently leaves the company before retirement age. Firms must set aside tax-deductible funds to meet these future benefit obligations, and the income on these assets is not taxed to either the corporations or the pension plan itself. Some firms fund all of their vested pension obligations, but many do not.

In 1980 there were an estimated 616,642 private pension plans in the United States, an enormous growth from the 14,671 plans in existence in 1951. Approximately 65% of plans in existence in 1980 were defined contribution. Defined-benefit plans, however, were much larger on the average and covered about three-quarters of the plan participants.

There are basically two approaches to determining the value of a corporation's defined-benefit pension obligation: the accrued-benefit method and the projected-benefit method. Accrued-benefit liabilities are essentially "shutdown" liabilities. They equal benefit obligations a plan would face if it terminated operation and paid off vested benefits and, in the case of total accrued-benefit liabilities, unvested benefits, using only past service and past levels of earnings to compute benefits. Projected benefit liabilities equal the present expected value of benefit payments payable to current participants, assuming the plan continues in operation and that service and earnings of active participants increase at projected rates, less the portion of that present expected value attributable to future service.

The vested accrued pension liability of a firm is an enforceable legal claim. However, in certain circumstances unvested accrued benefits also represent legal liabilities of the pension plan. Under ERISA, unvested accrued liabilities are residual claims on a terminating private plan, provided that the plan's assets exceed its vested accrued liabilities. Total and vested accrued liabilities are currently reported by most major corporations in accordance with the 1980 recommendation of the Financial Accounting Standards Board.[2]

Projected-benefit methods, on the other hand, allocate the firm's pension costs attributable to a worker according to a formula that ignores the legal accumulation of a worker's benefits. The various projected-benefit methods use different formulas for allocating costs between the past and the future. The proportion of the present expected value of future pension benefits attributable to past service under a given projected-benefit cost method is that method's projected liability.

Many economists and actuaries consider legal definitions of pension liability too narrow for purposes of judging the appropriate degree of pension funding or the true claim on plan sponsors. Legal pension claims—vested accrued benefits and, potentially, unvested accrued benefits—are paid, in practice, only in the case of plan termination. For ongoing pension plans that provide rapid growth in pension benefits as the worker accumulates more service and/or earns a larger wage, the assets required to fund projected liabilities will, in general, exceed those required to fund accrued liabilities based on past service and earnings experience.

For ongoing plans, projected benefits may represent implicit, if not legal, claims on plan sponsors. Contractual models of labor market behavior view workers and employers as entering into long-term agreements in which the worker provides a time path of labor services in exchange for a time path of total compensation. Within these models there need be little or no relationship between this year's labor effort and this year's compensation. In this context, projected pension benefits simply represent one component of the employer's long-term compensation obligation, and projected rather than accrued liabilities may be most relevant for considering the interactions of pensions and economic behavior. For example, young workers who consider joining a particular firm will consider the firm's projected pension benefit offer as well as its projected path of nonpension compensation in making their decision.

In contrast with this contractual view of labor markets, traditional spot labor market theories predict that new hires consider only their immediate wage and accrued pension compensation. For young workers covered by plans with long service requirements for vesting, the value of immediate pension accrual may be zero. If employers have effectively committed themselves to a long-term level of worker compensation including projected pension benefits, then it is projected rather than accrued unfunded liabilities that represent a claim on the plan sponsor's nonpension assets and future profits.

In a series of papers on this subject, Jeremy I. Bulow (1979, 1981a) has argued in favor of valuing the pension liability using the accrued-benefit approach even in the case where a plan termination or worker separation is not anticipated. Initially, he assumes a labor market in which an employee's total compensation in each period, salary plus pension accrual, equals the value of his marginal product. If the wage were set so that it plus the increase in promised pension benefits exceeded the employee's marginal product, it would pay for the firm to either terminate the plan or fire the employee. Because both employee and firm know this, they each assess their respective pension assets and liabilities at the "shutdown" value.

Alternatively, Bulow assumes a model with implicit labor contracts but where the size of the firm's implicit liability is uncorrelated with the structure of the firm's pension plan. He argues that firms which have defined-contribution pension plans (such as universities) or even no pension plan can have implicit contracts to pay old workers more than young workers just as easily as firms with defined-benefit plans. He argues that it is inconsistent to assume an implicit liability for firms with defined-benefit plans but not for other firms, unless one can show systematic differences in such firms. If any implicit liability is to be calculated, it should be based on the entire implicit contract between the worker and the firm rather than just the pension, so if a firm provides maternity or educational benefits which primarily go to younger workers or provides salary that is not proportional to marginal product, the firm should take these things into account in determining its projected liability. The projected-benefit pension cost methods are only right if it is assumed that the chosen projected-benefit path is tied to the difference between marginal product and explicit compensation each year.

Even if one agrees that the vested accrued liability is the relevant measure of pension indebtedness, there remains the issue of what interest rate should be used to compute the present value of the deferred life annuities owed to plan beneficiaries. On this issue there is a fundamental difference between the approach taken by actuaries and that taken by financial economists. Actuaries in principle choose a rate representing the yield expected to be achieved on the plan's assets in future years. Financial economists feel that the rate used to value a firm's pension liabilities ought to reflect the risk of those liabilities and not the risk of the plan's assets. Since the accrued pension entitlement is always known with certainty, the appropriate rate to use in computing its present value is the long-term riskless nominal rate.[3]

In practice, actuaries in recent years have used rates well below the long-term nominal riskless rates prevailing in the bond markets. But even using these below-market capitalization rates to evaluate their accrued-benefit liabilities, the majority of pension plans of major United States corporations appear to be adequately funded. Financial information for 1980, reported by approximately 1,000 of the largest corporations in the United States and compiled by the Financial Accounting Standards Board, shows an average assumed interest rate of 7% with a range of 4%–12% per year. Using these reported interest rates, just over half of these companies had pension assets whose market value exceeded their estimated total accrued liabilities. Adjusting the liabilities to reflect a uniform capitalization rate of 10% per year the proportion of fully funded or overfunded plans becomes 80% and at an interest rate of 12% this proportion becomes 90%.[4]

The Rights and Obligations in a Corporate Defined-Benefit Pension Plan

In the first chapter in this volume, "Who Owns the Assets in a Defined-Benefit Plan?" Jeremy I. Bulow and Myron S. Scholes take a position somewhat different from Bulow's earlier one. They question the idea that the assets held in trust by defined-benefit pension plans of large corporations are corporate assets and that the obligation to pay employees during retirement is a corporate liability similar to secured debt. They feel that this view, which implies that any difference between the value of pension assets and the value of the liability is a part of shareholders' equity, is overly simplistic. Instead, they believe that the employees and the stockholders share ownership of the pension fund. The equity stake of the employees stems from firm-specific human capital, which allows them to capture some of the rents of the corporation, and from the provisions of the Employee Retirement Income Security Act of 1974 (ERISA). Just as it is too simplistic to assume that in bankruptcy stockholders will receive nothing, Bulow and Scholes argue that it is too simplistic to assume that in the termination of an overfunded pension plan the workers would receive none of the surplus.

The effects of ERISA are also the subject of the second chapter in this volume, by Jeremy I. Bulow, Myron S. Scholes, and Peter Menell (BSM), "Economic Implications of ERISA." In it BSM claim that ERISA changed the ownership rights to defined-benefit plans through the establishment of minimum vesting and benefit accrual standards, the establishment of the benefit insurance program, and through the definition of fiduciary responsibility of plan administrators. BSM argue that despite these changes, the sharp increase in nominal interest rates since 1974 has significantly reduced the impact of ERISA by drastically reducing the present value of vested benefits. Without this increase in interest rates, the Pension Benefit Guaranty Corporation (PBGC), the insurance agency established to guarantee benefits, would have faced large liabilities on the terminations of pension plans. To prevent potentially huge increases in its liabilities in the future, BSM suggest that the PBGC could require employers to fully fund any increases in promised benefits and to hedge the benefits guaranteed by the PBGC.

In the third chapter in this volume, "Pensions as Severance Pay," Edward P. Lazear presents a model in which defined-benefit pension plans serve as a form of severance pay designed to ensure efficient labor mobility. He shows how pension values which vary with the age of retirement can make both workers and firms better off by moving the equilibrium compensation scheme in the direction of a perfect-information, first-best optimum. Assuming that in the later years of life wages exceed the marginal productivity of labor, pension values should decline with the age of retirement beyond a certain point in order to encourage workers to take early retirement. He finds support for this claim in data drawn from the 1980 Banker's Trust corporate pension plan study. Comparing these results with those from his earlier study using 1975 data, he finds that the ratio of early retirement pension value to normal retirement pension value has increased between 1975 and 1980.

The Impact of Taxes and ERISA on Corporate Pension Policy

A number of papers in the NBER pension project have dealt with the subject of optimal pension funding and asset allocation in the presence of corporate and personal taxes and ERISA. The first papers in this area were those of Fischer Black (1980a; also see Black 1980b) and Irwin Tepper (1981). The models in both papers imply that firms with defined-benefit pension plans can increase the value of the firm by funding or even overfunding their plans (even if this increases the firm's nonpension liabilities) and by investing the pension assets in what would normally be fully taxable bonds. Both of these results are due to the tax-shelter nature of pension plans and to their assumption that the assets of the plan are really owned by the firms rather than by its employees. The authors argue that in the absence of default risk the firm's liability to its vested workers is independent of the assets of the plan, and that it is ultimately the stockholders of the firm whose situation is affected by the investment results of the pension assets. In a subsequent paper, Bulow (1981b) looked at a somewhat broader set of assumptions, although in several cases he, too, found that bonds were the optimal asset for defined-benefit plans.

In the fourth chapter in this volume, "Optimal Funding and Asset Allocation Rules for Defined-Benefit Pension Plans," J. Michael Harrison and William S. Sharpe address this range of issues. Harrison and Sharpe explicitly examine default risk and the role of ERISA, as well as the tax considerations of the previous papers. They conclude that the current tax and insurance policies of the United States government regarding pensions make it optimal for firms to follow extreme funding and investment strategies. They show that, given the trade-off between the insurance and tax effect, the optimal policy for a firm would generally involve either (1) full funding plus investment solely in bonds, (2) minimum funding plus investment solely in stocks, or (3) full funding and investment solely in stocks.

In the fifth chapter in this volume, "Pension Funding, Pension Asset Allocation, and Corporate Finance: Evidence from Individual Company Data," Benjamin M. Friedman looks for systematic empirical relationships between the composition of a corporation's balance sheet and the management of its pension fund. Friedman uses a merged data set on individual companies assembled from Standard and Poor's Compustat files and from the United States Department of Labor's Form 5500 files.

The chief conclusion, on the basis of data for 7,828 pension plans sponsored by 1,836 companies and their subsidiaries, is that corporations do not manage the pension plans which they sponsor as if these plans had nothing to do with the corporation. Different responses appear to characterize firm's behavior in different contexts, but the evidence persistently indicates clear relationships between decisions about pension assets and liabilities and decisions about the other assets and liabilities of the firm. At the same time, the pattern of these relationships is, more often than not, inconsistent with the conclusions of the optimal pension funding/asset allocation models developed at the theoretical level by Black, Tepper, and Harrison and Sharpe. In addition, Friedman finds some evidence that corporations time their pension contributions so as to smooth their reported earnings, but earnings smoothing also does not provide an explanation for underfunding of pensions (as is often claimed) since such behavior is as prevalent among firms with fully funded as with underfunded plans.

Another aspect of pension asset allocation concerns the long-term nature of the commitment. In the sixth chapter in this volume, "Investing for the Short and the Long Term," Stanley Fischer considers how the relative riskiness of stocks and bonds changes with the length of the "holding period," defined as the length of time between successive portfolio revisions. He finds that in the United States the relative riskiness of stocks declines the longer the holding period because bill returns are more highly serially correlated than stock returns. But this does not greatly affect the optimal allocation between stocks and bonds. For typical untility functions, the optimal portfolio is very concentrated in stocks, although Fischer does not take account of the tax advantages of bonds discussed in the previous chapter.

Pension Obligations and Share Prices

In the seventh chapter in this volume, "Pension Funding Decisions, Interest Rate Assumptions, and Share Prices," Martin S. Feldstein and Randall Mørck attempt to assess the extent to which the market value of firms reflects accurately their unfunded pension obligations. The interest in this issue is in examining the efficiency of capital markets and in determining whether or not unfunded pensions depress national saving. If the unfunded liability is not reflected in a lower market value for the firm, the pension plan would create the appearance of an asset from the worker's point of view without a signal to the firm's owners that they are poorer. If, on the other hand, security values reflect the unfunded nature of the plan, the owners of the firm may save more on their own accounts to maintain their current wealth.

Using a new body of data on 132 firms, Feldstein and Mørck find that the market sets values that are related more closely to a pension obligation evaluated at a common standard interest rate than to the pension obligations as reported by the firms. This common interest rate, however, appears to be much lower than the long-term market interest rate prevailing at the time the sample was taken, implying that the present value of those liabilities is overstated. They also find evidence that the market may undervalue pension assets. This combination of overstated liabilities and understated assets may suggest that the expanding size of the private pension system may increase total savings by companies and their shareholders.

Inflation and Indexation

Much of the recent discussion about the relation between private pensions and inflation has emphasized the adverse impact that the unexpected rise in inflation during the past 15 years has had on pension recipients and on the performance of pension funds. Some of those who have commented on the problem have even concluded that the private pension system cannot survive in an inflationary economy. It is important, however, not to confuse the unfortunate consequences that followed when inflation caught pensioners and pension fund managers by surprise with the inability to adjust to future conditions, even uncertain future conditions.

In a previous study, Feldstein (1981a) concluded that a steady rate of inflation, far from destroying the pension system, would actually increase the share of total savings that goes into private pensions. The reason for this conclusion is that the advantage that the private pension has in exempting its portfolio income from taxation becomes greater when there is inflation. This, in turn, reflects the fact that individuals pay tax on the full nominal interest income that they earn on direct saving and therefore pay a tax per unit of capital that rises with the rate of inflation; in contrast, of course, since pensions pay no tax on their interest income, the tax differential per unit of capital rises with inflation. Similarly, individuals pay tax on nominal capital gains on stock (as well as on dividends), and this capital gains tax also implies a tax per unit of capital that rises with the rate of inflation. Thus, on both debt and equity, inflation increases the yield differential between household and pension funds in favor of pensions.

The uncertainty about future inflation makes long-term nominal contracts like private pensions extremely risky from the perspective of both the employees and the plan sponsor. Why, then, are private pensions not indexed? In the eighth chapter in this volume, "Should Private Pensions Be Indexed?" Feldstein offers a possible explanation: the availability of an optimal (or greater than optimal) amount of social security generally reduces the desired degree of indexing and, under a variety of conditions, makes it optimal to have no indexing at all in the private pension.

Indexation is also the subject of the ninth and tenth chapters in this volume. In "Observations on the Indexation of Old Age Pensions" Lawrence Summers concludes that alternative indexing arrangements may have far less impact on actual patterns of risk bearing than is usually thought to be the case and that insofar as the introduction of inflation indexing has real effects, there is no presumption that they are beneficial. The absence of indexed private pensions may not necessarily reflect market failure, but rather may reflect the tendency of competitive capital markets to allocate risks efficiently. Summers also points out that advocates of a large social security system may be opposed to the indexation of benefits because if indexation makes it more difficult to cut benefits in bad times, the level of indexed benefits offered in good times will be lower.

In his chapter, "On Consumption Indexed Public Pension Plans," Robert C. Merton considers the merits and feasibility of a mandatory fully funded savings plan in which required contributions and benefits are indexed to aggregate per capita consumption. He argues that people care about others and, among other things, will not let them starve in retirement. From this, we get a classical example of the "free-rider" problem which cannot be solved by the private markets but can be solved by an appropriately designed mandatory pension system.

A second argument in favor of such a system is the possibility of economies of scale in information costs. Virtually everyone faces the decision problem of how much to save for retirement and in what to invest those savings during their working years. If a pension plan were designed which reasonably approximated the plan which most individuals would choose if they were informed, then by making participation in the plan mandatory, the resources used in individual education and data gathering would be saved and the maximum benefits of pooling to reduce operating costs could be achieved.

Merton suggests aggregate per capita consumption as the appropriate base for indexation because of the known theoretical result that life-cycle investors will optimally hold portfolios whose returns are perfectly correlated with aggregate consumption. Although his analysis is made within the framework of a public pension plan, it applies equally well to organized private pension plans where participation is virtually mandatory and where individually designed programs are not practical. An additional feature of the plans examined is that they provide for life annuities during both the accumulation and retirement phases of the life cycles.

In the eleventh chapter in this volume, "Retirement Annuity Design in an Inflationary Climate," Zvi Bodie and James Pesando consider the desirability and feasibility of "performance" indexing as an alternative to price-level indexing of private pensions. They examine the tilt and risk-return characteristics of real retirement incomes provided by variable annuities tied to bills, bonds, and stocks and contrast them with conventional nominal annuities. Their analysis emphasizes the downward tilt and riskiness of the stream of real benefits provided by the conventional level-payment nominal annuity in an environment of high and variable rates of inflation. They also consider several innovations in annuity design, which have appeared in recent years in response to increased inflation uncertainty, and show them to be variants of the standard variable annuity. They interpret the ad hoc cost-of-living adjustments made by many large firms in recent years as a form of performance indexing.

Role of Social Security

In the twelfth chapter in this volume, "On the Role of Social Security as a Means for Efficient Risk Bearing in an Economy Where Human Capital Is Not Tradable," Robert C. Merton explores one possible economic function of a "pay-as-you-go" public retirement plan such as social security: to eliminate the inefficiencies caused by the nontradability of human capital.

Merton develops an intertemporal general equilibrium model of an economy with overlapping generations and two factors of production, labor and capital. He then uses it to analyze the economic inefficiencies caused by the nontradability of human capital and to derive a constrained Pareto-optimal system of taxes and transfers which "corrects" these inefficiencies. He shows that, in the absence of such a system, this market failure causes the equilibrium path of the economy to deviate from the optimum for two reasons. First, people cannot achieve their optimal life-cycle consumption program because early in life when most of their wealth is in the form of human capital they cannot consume as much as they would otherwise choose. Second, investors cannot achieve an optimal portfolio allocation of their savings. Not only will some investors be forced to bear more risk than they would choose in the absence of this market failure, but because factor shares are uncertain, the portfolios held by investors will be inefficient. The young are "forced" to invest "too much" of their savings in human capital and the old are "forced" to invest "too little" in human capital. Hence, all investors bear "factor-share" risk which, if human capital were tradable, could be diversified away. Merton shows that an optimal system of taxes and transfers not unlike the current social security system can eliminate this inefficiency, and, therefore, he suggests that a latent function of the present system may be to improve the efficiency of risk bearing in the economy.

Pensions and the Financial Status of the Aged

In the thirteenth chapter in this volume, "The Economic Status of the Elderly," Michael Hurd and John B. Shoven present a picture which contrasts sharply with some popularly held views. All of their calculations indicate that on average the elderly did relatively well economically over the decade of the 1970s and that they were not particularly vulnerable to inflation. The aggregate data show that incomes of the elderly increased faster than incomes of the rest of the population even though the labor force participation of the elderly declined. A substantial part of the elderly population was protected against inflation, and those who were highly vulnerable were concentrated among the wealthy, who were better able to tolerate the inflation risk.

Finally, in the fourteenth chapter in this volume, "Portfolio Composition and Pension Wealth: An Econometric Study," Louis Dicks-Mireaux and Mervyn A. King examine the impact of pension wealth on the composition of household asset holdings. Using cross-sectional data for 10,118 Canadian households, they found that whereas there seems to be an identifiable effect of pension wealth on total saving, the effect on portfolio composition was less significant and was mainly in terms of the number and combination of different assets held rather than in the amount of any given asset as a proportion of total wealth.

Appendix A: NBER Pension Papers

Author(s)	Title, Date, and Working Paper Number

Altman, Rosalind. "An Analysis of Occupational Pensions in Britain" (1980), no. S80-1

Black, Fischer. "The Tax Advantages of Pension Fund Investments in Bonds" (1980), no. 533

Blinder, Alan. "Private Pensions and Public Pensions: Theory and Fact" (1982), no. 902

Bodie, Zvi. "Investment Strategy in an Inflationary Environment" (1981), no. 701

————. "Purchasing Power Annuities: Financial Innovation for Stable Real Retirement Income in an Inflationary Environment" (1981), no. 442

Bodie, Zvi, and Pesando James. "Retirement Annuity Design in an Inflationary Climate" (1982), no. 896

Boskin, Michael J., and Hurd, Michael D. "The Effect of Social Security on Early Retirement" (1977), no. 204

Boskin, Michael J.; Avrin, Marcy; and Cone, Kenneth. "Modeling Alternative Solutions to the Long-Run Social Security Funding Problem" (1980), no. 583

Boskin, Michael J. "Social Security and Retirement Decisions" (1975), no. 107

Bulow, Jeremy I. "Analysis of Pension Funding under ERISA" (1979), no. 402

————. "Early Retirement Pension Benefits" (1981), no. 654

————. "The Effect of Inflation on the Private Pension System" (1981), no. C103

————. "Tax Aspects of Corporate Pension Funding Policy" (1981), no. 724

Bulow, Jeremy I., and Scholes, Myron S. "Who Owns the Assets in a Defined-Benefit Pension Plan?" (1982), no. 924

Bulow, Jeremy I.; Scholes, Myron S.; and Menell, Peter. "Economic Implications of ERISA" (1982), no. 927

Burtless, Gary, and Hausman, Jerry A. "Double Dipping: The Combined Effects of Social Security and Civil Service Pensions on Employee Retirement" (1981), no. 800

Dicks-Mireaux, Louis, and King, Mervyn A. "Portfolio Composition and Pension Wealth: An Econometric Study" (1982), no. 903

————. "Asset Holdings and the Life Cycle" (1981), no. 614

Eaton, Jonathon, and Rosen, Harvey S. "Agency, Delayed Compensation, and the Structure of Executive Remuneration" (1981), no. 777

Feldstein, Martin S. "Do Private Pensions Increase National Saving?" (1977), no. 186

————. "The Effect of Social Security on Private Savings: The Time Series Evidence" (1979), no. 314

————. "The Effect of Social Security on Saving" (1979), no. 334

————. "International Differences in Social Security and Saving" (1979), no. 355

————. "Private Pensions and Inflation" (1980), no. 568.

————. "Private Pensions as Corporate Debt" (1981), no. 703

————. "Should Private Pensions Be Indexed?" (1981), no. 787

————. "Social Security Benefits and the Accumulation of Preretirement Wealth" (1980), no. 477

Feldstein, Martin S. "Social Security, Induced Retirement, and Aggregate Capital Accumulation: A Correction and Updating" (1980), no. 579

Feldstein, Martin S., and Mørk, Randall. "Pension Funding Decisions, Interest Rate Assumptions and Share Prices" (1982), no. 938

Feldstein, Martin S., and Pellechio, Anthony. "Social Security and Household Wealth Accumulation: New Microeconomic Evidence" (1977), no. 206

————. "Social Security Wealth: The Impact of Alternative Inflation Adjustments" (1977). no. 212

Feldstein, Martin S., and Seligman, Stephanie. "Pension Funding, Share Prices, and National Saving" (1980), no. 509

Fischer, Stanley. "Investing for the Short and the Long Term" (1982), no. 922

Friedman, Benjamin M. "Pension Funding, Pension Asset Allocation, and Corporate Finance: Evidence from Individual Company Data" (1982), no. 957

Gersovitz, Mark. "Economic Consequences of Unfunded Vested Pension Benefits" (1982), no. 480

Harrison, J. Michael, and Sharpe, William S. "Optimal Funding and Asset Allocation Rules for Defined-Benefit Pension Plans" (1982), no. 935

Hurd, Michael, and Shoven, John B. "The Economic Status of the Elderly" (1982), no. 914

Hurd, Michael, and Boskin, Michael J. "The Effect of Social Security on Retirement in the Early 1970s" (1981), no. 659

Inman, Robert. "Public Pensions, Public Unions, and the Local Labor Budget" (1980), no. S80-9

Kotlikoff, Laurence J., and Spivak, Avia. "The Family as an Incomplete Annuities Market" (1979), no. 362

Kotlikoff, Laurence J., and Summers, Lawrence. "The Adequacy of Savings" (1981), no. 627

Lazear, Edward P. "Severance Pay, Pensions, and Efficient Mobility" (1982), no. 854

———. "Pensions as Severance Pay" (1982), no. 944

Merton, Robert C. "On the Role of Social Security as a Means for Efficient Risk-Bearing in an Economy Where Human Capital Is Not Tradeable" (1981), no. 743

———. "On Consumption-indexed Public Pension Plans" (1982), no. 910

Mitchell, Olivia S., and Fields, Gary S. "The Effects of Pensions and Earnings on Retirement: A Review Essay" (1981), no. 772

Pesando, James E. "Employee Valuation of Pension Claims and the Impact of Indexing Initiatives" (1981), no. 767

Shoven, John B. "An Evaluation of the Role of Factor Markets and Intensities in the Social Security Crisis: A Progress Report" (1977), no. 216

Summers, Lawrence. "Observations on the Indexation of Old Age Pensions" (1982), no. 1023

Taubman, Paul J. "Pensions and Mortality" (1981), no. 811

Tepper, Irwin "Taxation and Corporate Pension Policy" (1981), no. 661

Notes

1. See *Retirement Income Opportunities in an Aging America: Income Levels and Adequacy*, Employee Benefit Research Institute, 1982, p. vi.

2. When accrued benefits are calculated for company annual reports, nonvested accrued benefits are multiplied by a projection of the proportion of the benefits which will become vested. There are some other projections (e.g., with regard to early retirement) that make the currently used accrued-benefit methods less than pure.

3. See, e.g., Treynor (1977).

4. In adjusting the present value of accrued benefits to reflect market capitalization rates the following approximation was used:

$$a = b(r/m)^{.75},$$

where a = adjusted value of accrued benefits, b = book value of accrued benefits, r = book interest rate assumption, and m = market interest rate. The computations were done by Wayne Landsman under the direction of Jeremy Bulow, using data from the FASB Statement 33 Data Bank.

References

Black, F. 1980a. The tax advantages of pension fund investments in bonds. NBER Working Paper no. 533.

———. 1980b. The tax consequences of long-run pension policy. *Financial Analysts Journal* 36 (July/August): 21–28.

Bulow, J. I. 1979. Analysis of pension funding under ERISA. NBER Working Paper no. 402.

———. 1981a. The effect of inflation on the private pension system. NBER Working Paper no. C103.

———. 1981b. Tax aspects of corporate pension funding. NBER Working Paper no. 724.

Kotlikoff, L. J., and Smith, D. E., eds. 1983. *Pensions in the American economy*. Chicago: University of Chicago Press (for the National Bureau of Economic Research). Forthcoming.

Tepper, I. 1981. Taxation and corporate pension policy. NBER Working Paper no. 661.

Treynor, J. L. 1977. The principles of corporate pension finance. *Journal of Finance* 36 (2): 627–38.

1   Who Owns the Assets in a Defined-Benefit Pension Plan?

Jeremy I. Bulow and Myron S. Scholes

1.1 Introduction

Who owns the assets in the defined-benefit pension plans of corporations? Some may feel that this question is easy to answer: pension funds are legal entities separate from the corporation. This distinction was made more explicit with the enactment of the Employees Retirement Income Security Act of 1974 (ERISA). The provisions of the Act regulate the funding and investments of the fund as well as the benefits to employees. In addition, the Pension Benefit Guaranty Corporation (PBGC), which guarantees a level of benefits for employees, has the power to tax the corporation to secure the payment of pension benefits. The firm contributes to the pension plan, the administrators of the plan have responsibilities as other fiduciaries, and the employees receive benefits from the pension plan during their years in retirement. Although prior to the Act, employers had easier access to the assets of the fund, greater control over the funding and investing decisions, and could use the assets for corporate purposes, the provisions of the Act closed many routes to the assets of the fund.

Pension plans are too large and are growing too fast, however, for economists to be stopped by the literal description of the pension plan or for them not to try to strip away the legal form and to reveal the economics of defined-benefit pension plans. As explained in Bulow et al. (1983), there have been significant changes in the economics of the

Jeremy I. Bulow is associate professor, Stanford University Graduate School of Business, and a faculty research fellow of the National Bureau of Economic Research. Myron S. Scholes is Edward Eagle Brown Professor, Graduate School of Business, University of Chicago, and research associate, National Bureau of Economic Research.

We thank Eugene Fama and Merton Milles and the participants at the NBER Conference on Public and Private Pensions for their comments, expecially Jerry Green.

defined-benefit pension plan subsequent to the passage of ERISA. Currently, pension assets in all plans exceed $600 billion, while the assets in noninsured private pension plans exceed $300 billion. In recent years, pension contributions for Fortune 500 companies have averaged approximately 12% of pretax profits. These funds represent a large pool of assets: to define ownership to these assets is an important task.

Understanding the ownership of defined-benefit pension funds, however, is difficult. Early papers in the area by Sharpe (1976), Treynor et al. (1976), and Treynor (1977) considered that the pension trust was essentially an asset of the corporation. The liabilities to the employees were classified as essentially corporate obligations. Black (1976) argued that most of the risk of holding assets in a defined-benefit pension plan is borne by corporate stockholders. Bulow (1981) has argued that the pension promise is comparable to a discount bond: the current reduction in salary is the present value of the bond, and the future promise is the face amount of the bond. As a first approximation, the value of the corporate pension liability would then be only the accrued benefits, benefits that must be paid if the plan were terminated immediately.

Sharpe (1976), assuming a no-tax world, argued that it made little difference to the stockholders or the pension beneficiaries how the assets of the pension fund were allocated between bond and stock investments. With rational expectations neither group would expect to fool the other. Black (1980), Feldstein and Seligman (1981), and Tepper (1981) assume that retirement promises to employees are corporate liabilities with little risk and, most important, promises that are independent of the pension fund, in concluding that there were tax advantages to corporate stockholders of investing the assets of pension funds in bonds.

There are, however, flaws in this argument on various fronts, including the tax front. Sharpe and Harrison (1982) argue that with insurance provided by the PBGC and with taxation, the policy of the fund may shift toward either all stocks or all bonds within the fund. Miller and Scholes (1981) and Bulow (1982) argued that the pension claims of the employees were not independent of the value of the assets of the fund; some groups of employees consider that the assets in the defined-benefit plan belong to them, just as if the plan were a defined-contribution plan. Depending on the question to be answered, economists have assumed that different parties owned the pension fund.

In the last several years, however, many financial economists have come to the view that the pension plan of a large corporation is a corporate asset and the obligation to pay employees during retirement a corporate liability. This argument seems reasonable, since beneficiaries of a defined-benefit pension plan receive a pension based, in part, upon a percentage of their final salary with the firm, or receive a pension based on a fixed dollar amount multiplied by up to a maximum number of years of service with the firm. Although as a legal entity the pension fund is separate from the firm, employees look to the firm to pay their retirement benefits. These payments, therefore, have been assumed to be obligations of the corporation, promises to pay benefits to employees, similar in economic effect to promises to its other creditors. If benefits received by the employees are independent of the performance of the of the fund, or its assets, then the assets of the firm include the assets of the pension plan: both are the security for the pension claim. Tepper (1981) assumes this independence by treating the assets and liabilities of the pension fund no differently than assets and liabilities held on corporate account in constructing an augmented balance sheet of a corporation.

We want to contribute to the discussion of the issues in several ways. In the first section we discuss the implications of interpreting literally the provisions of a defined-benefit pension plan. Such an interpretation leads to some implausible conclusions even if the method used to account for pension benefits is the most consistent with accounting for other forms of employee compensation. These inconsistencies imply that when valuing the employee's claims on the pension fund it is necessary to look beyond the literal description of the compensation agreement.

In the second section of the chapter, we explore what can be learned from the form of the pension contract about the nature of compensation to the group of employees within the firm. The traditional view that stockholders set up forms of "implicit contracts" is rejected for the view that employees, within the salaried pension plan, should be looked at not as individuals but as a group. The group negotiates with the stockholders of the firm (the board of directors of the firm or its management representatives) over the division of the profits earned by the firm.

By considering the workers as members of a group, many of the anomalies considered in the first part of the chapter disappear. We conclude that viewing the pension fund and the corporate assets of a firm as a single consolidated account is too simplistic.

1.2 Who Owns the Pension Fund? A Dogmatic View of the Pension Covenants

At the start, we will consider only defined-benefit pension plans for salaried employees. Such plans are almost always well funded: if the plan were to terminate today, assets would be more than sufficient to assure all of the accrued vested benefits of the employees in the plan. As employees leave the firm, their pension wealth in the plan could be calculated easily by taking the present value of their vested benefits. As Bulow (1982) shows, the present value of vested benefits is the correct measure of pension wealth under either of two models of labor compensation: (1) a "marginal product model" and (2) an "orthogonal model."

In a marginal product model, an employee's total compensation each period is equal to marginal product, making little difference if the employee leaves or stays with the firm. It would be extremely tenuous to argue that the present value of the employees' vested benefits is not the correct measure of the employer's liability: future benefit accumulation is part of future compensation and is paid for by providing future services to the firm.

In an orthogonal model, the form of the pension plan is assumed to be independent of any deviations between employee compensation and their marginal product. Some recent work (e.g., Medoff and Abraham 1980) indicates that, after correcting for differences in marginal product, older workers may be paid more than younger workers. This does not mean, however, that these differences need be related in any way to the form of the pension plan. Stanford, for example, has a defined-contribution pension plan, yet it may be as "paternalistic" as Sunstrand Corporation with its defined-benefit plan. In both organizations, the young workers may be underpaid and the old workers might be overpaid. No one, however, would suggest that Stanford calculate a "projected liability" representing the amount of compensation the school will have to pay in excess of the present value of the future output of the employee, even though under the tenure system those liabilities are more explicit than those of a private firm.

For firms with defined-benefit pension plans, it does not make sense to calculate an implicit pension liability using projections of future salary scales and termination rates. In computing the liability of the firm to the beneficiaries of the plan, the liability should be no greater than the liability on terminating the pension fund. The liability should be unrelated to the form of the pension plan, whether the plan is of the defined-benefit or the defined-contribution type. Furthermore, since pension benefits represent less than 10% of total labor compensation, the calculation of a liability for implicit compensation by only using pension data would be subject to large errors in measurement.

Using these arguments, actuaries are justified in setting the value of the employees' pension equal to the present value of vested benefits, the benefits they retain on leaving the firm immediately. These are exactly the same benefits that employees would receive on the termination of a well-funded pension plan.

1.2.1   Anomalies in the Accrued-Benefit Method of Accounting for Pension Liabilities

We have found several ways, however, that accounting for pension wealth in this manner fails to reflect the present value of an employee's pension wealth. These anomalies make it difficult to accept the accrued-benefit method in total, without question or adjustments.

The anomalies that we have found that are most interesting include the following problems.

a) *Vesting occurs on discrete dates.* Until employees vest, they have no pension wealth; on "vesting day," however, their entire accrued benefits become part of their pension wealth. Under ERISA, in the most extreme form of vesting, if employees leave the firm with less that 10 years of service, they have no pension; however, after 10 years they are fully vested. No one would believe that employees accumulate their entire 10 years of pension wealth on the final day before vesting. Although this appears to be a serious deficiency, it is not as important as it might seem: the present value of the benefit is generally less than a few weeks' pay for a newly vested employee who is about 40 years old. If need be, the firm could pay salary that was fractionally less during the last year before vesting, knowing that the employee will consider loss of pension in deciding whether to stay with the firm.

Although the employee may receive salary that is independent of the day of vesting, this bonus is too small to invalidate using vested benefits as a proxy for pension wealth. We have better candidates to challenge the vested-benefit approach to valuing the pension benefit.

b) *Early retirement benefits.* Employees receive large lump sum benefits by remaining with the firm until the first date of early retirement. Many plans allow employees to retire early with benefits that are too high relative to the benefits received on remaining with the firm until normal retirement. For example, a plan may have the following provisions: (1) If the employee leaves before the early retirement date (e.g., age 55), the employee is eligible for a vested pension with benefits beginning at age 65; (2) if the employee stays until the early retirement date, the employee is eligible for perhaps 70% of a full pension, starting immediately; and (3) by staying until the early retirement date, the employee may become eligible for extended health benefits and periodic upward adjustments in pension benefits which are lost by those employees leaving the firm prior to the early retirement date. The employee's incentive to stay with the firm until the early retirement date may exceed one full year's salary.

Staying until early retirement has a dramatic effect on the employee's pension wealth. Looking strictly at vested benefits as a measure of pension wealth fails to account for the large jump on that one day. Employees may receive quite a few lump sum benefits during their careers, but none comparable to the gain achievable by staying with the firm until the date of early retirement. Clearly, those employees, soon to become eligible for early retirement, have substantial equity beyond their vested benefits (the benefits they would receive on leaving the firm before this important date).

To preserve comparability to the manner in which we account for other items, we still might choose to account for early retirement as a one-time windfall that is realized on reaching the date of retirement. For example, some employees at universities receive tuition benefits for children attending college; that item is expensed and not accrued throughout employment. Employees, however, do not de facto have such large lump sums payment as part of their compensation.

Early retirement provisions may in part be substitutes for severance pay. That is, employees who are fired before the date of early retirement might have a more generous severance arrangement than their colleagues. The early retirement date would still serve as a significant milestone; after that date, the employee would receive severance pay through pension in lieu of severance on retiring voluntarily. (Lazear [1982] has worked on a closely related question.)

c) *Lump sum distributions.* Lump sum distributions from pension plans have a significant effect on pension wealth. Many pension plans permit some or all retirees to take their pensions in a lump sum, with promised benefits that are discounted at low rates of interest. According to a recent survey, 90 of the 546 companies surveyed offered lump sum payment options while only assuming rates of interest that averaged around 6% (*New York Times,* April 5, 1981).

By using low rates of interest, the lump sum distribution has greater present value than receiving the pension through time. Therefore, at all dates prior to retirement, accrued benefits would be the present value of the lump sum. This has an interesting side effect: if the firm also uses a low rate of interest in valuing pension liabilities, then its book liability equals its literal valuation liability. There are, however, two major problems with this approach.

First, firms have a large degree of flexibility in changing the interest rate used in determining the lump sum. It may seem implausible that a firm could reduce the present value of its pension liabilities unilaterally by as much as 25% by changing its assumption on interest rates from 6% to 9%. Yet Texaco, American Airlines, and RCA Corporation are among corporations that have raised their interest rate in recent years, to the consternation of retiring employees (*Pensions and Investment Age,* May 10, 1982).

Second, firms have the power to decide whether a specific employee will be permitted to receive a lump sum benefit. For example, some plans make it easier for high-level executives, deemed to possess more financial acumen, to receive lump sums. At this stage of the analysis, however, it is puzzling that employees would give the firm so much discretion over the present value of their benefits. The vested benefit method of valuation does not allow for discretion of this type.

d) *Ad hoc increases in benefits.* Ad hoc increases in the benefits of pensioners appear to be a corporate giveaway. The vested-benefit method of valuation of pension benefits requires that future promises be known. Firms, however, grant ad hoc increases in benefits to already retired employees. These grants, made at random times during retirement, do not fit the vested-benefit approach to defining pension wealth.

e) Claims on pension assets. The stockholders have an equity position in the pension fund at least equal to the market value of the assets in the pension fund minus the present value of the liabilities of the fund. In addition, if the right to put the liabilities to the PBGC, the "pension put," has value, the stockholders have a more valuable claim. On the other hand, if the pension put has no value, a well-funded plan, then the stockholders are the sole gainers (losers) from increases (decreases) in the market value of the pension fund. The stockholders, not the employees, are concerned with the "wasting" of excess assets in a well-funded pension plan.

Yet recent events indicate that this clear separation of the claims on the assets in the plan is incorrect. For example, retirees of Grumman Corporation, not the stockholders, sued the trustees of the pension plan for wasting the assets of the pension fund by buying stock at a premium, presumably to prevent a takeover by LTV. With a vastly overfunded pension plan, it appears that the retirees were not injured; only the stockholders were hurt if they missed an opportunity to sell their stock at a higher price and if paying the premium was a waste of the excess assets of the plan. The benefits of retirees were still safe, and active workers may have been better off because their own pensions remained intact and their jobs may have become safer because of the antitakeover activity.

Also, under ERISA, the assets of the plan are to be managed for the sole benefit of the beneficiaries of the plan. The courts appear to follow this interpretation in defining the claimants to the assets of the plan. The Grumman case points to the difficulty in using the excess assets in the plan for corporate business purposes.

In another related case, the A&P Corporation terminated its pension plan. After negotiating with the union, and although no contract specified a division of the surplus, the surplus in the pension fund apparently will be split into two parts, with a substantial fraction going to the employees through increased benefits.

These anomalies lead us to conclude that the vested-benefit method for valuation of pension benefits does not give a complete picture. In actuality, employees have complex employment contracts with the firm, and the pension plan is only part of total compensation. To understand pension compensation, in addition to direct salary, we must also understand the various other aspects of the compensation package.

In the next section of the chapter we discuss a model of compensation that tries to explain how a firm could offer a compensation package that includes lumpy payments, such as the large bonus for staying until the date of early retirement. This analysis, we believe, gives us an insight into the nature of the claims of both the employees and the stockholders against the pension fund.

1.3 A Model of Labor Contracts

In the last section we showed that anomalies arise if we value pension benefits as termination benefits. In this section, we present an alternative model of the labor contract that reconciles many of these anomalies.

We eschew the standard "implicit contract" approach to labor relations, an approach where young workers are paid less than marginal product and old workers are paid more than marginal product because of some unwritten pact between the firm and the workers. Although some of the implicit contract models explaining the upward-sloping wage/tenure profile have been ingenious, such as the work by Harris and Holmstrom (1982), they typically depend on the firm honoring a noncontractual obligation to the employees. (Lazear [1979] has also contributed to this literature.) In a model such as Harris and Holmstrom's, it must be in the interest of the firm to renege on its implicit liabilities at some point, unless those liabilities can grow indefinitely by at least the interest rate (a possible Ponzi scheme). Although we present a model in which we expect to observe an upward-sloping wage/tenure profile, there is no reliance on an implicit labor contract.

In this model we study firms earning economic rents that, in part, go to the labor force. The labor force is able to extract some rents because the employees have developed some human capital specific to the firm. The firm cannot earn its rents without employing the workers, who have experience with the firm and who educate new and inexperienced workers. Each generation of workers is willing to take a low wage when young to gain experience and to become part of the group that negotiates a larger total wage bill. The older workers are essentially equity holders in the firm, and they sell their equity to the young workers. The sale takes place through differential wage rates: it cannot occur through sale to stockholders. There is no claim that can be sold in the market.

No generation of employees gets what is ex ante better than a fair deal; there is no queue for employment with the firm. Individual employees, however, accept low salaries because they are buying equity from other employees—not because of an implicit contract with the firm. The senior members of the organization, who at any moment possess the rents accruing to the labor force, are able to do as well via high salaries when old as they would if they could suddenly disembody the rents of the labor force and sell all future rents for their present value.

We distinguish three types of human capital. The first is fully transferable human capital, for example, the knowledge gained in earning an M.B.A. degree. Second is human capital specific to the individual, for example, an administrator who knows a tremendous amount about a particular company, with some of these skills not easily or at least quickly replicated at the firm. Third is firm-specific human capital, not unique to a particular individual and therefore shadow priced at the margin at zero. Although, if one employee leaves the firm, there is no loss in that the employee's marginal product is as high inside the firm as outside the firm, if a whole group of such employees left the firm all at once, there would be a loss to the firm. It is this third type of group human capital that we use in the model. Empirically, if we could observe the marginal product of these employees individually, it would be low. The marginal product of the group, however, is high. If employees negotiate their compensation as a group, either explicitly through union negotiations or implicitly through a management team, they are able to garner part of the "quasi" rents that are earned because of the firm-specific human capital of the group.

To illustrate these ideas and the concepts, we use a simple model and a numerical example. This will lead into our discussion of the ownership of the assets of the pension plan.

Assume that a firm is created that will last for four periods exactly and that the production function each period is as follows:

$$f(q_I, q_E) = 120 \ q_E^{1/2} + 40 \ q_I^{3/4} - 192$$

where q_E = quantity of experienced employees and q_I = quantity of inexperienced employees.

Assume that these employees only develop firm-specific human capital. The opportunity cost of working for the firm is the same regardless of the experience of the employee. For the purposes of the model, assume that in each period, W, the opportunity cost of each worker is 15.

Assume that no individual employee can be employed for more than two periods—one when inexperienced and one when experienced. In the first period there are no workers with experience. Finally, assume that the rate of interest, r, is 100%.

It can be shown that optimal employment would involve hiring 16 inexperienced employees in the first period and employing 16 experienced and 16 inexperienced employees in each of periods 2, 3, and 4. Under those circumstances, the marginal product of both experienced and inexperienced employees will be 15 (the market wage) in each period. The net present value of the project will be zero.

If individual employees acted as price takers, then all employees could receive a wage of 15 in every period. However, if the employees are able to negotiate their salaries as a group, they will be in a bilateral bargaining position with the stockholders of the firm (presumably through the board of directors or their representatives), and the experienced employees may be able to negotiate a higher level of compensation in period 1, 2, or 3.

For example, in period 4 the total income produced by the firm would be $120(16)^{1/2} + 40(16)^{3/4} - 192 = 608$. From this amount, each inexperienced employee would have to be paid 15 in a competitive labor market. The experienced employees, however, conceivably could negotiate any amount of salary between 15, at which level they would be indifferent to staying with the firm, and 23, at which level the stockholders would be indifferent to shutting down the firm.

Any assumption can be made about the expectations of the employees of how the bilateral negotiations for salary will be resolved in periods 2, 3, and 4. We can then calculate the expected total compensation of employees in each future period, the distribution of total compensation between experienced and inexperienced employees in each future period, and the salary that will have to be paid in the first period. For example, assume that everyone expects that in each period the employees will negotiate a compensation package under which they receive 25% of the rents earned by the firm. In each period, the opportunity cost of the 32 employees is 480 and the firm has gross income of 608; therefore, we assume that all parties expect the total compensation of the employees in the last three periods will be $480 + .25 (608 - 480)$, or 512.

In period 4, inexperienced employees will command a wage of 15 each. Therefore, the experienced employees will each receive $[512 - (16 \times 15)]/16 = 17$. In period 3, the inexperienced employees, expecting that they will receive 17 when old, will settle for a wage of 14 when young: the present value of their compensation will be the same as with a wage of 15 each year. Continuing backward, we can compute a table, as in table 1.1, of the expected salaries of the experienced and the inexperienced employees.

Because young employees expect to earn 18.50 in period 2 when they acquire experience, they will settle for 13.25 in period 1, which is 1.75 below the market salary. Given the wage in period 1 and the expected wage bill in periods 2, 3, and 4, the firm regards the investment as a zero net present value project. Instead, if in each period the firm were to pay market salaries to all of its employees, it would have cash flows of $- 112$, $+ 128$, $+ 128$, and $+ 128$. Because the stockholders must bargain with the employees in periods 1, 2, and 3, their expected share of the cash flows

Table 1.1   **Expected Salaries of Experienced and Inexperienced Employees**

Period	Experienced	Inexperienced
2	18.50	13.50
3	18.00	14.00
4	17.00	15.00

falls to +96 (75% of 128). Naturally the lower salary that the employees accept in the start-up phase of the enterprise reduces the initial cash outflow in that period from 112 to 84.

Essentially, in period 1 the inexperienced employees make an investment that is equal to 25% of the equity of the firm. At the end of the start-up phase of the enterprise, the firm will have a market value equal to only three-quarters of what it would be if the employees had no equity participation (loosely speaking, Tobin's q would be less than one).

The inexperienced employees settle for a salary of 13.25, which is 1.74 below the market salary, because they expect to earn an extra 3.50 the following period. Of this extra amount, 2.00 comes from the 32.00 in rents that are split among the 16 experienced employees, and 1.50 comes from selling the present value of their future share of the rents of the firms to the new young employees.

In the context of this model, representatives of the stockholders negotiate a total salary bill with the employee group. There are no implicit labor contracts—management and the employees are expected to negotiate as hard in each and every period. Nevertheless, there are some employees, generally the young and inexperienced, whose salaries are less than their marginal product, and some employees, generally the more senior and experienced, whose salaries are greater than their marginal product.

The model assumes that the employee group acquires an equity position within the firm, and the model assumes that they can sell these property rights only to new employees entering the firm. In the start-up phase of the firm, both the stockholders and the employee group might have provided the investment capital—the stockholders with direct investments, the employee group with reduced salaries. The firm earns rents that are shared over time through higher "dividends" to the employee group.

In this model of group compensation, we could observe large lumps of salary to selected members of the employee group at particular times, such as staying with the firm until early retirement day or receiving tuition for children attending college. As long as the total compensation bill is in line with previous negotiations, the stockholders do not object to paying a disproportionate amount to any one employee. Individual employees, therefore, need not worry about the stockholders trying to reduce their salaries at times when they become eligible to receive significant employee benefits.

While this model does not in itself explain why compensation should be parceled out in any particular form—it is hard to justify tuition benefits at universities without considering that in part these benefits are tax-exempt income—the model does open the door for individual compensation not equal to marginal product at each point in time.

In the next section, we discuss the implications of the model to answering the question of who owns the assets of a pension plan. The notion that the employee group has an equity share in the firm, a share that is sold to younger employees through a salary reduction plan, is important. Although this is equivalent to paying higher salaries to older workers, it separates the implicit contract notion from our notion of an equity participation.

1.4 Who Owns the Assets in a Defined-Benefit Pension Fund?

In the model above, the employees of the firm negotiate with the employer for a total compensation package and allocate compensation among members of the group according to marginal product, returns from previous equity investments, and purchases and sales of claims of the equity of the firm.

There are three important implications of this model for the ownership of the assets of the pension fund. First, the model appears to justify using defined-benefit pension plans. Under these plans, the present value of the pension accruals of the experienced, older employees is far greater than that of the accruals of the inexperienced, younger employees. If younger employees are buying the equity rights of older employees, a pension plan that skews pension savings to older employees might be preferred by both groups. Under a defined-contribution plan, however, employers are constrained to tie pension compensation to salary and not to make it directly dependent on age. The defined-benefit plan allows the younger employees to pay for equity shares at a slower rate, which they might prefer, and allows the older employees to defer, at the before-tax rate, the returns on the equity shares in the firm. Second, employers can aggregate over the many employees in the plan, to compute the liability of the firm, even if the individual's estimates of their own pension wealth do not aggregate to these totals. That is, the labor model does not require that individual employees be paid anything close to marginal product each period. The University of Chicago accounts, and reasonably at that, for the cost of its tuition benefit program by expensing the cash outlay each year. Individual employees, however, may include, and rightly so, some accrued tuition benefit wealth on their own personal balance sheets. To reconcile this seeming inconsistency, consider that the employee group owns part of the surplus generated by the university; employees with children approaching college age know that when their children become undergraduates, the university, acting as the agent, will give them a disproportionate share of the employee surplus. This allocation would be entirely consistent with how the employee group had determined to allocate the surplus among themselves. Similarly, in the pension area, that an employee will be eligible for early retirement next year, and therefore will have sharply increased vested benefits, means that the employee will estimate pension wealth at greatly in excess of current vested benefits. This employee, like the employee whose child is about to enter college, is in line to receive a disproportionate share of the equity claim of the employee group in the next year. Third, the group model of compensation implies that the surplus in the pension fund—plan assets less the present value of accrued benefits—is owned in part by the firm and in part by the employees.

The employees tradeoff current compensation for future compensation when they receive a promise of a pension. In our model, compensation is not as well defined: employees may be buying and selling equity rights as well as receiving the value of their marginal products. In a simple model of compensation, employees are just price takers, without any need to acquire experience with the firm. The trade-offs between current salary and a pension can be explained by using a defined contribution pension plan. In this plan, the employee gives up a dollar of current salary (before tax); this dollar is invested in a fund, such as a mutual fund (a CREF or a TIAA account). The retirement benefits of employees are uncertain to the extent of the risk they take in their investment account and up to changes in their marginal tax rate in the pre- and postretirement period. The firm acts as an agent, dividing salary between a check for the employee and a check for the retirement account; for the firm's tax purposes, the division of salary is irrelevant. Employees make their own funding and plan choices based on current and future consumption trade-offs, as well as the desire to assume risk. There is ample evidence that employees desire some risk in their pension accounts: university professors, presumably a representative group, albeit more risk averse, have placed approximately half of their defined contribution account money in common stocks, CREF, and the remainder in risky bonds and in risky mortgages, TIAA. For university professors, these pension accounts may represent the largest fraction of their savings in the form of stocks or bonds and, as explained in Miller and Scholes (1978), the contribution limits are so generous that professors may not need to hold common stock for retirement other than in their CREF account.

In early work, it was assumed that pension promise was like a bond contract, a nominal but definite promise to the employees of the firm. If there were some probability of defaulting on the bonds of the firm, the pension claim was of equal priority to these bonds. This assumption is not correct for several important reasons. On a strict termination basis, bondholders have a higher priority on the assets outside the fund; employees have a higher priority on the assets inside the fund. Assets in the fund increase the security of the pension claims of the employees. If to some extent, prior to ERISA, employers could use the assets in the pension fund for their own purposes, the provisions of ERISA made it more difficult for the firm's stockholders to obtain the surplus of the fund upon its termination. Furthermore, in our model, the employees own part of the surplus of the fund—group negotiations and ERISA give them increased bargaining power to obtain part of the surplus of the pension fund with and without plan termination. By analogy, just as bondholders seldom receive what their covenants entitle them to in bankruptcy, stockholders seldom receive what their covenants entitle them to in a plan termination.

The pension fund is not a savings account of the stockholders of the firm. Most corporate pension funds invest in bonds and stocks. Approximately 60% of the assets of pension funds are invested in common stock. Black (1980) and Tepper (1981), however, suggest that investing pension fund assets in bonds dominates these current investment policies. They assume that the pension fund and the pension promise are separate: the fund is an asset of the firm, the promise is a liability of the firm. Given this assumption, the stockholders are better off if the pension fund invests in bonds: (1) in the Black model, because the firm can keep its equity risk the same by substituting bonds for stocks in the fund and by leveraging by buying back common stock with newly issued bonds on corporate account—the bonds in the fund earn at the before-tax rate, while the offsetting bonds on corporate account require payments at the after-tax rate; (2) in the Tepper model, individual investors offset, on their own account, the change in the risk of their equity that results from substituting bonds for stocks in the pension fund. Both models use the Miller (1977) tax model—the equilibrium marginal after-tax rate of corporations is equal to the after-tax rate of individuals. Miller and Scholes (1981) and Bulow (1981) examine the crucial assumption of the independence of the assets in the pension plan from the promise of pension benefits to employees.

The tax models assume that employees do not make claims on the assets of the pension fund. If, in the extreme case, the bondholders and stockholders of the firm believed that the entire pension fund was owned by the employees, there would be no tax advantage to the firm to funding in bonds. The collateral security for the loan would be bad. With partial claims on the assets of the pension fund, the collateral security would be tainted. The equity model implies that the collateral security, if not bad, is at least tainted. With complicated equity claims on the assets of the pension fund, it might be difficult to write bond contracts that allow bondholders to extract the surplus in the pension plan to pay off debt claims.

As in Bulow et al. (1983), the Employees Retirement Income Security Act and the establishment of the Pension Benefit Guaranty Corporation changed the economics of the defined-benefit pension plan. If there were opportunities before ERISA to move assets from the pension account to the corporate account or to overfund the pension fund to obtain tax advangtages, ERISA has reduced these opportunities. Since employees, with claims on the assets of the pension fund, do not have redeemable claims, the PBGC serves to monitor the actions of corporate stockholders to preserve the rights of the pension beneficiaries. These property rights, and the power of the PBGC to enforce them, make it difficult and uncertain how to use the assets of the fund as collateral security on loan. Even employees in retirement look to the PBGC to secure rights to the assets of the fund.

Because it is possible to change the level of funding in the pension plan to some extent, as long as it is done slowly or without large changes, there is still a tax advantage to overfunding the pension plan. On the other hand, this implies that with large unanticipated changes in the circumstances of the firm, or with changes in the ERISA rules, the collateral security of the pension fund may be claimed by other than the bondholders of the firm.

That employees share an equity ownership in the firm may explain some of the other anomalies. Group negotiations prevent unilateral changes in interest rate assumptions that change the value of lump sum distributions. By thinking of the employees as negotiating as a group, we can understand and interpret the anomalous provisions of retirement plans, such as the early retirement and the lump sum payout provisions.

1.5 Conclusion

The assets of the pension fund are not necessarily the assets of the firm. This makes the question, "Who owns the assets in a defined-benefit pension plan?" more uncertain than if the assets were assets of the firm or if the fund were a defined-contribution plan and the assets belonged to the employees. In the augmented balance sheet model of pension finance, the stockholders own the assets in the pension plan. In the group model, the employees and the stockholders share ownership of these assets.

The employees, managing and running the firm, negotiate with the stockholders for a wage package; the wage package is distributed among the employees as current salary and as future pension (and other benefits). In part, the total wage is used by some members of the group to buy equity and to make investments from other members of the group.

To some extent, the stockholders of the firm may be able to overfund the pension fund to capture some tax advantages. By changing funding assumptions, employers adjust their contributions to the pension fund. It is unlikely, however, that the PBGC will allow large changes in the fund or in the company without notification; it is unlikely that pension beneficiaries will allow large changes (at least downward) in the value of the pension trust. In recent years, many companies, trying to change pension or corporate benefit policies, have been challenged by pension beneficiaries.

To use the pension trust as collateral for a loan is difficult for all but the most secure companies. No contract can be drafted; the claim must be a general obligation of the firm. The firm could change its policies at any time; pension beneficiaries and the PBGC could step in between the bondholders and the assets of the fund. The collateral security of the fund is bad or tainted. The stockholders would find it difficult to borrow on the assets on which others have a partial claim, namely, the pension beneficiaries.

With modern corporations, outside stockholders are risk takers and expect to be compensated for assuming capital risk. As Fama (1980) has argued, the internal management team, or employee group, is separate from the stockholders, other than through the board of directors of the firm. As long as stockholders earn a competitive rate of return on their holdings within the firm and the correct share of any new rents through investment, the shareholders are indifferent to how employees monitor each other within the firm. In the context of the large corporation, the pension plan could not be used as a device to monitor the actions of employees; in particular, for the young employee the pension plan is of little if any value.

The vast majority of large pension funds contain assets far in excess of the accrued benefits of the plan beneficiaries. A literal interpretation of pension covenants implies that the entire surplus within the fund belongs to the stockholders. We have seen, however, that if employees can negotiate as a group and if the provisions of ERISA are ambiguous as to whether the employees or the stockholders own the surplus, we cannot give a unique answer to the question, Who owns the assets in the pension plan?

Comment   Jerry Green

This is a very valuable contribution to the discussion about pension funding and the appropriate way to form firms' balance sheets in the presence of pension liabilities. It makes a single argument: the assets in the pension plan should be at least partially attributed to the pension beneficiaries because they have an implicit equity claim on the surplus generated by the firm, including the surplus in the pension account. In

Jerry Green is professor of economics at Harvard University and research associate, National Bureau of Economic Research.

addition, this chapter contains interesting discussion of pension-related issues, good factual material, and a review of the earlier work on ERISA by Bulow and on the integration of individual pension firm balance sheets by Scholes, Black, Tepper, and others.

This discussion will be organized as follows. First I will review the factual basis used by Bulow and Scholes for their main argument, then I will go over the theoretical aspects of their model, and finally I will offer my own comments.

Bulow and Scholes claim that many pensions grant extra increases to retirees, although not legally obligated to do so. This makes a prima facie case for their equity in the plan. They also cite two specific cases. The retirees of Grumman Corporation sued the plan for maladministration of its assets and were able to exert significant pressure in this respect, and, when the plan of the A&P Corporation terminated, the assets were divided and not kept entirely within the company.

In these cases the identifiability of workers with the firm meant that any action taken by the plan had implications, rational or not, for the expectations of current workers with respect to the future behavior of their employer. For example, in granting extra benefits to retirees, workers might justifiably believe that such benefits would be granted in the future, when they are retired, and therefore that their current wage demands could be reduced. I doubt if the same type of argument would apply to multiemployer plans because of the lack of close association between the administration of the plan and the locus of employment of the workers. More generally, labor market studies have shown that comparably skilled workers earn higher wages in industries that are healthier, growing faster, or cyclically stronger. In short, the labor market is not perfectly competitive, and human capital immobility or nontransferability is probably only a part of the story. Clearly, therefore, that part of compensation due to pension arrangements displays characteristics similar to the wage component.

On a theoretical level, Bulow and Scholes justify this behavior as the result of an implicit contract between the *collectivity* of workers and their employer. That is, it is the result of a bargaining agreement with two parties, in contrast to much of the implicit contracts literature, which treats the individual worker in long-term relationships with his firm. While it is true that any bargaining theory, at this level of generality, will lead to some form of "split the surplus," we are given neither an extensive form of the bargaining game nor enough information about the properties of the agreement to tie down exactly which point is achieved.

Finally, I would like to offer my comments on the Bulow-Scholes resolution of the paradox of aggregation in valuing pension liabilities. They assert that the liability of the corporation is the current level of vested benefits, whereas the pension asset of individuals is generally greater than their vested benefits because they are forecasting receiving benefits in the future which are not yet vested, but which should be counted in the present value of receipts from the plan. Their resolution is inconsistent with their general view of these plans as part of a long-term relationship in which the firm has a reputation at stake. The reason for valuing the liability at only the level of vested benefits is that the firm has an option of terminating the plan and recovering all assets in excess of the vested benefit level. (I am speaking here about well-funded plans.) But one must remember that the firm has its reputation at stake; indeed, that is why so many vastly overfunded plans continue, and only the rare exception is terminated.

I would say therefore that at the individual level, in a world of perfect certainty, the correct value for the pension asset is the present value of the benefits to be received. As the individual ages, this increases because future benefits are discounted less. In the presence of various kinds of uncertainties, this calculation has to be modified. In my opinion the principal modification is to introduce the option value that a worker has in remaining with his present employer. Those workers who have a better opportunity later, an opportunity which would cause them to lose some future benefits in their current plan, will weigh the value of such a move against the benefits to be forgone. Therefore, being employed by a firm entails a certain option, namely, the option to continue, and it is this option whose value must be at least equal to the future benefits to be received, even in excess of the vested level.

For a large firm in a relatively stable industry, individual firm leaving averages out. Therefore, the level of liability associated with a certain plan can be computed as the present value of the payments to be received by plan beneficiaries, reduced to the extent that there is some statistical attrition of this population.

In summary, Bulow and Scholes offer some fascinating discussion, but I feel that it is slightly at cross-purposes with itself. The long-term contracts/human capital view of pension valuation explains the sharing of fortunes that is observed. It does lead us to the view that, in a significant way, the workers have an equity claim on the firm, because the firm seeks to maintain its reputation as a "fair employer." But this very argument undermines the balance sheet calculation that the authors offer in connection with the aggregation paradox of pension valuation.

References

Arnott, R., and Gersovitz, M. 1980. Corporate financial structure and the funding of private pension plans. *Journal of Public Economics* 7 (April):231–47.

Barnow, B., and Ehrenberg, R. 1979. The costs of defined benefit pension plans and firm adjustments. *Quarterly Journal of Economics* 93 (November):523–40.

Black, F. 1976. The investment policy spectrum. *Financial Analysts Journal* (January/February), 23–31.

———. 1980. The tax consequences of long-run pension policy. *Financial Analysts Journal* (July/August), 3–10.

Bulow, J. 1979. Analysis of pension funding under ERISA. NBER Working Paper no. 402. November.

———. 1982. What are corporate pension liabilities? *Quarterly Journal of Economics* 97 (August):435–52.

———. 1981. Pension funding and investment policy. Stanford University Working Paper. October.

Bulow, J.; Scholes, M.; and Menell, P. 1983. Economic implications of ERISA. This volume, pp. 37–56.

Fama, E. 1980. Agency problems and the theory of the firm. *Journal of Political Economy* 88 (2):288–307.

Feldstein, M., and Seligman, S. 1981. Pension funding, share prices, and national savings. *Journal of Finance* 36 (September): 801–24.

Feldstein, M., and Summers, L. 1979. Inflation and the taxation of capital income in the corporate sector. *National Tax Journal* 32 (December): 445–70.

Goodman, H,; Munn, F.; Phillips, A.; and Vasarhelyi, M. 1981. *Illustrations and analysis of disclosures of pension information.* Financial Report Survey 22. New York: American Institute of Certified Public Accountants.

Harris, M., and Holmstrom, B. 1982. Ability, performance and wage dynamics. *Review of Economic Studies* 49 (3), no. 157: 315–34.

Lazear, Edward P. 1979. Why is there mandatory retirement? *Journal of Political Economy* 87 (December): 1261–64.

———. 1982. Pensions as severance pay. NBER Working Paper no. 944.

McGill, D. 1977. *Fundamentals of private pensions.* Homewood, Ill.: Irwin.

Medoff, J., and Abraham, K. 1980. Experience, performance and earnings. *Quarterly Journal of Economics* 95 (December): 703–36.

Miller, M. 1977. Debt and taxes. *Journal of Finance* 32 (May): 261–75.

Miller, M., and Scholes, M. 1981. Pension funding and corporate valuation. University of Chicago Working Paper.

———. 1978. Dividends and taxes. *Journal of Financial Economics* 6:333–64.

Sharpe, W. 1976. Corporate pension funding policy. *Journal of Financial Economics* 3 (June): 183–93.

Sharpe, W., and Harrison, M. 1982. Tax and investment considerations of ERISA. Stanford, Graduate School of Business. May.

Tepper, I. 1981. Taxation and corporate pension policy. *Journal of Finance* 36 (March): 1–13.

Tepper, I., and Affleck, A. 1974. Pension plan liabilities and corporate financial strategies. *Journal of Finance* (December): 1545–64.

Treynor, J. 1977. The principles of corporate pension finance. *Journal of Finance* 32 (May). 627–38.

Treynor, J.; Regan, P.; and Priest, W. 1976. *The financial reality of pension funding under ERISA.* Homewood, Ill.: Dow Jones–Irwin.

2   Economic Implications of ERISA

Jeremy I. Bulow, Myron S. Scholes, and Peter Menell

2.1   Introduction

On enacting the Employee Retirement Income Security Act (ERISA) in 1974, Congress changed the ownership rights to the assets of defined-benefit pension plans. These ownership rights were changed through the establishment of the benefit insurance program, the definition of fiduciary responsibility of plan administrators, and the minimum vesting and benefit accrual standards for plan beneficiaries.

If, in part, the intent of ERISA was to assure that the beneficiaries of virtually insolvent pension plans would receive adequate pension benefits, in recent years sharp increases in nominal rates of interest have blunted the extent of the impact of this policy. The enactment of ERISA created a huge liability to pay pension benefits, a liability that fell on the Pension Benefit Guaranty Corporation (PBGC), the agency established to insure pension benefits on the termination of corporate pension plans. As rates of interest rose, however, the PBGC found that the present value of its liabilities fell sharply, and that it no longer faced the likelihood of a funding crisis: it no longer faced a significant threat of multiple terminations of underfunded pension plans. Naturally, the PBGC will continue to guarantee its share of the benefits of the plans of corporations entering bankruptcy. Although significant in dollar amounts, these liabilities are small relative to the value of the claims on the PBGC on the enactment of ERISA.

Jeremy I. Bulow is associate professor, Stanford University Graduate School of Business, and a faculty research fellow of the National Bureau of Economic Research. Myron S. Scholes is Edward Eagle Brown Professor, Graduate School of Business, University of Chicago, and research associate, National Bureau of Economic Research. Peter Menell is affiliated with the Economics Department of Stanford University.

We thank the participants at the NBER Conference on Public and Private Pensions for their comments, especially Fischer Black and Richard Zeckhauser.

Under ERISA, rules constrain the uses of the assets in the pension fund; rules constrain the way the assets in the pension fund are managed; rules require audits and reports to government agencies, and rules require that insurance premiums be paid to the PBGC. The defined-benefit pension plan, however, remains as a viable alternative to other types of pension plans, such as a defined-contribution pension plan, the major competing alternative that is not subject to ERISA limitations. Balancing the increased costs of ERISA are rules that allow overfunding of the pension fund. By overfunding, the firm's stockholders earn the before-tax rate of return on the overfunded portion of the assets in the pension fund. With higher rates of interest, and with prospects in the late seventies and early eighties for decreasing corporate rates of tax, employers had powerful tax incentives to retain and to overfund defined-benefit pension plans. In addition, when the rules under ERISA were defined, revised, and understood, adjustment to them was relatively inexpensive, and in the end there were still as many "loopholes" with nearly as much potential to skew benefit accruals as before ERISA.

Although increases in the rate of interest limited the impact of ERISA by reducing the present value of pension liabilities, ERISA would have had an enormous impact if interest rates had remained unchanged or had fallen after the enactment of the Act. Without the reduction of pension liabilities, as a result of unexpected and high rates of interest, the PBGC would have faced a plight analogous to the plight that confronts the Federal Savings and Loan Insurance Corporation (FSLIC) with the same unexpected and high rates of interest. If interest rates had fallen in the late seventies, the liabilities of many plans would have increased to such an extent that employers would have had a far greater incentive to terminate their pension plans and pass the liabilities of their plans on to the PBGC. With the PBGC forced to assume these liabilities, its likely first response would have been to raise premiums. For employers with overfunded plans, however, increased premiums coupled with low rates of interest would have reduced the relative tax advantage of retaining defined-benefit pension plans. For the insurance system to have remained solvent, employers with overfunded plans would have had to agree to increase the subsidy to employers with underfunded and terminated plans. Faced with this prospect, many employers with overfunded plans would have selected out of ERISA coverage by switching to defined-contribution plans. Thus, a dramatic change in the Pension Reform Act would have been needed to prevent the ultimate collapse of the Pension Benefit Guaranty Corporation. Given the current opportunity, however, modest changes in the pension law could rectify the structural problems that could again cause damage, changes in the law that would reduce the value of terminating a pension plan.

In the first section of the chapter, we examine the economics of the pension funds and pension funding before the enactment of ERISA. We discuss the fundamental differences between plans that are overfunded and plans that are underfunded. We discuss possible reasons for establishing a defined-benefit plan and how these reasons affect corporate funding policy. The post-ERISA environment is analyzed in the second section of the chapter. The crucial plan termination rules are presented. We show how the effects of ERISA are different for overfunded plans than for underfunded plans. We emphasize the importance of the effects of changes in rates of interest to an understanding of the long-term economic effects of ERISA. In the final section, we analyze several approaches to changing the current pension law that could prevent future difficulties and provide viable long-term benefit insurance.

2.2   Defined-Benefit Pension Funds before ERISA

2.2.1   Pension Liabilities

Prior to the enactment of ERISA, pension liabilities were not liabilities of the firm. When a plan terminated, beneficiaries had claims on the assets of the pension fund only: if funds were insufficient to cover accrued liabilities, the beneficiaries of the plan had no recourse to the general assets of the firm. Whether terminating the plan caused redistribution from one group of participants to others or from participants to stockholders is ignored at this stage of the analysis. We assume that all parties have worked out arrangements to try to protect themselves against adverse agency problems.

When a plan terminated, the priority of claims on the assets in the fund was determined by the rules of the plan; for example, already retired workers might have had priority over active workers in the firm. The aggregate claim of all the beneficiaries could be expressed as:

(1) $$T = \min(F, V)$$

where T = benefits of beneficiaries if plan terminated, F = value of assets in the pension fund, and V = present value of vested benefits, discounted at the risk-free nominal interest rate. The claims of the pension beneficiaries could be looked at in two equivalent ways: (1) the beneficiaries "owned" the assets in the pension fund, but management had the option to call the assets in return for paying off the vested benefits of V, or (2) the stockholders "owned" the pension assets but had the right to "put" them to the participants in the plan in satisfaction of their claim V against the firm. To understand the value of these options, it was necessary to consider the interests of both the employer and the employee group, for example a union, in negotiating a new short-run labor contract when confronting a pension plan that was underfunded as contrasted to one that was overfunded.[1]

2.2.2   Underfunded Plans

Difficulty in Running an Underfunded Plan

Although there were circumstances under which plans could remain underfunded for long periods of time, pressures did exist for employers either to fund or to terminate defined-benefit pension plans. For a plan to remain underfunded required two important and sustainable conditions: (1) workers negotiated their salaries and benefits not individually but as a group, and (2) workers possessed firm-specific human capital—the present value of rents expected to be earned through future employment—that capital being greater in value than the value of the underfunding. To show that these were sufficient conditions, we will consider all four possible combinations of "worker negotiation" and "human capital."

Let

f_i = pension benefits to worker i if the plan terminates.

v_i = benefits to worker i on leaving the firm assuming the plan continues and pays off all vested benefits.

p_i = opportunity cost of worker i (present value of future compensation from alternative employment).

m_i = present value of future marginal product of worker i.

F = total amount of money in pension fund, (Σf_i).

V = present value of vested benefits, (Σv_i).

P = total worker present value, (Σp_i).

Individual Salary Negotiations and No Firm-Specific Human Capital

If the plan were never terminated, worker i would still earn p_i on leaving the firm but retain v_i in already accumulated pension benefits. Therefore, if the employer were to assure their pensions, workers would expect total future payments worth $P + V$. If the firm terminates the pension plan, however, the cost of its work force would be less, only $P + F$: each would receive a termination benefit of f_i and a salary of p_i. The employer has an incentive to terminate the underfunded pension plan.

Individual Salary Negotiations and Firm-Specific Human Capital

If the plan would never terminate, future compensation (including payouts of already earned pension benefits) would be negotiated as an amount between $p_i + v_i$ and $m_i + v_i$ for each worker. If the plan terminates, however, each worker receives only f_i and future compensation is bargained between p_i and m_i. Because $f_i \leq v_i$, under any standard bargaining solution, the employer would have at least as low a cost terminating the pension plan as continuing it.

Group Salary Negotiations and No Firm Specific Human Capital

With group negotiations and no firm-specific human capital, workers would not expect to receive more than $P + F$, the amount they would receive in pension benefits on termination of the underfunded pension fund. If the workers, however, were to believe that the plan would never terminate, and that they would receive v_i in benefits if they quit, they would stay with the firm only with a contract to pay each of them $p_i + v_i$, or a total of $P + V$. Therefore, the total cost to the firm would be greater continuing the underfunded plan. The only way that not terminating the plan could be profitable is if the firm could find a way, albeit unlikely, to maintain an equilibrium, where unfunded benefits (V-F) could somehow continue to grow at least at the interest rate.

Group Salary Negotiations and Firm Specific Human Capital

Assume that the workers, as a group, possess some firm-specific human capital. Define M as the present value of the workers' future output. $M \geq \Sigma m_i$, such that the marginal product of the total work force is greater than the sum of the marginal products of the individual workers (e.g., if a few workers were to quit there would be little if any loss, but if all the experienced workers left the firm there would be a large loss to the firm). With group bargaining, the threat point for the workers would be $P + F$, the amount they would earn if no new contract were signed and the plan terminated. Employers would be willing to pay no more than $M + F$; otherwise, terminating the plan and hiring new workers would be the better alternative. Individual workers, recognizing that the plan would continue, leave unless they receive at least $p_i + v_i$, or at least $P + V$ in aggregate. Although the final compensation package must be worth no less than $P + F$ and no more than $M + F$, it is conceivable that the package could be worth more than $P + V$. The firm need not terminate the plan. To value the liabilities of the pension plan, however, we can still use the value of the plan on a termination basis. The bargaining position of the firm is not impaired by the workers' knowing that the plan will never terminate.[2]

This analysis implies that salaried workers, who do not bargain explicitly as a group, are more likely to have pension funds that are funded than do union workers, who do bargain as a group. This is consistent with historical data. Even firms with difficult plans for salaried and for hourly workers invariably have better funded plans for the salaried workers.

Claims on Underfunded Plans

For simplicity, start by considering a plan that is so underfunded that there is no chance that F will exceed V by the end of the next labor contract. If no new contract is signed, and if the plan is terminated, the workers receive the money in the fund, F. If a new contract is signed, the value of the workers' claims at the end of the contract will be the value of the assets in the fund at that time: the value is a function of firm contributions, investment policy, and disbursements. In this situation, the firm's claim against the assets of the pension fund is of little, if any, value. The firm is concerned only with the contributions it is required to make to the plan in lieu of current salary to the workers.

The firm should be interested in negotiating only the pension contribution and should not be interested in the investment policy or the increases in vested benefits granted under the new contract. The only points on the "contract curve" involve the workers' setting investment and benefit policy however they please for "their" fund.[3]

Empirical work on testing these effects seems to bear out this analysis. Inman (1980), in a study of municipal pension plans, estimated that there is a significant difference between how workers value extra vested benefits in greatly underfunded plans and how they value benefits in well-funded plans. They ascribe little value to promises of increased benefits if their plan is underfunded.

Anecdotal evidence also supports this view. For example, as part of their financial concessions to a hard-pressed New York City, union representatives allowed the city, albeit for possible other payments, to buy city securities with the assets in the union pension funds and to do so at more than market prices. If the fund were overfunded the workers would have valued their pension as V, the vested benefits, and the reduction of the value of the assets in the pension plan would have been costless for them and of no benefit to the city. That the employees and the city officials felt that the purchase of city bonds at below market rates of interest was a genuine concession indicates that the value of the claims in underfunded plans depends crucially on the value of the fund, F.

Summary of Underfunded Plans

Before ERISA, when F was far below V, contract negotiations centered on contributions to the fund. Workers gained when the value of the fund increased and lost when the value of the fund decreased. The fund belonged to the workers. Although the value of vested benefits, V, was computed by discounting vested benefits at the riskless rate of interest, and V changed with changes in interest rates, a change in V might not have implied a transfer of assets to either the firm or the workers.

2.2.3 Overfunded Plans

The second polar case concerns a plan that was well funded and could cover its vested benefits. Since the minimum of F and V was V, negotiations centered on granting additional benefits, increasing V. For these plans, employees were not concerned with changes in the assumed interest rate; they were not affected by a reduction in contributions to the pension fund—benefits would still have been valued at V despite the inframarginal reduction in F. Plan participants were not concerned with the investment policy of the fund; the stockholders, however, as residual claimants were concerned with investment policy.

In an overfunded plan the risk of the plan, (risk in F), was borne by the stockholders of the firm. The value of the pension claims, V, remained approximately the same with changes in the value of the assets in the plan. Unanticipated changes in V, however, mainly due to changes in interest rates, represented transfers between the employees and the stockholders.

2.2.4 Why Have a Defined-Benefit Pension Plan?

Defined-benefit pension plans are more complicated to analyze than defined-contribution pension plans. There is little literature on valuing pension liabilities in a defined contribution plan—everyone knows that at any given time the value of a pension in a defined-contribution plan is simply the amount of wealth currently in the plan. No complicated actuarial methods are needed to allocate defined-contribution pension costs—simply, the costs in any year are the contributions for that year. The valuation of defined-benefit pension liabilities, however, has received significant attention over the past five years, and there still is uncertainty about the correct method to value these benefits.

Given that defined-benefit plans are complicated, why do so many firms use these plans? Prior to ERISA, there were at least four reasons why it was in the interests of corporations to use these plans. First, defined-benefit plans were used to shelter income from the corporate tax. A defined-contribution plan is always funded fully—never overfunded or underfunded. If there is a tax advantage to overfunding a pension plan, the advantage could only be gained through having a defined-benefit plan.

How the tax advantage to overfunding the pension plan comes into being depends on the model of capital market equilibrium. Since in a Miller (1977) model there is no advantage to issuing corporate debt—in equilibrium the effective personal and corporate brackets are the same— the tax advantage arises from holding bonds in the pension fund that earn at the pretax corporate rate. In the "debt capacity" model, the tax advantage comes from issuing debt on corporate account. Holding extra assets in the pension fund increases debt capacity. In addition, with expectations of a falling corporate tax rate, there is an incentive to overfund the plan, at least for corporations paying taxes.

Before ERISA, however, the annual tax savings possible through overfunding were limited. Nominal interest rates were low, and prospects were not as bright for a reduction in the corporate rate of tax. With low rates of interest it was difficult to understate the interest assumption to increase the funding of the plan. Additionally, the incentive to accelerate contributions to a pension plan was significantly less than with high rates of interest.

It was, however, relatively easy to move money into and out of a pension fund—there were no minimum funding standards. Since the tax advantage of overfunding belonged to the stockholders, the ease of moving the excess between the pension fund and the corporate account made the location of the money important only for tax purposes. There were many examples of firms moving money into and out of their plans (e.g., U.S. Steel in 1955).

Second, a defined-benefit plan can be used to leverage total compensation. Since pension benefits are tied to final average salary, an increase in salary of 1% can increase total compensation (pension plus salary) by more than 1%.

Third, there may be information conveyed by the form of the pension plan. For example, workers might receive early retirement benefits in lieu of severance pay. With a defined-benefit plan, the firm accumulates severance pay in a tax-free account, and formalizes the arrangement with workers. Workers, leaving the firm early, know what severance pay they will receive and that they will earn it whether they quit or are fired by the firm.

As a last point, Bulow (1982) has shown that most accruals of benefits in a pension fund are credited to the older workers. The defined-benefit plan provides an easy way to skew pension compensation toward older workers while still appearing to be somewhat evenhanded in the treatment of all workers. Although no one is necessarily fooled by this approach, older workers do tend to save more for retirement than younger workers. It is extremely difficult to skew benefits in a defined-contribution plan. Expanding on this theme, some have argued that these plans, being complicated, have been used to fool workers and government officials and to smoothe corporate earnings.

2.2.5 Summary of Pre-ERISA Environment

Before the enactment of ERISA, workers in effect owned the assets of the underfunded pension plans; the stockholders owned the assets in excess of funding requirements in the overfunded pension plans. Only the plans for organized labor could remain underfunded for any length of time without being terminated.

The overfunded plans, on the other hand, could be used to shelter funds from tax for it was fairly easy to move funds between the pension fund and the corporation, and vice versa. The tax advantage, however, was seldom great; interest rates before 1974 were relatively low. In addition to any tax advantage, defined-benefit plans could be used to lever compensation, to accumulate a form of severance pay, or to skew pension compensation toward older workers.

2.3 Defined-Benefit Pension Plans after ERISA

With ERISA, the legal claims of beneficiaries and of employers changed. Most important was the introduction of a form of plan termination "insurance" that guaranteed approximately 85% of all vested benefits. With this insurance, beneficiaries of underfunded plans, mostly members of organized labor, gained at the expense of the PBGC. If interest rates had not risen, sharply reducing the value of these claims, the PBGC would have faced many more plan terminations than actually have occurred since the enactment of ERISA. To understand how to reform the rules and to prevent a possible collapse in the future, we will explain the economic effects of the rules for terminating a pension plan.

In addition to promulgating the rules for terminating a plan, ERISA also tightened the standards that apply to a fiduciary managing a pension fund. A major effect of these changes has been to restrict the movement of assets to the corporation from the pension plan. With these restrictions it became more costly to overfund and to pull back the funds as needed, just as the level of the interest rate made it more advantageous to overfund the plan. ERISA, however, failed in taking aim at curtailing "backloading"—the skewing of benefit accruals toward long-term employees.

2.3.1 Pension Liabilities after ERISA

We use the following notation to describe the rules mandated by ERISA: A = accrued benefits, G = guaranteed benefits, E = "net worth" of the firm, F = value of the assets in the pension fund, T = value of the worker's claim on termination of the fund, $PBGCL$ = liability of PBGC on termination of the fund, and FL = liability of firm on termination of the fund.

Accrued benefits are the sum of vested and nonvested benefits. Guaranteed benefits differ from vested benefits in several respects: (1) there is a maximum to the amount guaranteed each worker in the plan; (2) the guarantee of benefits arising from an amendment to a plan is phased in over 5 years (ERISA, Sec. 4022[b][1] and [8]); (3) ancillary benefits such as death benefits are not guaranteed; and (4) the PBGC is not required to grant lump sum payments or early retirement benefits if the present value of these benefits exceeds the present value of normal retirement benefits (PBGC Opinion Letters 75-33 and 77-141). From current PBGC experience, it guarantees approximately 85% of the vested benefits of employees in covered plans that were terminated with deficits.[4]

Under ERISA Section 4062, the employer maintaining an underfunded plan at termination is liable for up to 30% of the "net worth" of the corporation. This section states that "net worth is determined on whatever basis best reflects, in the determination of the Corporation

(PBGC), the current status of the employer's operations and prospects at the time chosen for determining the net worth of the employer." The PBGC appears to be able to use any method of valuation to secure its guarantees. Under ERISA, then,

(2) $$T = \max[G, \min(A,F)]$$

(3) $$FL = \min\{A - F, \max[0, \min(G - F, .3E)]\}$$

(4) $$PBGCL = \min(0, F + .3E - G).$$

Note that $T - FL - PBGCL = F$; the total value of all claims against the fund add to the amount in the fund.

Overfunded Plans

If a plan is overfunded, $F > A$, ERISA has little direct impact other than the requirement that the employers pay annual insurance against plan termination (currently $2.60 per employee). The main impact of the Act was to require employers to adhere to rigorous standards when acting in the capacity of a fiduciary for the defined-benefit plan. Although the firm owns the excess assets in the fund, it is restricted greatly in its ability to use these assets. ERISA Section 4044 (d)(1) states that any residual assets in a terminated plan revert to the employer only if the pension plan explicitly provides for such a distribution in termination. Thus, in many cases the PBGC has contended that excess assets should go to plan beneficiaries. Despite these restrictions, employers are still able to withdraw funds from pension plans by at least the following indirect methods: (1) by making small reductions each year in the amounts contributed to the plan; (2) by increasing the fraction of total compensation in the form of promised pensions; or (3) by increasing early retirement benefits. These routes, however, are not as clear-cut and fast as some might like, especially the creditors of the firm.

Underfunded Plans

ERISA brought about major changes for plans that were underfunded, that is, plans for which $F < A$. Beneficiaries of plans that were underfunded to the extent that the PBGC would bear some residual liability on termination, $(F + .3E < G)$, and that applies mainly to union plans, found that their benefits were raised to G: an amount independent of the assets in the plan. The PBGC assumed the risk of a default, while previously union members bore this risk. A literal interpretation of the rules implies that a firm can terminate its plan and require that the PBGC pay up the amount $G - F - .3E$ to members of the union. The firm has an option to terminate its plan; the exercise value of the option is the $\max(0, G - F - .3E)$. Although the pension put may be valuable, the PBGC can reduce its value to zero by requiring the firm to shore up the plan or by taking over the plan as soon as G exceeds F or the put becomes valuable. The PBGC, however, may not move quickly to take over a firm because of the cost of assuming 30% of the equity of the firm or the cost of reorganizing the firm. This has resulted in a degree of uncertainty about how the PBGC responds when a pension fund becomes greatly under-funded. The PBGC may forbear for a period of time and not act to shut down the plan: the put option becomes difficult to value.

2.3.2 Why Not Terminate a Defined-Benefit Pension Plan?

By enacting ERISA, Congress made the PBGC immediately liable for the unfunded guaranteed benefits that could not be covered by 30% of a firm's net worth. For those firms with overfunded plans, the insurance premium is akin to a tax, unless there was an expectation that the PBGC would forbear in the future or that the plans had benefits over defined-contribution plans that exceeded the insurance costs. Since the PBGC does forbear, the reasons that a plan does not terminate include: (i) the firm loses the possibility of being liable for less than 30% of its "net worth"; it may be more profitable to hold its option than to exercise it; (ii) "cash flow" considerations make continuation for the coming period profitable. To show this, let G_t, G_{t+1} = value of guaranteed benefits in periods t and $t+1$; D_{t+1} = dividends paid by the firm in period $t+1$; P_{t+1} = payouts by pension fund of guaranteed benefits in period $t+1$; r = riskless rate of interest; and C_{t+1} = contributions to the plan in period $t+1$. Then if

$$(5) \qquad G_{t+1} + P_{t+1} - (1+r)G_t + D_{t+1} - C_{t+1} > 0,$$

it pays to delay termination, even if termination is likely to occur in the future. The pension compensation from continuing the plan another period, $G_{t+1} + P_{t+1} - (1+r)G_t$, and the reduction in the value of the PBGC's equity claim through dividend payouts exceed the required pension contribution of the firm. By continuing the plan, the workers and stockholders both gain at the expense of the PBGC.

The value of the reputation of a firm might also make managers pause before terminating a plan. For an overfunded plan there is no problem. Other pension benefits could be substituted and employees would be as well off as with the defined-benefit plan. With an underfunded plan, a termination, with a surrender of 30% of the net worth of the firm, might result in a backlash from its workers, from its customers, and from its creditors.

Difficulties in Applying ERISA

Although the potential for huge plan terminations existed in the mid-seventies, there were fewer terminations than the analysis might suggest. On the enactment of the Act, according to a strict interpretation of the rules of ERISA, the PBGC had a large and mostly unfunded liability. To some extent, the PBGC may have been slightly better off because it was ambiguous whether a firm could terminate an underfunded pension plan, give up 30% of its net worth, and continue in business. It was also unclear what the latitude of the PBGC was in defining what constitutes "net worth." In PBGC opinion letter 80-5, a subsidiary of a firm submitted a request for waiver of liability on terminating an underfunded plan because it had negative worth. The waiver was denied on the grounds that the parent of the subsidiary showed adequate book and retained earnings. In that opinion letter, the PBGC argued that in determining the net worth of a business it could look beyond book value and use other factors to establish the value of the business as a going concern. In PBGC opinion letter 80-6, the PBGC stated that "net worth," as used in Section 4062(b) of ERISA, refers to an employer's fair market value, which in many cases may differ significantly from an employer's balance sheet or appraised value. Naturally, the PBGC has argued that in passing ERISA, the intent of Congress was not to bail out underfunded pension plans. One important case involved Alloytek, a firm that attempted to terminate its underfunded pension plan and to start a new plan with the exact same benefits as the current plan. The firm had a negative book value, and the shares of its stock were not traded; the firm argued that its "net worth" was zero. The issue was whether a going concern can terminate an underfunded plan at the expense of the PBGC. The settlement of the case was highly favorable to Alloytek and should lead to some immediate reforms in the pension law.

The definition of net worth is a major issue of current pension fund litigation. There is enough ambiguity in interpreting "net worth" to make it unclear what "net worth" really applies in defining the liability of the firm. For example, Penn-Dixie, a bankrupt firm, negotiated a large payoff to the PBGC as part of its plan of reorganization. Even with a bankrupt firm the PBGC may have a claim closer to that of a creditor than that of an equity owner. This claim as a creditor may arise because the firm often violates a provision of ERISA if it is near bankruptcy; for example, by falling behind in contributions.

Another major issue of definition arises in picking a rate of interest at which to discount the future benefits to calculate the guaranteed benefits, G. The PBGC calculates its interest rates using a survey of annuity rates offered by major insurance companies, subtracts the expense and profit rates of the insurance company, and adjusts for its own expense rates. On terminating plans, employers have the following options: (1) let the PBGC take over the assets of the plan along with the liabilities; (2) value the liabilities according to PBGC rates, or (3) buy out some of the liabilities through private contracting with insurance companies. Even though the PBGC rates of interest are below market rates, increasing the value of the guarantees, most employers have opted to have the PBGC take over the assets and liabilities of their plans.

We suspect the reason for this is that many of the plans that have terminated were the smaller plans, for which an insurance company would add administrative charges to the rate of interest to cover its own expenses. If a large plan terminates it may do better by buying insurance in the market; if not, the low interest rate assumptions have interesting implications. Using a low rate of interest overstates the value of the guaranteed benefits. By overstating these benefits the PBGC can force a firm with insufficient assets in the pension fund to pay up a greater percentage of the value of its equity (up to 30%) on terminating the pension fund. Terminating a pension fund may be more costly than the rules suggest.

2.3.3   Summary of Effects of ERISA on Underfunded Pension Plans

By guaranteeing the pension benefits, ERISA transferred resources to the beneficiaries of underfunded pension plans. This transfer came partly at the expense of the equity holders of the firm, up to 30% of the security of their equity value, and partly at the expense of the PBGC, which is required to make up the difference between guaranteed benefits and the liability of the firm. In the short run, underfunded plans would not have had an incentive to terminate because of the value of the "put" option. A plan termination under ERISA, however, does not imply that an employer abrogates pension obligations to its employees. It may mean simply that the firm changes to a different type of plan (e.g., a defined-contribution plan). Thus terminating a plan is not necessarily a major disruption within the firm; it may have no effect on the reputation of the employer.

Most terminations were by fully funded plans. This does not mean that the PBGC was financially sound at its creation. Remember that increases in rates of interest reduced the present value of the promise to the beneficiaries of pension plans guaranteed by the PBGC. At the end of 1980, using a sample of 682 large corporations with defined-benefit plans, we found that only five firms had liabilities that would require PBGC payments. The five were Chrysler, Uniroyal, Wheeling-Pittsburgh, Braniff, and Cyclops. (Our sample did not include International Harvester, and Braniff has declared bankruptcy.) To estimate the liability, we used 1980 year-end market values of the firms in the sample, an 11% rate of interest, and the current relation between guaranteed benefits and reported benefits, $G = .85 V$ (firm rate of interest$/.11)^{.75}$. We were forced to use the consolidated liability, V, in making these estimates because some firms have both a union and a salaried plan where union plans tend to be vastly underfunded and salaried plans are usually well funded (e.g.,

Chrysler). Consolidation understates the liability of the PBGC. Nevertheless, interest rates have limited the problem of the PBGC to only a few firms. In fact, using only the assets in their pension plans to cover the guarantee, only 25 pension plans had guaranteed benefits in excess of the assets in the plans. Therefore, even with bankruptcies of a few major firms, it becomes clear why the frequency of savings and loan association bankruptcies and the status of the FSLIC were salient issues in public policy relative to the solvency of pension plans and the PBGC's ability to guarantee benefits in the early 1980s.

An interesting side effect of the ERISA guarantee is that negotiations of new labor contracts have switched their emphasis from contributions to benefits. Before ERISA, the union would have rejected a Chrysler plan to postpone indefinitely making any contributions to the pension plan. Recently the firm negotiated such delays for its underfunded hourly plan without objection. Negotiations are primarily over benefits that increase the amount of the guarantee.

2.3.4 Summary of Effects of ERISA on Overfunded Plans

One major effect of ERISA has been to increase the cost to the employer of using defined-benefit plans. Insurance premiums are required, and the new fiduciary rules make defined-benefit pension plans less flexible. Balancing this, however, are tax advantages of overfunding a defined-benefit pension plan. Whenever rates of interest are high or prospects for tax rates are lower, employers have an incentive to continue using a defined-benefit pension plan.

A firm can increase the amount of overfunding in the plan simply by not altering its assumptions about the rate of interest used to calculate the present value of the benefits. Although IBM, for example, is approximately fully funded on its books, IBM uses only a 5.5% rate of interest. Using current interest rates, its pension plan is overfunded by approximately $3 billion. Because firms assume low interest rates and modify these assumptions infrequently, increases in the market rate of interest tend to increase the amount of overfunding possible in a plan.

Balancing the benefits of overfunding, however, are the new rules that fiduciaries must follow in managing the assets of the fund. These rules obscure the ownership of the excess assets in the pension fund. ERISA has made it more difficult to borrow against the assets in the pension fund. Some firms thus may be reluctant to overfund, and this may help explain why many firms reduce their accumulations in the fund by changing their actuarial assumptions even though they did not need to make the change. About 15% of the more than 1,000 firms subject to FASB inflation-accounting rules of disclosure changed their actuarial assumptions in 1980, though not all changed their interest rate assumption.

2.3.5 Ineffectiveness of Other ERISA Provisions

ERISA requires that pensions of employees vest according to minimum vesting rules. Another stated objective of ERISA is to minimize the backloading of benefits. "Backloading" is the practice of having a benefit formula that biases the pension benefits in favor of the long-term employees. For example, a plan might give a worker a pension equal to one-half of one percent of final salary times the number of years worked up to 20 plus 2% of salary times the number of years worked beyond the 20 years. Under current law, however, the annual rate of accrual cannot be more that 4/3 as great in future years than in the current year (ERISA Sec. 204 [b][1][B]).

It is still possible, however, to backload. Backloading of a substantial amount can occur by using the rules for integration with social security and by using the high interest rates. As shown by Bulow (1982), if the provisions of a plan state that a worker will receive a fixed percentage of final salary times the number of years worked, then pension accruals are highly skewed toward the last years with the firm. McGill (1977) explains that by using the formulas for integrating social security with pension benefits under ERISA, a disproportionate share of the accrued benefits of any worker leaving the firm at a young age or any worker leaving after a short duration can be eliminated by integration with social security. Although it is easy to skew benefits in a defined-benefit plan, it is difficult to skew benefits in a defined-contribution plan. The designers of pension plans might use this feature to better fashion the plan to the needs of the beneficiaries.

2.4 Possibilities for Reform of ERISA

The PBGC has a direct interest only in plan funding, portfolio allocation, and benefit accrual decisions: these decisions affect the value of the "pension put." As we have discussed, the pension put is currently "out of the money" for all but a few plans. Modest changes in the funding and portfolio allocation rules will ensure that the PBGC will not be as vulnerable to plan terminations as it was in the mid-1970s.

Under ERISA, the PBGC technically has the power to terminate any plan as soon as it feels there is a danger that if a plan terminates it would be liable to pay benefits (ERISA Sec. 4042[a]). Since the exercise value of the pension put to the corporation is $\max(0, G - F - .3E)$, the PBGC, by following the mandate literally, could make the value of the pension put equal to zero by terminating the plan when $G = F + .3E$. If such a policy were followed, pension insurance would be of no value to most firms. The only reason that firms would continue to pay the insurance premium would be to maintain the tax advantage of a qualified defined-benefit pension plan.

Actually, the PBGC has a policy of forbearance: it does not terminate many plans. In any event, it would probably have some difficulty in the courts if it tried to terminate a plan that was meeting the minimum ERISA funding standards. Also, the PBGC is not equipped to take over large numbers of pension plans, nor does it view the taking over of plans as being the intent of Congress.

If the PBGC does forbear in not terminating plans, its role changes to that of the pension fund monitor. As a price for not immediately terminating insufficient plans, the PBGC could require funding and investment policies that reduce the value of the pension put or at least keep it from becoming too valuable. Three types of changes can protect the PBGC, and they will not interfere to any extent with the management of the pension fund.

First, the PBGC could require better matching of pension fund assets and liabilities for firms where $F + .3E$ is not significantly greater than G. For a firm as well funded, and with as much equity as IBM, the PBGC does not care about funding policy; the probability is close to one that $F + .3E$ (about \$26 billion for IBM) will remain above G (approximately \$2 billion for IBM). For other firms, however, a decrease in interest rates and in the stock market could create a large liability for the PBGC. For these firms, the PBGC could require that plan assets be used to "hedge" the *guaranteed benefits*. Because the guaranteed benefits are almost entirely annuities and deferred annuities, the appropriate hedge appears to be long-term bonds with a duration similar to that of the pension liabilities.

Second, the rules could be changed for funding benefits that arise from amending the pension plan. Hourly plans are able to remain perpetually underfunded because each time the fixed nominal pension benefits are increased, the increase is funded over a period of 10–30 years, while the benefits are guaranteed over a period of only 5 years. With this rule, a firm may be able to increase its unfunded guaranteed benefits perpetually. If not immediately, then, firms could be required to fund benefits over 5 years, and at the same rate as the benefits become guaranteed.

Third, consolidating plans within a firm reduces the risk of plan terminations. That is, if a plan were terminated with insufficient assets within the plan (e.g., a plan for hourly workers), the PBGC could have the right to consolidate other plans within the firm (e.g., an overfunded salaried plan).

With so many plans in good financial health, these changes would have a minimal short-term effect on most firms. By adopting these safeguards now, however, the PBGC can dramatically reduce its potential for disaster in the future.

Notes

1. For union plans, we include only single-employer plans. Thus, plans run by the union, multiemployer plans, are excluded in the analysis. We assume that all benefits are vested, and we ignore that workers accrue benefits and become vested only after a number of years of employment with the firm. Although vested benefits are assumed to be paid in a lump sum at retirement, most pension plans have insurance features in that workers receive monthly payments for life. We assume that an insurance company sells a guaranteed life annuity to the firm.

2. It is uncertain why union representatives preferred to negotiate the sharing of the difference between $M + F$ and $P + F$, in part, as $V > F$. It may be that as long as the union controlled the process of bargaining this was an efficient mechanism to transfer ownership rights of the human capital of the group, a transfer to the younger workers who assume the rights for the future. Older workers and union representatives might skew benefits to themselves, yet this might have been efficient if younger workers and older workers had worked this out as a way to transfer these ownership rights. Changes in the rate of interest may affect the value of the "loans" through changes in V as the transfers took place; however, the firm may not have been involved directly. (See Bulow and Scholes, Who Owns the Assets in a Defined-Benefit Pension Plan?, this volume.)

3. Expanding on 2, if sharing includes an underfunded pension plan, employers were not at a competitive disadvantage because they lost tax benefits. The employees, in part, owned "stock" in the firm through their share of the difference between M and P. If the assets of a pension fund include the stock of the firm employing the workers, as in this case, there is no tax disadvantage to an underfunded pension plan. This follows, because dealings in the firm's stock for corporate purposes, sales and repurchases, do not result in any tax at the corporate level—the stockholders earn the before-tax rate of return on dealings in their own stock.

4. The PBGC considers accrued benefits to be the same as vested benefits; it assumes that everyone in the fund is fully vested on joining the plan. This treatment differs from the Financial Accounting Standard Board rules, which require a probability weighting on the vesting of benefits, an expected value calculation. For most plans, the difference is small in this accounting treatment. Maximum benefits are nominal benefits, limits that are set each year with changes in social security benefits. If workers in a plan that terminates in 1982 receive the maximum guaranteed benefit, approximately $1380 per month, they will receive $1380 per month on retirement, whether it is next year or 20 years hence. The maximum benefit is raised each year and applies only to plans that terminate in that year.

Comment   Richard J. Zeckhauser

Imagine a board game called Pensions. Some players represent firms, others are unionized workers, still others are nonunionized workers. One woebegone soul would be assigned to play the part of the Pension Benefit Guaranty Corporation (PBGC), whose behavior is constrained by rules defined by Congress in ERISA. The principal contribution of Bulow,

Richard J. Zeckhauser is professor of political economy, John F. Kennedy School of Government, Harvard University, and research associate, National Bureau of Economic Research.

Scholes, and Menell is to devise such a game and provide a strategy manual for it.

Pensions employs real concepts, such as human capital and defined-benefit contribution plans. Its chance cards represent actual events, such as the Chrysler bail-out and the coerced purchase of city bonds by New York municipal workers. And the game, as played according to the clearly formulated strategies of the authors, highlights important forces and tendencies in the real world.

The central lesson in their strategy manual is a simple one: When you provide insurance, as ERISA does for defined-benefit pension liabilities, moral hazard will generate more of the insured-against event, in this case pension defaults. Underfunding is linked to such defaults as fast driving is to auto accidents. Unexpected low interest rates, which raise the present value of future liabilities, parallel unexpectedly slippery weather conditions. There is even the possibility of deliberate plan terminations reminiscent of arson for insurance.

How have the players been doing? The authors are quite clear. ERISA endowed the PBGC with a disastrous set of permissible strategies. In terms of expected value, the guarantees associated with the passage of ERISA represent a vast windfall for the beneficiaries of underfunded pension plans. Companies and workers were given an entitlement to gang up on the Pension Benefit Guaranty Corporation. Firms would terminate their plans, and their employees would promise not to think less well of the firm. Stockholders, so the authors tell us, also contributed to this windfall. Some lost substantial portions, up to 30% of their equity value. Like the financial press, these equity holders were naive about the implications of ERISA; few even lobbied hard against its passage. In the event, ERISA and its captive partner the PBGC have been fortunate. A chance card led to an unexpected period of sustained high interest rates. The present values of the liabilities in defined-benefit pension plans have been dramatically reduced, removing (temporarily) the incentive for strategic terminations of underfunded plans.

Because of that chance card, the authors' predictions of calamities for the PBGC, vast shufflles of wealth, strategic terminations of pension plans, and the like cannot be verified. Alas for science. That card also provides the authors a defense against the charge of Chicken Littledom.

The authors suggest some changes in the operations of the Pension Benefit Guaranty Corporation that will "dramatically reduce its potential for disaster." The basic principle they espouse is stricter standards. They prescribe mechanisms to police the portfolios of firms, requiring the funding of benefits over shorter times and the consolidation of plans within a firm should a termination be proposed.

The PBGC probably could enforce such provisions, were they law, though the administrative overhead would be substantial. In any crucial case, it is doubtful whether it could be as stringent as it would like to pretend it would be. It is highly unlikely that a company in trouble, with a pension plan in trouble, would ever be forced into a still more precarious state by a government agency requiring it to put more money into pension assets. With the government as pension guarantor, the workers and management constitute a natural alliance whose primary purpose would be to gain relief from requirements to reduce underfunding. As the Chrysler experience illustrates, such an alliance would be politically powerful in times of crisis.

Should the PBGC enforce these provisions? I would argue probably not, for three reasons. First, the level and manner of pension funding have significant consequences for the operation of capital markets. These proposals would constitute one more intervention in such markets, imposing possibly stringent regulations yet ignoring a most important area of consequence, namely, their effect on capital flows. Second, the heterogeneity of conditions among firms and workers, which the authors describe insightfully, suggests that pricing, not regulation, should be the preferred mechanism for ensuring the solvency of pension funds. Pricing, which responds continuously to all conditions in a pension fund, will influence all decisions affecting all pension funds, whether over- or underfunded. Regulation, in contrast, only influences funds close to not meeting the required standards. Third, the proposed provisions ignore the issue of what entity is best suited to oversee pension funds. With a pricing solution, firms would have to convince competing insurers, not regulatory authorities, that an investment approach or funding strategy is secure. Even if political realities are such that the government must remain the insurer of pension solvency, a pricing approach would seem far superior to regulation.

Bulow, Scholes, and Mennell, experts in finance, create a game defined almost exclusively in terms of the financial provisions and inducements of the pension regulatory system. If there were security markets for pension entitlements and liabilities, this game might well capture the salient elements of the real world, for a few experts could reap a fortune bringing the pensions market into equilibrium. Equilibrium would thus be assured. In fact, pension entitlements are not traded and liabilities are bundled with the other assets and liabilities of the firm. The real pensions game depends on the behavior of participants, who focus, at times myopically, on surface manifestations, such as effects on labor markets and reputations, in part because that is where other participants are looking.

References

Arnott, R., and Gersovitz, M. 1980. Corporate financial structure and the funding of private pension plans. *Journal of Public Economics* 7 (April): 231–47.

Barnow, B., and Ehrenberg, R. 1979. The costs of defined benefit pension plans and firm adjustments. *Quarterly Journal of Economics* 93 (November): 523–40.

Black, F. 1980. The tax consequences of long-run pension policy. *Financial Analysts Journal* (July/August), 3–10.

———.1976. The investment policy spectrum. *Financial Analysts Journal* (January/February), 23–31.

Bulow, J. 1979. Analysis of pension funding under ERISA. NBER Working Paper no. 402.

———. 1982. What are corporate pension liabilities? *Quarterly Journal of Economics* 97 (August): 435–52.

———. 1981. Pension funding and investment policy. Stanford University Working Paper, October.

Feldstein, M., and Summers, L. 1979. Inflation and the taxation of capital income in the corporate sector. *National Tax Journal* 32 (December): 445–70.

Feldstein, M., and Seligman, S. 1981. Pension funding, share prices, and national savings. *Journal of Finance* 36 (September): 801–24.

Goodman, H.; Munn, F.; Phillips, A.; and Vasarhelyi, M. 1981. *Illustrations and analysis of disclosures of pension information.* Financial Report Survey 22. New York: American Institute of Certified Public Accountants.

Inman, Robert. 1980. Public pensions, public unions, and the local labor budget. NBER Summer Institute Paper no. 80-9, December.

McGill, D. 1977. *Fundamentals of private pension.* Homewood, Ill.: Irwin.

Miller, M. 1977. Debt and taxes. *Journal of Finance* 32 (May): 261–275.

Miller, M., and Scholes, M. 1981. Pension funding and corporate valuation. University of Chicago Working Paper.

Pension Benefit Guaranty Corporation. 1976. Premium requirements for the singles employer basic benefits insurance program. Part II.

Sharpe, W. 1976. Corporate pension funding policy. *Journal of Financial Economics* 3 (June): 183–93.

Tepper, I. 1981. Taxation and corporate pension policy. *Journal of Finance* 36 (March): 1–13.

Tepper, I., and Affleck, A. 1974. Pension plan liabilities and corporate financial strategies. *Journal of Finance* (December): 1549–64.

Treynor, J. 1977. The principles of corporate pension finance. *Journal of Finance* 32 (May): 627–38.

Treynor, J.; Regan, P.; and Priest, W. 1976. *The financial reality of pension funding under ERISA.* Homewood, Ill.: Dow Jones-Irwin.

3   Pensions as Severance Pay

Edward P. Lazear

When wages equal marginal product and workers are risk neutral, severance pay is not merely superfluous—it is harmful. However, when either of these conditions is violated severance pay becomes an important part of an optimal compensation scheme. For example, if the contemporaneous wage exceeds marginal product then workers prefer to remain with the firm even when it is inefficient to do so. Severance pay causes the worker to leave the job more frequently, and a judiciously chosen combination of wage and severance pay can induce efficient quitting behavior.

Pensions which vary with the date of retirement can be thought of as a form of severance pay. If the expected present value of the pension declines with later retirement, then the worker sacrifices some benefits to remain on the job. Stated conversely, firms appear to be willing to pay a larger pension value (stock, not flow, of course) to workers who retire early. These larger pensions can be interpreted as severance pay because they induce the worker to leave the job more frequently than he would in the absence of such a structure.

This view of pensions is quite different from the one that holds that pensions are a way to save at before-tax rather than after-tax rates of interest. Although there must be some truth to the notion that pensions function as a tax-free savings account, this view alone is inconsistent with the finding (presented below) that the expected value of the pension stream declines with increased age of retirement. Since nothing is withdrawn explicitly from the account until retirement, the value of pension benefits should be strictly increasing with age of retirement under the

Edward P. Lazear is professor of industrial relations, University of Chicago Graduate School of Business, and research associate, National Bureau of Economic Research.

Helpful comments by David Wise are gratefully acknowledged.

savings account interpretation of pensions. The widespread existence of pensions which decline with age of retirement is evidence for the notion that pensions act as a form of severance pay to ensure efficient labor mobility.

Below, a theory of severance pay is presented and specific implications of that theory to pensions are derived. The theory is tested using data which I generated using the 1980 Bankers' Trust *Corporate Pension Plans Study*. The results are then compared to those obtained using a similar data set for 1975 which was analyzed in a previous study (Lazear 1982).

The major findings are:

1. Although severance pay does not always guarantee efficient labor mobility, appropriately chosen severance pay moves the economy in the direction of the perfect information optimum under almost all circumstances.

2. Most major pension plans in both 1975 and 1980 paid a larger expected present value of pension benefits for early retirement. This is consistent with the view that pensions act as severance pay but inconsistent with the notion that pensions are merely a tax-deferred savings account.

3. The structure of pensions between 1975 and 1980 does not appear to have changed dramatically. Either ERISA's (1974) effect was almost fully captured by the 1975 data or it did not have a significant effect on pension values.

4. There was about a 50% increase in the average nominal value of pensions across the board between 1975 and 1980. Additionally, there was over a 100% increase in the value of pensions taken 10 years before the date of normal retirement for pattern skews. This may have been a reaction to changes in the Age Discrimination in Employment Act which restricted mandatory retirement clauses.

The Model

The first task is to derive a simple model of severance pay.[1] To begin, consider a two-period world in which workers are risk neutral. The terms of trade between the worker and firm are set in period 0 and work, if it occurs at all, takes place during period 1. For the moment, we do not elaborate the reasons for setting up a contractual arrangement when a spot market might appear to perform as well or better. Simply take the two-period construct as given.

Define the wage at which trade occurs in period 1 as W, the worker's value to the firm as V, and the value of his alternative use of time as A. If work takes place, the worker receives W, but work does not occur in the event of a "quit" or "layoff," each of which is determined unilaterally. A worker quits if and only if $A > W$ and the firm lays the worker off if and only if $V < W$.

Work is efficient whenever $A < V$. Under these circumstances, appropriate transfers could make all parties better off if work occurs. But if W equals neither A nor V, work will not always occur when it is efficient. To see this, consider figure 3.1. Work is efficient whenever the realization of V, A lies to the southeast of the $A = V$ line. Suppose that the wage which is negotiated is W. The worker quits whenever $A > W$ or whenever the realization of A is above the horizontal line at W. Some of these quits are efficient since the worker quits when $A > W > V$ and when $A > V > W$, both of which imply that $A > V$ so that the separation should occur. But some of those quits are inefficient since the worker also quits when $V > A > W$. These points are shown in the triangle labeled "inefficient quits." The problem is that the worker can unilaterally deter-

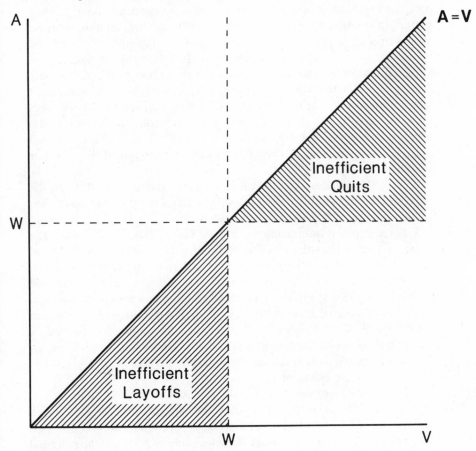

Fig. 3.1

mine a separation and he has no incentive to take into account the fact that although his alternatives are relatively good, he is worth even more to society at his current job.

The converse is also true. The firm unilaterally determines that a layoff occurs whenever $V < W$. In the diagram, layoffs occur whenever the realization of V is to the left of the vertical line at $V = W$. Some of these layoffs are efficient because the firm lays the worker off when $W > A > V$ and when $A > W > V$, both of which imply that $A > V$. Thus a separation should occur. But some are inefficient because the firm also lays workers off when $W > V > A$, shown in the triangle labeled "inefficient layoffs." The problem here is that the firm can unilaterally determine a separation, and it has no incentive to take into account the fact that although the worker is worth little to the firm his alternative use of time is even lower.

Labor market situations seem to resemble this simple set-up. Workers have better information about their alternatives than firms and firms have better information about the worker's worth to the firm than the worker. Wages or wage profiles are somewhat rigidly fixed in advance so that the bilateral monopoly situation which arises after the value of A and V are known does not lead to costly negotiation about how rent is to be split.

Now consider the role of severance pay. Suppose that the agreement which is negotiated at time zero includes the provision that work takes place at wage W, but that a payment S is made from firm to worker if a separation occurs.[2] The worker quits if and only if $A + S > W$ or if and only if $A > W - S$. The firm lays the worker off if and only if $W - V > S$ or if and only if $V > W - S$.

If both W and S are free to vary, severance pay adds nothing to the analysis. We can simply define $W^* = W - S$ and the previous discussion carries over perfectly to this case as well.

Severance pay is interesting when W or S is not free to vary so that the wage that minimizes the loss due to inefficient separation either is not feasible or is undesirable by some other criterion. In the static context, the division of rent provides a motivation for a separate wage and severance pay. Since $V > A$ automatically implies that rent is generated as the result of trade, that rent must be split up. It is desirable that the way in which rent is shared should not affect the allocation of resources. A two-part wage is sufficient to bring this about. The worker receives S even if no work occurs, so $W - S$ is the marginal payment for work and it is this value that affects behavior.

For example, suppose that $V = \bar{V}$ were known with certainty by all parties. Then if $g(A)$ is the density of A, the expected rent associated with the activity is $\bar{V} - \int_{-\infty}^{\bar{V}} A\, g(A)dA$ if no inefficient separation occurs. This value can be realized only if work occurs whenever $A < \bar{V}$. If the marginal payment to work is set equal to $\bar{V}$, a layoff never occurs and quits occur if and only if $A > \bar{V}$. Thus, $W - S = \bar{V}$ is efficient. The split of the rent is a bargaining problem, but it is clear that any level of S chosen is consistent with $W - S = \bar{V}$ because W is free to vary. Thus, the rent-sharing arrangement pays S and the additional degree of freedom provided by W ensures separation efficiency.

A pension can be thought of as this most simple form of severance pay. After signing the contract (becoming vested, perhaps), the worker can quit and receive the pension S, or he can continue to work in which case he receives $W - S$ for work plus a pension of S upon retirement. Below, we enrich the definition of severance pay to encompass the more elaborate forms that pensions take, but the simple notion that a pension may function as a form of severance pay remains.

In this static context, the timing of S is inconsequential. It can be paid during period zero or after period one so that the term "severance pay" may be somewhat misleading. In the dynamic context, the timing of the payment may be crucial. The fact that contracts are not costlessly enforced seems to be a major part of the story and it is this aspect of the problem that makes it necessary that the lump sum part of payment, the severance pay, be paid after employment ceases.

One situation in which it is important that severance pay follow employment arises when effort cannot be monitored costlessly. As has been argued elsewhere (Becker and Stigler 1974; Lazear 1979, 1981), deferred compensation can act as an incentive device to bring about an efficient amount of effort on the job. A pension given on retirement may be regarded as a reward for service well done, and the existence of such a reward induces workers to avoid shirking over their work lives. But a pension awarded only on retirement is not, in general, the best way to produce this result. I have shown that under a number of circumstances it is preferable to combine some pension on retirement with an age-earnings profile which rises more rapidly than worker productivity.

The difficulty associated with steeply rising age-earnings profiles is that they distort the labor supply/separation decision. Mandatory retirement is one institutional adaptation which has arisen to alleviate the harmful effects of that distortion. But the problem is one which affects the worker and firm in all periods of their partnership and is not specific to retirement. In the vocabulary of the earlier discussion, if W exceeds V, then the worker will not leave the job when it is efficient for him to do so. The firm, on the other hand, is too anxious to rid itself of the worker. If V is known to both worker and firm, then it is easy to set up an arrangement that will guarantee both optimal effort and efficient separation. That scheme involves the use of an upward-sloping age-earnings profile with some pension after retirement at the normal age. All separations are initiated by workers except in the case of effort below the required level. Under that circumstance, the worker is fired and loses the right to draw high future salary and perhaps some pension device since the expected present value of the pension, and therefore of the severance pay, varies with age of retirement. Let us formalize the approach.

We broaden our model to consider a situation in which workers remain with a particular firm for a number of periods. Define T as the period of "normal" retirement. (As will be argued below, "normal" retirement is nothing more than the modal age of retirement because, with efficient severance pay, workers leave the firm appropriately.) A typical profile with wage not equal to marginal product is shown in figure 3.2. Here wage, labeled W, starts out below worker's marginal product, V, and then rises above it. The distortion occurs because the worker reacts to the relationship between his alternative, A, and W, rather than to the relationship between his alternative, A, and marginal product, V. Severance pay can eliminate the distortion.

Utility maximization implies that a worker quits and accepts severance pay if two conditions hold: (1) the present value of severance pay plus the alternative stream exceeds the present value of the wage stream in the current firm and (2) the worker cannot do even better by delaying his retirement to some time in the future.[3] In period $T - 1$, the worker retires if

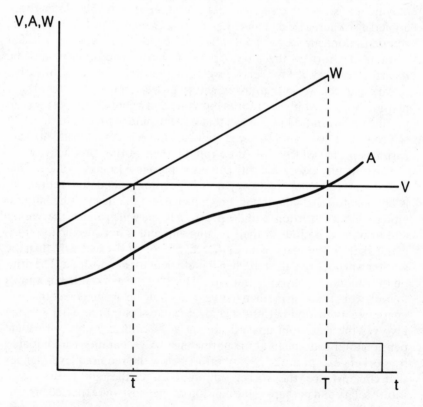

Fig. 3.2

$$(1) \qquad A_{T-1} + S_{T-1} \sum_{\tau=0}^{K+1} \frac{1}{(1+r)^{\tau}} > W_{T-1}$$

$$+ \left(\frac{1}{1+r}\right) S_T \sum_{\tau=0}^{K} \frac{1}{(1+r)^{\tau}}$$

where K is the number of years beyond normal retirement age that the individual lives, S_t is the annual pension payment received from t until death if the worker retires at t, and r is the discount rate.

To induce efficient quitting behavior, it is necessary that the l.h.s. of (1) exceeds the r.h.s. of (1) if and only if $A_{T-1} > V_{T-1}$. If $P_{T-1} \equiv S_{T-1} \sum_{\tau=0}^{K+1} 1/(1+r)^{\tau}$ and $P_T \equiv S_T \sum_{\tau=0}^{K} 1/(1+r)^{\tau}$, then choose P_T and P_{T-1} so that

$$(2) \qquad P_{T-1} - \left(\frac{1}{1+r}\right) P_T = W_{T-1} - V_{T-1}.$$

Substitution of (2) into (1) yields the necessary and sufficient condition that the worker quits if

$$A_{T-1} + W_{T-1} - V_{T-1} > W_{T-1}$$

or

$$(3) \qquad A_{T-1} > V_{T-1}.$$

Since this is the efficiency condition, the severance pay arrangement results in efficient turnover.

Now consider that decision at $T-2$. The worker resigns at $T-2$ if and only if two conditions hold: First, the present value of retiring at $T-2$ and receiving severance pay must exceed the present value of continuing to work until $T-1$ and retiring then, taking the $T-1$ severance pay. Second, the present value of retiring at $T-2$ with severance pay must exceed the present value of working until T and taking the normal pension. If we make the assumption that $A_t > V_t$ implies $A_{t'} > V_{t'}$ for $t' > t$, then the second condition becomes redundant (demonstrated below).

Consider the first condition: A worker retires at $T-2$ rather than at $T-1$ if and only if

$$(4) \qquad \begin{aligned} & A_{T-2} + \frac{E_{T-2}(A_{T-1})}{1+r} + S_{T-2} \sum_{\tau=0}^{K+2} \frac{1}{(1+r)^{\tau}} > W_{T-2} \\ & + \frac{E_{T-2}(A_{T-1})}{1+r} + \frac{S_{T-1}}{1+r} \sum_{\tau=0}^{K+1} \frac{1}{(1+r)^{\tau}}, \end{aligned}$$

where $E_{T-1}(A_{T-1})$ is the expectation of the alternative wage offer at $T-2$ given the information at $T-2$.

For efficiency, it is necessary that the l.h.s. of (4) exceed the r.h.s. if and only if $A_{T-2} > V_{T-2}$ (which by assumption, implies $A_{T-1} > V_{T-1}$). An efficient pension plan sets

$$P_{T-2} - \frac{1}{(1+r)} P_{T-1} = W_{T-2} - V_{T-2},$$

or

(5)

$$\frac{S_{T-2} \sum\limits_{\tau=0}^{K+2} \left(\frac{1}{1+r}\right)^{\tau} - \frac{S_{T-1}}{1+r}}{\sum\limits_{\tau=0}^{K+1} \left(\frac{1}{1+r}\right)^{\tau}} = W_{T-2} - V_{T-2}.$$

To see this, substitute (5) into (4). The worker opts to leave if and only if

(6) $$A_{T-2} + W_{T-2} - V_{T-2} > W_{T-2}$$

or if $A_{T-2} > V_{T-2}$, which is the efficiency condition.

Note also that if $A_{T-2} > V_{T-2}$, the worker chooses retirement at $T-2$ over retirement at T. The second condition is redundant. Since $A_{T-2} > V_{T-2}$ implies $A_{T-1} > V_{T-1}$, the efficient pension plan already ensures that inequality (3) holds as well. Since the efficient pension at $T-1$ induced retirement at $T-1$ whenever $A_{T-1} > V_{T-1}$, it is clear that retirement at $T-2$ dominates retirement at $T-1$.

This provides a general statement of the efficient pension:

(7) $$P_{T-i} - \frac{P_{T-i+1}}{1+r} = W_{T-i} - V_{T-i}$$

or

(7′)

$$\frac{S_{T-i} \sum\limits_{\tau=0}^{K+i} \left(\frac{1}{1+r}\right)^{\tau} - \frac{1}{1+r} S_{T-i+1}}{\sum\limits_{\tau=0}^{K+i-1} \left(\frac{1}{1+r}\right)^{\tau}} = W_{T-i} - V_{T-i}$$

so

(8) $$P_{T-i} = \sum_{\tau=1}^{i} (W_{T-\tau} - V_{T-\tau}) \left(\frac{1}{1+r}\right)^{i-\tau} + \frac{P_T}{(1+r)^i}.$$

The terminal value, P_T, is exogenous to this problem. It might be the optimal pension to prevent shirking in the final period before retirement or simply a rent-sharing parameter.

It is through equations (7) and (8) that we derive our results. If the wages of old workers exceed their marginal products, then the present value of the pension falls as the age of retirement rises (eq. [7]). Similarly, equation (7) provides us with an estimate of the difference between W and V at each point in time because P_{T-i} and P_{T-i+1} are observed.

The case of postponed retirement is equivalent. Normal retirement is not special once we allow pension benefits to vary with the date of retirement. The date of "normal retirement" is likely to be the date of modal retirement. In almost all cases that age is 65 and corresponds to the start of social security payments because the social security earnings test causes the $A(t)$ function to take a discrete jump upward at age 65. Except for this detail, the analysis of postponed retirement is similar. The worker's choice is still reflected by (1) so all holds as above with a replacement of subscripts. If j is the number of years after normal retirement, then retirement occurs if and only if

$$A_{T+j} + S_{T+j} \sum_{\tau=0}^{K-j} \left(\frac{1}{1+r}\right)^{\tau} > W_{T+j}$$

(1')

$$+ \frac{S_{T+j+1}}{1+r} \sum_{\tau=0}^{K-(j+1)} \left(\frac{1}{1+r}\right)^{\tau}.$$

Equations (7), (7'), and (8) follow correspondingly, so that an estimate of $W - V$ can be obtained for those years after T as well by examining the way in which pension benefits decline in late retirement.

Let us summarize this section. The pension which acts as severance pay reduces the true wage to V when we take into account the way that the pension value falls with experience. Since the pension is not paid if the separation is punishment for too little effort, incentives are maintained while efficient turnover is produced. Employers are willing to buy out of a long term contract if the wage rate exceeds VMP. The amount that employers are willing to pay reveals something about the difference between W and V. Pensions may act as a buyout. If the value of the pension declines with the age of retirement, this suggests that the pension plays the role of severance pay.

3.1.1 Less Than Perfect Separation Efficiency

The model discussed earlier allowed V to be random and unknown by both parties. Under these circumstances, one instrument—in this case the pension stream $P(t)$—is not sufficient to eliminate all inefficient separation. The reason is that when the firm uniquely knows the value of the worker to the firm, the only way to make that information useful is to give the firm some discretion over when work occurs. But to do this immediately creates a problem, because the firm is anxious to sever the worker whenever $V < W - S$. This leads to situations where $A < V < W - S$, so that a layoff occurs when a separation is inefficient.

The introduction of a second instrument can alleviate some of this difficulty. If different amounts of severance pay are paid depending upon who initiates the separation, some inefficient layoffs and quits can be eliminated. This raises two difficulties. First, it creates a situation where each side tries to induce the other to initiate the separation. Second, it generates inefficient retention as a biproduct. This occurs when $W - L < V < A < W - Q$, where Q is what is paid to the worker as severance pay if the worker initiates the separation and L is what is paid to the worker if the firm initiates the separation. If $L = Q$ this condition can never hold, but for $L > Q$, inefficient retention occurs. This is discussed in depth in Hall and Lazear (1982). It is also shown that it is never optimal to select $L < Q$ because this results in needless inefficient separations. Perhaps because of these difficulties and those associated with determining who actually initiated the separation, pensions rarely vary with the identity of the initiating party.

3.1.2   Vesting

Vesting is an issue that always arises when pensions are discussed. This seems especially relevant when one of the arguments for incorporating a pension into the generalized compensation plan relates to incentives for increased effort or reduced turnover. It is sometimes suggested that nonvested pensions can reduce worker turnover whereas vested pensions cannot. The model in the previous section should make clear that "vesting" in and of itself has little meaning.

Vesting guarantees that a worker is entitled to receive currently accrued benefits. But currently accrued benefits may be small indeed until the last few years before retirement. There are a number of reasons which all derive from the large number of degrees of freedom inherent in setting up a benefit formula. First, many benefit formulas depend upon final salary or an average of salaries earned in the last few years before retirement. Because salary grows with age and, in an inflationary period, with chronological time, the benefits received by a worker who leaves the firm at age 30 may be much smaller than those received by the same worker if he leaves at age 65. Second, because length of service affects benefits, formulas can be specified to make the accrual rate a convex function of years of service, placing a premium on long tenure. Third, as Bulow points out, a worker who is vested but below the age at which early retirement benefits can be received earns a promise of a pension at normal retirement age, not the benefits themselves. Because of the higher value of pensions taken on early retirement, remaining with the firm at least until the age of early retirement election is generally lucrative.

In the same vein, the tendency of many plans to gear pension benefits to final salary is evidence for the incentive role of pensions. Most other rationalizations for pensions (discussed below) at best gear pensions to a lifetime average rather than to an average of final salaries. Since final salary can be adjusted to reflect worker effort, hours worked, and productivity, the multiplier effect on the pension value may provide significant incentives for workers to maintain effort and a high level of hours worked during those final years.

3.2 The Empirical Analysis

3.2.1 Data

The data for this analysis were constructed using two sources: the Bankers' Trust *Study of Corporate Pension Plans 1975* and the Bankers' Trust *Corporate Pension Plan Study (1980)*. Each of these studies consists of a detailed verbal description of the pension plans of over 200 of the nation's largest corporations. The data sets apply to approximately 8–10 million workers, and this comprises about one-fourth of the entire covered population.

Firms are not identified by name in the descriptions. However, enough detail is given about each firm so that it is possible to match up firms in the 1975 and 1980 samples. For example, the descriptions report the industry in which the firm produces, the date at which the pension plan was adopted and amended, and the number and types of employees covered by the plan. Screening on the basis of these and other criteria resulted in a longitudinal data set of 70 matched firms for the two years in addition to the two cross sections of 200 + firms for each year.

The major empirical task was to convert the verbal descriptions into machine-readable data. This required setting up a coding system that was specific enough to capture all of the essential detail associated with each plan. It was then necessary to write a program which calculates the present value of pension benefits at each age of retirement. A brief summary of that approach follows.

Pension benefit formulas assume three different types. The two most common fall under the rubric of defined-benefit plans. A defined-benefit plan specifies the pension flow as a fixed payment determined by some formula. The pattern plan awards a flat dollar amount per year worked to the recipient on retirement. The conventional plan calculates the pension benefit flow from a formula which depends on years of service and some average salary. In contrast to the defined-benefit plans are the defined-contribution plans in which the employer (or employee) contributes a specified amount each year during the work life to a pension fund. The flow of pension benefits that the worker receives upon retirement is then a function of the market value of that fund. The defined-contribution plan is much less frequently used than is either the pattern plan or the conventional plan.

In order to test the theory exposited above, it is necessary to obtain estimates of the expected present value of pension benefits for each potential year of retirement. Specifically, the way in which pension values vary with age of retirement must be calculated. Some plans do not permit the individual to receive early retirement benefits or only permit early retirement up to a given number of years before the normal date. This means that in order to perform the necessary comparisons, sometimes plans had to be deleted from the relevant sample so that the entire series of retirement values would be valid.

It is important to realize that there are no real individuals in this sample. Since the data sets discussed above are descriptions of pension plans, the "individuals" below are hypothetical ones, created to perform the necessary simulation exercises. For each plan, for each of the two years, 12 "typical" employees were created, having all combinations of salary on normal retirement of $9,000, $15,000, $25,000 and $50,000 and of tenure of 10, 20, and 30 years in 1975 and 20, 30, and 40 years in 1980. Much of the analysis below relates to these 2,928 "individuals" from 244 plans in 1975 and to the 2,712 "individuals" from the 226 plans in 1980. Because this simulation exercise was computationally expensive, a representative group was selected having salary of $25,000 and tenure of 30 years on normal retirement. Many of the comparative statics results below are derived from an examination of the individuals in this representative sample.

In order to calculate the expected present value of retirement at each age, two steps must be taken. First, for any hypothetical employee, the pension flow that he receives on retirement in any given year must be calculated. Second, that flow must be converted into an expected present value by discounting it appropriately and by taking into account the age-specific death rates. Even the first step is far from straightforward.

Most plans have many restrictions on the maximum amount which can be accrued, and many provide for minimum benefits. Additionally, a number reduce pension benefits by some fraction of the social security benefits to which some basic class is entitled. Moreover, a number of plans provide supplements for retirement before the social security eligibility age. Sometimes these supplements relate directly to social security payments; at other times they depend on the individual's salary or benefit level.

Other restrictions have to do with vesting requirements, with the maximum age at which the individual begins employment, and with the minimum number of years served before the basic accrual or particular supplements are applicable. The accrual rate, or flat dollar amount per year to which the individual is entitled, is often a nonlinear function of tenure and salary, and these kinks had to be programmed into the calculations.

In calculating retirement benefits, assumptions about wage growth for older workers are crucial. All plans which are based on salary compute some average of annual earnings over some relevant period. Therefore, it is nominal earnings growth that will affect the pension values. Elsewhere (Lazear 1981) I estimated earnings growth and found something that is well known among labor economists: earnings growth is often negative in final years because hours of work decline (primarily for health reasons) in the final years before retirement. In the sample I examined, based on CPS data from the mid 1970s, the estimate of earnings growth for a particular synthetic cohort was anywhere from -2% to -13% depending on how the sample was selected. Because more rapid wage growth will tend to make pension values increase with the age of retirement, selecting higher rates of wage growth tends to push the results against the theory of this chapter. To be conservative, I selected a wage growth rate of zero for most of the analysis and also recalculated pension benefits with a growth rate of positive 5%, well above that actually observed in the data.

Since all values are nominal, the nominal interest rate should be used as the discount factor. For most of the analysis 10% was used, but 15% and 5% were also tried in order to ascertain the sensitivity of the results to the choice of discount rate. Although varying the rates had some effects, it did not alter the qualitative conclusions.

Finally, in performing the actuarial correction, it was necessary to choose a life table. The 1975 life table for Americans was used for the 1975 sample and the 1978 table was used for the 1980 sample. Both were obtained from the U.S. Vital Statistics. The choice of table turns out to be the least crucial part of the analysis. Values do not vary greatly from year to year and discounting makes what small differences there are unimportant. What is important, however, is the possibility that early retirees do not have the same life expectancy of normal retirees. It is likely that many individuals retire early as the result of poor health and consequently have higher age-specific death rates. If this is true, then ignoring those differences will tend to bias the results in the direction of higher pension values for early retirees than is actually the case.

3.2.2   Findings

We start by discussing the data from the 1980 sample. Table 3.1 contains some descriptive statistics. Notice that there is a tremendous amount of variation in the present value of pension benefits even within each salary-tenure group. For all "workers" taken together the standard deviation is as large as the mean. Within each salary-tenure group, the standard deviation is around half of the mean. A simple rule of thumb suggests that the mean pension value is about one-thirteenth of the product of final salary and tenure at retirement. It is somewhat more than this for very low-salary workers and slightly less than this for high-salary workers. This reflects the provisions for both maximum and minimum pension values which make the benefit structure progressive.

Table 3.1 **1980 Data: Moments of the Expected Present Value of Normal Retirement Benefits (Sample Selection Criterion: EPV − 0 Valid)**

Salary ($)	Tenure (Years)	Mean	Standard Deviation	N
9,000	20	17,102	8,063	218
9,000	30	25,209	11,144	220
9,000	40	32,676	14,610	221
15,000	20	23,054	10,597	220
15,000	30	34,167	14,100	220
15,000	40	44,020	18,027	221
25,000	20	37,367	19,140	221
25,000	30	55,353	26,110	221
25,000	40	70,779	32,897	221
50,000	20	75,730	44,270	221
50,000	30	111,368	61,755	221
50,000	40	140,551	77,253	221
All		55,690	50,636	2,646

Before going further, it is interesting to compare this to the cross section from 1975. Those data are presented in table 3.2. Although the average pension value is smaller in 1975 than in 1980, this is the result of differences across groups. The 1975 data are constructed using hypothetical workers with 10, 20, and 30 years of tenure, whereas the 1980 data are constructed using hypothetical workers with 20, 30, and 40 years of tenure. In fact, within each comparable salary-tenure group, the values

Table 3.2 **1975 Data: Moments of Expected Present Value of Normal Retirement Benefits (Sample Criterion: EPV − 0 Valid)**

Salary ($)	Tenure (Years)	Mean	Standard Deviation	N
9,000	10	10,624	3,921	192
9,000	20	20,864	7,700	194
9,000	30	30,403	11,411	183
15,000	10	16,416	7,008	194
15,000	20	31,359	14,116	204
15,000	30	47,369	20,118	186
25,000	10	26,125	13,869	199
25,000	20	51,337	26,328	206
25,000	30	76,989	39,165	188
50,000	10	50,931	31,338	205
50,000	20	101,462	60,683	206
50,000	30	151,337	90,222	188
All		55,690	50,636	2,646

for 1975 are significantly higher than those for 1980. We defer until later discussion of the reasons for this pattern. Another interesting difference is that the pattern is significantly less progressive in 1975 than in 1980. In 1975, the rule that the pension value equals about one-tenth of the product of final salary and tenure seems to hold across all salary levels with only slight traces of progressivity.

These findings do not suggest that pensions were larger in 1975 than in 1980. There are two main reasons: First, firms are not matched across years in these tables, so that some of the difference may simply reflect random sample variations. Second, final salaries were substantially higher in 1980 than in 1975, so the relevant comparison is not necessarily the one that holds salary level constant.

In the context of the model, the most important results relate to the way in which pension values vary with the age of retirement. Tables 3.3–3.5 select those "individuals" in the 1980 sample who were permitted to retire at least 10 years before the normal age and trace the mean present value of pensions for that group. EPV $-$ 10 refers to the expected present value of retiring 10 years before the normal age, and similarly for EPV $-$ 9 . . . EPV $-$ 1. EPV $-$ 0 is the present value of retiring at normal age. The tables are broken down by pension benefit formula type and then by salary and tenure level.

First examine table 3.3, which relates to conventional plans. Note that for all tenure-salary groups, the value of early retirement exceeds that of normal retirement (EPV $-$ 10 $>$ EPV $-$ 9 $>$ . . . $>$ EPR $-$ 1 $>$ EPV $-$ 0). For ease of reading, ERAT(t) is defined as EPV(t)/EPR0, so that ERAT $>$ 1 for all $t < 0$. This evidence supports the major prediction of the model: The expected present value of pension benefits declines as the age of retirement increases. Firms actually do "buy out" workers who retire early with higher pensions. As such, the interpretation that pensions act as severance pay is consistent with these results.

Further, ERAT $-$ 10 increases with tenure and salary. The buy-out is larger, not only in absolute terms, but also in relative terms for employees of longer service and of higher salaries. This is consistent with the interpretation that an upward-sloping age-earnings profile acts as an incentive device.

This is most easily seen by examining WVDIFF $-$ 10 . . . WVDIFF $-$ 1. WVDIFF(t) is defined as $W_{T-t} - V_{T-t}$ and is calculated using the relationship shown in equation (7). WVDIFF $>$ 0 implies that the worker is being paid more than his marginal product, and it results whenever $P_{T-i} > P_{T-i+1}$. WVDIFF $-$ 1/SALARY is the ratio of over-payment during the final year before retirement. That ratio goes from 1/6 for workers in the group with salary = 9,000, tenure = 20 to 1/2 for workers in the group with salary = 50,000, tenure = 40. This result has a nice interpretation.

Table 3.3   1980 Expected Present Value of Pension Benefits: Defined-Benefit
                   Conventional Plans
                   (Sample: Valid EPV − 10 . . . EPV − 0)

Variable	Final Salary $9,000			Final Salary $15,000		
	20-Year Tenure	30-Year Tenure	40-Year Tenure	20-Year Tenure	30-Year Tenure	40-Year Tenure
EPV − 10	27,225	50,845	73,959	35,384	66,875	97,232
EPV − 9	26,911	48,451	69,381	35,391	64,506	92,318
EPV − 8	26,392	45,905	64,904	35,116	61,886	87,459
EPV − 7	25,684	43,266	60,506	34,603	59,074	83,620
EPV − 6	24,856	40,687	56,288	33,945	56,211	77,814
EPV − 5	23,868	38,216	52,277	33,162	53,484	73,241
EPV − 4	22,752	35,594	48,218	32,058	50,344	68,345
EPV − 3	21,496	32,993	44,277	30,634	47,113	63,512
EPV − 2	20,089	30,311	40,347	28,890	43,598	58,377
EPV − 1	18,699	27,785	36,690	27,146	40,278	53,594
EPV − 0	17,032	24,839	31,624	24,846	36,166	45,962
ERAT − 10	1.617	2.131	2.517	1.550	2.122	2.542
ERAT − 9	1.609	2.038	2.372	1.553	2.041	2.407
ERAT − 8	1.587	1.939	2.228	1.541	1.955	2.274
ERAT − 7	1.552	1.835	2.085	1.519	1.865	2.143
ERAT − 6	1.509	1.733	1.946	1.490	1.773	2.013
ERAT − 5	1.453	1.636	1.815	1.456	1.686	1.891
ERAT − 4	1.389	1.528	1.679	1.409	1.587	1.762
ERAT − 3	1.317	1.421	1.547	1.349	1.485	1.636
ERAT − 2	1.234	1.307	1.412	1.274	1.373	1.502
ERAT − 1	1.151	1.201	1.287	1.198	1.268	1.377
ERAT − 0	1.000	1.000	1.000	1.000	1.000	1.000
WVDIFF − 10	121	922	1,764	− 2	913	1,894
WVDIFF − 9	220	1,079	1,898	116	1,111	2,060
WVDIFF − 8	330	1,231	2,051	238	1,311	2,257
WVDIFF − 7	424	1,323	2,164	337	1,469	2,466
WVDIFF − 6	557	1,394	2,264	441	1,539	2,581
WVDIFF − 5	693	1,628	2,519	685	1,949	3,040
WVDIFF − 4	857	1,776	2,691	972	2,206	3,300
WVDIFF − 3	1,056	2,015	2,952	1,310	2,640	3,857
WVDIFF − 2	1,148	2,087	3,022	1,441	2,743	3,952
WVDIFF − 1	1,515	2,678	4,605	2,090	3,738	6,938
NORMAL	2,911	4,267	5,282	4,759	6,994	8,679
N	133	133	134	140	141	144

First consider tenure: Individuals with shorter tenure are those who initiated their employment with the firm more recently. In the context of figure 3.2, those workers are less likely to have wages which exceed their marginal products. As the result, the buy-out should be smaller. In fact, for individuals whose tenure is below $\bar{T}$ in figure 3.2, the buy-out should

Final Salary $25,000			Final Salary $50,000		
20-Year Tenure	30-Year Tenure	40-Year Tenure	20-Year Tenure	30-Year Tenure	40-Year Tenure
55,958	107,585	158,225	115,633	226,685	332,604
56,822	105,111	151,713	118,342	222,374	319,890
57,200	101,951	144,918	119,778	216,465	306,211
57,081	98,212	137,902	120,120	209,160	291,814
56,522	94,213	130,778	119,398	201,062	276,943
55,604	90,176	123,844	117,706	192,441	261,907
54,142	85,524	116,234	114,845	182,598	245,945
52,165	80,656	108,553	110,988	172,413	229,942
49,549	75,143	100,236	105,770	160,908	212,544
46,903	69,863	92,429	100,288	149,675	195,920
43,244	63,165	79,476	92,555	135,577	168,913
1.601	2.285	2.836	1.972	2.993	3.816
1.619	2.212	2.694	1.996	2.887	3.609
1.623	2.129	2.550	2.000	2.770	3.401
1.612	2.039	2.406	1.985	2.644	3.194
1.590	1.944	2.263	1.953	2.512	2.989
1.557	1.850	2.126	1.908	2.378	2.789
1.512	1.747	1.982	1.847	2.236	2.590
1.456	1.641	1.840	1.776	2.094	2.395
1.380	1.522	1.689	1.680	1.936	2.192
1.303	1.408	1.549	1.581	1.784	2.000
1.000	1.000	1.000	1.000	1.000	1.000
−332	953	2,510	−1,044	1,661	4,901
−160	1,340	2,881	−609	2,506	5,801
55	1,744	3,272	−159	3,408	6,716
286	2,052	3,655	370	4,155	7,641
518	2,278	3,914	955	4,866	8,476
908	2,888	4,725	1,776	6,112	9,910
1,350	3,324	5,245	2,634	6,956	10,930
1,964	4,141	6,249	3,920	8,644	13,071
2,187	4,363	6,451	4,531	9,282	13,738
3,326	6,089	11,775	7,029	12,816	24,551
7,885	11,608	14,363	15,783	23,258	28,787
141	144	144	143	144	144

actually be negative. (Although this occurs in a significant number of cases, it does not occur frequently enough to make the means display an increasing pattern.)

Second, high-salary workers are those most likely to be performing jobs where wage incentive schemes are useful. Since those may be the

Table 3.4   1980 Expected Value of Pension Benefits: Defined-Contribution
             Pattern Plans
             (Benefits are Independent of Final Salary)

Variable	20-Year Tenure	30-Year Tenure	40-Year Tenure
EPV – 10	20,450	40,651	64,349
EPV – 9	21,085	40,103	61,913
EPV – 8	21,513	39,296	59,276
EPV – 7	21,704	38,262	56,477
EPV – 6	21,667	37,031	53,554
EPV – 5	21,454	36,164	51,868
EPV – 4	21,053	34,485	48,489
EPV – 3	20,498	32,716	45,117
EPV – 2	19,730	30,752	41,577
EPV – 1	18,863	28,767	38,430
EPV – 0	17,982	26,876	35,361
ERAT – 10	1.113	1.491	1.810
ERAT – 9	1.150	1.473	1.743
ERAT – 8	1.176	1.446	1.670
ERAT – 7	1.189	1.410	1.592
ERAT – 6	1.190	1.367	1.510
ERAT – 5	1.180	1.334	1.461
ERAT – 4	1.161	1.274	1.367
ERAT – 3	1.132	1.210	1.272
ERAT – 2	1.092	1.140	1.173
ERAT – 1	1.047	1.068	1.085
ERAT – 0	1.000	1.000	1.000
WVDIFF – 10	– 244	211	939
WVDIFF – 9	– 181	342	1,118
WVDIFF – 8	– 89	482	1,305
WVDIFF – 7	13	631	1,500
WVDIFF – 6	126	489	951
WVDIFF – 5	249	1,042	2,098
WVDIFF – 4	378	1,208	2,303
WVDIFF – 3	577	1,475	2,659
WVDIFF – 2	716	1,640	2,600
WVDIFF – 1	801	1,718	2,789
NORMAL	2,766	4,123	5,421
N	38	38	38

jobs which are most difficult to monitor, a large penalty in the form of lost earnings is likely to be an integral part of the optimal compensation profile for these workers.

These points are also supported by consideration of table 3.4, which relates to pattern plan workers. It is also true that the general tendency is for the pension value to decline with age of retirement. But the decline does not seem to be as pronounced for these employees as for those with conventional plans. In fact, for those with only 20 years of experience at normal retirement, the means of WVDIFF − 10, WVDIFF − 9, and WVDIFF − 8 are actually positive, reflecting location in terms of figure 3.2 before $\bar{t}$. Since most of these workers are blue-collar workers where more direct monitoring is possible, it is not surprising that the wages conform more to marginal product for these workers than for their higher-level counterparts.

Finally, table 3.5 reports defined-contribution plans. We hesitate to draw any significant conclusions from this table for two reasons. First, there are so few observations. Second, the Bankers' Trust studies do not really report the appropriate information for defined-contribution plans, so these calculations are more likely to be a function of interpretations made by them and by me. The one obvious feature is that definitionally a defined-contribution plan cannot decline in present value with age of retirement because the worker is always entitled to the present value of his contributions. Since contributions are never negative, that value must grow with age of retirement (although not necessarily at the same rate).

It is also true that pensions associated with retirement after the normal age should follow the same pattern of decline with age. Most of the sample was subject to mandatory retirement, but 13 conventional plans did allow the worker to elect to remain beyond the date of normal retirement. Table 3.6 presents information on those individuals. Since the pattern is similar across salary and tenure groups, we only report those calculations for a representative group with salary = 25,000 and tenure = 30. The pattern of declining pension values is the same and smooth both before and after normal retirement.

It is interesting that this group for which there is no mandatory retirement has more steeply declining pensions than the group which does not distinguish on the basis of mandatory retirement. Compare ERAT(t) in table 3.6 with that for the corresponding group (salary = 30,000, tenure = 30) in tables 3.3–3.5 and it is clear that pensions decline more rapidly in table 3.6. This suggests that reductions in pensions are an alternative to mandatory retirement.[4]

The 1975 cross section provides a basis for comparison. Results for the representative group are reported in table 3.7. In comparing these values with those for the appropriate groups in tables 3.3–3.5 two things stand out. First, for pattern plans, the pensions are higher in the 1980 cross section than in the 1975 cross section, while the reverse is true for conventional plans. Second, the decline in pension value with age of retirement is sharper in 1975 than in 1980 for pattern plans while the reverse is true for conventional plans. We defer attempts to explain these findings until after discussion of the matched sample because these differences may simply reflect random sampling variation across firms rather than trends over time.

Table 3.5   **1980 Expected Present Value of Pension Benefits:**
Defined-Contribution Conventional Plans
(Sample: Valid EPV − 10 . . . EPV − 0)

	Final Salary $9,000			Final Salary $15,000		
Variable	20-Year Tenure	30-Year Tenure	40-Year Tenure	20-Year Tenure	30-Year Tenure	40-Year Tenure
EPV − 10	12,673	25,346	38,019	18,342	36,685	55,028
EPV − 9	14,915	28,475	42,035	21,588	41,214	60,840
EPV − 8	17,256	31,636	46,016	24,975	45,789	66,602
EPV − 7	19,670	34,800	49,931	28,469	50,369	72,269
EPV − 6	22,131	37,940	53,749	32,033	54,913	77,794
EPV − 5	24,615	41,025	57,435	35,627	59,379	83,130
EPV − 4	26,280	42,705	59,130	38,037	61,810	85,584
EPV − 3	27,865	44,257	60,649	40,332	64,056	87,781
EPV − 2	28,500	44,334	60,168	41,251	64,168	87,086
EPV − 1	28,995	44,255	59,516	41,966	64,054	86,142
EPV − 0	29,344	44,016	58,689	42,472	63,708	84,944
ERAT − 10	0.431	0.575	0.647	0.431	0.575	0.647
ERAT − 9	0.508	0.646	0.716	0.508	0.646	0.716
ERAT − 8	0.588	0.718	0.784	0,588	0.718	0.784
ERAT − 7	0.670	0.790	0.850	0.670	0.790	0.850
ERAT − 6	0.754	0.861	0.915	0.754	0.861	0.915
ERAT − 5	0.838	0.932	0.978	0.838	0.932	0.978
ERAT − 4	0.895	0.970	1.007	0.895	0.970	1.007
ERAT − 3	0.949	1.005	1.033	0.949	1.005	1.033
ERAT − 2	0.971	1.007	1.025	0.971	1.007	1.025
ERAT − 1	0.988	1.005	1.014	0.988	1.005	1.014
ERAT − 0	1.000	1.000	1.000	1.000	1.000	1.000
WVDIFF − 10	− 864	− 1,206	− 1,548	− 1,251	− 1,745	− 2,240
WVDIFF − 9	− 992	− 1,340	− 1,688	− 1,436	− 1,940	− 2,443
WVDIFF − 8	− 1,126	− 1,476	− 1,826	− 1,629	− 2,136	− 2,643
WVDIFF − 7	− 1,263	− 1,611	− 1,958	− 1,828	− 2,331	− 2,835
WVDIFF − 6	− 1,401	− 1,741	− 2,081	− 2,028	− 2,520	− 3,012
WVDIFF − 5	− 1,033	− 1,043	− 1,052	− 1,496	− 1,509	− 1,523
WVDIFF − 4	− 1,082	− 1,059	− 1,036	− 1,567	− 1,534	− 1,500
WVDIFF − 3	− 477	− 58	360	− 690	− 84	522
WVDIFF − 2	− 408	65	539	− 591	94	780
WVDIFF − 1	− 317	217	752	− 459	314	1,088
NORMAL	4,560	6,840	9,120	6,600	9,900	13,200
N	1	1	1	1	1	1

[7]

The one obvious feature is again that the expected present value of pension benefits declines with increases in the age of retirement. Both years provide strong support of that conclusion. Again, this is consistent with the idea that pensions function as severance pay in an efficient compensation scheme.

Final Salary $25,000			Final Salary $50,000		
20-Year Tenure	30-Year Tenure	40-Year Tenure	20-Year Tenure	30-Year Tenure	40-Year Tenure
79,855	92,130	104,405	110,490	130,873	151,256
74,546	87,680	103,924	104,846	127,313	150,007
70,081	84,009	112,287	100,447	124,857	156,816
66,364	83,964	120,471	97,148	123,350	170,478
63,310	90,640	128,407	94,808	129,091	183,789
60,836	97,162	136,028	93,295	139,642	196,637
62,885	102,189	141,492	91,610	148,476	206,947
67,321	106,923	146,524	98,781	156,887	216,587
70,731	110,026	149,322	105,018	163,361	223,525
73,865	112,742	151,618	110,929	169,314	229,722
76,686	115,029	153,372	116,434	174,652	235,071
0.916	0.754	0.673	0.760	0.654	0.597
0.876	0.738	0.685	0.747	0.661	0.614
0.846	0.727	0.742	0.744	0.673	0.655
0.825	0.742	0.798	0.748	0.689	0.717
0.810	0.803	0.853	0.759	0.734	0.777
0.802	0.862	0.905	0.775	0.798	0.835
0.835	0.905	0.940	0.786	0.850	0.880
0.892	0.945	0.971	0.849	0.899	0.923
0.932	0.966	0.984	0.902	0.936	0.952
0.968	0.985	0.993	0.953	0.969	0.977
1.000	1.000	1.000	1.000	1.000	1.000
2,046	1,715	185	2,175	1,372	481
1,893	1,557	−3,546	1,865	1,041	−2,887
1,733	20	−3,817	1,539	702	−6,373
1,567	−3,425	−4,072	1,200	−2,945	−6,830
1,396	−3,681	−4,301	853	−5,956	−7,252
−1,272	−3,121	−3,393	1,046	−5,484	−6,401
−3,030	−3,233	−3,436	−4,897	−5,745	−6,583
−2,561	−2,331	−2,101	−4,686	−4,864	−5,213
−2,590	−2,244	−1,898	−4,885	−4,919	−5,121
−2,564	−2,079	−1,594	−5,004	−4,852	−4,863
11,916	17,875	23,833	18,777	28,166	37,555
2	2	2	3	3	3

There are some obvious institutional differences between the 1980 period and 1975. The most obvious is that the primary social security benefit, against which many benefit formulas are offset, increased between 1975 and 1980. In order to determine the effect of social security on the calculations, the 1980 analysis was repeated, plugging in the 1975

Table 3.6   **1980 Expected Present Value of Pension Benefits: Defined-Benefit Conventional Plans**
(Sample: Valid EPV − 10 through EPV + 10)
Salary = $25,000, Tenure = 30 Years

Variable	Value	Variable	Value
EPV − 10	172,152	ERAT − 10	1.837
EPV − 9	164,207	ERAT − 9	1.755
EPV − 8	155,953	ERAT − 8	1.670
EPV − 7	147,497	ERAT − 7	1.583
EPV − 6	139,459	ERAT − 6	1.499
EPV − 5	131,337	ERAT − 5	1.415
EPV − 4	123,435	ERAT − 4	1.335
EPV − 3	115,517	ERAT − 3	1.253
EPV − 2	107,090	ERAT − 2	1.167
EPV − 1	98,892	ERAT − 1	1.083
EPV − 0	90,864	ERAT − 0	1.000
EPV + 1	81,761	ERAT + 1	0.899
EPV + 2	73,155	ERAT + 2	0.805
EPV + 3	65,256	ERAT + 3	0.719
EPV + 4	57,955	ERAT + 4	0.639
EPV + 5	51,232	ERAT + 5	0.565
EPV + 6	45,070	ERAT + 6	0.497
EPV + 7	39,446	ERAT + 7	0.435
EPV + 8	34,337	ERAT + 8	0.379
EPV + 9	29,718	ERAT + 9	0.328
EPV + 10	25,562	ERAT + 10	0.282
$N = 13$			

primary social security formula. Since that value was lower than the 1980 value, pensions increased. That is, some benefit formulas usually subtract some fraction of social security benefits from pension payments. Over time the amount subtracted has increased. Table 3.8 (col. 2) presents the results for the representative group (salary = 25,000, tenure = 30).

Pension benefits for 1980 in column 2 with the 1975 social security formula are about 7% higher than those using the 1980 formula for conventional plans. Although it is difficult to state the increase in primary social security benefits as a scalar, for the average worker that increase amounted to 68%. Thus the "elasticity" of the mean of pension benefits with respect to social security benefits is 0.1. It is less than one primarily for two reasons: First, not all plans offset social security payments. Second, even those that do offset benefits do not do so fully. No pattern plans had social security offset provisions.

A general point is that, because of the way that benefits are offset against social security primary benefits, any change in those benefits has major impacts on pensions and therefore on retirement and tax revenues. We do not explore those implications here.

Table 3.7   1975 Expected Present Value of Pension Benefits
                 (Sample: Valid EPV − 10 . . . EPV − 0)

| | Group | | |
| | Defined Benefits | | Defined Contribution |
Variable	Conventional	Pattern	
EPV − 10	125,113	33,779	62,454
EPV − 9	120,062	32,585	62,016
EPV − 8	114,846	31,215	62,273
EPV − 7	109,373	29,698	64,556
EPV − 6	103,770	28,059	67,358
EPV − 5	98,161	26,831	70,045
EPV − 4	92,247	25,215	72,904
EPV − 3	86,338	23,692	75,589
EPV − 2	80,283	22,017	77,623
EPV − 1	74,422	20,478	79,395
EPV − 0	65,962	19,007	80,441
ERAT − 10	2.052	1.764	0.782
ERAT − 9	1.990	1.703	0.779
ERAT − 8	1.922	1.633	0.785
ERAT − 7	1.848	1.555	0.812
ERAT − 6	1.768	1.471	0.846
ERAT − 5	1.686	1.407	0.878
ERAT − 4	1.596	1.323	0.913
ERAT − 3	1.505	1.244	0.945
ERAT − 2	1.409	1.157	0.969
ERAT − 1	1.314	1.077	0.989
$N =$	127	42	11

The rate of inflation, wage growth, and nominal interest rates were different in 1980 than they were in 1975. In fact, one could argue that earnings growth of 5% per year for old workers and a nominal rate of interest of 15% are more reasonable. Column 3 of table 3.8 reports the results on the 1980 data using these assumptions.

Although the values change somewhat, the qualitative conclusions remain essentially unchanged. Pension values decline significantly with age. Incidentally, the reason that values are so much lower for conventional plans under the revised assumptions is that wage growth of 5% implies that an individual who retires 10 years early has a salary of $15,348 rather than $25,000. Since conventional plans are contingent on final salary, benefits fall. At normal retirement, values are lower because of higher discount rates. Only the latter consideration affects pattern plans, causing their decline to be steepened substantially. The reasoning is not quite so straightforward, however, since these are means of highly nonlinear functions.[5]

Finally, as a last check on the robustness of the results, the analysis was

Table 3.8   **1980 Expected Present Value of Pensions: Comparative Analysis**
(Sample: Valid EPV – 10 . . . EPV – 0)

Salary = $25,000, Tenure = 30 Years

| | Defined-Benefit Conventional Plan | | | |
Variable	Wage Growth = 0 r = .1 Social Security = 1980 (1)	Wage Growth = 0 r = .1 Social Security = 1975 (2)	Wage Growth = 5% r = .15 Social Security = 1980 (3)	Wage Growth = 0 r = .05 Social Security = 1980 (4)
EPV – 10	107,585	115,384	75,317	98,194
EPV – 9	10,511	112,624	72,110	99,791
EPV – 8	101,951	109,222	68,908	100,673
EPV – 7	98,212	105,190	65,751	100,866
EPV – 6	94,213	100,945	62,739	100,629
EPV – 5	90,176	96,537	60,051	100,129
EPV – 4	85,524	91,512	56,973	98,769
EPV – 3	80,656	86,313	53,779	96,880
EPV – 2	75,143	80,482	50,347	93,876
EPV – 1	69,863	74,810	47,206	90,727
EPV – 0	63,165	67,749	43,452	85,261
ERAT – 10	2.285	2.297	2.197	1.548
ERAT – 9	2.212	2.221	2.070	1.558
ERAT – 8	2.129	2.137	1.949	1.559
ERAT – 7	2.039	2.045	1.835	1.553
ERAT – 6	1.944	1.949	1.728	1.540
ERAT – 5	1.850	1.852	1.632	1.523
ERAT – 4	1.747	1.748	1.531	1.496
ERAT – 3	1.641	1.641	1.431	1.461
ERAT – 2	1.522	1.523	1.326	1.409
ERAT – 1	1.408	1.408	1.231	1.355
ERAT – 0	1.000	1.000	1.000	1.000
N = 144	144	144	137	144

Table 3.9 **1980 Expected Present Value of Pensions: Comparative Analysis**
(Sample: Valid EPV–10 . . . EPV–0)

Salary = $25,000, Tenure = 30 Years

| | Defined-Benefit Pattern Plan | | | |
| | Wage Growth = 0 $r = .1$ Social Security = 1980 (1) | Wage Growth = 0 $r = .1$ Social Security = 1975 (2) | Wage Growth = 5% $r = .15$ Social Security = 1980 (3) | Wage Growth = 0 $r = .05$ Social Security = 1980 (4) |
Variable				
EPV – 10	40,651	40,651	48,189	37,328
EPV – 9	40,103	40,103	45,650	38,291
EPV – 8	39,296	39,296	42,961	39,011
EPV – 7	38,262	38,262	40,178	39,489
EPV – 6	37,031	37,031	37,353	39,728
EPV – 5	36,164	36,164	35,134	40,201
EPV – 4	34,485	34,485	32,180	39,859
EPV – 3	32,716	32,716	29,326	39,314
EPV – 2	30,752	30,752	26,481	38,447
EPV – 1	28,767	28,767	23,797	37,358
EPV – 0	26,876	26,876	21,379	36,247
ERAT – 10	1.491	1.491	2.222	1.015
ERAT – 9	1.473	1.473	2.109	1.043
ERAT – 8	1.446	1.446	1.988	1.064
ERAT – 7	1.410	1.410	1.862	1.079
ERAT – 6	1.367	1.367	1.733	1.087
ERAT – 5	1.334	1.334	1.629	1.100
ERAT – 4	1.274	1.274	1.494	1.092
ERAT – 3	1.210	1.210	1.364	1.079
ERAT – 2	1.140	1.140	1.234	1.056
ERAT – 1	1.068	1.068	1.111	1.028
ERAT – 0	1.000	1.000	1.000	1.000

$N = 38$

repeated under the assumption that the nominal interest rate was only 5%. Column 4 of table 3.8 contains those results.

With a nominal interest rate of 5%, the decline in pension value does not occur until about 6 years before normal retirement for the representative group. However, for groups with longer tenure (= 40) the decline occurs throughout the period for conventional plans and during the last 9 years for pattern plans. Moreover, in 1980 a nominal discount rate of 5% is surely well below the feasible range since short rates were above 20% and 30-year mortgage rates were around 16%. It is difficult to believe that 5% was the anticipated discount rate.

3.2.3   The Matched Sample

Any of the differences noted above may have been the result of random differences in the cross section rather than true time variations. To eliminate that source of confusion, 70 plans have been matched across the two years. This section reports findings based on that sample. The results are presented in table 3.10.

The major changes occured for pattern plans. In the matched sample, there was an increase in pension values of about 50% for normal retirement and over 100% for retirement 10 years early. Since pattern plans are independent of final salary, it is not surprising that their values should increase in nominal terms over the period. However, two points are interesting. First, certainly for early retirement, but even for normal retirement the increase probably exceeds the increase in prices so that some of the gain is real, not nominal. Second, the decline in pension benefits with early retirement seems to have steepened sharply over the 5-year period, reflected in the 100 + % gain for early and only 50 + % gain for normal retirement.

Again, this may reflect a substitution of pension reductions for mandatory retirement in light of changes in the Age Discrimination in Employment Act. Of course, if pensions acted perfectly as an efficient severance pay device there would be no need for mandatory retirement at all. The inability to induce both efficient layoffs and quitting simultaneously provides a role for mandatory retirement and its restriction works in the direction of inducing more worker-initiated separations.

The results for conventional plans suggest a different pattern. Although differences are small, the benefits have, if anything, declined over time. This should not be taken at face value. More than this decline can be attributed to changes in social security. The maximum decline here is less than 5% and the mean decline due to social security was estimated at 7%. But more important is that conventional plans depend on final salary which increases over time with inflation. This table makes comparisons based on equality of salary in nominal terms. But using the

Table 3.10   **Matched Data: Pension Values**
              (Sample: Valid EPV − 10 . . . EPV − 0)
              Salary = $25,000, Tenure = 30 Years

Years before Normal Retirement	EPV80	EPV75	EPV80 − EPV75
	Conventional plans		
EPV − 10	99,981	102,380	− 2,399
EPV − 9	97,554	98,815	− 1,261
EPV − 8	94,583	94,874	− 290
EPV − 7	91,241	92,823	− 1,581
EPV − 6	87,617	88,272	− 654
EPV − 5	84,049	86,952	− 2,902
EPV − 4	79,727	82,376	− 2,649
EPV − 3	75,201	79,034	− 3,832
EPV − 2	70,260	73,616	− 3,355
EPV − 1	65,715	68,334	− 2,618
EPV − 0	61,232	61,907	− 675
N = 19			
	Pattern plans		
EPV − 10	43,097	20,199	22,898
EPV − 9	42,476	20,179	22,296
EPV − 8	41,583	23,283	18,300
EPV − 7	40,451	22,842	17,609
EPV − 6	39,112	22,261	16,851
EPV − 5	38,660	25,111	13,548
EPV − 4	36,737	23,818	12,918
EPV − 3	34,729	22,724	12,005
EPV − 2	32,505	21,272	11,233
EPV − 1	30,274	19,925	10,349
EPV − 0			

information in tables 3.3–3.5 we can adjust the pension benefits to take this into account.

At tenure = 30, an increase in salary from $25,000 to $50,000 increases normal retirement value by (135,577 − 63,165)/63,165, or 114%. Therefore we can estimate that each dollar increase in final salary at tenure = 30 increases normal retirement pension value by $1.14. If the average final salary in these firms grew say 30% over the 5-year period, normal pension value would be expected to increase from $61,907 in 1975 to (61,232)(1.30)(1.14) = $90,745 in 1980. This would be an increase of 47%. This increase is about the same as that for pattern plans over the same period.

A similar exercise can be performed to correct the present value of retirement 10 years early. Under the same assumptions, this results in an estimated pension value of 143,886 in 1980 based on the 1975 salary of

$25,000. This is an increase of 40%, so the steepening of the decline in pension values for pattern plans does not seem to be duplicated for conventional plans.[6]

Summarizing, pattern plans on average pay 50% more at normal retirement and 100% more on retirement 10 years early than they did in 1975. In both years and under any reasonable assumptions, the expected present value of pensions tends to decline with increases in the age of retirement.

3.3   An Alternative Explanation and Other Issues

Throughout the model it was assumed that workers were risk neutral. However, if workers are risk averse, then another explanation for the decline in pension value with age of retirement is available. When a worker begins employment, he may not know whether or not he will become ill and be forced to retire before the normal age. Because illness is a bad event, workers may wish to insure against that contingency by paying higher pensions to early retirees.

At some levels, this story is not inconsistent with the model. Equations (1)–(7) would have to be modified to take utility rather than alternative use of time into account. But the pension still acts as severance pay and induces workers to leave when appropriate. "Appropriate" carries a different meaning, however. Now, workers cannot be induced to leave if and only if the alternative use of time exceeds the value of the worker to the firm. To do so destroys the role of severance pay as an insurance device. This well-known result appears in many places,[7] but its point carries with it two implications for this analysis. First, severance pay does not induce efficient separation in the sense of a first best, perfect information optimum. Second, and as the result, the decline in pension value with retirement age is not an accurate measure of the difference between wage and marginal product. In fact, it overstates that value because some of the payment for early retirement is insurance.

There are a number of arguments which suggest that the insurance story is somewhat less plausible. First, there are other forms of insurance, some provided by the firm and others by a third party, which seem to be set up explicitly to handle these contingencies. Health insurance and, more to the point, disability insurance perform exactly those functions. It is not clear why a declining pension value should be required to play the same role.

Second, if pensions act as insurance, one would think that there would be no reason to prevent workers from taking them early. But most pension plans severely limit the age of early retirement. This is not true in general for health insurance and disability insurance. If pensions are an incentive device, it is easier to rationalize the unwillingness to pay pensions to early retirees.

Third, most pensions that are based on salary use the final few years' salary as the basis of computation. If insurance were the motive, a lifetime average which more closely reflects expected permanent income would be appropriate. In fact, with insurance a case could be made for a negative relationship between final salary and pension, given lifetime income, because of the inability of the older disabled worker to adjust to the fall in income.

Fourth, the decline in pension values is steepest for high-income, white-collar workers who have conventional rather than pattern plans. Yet one might argue that it is the blue-collar workers who have both riskier jobs and fewer alternative forms of insurance. Although insurance may be a partial motive for pension values which decline with age of retirement, it seems difficult to believe that this is a major factor in the explanation.

3.4 Conclusion

The expected present value of pension benefits generally declines with the age of retirement. This phenomenon is easily explained if one views the pensions as a form of severance pay rather than as a tax-deferred savings account. Further, the real value of pension benefits has remained constant or increased in real terms over the period between 1975 and 1980 even though the same is probably not true for older workers' real earnings. Finally, there is some evidence to suggest that higher pensions for early retirement are being used as a substitute for mandatory retirement clauses in labor contracts.

Notes

1. This analysis marries the models presented in Lazear (1981) and Hall and Lazear (1982).

2. A more general formulation allows the severance payment to vary with the identity of the party who initiates the separation. Hall and Lazear (1982) consider this case and discuss its drawbacks.

3. That the entire remaining stream must be examined is recognized in Fields and Mitchell (1981). Bulow (1981) also points out (as my calculations implicitly do) that the "true" current wage also includes the value of changing the pension as the result of working that period.

4. See also Burkhauser and Quinn (1981).

5. E.g., for some ages the mean rises even though no one plan ever rose. The nonlinearities make some plans fall by less than others.

6. There was only one matched defined-contribution plan.

7. To name a few, see Azariadis (1980), Arnott and Stiglitz (1981), Green (1981), Green and Kahn (1981), Grossman and Hart (1981a, 1981b).

Comment   David A. Wise

Through a substantial coding effort, Lazear has computerized the stipulations of a number of pension plans. Having done this, he has been able to compare the provisions of the plans with the predictions suggested by his theory. Although the idea is straightforward, the implementation of it is not simple, and, indeed, the data set that Lazear has created is interesting in its own right. The data are consistent with the theory. The chapter gives us a major piece of information: once the age of early retirement is reached, annual "earnings" in the form of pension benefits decline with additional years of employment, according to the provisions of a large group of pension plans.

Without Lazear's theory, I believe a standard prediction would be that workers are paid more than their marginal products early in their working lives, then less than their marginal products, and finally more than their marginal products toward the end of their working careers. That they are paid more late in life creates an incentive for them to continue working. Mandatory retirement is one way of bringing overpayment to an end. In any case, firms under this scenario have an incentive to get older workers to retire before the mandatory retirement age. What Lazear has added to this story is that judicious selection of pension parameters could theoretically tend to produce more efficient quitting. This is done by reducing retirement benefits from one year to the next in such a way as to just offset the difference between the wage rate and the marginal product during that year. The net marginal wage faced by the worker is equal to his marginal product, and thus it leads to efficient quitting decisions. Guided by this interpretation, Lazear's data seem to indicate that the divergence between wage and marginal product in these late years increases with age. At least this seems to be true for persons on defined-benefit plans. However, it seems not generally to be the case with respect to defined-contribution plans.

Again, using Lazear's interpretation of the data, it also turns out that the difference between wage and marginal product is greater for workers with long tenure with the firm and also for those with higher salaries. The possibility that short tenured workers may be paid less than their marginal product seems plausible to me, but the reasoning for higher-salary workers is to me more questionable. Lazear has argued that relative to blue-collar workers it is more difficult to monitor the performance of higher-salary workers and therefore in part the higher salary is a necessary incentive. On the other hand, in my limited experience with a large

David A. Wise is John F. Stambaugh Professor of Political Economy, John F. Kennedy School of Government, Harvard University, and research associate, National Bureau of Economic Research.

corporation, it was made clear to me that the highest-paid workers were the easiest to monitor and indeed that the firm cared relatively little about managers below middle management and would not normally take steps to fire them even if they were performing poorly. On the other hand, the claim was that the performance of people at higher levels of management was obvious from the performance of their divisions and that these people were paid more in part because their marginal contributions to the firm were potentially high. Also, it was claimed that these people would be dismissed if their performance did not live up to expectations.

Now let me say a bit more about the possible interpretations of the data. I agree with Lazear that the data seem to be inconsistent with a savings motivation for pensions, at least in the main.

I am not so sure, however, that the data are inconsistent with an insurance motive for pensions. People who retire early often say that they do so because of health status. Presumably persons believe that should poor health necessitate early retirement they would need higher benefits than if this contingency were not to arise. There are, of course, other insurance schemes that are more directly related to health than general retirement plans are, but to get disability insurance one presumably has to demonstrate disability. Declining health status may mitigate against working, yet a person may not be disabled in a strict sense and thus may want the added insurance of a retirement plan. There is, of course, a moral hazard problem when retirement benefits are allowed to act as insurance, which is, of course, what disability verification tries to guard against.

This leads me to wonder how Lazear's theory relates to individual differences among workers. Is the same scheme to apply to all? It does not seem to me that existing pension plans can reduce benefits in accordance with individual differences in marginal product versus wage. I am reminded of this difference because of the experience of a large Boston corporation that recently wanted to reduce its work force. The firm presumably set out to do this by a judicious selection of severance pay determined worker by worker, or at least based on individual work histories. After the fact, the firm apparently found that their incentive scheme was not—at least to the extent that it wished—encouraging those that they wanted to retain to stay, and those that they did not want to retain to leave. I wonder how pension plans in the aggregate could be expected to perform in this respect.

It is also interesting that Lazear's data seem to be consistent with his theory with respect to defined-benefit plans but the data on defined-contribution plans apparently are not. Does this mean that firms with defined-contribution plans have different lifetime salary structures of different implicit contracts with workers or that they have different work settings such that appropriate incentive schemes are different from those that apply in firms with defined-benefit plans? For example, construction workers may typically have defined-contribution plans while auto firm employees may have defined-benefit plans. Since the normal job tenure of the two groups is typically very different, the incentives of their pension plans might also be expected to differ. Also, the plans selected by Lazear for analysis are those that allow early retirement. Could it be that firms that allow early retirement are those that would like to dismiss some older workers and thus have pension plans that are consistent with this goal?

Along these lines, I think it would be interesting to compare salary structures in the relatively recent past, when pensions were much less prevalent than they are today, with salary structures that exist today. In particular, could one demonstrate that the divergence between wage and marginal product of older workers is greater now than it used to be? Finally, it seems to me that Lazear's evidence suggests the advantages that could be gained from longitudinal microdata that match individual salary trajectories and turnover (quitting) with pension plan parameters.

In summary: Lazear's chapter has contributed a major piece of information to our knowledge about pension plans. Together with his theory, this information helps us to understand a possible role of pensions: to encourage efficient retirement. A major portion of the plans considered by Lazear do appear to be consistent with this role, although others apparently are not. Thus the chapter raises several interesting issues for future investigation.

References

Arnott, R., and Stiglitz, J. 1981. Labor turnover, wage structures, and moral hazard: The inefficiency of competitive markets. Econometric Research Program no. 289.

Azariadis, C. 1980. Employment with asymmetric information. CARESS Working Paper no. 80–22.

Bankers' Trust Study of Corporate Pension Plans. 1976. New York: Bankers' Trust.

————. 1980. Corporate pension plan study. New York: Bankers' Trust.

Becker, G. S., and Stigler, G. J. 1974. Law enforcement, malfeasance, and compensation of enforcers. *Journal of Legal Studies* 3:1–18.

Bulow, J. 1981. Early retirement pension benefits. NBER Working Paper no. 654.

Burkhauser, R., and Quinn, J. 1981. The effect of pension plans on the pattern of life cycle consumption.

Current Population Survey. 1974, 1976.

Fields, G., and Mitchell, O. 1981. Pensions and optimal retirement behavior. NYSSILR Working Paper no. 27.

Green, J. 1981. Wage employment contracts. HIER Discussion Paper no. 807.

Green, J., and Kahn, C. 1981. Wage-employment contracts: Global results. NBER Working Paper no. 675.

Grossman, S., and Hart, O. 1981*a*. Implicit contracts, moral hazard and unemployment. *American Economic Review.* 71 (May):301–7.

———. 1981*b*. Implicit contracts under asymmetric information. University of Chicago Graduate School of Business (February).

Hall, R. E., and Lazear, E. 1982. The excess sensitivity of layoffs and quits to demand. University of Chicago Graduate School of Business.

Lazear, E. P. 1979. Why is there mandatory retirement? *Journal of Political Economy* 87 (December): 1261–64.

———. 1981. Agency, earnings profiles, productivity and hours restrictions. *American Economic Review* 71, 4 (September): 606–20.

———. 1982. Severance pay, pensions and efficient mobility. University of Chicago, Graduate School of Business. June.

4 Optimal Funding and Asset Allocation Rules for Defined-Benefit Pension Plans

J. Michael Harrison and William F. Sharpe

4.1 Introduction

Considerable attention has been devoted to the funding of defined-benefit pension plans. Both the level of funding and the allocation of fund assets have been considered from the viewpoints of various interested parties (beneficiaries, corporate managers, corporate shareholders, and the Pension Benefit Guaranty Corporation). Both practical and theoretical investigations have tended to characterize the asset allocation decision as one of choosing an appropriate "bond-stock mix."

Sharpe (1976) showed that, in the absence of taxes, if the parties bearing the cost of possible default behave rationally, neither the asset allocation decision nor the funding decision may affect the wealth of corporate shareholders. On the other hand, if some parties do not require compensation for actions that increase the risk of default, the optimal policy from the viewpoint of corporate shareholders may involve funding as little as possible and using asset allocation to maximize default risk.

Two important papers, by Black (1980) and Tepper (1981), consider the effects of current tax law, assuming that there is no probability of default.[1] Under these conditions shareholder wealth may be maximized by funding to the greatest possible extent and holding assets (such as bonds) taxed highly for other investors. This chapter considers a world in which pension funds may default, the cost of the associated risk of default is not borne fully by the sponsoring corporation, and there are differential tax effects. We explore ways in which the wealth of the shareholders

J. Michael Harrison is professor of decision sciences, Stanford University Graduate School of Business. William F. Sharpe is professor of finance, Stanford University Graduate School of Business and research associate, National Bureau of Economic Research.

The comments and suggestions of Jeremy Bulow, Myron Scholes, and Robert Litzenberger are gratefully acknowledged.

of a corporation sponsoring a pension plan might be increased if the Internal Revenue Service (IRS) and the Pension Benefit Guaranty Corporation (PBGC) follow simple (and naive) policies. This analysis suggests that the two agencies may want to consider more complex rules. Optimal policy for the PBGC is discussed briefly in Sharpe (1976); Tepper (1982) describes some of the issues involved in setting tax policy. We do not explore such issues here. Instead, we hope to provide useful inputs for addressing these more fundamental questions.

4.2 The General Problem

Throughout we will deal with a defined-benefit plan. An initial decision must be made concerning the amount of assets in the plan. Following this decision, we assume that the plan will be frozen. That is, no further benefits will accrue and no further contributions will be made. In addition to the decision concerning the level of initial assets, decisions must be made in subsequent periods concerning the allocation of assets among alternative investment instruments. The former is termed the *funding decision*, the latter are *asset allocation decisions*. All may be constrained by legal, regulatory, or other restrictions.

The liabilities of a frozen defined-benefit plan can be described by a vector of benefit payments $B_1, B_2, \ldots, B_T$ to be paid from the fund at times $1, 2, \ldots T$ if possible. We assume these are known with certainty.[2] At each time t, the current market value of the fund's assets is compared with the benefits then due. If assets exceed required payments, the benefits are paid and the remaining assets reinvested. If not, no further benefits are paid by the fund. If all benefits have been paid at date T, the remaining assets revert to the sponsoring corporation. Beneficiaries may be insured in whole or in part against default, but we assume that neither insurance premia nor wages paid by the corporation are affected by the level of funding or the allocation of fund assets. Moreover, we assume that the goal of those making these decisions is to maximize the wealth of corporate shareholders.[3]

4.2.1 Valuation of Contingent Claims

To represent a market with "tax effects" we employ a modified version of the state-preference approach used by Litzenberger and Van Horne (1978). Individual investors can purchase claims to receive income contingent on the occurrence of alternative states of the world. However, different kinds of payments may be taxed differently for at least some investors. Thus a claim for a capital-gain dollar contingent on state s may be valued differently in the market than one for a dividend dollar contingent on the same state. Given M such types of dollars and N states of the world, we assume that it is possible, explicitly or implicitly, for individual investors to puchase all $M \times N$ primitive (Arrow-Debreu) contingent claims. This is similar to, but not the same as, the familiar complete-markets approach. The latter typically assumes that existing securities span the space of state-contingent claims and that unlimited short sales with no impounds and full use of the proceeds are possible. In a taxable world, if this were possible, riskless tax arbitrage between two investors in different tax brackets could occur, as shown by Schaefer (1978). Thus we implicitly assume the existence of boundaries on holdings and/or tax treatment.

We assume that at time T the residual value of the fund, R (which will be zero if the fund has defaulted), will be used to pay shareholders. The amount may be subject to corporate tax, leaving less than R to be paid out. Let $R(s)$ = the residual value if state s occurs; t^c = the corporate tax rate, assumed to be independent of s and $R(s)$; and $v^a(s)$ = the present value of a dollar paid to the corporation's shareholders in state s. If the residual is to be paid in the form of dividends, $v^a(s)$ will be the market price for a dividend dollar in state s; if the residual is to be paid in capital gains, $v^a(s)$ will be the market price of a capital-gains dollar in state s. We assume only that the form each distribution would take is known and that the $v^a(s)$ values are selected accordingly.

Letting $v(s) = v^a(s)(1 - t^c)$, the present value of $R(s)$ is $V(s) = v(s)R(s)$. Henceforth we will focus on the $v(s)$ values, with $v(1), \ldots, v(N)$ termed the *valuation function*.

Given a set of possible residual values $R(1), \ldots, R(N)$ the value of the pension fund for the corporate shareholders will be $V = \Sigma_s V(s) = \Sigma_s [v(s)R(s)]$. We assume that the objective of those making the decisions concerning the fund is to maximize V, given some valuation function $v(1), \ldots, v(N)$. A key ingredient in our analysis is the assumption that neither the corporate taxes nor the personal taxes paid on $R(s)$ will be related to the choice of investments made by the managers of the pension fund. For example, the eventual taxes paid if a dividend dollar is received within the pension fund in a given state of the world would be the same as those paid if a capital-gains dollar had been received within the fund in the same circumstances. A dollar received in the pension fund in a given state of the world thus has the same value for the corporation's shareholders, whatever its type. However, the present price of a claim to receive such a dollar may depend on its type. Thus the presence of differential tax treatment will influence the relative attractiveness of alternative instruments, even for a tax-exempt pension fund.

4.2.2   Choice of Assets

While individuals may have some flexibility in their choice of state-contingent payments, we assume that the pension fund must choose from a limited set of combinations of such claims. The fund manager's choice set thus does not span the set of state-contingent claims. In the next part of the chapter we consider a choice between two instruments (e.g. bonds and stocks) in a one-period setting. We show that in this case one of two extreme funding policies (fund either as much or as little as possible) will be optimal, as will one of two extreme asset allocation policies (invest either in bonds or in stocks but not in both). Later we obtain analogous results in a setting involving many periods and many assets. We then address the issue raised by Black and Tepper: given two instruments, bonds and stocks, with different tax status and different risks, we show that an all-bond, maximum-funding policy may not be optimal. The final section of the chapter provides suggestions for future research.

4.3   One Period and Two Assets

We begin with the asset allocation decision. Consider a pension plan with A dollars to invest. This may be used to purchase either or both of two types of assets. One unit of asset 1 can be purchased for one dollar and will pay $D^1(s)$ dollars one period hence if the state of the world is s. Similarly, one unit of asset 2 can be purchased for one dollar and will pay $D^2(s)$ dollars in one period if state s occurs. We assume a simple regulatory setting in which the plan's managers may select a value of X between X_{min} and X_{max}, where $X =$ the proportion of the fund's assets to be invested in asset 2. We also assume that there are no transactions costs.

The value of assets one period hence will be $(1 - X)$ $AD^1(s) + XAD^2(s)$. At the end of the period, a benefit of B dollars must be paid out of the fund's assets if possible. The amount (if any) left for taxes and payments to shareholders will be $R(A, X, s)$ $= [(1 - X)AD^1(s) + XAD^2(s) - B]^+$, where $[z]^+$ denotes z if $z \geq 0$ and zero if $z < 0$. Assume that neither the firm's wage bill nor its insurance premium is a function of X or A.[4] The amount of the residual claim in state s is $R(A, X, s) = \{A[D^1(s) + X(D^2(s) - D^1(s))] - B\}^+$. The goal is to maximize the value of the residual claim $V = \Sigma_s \, v(s) \, R(A, X, s)$ by choosing feasible values of A and X.

Let

$$V(s) = v(s)R(A, X, s)$$
$$= v(s)\{A[D^1(s) + X(D^2(s) - D^1(s))] - B\}^+.$$

Figure 4.1 plots $V(s)$ as a function of X, given A, for three cases: (1) a state in which asset 2 underperforms asset 1, (2) a state in which the two assets have equal payoffs, and (3) a state in which asset 2 outperforms asset 1. A key observation is that the function is (weakly) convex from above—going from left to right the slope never decreases. Note that V is simply the sum over states of such components of value: $V = \Sigma_s V(s)$. Thus it must also be weakly convex from above. It follows that, given A,

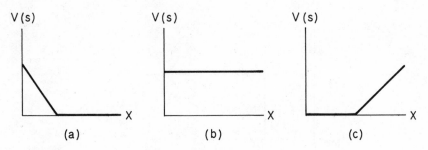

Fig. 4.1   Convexity of $V(s)$ as a function of X.

shareholder wealth will be maximized at either X_{min} or X_{max}, but every interior feasible value of X will be dominated. Depending on the situation, all funds should be invested in either asset 1 or asset 2. *No* mixed solutions will be optimal.

Now consider the question of the appropriate funding level. Assets invested in a pension fund must come from somewhere. Corporate projects must be forgone, funds must be raised from bondholders or stockholders, etc. For simplicity, assume that dollars not invested in the fund will be used to finance an investment that will pay $D^c(s)$ dollars one period hence if the state of the world is s, and that such payoffs will be taxed in the same manner as those obtained as residual values from the pension fund. Then the opportunity cost of an investment of A dollars in the fund will be $A \sum_s [v(s) D^c(s)] = A V^c$, where V^c = the present value of one dollar invested in corporate assets (at the margin, one dollar) and the net present value of the pension fund to the shareholders will be $V^n = \sum_s [V(s) - v(s)D^c(s)]$. Equivalently stated, $V^n = \sum_s V^n(s)$, where $V^n(s) = v(s)\{[Ar(s) - B]^+ - AD^c(s)\}$ and $r(s) = (1 - X)D^1(s) + XD^2(s)$. The value of V^n will typically be negative; thus $(-V^n)$ can be interpreted as the cost of the pension plan. We assume that the goal is to maximize the former value (i.e., to minimize the cost of the plan).

Figure 4.2 shows the assumed regulatory climate. The fund may choose a value of A between A_{min} and A_{max} and a value of X between X_{min} and X_{max}. The value of A_{max} might correspond to ERISA's full funding limitation and A_{min} to its minimum funding standard. The values of X_{min} and X_{max} are intended to represent a naive policy on the part of the PBGC concerning prudent management of the fund. In this simple case the feasible region has four corners. In Section 4.4 we consider a somewhat broader class of regulatory policies; however, the assumption is retained that the feasible region is convex, with linear borders.

Figure 4.3 plots $V^n(s)$ as a function of A, given X, for three cases: (1) a state in which pension assets do better than corporate assets, (2) a state in which the two types of assets do equally well, and (3) a state in which

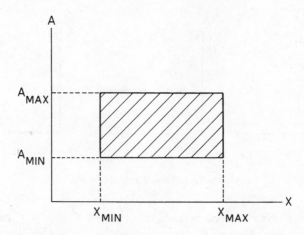

Fig. 4.2   The feasible region with simple regulatory constraints.

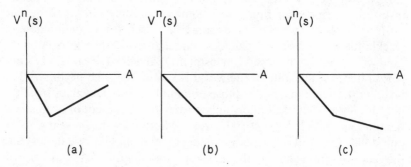

Fig. 4.3   Convexity of $V^n(s)$ as a function of A.

pension assets underperform corporate assets. This function is also (weakly) convex from above. And, since V^n is the sum over states of such components of value, it too must be weakly convex from above. It follows that, give X, shareholder wealth will be maximized at either A_{min} or A_{max} but every interior feasible value of A will be dominated. Depending on the situation, one should fund a plan as much or as little as possible.

Given A, an extreme value of X should be chosen. Given X, an extreme value of A should be chosen. The overall optimum thus involves an extreme value of A and an extreme value of X. In figure 4.2, all positions but those at the corners of the feasible region will be dominated.

4.4   Many Periods and Many Assets

Consider now a more general problem with defined benefits $B_1, \ldots, B_T$ payable at times $1, \ldots, T$. Further suppose that the pension plan can invest in K assets, indexed by $k = 1, \ldots, K$. Generalizing the notation used earlier, we denote by D_t^k the return at time t to a dollar invested at time $t - 1$ in security k. Of course D_t^k further depends on the state s, but it will be convenient to suppress this dependence initially.

Next let X_t^k denote the fraction of the pension plan's wealth that is invested in security k between times $t - 1$ and t, and define

$$(1) \qquad M_t = \sum_{k=1}^{K} X_t D_t^k \quad \text{for } t = 1, \ldots, T.$$

If a total of Z dollars is invested at time $t - 1$, the wealth of the pension fund at time t, before payment of benefits, will be ZM_t. We call M_t the pension fund's *investment multiplier* for period t. The portfolio proportions X_t^k are decision variables and can depend on the state s through information that is available at time $t - 1$ (see below), but we suppress this dependence for the moment. The pension fund manager's other decision variable is the initial investment level A. We denote by W_t the wealth of the pension fund at time t, immediately after payment of benefits. These wealth levels W_t can be expressed in terms of the initial investment level A and portfolio proportions X_t^k by the recursive formula

$$(2) \qquad W_t = (W_{t-1} M_t - B_t)^+ \quad \text{for } t = 1, \ldots, T$$

with $W_0 = A$ by convention.

PROPOSITION: The residual wealth $R = W_T$ is a convex function of each multiplier M_t alone, holding the other multipliers, the benefit obligations, and the initial investment level fixed. Furthermore, R is a convex function of the initial investment level A, holding all else fixed.

PROOF: Let t be arbitrary, let $M_t' \geq = 0$ and $M_t'' \geq = 0$ be two possible values for the multiplier in period t, and set $M_t = .5M_t' + .5M_t''$. Let $W_1', \ldots, W_T'$ be defined by (2), with M_t' in place of M_t (plus the convention $W_0' = A$), and let $W_0'', W_1'', \ldots, W_T''$ be defined similarly. To prove the first statement of the proposition, we need to show that $W_T \leq .5W_T' + .5W_T''$. Obviously $W_i = W_i' = W_i''$ for $i = 0, \ldots, t - 1$. Then

$$
\begin{aligned}
W_t &= (W_{t-1} M_t - B_t)^+ = [W_t(.5M_t' + .5M_t'') - B_t]^+ \\
&= [.5(W_{t-1} M_t' - B_t) + .5(W_{t-1} M_t'' - B_t)]^+ \\
(3) \qquad &\leq .5(W_{t-1} M_t' - B_t)^+ + .5(W_{t-1} M_t'' - B_t)^+ \\
&= .5W_t' + .5W_t'',
\end{aligned}
$$

because $(\cdot)^+$ is a convex function. But $(\cdot)^+$ is also an increasing function, so from (3) we have next that

$$
\begin{aligned}
W_{t+1} &= (W_t M_{t+1} - B_{t+1})^+ \\
(4) \qquad &\leq [(.5W_t' + .5W_t'') M_{t+1} - B_{t+1}]^+ \\
&= [.5(W_t' M_{t+1} - B_{t+1}) + .5(W_t'' M_{t+1} - B_{t+1})]^+.
\end{aligned}
$$

Using again the convexity of $(\cdot)^+$,

(5)
$$[.5(W_t' M_{t+1} - B_{t+1}) + .5(W_t'' M_{t+1} - B_{t+1})]^+$$
$$\leqq .5(W_t' M_{t+1} - B_{t+1})^+ + .5(W_t'' M_{t+1} - B_{t+1})^+$$
$$= .5W_{t+1}' + .5W_{t+1}''.$$

Combining (4) and (5) gives $W_{t+1} \leqq .5W_{t+1}' + .5W_{t+1}''$, and one can obviously continue in this way to prove by induction that $W_T \leqq .5W_T' = .5W_T''$. This completes the proof of the first statement.

To prove that W_T is a convex function of the investment level, let $A' \geqq 0$ and $A'' \geqq 0$ be arbitrary, and set $A = .5A' + .5A''$. Set $W_0' = A'$ and $W_0'' = A''$ and define W_t, W_t', and W_t'' in the obvious way for $t = 1, \ldots, T$. We need to show that $W_T \leqq .5W_T' + .5W_T''$. Steps (4) and (5) above can be used inductively to prove the stronger result that $W_t \leqq .5W_t' + .5W_t''$ for all $t = 1, \ldots, T$. Thus the proof of the proposition is complete.

4.4.1   Formulation of the Fund Manager's Problem

We assume that the pension fund manager wants to select an initial funding level A and relative portfolio proportions X_t^k so as to maximize the valuation of the residual claim $R = W_T$ subject to regulatory limitations imposed on the initial funding level or fund allocation among assets. One must also specify the fund manager's capability to adjust the allocation dynamically in response to information received. The latter aspect makes formal representation to multiperiod problems fundamentally more complex than single-period problems. We will adopt a rather abstract representation of the manager's optimization problem, but one that is well suited to our objectives.

Let Ω be the set of all states s that might pertain at time T. A trading strategy will be formally defined as a collection $(A, X_1, \ldots, X_T)$ where A is a constant, $X_1 = (X_1^1, \ldots, X_1^K)$ is a vector whose components sum to one, and, for $t = 2, \ldots, T$, $X_t = [X_t^1(s), \ldots, X_t^K(s)]$ is a vector of functions whose components sum to one for every state s.

One interprets $X_t^k(s)$ as the fraction of the fund's wealth to be invested in security k during period t if state s prevails, and it is obviously necessary to restrict the way in which this fraction may depend on s. We take as given a sequence $P_1, \ldots, P_{T-1}$ of successively finer partitions of Ω, with cells of the partition P_t representing those events whose occurrence or nonoccurrence will be known at time t. In addition to the restrictions stated above, it is required that X_t (viewed as a vector-valued function of s) be measurable with respect to P_{t-1}, meaning that $X_t(s) = X_t(s')$ whenever s and s' lie in the same cell of the partition P_{t-1}.

To complete the formulation, we require that $A \, \varepsilon \, I$ and that $X_t(s) \varepsilon \Delta$ for all $t = 1, \ldots, T$ and $s \varepsilon \Omega$, where I is a compact interval and Δ is a set to be described shortly. As in the model of Section 4.2, I is the interval between a lower funding limit imposed by the PBGC and an upper limit imposed by the IRS, while Δ is the set of all asset distributions (relative portfolio proportions) that are judged by the PBGC to be prudent. For the two-asset model of Section 4.2 we took Δ to be the set of all pairs (X^1, X^2) such that $X_{min} \leq X^1 \leq X_{max}$ and $X^1 + X^2 = 1$. For the general setting we assume that Δ is the bounded solution set of some finite system of linear inequalities and equalities, including the requirement $X^1 + \ldots + X^K = 1$. (Thus Δ is a compact, convex, polyhedral set and has a finite number of extreme points.)

The preceding paragraph contains a strong assumption. We are assuming that the definition of a prudent asset distribution does not depend on the initial funding level A, and more generally does not depend on the success enjoyed by the fund's investments up to an intermediate decision point. This assumption is essential in all that follows, although Δ can be allowed to depend on t and even s (subject to measurability restrictions) without substantially changing our analysis.

For $t = 1, \ldots, T$, let Γ_t be the set of all functions X_t that map Ω into Δ and are measurable with respect to P_{t-1}. The preceding discussion may be summarized as follows. The pension fund manager must choose $A \varepsilon I$, $X_1 \varepsilon \Gamma_1, \ldots, X_T \varepsilon \Gamma_T$ so as to maximize

$$(6) \qquad V = \sum_s v(s) \, [R(s) - AD^c(s)],$$

where $v(\cdot)$ is the valuation function discussed in Section 4.2 and $R(s)$ is defined in terms of A and the relative portfolio proportions $X_t^k(s)$ as at the beginning of this section. Ours is not a standard dynamic programming formulation of the fund manager's sequential decision problem. In particular, we have made no explicit mention of the way current portfolio decisions may depend on the fund wealth carried forward from previous periods. By coordinating the way successive portfolio descriptions $X_1, \ldots, X_T$ are made to depend on s, however, one can synthesize any desired dependency of current decisions on past success or failure. Our formulation is completely equivalent to the standard one. For future reference, we observe that this problem does have an optimal solution (the supremum is attained) because it amounts to maximization of a continuous function over a compact subset of a finite-dimensional Euclidean space.

4.4.2   Optimality of Extremal Strategies

Hereafter we denote by $x = (x^1, \ldots, x^K)$ a generic element of Δ, by $y = (y^1, \ldots, y^K)$ a generic extreme point of Δ, and by E the (finite) set of all such extreme points y. Since Δ is a compact, convex, polyhedral set by assumption, each point $x \varepsilon \Delta$ can be written as a convex combination of the extreme points $y \varepsilon E$. That is, there exist *nonnegative* weights $[a(y), y \varepsilon E]$ such that $\sum_y a(y) = 1$ and

(7) $$x = \sum_y a(y) y$$

or, equivalently,

(8) $$x^k = \sum_y a(y) y^k, \text{ for } k = 1, \ldots, K.$$

A strategy $(A, X_1, \ldots, X_T)$ for the fund manager's optimization problem is said to be extremal if A is an endpoint (extreme point) of the interval I and $X_t(s) \varepsilon E$ for each state s and each $t = 1, \ldots, T$. Incidentally, a single strategy component X_t will be called extremal if $X_t(s) \varepsilon E$ for all states s.

It is the pupose of this subsection to prove there exists an optimal strategy which is extremal. Toward that end, first let $(A, X_1, \ldots, X_T)$ be an arbitrary feasible strategy. Adding a notational dependence on A for emphasis, let $R(A, s) = W_T(A, s)$ be defined in terms of A and the relative portfolio proportions $X_t^k(s)$ as at the beginning of this section, and then let $V(A)$ be defined in terms of $R(A, s)$ by (6). The Proposition shows that $R(A, s)$ is a convex function of A for each fixed s, and it follows immediately, because the contingent claim valuations $v(s)$ are nonnegative, that $V(A)$ is convex. Thus $V(A)$ will be maximized by taking A to be an endpoint of the feasible interval I. To repeat, the valuation associated with an arbitrary feasible strategy can be increased (or at least not decreased) by moving A to one of the extreme points of I, leaving $X_1, \ldots, X_T$ fixed.

We now argue that a similar improvement can be effected by substituting for any of the strategy components X_t a well-chosen extremal strategy component. Again let $(A, X_1, \ldots, X_T)$ be arbitrary, fix a period t, and let S be any cell of the partition P_{t-1}. Then there exists a point $x \varepsilon \Delta$ such that $X_t(s) = x$ for all $s \varepsilon S$. Adding a notational dependence on x for emphasis, let us set

(9) $$M_t(s, x) = \sum_{k=1}^{K} X_t^k(s) D_t^k(s).$$

$$= \sum_{k=1}^{K} x^k D_t^k(s) \text{ for } s \varepsilon S.$$

Then $R(s, x) = W_T(s, x)$ is defined in terms of $M_t(s, x)$ for states $s \varepsilon S$ as at the beginning of this section, and we set $V(S, x) = \sum_{s \varepsilon S} v(s)[R(s, x) - AD^c(s)]$. Obviously $V(S, x)$ is the contribution to the total valuation V made by states in cell S, and it is only the contribution from these states that is affected by our choice of x.

Recall that x can be represented in terms of the extremal points y via (7), and we now consider how the partial valuation $V(S)$ would be affected if we were to replace x by some $y \varepsilon E$. By analogy with (9), let

(10) $$M_t(s, y) = \sum_{k=1}^{K} y D_t^k(s) \text{ for } y \varepsilon E \text{ and } s \varepsilon S,$$

and then let $R(s, y)$ and $V(S, y)$ be defined in terms of $M_t(s, y)$ in the obvious way. From (7), (9), and (10), we have

$$(11) \qquad M_t(s, x) = \Sigma_{y \varepsilon E} a(y) M_t(s, y) \text{ for } s \varepsilon S.$$

The Proposition says that $R = W_T$ is a convex function of M_t, so (11) implies

$$(12) \qquad R(s, x) \leqq \Sigma_{y \varepsilon E} a(y) R(s, y) \text{ for } s \varepsilon S,$$

and hence, because $v(s) \geqq 0$ for all $s \varepsilon S$,

$$(13) \qquad V(S, x) \leqq \Sigma_{y \varepsilon S} a(y) V(S, y).$$

Obviously (13) can only hold if $V(S, y) \geqq V(S, x)$ for at least one extreme point y, so we can increase (or at least not decrease) $V(s)$ by substituting this y for x in our specification of the strategy component X_t. Repeating this argument for each cell of the partition P_{t-1}, we come to the following: one can increase the overall valuation $V = \Sigma_s V(s)$, or at least not decrease it, by substituting for X_t an extremal strategy component X_t^*.

The proof that there exists an extremal optimal policy is now essentially complete. We know that there exists an optimal solution $(A, X_1, \ldots, X_T)$. But one can substitute for A an extremal investment level A^*, then substitute for X_1 a well-chosen extremal strategy component $X_1^*, \ldots$, then substitute for X_T a well-chosen extremal strategy component X_T^*, without ever decreasing the total valuation. Absolutely essential to this argument is the assumption that one can take A to be any point in the interval I and X_t to be any element of Γ_t, regardless of how the other componenets of the overall strategy have been selected.

4.5 Bonds versus Stocks

We turn now to the issues raised by Black (1980) and Tepper (1981). Given a choice between bonds and stocks and a range of permissible funding levels, what policies will be optimal for corporate shareholders? To analyze these issues, we will use the simple one-period, two-asset setting of Section 4.3.

Key to the Black-Tepper argument is the superiority of pension fund investment over corporate investment and, within the pension fund, the superiority of bonds (here, asset 1) over stocks (asset 2). In our notation this assumption takes the form

$$(14) \qquad \Sigma_s v(s) D^1(s) > \Sigma_s v(s) D^2(s) > \Sigma_s v(s) D^c(s).$$

From (14) it is easy to deduce the following: if all feasible (A, X) combinations provide adequate coverage to pay every beneficiary in full in every state of the world, the optimal solution will involve full funding $(A = A_{\max})$ and investment solely in bonds $(X = 0)$. The argument goes as follows. Since there will be no default in any state, the positive part

$([\cdot]^+)$ notation becomes redundant and the value of the residual can be written as

$$V^n = \sum_s v(s)[Ar(s)] - \sum_s v(s)B - A\sum_s v(s)D^c(s)$$
$$= A[\sum_s v(s)r(s) - \sum_s v(s)D^c(s)] - B\sum_s v(s).$$

Note that at $X = 0$, $\Sigma_s v(s)r(s) = \Sigma_s v(s)D^1(s)$ and at $X = 1$, $\Sigma_s v(s)r(s) = \Sigma_s v(s)D^2(s)$. Given the tax effects, the expression in brackets is clearly maximized at $X = 0$. Moreover, at $X = 0$ this expression is positive. Conditional on the choice of an optimal X value, V^n is thus maximized at $A = A_{max}$. This is the conclusion reached by Black and Tepper. Our setting is different—we rely on a market structure, while they use arbitrage arguments that require explicit offsetting actions—but the conclusions are the same.

The Black-Tepper result involves the use of pension funding and investment in bonds to take advantage of an asymmetric tax structure. Policies that involve possible default by the fund provide a way to take advantage of possible asymmetric behavior on the part of the PBGC, the insurer of pension benefits. If stocks are more effective than bonds in this role, and if the feasible (A, X) region includes combinations that make default possible, the Black-Tepper strategy may not maximize shareholder wealth. The matter is not straightforward, even in this very simple setting. The value of the insurance depends on the relationship between the payoffs over states of fund assets and benefits. It is entirely possible that a risky bond might provide both tax benefits and a large value for the insurance. In effect, we are assuming that the manager will consider both the tax effect and the insurance effect of decisions concerning funding and investment. Our previous results indicate that in our setting, the optimal policy will involve an extreme point in the feasible (A, X) space, whether the choice of bonds versus stocks involves a trade-off of these two effects or not. It is instructive, however, to examine a very simple case in which there is such a trade-off.

Assume that the payoffs from the two instruments are $D^1(1) = 1.1$, $D^1(2) = 1.1$ (bonds) and $D^2(1) = 1.2$, $D^2(2) = .1$ (stocks). The valuation function is $v(1) = .85, v(2) = .10$. We assume that $\Sigma_s v(s)D^c(s) = 1$. Note that there is a tax effect, since $\Sigma_s v(s)D^1(s) = 1.045$, $\Sigma_s v(s)D^2(s) = 1.030$, and $\Sigma_s v(s)D^c(s) = 1.000$. Benefits are 110, regardless of state, and regulatory constraints are $A_{max} = 120$, $A_{min} = 100$, $X_{max} = 1.0$, and $X_{min} = 0.0$.[5] Note that investment solely in bonds will cover benefit payments in every state, even at the minimum feasible funding level. Thus the value of the insurance will increase with X.

Figure 4.4 shows the feasible region and the value of V^n at each corner (as indicated earlier, the absolute value can be interpreted as the cost of the pension plan). One might think that, given the trade-off between the insurance and tax effects, and our previous results, the optimal policy

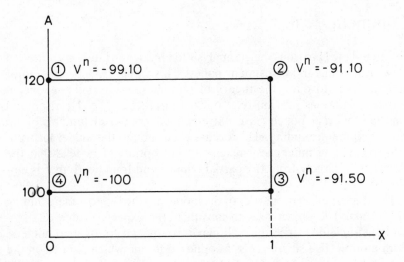

Fig. 4.4   Values of V^n at the four corners of the feasible region.

would involve either full funding plus investment in bonds (corner 1 in fig. 4.4) or minimum funding plus investment in stocks (corner 3 in fig. 4.4). However, as our example shows, this need not be the case. Here the cost of the plan is minimized by a policy involving full funding and investment solely in stocks (corner 2).

4.6. Summary and Conclusions

The main conclusion of this chapter is the indication that a fund manager should focus on extreme funding and investment strategies if our assumptions about regulatory constraints are valid. The IRS and the PBGC, on the other hand, may want to adopt regulatory policies such that the fund manager's optimal strategies will be more consistent with broader social objectives.

Notes

1. Tepper makes this assumption explicitly, Black implicitly.
2. Since the only source of uncertainty is mortality, appeal may be made to the law of large numbers for justification.
3. This rules out decisions made to maximize the utility of risk-averse managers or shareholders who are unable to diversify sufficiently to regard the decision as one of maximizing current wealth.
4. Realistically, given ERISA and the behavior of the PBGC.
5. Given the contingent liability of the corporate sponsor under ERISA, the values of A should include 30% of the corporation's net worth. With this interpretation, our numeric example is not overly fanciful.

Comment   Irwin Tepper

I expected the Harrison-Sharpe analysis to produce an interior solution to pension funding and investment policy. This would have been a major finding since, to date, the theory of optimal pension policy is one of extremal solutions, obviously at odds with practice. Yet Harrison and Sharpe's optimal policies are extremal: all bonds/full funding or all stocks/minimum funding. This occurs even though the model incorporates competing influences—taxes and put options. I believe that the results stem largely from the partial equilibrium framework that is employed.

The single-period properties of the model are the key to understanding the results. The objective is to maximize the expected value of state-contingent claims, since this will maximize the wealth of shareholders. With an objective such as this, as opposed to one which focuses on the expected utility (and which would exhibit diminishing marginal utility of wealth), it is clear that this is a partial equilibrium approach. The valuation factors applied to the cash flows bear the burden of reflecting the general equilibrium prices. These valuation factors are set up to indirectly represent shareholder opportunities and the impact of other corporate assets and liabilities on pension plan decisions. In particular, the tax effects are embedded in these valuation factors. The valuation factors do not change in response to a policy decision for the pension plan. In a general equilibrium approach the other assets and liabilities of the firm and of its shareholders are explicitly introduced and optimal policies are identified by examining shifts in the distribution of holdings among these entities. All of this is analogous to the traditional approach to capital structure as it contrasts with Miller-Modigliani analysis. In the Miller-Modigliani world changes in the cost of capital in response to capital structure changes reflect the market opportunities of the shareholders. In more traditional work, the cost of capital changes because of changes in the profile of returns from the firm.

The essential trade-off in the Harrison-Sharpe chapter is between tax benefits and default risk. In this regard, a key assumption is that the cost of potential default is not fully borne by the company. The IRS and the PBGC follow simple and naive policies. Insurance premia and wages are unaffected by funding and/or asset allocation decisions. These assumptions, which are not rational, might match reality fairly closely, also contribute to the extremal policies.

I am not surprised that the single-period solution properties carry over into the multiperiod world, although this is a major result. In order to get

Irwin Tepper is affiliated with Irwin Tepper Associates, Newton, Massachusetts.

this to happen the authors do not have wealth appearing in the value functions, and there are no intermediate contributions.

The search will continue to find a rationalization for the interior policies that exist in the real world. It is likely that some form of managerial discretion model in a world of imperfect markets will produce a result more comforting to those who believe that current practice is rational. The central problem, I think, is that theory assumes a complete integration of firms' assets and liabilities with those of the pension plans they sponsor. It also assumes integration with the assets and liabilities of shareholders and of beneficiaries. Yet companies do not manage their plans in this framework. They do not look at equity risk in the pension plan as a substitute for equity exposure on the corporate balance sheet. They do not think of arbitraging pension assets against corporate liabilities. It is these fundamental differences between theory and practice that must be met head on if progress is to be made in the development of a more satisfactory explanation of pension practice as it currently exists.

References

Black, F. 1980. The tax consequences of long-run pension policy. *Financial Analysts' Journal* 36 (4): 21–28.

Litzenberger, R. H., and Van Horne, J. 1978. Elimination of the double taxation of dividends and corporate financial policy. *Journal of Finance* 33:737–49.

Schaefer, S. 1978. Taxes and security market equilibrium. Stanford University Graduate School of Business Research Paper no. 568.

Sharpe, W. F. 1976. Corporate pension funding policy. *Journal of Financial Economics* 3:183–94.

Tepper, I. 1981. Taxation and corporate pension policy. *Journal of Finance* 36 (1): 1–13.

———. 1982. The future of private pension funding. *Financial Analysts' Journal* 38 (1): 25–31.

5 Pension Funding, Pension Asset Allocation, and Corporate Finance: Evidence from Individual Company Data

Benjamin M. Friedman

Private pension funds now constitute one of the largest pools of investment assets in the United States. Their total assets exceed $300 billion, and for the foreseeable future they are almost certain to grow still further in relation to the overall size of the United States financial markets. These funds already comprise by far the largest major category of institutional investor in the United States corporate equity market and the second largest (after the life insurance industry) in the corporate bond market. As private pension funds continue to account for a steadily growing share of these key markets, their behavior becomes increasingly important to the understanding of how the United States financial markets determine the yields on, and prices of, financial assets.

At the same time, both the assets held by private pension plans and these plans' liabilities for future benefit payments are now large—and growing—in relation to the nonpension assets and liabilities of the United States private business sector. Many major corporations' pension assets and pension liabilities represent substantial fractions of the net worth of the company, and in some cases even bulk large in comparison to the company's total assets. Because corporate equity shares therefore represent ownership claims on two pools of assets, and obligations via two sets of liabilities, shareholders clearly have a direct interest in the company's pension plan in addition to the quantities that appear on its balance sheet. The larger are the assets and liabilities of the company's pension plan, the

Benjamin M. Friedman is professor of economics, Harvard University, and research associate of the National Bureau of Economic Research.

I am grateful to Arturo Estrella and Joyce Manchester for research assistance; to them, Jay Light, and the members of the NBER study of public and private pensions, including especially Fischer Black, for many helpful discussions and for comments on an earlier draft; and to the National Bureau of Economic Research and the Alfred P. Sloan Foundation for research support.

greater is their role, along with the nonpension assets and liabilities, in determining the sponsoring company's overall risk-return prospects. Hence private pension plans increasingly matter not just for employees but for corporations' shareholders and, in the event of default, for corporations' creditors.

The growing importance of pension plans' assets and liabilities for nearly all constituencies within a typical corporation raises the possibility that the corporation's overall financial position and prospects may influence its strategy for funding its pension liabilities, as well as its subsequent allocation of these funds among alternative investment assets, in any of a number of ways. Companies may use unfunded pension liabilities as a substitute for credit market debt, or to extend overall indebtedness in conjunction with credit market debt. Similarly, companies may invest pension assets so as to mitigate, or to compound, the leverage and other risk-determining characteristics of their business. Then, too, there may be no connection at all—perhaps because managements feel a responsibility to subordinate the corporation's interest in its pension plan to the interests of the plan's beneficiaries.

Moreover, as private pension assets and liabilities continue to grow in relation to the balance sheet of the typical corporation, the possibility arises that the connection between corporate finance and pensions may be as relevant for understanding the former as the latter. If companies face limitations on the management of their pension assets and liabilities (as they do under the 1974 Employee Retirement Income Security Act), or if the treatment for tax purposes of any specific asset or liability depends on whether if falls within the pension (as it does under the current United States Tax Code), then the desired positioning of the company's consolidated pension plan and balance sheet may not be attainable solely through actions executed in the pension plan. In such circumstances companies may take at least some features of (or constraints on) the pension plan as given in making decisions about the structure of their other assets and liabilities. More generally, a company may act so as to determine the structure of its pension plan and that of its balance sheet jointly.

The object of this chapter is to test empirically for interrelationships along just these lines between United States corporations' management of their pension plans and their management of the more familiar aspects of corporate financial structure. One motivation underlying this effort is to subject to empirical scrutiny some of the theoretical hypotheses that have already emerged in the nascent literature of private pensions and corporate finance. In addition, the goal is to examine the data more broadly, to allow other regularities to appear which may be suggestive in the further development of theory describing these aspects of corporations' financial behavior.

Because of the overwhelming heterogeneity of both pension arrangements and financial structure within the United States corporate business sector, and because of the profusion of powerful economic, regulatory, and other institutional influences that have shaped the pension and general corporate financial environments in recent years, any attempt to conduct such an investigation using aggregated time-series data would be of limited value. Instead, the analysis undertaken here relies on individual company data assembled from the pension plan information that each plan sponsor provides to the Internal Revenue Service and the United States Department of Labor on Form 5500, used in conjunction with additional conventional individual company financial statistics contained in the Standard and Poor's Compustat file. The pension data are for plan year 1977, the only year for which a nearly complete Form 5500 file exists as of the time of writing.

Section 5.1 describes the data and indicates the procedures used for such steps as within-firm aggregation of multiple pension plans, merging of the Form 5500 and Compustat files, and treatment of corporate parent-subsidiary relationships. Section 5.2, which focuses on pension funding strategy, presents the results of a series of tests for relationships between corporations' funding of their pension liabilities (the total of which is taken as given here) and other characteristics of the respective firms' business and balance sheet (also taken as given). Section 5.3, also on pension funding strategy, digresses to examine the results of tests of the familiar hypothesis that corporations' decisions in this regard are oriented not to achieving fundamental financial objectives but to smoothing their reported earnings statements over time. Section 5.4, which focuses on pension asset allocations, presents the results of a series of tests for relationships between corporations' investment of their pension assets (the total of which is taken as given here) and other characteristics of the firms' business and balance sheet (also taken as given). Section 5.5 generalizes the line of investigation pursued in section 5.2 by presenting results of tests for a joint relationship between pension funding strategy and the corporation's balance sheet, thereby allowing for the possibility that balance sheet decisions may not be predetermined with respect to pension funding decisions. Section 5.6 briefly summarizes the chapter's principal conclusions, highlights some important caveats, and indicates directions for potential future research.

5.1   The Data

The Employee Retirement Income Security Act of 1974 requires each pension benefit plan sponsored by a United States corporation to file a report annually, with the Internal Revenue Service and the Department of Labor, on Form 5500 (or Form 5500-C if the plan covers 100 or fewer participants). The form includes information about the plan's benefit structure, income and expenses for the year, beginning-of-year and end-of-year assets broken down into a substantial detail of investment categories, and the number and current status of participants in the plan. Each defined-benefit plan must also file Form 5500 Schedule B, which provides actuarial information about the plan's accrued liabilities, including its vested and nonvested liabilities separately, together with other related items. The Appendix shows the format of Form 5500 and Schedule B.

The 1977 Employee Benefit Plan Sample File contains all 29,120 Form 5500 returns submitted for plan year 1977 and processed by the Internal Revenue Service between July 1, 1978, and June 30, 1979.[1] Those returns constituted 77.5% of the Form 5500 returns ultimately submitted for plan year 1977. The 22.5% of the returns that are missing from the file are heavily concentrated among smaller plans (as measured by asset size), however.[2] Of the 29,120 returns included in the file, 4,694 either pertained to plans sponsored by nonprofit organizations or reported zero assets. The remaining 24,426 returns form the basic sample used in this chapter.

Table 5.1 shows the distribution of assets across this sample of 24,426 plans. The combined assets for all 24,426 totaled $222 billion.[3] The great majority of this $222 billion was concentrated in a small fraction of the plans. Nearly one-half of the plans had less than $1 million in assets, and more than four-fifths had less than $5 million. By contrast, the 22 plans with more than $1 billion in assets together accounted for almost one-fifth of the total, and the 55 plans with more than $500 million together accounted for almost one-third.[4]

Because many companies sponsor more than one pension plan—one plan for salaried staff and another for wage earners, for example—the 24,426 plans in the sample represented only 15,098 sponsoring corporations.[5] For purposes of testing hypotheses about relationships between pension asset and liability decisions and corporate financial behavior in the conventional sense, what presumably matters is not the assets or liabilities of any one of a corporation's pension plans but the combined assets and liabilities of all plans that it sponsors. Table 5.2 shows the distribution of the $222 billion in total assets across the 15,098 sponsoring firms in the sample. As one might expect, aggregating all plans sponsored by a single firm shifts the distribution toward larger assets for each observation, although the effect is quantitatively small.

The most common form of pension plan in the United States is the defined-benefit plan, but other forms (primarily the defined-contribution plan) exist as well. The distinction is relevant because the concept of pension "liabilities" has meaning only for defined-benefit plans. For the same reason, shareholders in a corporation have no direct financial

Table 5.1   Asset Distribution of Disaggregated Sample: All For-Profit Sponsors

Asset Size	Distribution of Plans				Distribution of Assets			
	Number	%	Cumulative Number	Cumulative %	Amount	Cumulative Amount	%	Cumulative %
0–0.5	7,384	30.2	7,384	30.2	1.9	1.9	0.9	0.9
0.5–1.0	4,127	16.9	11,511	47.1	3.2	5.1	1.4	2.3
1–5	8,414	34.4	19,925	81.6	19.7	24.8	8.8	11.2
5–10	1,864	7.6	21,789	89.2	13.1	37.9	5.9	17.1
10–25	1,368	5.6	23,157	94.8	21.4	59.4	9.7	26.7
25–50	600	2.5	23,757	97.3	21.3	80.6	9.6	36.3
50–100	335	1.4	24,092	98.6	23.7	104.4	10.7	47.0
100–250	218	0.9	24,310	99.5	33.1	137.5	14.9	61.9
250–500	61	0.3	24,371	99.8	21.3	158.8	9.6	71.5
500–1,000	33	0.1	24,404	99.9	23.4	182.2	10.5	82.0
Over 1,000	22	0.1	24,426	100.0	40.0	222.2	18.0	100.0

Note: Asset size categories are in millions of dollars; asset amounts are in billions of dollars.

Table 5.2   Asset Distribution of Aggregated Sample: All For-Profit Sponsors

	Distribution of Sponsors				Distribution of Assets			
Asset Size	Number	Cumulative Number	%	Cumulative %	Amount	Cumulative Amount	%	Cumulative %
0–0.5	3,893	3,893	25.8	25.8	1.1	1.1	0.5	0.5
0.5–1.0	2,389	6,282	15.8	41.6	1.9	2.9	0.8	1.3
1–5	5,308	11,590	35.2	76.8	12.6	15.5	5.7	7.0
5–10	1,301	12,891	8.6	85.4	9.2	24.7	4.1	11.1
10–25	1,036	13,927	6.9	92.2	16.5	41.2	7.4	18.5
25–50	491	14,418	3.3	95.5	17.2	58.4	7.7	26.3
50–100	296	14,714	2.0	97.5	20.6	78.9	9.3	35.5
100–250	246	14,960	1.6	99.1	36.7	115.6	16.5	52.0
250–500	73	15,033	0.5	99.6	25.6	141.3	11.5	63.6
500–1,000	38	15,071	0.3	99.8	26.1	167.3	11.7	75.3
Over 1,000	27	15,098	0.2	100.0	54.8	222.2	24.7	100.0

Note: Asset size categories are in millions of dollars; asset amounts are in billions of dollars.

interest in how the assets of a defined-contribution plan perform. Of the 24,426 plans in table 5.1, 16,200 sponsored by 10,470 different companies, and with $165 billion in assets, were defined-benefit plans. Nevertheless, 856 of these plans failed to file Schedule B in time for the Internal Revenue Service to process it, along with the corresponding Form 5500 return, before June 30, 1979. The remaining 15,344 plans, sponsored by 9,899 companies, reported $152 billion in combined assets. Table 5.3 shows the distribution of these assets across the 9,899 firms.

The information contained in Form 5500 is insufficient, of course, to facilitate tests of hypotheses about relationships between pension asset and liability decisions and corporate finance decisions in the conventional sense. Some source of information about each sponsoring company's balance sheet, as well as its income statement and other aspects of its financial situation, is also necessary. Because many of the 15,098 companies sponsoring pension plans included in the 1977 Form 5500 sample are either small or closely held, however, obtaining such information on a comprehensive basis would be impractical if not impossible. By contrast, most of the larger companies are included in the Standard and Poor's Compustat file. A systematic search, based on a computer procedure supplemented with "by hand" inspection, revealed 1,690 corporations included in the Compustat file that were sponsors of 5,788 pension plans included in the 1977 Form 5500 sample.[6]

Even so, simply matching Compustat firms with pension plan sponsors would still be inadequate. The Compustat file reports balance sheets and earnings statements for each included corporation on a consolidated basis—that is, including all of the corporation's wholly owned subsidiaries. From the perspective of analyzing corporate financial behavior at the level of the relationships posited in this investigation, consolidation is presumably the correct procedure. Matching Compustat firms with pension plan sponsors would be inadequate, therefore, without also consolidating plans sponsored by each Compustat firm with plans sponsored by its subsidiaries (if any). A laborious "by hand" search revealed that 593 Compustat firms were sponsors—not directly but through subsidiaries—of 2,040 pension plans included in the 1977 Form 5500 sample.[7] Of the 593 Compustat firms sponsoring pension plans through subsidiaries, 447 also sponsored one or more plans directly.

The fully aggregated and consolidated sample available for use in testing for relationships between pension decisions and corporate financial decisions therefore consists of 7,828 pension plans (including defined-benefit as well as other plans, and, among defined-benefit plans, those that did and did not file Schedule B), with $153 billion in combined assets, sponsored by 1,836 consolidated companies.[8] Table 5.4 shows the distribution of this $153 billion of assets across the 1,836 firms. Of the 7,828 plans sponsored by consolidated Compustat companies, 5,836 were de-

Table 5.3　Asset Distribution of Aggregated Sample: Defined-Benefit Plans Only

Asset Size	Distribution of Sponsors				Distribution of Assets			
	Number	Cumulative Number	%	Cumulative %	Amount	Cumulative Amount	%	Cumulative %
0–0.5	2,398	2,398	24.2	24.2	0.7	0.7	0.4	0.4
0.5–1.0	1,498	3,896	15.1	39.4	1.2	1.8	0.8	1.2
1–5	3,414	7,310	34.5	73.8	8.2	10.0	5.4	6.6
5–10	923	8,233	9.3	83.1	6.5	16.5	4.3	10.9
10–25	776	9,009	7.8	91.0	12.3	28.8	8.1	19.0
25–50	388	9,397	3.9	94.9	13.8	42.6	9.1	28.0
50–100	240	9,637	2.4	97.4	16.9	59.5	11.2	39.2
100–250	164	9,801	1.7	99.0	24.9	84.4	16.4	55.6
250–500	53	9,854	0.5	99.5	18.6	103.0	12.3	67.9
500–1,000	30	9,884	0.3	99.8	20.9	124.0	13.8	81.7
Over 1,000	15	9,899	0.2	100.0	27.8	151.8	18.3	100.0

Note: Asset size categories are in millions of dollars; asset amounts are in billions of dollars.

Table 5.4   **Asset Distribution of Aggregated and Consolidated Sample: All Compustat Sponsors**

Asset Size	Distribution of Sponsors				Distribution of Assets			
	Number	Cumulative Number	%	Cumulative %	Amount	Cumulative Amount	%	Cumulative %
0–0.5	87	87	4.7	4.7	0.0	0.0	0.0	0.0
0.5–1.0	108	195	5.9	10.6	0.1	0.1	0.1	0.1
1–5	389	584	21.2	31.8	1.0	1.1	0.7	0.8
5–10	243	827	13.2	45.0	1.8	2.9	1.2	1.9
10–25	317	1,144	17.3	62.3	5.2	8.1	3.4	5.3
25–50	226	1,370	12.3	74.6	8.0	16.2	5.3	10.6
50–100	180	1,550	9.8	84.4	12.6	28.8	8.2	18.8
100–250	180	1,730	9.8	94.2	27.4	56.2	18.0	36.8
250–500	59	1,789	3.2	97.4	20.4	76.6	13.4	50.2
500–1,000	28	1,817	1.5	99.0	19.2	95.8	12.6	62.7
1,000–5,000	18	1,835	1.0	99.9	38.5	134.3	25.2	87.9
Over 5,000	1	1,836	0.1	100.0	18.4	152.7	12.1	100.0

Note: Asset size categories are in millions of dollars; asset amounts are in billions of dollars.

Table 5.5   Asset Distribution of Aggregated Sample: Defined-Benefit Plans Only, All Compustat Sponsors

Asset Size	Distribution of Sponsors				Distribution of Assets			
	Number	Cumulative Number	%	Cumulative %	Amount	Cumulative Amount	%	Cumulative %
0–0.5	87	87	5.6	5.6	0.0	0.0	0.0	0.0
0.5–1.0	78	165	5.0	10.6	0.1	0.1	0.1	0.1
1–5	342	507	22.0	32.7	0.9	1.0	0.9	0.9
5–10	204	711	13.1	45.8	1.5	2.5	1.3	2.3
10–25	283	944	18.2	64.0	4.7	7.2	4.3	6.5
25–50	187	1,181	12.0	76.1	6.6	13.8	6.0	12.5
50–100	170	1,351	11.0	87.0	12.2	26.0	11.1	23.6
100–250	128	1,479	8.2	95.3	20.0	46.0	18.1	41.8
250–500	44	1,523	2.8	98.1	15.9	61.8	14.4	56.2
500–1,000	18	1,541	1.2	99.3	12.7	74.5	11.5	67.7
1,000–5,000	10	1,551	0.6	99.9	19.2	93.7	17.5	85.1
Over 5,000	1	1,552	0.1	100.0	16.4	110.1	14.9	100.0

Note: Asset size categories are in millions of dollars; asset amounts are in billions of dollars.

fined-benefit plans, of which 5,670 filed Schedule B in time for Internal Revenue Service processing. Table 5.5 shows the distribution of these 5,670 plans' $110 billion of assets across the plans' 1,552 sponsoring firms. A comparison of tables 5.2 and 5.4, and of tables 5.3 and 5.5, shows that the result of not only consolidating subsidiaries into parent companies but also excluding all plans not sponsored by a Compustat firm (even through a subsidiary) is to shift the distribution further toward larger dollar amounts per company.[9]

5.2 Pension Funding Strategy

In the most abstract conception of the incorporated firm, the assets and liabilities of a corporation's defined-benefit pension plan(s) are just like the assets and liabilities that appear on its balance sheet. Shareholders own both sets of assets, and they are responsible (to the extent of their equity) for both sets of liabilities. Whether the firm's management acts so as to maximize the share price, to maximize expected profits, or to achieve yet some other objective, there is no need to distinguish between one pool of assets and the other or between one group of liabilities and the other.

Such an abstraction may fail to describe the world of United States corporations and their sponsored pension plans for several well-known reasons.[10] At the most practical level, the firm's flexibility on the pension liability side is usually severely limited. Conventions of labor market practice, reinforced by legal requirements and often by collective bargaining agreements, restrict the range within which a firm and its workers can divide total labor costs between current and deferred compensation. To the extent that the firm's basic pension liabilities are predetermined from the perspective of financial decision making, therefore, its choice of pension "liabilities" in this context refers only to that part of the basic actuarial liability in excess of the amount of assets committed to the pension fund. Hence decisions about pension "liabilities" in this sense are really decisions about pension assets. Moreover, the firm's flexibility is limited here, too, in that its pension funding position must meet standards specified by the Employee Retirement Income Security Act.[11]

Wholly apart from such constraints, a variety of considerations may lead the firm to see pension assets and liabilities as less than perfect substitutes for its other assets and liabilities. First, the implicit cost of "borrowing" by less than fully funding pension liabilities need not be identical, either before or after taxes, to the explicit cost of borrowing in the credit market. In the extreme, the former "source of funds" may be available at times when the latter is not. Even under ordinary circumstances, the scheduling of the "debt service" associated with the two kinds of liabilities may differ in important ways. A second distinction is that pension liabilities, unlike the firm's other liabilities in most circumstances, are insured in a way that limits the firm's exposure. The Pension Benefit Guaranty Corporation insures corporations' pension liabilities in full but, in the event of default, has a claim on only one-third of the firm's assets. The tax treatment of pension plans provides a third reason why the simple abstraction, in which one asset or liability is just like any other, may not apply to actual corporations. Payments of funds into the pension plan are deductible from the firm's income for tax purposes, and earnings on assets held in the pension plan are excluded from taxable income. Finally—although these four factors do not exhaust the possible reasons for distinguishing pension versus other assets and liabilities—shareholders and potential shareholders may be more fully aware of that part of a firm's liabilities which actually appears on its balance sheet.[12]

For all of these familiar reasons, therefore, a corporation may not behave as if it is indifferent between pension and other assets, or between pension and other liabilities. Hence, instead of the usual net worth constraint,

$$(1) \qquad TA - TL = NW,$$

where TA and TL are the firm's total assets and total liabilities, respectively, and NW is net worth (assumed to be predetermined as of any specific time), the more relevant expression is

$$(2) \qquad PA + BA - PL - BL = NW,$$

where PA and PL distinguish the assets and liabilities of the firms's defined-benefit pension plan(s), while BA and BL represent the assets and liabilities that appear on the firm's balance sheet.[13]

If the firm were free to choose simultaneously each of these four quantities, subject only to the net worth constraint, then its consolidated "portfolio" behavior would take the familiar form

$$(3) \qquad \frac{1}{NW} \begin{bmatrix} PA \\ BA \\ -PL \\ -BL \end{bmatrix} = \alpha + B\mathbf{X},$$

where $\mathbf{X}$ is a vector of external factors determining the firm's responses, α is a vector of coefficients summing to unity, and B is a matrix of coefficients with zero column sums. The most familiar empirical application of this conception is in a time-series context, in which $\mathbf{X}$ would include primarily (often exclusively) the expected yields on the respective assets and liabilities. By contrast, in a cross-section context the elements of $\mathbf{X}$ are firm-specific factors that are taken to be predetermined with respect to the firm's portfolio choice in the one time period under observation, and that (at least potentially) influence that choice. To the extent that some of the firm's portfolio choices are predetermined with respect to others, however, some of the elements within the left-hand side of (3) belong more properly on the right. If the firm decides on its pension assets and liabilities only secondarily, after deciding on its other liabilities, then PA and PL may depend on BA and BL as well as the other factors included within X.

One question that immediately arises in this context is whether firms have fixed targets for their total liabilities ($PL + BL$) so that they take on fewer pension liabilities as they have more liabilities on their balance sheets or, alternatively, whether they systematically use PL and BL together to achieve greater or smaller total leverage. Put in another way, the question is whether the firm treats pension liabilities and other liabilities as substitutes or complements, although the sense of substitutability versus complementarity involved here differs somewhat from the usual one in which vector $\mathbf{X}$ includes specific time-varying yields associated with PL and BL.

The evidence from the 1977 Form 5500 sample is consistent with complementarity of PL and BL in this sense. Estimating the cross-section regression

$$(4) \qquad \frac{PL}{NW} = \alpha + \gamma \frac{BL}{NW}$$

for the sample of all consolidated Compustat firms with defined-benefit plans filing Schedule B yields $\gamma = .17$, with t-statistic 7.8 ($\overline{R}^2 = .04$).[14] For the subsample in which each firm's pension plan is sufficiently important in its overall structure that pension liabilities amount to at least 3% of the firm's total assets, the result is $\gamma = .26$, with t-statistic 6.4 ($\overline{R}^2 = .07$). For the further subsample in which $PL/TA \geq .10$, the result is $\gamma = .50$, with t-statistic 7.9 ($\overline{R}^2 = .17$).

Further analysis that controls for other influences in the spirit of (3), while maintaining the assumption that BL is predetermined with respect to PL, supports this conclusion. Table 5.6 reports estimation results for a series of regressions of the form

$$(5) \qquad \frac{PL}{NW} = \alpha + \gamma \frac{BL}{NW} + \beta X$$

where X is, in turn, each of a series of variables describing the firm and its operating environment. Once again, the positive relationship between pension and other liabilities (both scaled by net worth) holds up regardless of the choice of additional controlling variables.

The specific results for the partial effects of the several controlling variables are also interesting in some cases. Neither the growth rate nor

Table 5.6   Relationship between Pension Liabilities and Other Liabilities

Control Variable	Full Sample		$PL/TA \geq .10$ Subsample	
	γ	β	γ	β
$\rho(EBIT)$	.17	.32	.51	$-.46$
	(7.5)	(0.4)	(7.6)	(-0.2)
$\sigma(EBIT)$	.17	.14	.51	1.20
	(7.5)	(0.4)	(7.9)	(1.1)
E/BA	.20	.60	.55	1.15
	(6.7)	(3.1)	(6.8)	(2.0)
$\mu(E/BA)$	.16	.17	.46	.20
	(5.6)	(0.6)	(6.0)	(0.2)
$\sigma(E/BA)$	.15	$-.81$	.46	$-.46$
	(6.1)	(-1.9)	(6.8)	(-0.3)
$\mu(T/E)$	.15	.00	.46	.06
	(6.5)	(0.4)	(6.9)	(1.0)
$\mu(L/S)$	.20	.23	.66	.21
	(5.6)	(2.0)	(5.7)	(0.6)
AGE	.15	$-.44$	.44	$-.26$
	(6.1)	(-5.6)	(6.6)	(-1.2)

Note: Results shown are estimated coefficients (and t-statistics) for the regression $PL/NW = \alpha + \gamma(BL/NW) + \beta X$, where $\rho(EBIT) = $ 10-year growth rate of earnings before interest and taxes; $\sigma(EBIT) = $ 10-year normalized standard deviation of EBIT around its growth trend; $E/BA = $ ratio of earnings to nonpension assets; $\mu(E/BA) = $ 10-year mean of E/BA; $\sigma(E/BA) = $ 10-year standard deviation of E/BA around $\mu(E/BA)$; $\mu(T/E) = $ 5-year mean of ratio of taxes paid to before-tax earnings; $\mu(L/S) = $ 5-year mean of ratio of labor and related expenses to net sales; and $AGE = $ ratio of pension plan participants currently employed to all plan participants.

the trend-adjusted variability of the firm's earnings had a significant effect on its pension liabilities. The 1977 rate of return on assets affected pension liabilities positively, but the mean rate of return over the past 10 years did not. The negative effect of the volatility of rate of return was marginally significant in the full sample, but not in the subsample with large pension liabilities relative to the firm's total assets. The firm's tax status had no significant effect. As would be expected, the firm's labor intensiveness affected pension liabilities positively, and the fraction of the firm's pension plan participants who were still employed affected pension liabilities negatively; but both effects were significant in the full sample only.

The failure of so many basic aspects of the firm's risk and return situation to affect its pension liabilities supports the suggestion, made above, that the firm does not actually choose PL in the usual portfolio sense. Instead, the firm may take PL as given—by labor market considerations, for example—so that its actual choice in this context is simply how much of its pension liabilities to fund. If the firm were free to choose in this context, its portfolio problem would take the form

$$(6) \qquad \frac{1}{NW} \begin{bmatrix} BA \\ -BL \\ -(PL - PA) \end{bmatrix} = \alpha + B\mathbf{X}.$$

Moreover, if the firm decides only secondarily on its unfunded pension liabilities (that is, on its pension assets in this context), then again the possibility arises that $(PL - PA)$ depends on BA and BL as well as on any or all of the other factors included within $\mathbf{X}$.

The parallel question in this context is whether firms with large amounts of debt on their balance sheet choose to have greater or smaller amounts of unfunded liabilities. In this form the question bears a direct connection to at least one prominent line of theoretical analysis of how corporations' pension funding decisions depend on their financial condition. In particular, Sharpe (1976) has suggested that an important rationale for firms to fund their pension plans less than fully is the value of the insurance provided by the Pension Benefit Guaranty Corporation (PBGC).[15] In Sharpe's analysis the insurance written by the PBGC is equivalent to a put option, and the firm's incentive is to maximize the value of the put. A major implication of this line of reasoning is that the firms for which the probability of bankruptcy is nontrivial have an incentive to underfund their pension plans. The more highly levered a firm is, therefore—that is, the larger is BL relative to NW, all other considerations equal—the greater is the firm's incentive to underfund its pension plan. In terms of the current analysis, therefore, the Sharpe hypothesis suggests that BL and $(PL - PA)$ are complements.

The evidence from the 1977 Form 5500 sample is consistent with complementarity not only of BL and PL, as in (4), but also of BL and $(PL - PA)$. Hence the data are consistent with Sharpe's analysis of the pension funding decision. Estimating the cross-section regression

$$(7) \qquad \frac{PL - PA}{NW} = \alpha + \gamma \frac{BL}{NW}$$

for the full sample yields $\gamma = .14$, with t-statistic 10.1 ($\bar{R}^2 = .07$).[16] For the subsample of firms with $PL/TA \geq .03$, the corresponding results are $\gamma = .25$, with t-statistic 9.3 ($\bar{R}^2 = .13$). For the subsample with $PL/TA \geq .10$, the results are $\gamma = .44$, with t-statistic 10.8 ($\bar{R}^2 = .27$).

Table 5.7 shows estimation results, comparable to those in table 5.6, for a parallel series of regressions

$$(8) \qquad \frac{PL - PA}{NW} = \alpha + \gamma \frac{BL}{NW} + \beta X$$

Table 5.7   **Relationship between Unfunded Pension Liabilities and Other Liabilities**

Control Variable	Full Sample		$PL/TA \geq .10$ Subsample	
	γ	β	γ	β
$\rho(EBIT)$	.14	.13	.45	$-.82$
	(9.6)	(0.3)	(10.2)	(-0.4)
$\sigma(EBIT)$	.14	.17	.45	1.05
	(9.7)	(0.8)	(10.8)	(1.3)
E/BA	.15	.35	.48	.88
	(7.3)	(2.7)	(8.1)	(2.1)
$\mu(E/BA)$	.12	.12	.42	.25
	(6.5)	(0.7)	(7.5)	(0.4)
$\sigma(E/BA)$	.12	$-.32$	.41	.11
	(7.0)	(-1.1)	(8.4)	(0.1)
$\mu(T/E)$	.11	.00	.39	.05
	(7.2)	(0.4)	(8.2)	(1.1)
$\mu(L/S)$	.16	.16	.53	.30
	(7.4)	(2.1)	(8.0)	(1.1)
AGE	.12	$-.31$	.39	$-.37$
	(7.1)	(-6.0)	(8.1)	(-2.4)

Note: Results shown are estimated coefficients (and t-statistics) for the regression $(PL - PA)/NW = \alpha + \gamma(BL/NW) + \beta X$. See table 5.6 for definitions of variable symbols.

that differ only in the assumption that the firm's choice variable is unfunded pension liabilities rather than total pension liabilities. Here Sharpe's analysis implies that aspects of the firm's operating environment that affect its probability of bankruptcy—variability of earnings, for example—should also increase the firm's incentive to underfund its pension. Once again, the strong positive relationship between (unfunded) pension liabilities and the firm's other liabilities holds up regardless of the controlling variable. The results for the effects of the individual controlling variables are again about as in table 5.6. In particular, neither volatility of earnings nor volatility of rate of return exhibits the significant positive effect that would be consistent with Sharpe's hypothesis.

Finally, the form of both (7) and (8) assumes not only that the firm takes its pension liabilities as given in deciding on pension funding but also that the firm takes decisions solely on the difference $(PL - PA)$ irrespective of either individual amount. In other words, (7) and (8) are equivalent, respectively, to

(9)
$$\frac{PA}{NW} = \alpha + \delta \frac{PL}{NW} + \gamma \frac{BL}{NW}$$

and

(10) $$\frac{PA}{NW} = \alpha + \delta\frac{PL}{NW} + \gamma\frac{BL}{NW} + \beta X$$

subject to the constraint $\delta = 1$. The data consistently reject this constraint, however. Estimating (9) for the full sample yields $\delta = .60$ and $\gamma = -.06$, with respective t-statistics 42.8 and -4.9 ($\bar{R}^2 = .59$).[17] For the subsample with $PL/TA \geq .03$, the corresponding results are $\delta = .63$ and $\gamma = -.09$, with respective t-statistics 32.8 and -4.4 ($\bar{R}^2 = .66$). For the subsample with $PL/TA \geq .10$, the results are $\delta = .66$ and $\gamma = -.16$, with respective t-statistics 22.6 and -4.7 ($\bar{R}^2 = .64$). The results of estimating (10) with any of the control variables shown in tables 5.6 and 5.7 indicate similar values for δ and γ, and β values that are again consistent with those found in estimating (5) and (8).

Hence the firm-to-firm variation in pension funding does not simply reflect individual firms' decisions strictly about their unfunded liabilities. At the margin, with other factors equal, a firm with an additional $1 of pension liabilities typically funds only about 60¢ more in pension assets. This marginal funding rate—marginal from one firm to the next, that is, rather than for one firm over time—is also just equal to the average funding ratio (.62) for all firms in the sample. In addition, the consistent finding of a negative γ value in (9) and (10) indicates that firms with greater amounts of nonpension liabilities fund their pension liabilities less fully, to the extent of about a 10¢ reduction in pension funding for each $1 of additional nonpension liabilities. This result is again consistent with Sharpe's analysis of the pension funding decision in the context of the value of the put to the PBGC.

The main conclusions that emerge from this consideration of the firm's choice of pension liabilities and funding, on the assumption that the asset and liability totals on the firm's balance sheet are predetermined with respect to its pension decisions, are (1) that pension liabilities, either in total or in excess of funding, depend positively on the firm's other liabilities; (2) that firms do not make decisions simply with respect to their unfunded pension liabilities, but instead fund pension liabilities less than one-for-one at the margin; (3) that funding of the firm's pension liabilities depends negatively on its other liabilities; and (4) that, apart from labor-specific characteristics like the firm's labor intensiveness and the working-retired status of its labor force, basic aspects of the firm's risk and return position have no apparent effect on its choice of either total or unfunded pension liabilities.

5.3 The Earnings-Smoothing Hypothesis

The discussion of pension funding strategy in Section 5.2 focuses on fundamental aspects of portfolio behavior: substitutability versus complementarity of pension and other liabilities, the degree to which pension assets offset pension liabilities, and the role of other measures of risk and return confronting the firm. From the perspective of any familiar theory of corporate financial behavior, these considerations and others like them are the principal determinants of the firm's pension decisions.

By contrast, discussions of pension funding strategy by corporate practitioners often emphasize different factors. In particular, in seeking to explain why so many firms underfund their pension plans despite apparent tax incentives to fund fully, corporate financial officers and other financial market participants frequently cite the "hidden" nature of pension liabilities. Because the pension plan is off the balance sheet, shareholders and others may be at least partly unaware of the associated liabilities. The most obvious implication of this assertion is that a firm may be able to raise its share price by substituting pension liabilities for liabilities that appear on the balance sheet, but recent research on the relationship between stock prices and pension liabilities has provided evidence that typically warrants rejecting this proposition.[18]

A further implication of the idea that pension assets and liabilities are hidden is that shareholders and other interested persons may judge the firm's performance by its reported earnings rather than by more comprehensive flow measures. Because contributions to a firm's pension plan reduce its reported earnings in the same way as any other expense item, control over the timing of pension contributions enables firms to influence the time path of reported earnings. To the extent that the management seeks to report smoothly growing earnings over time, therefore, it may want to increase pension contributions when business is strong and reduce them when business is weak. Such actions need not change the total amount contributed to the pension plan over time. Indeed, in the broader context that consolidates the firm's pension assets and liabilities with its other assets and liabilities, such actions change nothing at all. They have a purpose only if some constituency, whose actions matter to the corporation, focuses on the time path of reported earnings.

This earnings-smoothing hypothesis provides a potential explanation for the pension underfunding puzzle to the extent that firms with unfunded pension liabilities have more flexibility to adjust the timing of their pension contributions than do firms with fully funded pensions. Restrictions on prefunding unaccrued pension liabilities prevent a firm with a fully funded pension from making extraordinary increases in contributions, and firms that simply decide to fund fully choose thereby to forgo using the potential flexibility in the opposite direction.

Data from the 1977 Form 5500 sample provide evidence indicating that firms typically do manage earnings in this way. For the entire sample of firms with defined-benefit plans, 70.0% had before-tax reported earnings streams that were smoother, as measured by the normalized 10-year standard deviation around trend, than the corresponding consolidated earnings including pension contributions. On an after-tax basis, with the included pension contributions adjusted for additional taxes that the firm would otherwise have paid, 70.5% of firms had smoother reported earnings than consolidated earnings.

Nevertheless, the data provide almost no support for the claim that firms with underfunded pension liabilities are more likely to manage their reported earnings in this way. Table 5.8 shows the percentages of firms with smoother reported than consolidated earnings, comparable to the percentages reported above, for a breakdown of the full sample according to the ratio of pension assets to pension liabilities. If anything, these distributions seem to indicate that firms with underfunded pension liabilities are *less* likely to engage in smoothing their reported earnings by managing their pension contributions. Only for the two extreme subsamples—with funding ratios below .10 or above .90—does the relationship go in the hypothesized direction.

A more systematic examination of the data confirms this impression. Estimating the regression

$$(11) \qquad \frac{\sigma(E)}{\sigma(E + PC)} = \alpha + \beta \frac{PA}{PL},$$

where $\sigma(E)$ and $\sigma(E + PC)$ are the normalized 10-year standard deviations of reported earnings and consolidated earnings, respectively, yields a value of β which is positive, as hypothesized, but negligibly small and with t-statistic less than 0.1. The results for the relationship based on after-tax earnings are analogous.

In sum, the evidence does show substantial prevalence of the timing of pension contributions so as to smooth reported earnings, but it does not support the hypothesis that this practice is related to the funding status of

Table 5.8   Relationship between Earnings Smoothing and Pension Funding

	Percentage Showing Smoother Reported than Consolidated Earnings	
Funding Ratio	Before Tax	After Tax
0–.1	64.3	78.6
.1–.2	50.0	66.7
.2–.3	53.3	53.3
.3–.4	69.0	66.7
.4–.5	77.6	77.6
.5–.6	73.6	75.7
.6–.7	71.0	70.2
.7–.8	69.8	70.6
.8–.9	77.1	72.9
.9–1.0	58.6	60.6

firms' pensions. The explanation for the underfunding puzzle apparently lies elsewhere.

5.4 Pension Asset Allocations

Private pension plans invest their assets in a way unlike any other major category of institutional investors. For the aggregate of all pension plans, nearly two-thirds of all assets held are corporate equities. Among other major investor groups (apart from mutual funds), the corresponding fractions are about one-fifth equities for the public pension plans sponsored by state and local governments, one-sixth equities for fire and casualty insurance companies, and one-ninth equities for life insurance companies (even including some "separate accounts").[19] Clearly there is something unique about the investment choices made by private pension plans.

To the extent that the assets in a corporation's defined-benefit pension plan "belong" to the sponsoring firm's shareholders, in the sense that they and not the plan's beneficiaries stand to gain or lose according to the assets' return, the heavy concentration of private pension assets in equities is not surprising.[20] By holding the corporation's shares in the first place, shareholders have already expressed the desire for an equity investment. Because of the pension plan(s) that the firm sponsors, however, each such investment represents ownership in two pools of assets. If the firm's pension plan holds debt securities instead of equities, then the shareholder's investment is no longer a pure (or even levered) equity but a mixture of debt and equity claims.

In the simplest abstraction like that used to motivate the discussion in section 5.2, a corporation would not hold its pension assets in any form other than the ordinary assets of its business—that is, in its own stock. Legal restrictions preclude holding pension assets entirely in this form, however, and also impose "prudence" standards that many firms interpret to preclude investing pension assets entirely in equity securities even on a fully diversified basis. Once again, therefore, the extreme simplification does not adequately describe the behavior of actual corporations and the pension plans that they sponsor. In addition, tax considerations appear to favor holding equity assets outside the pension plan and debt assets in the plan.[21]

The discussion in section 5.2 emphasizes the role of the firm's pension assets and liabilities, along with the assets and liabilities on its balance sheet, in determining its overall risk and return posture. The allocation of the pension assets among alternative investment vehicles is a further element in this calculus. For example, borrowing in the credit market to finance additional (tax-deduction augmented) pension contributions has essentially no risk implications for the firm if the pension plan then invests these funds in debt securities, but such an action increases the firm's risk if the pension plan invests in equities.[22]

The dependence of the firm's risk and return posture on the allocation of its pension assets raises in turn the possibility that these allocations may depend on the firm's asset-liability structure in the sense of either (1) or (2) above, or on other characteristics of the firm's business and financial situation as introduced in (3), or on both. Sharpe's analysis described in section 5.2, for example, suggests that firms with nontrivial probability of bankruptcy have an incentive to maximize the value of the effective put to the PBGC. In the context of pension asset allocation decisions, therefore, the Sharpe hypothesis is that firms bearing greater overall risk will tend to invest their pension assets more in equities. Hence the more highly levered a firm is (as measured by debt on the balance sheet or by unfunded pension liabilities), or the greater is its risk exposure in other regards, the greater is the firm's incentive to invest its pension assets in equities.

In the simple context of (3), the question of pension asset allocation represents simply a disaggregation within the pension asset total PA. By contrast, if the total amount of pension assets is predetermined with respect to the allocation—as seems plausible in the context of most corporations' decision procedures—then PA is the constraining variable and the portfolio choice problem is of the form

$$(12) \qquad \frac{1}{PA} \begin{bmatrix} PA_1 \\ PA_2 \\ \vdots \\ PA_N \end{bmatrix} = \alpha + B\mathbf{X},$$

where the PA_i are specific forms of pension assets and α and B are again as in (3). Table 5.9 presents the results of estimating this relationship, for the sample of all Compustat firms sponsoring defined benefit plans, in the somewhat different form

$$(13) \qquad \frac{1}{BA} \begin{bmatrix} PAE \\ PAD \\ PAO \end{bmatrix} = \alpha + \gamma \frac{PA}{BA} + \beta X,$$

where PAE, PAD, and PAO are pension assets in defined-benefit plans, held in equities, debt securities, and other investment vehicles, repectively, α is a vector of coefficients summing to zero, and γ is a vector of coefficients summing to unity.

The one result that stands out in table 5.9 is the negative relationship between the allocation of pension assets to equities and the variability of

Table 5.9   Determinants of Pension Portfolio Allocation

Control Variable	PAE/BA		PAD/BA		PAO/BA	
	γ	β	γ	β	γ	β
$\rho(EBIT)$	.31	$-.18$	.37	.11	.32	.07
	(58.1)	(-0.6)	(51.7)	(0.3)	(41.3)	(0.2)
$\sigma(EBIT)$	.31	$-.29$	.37	.05	.32	.24
	(58.3)	(-2.5)	(51.6)	(0.3)	(41.2)	(1.4)
$\mu(T/E)$	.30	.00	.37	.00	.33	$-.00$
	(55.1)	(0.3)	(49.8)	(0.2)	(39.8)	(-0.4)
AGE	.31	$-.01$	.37	.02	.32	$-.00$
	(58.1)	(-0.5)	(51.7)	(0.5)	(41.4)	(-0.1)
PA/PL	.30	.00	.41	.00	.29	$-.00$
	(39.3)	(0.3)	(41.6)	(0.1)	(28.8)	(-0.3)

Note: Results shown are estimated coefficients (and t-statistics) for the regression $PA_i/BA = \alpha + \gamma(PA/BA) + \beta X$. See table 5.6 for definitions of variable symbols.

the firm's earnings relative to trend—a result that is directly counter to the implication of Sharpe's hypothesis. Moreover, this result holds regardless of the definition of earnings used (before tax, after tax, with or without consolidation of pension contributions, etc.), and it also holds for subsamples limited according to the importance of pension assets in the firm's overall asset structure.[23] Hence firms with greater business risk, as measured by greater volatility of earnings, systematically seek to offset at least part of that risk by investing their pension assets in instruments *other* than equities.

It is interesting that several measures included in table 5.9 do not appear to affect pension asset allocations. Despite the incentives for taxable firms to hold high-yield assets in their pension plans and low-yield assets on their balance sheets, as emphasized by Black (1980) and Tepper (1981), the firm's tax status over the past 5 years has no apparent impact at this level. Similarly, although the age and related structure of the pension plan's beneficiary population affects the time profile of liabilities under the plan, the current employment ratio also has no effect. Finally, the firm's overall pension funding ratio has no noticeable effect either— again in apparent contradiction of Sharpe's analysis.

It is also useful to note how two specific aspects of the results shown in table 5.9 carry over to the larger sample including Compustat firms' defined-contribution plans as well as their defined-benefit plans. First, the negative relationship between earnings volatility and the equity allocation is smaller in absolute magnitude, but statistically more significant, in the broader sample.[24] With $\sigma(EBIT)$ as the control variable in (13), the estimated value of β in the equity equation is $-.11$, with

t-statistic -4.0 ($\bar{R}^2 = .60$). Second, although the current employment ratio of the beneficiary population does not matter in the defined-benefit-only sample, it does in the broader sample. With AGE as the control variable, the estimated value of β in the equity equation is .014, with t-statistic 2.1 ($\bar{R}^2 = .60$).[25] Because a large AGE ratio typically reflects a younger beneficiary population, a positive β value means that plans with younger workers are typically more heavily invested in equities. Hence pension plans in which the beneficiaries stand to gain or lose according to the return on the plan's invested assets do take account of the beneficiary population's age structure in making asset allocation decisions, even though plans in which the firm's shareholders stand to gain or lose from the assets' return do not.[26]

The pension asset allocation and the pension funding ratio are two major determinants of prospective risk and return for many firms. A third important element in the risk and return structure, of course, is the debt on the firm's balance sheet. The relationship among these several components raises the possibility, therefore, that the firm's allocation of its pension assets may also depend on its basic leverage. A relationship consistent with the risk-offsetting strategy reported above, for example, would be for highly levered firms to offset some of their leverage by holding debt securities in their defined-benefit pension plans.[27] Alternatively, under either Sharpe's PBGC put hypothesis or some form of "general aggressiveness" hypothesis, firms content to have a more leveraged position, as indicated by the liabilities on their balance sheets, might further extend that risk posture by investing their pension assets in equities.

Table 5.10 presents the results of an attempt to examine this question in compact form by estimating the regression

$$(14) \qquad \frac{PAD}{PAD + PAE} = \alpha + \gamma \frac{BL}{BL + BEQ} + \beta X,$$

where BEQ is the book value of equity on the firm's balance sheet, and all other variables are as before. The estimated value of γ is consistently positive, in contradiction to either the Sharpe hypothesis or a "general aggressiveness" hypothesis, indicating instead that firms with more highly levered balance sheets have some tendency to offset that leverage by investing more of their pension assets in debt securities.[28] Somewhat surprisingly, however, this positive relationship is statistically significant (and larger) in the broader sample including defined-contribution plans but not in the sample limited to defined-benefit plans.

The estimated β values shown in table 5.10 support and extend the findings shown in table 5.9 in several ways. First, the allocation of pension assets to debt securities is positively related to any measure of the variability of earnings. It is interesting that this effect, too, is always

Table 5.10   Relationship between Pension Asset Allocation and Firm Leverage

Control Variable	Defined Benefit Only		All Pension Plans	
	γ	β	γ	β
$\rho(EBIT)$	.05	$-.23$	.09	.07
	(0.9)	(-0.3)	(1.9)	(0.1)
$\sigma(EBIT)$	.05	1.31	.09	1.86
	(1.1)	(3.6)	(2.0)	(5.7)
$\mu(E/BA)$	.02	$-.25$	.02	$-.55$
	(0.4)	(-0.8)	(0.4)	(-1.9)
$\sigma(E/BA)$	.05	1.77	.09	2.96
	(1.1)	(3.8)	(2.0)	(6.9)
$\mu(E/EQ)$	.04	$-.08$	.07	$-.11$
	(0.7)	(-2.1)	(1.5)	(-2.6)
$\sigma(E/EQ)$	.04	.03	.07	.04
	(0.8)	(1.9)	(1.6)	(2.3)
$\mu(T/E)$	.10	.00	.17	.00
	(2.0)	(0.5)	(3.8)	(0.4)
AGE	.05	.22	.08	.14
	(1.0)	(2.6)	(1.9)	(1.8)

Note: Results shown are estimated coefficients (and *t*-statistics) for the regression $PAD/(PAD + PAE) = \alpha + \gamma[BL/(BL + BEQ)] + \beta X$, where E/EQ = ratio of earnings to book value of equity; $\mu(E/EQ)$ = 10-year mean of E/EQ; and $\sigma(E/EQ)$ = 10-year standard deviation of E/EQ around $\mu(E/EQ)$. See table 5.6 for definitions of other variable symbols.

larger and more highly significant in the broader sample. Second, firms with high rates of return (to either assets or book equity) tend to invest their pension assets more in equities and less in debt securities. Third, the firm's tax status apparently has no independent impact on pension asset allocation, although allowing for it about doubles the estimated magnitude of the effect of balance sheet leverage. Fourth, after allowance for balance sheet leverage, firms with younger pension beneficiary populations tend to invest more in debt securities and less in equities, although the estimated effect is smaller (as would be expected) and statistically insignificant in the broader sample including defined-contribution plans.

The main conclusions of this analysis of the allocation of pension assets, on the assumption that not only the pension asset total but also the other principal elements of the firm's asset and liability structure are predetermined with respect to that allocation choice, are (1) that firms with more volatile earnings invest pension assets so as to offset their ordinary business risk by holding less equity and more debt securities in the pension; (2) that firms with more highly leveraged balance sheets invest pension assets so as to offset this risk too, again by holding less equity and more debt securities in the pension; (3) that firms earning high rates of return adopt the opposite allocation strategy, investing pension assets more in equities and less in debt securities; and (4) that firms' pension asset allocation decisions also depend on the current employment status of the pension beneficiary population, with employed (hence presumably younger) beneficiaries leading firms with defined-benefit plans to invest pension assets less in equity and more in debt securities but with just the opposite effect for defined-contribution plans.

5.5   The Corporate Balance Sheet

The empirical analysis undertaken in sections 5.2 and 5.4 considers first the firm's pension funding strategy, and then its pension asset allocation, on the assumption that the amount and nature of assets and liabilities on the firm's balance sheet are predetermined with respect to decisions about the firm's pension. Such a secondary role for pension decisions in corporate financial structures may be plausible when the sums involved are small in relation to the sponsoring firm's ordinary business assets and liabilities. In an increasing number of corporations, however, pension liabilities (and pension assets too, if the liabilities are fully funded) are large in comparison to the assets and liabilities that appear on the firm's balance sheet. Moreover, pensions are continuing to grow more rapidly than general corporate assets or liabilities. The larger pensions become, the more likely it is that firms make decisions about their pension assets and liabilities and their other assets and liabilities jointly.

As the discussion in section 5.2 already emphasizes, the combination of legal requirements and established labor market practices sharply restricts many firms' flexibility with respect to their pension liabilities. In considering possible interrelationships by which the firm's pension assets and liabilities affect its ordinary business decisions, therefore, a useful place to begin is the possibility that the direction of influence in (4) and (5) above is backward. Estimating the reverse relationship, in which the firm takes its pension liabilities as given in deciding how much to borrow on its balance sheet,

$$(15) \qquad \frac{BL}{NW} = \alpha + \gamma \frac{PL}{NW}$$

yields $\gamma = .26$, with t-statistic 7.8 ($\bar{R}^2 = .04$), for the sample of all Compustat firms sponsoring defined-benefit plans, and $\gamma = .34$, with t-statistic 7.9 ($\bar{R}^2 = .17$), for the subsample in which each firm's pension liabilities equal at least one-tenth of its total assets.[29]

That estimating (4) in the reverse order (15) again leads to a significant positive relationship is hardly surprising. What is more interesting is that the positive partial relationship between pension liabilities and other liabilities—that is, the relationship after allowance for other controlling variables—also holds up on reversal of the ordering. Table 5.11 presents results, analogous to those in table 5.6, of estimating the reverse of (5),

$$(16) \qquad \frac{BL}{NW} = a + \gamma \frac{PL}{NW} + \beta X,$$

for the full sample and the sample with $PL/TA \geq .10$. Once again, the strong positive value of γ appears regardless of the choice of controlling variable.

Although the focus of this chapter is not on corporations' debt issuance, except in its relation to their sponsored pension plans, it is interesting nevertheless to notice several of the β values in table 5.11. First, the growth of earnings had no effect on pension liabilities in (5), but earnings growth negatively affects other liabilities in (16). This result also holds for other definitions of earnings. Second, the mean rate of return either on assets or on equity (not shown in the table) had no effect on pension liabilities in (5), but mean returns negatively affect other liabili-

Table 5.11   **Relationship between Balance Sheet Liabilities and Pension Liabilities**

Control Variable	Full Sample		$PL/TA \geq .10$ Subsample	
	γ	β	γ	β
$\rho(EBIT)$	.25	−5.62	.32	−8.45
	(7.5)	(−6.5)	(7.6)	(−4.0)
$\sigma(EBIT)$	.26	.40	.34	−.92
	(7.5)	(1.0)	(7.9)	(−1.0)
E/BA	.22	−3.52	.28	−3.77
	(6.9)	(−20.6)	(6.8)	(−11.1)
$\mu(E/BA)$	.20	−4.11	.27	−4.66
	(5.6)	(−15.5)	(6.0)	(−8.6)
$\sigma(E/BA)$	.24	1.20	.34	1.54
	(6.1)	(2.3)	(6.8)	(1.1)
$\mu(T/E)$	.24	.00	.33	−.02
	(6.5)	(0.1)	(6.9)	(−0.5)
$\mu(L/S)$	.28	−.33	.30	−.63
	(5.6)	(−2.4)	(5.7)	(−2.5)
AGE	.24	.12	.33	−.28
	(6.1)	(1.2)	(6.6)	(−1.5)

Note: Results shown are estimated coefficients (and t-statistics) for the regression $BL/NW = \alpha + \gamma(PL/NW) + \beta X$. See table 5.6 for definitions of variable symbols.

ties in (16). Third, the variability of the firm's rate of return affected pension liabilities negatively in (5), but return variability affects other liabilities positively in (16), at least in the full sample.[30] Fourth, labor intensity affected pension liabilities positively in (5), at least in the full sample, but labor intensity affects other liabilities negatively in (16). Each of these influences is familiar in the literature on corporate choice of capital structures, and these results would perhaps be of interest in an investigation of that subject. In the context of this chapter's focus on pensions, the main point is simply that the positive partial relationship between pension liabilities and other liabilities holds up after allowance for any of these separate effects.

Similar conclusions follow from reversing the order of (7) and (8), which treat not total pension liabilities but only the unfunded portion as the relevant measure. Estimating the reverse relationship

$$(17) \qquad \frac{BL}{NW} = \alpha + \gamma \frac{PL - PA}{NW}$$

yields $\gamma = .50$, with t-statistic 10.1 ($\bar{R}^2 = .07$), for the full sample and $\gamma = .61$, with t-statistic 10.8 ($\bar{R}^2 = .27$), for the $PL/TA \geq .10$ subsample.[31] Controlling for additional influences by estimating the regression

$$(18) \qquad \frac{BL}{NW} = \alpha + \gamma \frac{PL - PA}{NW} + \beta X$$

also yields consistently positive γ values, and β values roughly in line with those shown in table 5.11 and discussed above.

Once again, it is useful to examine whether pension liabilities and assets matter separately in this context, or whether what matters is only the difference, as in (17) and (18). Estimating the regression

$$(19) \qquad \frac{BL}{NW} = \alpha + \gamma \frac{PL}{NW} + \delta \frac{PA}{NW}$$

for the full sample yields $\gamma = .49$ and $\delta = -.51$, with respective t-statistics 4.8 and -2.7 ($\bar{R}^2 = .05$). For the $PL/TA \geq .10$ sample, the corresponding results are $\gamma = .58$ and $\delta = -.54$, with respective t-statistics 6.1 and -3.1 ($\bar{R}^2 = .17$). To the extent that firms make borrowing decisions in light of their pension assets and liabilities, therefore, what matters is just the unfunded pension liabilities.[32] Moreover, these results too hold up in the presence of other controlling variables like those included in table 5.10.

Finally, if firms decide on their pension assets and liabilities and on their other assets and liabilities in a fully joint way, then neither the direction of influence assumed in the regressions presented in section 5.2 nor that assumed in (15)–(19) is strictly correct. Instead, a fully simultaneous portfolio choice like that in (3)—or, if only unfunded pension liabilities matter, (6)—would be the correct way to view the firm's decision process. Table 5.12 presents results (values of β) for estimating (3) directly, using one independent variable at a time. These results add little to the analysis above, however. With the somewhat marginal exception of the earnings volatility measure, the estimation of the full portfolio choice model does not reveal influences that affect both the pension and the balance sheet.[33]

The main conclusions of this analysis of the relationship between the firm's borrowing decisions and its pension assets and liabilities are (1) that the amount of liabilities on the firm's balance sheet is positively related to the firm's pension liabilities and (2) that what matters for the determination of balance sheet liabilities in this context is just the firm's unfunded pension liabilities rather than its pension assets and liabilities separately.

5.6 Concluding Remarks

The final paragraph in each of sections 5.2–5.5 summarizes in capsule form the principal specific empirical findings of this chapter, and there is no need to restate each one here. The unifying overall conclusion from the data is that United States corporations do not manage the pension plans which they sponsor as if these plans had nothing to do with the corporation. Different responses appear to characterize firms' behavior in different contexts, but the evidence persistently indicates clear relationships between decisions about pension assets and liabilities and decisions about the other assets and liabilities of the firm. At the same time, the pattern of these relationships is, more often than not, inconsistent with familiar hypotheses that have emerged thus far in the theoretical literature analyzing pension aspects of corporate finance.

At least three caveats are important, however. The most significant is that the measurement of pension liabilities is hardly uniform across firms. To the extent that each corporation's management believes that the value it reports for liabilities on Form 5500 Schedule B is the best available measure of the firm's actual commitment or exposure, firm-to-firm variation in actuarial assumptions need not affect the analysis here. If managements make allowance for the differing actuarial assumptions, however, then this analysis neglects a potentially important element.[34] Further potential problems of a related nature also arise in connection with the date and the method chosen for Schedule B valuation of pension assets.

The second major caveat stems from the use in this chapter of fully consolidated firm data, incorporating all wholly owned subsidiaries, whenever possible. No doubt many parent corporations do adopt a consolidated approach to financial management. Even so, the possibility remains that many firms handle such matters as pension decisions in a decentralized way, or that some of the parent-subsidiary relationships

Table 5.12   **Full Portfolio Treatment of the**
                        Pension and Balance Sheet

Control Variable	BL/NW	BA/NW	PL/NW	PA/NW
ρ(*EBIT*)	−7.32	−8.26	−1.15	−.21
	(−5.5)	(−5.2)	(−1.0)	(−0.3)
σ(*EBIT*)	.91	1.63	1.45	.72
	(1.6)	(2.5)	(2.9)	(2.7)
E/BA	−4.10	−4.42	−0.23	0.08
	(−16.8)	(−14.0)	(−0.8)	(0.5)
μ(*E/BA*)	−4.94	−5.42	−.62	−.14
	(−12.7)	(−11.1)	(−1.5)	(−0.6)
σ(*E/BA*)	2.21	−2.16	−.46	−.41
	(2.8)	(−2.2)	(−0.6)	(−1.0)
μ(*T/E*)	−.01	−.01	−.00	−.00
	(−0.5)	(−0.4)	(−0.1)	(−0.2)
μ(*L/S*)	−.08	.22	.74	.45
	(−0.4)	(1.0)	(4.7)	(5.1)
AGE	.13	−.28	−.68	−.28
	(0.9)	(−1.6)	(−5.2)	(−3.8)

Note: Results shown are estimated coefficients (and *t*-statistics) for the regression

$$\frac{1}{NW}\begin{bmatrix} BL \\ BA \\ PL \\ PA \end{bmatrix} = \alpha + X\beta.$$

See table 5.6 for definitions of variable symbols.

consolidated here were then (and may still be) too recent to have had much impact on the structure of the subsidiaries' pension assets and liabilities.

The third reason for caution in interpreting the results presented here is simply that they reflect evidence from a cross section of firms (a quite comprehensive cross section, to be sure) in one year only. Despite its portfolio-theoretic approach, therefore, the analysis entirely omits any account of effects due to changing yield relationships over time. For the same reason, the analysis is also subject to all of the usual problems associated with observing only one point in time. Was 1977 a "typical" year in any or all of the many senses that matter here? It is never possible to answer such a question adequately. At the least, however, the Employee Retirement Income Security Act and the Pension Benefit Guaranty Corporation were both very recent as of 1977, and neither may yet have had its full impact on corporations' behavior.

Each of these three reservations about the analysis presented in this chapter points to potentially fruitful directions for further empirical research. Taking account of cross-firm variation in pension actuarial decisions, more carefully treating the range of possible parent-subsidiary relationships, and working with additional data as they become available would all be major extensions of this work which could importantly alter the conclusions reached. No doubt additional lines of investigation would provide new insights also. This chapter only begins to analyze the interrelationships connecting private pensions and corporate finance. As private pensions continue to grow, in both absolute and relative terms, those interrelationships will almost surely become more powerful and more important for understanding financial behavior.

Appendix

Form **5500** Department of the Treasury Internal Revenue Service Department of Labor Pension and Welfare Benefit Programs Pension Benefit Guaranty Corporation	**Annual Return/Report of Employee Benefit Plan** **(With 100 or more participants)** This form is required to be filed under sections 104 and 4065 of the Employee Retirement Income Security Act of 1974 and sections 6057(b) and 6058(a) of the Internal Revenue Code, referred to as the Code.	1**977** This Form is Open to Public Inspection

For the calendar plan year 1977 or fiscal plan year beginning _____ , 1977 and ending _____ , 19 ____

File original of this form, including schedules and attachments, completed in ink or type.

▶ Keogh (H.R. 10) plans with fewer than 100 participants and with at least one owner-employee participant **do not file this form.**
   File Form 5500–K instead.

▶ Other pension benefit plans and certain welfare benefit plans with fewer than 100 participants **do not file this form.** File Form
   5500–C instead.

▶ Welfare benefit plans with 100 or more participants complete only items 1 through 16 and item 22.

▶ Pension benefit plans, unless otherwise excepted, complete all items. Annuity arrangements of certain exempt organizations and
   individual retirement account trusts of employers complete only items 1 through 6, 9 and 10.

▶ Government plans and church plans (not electing coverage under section 410(d) of the Code) complete only items 1 through 7,
   9, 10(a), (b), (c), (d), 11 and 17.

▶ Plan number—Your 3 digit plan number must be entered in item 5(c); see instruction 5(c) for explanation of "plan number."

▶ If any item does not apply, enter "N/A."

1 (a) Name of plan sponsor (employer if for a single employer plan)	1 (b) Employer identification number
Address (number and street)	1 (c) Telephone number of sponsor ( )
City or town, State and ZIP code	1 (d) Employer taxable year ends Month Day Year 19
2 (a) Name of plan administrator (if other than plan sponsor)	1 (e) Business code number
Address (number and street)	2 (b) Administrator's employer identification no.
City or town, State and ZIP code	2 (c) Telephone number of administrator ( )

3 Name, address and identification number of ☐ plan sponsor and/or ☐ plan administrator as they appeared on the last return/
report filed for this plan if not the same as in 1 or 2 above ▶ --

4 Check appropriate box to indicate the type of plan entity (check only one box):

(a) ☐ Single-employer plan   **(c)** ☐ Multiemployer plan   **(e)** ☐ Multiple-employer plan (other)

(b) ☐ Plan of controlled group of corporations **(d)** ☐ Multiple-employer-collec- **(f)** ☐ Group insurance arrangement (of
   or common control employers   tively-bargained plan   welfare plans)

5 (a) (i) Name of plan	5 (b) Effective date of plan
(ii) ☐ Check if changed since last return/report	5 (c) Enter three digit plan number ▶

6 Check at least one item in (a) or (b) and applicable items in (c). Item (d) on page 2 must be completed:

(a) Welfare benefit plan: (i) ☐ Health insurance   (ii) ☐ Life insurance   (iii) ☐ Supplemental unemployment
   (iv) ☐ Other (specify) ▶ --

(b) Pension benefit plan:

   (i)   Defined benefit plan—(Indicate type of defined benefit plan below):
      (A) ☐ Fixed benefit   (B) ☐ Unit benefit   (C) ☐ Flat benefit   (D) ☐ Other (specify) ▶ --------------

   (ii) Defined contribution plan—(indicate type of defined contribution plan below):
      (A) ☐ Profit-sharing   (B) ☐ Stock bonus   (C) ☐ Target benefit   (D) ☐ Other money purchase
      (E) ☐ Other (specify) ▶ --

   (iii) ☐ Defined benefit plan with benefits based partly on balance of separate account of participant (section 414(k) of the
      Code)

   (iv) ☐ Annuity arrangement of a certain exempt organization (section 403(b)(1) of the Code)

   (v)   ☐ Custodial account for regulated investment company stock (section 403(b)(7) of the Code)

   (vi) ☐ Trust treated as an individual retirement account (section 408(c) of the Code)

   (vii) ☐ Employee stock ownership plan not part of a qualified plan (section 301(d) of the Tax Reduction Act of 1975)

   (viii)☐ Other (specify) ▶

Under penalties of perjury and other penalties set forth in the instructions, I declare that I have examined this report, including accompanying schedules and statements, and
to the best of my knowledge and belief, it is true, correct, and complete.

Date ▶ ....   Signature of employer/plan sponsor ▶ ....

Date ▶ ....   Signature of plan administrator ▶ ....

Form 5500 (1977)   Page **2**

(c) Other plan features: *(i)* ☐ Thrift-savings   *(ii)* ☐ Keogh (H.R. 10) plan
   (iii) ☐ Employee stock ownership as part of a qualified plan (check only if you checked a box in (b)(ii) above)
(d) Is this a defined benefit plan covered under the Pension Benefit Guaranty Corporation
   termination insurance program? . . . . ☐ Yes ☐ No ☐ Not determined

7 Number of participants as of the end of the plan year (welfare plans complete only (a)(iv), (b), (c) and (d)):
   (a) Active participants (employed or carried as active) *(i)* Number fully vested . .
                                              (ii) Number partially vested .
                                              (iii) Number nonvested . . .
                                              (iv) Total . . . .
   (b) Retired or separated participants receiving benefits . . . .
   (c) Retired or separated participants entitled to future benefits . . . .
   (d) Subtotal, sum of (a), (b) and (c) . . . .
   (e) Deceased participants whose beneficiaries are receiving or are entitled to receive benefits . . . .
   (f) Total, (d) plus (e) . . . .

	Yes	No

   (g) During the plan year, was any participant(s) separated from service with a deferred vested benefit? . . . . .
      If "Yes," see instructions.
8 Plan amendment information (welfare plans complete only (a), (b)(i) and (c)):
   (a) Was any amendment to this plan adopted in this plan year? . . . .
   (b) If "Yes," *(i)* And if a material modification, has a summary description of this modification—
      (A) Been sent to plan participants? . . . .
      (B) Been filed with DOL? . . . .
      (ii) Does any such amendment result in the reduction of the accrued benefit of any participant under the plan? . .
      (iii) Will amendment result in a reduction of current or future benefits? . . . .
      (iv) Has a determination letter been requested from IRS with respect to such amendment? . . . .
   (c) Enter the date the most recent amendment was adopted . . ▶ Month   Day   Year
9 Plan termination information (welfare plans complete only (a), (b), (c) and (f)):
   (a) Was this plan terminated during this plan year or any prior plan year? . . . .
   (b) If "Yes," were all trust assets distributed to participants or beneficiaries or transferred to another plan? . .
   (c) Was a resolution to terminate this plan adopted during this plan year or any prior plan year? . . . .
   (d) If (a) or (c) is "Yes," have you received a favorable determination letter from IRS with respect to such termination? . . . . .
   (e) If (d) is "No," has a determination letter been requested from IRS? . . . .
   (f) If (a) or (c) is "Yes," have participants and beneficiaries been notified of the termination or the proposed termination? . . . .
10 (a) In this plan year, was this plan merged or consolidated into another plan or were assets or liabilities transferred to another plan? . .
      If "Yes," identify other plan(s):

(b) Name of plan(s) ▶	(c) Employer identification number(s)	(d) Plan number(s)

   (e) Has Form 5310 been filed with IRS? . . . . ☐ Yes ☐ No
11 Indicate funding arrangement:
   (a) ☐ Trust (benefits provided in whole from trust funds)
   (b) ☐ Trust or arrangement providing benefits partially through insurance and/or annuity contracts
   (c) ☐ Trust or arrangement providing benefits exclusively through insurance and/or annuity contracts
   (d) ☐ Custodial account described in section 401(f) of the Code and not included in (c) above
   (e) ☐ Other (specify) ▶
   (f) If (b) or (c) is checked, enter the number of Schedule A's (Form 5500) which are attached . . . . . . ▶
12 Did any person who rendered services to the plan receive, directly or indirectly, compensation **from the plan** in the plan year? . . ☐ Yes ☐ No
   If "Yes," furnish the following information:

a. Name	b. Official plan position	c. Relationship to employer, employee organization or person known to be a party-in-interest	d. Gross salary or allowances paid by plan	e. Fees and commissions paid by plan	f. Nature of service code (see Instructions)

Form 5500 (1977)   Page **3**

13 Plan assets and liabilities at the beginning and the end of the plan year (list all assets and liabilities at current value). If plan is funded entirely by allocated insurance contracts for which no trust is involved, check box and do not complete this item . . ☐
  Note: *Include all plan assets and liabilities of a trust or separately maintained fund. (If more than one trust/fund, report on a combined basis.) Include unallocated, but not allocated, insurance contracts. Round off amounts to nearest dollar.*

Assets	a. Beginning of year	b. End of year
(a) Cash: *(i)* On hand		
(ii) In bank: (A) Certificates of deposit		
(B) Other interest bearing		
(C) Noninterest bearing		
(iii) Total cash		
(b) Receivables: *(i)* Employer contributions		
(ii) Employee contributions		
(iii) Other		
(iv) Reserve for doubtful accounts		
(v) Net receivables, sum of (i), (ii) and (iii) minus (iv)		
(c) General investments other than party-in-interest investments:		
(i) U.S. Government securities:		
(A) Long term		
(B) Short term		
(ii) State and municipal securities		
(iii) Corporate debt instruments:		
(A) Long term		
(B) Short term		
(iv) Corporate stocks: (A) Preferred		
(B) Common		
(v) Shares of a registered investment company		
(vi) Real estate		
(vii) Mortgages		
(viii) Loans other than mortgages		
(ix) Value of interest in pooled fund(s)		
(x) Other investments		
(xi) Total general investments, sum of (i) through (x)		
(d) Party-in-interest investments:		
(i) Corporate debt instruments		
(ii) Corporate stocks: (A) Preferred		
(B) Common		
(iii) Real estate		
(iv) Mortgages		
(v) Loans other than mortgages		
(vi) Other investments		
(vii) Total party-in-interest investments, sum of (i) through (vi)		
(e) Buildings and other depreciable property		
(f) Value of unallocated insurance contracts:		
(i) Separate accounts		
(ii) Other		
(iii) Total, (i) plus (ii)		
(g) Other assets		
(h) Total assets, sum of (a)(iii), (b)(v), (c)(xi), (d)(vii), (e), (f)(iii) and (g)		
Liabilities		
(i) Payables: *(i)* Plan claims		
(ii) Other payables		
(iii) Total payables, (i) plus (ii)		
(j) Acquisition indebtedness		
(k) Other liabilities		
(l) Total liabilities, sum of (i)(iii), (j) and (k)		
(m) Net assets, (h) less (l)		
(n) During the plan year what were the:		
(i) Total cost of acquisitions for common stock?		
(ii) Total proceeds from dispositions of common stock?		

Form 5500 (1977)   Page **4**

14 Plan income, expenses and changes in net assets for the plan year:

Note: *Include all income and expenses of a trust(s) or separately maintained fund(s). Round off amounts to nearest dollar.*

Income	a. Amount	b. Total
(a) Contributions received or receivable in cash from—		
(i) Employer(s) (including contributions on behalf of self-employed individuals)		
(ii) Employees		
(iii) Others		
(b) Noncash contributions (specify nature and by whom made) ▶		
(c) Total contributions, sum of (a) and (b)		
(d) Earnings from investments—		
(i) Interest		
(ii) Dividends		
(iii) Rents		
(iv) Royalties		
(e) Net realized gain (loss) on sale or exchange of assets—		
(i) Aggregate proceeds		
(ii) Aggregate costs		
(f) Other income (specify) ▶		
(g) Total income, sum of (c) through (f)		

Expenses	a. Amount	b. Total
(h) Distribution of benefits and payments to provide benefits—		
(i) Directly to participants or their beneficiaries		
(ii) To insurance carrier or similar organization for provision of benefits		
(iii) To other organizations or individuals providing welfare benefits		
(i) Interest expense		
(j) Administrative expenses—		
(i) Salaries and allowances		
(ii) Fees and commissions		
(iii) Insurance premiums for Pension Benefit Guaranty Corporation		
(iv) Insurance premiums for fiduciary insurance other than bonding		
(v) Other administrative expenses		
(k) Other expenses (specify) ▶		
(l) Total expenses, sum of (h) through (k)		
(m) Net income (expenses), (g) minus (l)		

(n) Change in net assets—	a. Amount	b. Total
(i) Unrealized appreciation (depreciation) of assets		
(ii) Other changes (specify) ▶		
(o) Net increase (decrease) in net assets for the year, (m) plus (n)		
(p) Net assets at beginning of year, line 13(m), column a		
(q) Net assets at end of year, (o) plus (p) (equals line 13(m), column b)		

15 Has there been any change since the last report in the appointment of any trustee, accountant, insurance carrier, enrolled actuary, administrator, investment manager or custodian? | Yes | No |

If "Yes," explain and include the name, position, address and telephone number of the individual who left or was removed by the plan ▶ _____

_____

_____

_____

_____

_____

_____

_____

_____

_____

_____

Form 5500 (1977)   Page **5**

	Yes	No
16 Bonding:		

(a) Was the plan insured by a fidelity bond against losses through fraud or dishonesty? . . . .

(b) If "Yes," enter the maximum amount of loss recoverable ▶ ....

(c) Enter the name of the surety company ▶ ....

(d) Does the plan, or a known party-in-interest with respect to the plan, have any control or significant financial interest, direct or indirect, in the surety company or its agents or brokers? . . . .

(e) If the plan is not insured by a fidelity bond, explain why not ▶ ....

(f) In the current plan year was any loss to the plan caused by the fraud or dishonesty of any plan official or employee of the plan or of other person handling funds of the plan? . . . .
If "Yes," see specific instructions.

17 Information about employees of employer at end of the plan year (Plans not purporting to satisfy the percentage tests of section 410(b)(1)(A) of the Code complete only (a) below and see specific instructions):

(a) Total number of employees . . . .

(b) Number of employees excluded under the plan—

    (i) Minimum age or years of service . . . .

    (ii) Employees on whose behalf retirement benefits were the subject of collective bargaining . . .

    (iii) Nonresident aliens who receive no earned income from United States sources . . . .

    (iv) Total excluded, sum of (i), (ii) and (iii) . . . .

(c) Total number of employees not excluded, (a) less (b)(iv) . . . .

(d) Employees ineligible (specify reason) ▶ ....

(e) Employees eligible to participate, (c) less (d) . . . .

(f) Employees eligible but not participating . . . .

(g) Employees participating, (e) less (f) . . . .

	Yes	No
18 Is this plan an adoption of a:		

(a) ☐ Master/prototype,   **(b)** ☐ Field prototype,   **(c)** ☐ Pattern or   **(d)** ☐ Model plan? . . .
If "Yes," enter the four or eight digit IRS serial number (see instructions) ▶

19 (a) Is it intended that this plan qualify under section 401(a) or 405 of the Code? . . . .

    (b) Have you requested or received a determination letter from the IRS for this plan? . . . .

20 If plan is integrated, check appropriate box:

(a) ☐ Social security   **(b)** ☐ Railroad retirement   **(c)** ☐ Other

21 (a) Is this a defined benefit plan subject to the minimum funding standards for this plan year? . . . .
If "Yes," attach Schedule B (Form 5500).

(b) Is this a defined contribution plan, i.e., money purchase or target benefit, subject to the minimum funding standards? (If a waiver was granted, see instructions.) . . . .
If "Yes," complete (i), (ii) and (iii) below:

    (i) Amount of employer contribution required for the plan year under section 412 of the Code . . .

    (ii) Amount of contribution paid by the employer for the plan year . . . .
        Enter date of last payment by employer . . . . . ▶ Month .... Day .... Year ....

    (iii) Funding deficiency, excess, if any, of (i) over (ii) . . . .

	Yes	No

22 The following questions relate to the plan year. If (a)(i), (ii), (iii), (iv) or (v) is checked "Yes," schedules of such items in the format set forth in the instructions are required to be attached to this form.

(a) (i) Did the plan have assets held for investment? . . . .

    (ii) Did any non-exempt transaction involving plan assets involve a party known to be a party-in-interest? . .

    (iii) Were any loans by the plan or fixed income obligations due the plan in default as of the close of the plan year or classified during the year as uncollectable? . . . .

    (iv) Were any leases to which the plan was a party in default or classified during the year as uncollectable? . .

    (v) Were any plan transactions or series of transactions in excess of 3% of the current value of plan assets? .

(b) The accountant's opinion is ☐ not required or ☐ required, attached to this form, and is—

    (i) ☐ Unqualified

    (ii) ☐ Qualified

    (iii) ☐ Adverse

    (iv) ☐ Other (explain)

Form 5500 (1977)   Page **6**

23 Complete this item only if you answered "Yes," to Item 6(d)

	Yes	No
Did one or more of the reportable events or other events requiring notice to the Pension Benefit Guaranty Corporation occur during this plan year?	░░░	░░░

If "Yes," complete (a) through (h) below.

	Yes	No
(a) Notification by the Internal Revenue Service that the plan has ceased to be a plan as described in Section 4021(a)(2) of ERISA or a determination by the Secretary of Labor of non-compliance with Title I of ERISA . .	░░░	░░░
(b) A decrease in active participants to the extent specified in the instructions		
(c) A determination by the Internal Revenue Service that there has been a termination or partial termination of the plan within the meaning of Section 411(d)(3) of the Code	░░░	░░░
(d) An inability to pay benefits when due		
(e) A distribution to a Substantial Owner to the extent specified in the instructions		
(f) An alternative method of compliance has been prescribed for this plan by the Secretary of Labor under Section 110 of ERISA	░░░	░░░
(g) A cessation of operations at a facility to the extent specified in the instructions		
(h) A withdrawal of a substantial employer		

If additional space is required for any item, attach additional sheets the same size as this form.

SCHEDULE B (Form 5500)	**Actuarial Information**	1977
Department of the Treasury Internal Revenue Service Department of Labor Pension and Welfare Benefit Programs Pension Benefit Guaranty Corporation	This schedule is required to be filed under section 104 of the Employee Retirement Income Security Act of 1974, referred to as ERISA, and section 6059(a) of the Internal Revenue Code, referred to as the Code. ▶ **Attach to Forms 5500, 5500–C and 5500–K if applicable.**	This Form is Open to Public Inspection

For plan year beginning _____ , 1977 and ending _____ , 19 _____

▶ Please complete every applicable item on this form. If an item does not apply, enter "N/A."
▶ Round off amounts to nearest dollar.

Name of plan sponsor as shown on line 1(a) of Form 5500, 5500–C or 5500–K	Employer identification number

Name of plan	Enter three digit plan number ▶			Yes	No

1 Has a waiver of a funding deficiency for the current plan year been approved by the IRS? . . . .

  If "Yes," attach a copy of the IRS approval letter.

2 Is a waived funding deficiency of a prior plan year being amortized in the current year? . . . .

3 Have any of the periods of amortization for charges described in section 412(b)(2)(B) of the Code been extended by DOL? . . . . .

  If "Yes," attach a copy of the DOL approval of extension letter.

4 (a) Has the shortfall funding method been used? . . . .

  (b) *(i)* If (a) is "Yes," has the deferral of the amortization of the shortfall gain (loss), beyond the plan year following the year in which the shortfall gain (loss) arose, been elected? . . . .

  (ii) If (a) is "Yes," has the deferral of the amortization of the actuarial gain (loss), beyond the first plan year after valuation, been elected? . . . .

5 Actuarial method and operational information: **(a)** Enter most recent actuarial valuation date ▶ _____

  (b) Enter date(s) and amount of contributions received this plan year for prior plan years and not previously reported:

  Date(s) ▶ _____ , Amount ▶

  (c) Accumulated funding deficiency at end of plan year (amount of contribution certified by the actuary as necessary to reduce the funding deficiency to zero), from 7(m) or 8(g) . . . .

  (d) *(i)* Accrued liabilities as of (enter date) ▶ _____

  (ii) Value of assets as determined for funding standard account . . . .

  (iii) Unfunded accrued liability . . . .

  (e) Value of vested benefits (if calculated) . . . .

  (f) Current value of the assets accumulated in the plan as of (enter date) ▶ _____

  (g) Number of persons covered (included in the most recent actuarial valuation): *(i)* Active participants . .

  (ii) Terminated participants with vested benefits . . . .

  (iii) Retired participants and beneficiaries of deceased participants . . . .

  (h) *(i)* Actuarial gains or (losses) for period ending ▶ _____

  (ii) Shortfall gains or (losses) for period ending ▶ _____

  (i) Attach a statement of actuarial assumptions and methods used to determine *(i)* the normal cost and liabilities shown on lines 7(b) or 8(b) and 5(d)(i), and *(ii)* the value of assets shown on line 5(d)(ii). The statement is to include a summary of the principal eligibility and benefit provisions upon which the valuation was based, an identification of benefits not included in the calculation, and other facts, such as, any change in actuarial assumptions or cost methods and justifications for any such change. Include also such other information, if any, needed to fully and fairly disclose the actuarial position of the plan.

6 Contributions made to the plan for the plan year by employer(s) and employees:

(a) Month Year	(b) Amount paid by employer	(c) Amount paid by employees	(a) Month Year	(b) Amount paid by employer	(c) Amount paid by employees
		Total . . .			

Statement by enrolled actuary (see instructions before signing):

  To the best of my knowledge, the information supplied in this schedule and on the accompanying statement, if any, is complete and accurate, and in my opinion the assumptions used in the aggregate (a) are reasonably related to the experience of the plan and to reasonable expectations, and (b) represent my best estimate of anticipated experience under the plan.

_____ _____
Signature of actuary   Date

_____ _____
Print or type name of actuary   Enrollment number

_____ _____
Address   Telephone number (including area code)

7 Funding standard account statement for plan year ending ▶ .... |

Charges to funding standard account:

(a) Prior year funding deficiency, if any . . . . | _____

(b) Employer's normal cost for plan year . . . . | _____

(c) Amortization charges (outstanding balance at beginning of plan year ▶ $......................) . . . . . | _____

(d) Interest on (a), (b) and (c) . . . . | _____

(e) Total charge, sum of (a) through (d) . . . . | _____

Credits to funding standard account:

(f) Prior year credit balance, if any . . . . | _____

(g) (i) Employer contributions (total from column (b) of item 6) . . . . | _____

(ii) Employer contributions received this plan year for prior plan years and not previously reported . . . | _____

(h) Amortization credits (outstanding balance at beginning of plan year ▶ $......................) . . . . | _____

(i) Interest on (f), (g) and (h) . . . . | _____

(j) Other (specify) ▶.. | _____

(k) Total credits, sum of (f) through (j) . . . . | _____

Balance:

(l) Credit balance, excess, if any, of (k) over (e) . . . . | _____

(m) Funding deficiency, excess, if any, of (e) over (k) . . . . | _____

8 Alternative minimum funding standard account (omit if not used):

(a) Was the entry age normal cost method used to determine entries in item 7 above? . . . . ☐ Yes ☐ No

If "No," omit (b) through (g) below.

(b) Normal cost . . . . | _____

(c) Excess, if any, of value of accrued benefits over market value of assets . . . . | _____

(d) Interest on (b) and (c) . . . . | _____

(e) Employer contributions (total from column (b) of item 6) . . . . | _____

(f) Interest on (e) . . . . | _____

(g) Funding deficiency, excess, if any, of the sum of (b) through (d) over the sum of (e) and (f) . . . . . | _____

Instructions

Who Must File.—The employer or plan administrator of a defined benefit plan that is subject to the minimum funding standards (see section 412 of the Code and Part 3 of Title I of ERISA) must file this schedule as an attachment to the annual return/report filed for plan years beginning on or after January 1, 1976. Plans maintained on January 1, 1974, pursuant to one or more collective bargaining agreements entered into before September 2, 1974, are not subject to the minimum funding standards for plan years beginning before the earlier of the termination of the collective bargaining agreement(s) or January 1, 1981.

For split-funded plans, the costs and contributions reported on Schedule B should include those relating to both trust funds and insurance carriers.

Specific Instructions

(References are to line items on the form.)

4(a) A collectively bargained plan only may elect the shortfall funding method (see regulations under section 412 of the Code). Advance approval from the IRS of the election of the shortfall method of funding is NOT required if it is first adopted on or before the later of (i) the first plan year to which section 412 of the Code applies or (ii) the last plan year commencing before December 31, 1980. However, advance approval from IRS is required, or application at a later time or if discontinued.

4(b) Advance approval from IRS of the election to defer the amortization of the shortfall gain (loss) and/or the amortization of the actuarial gain (loss) is required for a plan year, subsequent to the first plan year to which the shortfall method applies. Advance approval from IRS is required for discontinuance.

5(a) The valuation for a plan year may be as of any date in the year, including the first and last. Valuations must be performed within the period specified by section 103(d) of ERISA and section 6059(a) of the Code.

5(b) Not applicable to the first plan year to which the minimum funding standards apply.

5(c) Insert amount from item 7(m). However, if the alternative method is elected, and item 8(g) is smaller than item 7(m), enter the amount from item 8(g). File Form 5330 with the Internal Revenue Service to pay the 5% excise tax on the funding deficiency.

5(d) Amounts in 5(d) should all be as of the same date which should be the date of the end of the plan year or date as of which the most recent actuarial valuation was made. If amounts are not as of the date of the most recent actuarial valuation, indicate in the statement of actuarial assumptions and methods (as required by 5(i)) how the amounts in 5(d) were determined. Liabilities fully funded by annuity and insurance contracts other than any contract funds not allocated to individuals may be omitted from both items 5(d)(i) and 5(d)(ii).

5(d)(i) If the aggregate cost or frozen initial liability method is used, enter "N/A."

5(d)(ii) Determine the value of assets in accordance with section 412(c)(2) of the Code or 302(c)(2) of ERISA.

5(d)(iii) If the aggregate cost or frozen initial liability method is used, enter "N/A."

5(f) This should be as of the same date as 5(d) or, if not, the method of adjustment between the two dates should be indicated in 5(i).

5(h)(i) If the aggregate cost or frozen initial liability method is used, enter "N/A."

5(h)(ii) For the methods to be used to determine the shortfall gain (loss) see the regulations under section 412 of the Code.

5(i) A summary of one page or less of plan provisions will ordinarily be adequate. For the first year for which Schedule B is required to be filed, no change in the actuarial method or assumptions needs to the noted or justified. In subsequent years, a change in actuarial method or plan year requires IRS approval. Actuarial methods should be described in accordance with section 3(31) of ERISA as accrued benefit cost (or unit credit), entry age normal cost, individual level premium, aggregate cost, attained age normal cost or frozen initial liability, where those terms are applicable. If the shortfall method of funding is used, all pertinent facts relating to funding peculiar to this method should be included in the statement.

6 Show all employer and employee contributions for the plan year, and employer contributions made not later than 2½ months (or such later date allowed under section 412(c)(10) of the Code and section 302(c)(10) of ERISA) after the end of the plan year.

Statement by enrolled actuary.—In lieu of signing the statement, an enrolled actuary may attach a signed statement containing the name, address, enrollment number, telephone number and the actuary's opinion that the assumptions used in preparing Schedule B are in the aggregate reasonably related to the experience of the plan and to reasonable expectations, and represent his or her best estimate of anticipated experience under the plan and to the best of his or her knowledge the report is complete and accurate. In addition, the actuary may offer any other comments related to the information contained in Schedule B.

7 Under the shortfall method of funding, the Normal Cost in the funding standard account, is the charge per unit of production (or per unit of service) multiplied by the actual number of units of production (or units of service) which occurred during the plan year. Each amortization installment in the funding standard account is similarly calculated. For a plan maintained by more than one employer, the amortization of the shortfall gain (loss) and the actuarial gain (loss) may be deferred. See regulations under section 412 of the Code.

7(b) If no valuation was made for the current year, enter the normal cost calculated in the most recent actuarial valuation, or the estimated cost for the current year based on such valuation. If amounts are not as of the date of the most recent actuarial valuation, indicate in the statement of actuarial assumptions and methods (as required by 5(i)) how the amounts shown were determined.

8(a) If the entry age normal cost method was not used to determine the entries in item 7, the alternative minimum funding standard account may not be used.

8(c) The value of accrued benefits should exclude benefits accrued for the current plan year. The market value of assets should be reduced by the amount of any contributions for the current plan year.

Notes

1. The 1977 "plan year" for purposes of Form 5500 is either the 1977 calendar year or the plan's fiscal year beginning in 1977. The plan sponsor has until 7 months after the plan year ends to file the return.

2. A one-by-one inspection of the 384 plans reporting over $100 million in assets suggested few obvious omissions among large corporate sponsors.

3. By contrast, the Federal Reserve System's flow-of-funds accounts reported total assets of private pension funds as $178 billion at year end 1977 and $198 billion at year end 1978. The Form 5500 data therefore confirm the widely acknowledged underreporting in the flow-of-funds sample.

4. The largest single plan, sponsored by General Electric, reported assets of $3.8 billion.

5. The great majority of companies sponsor five or fewer plans. The largest number of plans sponsored by any one company (excluding subsidiaries) was 63.

6. The computer program that searches for Compustat matches was developed by Clint Cummins; I am grateful to him for making the program available.

7. The key to this part of the matching process was the *Directory of Corporate Affiliations 1978* (Skokie, Ill.: National Register Publishing Co., 1978). It would be difficult to overestimate the amount of painstaking effort devoted to this task by Arturo Estrella and Joyce Manchester.

8. Of the 1,836 consolidated plan sponsors, 1,571 sponsored defined-benefit plans.

9. The pension sponsor with the largest amount of pension assets on a consolidated basis was American Telephone and Telegraph, with $18.4 billion in assets held in three plans sponsored by the parent company and 26 plans sponsored by subsidiaries.

10. See, for example, the work of Sharpe (1976), Oldfield (1977), Black (1980), Feldstein and Seligman (1981), Scholes (1981), and Tepper (1981).

11. In many situations, a corporation's principal means of flexibility in this regard is its ability to choose what assumptions (interest rate, inflation rate, etc.) to use in calculating the actuarial value of the liabilities to be funded. See, for example, Tepper and Affleck (1974). A careful empirical study of corporations' behavior in this regard represents a potentially fruitful line of research, but one that lies beyond the scope of this chapter; see sec. 5.6 below.

12. United States corporations must report, as a footnote to the balance sheet, the difference between vested pension liabilities and the level of pension funding. Neither total need be stated individually, nor need the corporation report its nonvested liabilities at all (except on Form 5500 Schedule B).

13. Whatever off-balance-sheet assets and liabilities the firm has, apart from PA and PL, are included in BA and BL for purposes of this chapter. See also note 34 below on the definition of PL.

14. The sample for this regression, and those reported in the following discussion, omits 13 firms for which net worth is sufficiently small that either PL/NW or FL/NW exceeds 3.0. The result of a significant positive relationship also appears (although with smaller γ values) when VL, the firm's vested pension liabilities only, is used in place of total pension liabilities PL. (The simple correlation between VL and PL within the total sample is .89.) It is interesting to note that regressions of the form (4) and also (5) below, estimated with BA instead of NW as the scale variable, typically show a small *negative* value of γ which is marginally significant at the .05 level. By contrast, most of the results reported in this chapter are essentially invariant to the choice of NW or BA as the scale variable; see note 16 below for the one other case in which this choice makes a substantive difference.

15. See also the chapter by Harrison and Sharpe in this volume.

16. Defined-benefit plans report total assets explicitly on Form 5500 and implicitly (as the difference between liabilities and unfunded liabilities) on Schedule B. The two asset measures need not coincide. For the 1977 sample, the simple correlation between the two is

.92 in the disaggregated sample and .95 in the aggregated sample. The results reported here and below rely on the asset measure implicit in Schedule B because it is more likely to be consistent with the liability measure. Here, as in (4), using vested liabilities VL in place of PL also consistently results in a significant positive relationship but with smaller γ values. In the regressions of the form (7) as well as (8) below, replacing NW by BA as the scale variable typically leads to small (in absolute value) values of γ, of either sign, that are not statistically significant; see 14 above.

17. The t-statistic associated with the explicit test of the null hypothesis $\delta = 1$ is 28.2, easily warranting rejection at any plausible confidence level. For the two subsample regressions described immediately below, the analogous t-statistics are 19.2 and 11.9, respectively.

18. See esp. Oldfield (1977) and Feldstein and Seligman (1981), as well as the chapter by Feldstein and Mørck in this volume. It is always possible, of course, that managements make decisions on the basis of believing that they can affect the share price in this way even if that belief is false.

19. These aggregate data are from the Federal Reserve System's flow-of-funds accounts for year end 1980. Although the proportions vary over time, primarily as a result of fluctuations in equity prices, the 1980 values are not atypical.

20. See Pesando (1981) for evidence on beneficiaries' implicit sharing in these returns, however.

21. See Black (1980) and Tepper (1981).

22. This statement abstracts from such factors as risk and maturity differences between the debt issued and the debt held.

23. For the subsample of firms with $PA/BA \geq .03$, the β value for $\sigma(EBIT)$ in the equity equation is $-.37$, with t-statistic -2.5; for the subsample with $PA/BA \geq .10$, it is $-.75$, with t-statistic -2.2.

24. Again this result carries over to all measures of earnings.

25. The corresponding β values in the PAD and PAO equations are both negative, though not statistically significant.

26. This distinction between equity investment in the accumulation and the annuity phases of defined-contribution pension plans corresponds to what many participants in TIAA-CREF voluntarily elect when they switch their pension reserves from CREF to TIAA at or near the time of retirement.

27. If the observations in the sample corresponded to different dates for the same firm, then a positive relationship between balance sheet leverage and pension asset allocations to debt securities would be evidence that firms behaved over time as Black (1980) and Tepper (1981) have suggested that they should for tax reasons. In a cross-section sample, however, no such inference would be warranted. At most, a positive cross-section relationship would indicate differences among firms in their extent of implementation of Black and Tepper's advice.

28. This positive relationship is opposite to what I found in earlier work based on a limited sample of Form 5500 and related data for plan year 1976.

29. Using vested liabilities VL in place of PL in (15) does not substantially affect the estimated γ values but does reduce the associated t-statistics; for the two samples reported above the results based on VL are, respectively, $\gamma = .31$, with t-statistic 6.4 ($\bar{R}^2 = .03$), and $\gamma = .26$, with t-statistic 5.0 ($\bar{R}^2 = .07$).

30. The variability of the rate of return on equity affects other liabilities negatively in both the full sample and the $PL/TA \geq .10$ subsample.

31. Using vested liabilities VL in place of PL in (17) also consistently results in a significant positive relationship but with smaller γ values.

32. These results apply to the Schedule B value of assets. For the Form 5500 asset totals, which need not have the same date as the liabilities reported in Schedule B, the corresponding results are $\gamma = .46$ and $\delta = -.32$, with respective t-statistics 8.9 and -4.9 ($\bar{R}^2 = .06$) for

the full sample, and $\gamma = .58$ and $\delta = -.40$, with respective t-statistics 8.7 and -4.7 ($\bar{R}^2 = .23$) for the subsample.

33. The results for estimating (6) are comparable.

34. As Jay O. Light points out in his discussion in this volume, there is also a problem if managements use differing actuarial concepts in defining pension "liabilities"—or, even if a single concept is used, if that concept differs importantly from that assumed here. The concept of pension liabilities used here (as in all of the previous literature cited above) is the actuarial present discounted value of accrued obligations for future benefit payments. This concept is identical to the notion of "actuarial present value of accumulated plan benefits" as defined by the Financial Accounting Standards Board (FASB) in its *Statement No. 35*, adopted March 1980 (see esp. pp. 6–9). What matters here, however, is what concepts managements used at the time they submitted their companies' reports for the 1977 plan year. On the basis of a close reading of the pension handbooks and texts available at that time, as well as the few available surveys of pension actuarial practice, it is not possible to determine whether—or to what extent—managements relied on the concept used here, which was later formalized by FASB-35, or the different net concept suggested by Light, or yet some other interpretation. The question does bear importantly on the empirical work in this chapter, as well as in all other empirical studies involving pension liability data before FASB-35.

Comment   Jay O. Light

First, I would like to congratulate Benjamin M. Friedman for a difficult empirical task well done. I hesitate to imagine just how many man-months were absorbed in preparing the basic data, but they must have been quite a few. The resultant data base has already furnished useful insights in Friedman's chapter, and I trust that it will continue to do so.

Friedman's chapter is a first exploratory trip through the data, searching for important relationships among corporate pension funding policy, the allocation of pension fund assets, corporate capital structure, and the characteristics of the underlying firms. It is the most thorough attempt I know to find such relationships using the detailed Form 5500 data, and as such it is an important work.

I propose to comment on several of what I think are the most interesting sections of the chapter. For each section, I will state the empirical results that might have been predicted on the basis of extant pension theories and the actual empirical results that were obtained. I will then tell some stories that might help to rationalize some of the observed empirical phenomena.

Before embarking on these tasks, let me first urge the reader to be cautious of Friedman's results and, perhaps more important, of my own comments. The financial decisions being investigated (funding policy, pension investment policy, and capital structure policy) are all, in princi-

Jay O. Light is professor, Harvard University Graduate School of Business Administration.

ple at least, simultaneous decisions. Causality is therefore very unclear, and the same cross-sectional results can be rationalized by a variety of quite different stories. More important, in this area our principal theoretical insights seem to point toward extremal policies (see, for example, the Harrison and Sharpe chapter in this volume). Interpreting cross-sectional regression results in the light of these extremal hypotheses is particularly difficult.

The Asset Allocation Results

With these words of caution, let me discuss what I find to be Friedman's most interesting results: the relationship of the pension fund's asset mix to other variables.

As a first step, let us speculate about what empirical relationships we would have expected to find on the basis of extant theory. The most convincing piece of theory is the tax-based argument (Black 1980; Tepper 1981), which essentially maintains that 100% of the fund's investments should be in the most heavily taxed asset, in this case presumably bonds. Note that this theory tells us only that the asset allocation should be an extreme choice. It does not predict what the *cross-sectional* empirical results presented in Friedman's chapter should look like. Indeed, we do not need cross-sectional results to test the tax-based theory. We know that very few firms invest their pension funds exclusively in bonds. To the contrary, most firms maintain a mixed portfolio, often weighted somewhat more heavily toward equities. Thus, very simple and well-known evidence shows that tax-based theories do not explain actual pension fund allocations.

To structure a theory-based hypothesis for the cross-sectional results, we must construct an augmented theory which states why firms might depart from the tax-based all-bonds strategy. The most likely candidate for such an augmented theory is the joint consideration of tax factors and the value of the put to the PBGC. (Friedman calls this latter effect the "Sharpe hypothesis.") For example, we might hypothesize that firms for whom the PBGC *put* is more valuable (that is, more in the money) will hold more of the most volatile asset, presumably common stocks, and vice versa.[1] The PBGC put is likely to be more valuable for underfunded plans, for unprofitable companies or companies with high profit variability, or for companies with more debt. We would thus expect the following kinds of companies to hold more common stocks in their pension portfolios: companies with underfunded pension plans, less profitable companies, companies with higher earnings variability, and companies with more debt.

Unfortunately, the actual empirical results confirm none of these hypotheses, as Friedman's excellent discussion points out. Surprisingly, there is no significant correlation between the funding of a plan and the allocation of assets within the fund.[2] There was a significant correlation of asset allocation with the other variables, but the opposite of that hypothesized above. In short, less profitable companies with more debt and higher earnings variability tended to hold somewhat less common stock in their pension funds, not more.

Why is that? The empirical results are consistent with a "risk-offsetting story," rather than with the theory discussed above. Corporations seem to manage their pension fund asset allocations to counterbalance the risks stemming from product markets or financial structure, so as to more nearly equalize total risk across firms at any given point in time. To some extent, this large sample result merely confirms anecdotal advice that can often be overheard from pension officers; namely, the riskier the company, the safer the pension fund should be. It is not at all clear, however, whether it is risk to the company, or to the pension beneficiaries, or to the agents themselves (i.e., the pension officers) that decision makers endeavor to offset, though these are all affected by the asset choice. Nonetheless, this empirical study demonstrates that risk offsetting appears to be a central feature of asset allocation.

Pension Funding and Capital Structure

The other results I will discuss here are the observed relationships between the degree of pension funding, capital structure, and other attributes of the firm. I have two small but nagging concerns about this set of results.

First, the measures of funding that are used are derived from the item "Accrued Liabilities" reported on Schedule B, Form 5500, entitled "Actuarial Information." It is not clear to me that this definition of pension liabilities is really measuring what one might first imagine, and the labels and definitions here can be quite misleading. The structure of Schedule B suggests that this "accrued liabilities" item is the calculation used in determining the actual funding contributions for the plan, rather than, for example, the "actuarial present value of accumulated plan benefits" currently required by FASB 35. More particularly, "accrued liabilities" in the language of the actuary is often used to mean the *present value* of what past contributions should have been had the current actuarial method, actuarial assumptions, and benefit levels been in effect during all past time periods. "Accrued liabilities" in this sense, when compared to the value of the fund's assets, determine the "unfunded liability," the measure of the extent to which the fund's assets are such that the pension fund is on the "funding trajectory" specified by the particular funding method. Unfortunately, however, this definition of "accrued liabilities" is dependent on the funding method selected by the firm, as well as on the actuarial assumptions used (such as discount rate). Thus, two firms in the identical economic position vis-à-vis their projected benefits may report substantially different "accrued liabilities," and vice versa, introducing a source of possible distortion in the data. Unfortunately, we do not know for sure what firms recorded under the item "accrued liabilities" on the Form 5500. The pension liability information currently being reported for more recent years since introduction of the new FASB 35 will allow us to be more confident that we have a cross-sectionally consistent measure of pension liabilities.

Second, several of the empirical results reported by Friedman stem from regressions where net worth is used as the scale (or deflating) variable. Clearly, because firms are quite different in size, some scaling is necessary. However, net worth is a relatively troublesome choice for this scale variable, for it is a residual quantity which can become quite small.[3] It thus could possibly introduce some spurious correlation into the regression results. Friedman's note 14 suggests that he was sensitive to this potential problem and omitted some observations to attempt to limit its effect. Nonetheless, several of the key empirical results would have reversed sign had another scale variable, other than net worth, been used (see Friedman's notes 14 and 16). Given some misgivings about net worth on a priori grounds, the sensitivity of results to the choice of scale variable is a little troubling.

Having raised these two concerns, let me discuss the actual funding results. As to theory, the tax-based arguments would suggest that pension funds should always be as fully funded as possible, consistent of course with IRS regulations. But to interpret cross-sectional tests, we once again need an augmented theory which allows us to hypothesize why firms might depart from policy of full funding. The most likely candidate, as Friedman points out, is the put to the PBGC. A hypothesis stemming from this conjecture would be that riskier firms should have bigger unfunded liabilities. Firms with low profitability, or variable profitability, might well be thought of as riskier firms, and we might expect them to have bigger unfunded liabilities. Unfortunately, the empirical results (see, for example, table 5.7) suggest that this is not the case. Indeed, the results, while generally not statistically significant, have the opposite sign.

There is, however, one rather intriguing result here: the more debt a company has on its balance sheet, the larger its unfunded liabilities are. And there are several alternative explanations of this result. First, and most simply, we can think of unfunded liabilities as merely another form of corporate borrowing. When a company needs to borrow, we might argue, it tends to borrow in two ways: from the capital markets, which is shown on the balance sheet, and from its pension fund, which is shown as unfunded pension liabilities.

Second, this result could be interpreted, as Friedman suggests, as empirical support for the Sharpe hypothesis about the value of the PBGC put. Finally, I might offer the following agency explanation. When a company has more debt, it tends to be managed somewhat more in the interests of current (and possibly future) creditors. Stepping back from the problem for a moment, the tax-based arguments (Black 1980; Tepper 1981) really just maintain that the interests of pension beneficiaries and shareholders are collinear. Ignoring the put to the PBGC, both of these groups want the pension fund fully funded and invested in bonds, the beneficiaries to maximize their collateral, and the shareholders to maximize their tax benefits. In whose interests, however, would it be to underfund the plan? Who are the losers when we fully fund? The creditors are the most important set of apparent losers. By funding the pension liabilities, we collateralize these liabilities to the detriment of liabilities of the company. Consequently, if creditors could dictate corporate pension policy, they would clearly be interested in underfunding the plan but investing the pension fund in bonds. Interestingly, what we observe in the empirical data is that the more debt a company has, the bigger its unfunded liabilities (table 5.7 and [17]) and the more bonds it holds in the pension fund (table 5.10). It is possible that we are observing an agency phenomenon here, reflecting the influence and interests of creditors on the financial policies of highly leveraged companies.

Conclusion

Benjamin Friedman's chapter in this volume has expanded our knowledge of how companies actually manage their pension policies and is therefore an important contribution. We hope that future studies will pursue this same goal.

For the present, however, we are left in a somewhat unsatisfactory state. The tax-based arguments of Black (1980) and Tepper (1981) suggest that firms should fully fund their pensions and invest the accumulated pension funds solely in bonds. Unfortunately, they do not. The Sharpe hypothesis suggests a rational economic reason why firms might be departing from these extremal policies: the value of the put to the PBGC. Unfortunately, while several of the cross-sectional regressions reported in this chapter are consistent with this hypothesis, others are not. In short, our evolving theories of pension policy and our evolving understanding of reality are at odds with one another in several important respects.

Notes

1. This is an empirically testable proposition using cross-sectional regressions if firms adopt extremal asset allocations (as suggested by Harrison and Sharpe) or if they adopt interior mixed allocations—as, in fact, we know they actually do.

2. See my later discussion of the funding variable used in the data base.

3. "Net worth," as defined by Friedman, is not only net of corporate debt but net of unfunded pension liabilities as well (see eq. [2]), so it can become quite small—indeed, conceivably negative.

References

Black, F., 1980. The tax consequences of long-run pension policy. *Financial Analysts Journal* 36: 25–31.

Feldstein, M., and Seligman, S. 1981. Pension funding, share prices, and national savings. *Journal of Finance* 36: 801–24.

Oldfield, G. S. 1977. Financial aspects of the private pension system. *Journal of Money, Credit and Banking* 9: 48–54.

Pesando, J. E. 1981. Employee valuation of pension claims and the impact of indexing initiatives. NBER Working Paper no. 767.

Scholes, M. 1981. Investigation of the Tepper/Black funding and allocation theory. Mimeographed. Chicago: University of Chicago, Graduate School of Business.

Sharpe, W. F. 1976. Corporate pension funding policy. *Journal of Financial Economics* 3: 183–93.

Tepper, I. 1981. Taxation and corporate pension policy. *Journal of Finance* 36: 1–14.

Tepper, I., and Affleck, A. R. P. 1974. Pension plan liabilities and corporate financial strategies. *Journal of Finance* 29: 1549–64.

6   Investing for the Short and the Long Term

Stanley Fischer

The expected real monthly return on Treasury bills is serially correlated, by some estimates following a random walk.[1] Expected real returns on stocks have a different dynamics. This means that the relative risk characteristics of stocks and bills differ depending on how long they are held.

For example, suppose that the expected real returns on Treasury bills are highly serially correlated and that expected real returns on stocks are less serially correlated. It is known that the variance of unexpected real returns on stocks, looking ahead one month, is about one hundred times the variance of the unexpected real return on bills. Stocks are of course much riskier than bills in the short run of a month.

Now consider an investor making a long-term portfolio decision to allocate his wealth between two mutual funds—a bill fund and a stock fund—with the proceeds being automatically reinvested in the fund in which they originate. Given the assumed serial correlation properties of asset returns, the longer the investment period, the less risky are stocks relative to bills.

Three questions are taken up in this chapter: (1) How does the term structure of risk arising from differences in the dynamics of asset returns affect optimal investment behavior? (2) What is the evidence on the dynamics of returns on stocks and bills in the United States? (3) Given the returns dynamics estimated in the paper, how do optimal portfolios change with the length of the holding period?

Stanley Fischer is professor of economics, Massachusetts Institute of Technology, and a research associate of the National Bureau of Economic Research. Part of the work for this paper was done while he was a visiting scholar at the Hoover Institution.

I am grateful to Sudipto Bhattacharya, Fischer Black, Barry Goldman, Hayne Leland, Thomas MaCurdy, and Robert Merton for helpful comments and discussions, and to Jeffrey Miron for excellent research assistance. Financial support was provided by the National Science Foundation and the Hoover Institution.

In section 6.1 I distinguish between the *horizon* of the investor and the *portfolio holding period* and briefly review known results on the effects of the horizon on the investment decision. In section 6.2 I set out the dynamics of asset returns and uncertainty about those returns as a function of the length of the holding period of an asset. Optimal mean-variance portfolios for investors choosing between two assets each with returns following a first-order autoregressive process are calculated in section 6.3. The dynamics of returns on stocks and bills are described in section 6.4, using United States data since 1926. Section 6.5 presents the results of simulations of optimal portfolios for holding periods of different lengths, given the dynamics described in section 6.4. Section 6.6 contains comments on the applicability of the analysis to pension investing. Concluding remarks are in section 6.7.

6.1 The Investment Horizon and the Portfolio Holding Period

Consider an investor maximizing the intertemporal utility function

$$(1) \qquad V(\ ) = \theta E_0 \int_0^T e^{-\delta t} U[C(t)] dt + (1 - \theta) E_0 B[W(T)],$$

where $C(t)$ is the rate of consumption at time t, $U[C(t)]$ is the instantaneous utility function, δ is the discount rate, $W(T)$ is real wealth at time T, $B(\ )$ is a utility of bequests function, and θ is a constant, $0 \le \theta \le 1$.

Suppose first that θ is equal to zero, so that the individual maximizes only the expected utility of bequests $E_0 B[W(T)]$. In this case T is the *investment horizon*. The function $B(\ )$ is also called the terminal utility of wealth function. Research on growth and turnpike portfolios (for example, Hakansson 1971, 1974; Leland 1972; Merton and Samuelson 1974; Ross 1974) has examined the effects of the length of the investor's horizon on optimal portfolio composition. The main question here is whether as the horizon lengthens all investors tend to hold the same portfolio—the general answer is no. There is a further question whether investors should or might want to maximize the expected growth rate of the value of the portfolio (subject to no short sales); again, the answer is in general no.

The investor's *holding period* is the interval of time between successive portfolio actions.[2] At one extreme, the investor may have an arbitrarily short holding period, engaging in continuous trading to rebalance the portfolio. At the other extreme, the investor may make his only portfolio decision at time zero and thereafter not be able to adjust the portfolio's composition. The important point is that the investor does not respond within the holding period to changes in actual and desired portfolio composition resulting from the behavior of asset returns.

For any given holding period, the individual solves the optimal portfolio problem from the recursion relations

(2) $\qquad J[W(t)] = \max E_t\{J[W(t + \Delta)]\},\ 0 \le t < T,$

with $J[W(T - \Delta)] = \max E_{T-\Delta} B[W(T)]$. In (2) $J(\ \ )$ is the indirect or derived utility function, and Δ is the length of the holding period. The maximization is conducted with respect to the composition of the portfolio.

Research on myopia in portfolio choice, by Mossin (1968), Hakansson (1970), and Samuelson (1969), considers the circumstances under which the investor's optimal portfolio is, for any given holding period, independent of the horizon. For utility functions with constant absolute or relative risk aversion, the investor's portfolio decision is independent of the length of the horizon, depending only on wealth. But, as shown by Goldman (1979), the composition of the optimal portfolio is *not* independent of the holding period, even when utility functions have constant relative risk aversion.

The holding period for an individual managing his own portfolio is likely to be finite but not constant. Portfolio rebalancing will be undertaken only at discrete intervals because it is costly. But the interval is not fixed because the need for rebalancing varies with the behavior of asset prices.

An investor who saves through regular contributions to a retirement fund, for which he specifies the breakdown of his portfolio between equities and bonds, may formally be permitted to change the composition of his retirement portfolio only once a year or every few years. However, if such an individual also has discretionary portfolio assets, he can effectively rebalance his portfolio more frequently than the rules of the retirement fund formally permit. He does this by using the discretionary funds to offset movements in portfolio composition in the retirement funds.

When the possibility of consuming at intermediate dates, $t < T$, is reinstated by setting θ in (1) at a value other than zero, the notion of the horizon loses its crispness. Date T is still the horizon in the sense that the individual looks no further ahead than T. But now events that occur at $t < T$ matter not only because they affect the situation at T but also because consumption at t and later depends on the state of the world at time t. Despite the ambiguity, I continue to refer to T as the horizon.

The notion of the portfolio holding period retains its meaning, however. Even if consumption is continuous, optimal portfolio behavior may involve infrequent rebalancing of the portfolio. Inventories of goods and liquid assets are used to finance consumption within the holding period, while the investment portfolio is rebalanced at discrete intervals.

The optimizing problem of the investor-consumer is again solved as in (2), with the aid of recursion relations and an indirect utility function. For any given frequency with which decisions are made, questions about myopia in portfolio behavior receive the same answers as they do without intermediate consumption.

I do not in this chapter analyze optimal investment strategy for an individual faced with costs of portfolio management and given dynamic properties of asset returns. Optimal strategy in such a case will involve a finite but not constant holding period. Instead, I study the simpler problem in which the holding period is given. My analysis focuses on the effects of the length of the holding period on the optimal composition of the portfolio when asset returns are serially correlated.[3] I assume that there are a significant number of individuals for whom the portfolio holding period is on the order of months or even years. For such individuals the distinction between the short-run and the long-run properties of asset returns may be important.

6.2 Rates of Return and the Length of the Holding Period

In this section I briefly examine the distribution of per period rates of return on an asset as a function of the number of periods for which it is held. The returns are assumed to follow a stable first-order autoregressive process.

Suppose the rate of return on an asset, r_t, is described by

$$(3) \qquad \ln(1 + r_t) \equiv x_t = \alpha + \beta x_{t-1} + \varepsilon_t,$$

where ε_t is serially uncorrelated and normally distributed with expectation zero and variance σ_ε^2.

Let W_N be the amount obtained by buying one dollar of the asset at the beginning of period 1 and reinvesting the returns for N periods. Then

$$(4) \qquad \ln W_N = \ln \Pi_1^N (1 + r_i)$$
$$= \Sigma_1^N x_i .$$

From (3) and (4),

$$(5) \quad \ln W_N = \frac{N\alpha}{1-\beta} + \frac{\beta(1-\beta^N)}{1-\beta}(x_0 - \alpha) + \Sigma_1^N \varepsilon_i \left(\frac{1-\beta^{N+1-i}}{1-\beta} \right).$$

W_N is therefore lognormally distributed, with

$$(6) \qquad E(\ln W_N | x_0) = \frac{N\alpha}{1-\beta} + \frac{\beta(1-\beta^N)}{1-\beta}(x_0 - \alpha) \equiv m_N$$

and

$$(7) \quad \text{var}(\ln W_N | x_0) = \frac{\sigma_\varepsilon^2}{(1-\beta)^2} \left\{ N - \frac{\beta(1-\beta^N)}{1-\beta} \left[2 - \frac{\beta(1+\beta^N)}{1+\beta} \right] \right\} \equiv s_N^2 .$$

The expectation and variance of terminal wealth, W_N, are given by

$$(8) \qquad E(W_N | x_0) = e^{m_N + s_N^2}$$

and

(9)
$$\text{var}(W_N|x_0) = e^{2m_N + s_N^2}(e^{s_N^2} - 1).$$

Now define the expected rate of return per period on an N-period investment, $\mu(N)$, by

(10)
$$N\mu(N) \equiv m_N.$$

The variance of the per period return, $\sigma^2(N)$, is defined by

(11)
$$N\sigma^2(N) \equiv s_N^2.$$

Asymptotically, the per period expected rate of return is just $[\alpha/(1-\beta)]$, with the additional term in (6) reflecting the effect on expected returns of initial conditions.

The per period variance of returns goes asymptotically to

(12)
$$\lim_{N\to\infty} \sigma^2(N) = \frac{\sigma_\varepsilon^2}{(1-\beta)^2}.$$

For $N = 1$, of course,

(13)
$$\sigma^2(1) = \sigma_\varepsilon^2.$$

Thus the variance of the per period rate of return on an asset increases by a factor of $(1-\beta)^{-2}$ as the number of periods for which it is held rises from one to many. For a highly autocorrelated series, $\beta = .9$, the ratio of the asymptotic to the one-period variance of the per period return is 100.

Table 6.1 shows how the variance of the per period rate of return changes with the number of periods for a first-order autoregressive process, for alternative values of β. The effects of the serial correlation on the variance of the per period return are highly nonlinear in the parameter β.

Table 6.1   **Variance of per Period Returns for a First-Order Autoregressive Process**

N	$\beta = 0.95$	$\beta = 0.9$	$\beta = 0.75$	$\beta = 0.5$
1	1.0	1.0	1.0	1.0
2	2.4	2.3	2.0	1.6
3	4.3	4.0	3.1	2.1
6	12.5	10.4	6.2	2.9
12	36.2	25.1	10.0	3.4
24	92.7	48.6	12.9	3.7
48	186.9	71.6	14.4	3.9
120	304.5	88.6	15.4	3.9

Note: Entries show variances of per period returns for holding period of length N relative to variance for one period.

6.3   Minimum Variance and Optimal Mean-Variance Portfolios

In this section I examine minimum variance and optimal mean-variance portfolios when asset returns follow first-order autoregressive processes like (3). The consumer-investor is understood to be maximizing an intertemporal utility function with indirect utility function that is quadratic in the portfolio return, and with portfolio holding period of length N.

Suppose there are two assets, 1 and 2, with returns described by

$$(14) \qquad x_{i,t} = \alpha_i + \beta_i x_{i,t-1} + \varepsilon_{it}, \qquad i = 1, 2,$$

with $E(\varepsilon_{1t}\varepsilon_{2t}) = \sigma_{12}$ and variances of ε_i denoted σ_i^2.

Define the variance of the per period rate of return for each asset by $\sigma_i^2(N)$, as in (11).[4] Let w be the share of the first asset in the portfolio and define the variance of the portfolio rate of return as

$$(15) \quad \sigma_P^2(N) = w^2 \sigma_1^2(N) + 2w(1-w)\sigma_{12}(N) + (1-w)^2 \sigma_2^2(N),$$

where $\sigma_{12}(N)$ is the covariance of the per period rates of return, given by

$$
(16) \quad N\sigma_{12}(N) = E\left[\Sigma_1^N \varepsilon_{1i}\left(\frac{1 - \beta_1^{N+1-i}}{1 - \beta_1}\right)\Sigma_1^N \varepsilon_{2i}\left(\frac{1 - \beta_2^{N+1-i}}{1 - \beta_2}\right)\right]
$$

$$
= \frac{\sigma_{12}}{(1 - \beta_1)(1 - \beta_2)}[N - f(N)]
$$

where

$$
f(N) \equiv (1 - \beta_1\beta_2)[\beta_1(1 - \beta_2)(1 - \beta_1^{N+1}) + \beta_2(1 - \beta_1)(1 - \beta_2^{N+1})]
$$
$$
+ \beta_1\beta_2(1 - \beta_1)(1 - \beta_2)[1 - (\beta_1\beta_2)^{N+1}].
$$

6.3.1   The Minimum Variance Portfolio

The minimum variance portfolio is given by

$$(17) \qquad w^*(N) = \frac{\sigma_2^2(N) - \sigma_{12}(N)}{\sigma_1^2(N) - 2\sigma_{12}(N) + \sigma_2^2(N)}.$$

In particular,

$$(18) \qquad w^*(1) = \frac{\sigma_2^2 - \sigma_{12}}{\sigma_1^2 - 2\sigma_{12} + \sigma_2^2}$$

and

$$(19) \quad w^*(\infty) = \frac{(1 - \beta_1)^2 \sigma_2^2 - (1 - \beta_1)(1 - \beta_2)\sigma_{12}}{(1 - \beta_2)^2 \sigma_1^2 - 2(1 - \beta_1)(1 - \beta_2)\sigma_{12} + (1 - \beta_1)^2 \sigma_2^2}.$$

The difference between the one-period and asymptotic minimum variance portfolios depends largely on $\beta_2 - \beta_1$:

$$(20) \qquad w^*(\infty) - w^*(1) = \frac{(\beta_2 - \beta_1)\{\sigma_1^2(1 - \beta_2)[\sigma_2^2 - \sigma_{12}] + \sigma_2^2(1 - \beta_1)(\sigma_1^2 - \sigma_{12})\}}{D_1 D_\infty},$$

where D_1 and D_∞ are the denominators of the expressions in (18) and (19), respectively.

For both β_1 and β_2 less than one in absolute value, and for zero covariance of asset returns ($\sigma_{12} = 0$), the minimum variance portfolio moves toward or away from stocks as the holding period lengthens, depending only on the sign of ($\beta_2 - \beta_1$). When asset returns are positively correlated ($\sigma_{12} > 0$), the direction of the shift in the minimum variance portfolio apparently becomes less certain. However, for stocks as the riskier asset (so $\sigma_1^2 > \sigma_{12}$) and provided $w^*(1)$ is positive (so $\sigma_2^2 > \sigma_{12}$), the direction of shift is of the same sign as ($\beta_2 - \beta_1$).

The composition of the minimum variance portfolio may be highly sensitive to the length of the holding period. To take a simple example, in which asset 1 should be thought of as stocks, assume that $\sigma_{\varepsilon 1}^2 = 99\sigma_{\varepsilon 2}^2$, $\sigma_{12} = 0$, $\beta_1 = 0$, and $\beta_2 = .9$. Then $w^*(1) = .01$ and $w^*(\infty) = .50$. As the holding period lengthens in this case, stocks take up a larger part of the minimum variance portfolio. It takes a holding period of 19 periods for the optimal share of the first asset in the portfolio to reach 25%. The 47.5% mark is reached only after 131 periods.

6.3.2 Mean-Variance Portfolios

Although the usual justifications for mean-variance portfolio analysis do not apply when portfolio decisions are made for the long term, it is instructive briefly to consider optimal mean-variance portfolios as a function of the decision period. If utility is defined as a function of the mean and variance of the portfolio returns, the optimal proportion of the first asset in the portfolio is

$$(21) \qquad w^{**}(N) = A\left[\frac{\mu_1(N) - \mu_2(N)}{\sigma_1^2(N) - 2\sigma_{12}(N) + \sigma_2^2(N)}\right] + w^*(N),$$

where A is a measure of risk tolerance and $\mu_i(N)$ is the expected per period return on asset i.

In (21) we interpret the first asset as the stock, which has a higher expected return than bills. Two forces act on the portfolio as the horizon changes. In the first (excess return) term on the right-hand side of (21), the numerator stays constant as N increases while the denominator increases with N. Thus the asset holder will want to hold less of the stock when the riskiness of the excess return on stocks rises relative to the expected return, as the holding period lengthens. Second, as seen above, the share of the stock in the minimum variance portfolio, $w^*(N)$, changes as the holding period N increases.

For $\beta_2 > \beta_1$, the two portfolio effects—that through the first, excess return, term and that through the minimum variance portfolio—work in opposite directions. Thus the effects of changes in the holding period on the composition of the portfolio will be ambiguous for this mean-variance case, if $\beta_2 > \beta_1$. The net effect on the portfolio will depend on the parameters of the stochastic processes describing asset returns and on the investor's risk tolerance. The presumption is that if $\beta_2 >> \beta_1$, the shift in the portfolio will be toward stocks as the holding period lengthens, but if the serial correlation properties of the returns on the two assets are similar, it is less certain which way the portfolio will shift with the holding period.

6.3.3   Constant Relative Risk Aversion Portfolios

Mean-variance portfolio analysis is difficult to justify when the holding period is long. But it turns out that ambiguities similar to those noted above emerge when utility functions are isoelastic and asset returns follow diffusion processes.

Goldman (1979) has shown, for isoelastic utility functions, that portfolios become less diversified as the holding period lengthens when asset returns are generated by diffusion processes with no serial correlation. Portfolio proportions move away from one-half toward undiversified positions as the holding period lengthens.

When serial correlation of asset returns is introduced, there is an effect additional to that of Goldman on the composition of the portfolio (Fischer 1982). As the relative risk of assets changes with the holding period, the composition of the portfolio changes for that reason as well as the Goldman effect. The net effect depends on the relative strengths of the Goldman effect and the risk-aversion effect.

Portfolio analysis thus cannot unambiguously describe the effects of changes in the holding period on the composition of the portfolio. The effects depend on both the facts—the stochastic processes describing asset returns—and the investor's preferences. In the next section we turn to the facts.

6.4   Asset Returns

Although knowledge of the stochastic processes generating asset returns is essential to portfolio behavior, there is no consensus on what these processes are. Nor are there well-known competing estimates of the stochastic processes. In this section I first present evidence that there are both serial correlation in bill returns and differential returns dynamics of bill and stock returns. Then I present three alternative estimates of the stochastic processes generating asset returns.

Method 1 estimates a simple autoregressive model for real bill returns and then treats the real return on stocks as a function of the anticipated real rate on bills and lagged stock returns. This method has been used by Fama and Gibbons (1982).

Method 2 estimates a complete monthly vector autoregressive model of the economy, including stock and bill returns among the variables in the model. The vector autoregressive model implies the dynamics of stock and bill returns. Because the rate of inflation, growth rate of industrial production, and rate of money growth are included in the model, the dynamics of asset returns is potentially richer than in the simpler constrained processes estimated by method 1.

Both methods 1 and 2 at times imply that the expected real return on bills exceeds that on stocks. Method 3 therefore imposes a constraint, of a type implied by the capital asset pricing model, on the processes generating the returns.

This section ends with a comparison of the alternative estimates of returns.

6.4.1   Differential Returns Dynamics

Simple time-series properties of realized real rates of return on stocks and Treasury bills are suggested by table 6.2. Stock and bill returns are monthly Ibbotson-Sinquefield data from the Center for Research in Security Prices; stock returns are from the Standard and Poor's Composite Index. Real rates of return are calculated from the nonseasonally adjusted consumer price index.[5] Returns are measured as logarithms of one plus the return. Returns for more than one month are compounded for nonoverlapping periods.

The essential point made by table 6.2 is that the relative riskiness of stock returns falls with the length of the holding period. For data covering the entire 1926–80 period, the per period variance of returns on stocks is 100 times that on bills over a one-month holding period; over a one-year holding period, the variance of returns on stocks is 20 times greater than that on bills. The ratio of variances over 5-year holding periods is only 4.4, though this number should be treated with caution because it is based on only 11 5-year periods. A similar, though less dramatic, pattern holds over the 1948–80 period.[6] I will from this point on work with monthly data for the period 1948–80.

The per period variances in table 6.2 suggest both that stock returns are (approximately) serially uncorrelated and that bill returns are positively serially correlated. If stock returns were i.i.d., the per period variance would be independent of the length of the holding period. As it is, the per

Table 6.2   Real Monthly Returns on Stocks and Bills

	1926–80			1948–80		
	Stocks (1)	Bills (2)	Ratio (1)/(2)	Stocks (1)	Bills (2)	Ratio (1)/(2)
Mean return	.00511	− .00008		.00593	.00003	
Variance of returns per month						
1-month holding period	.362	.00353	102.5	.160	.00098	164.3
2-month holding period	.402	.00547	73.5	.164	.00140	117.2
4-month holding period	.355	.00826	43.0	.192	.00177	108.8
12-month holding period	.381	.01649	23.1	.192	.00330	58.3
60-month holding period	(.188	.04322	4.4)	(.326	.00683	47.7)

Note: The variances should all be multiplied by .01. Stock and bill returns are from the Ibbotson-Sinquefield File, Center for Research in Security Prices, University of Chicago; real returns are calculated using seasonally unadjusted CPI. Parentheses in last row of table are a reminder that statistics are based on only 11 and six data points, respectively.

period variance for stocks increases slightly with the length of the holding period. The per period variance of returns on bills rises more sharply with the length of the period.

Autocorrelation functions for real stock and bill returns are presented in table 6.3. Bill returns are significantly serially correlated, whereas stock returns are not. The autocorrelation function for bills suggests that the stochastic process for bill returns is something other than a first-order autoregression.

I now present three sets of estimates of the stochastic processes generating asset returns. Each method allows for correlation of stock and bill returns; such correlations can have a major impact on portfolio decisions. It will become clear below that method 3 is the preferred estimation method in this chapter, but methods 1 and 2 are included since they either have already appeared in the literature or else are typical of methods currently used to generate expectations.

6.4.2   Estimation Methods

Method 1

The first method of estimating bill and stock returns dynamics is that of Fama and Gibbons (1982). The procedure is first to estimate a simple ARMA model for real bill returns and then to relate stock returns to expected bill returns. The rationale for this approach is that models of capital asset pricing imply that expected real returns on stocks are related to expected returns on bills.

Table 6.4 presents estimates of a twelfth-order autoregressive process for the real bill rate, using data from the period 1948:2–1980:12. The

Table 6.3   Autocorrelation Functions, Real Monthly Returns on Stocks and Bills, 1948:2–1980:12

	Lag 1	Lag 2	Lag 3	Lag 4	Lag 5	Lag 6	Lag 7	Lag 8	Lag 9	Lag 10	Lag 11	Lag 12
Real bill rate	.39	.29	.22	.10	.09	.05	.05	.14	.15	.14	.14	.13
Real stock return	.03	-.01	.07	.10	.11	-.07	-.03	-.02	.06	-.03	.02	.08

	Lag 13	Lag 14	Lag 15	Lag 16	Lag 17	Lag 18	Lag 19	Lag 20	Lag 21	Lag 22	Lag 23	Lag 24
Real bill rate	.03	.04	.06	.06	-.01	-.05	-.10	0	0	.01	.05	.04
Real stock return	-.01	-.07	0	.03	.02	-.04	-.05	0	-.05	-.02	-.02	-.04

Notes: Real returns are calculated using seasonally unadjusted CPI; patterns using seasonally adjusted CPI show somewhat higher autocorrelations for real bill rates, no change for stocks. Standard error of coefficients is .05. (There are 395 observations.)

Table 6.4   **Bill and Stock Returns, Method 1, 1948:2–1980:12**

Equation (R1): Real Bill Rate[a]

Lag 1	Lag 2	Lag 3	Lag 4	Lag 5	Lag 6
.25	.10	.11	.04	−.03	−.06
(1.89)	(1.84)	(2.09)	(0.69)	(−0.55)	(−1.20)

Lag 7	Lag 8	Lag 9	Lag 10	Lag 11	Lag 12
.06	.10	.07	.09	−.11	−.05
(1.27)	(1.95)	(1.51)	(1.80)	(−2.30)	(−1.05)

Equation (R2): Real Stock Rate[b]

$$RS_t = .0057 + 3.03 \,_{t-1}RB_t + .019 \, RS_{t-1}$$
$$\quad\;\; (2.83) \quad (2.33) \qquad (0.38)$$

Note: $_{t-1}R_t$ is the expectation of RB_t formed at the end of period $t-1$, using eq. (R1). Numbers in parentheses are t-statistics.
[a]Regressed on constant, 11 seasonal dummy variables, and 12 lags of real bill rate. $\bar{R}^2 = .20$, SEE $= .0028$, D-W $= 1.92$, $Q = 59.7$.
[b]$\bar{R}^2 = .0097$, SEE $= .0398$, D-W $= 1.99$, $Q = 61.5$.

length of the autoregression was chosen to eliminate serial correlation in the residuals, as indicated by the Q-statistic. More parsimonious representations using moving average as well as autoregressive parameters did not improve on the properties of the real bill rate equation.[7]

The real return on stocks is then regressed on the expected return on bills, as computed in regression (R1). The real return on stocks is significantly positively related to the ex ante real return on bills. The share of the variance of realized stock returns accounted for by movements in the expected bill rate is however less than 1%. The standard error of estimate of the stock rate of return over the next month is almost 4%, at a monthly rate. Thus actual movements in real stock returns are hardly at all the result of changes in the expected rate, at least according to the estimates presented in table 6.4.

As a result of the constraints under which the stock and bill returns processes are estimated, the ex ante rates of return on stocks and bills follow very similar stochastic processes. The first-order autocorrelations of ex ante bill and stock returns are both about .7.

Method 2

Method 2 estimates a monthly five-variable vector autoregressive model of the United States economy for the period 1948:2–1980:12. The five variables are the rate of money growth (M1-B), the rate of inflation (CPI), the rate of growth of industrial production, the nominal bill rate, and real stock returns. Variables are not seasonally adjusted.

A vector autoregressive model (Sims 1980) imposes a minimum of theory in estimating dynamic equations. All variables are modeled as endogenous, lags are made long enough to eliminate any serial correlation of residuals in estimated equations, and no zero restrictions are imposed on coefficients beyond those implied by the choice of variables to include in the model and the length of lag.

The form of the model is

$$(22) \qquad\qquad \mathbf{X}_t = \sum_{i=1}^{I} A_i X_{t-1-i} + \mathbf{u}_t ,$$

where $\mathbf{X}_t$ is the vector of (in this case five) included variables, the maximal lag length I has to be specified, the coefficients in the A matrices are to be estimated, and $\mathbf{u}_t$ is a white-noise vector of disturbances that may be contemporaneously correlated.

In the model estimated here the lag length was taken to be 12, both to eliminate serial correlation of residuals and to pick up any potential residual seasonal patterns that were not eliminated by the presence of seasonal dummy variables in each of the five equations. The Box-Pierce Q-statistic was used to indicate serial correlation.[8]

The lag coefficients were estimated imposing a Bayes-Litterman prior (Litterman 1980). The prior is that the model is purely first-order autoregressive, with each variable following a random walk. Thus priors are that the coefficient of the first own lag in each equation is unity and all other lag coefficients are zero.[9] Prior estimates of the standard deviations of the lag coefficients are that the standard deviations fall geometrically, with an imposed decay coefficient of .9. The standard deviation for the first own lag coefficient is estimated from a first-order autoregression. Standard deviations on coefficients of all other variables in an equation follow the same decay pattern as those on the own variable, but with standard deviations that are half those on the own variables.

The prior restrictions, which are tighter at the longer lags, reflect a general presumption that economic systems are low-order autoregressions. The priors typically prevent the alternation of coefficients that would be expected in any system in which the regressors are highly collinear.

Summary statistics from the five equations are presented in table 6.5. The regressions themselves contain too many parameters to be presented. The most striking feature of the system is the inability to predict stock returns well using the vector autoregressive approach. The F-statistic for the regression as a whole is not significant at the 5% level, though it is significant at the 10% level.

Table 6.5   **Method 2, Five-Variable Monthly Vector Autoregressive Model**

Equation (R3):   *Real Stock Returns*
$\bar{R}^2 = .15$ SEE = .0369   D-W = 2.00
$Q = 42.9$ (significance level = .92)
F-statistics for sums of coefficients on each variable are not significant at 10% level for any of the variables. *F*-statistics for all coefficients not significant at 5% level.

(R4)   *Nominal Bill Returns*
$\bar{R}^2 = .95$ SEE = .00051   D-W = 1.98
$Q = 40.9$ (significance level = .95)
F-statistics show strong significance of lagged bill returns; no other variables significant at 10% level.

(R5)   *CPI Inflation Rate*
$\bar{R}^2 = .59$ SEE = .00256   D-W = 1.98
$Q = 58.5$ (significance level = .42)
F-statistics show strong significance of lagged inflation rate; lagged nominal bill rates are significant at 2% level, lagged money growth at 6% level. Sum of coefficients for each of these three variables is positive.

(R6)   *Growth Rate of Industrial Production*
$\bar{R}^2 = .85$ SEE = .0116   D-W = 2.05
$Q = 30.4$ (significance level = .998)
Lagged stock returns, lagged industrial production and lagged money growth are all significant at 5% level. Sum of lagged coefficients is positive for all three variables.

(R7)   *Growth Rate of Money*
$\bar{R}^2 = .92$ SEE = .0040   D-W = 1.99
$Q = 49.1$ (significance level = .76)
F-statistics show sum of coefficients on lagged nominal interest rates and lagged money growth strongly significant. Lagged stock prices have significance level of .08. Sum of lagged coefficients positive for all three variables. Coefficients on bill rate lagged one and two periods are both negative.

A vector autoregressive model of the type estimated here should be viewed as a statistically sophisticated extension of single-variable time-series forecasting methods. No attempt is made to estimate structural relations. The hypothesis implicit in the use of such models for forecasting purposes is that the underlying economic structure, including policy response functions, is stable. This approach is as vulnerable as more traditional econometric models to the Lucas policy evaluation critique that coefficients will change if policy rules change.

The model was used to form within-sample one-period-ahead forecasts of real rates of return on stocks and bills. These predicted rates are serially correlated. The first autocorrelation of the *real* return on bills (equal to the nominal rate of interest minus the predicted inflation rate) is .61. The first autocorrelation of the predicted return on stocks is .34. However, there is a seasonal pattern in stock returns, resulting in a twelfth-order autocorrelation of .56. The predicted rates of return on stocks have a high standard deviation, equal to 1.3% *per month*. The standard deviation of predicted real bill returns is 0.2% per month.

The high variability of the ex ante stock rate also produces occasions on which the expected return on stocks is lower than the expected return on bills. Rather than attempt to correct this problem by tightening the priors on the lag coefficients in the stock returns equation, I imposed a constraint of a type implied by the capital asset pricing model. This leads to method 3 for estimating bill and stock returns.

Method 3

Method 3 estimates a vector autoregressive model to generate expected real returns on bills and then uses the one-period-ahead forecast of the real bill rate from that model to estimate an equation for the predicted real return on stocks. The assumption is that

$$(23) \qquad _{t-1}RS_t - {}_{t-1}RB_t = a_{t-1}s_t^2 + e_t.$$

In (23), the left-hand-side variables are the expected real returns on stocks and bills, respectively. The variable $_{t-1}s_t^2$ is the expected or estimated variance of the excess return on the market. The variable e_t is random, and a is a parameter to be estimated.

Equation (23) is not exact, because the capital asset pricing model does not imply a constant value of the parameter a when the opportunity set is changing. The error term is included to reflect such changes. The coefficient a is estimated using the assumption that expectations of stock returns are rational. With rational expectations,

$$(24) \qquad RS_t = {}_{t-1}RS_t + v_t,$$

where v_t is a serially uncorrelated error term with expectation zero. Substituting (24) into (23), we obtain the estimated equation

$$(25) \qquad RS_t - {}_{t-1}RB_t = a_{t-1}s_t^2 + e_t - v_t.$$

Some comments on (25). First, the structure of the error term in (25), or equivalently the form in which (25) is estimated, is not known or determined by a priori considerations. It is possible that e_t is heteroscedastic[10] and that the implicit assumption made in moving from (24) to (25) about the variance of v_t is inappropriate. Estimation of (25) in the alternative form

$$(25') \qquad \frac{RS_t - {}_{t-1}RB_t}{{}_{t-1}s_t^2} = a + \hat{e}_t - \hat{v}_t.$$

hardly affected the estimate of a, to be reported in table 6.6 below.

Second, (25) is constrained not to allow a constant. When a constant is added on the right-hand side, the constant is small and insignificant, the estimate of a falls a little, but a loses its statistical significance.

Third, it is necessary in (25) to use an estimate of the variance of the excess return on the market.[11] I experimented with variances of lagged realized stock returns over 12, 24, and 36 months. There were no major differences in the estimates of a. The final choice was the 36-month moving variance.[12]

Table 6.6 contains details of the estimated vector autoregressive system and of (R12), which is the estimated version of (25). The vector autoregressive system contains four variables, those of the previous section excluding the real return on stocks. Because real stock returns did not appear significantly in other equations in the five-variable model, the equations for the four-variable model are very similar to those estimated in method 2.

The estimate of a in (R12) is significantly different from zero. The predictive power for real stock returns of an equation like (R12) is of course extremely small. The implied value of the coefficient of relative

Table 6.6   Method 3, Estimated Four-Variable Vector Autoregressive Model and Stock Returns Equation

(R8) *Nominal Bill Returns*
$\bar{R}^2 = .94$ SEE = .00051   D-W = 1.97
                                              $Q = 43.5$ (significance level = .91)
F-statistics show strong significance of lagged bill returns; significance level for inflation variables is .11.

(R9) *CPI Inflation Rate*
$\bar{R}^2 = .58$ SEE = .00259   D-W = 1.99
                                              $Q = 56.0$ (significance level = .51)
Coefficients on lagged bill returns and lagged inflation are strongly significant; significance level for money variables is .08.

(R10) *Industrial Production*
$\bar{R}^2 = .84$ SEE = 0.0119   D-W = 2.04
                                              $Q = 31.6$ (significance level = .998)
Coefficients on lagged industrial production and money are strongly significant.

(R11) *Growth Rate of Money*
$\bar{R}^2 = .91$ SEE = .00408   D-W = 2.00
                                              $Q = 49.5$ (significance level = .75)
Lagged bill rates, industrial production, and money are significant at 5% level. Sum of coefficients on bill rate is positive; first two coefficients are large and negative. Sum of coefficients on industrial production is positive.

(R12) *Real Stock Returns*
$$RS_t = {}_{t-1}RB_t + 3.42 \, {}_{t-1}s_t^2$$
$$(2.94)$$
$\bar{R}^2 = .000046$ SEE = 0.0399   D-W = 1.95
                                              $Q = 59.7$ (significance level = .38)
Variables are: ${}_{t-1}RB_t$ is expected *real* return on bills, equal to nominal rate minus ${}_{t-1}\pi_t$, the expected inflation rate from (R9). ${}_{t-1}s_t^2$ is the variance of real stock returns over the previous 36 months. t-statistics in parentheses.

risk aversion is about 3, corresponding to a utility function of the form $(-W)^{-2}$.

The expected real rate of return on stocks is now highly serially correlated. This is in large part a result of the serial correlation built into the method of creating the variance. The first autocorrelation for expected stock returns is .83. That for bills is 0.62, approximately the same as for method 2. The standard deviation of the expected real rate on stocks is now only 0.27% per month; that for bills is 0.18% per month. Expected stock returns always exceed expected bill returns, though the premium certainly varies. The highest premium is recorded in 1976 and is equal to 1.2% per month. The lowest premium occurs in early 1966 and is only 0.17% per month. If such variation is too large to be plausible, the source of the difficulty is no doubt to be traced to the variance estimator.

The purpose of estimating the alternative forecasting models is to use them in examining portfolio selection over different holding periods. In the next section, I use methods 2 and 3 to simulate the behavior of different portfolios over one- and 60-period holding periods.

6.5 Simulated Portfolio Results

The stochastic processes for bill and stock returns implied by methods 2 and 3 in the previous section were used in simulating the behavior of alternative portfolios over holding periods of one month and 60 months. The utility function was taken to be isoelastic, of the form

$$(26) \qquad J(W_t) = W_t^{\gamma}/\gamma, \gamma < 1.$$

For $\gamma = 0$, we have the logarithmic utility function. The smaller is γ, the more risk averse the individual.

Four alternative utility functions were used to evaluate portfolio performance. They were the logarithm, $\gamma = -1.5, \gamma = -4$, and $\gamma = -10$. The last utility function has risk aversion well beyond any that is usually estimated. It is included because the less risk-averse utility functions show little inclination toward portfolio diversification.

The simulation procedure is to set each model off with starting conditions that are equal to historical means of the relevant variables over the estimation period. Drawings of the additive error terms in each equation are then made and first-period values of the variables in the simulation recorded. The process then repeats, with updated values of lagged variables (in the 60-period simulation) and keeps doing so to the end of the holding period.

Portfolios are allocated between bills and stocks, on a grid of 0.05, running from all stocks to all bills. The total return accumulated over the holding period by one dollar invested in each asset and the terminal wealth and utility obtained from each portfolio choice for each utility function are recorded for each simulation. There were 10,000 simulations of the portfolios generated using the stochastic processes of model 2, and 2,500 of the portfolios generated using model 3. The mean of the utility level attained under each portfolio choice for each set of simulations is calculated and taken to be an estimate of expected utility.

Because mean asset returns initially differed over the one-month and 60-month holding periods, the means of the returns on both bonds and stocks were adjusted in the one-month-holding-period simulations to be the same as those in the 60-month simulations. The identity of the reported means of asset returns in one- and 60-month simulations in each table is thus the result of calculation and not chance.

The simulated optimal portfolios in table 6.7 are heavily in stocks for both short and long horizons. Diversification only occurs for utility functions with high risk aversion. The most interesting result in the table, from the viewpoint of this discussion, is that lengthening the holding period shifts the portfolio *toward* bills, rather than away from them, for the highly risk-averse investors. These investors are probably reacting to the increasing riskiness of the excess return on stocks over the return on bills, even though the relative riskiness of stocks is falling. A second factor that may account for the result is that the covariance of bill and stock returns can move investors into bills as the horizon lengthens, even if the relative riskiness of bills is rising (Fischer 1982).

The results of 2,500 simulations made using the dynamics of method 3 estimates are shown in table 6.8. The levels of the optimal portfolios are very similar to those in table 6.7. This is to be expected since the interactions between stock returns and the rest of the system in method 2 were minimal.

Table 6.7   **Simulated Optimal Portfolios, Method 2**

Holding Period	Utility Function			
	$\ell n\ W$	$-W^{-1.5}$	$-W^{-4}$	$-W^{-10}$
1 month	1	1	1	.45
60 months	1	1	.85	.4

Statistics	Mean Bill Return per Month	Mean Stock Return per Month	Variance of Bill Return per Month (1)	Variance of Stock Return per Month (2)	(2)/(1)
1 month	$.160 \times 10^{-3}$	.00600	$.640 \times 10^{-5}$	.00125	195.3
60 months	$.160 \times 10^{-3}$	.00600	$.341 \times 10^{-4}$	.00163	47.9

Notes: Entries in first two rows are shares of stocks in optimal portfolio. There were 10,000 replications.

Table 6.8   **Simulated Optimal Portfolios, Method 3**

Holding Period	Utility Function			
	$\ell n\ W$	$-W^{-1.5}$	$-W^{-4}$	$-W^{-10}$
1 month	1	1	.75	.35
60 months	1	1	.80	.35

Statistics	Mean Bill Return per Month	Mean Stock Return per Month	Variance of Bill Return per Month (1)	Variance of Stock Return per Month (2)	(2)/(1)
1 month	.00013	.00546	$.633 \times 10^{-5}$	.00162	256.4
60 months	.00013	.00546	$.330 \times 10^{-4}$	.00159	48.1

Notes: Entries in first two rows are shares of stocks in optimal portfolios. There were 2,500 replications.

However, the effects of the holding period on the optimal portfolio are now different from those in table 7. For all but one utility function, there is no change in the portfolio as the holding period changes. For the utility function $(-W)^{-4}$, the portfolio actually moves toward *stocks* as the holding period lengthens. This is more in accord with the intuition suggested by the discussion of Section 6.1, but it is not a strong effect. The effect is not a quirk of rounding, though. A search for optimal portfolios over a finer grid located the optimum for a one-month holding period at a share of .745 for stocks; for a 60-month holding period the optimum was .795.

There are two main conclusions from these simulations.

1. The differential dynamics of asset returns does not cause optimal portfolios to change dramatically with the length of the holding period. The direction of movement depends on the stochastic process generating portfolio returns. Because the stochastic process for method 3 is more soundly based, the results for this method should receive more weight. These indicate that the portfolio moves, if at all, toward stocks as the holding period lengthens.

2. For the specified utility functions, and given the historical behavior of stock and bill returns, portfolios are heavily in stocks.[13] Indeed, for utility functions consistent with estimated coefficients of risk aversion, portfolios are entirely in stocks.[14]

6.6   Pension Investments

Individuals investing in pension or retirement funds are investing for a long horizon. In some cases they are also, formally, investing for a long holding period, since the portfolio proportions may be changed only at discrete intervals, typically a year. The possibility that optimal portfolios differ depending on the holding period is relevant to such investing.

If the investor has other discretionary assets, he can use them to offset movements in the composition of the pension or retirement portfolio within the holding period for the latter portfolio. He may be able effectively to rebalance the portfolio continuously. Given the composition of the retirement portfolio, the individual's discretionary portfolio will hedge against changes in the retirement portfolio composition. But for those for whom the pension fund is the only asset, the holding period may be of the order of a year or several years.

Pension funds looking to create desirable long-term stock portfolios may also be concerned about the term structure of risk, something of which they are of course aware in the case of bonds. It is quite possible that some stocks may have relatively better long-term than short-term risk characteristics—though that cannot be demonstrated at the aggregate level of this chapter.

6.7   Summary

This chapter introduces the notion of the differential term structure of risk between stocks and bonds and then estimates stochastic processes for the generation of bill and aggregate stock returns. The stochastic process estimates are to be regarded as tentative, for it is clear that there are major problems in estimating these returns. Despite the difficulty, estimates of such processes are essential for making informed portfolio choices.

The raw data and the estimated processes show more serial correlation of bill returns than of stock returns. But estimated bill returns are not sufficiently highly serially correlated relative to stock returns to make them anywhere near as risky as stocks for even long holding periods.

The estimated returns processes are then used in stochastic simulations to estimate optimal portfolio proportions over different holding periods. There are two interesting findings. First, optimal portfolios change little as the holding period changes. The direction of movement depends on the estimated dynamic process for stock returns. Indeed, one of the implicit findings of this chapter is the lack of agreed or acceptable estimates of these dynamic processes. Second, and very striking, optimal portfolios for what are thought of as typical utility functions are very heavily in stocks.

Notes

1. The random walk hypothesis is not rejected by Nelson and Schwert (1977), Garbade and Wachtel (1978), and Fama and Gibbons (1982).

2. The terminology is slightly awkward. An alternative term is the portfolio decision period, which however is potentially misleading since for certain utility functions the investor keeps the portfolio composition fixed, and thus need make only one investment decision. Goldman (1979) uses the term "revision period."

3. Goldman has analyzed this question when asset returns are not serially correlated.

4. Note that x_t is the logarithm of one plus the rate of return, so that the variance is that of the logarithmic returns on the portfolio.

5. Use of the seasonally adjusted price index does not much affect the results.

6. There is one period in which the pattern seen in table 6.2 is absent, in that relative riskiness is independent of the holding period. This is the 1953–71 period—the period over which Fama (1975) showed the real interest rate on bills was constant.

7. There is a question about the interpretation to be placed on the coefficients in regression (R1). Suppose, as is assumed by Fama and Gibbons (1982), that the stochastic process generating real bill returns is one between expected real rates. Thus,

(F1) $$_{t-1}RB_t = a + b_{t-2}RB_{t-1} + e_t,$$

where a and b are constants and $_{t-i}RB_{t-i+1}$ is the expected bill rate. Given that, under rational expectations,

(F2) $$RB_t = {}_{t-1}RB_t + v_t,$$

where v_t is serially uncorrelated, there is an error in variables problem when (F1) is estimated using realized bill rates of return. The estimated coefficient $\hat{b}$ is biased downward from the true b if (F1) is estimated as a first-order autoregression.

If one is willing to assert a priori that the true relation is a first-order autoregression, the coefficient b can be identified by estimating a $(1, 1)$ ARMA model for the realized bill rate. It was by using a restriction of this type that Fama and Gibbons concluded that the ex ante bill rate follows a random walk—they were not able to reject the hypothesis that b in (F1) was equal to one. However, separate knowledge of the coefficient b is not needed to form optimal forecasts of the real bill rate when there are errors in variables and no information other than realized bill rates to identify the expected real rate. The optimal forecast is obtained from the appropriate ARMA regression on *realized* bill rates. Thus, from a forecasting viewpoint the interpretation of the coefficients in (R1) is not important.

8. The need for a twelfth-order system arose from the presence of serial correlation in the money growth equation residuals for shorter lags.

9. An exception was made for stocks, for which the prior was that returns were white noise plus a mean.

10. This possibility has been emphasized by Merton (1980) in his exploratory estimation of market returns.

11. Fools rush in, despite the good example of Black (1976). The hope is that this foolishness will encourage those less foolish to do better.

12. The assumption that the estimated stock market variance is formed in this way is obviously crude. In work in progress, Olivier Blanchard and I are attempting to provide a more sophisticated model for the variance.

13. The results of the simulations are consistent with typical estimates of coefficients of relative risk aversion as being around 2. These estimates are based on the market risk premium. In equilibrium, the desired portfolio for the "market" must be the market portfolio, in which Treasury bills play only a small part. Hence the simulated optimal portfolios should have only a small share of Treasury bills.

14. What about taxes, it may be asked. The assumption is that the asset returns are untaxed. Alternative assumptions about taxation could be incorporated in future simulations of optimal portfolios.

Comment   Fischer Black

I will start by restating some of Stanley Fischer's points in my own words. Then I will ask some of the questions that his analysis raised in my own mind.

Assume that you have a portfolio containing a single kind of security, like stocks or bills, and that you put all returns from the portfolio back into the portfolio. You reinvest all dividends or interest payments in shares of the same portfolio. Let us look at the variance of the value of this portfolio at the end of a period of fixed length. No matter how long the period is, the variance will be higher for a portfolio of stocks than for a portfolio of bills. Now let us set the length of the period at zero and raise it gradually. The variance will increase for any portfolio. It will increase faster in percentage terms for a portfolio of bills than for a portfolio of stocks. In arithmetic terms, it will increase faster for stocks than for bills.

Assume one person has high fixed transaction costs for going into or out of stocks while another person does not. The first person will face a higher cost of adjusting her portfolio as conditions change. She will not be able to move freely between stocks and bills. Then she will want to hold less in stocks, on average, than the second person. This is true whether or not part of her portfolio is in a defined-contribution pension fund. In equilibrium, the average person will hold the market portfolio of all risky assets. A more risk-averse person will mix the market portfolio with lending, perhaps by holding a portfolio of bills, while a less risk-averse person will mix the market portfolio with borrowing. These points I understand. Other points raised questions in my mind. Some of the questions that came to me are as follows.

Why should an investor be interested in a portfolio strategy with reinvestment of all returns in a single kind of security or a mix of two such strategies? Because a limited number of defined-contribution pension plans currently impose it on their participants? Why not consider a broader class of strategies?

Why should anyone have high fixed transaction costs or a long holding period? Aren't transaction costs on no-load mutual funds negligible? Can't transfers be made frequently between two such funds in a single family of funds? Are the costs of deciding to make such transfers high, at

Fischer Black is professor of finance at Massachusetts Institute of Technology and research associate, National Bureau of Economic Research.

the margin? Do most people have their marginal savings in pension claims that are hard to adjust?

Why is the investigator interested in any model other than a generalization of equation (23)? Shouldn't a sensible model say that the expected return on stocks changes in response to changes in risk and past returns and other shocks and then drifts gradually back toward a mean? Shouldn't the mean itself depend on risk and other observables?

Why should we model an individual as caring about his real bequest? If he doesn't have children or care about them, he won't derive utility from bequests. If he cares about his children, won't his utility simply depend on their utility? For this paper, it does not matter much which assumption is made, but doesn't it matter in other contexts?

When one maximizes an expected utility function with consumption at various times and the utility of children, and when transaction costs are zero, investing for the short term and investing for the long term cease to be distinct, as Stanley Fischer noted at the end of the first section of his chapter.

References

Black, F. 1976. Studies of stock price volatility changes. In *Proceedings of the business and economic statistics section*, American Statistical Association, Washington, D.C.

Fama, E. 1975. Short-term interest rates as predictors of inflation. *American Economic Review* 65 (June):269–82.

Fama, E., and Gibbons, M. 1982. Inflation, real returns and capital investment. *Journal of Monetary Economics* 9 (May):297–324.

Fischer, S. 1982. Serial correlation properties of asset returns and optimal investment strategies. Unpublished paper, Department of Economics, MIT.

Garbade, K., and Wachtel, P. 1978. Time variation in the relationship between inflation and interest rates. *Journal of Monetary Economics* 4 (November): 755–66.

Goldman, M. B. 1979. Anti-diversification, or optimal programs for infrequently revised portfolios. *Journal of Finance* 34 (May): 505–16.

Hakansson, N. 1970. Optimal investment and consumption strategies under risk for a class of utility functions. *Econometrica* 38: 587–607.

———. 1971. Multi-period mean-variance analysis: Toward a general theory of portfolio choice. *Journal of Finance* 26:857–84.

———. 1974. Convergence to isoelastic utility and policy in multiperiod portfolio choice. *Journal of Financial Economics* 1:201–24.

Leland, H. 1972. On turnpike portfolios. In *Mathematical methods in investment and finance*, ed. G. P. Szego and K. Shell. New York: American Elsevier.

Litterman, R. 1980. A Bayesian procedure for forecasting with vector autoregressions. (Unpublished paper.) Federal Reserve Bank of Minneapolis.

Merton R. 1980. On estimating the expected return on the market. *Journal of Financial Economics* 8: 323–61.

Merton, R., and Samuelson, P. A. 1974. Fallacy of the log-normal approximation to optimal portfolio decision-making over many periods. *Journal of Financial Economics* 1: 67–94.

Mossin, J. 1968. Optimal multiperiod portfolio policies. *Journal of Business* 41: 215–29.

Nelson, C., and Schwert, G. W. 1977. On testing the hypothesis that the real rate of interest is constant. *American Economic Review* 67 (June): 478–86.

Ross, Stephen. 1974. Portfolio turnpike theorems for constant policies. *Journal of Financial Economics* 1: 171–98.

Samuelson, P. 1969. Portfolio selection by dynamic stochastic programming. *Review of Economics and Statistics* 60 (August): 239–46.

Sims, C. 1980. Macroeconomics and reality. *Econometrica* 48 (January): 1–40.

7   Pension Funding Decisions, Interest Rate Assumptions, and Share Prices

Martin Feldstein and Randall Mørck

The effect of pension obligations on share prices is of intrinsic interest to anyone concerned with the efficiency of capital markets and the nature of corporate financial decisions. More generally, however, the ability of share prices to reflect unfunded pension obligations is an important link in the effect of private pensions on national saving (Feldstein 1978a). If unfunded obligations are not fully reflected in share prices, the equity owners will be induced to increase their consumption incorrectly and national saving will be lower than it would be with correct perceptions.

In this chapter we use a new body of data on corporate pensions to evaluate how unfunded pension liabilities influence the value of corporate equities and to begin an empirical examination of the corporate decision not to fund pension obligations fully. The important and novel feature of the new data is information on the interest rate assumed by each firm in evaluating the present value of its pension obligations.[1] Before such interest rate information became available, it was difficult to interpret and compare differences among firms in the extent of unfunded pension obligations. In a previous study, Feldstein and Seligman (1981) warned that the heterogeneity of interest rate assumptions was the source of a potentially serious problem in measuring the key variable in their study of the effect of unfunded pension liabilities on share prices.[2] The new data make it possible to assess the importance of this source of bias and to examine whether the market takes the differences in interest rate assumptions into account in evaluating pension liabilities.

Martin Feldstein is professor of economics, Harvard University, and past president of the National Bureau of Economic Research. Randall Mørck is affiliated with Harvard University and the National Bureau of Economic Research.

We are grateful to members of the NBER study of public and private pensions for comments and discussion, especially to Jeremy Bulow, Stewart Myers, and Lawrence Summers.

To understand the link between national saving and the effect of pension obligations on share prices, it is useful to consider the effect of a firm that obtains lower present wages in exchange for a promise of future pension benefits with the same present value but does not fund the resulting pension obligation. As a result, the firm reports higher earnings and adds the earnings to its capital stock. Over time, the firm's capital stock is increased by an amount equal to its unfunded pension obligation. If shareholders correctly perceive the unfunded obligation, they will recognize that the change in the form of employee compensation has not made the shareholders any wealthier, and their consumption will remain unchanged. The net effect of the pension on national saving will therefore be the difference between the firm's additional retained earnings and the reduction in the employee's direct personal saving that is induced by the promise of retirement benefits.[3] If, however, the share price understates the unfunded pension obligation, shareholders will regard themselves as wealthier, increase their consumption, and thus reduce national saving by a corresponding amount.[4]

The effect of unfunded pension obligations has attracted attention not only because a significant fraction of the pension obligations of some firms is now unfunded but also because alternative legal funding requirements could increase the extent to which pension obligations are not explicitly funded. Current Employee Retirement Income Security Act and tax rules require companies to fund their pension obligations over a period of years and permit a deduction in the calculation of taxable income only for the amount contributed to a fund. An alternative rule would be a "book reserving" system in which a firm would not be obliged to fund its pension obligation but could deduct for tax purposes the present value of a pension obligation that it assumes even if it does not fund that obligation as long as it reports the obligation on its "books" (i.e., balance sheet) and finds an appropriate organization like an insurance company or bank to "guarantee" that pension obligation. The national savings impact of unfunded pensions of this type would depend on the ability of share prices to reflect the accumulating liability and therefore to prevent shareholders from increasing their consumption in response to the apparent but artificial increase in the net assets of the firm.

In considering a firm's pension obligations, it is important to distinguish vested benefits from other types of expected pension payments. The vested benefits are those that will be paid to existing retirees and that would have to be paid to current employees even if they left the firm immediately. In addition to these vested benefits, there are also two other types of benefits that a firm or its shareholders might take into account. First, "unvested accrued pension benefits" refer to the benefits that current employees have earned on the basis of their service with the firm but which have not yet become vested. Second, firms also look ahead and, on the basis of expected employee turnover and projected wages, estimate the pension benefits that current employees are likely to receive when they retire. Firms may use this very broad concept of benefits based on past and future employment for the purpose of determining the tax-deductible contributions that they can make to their pension fund. Pension assets can therefore exceed both vested pension liabilities and total past service liabilities.

Focusing on the vested pension benefits is important for two reasons. First, vested benefits are the only legal obligation of the firm and have been the principal concern of financial analysts who discuss pension obligations. Moreover, as Bulow (1979, 1982) has explained, the cost to the firm of any nonvested pension benefits can in principle be offset by corresponding reductions in wage payments as those benefits become vested. However, as Feldstein and Seligman (1981) note, it is not clear to what extent such wage adjustments are actually made in practice or taken into account by financial analysts. It is noteworthy, though, that while firms are required to report values for vested benefit obligations and sometimes report values for other past service liabilities, the broader measure of total expected liabilities is not reported.

Most of the estimates presented in this chapter refer to the difference between vested pension liabilities and pension assets. The "unfunded vested pension liability" (UVPL) reported by the firms in our sample is in fact negative for more than two-thirds of the firms in our basic sample (92 of 132 firms reported negative UVPL), implying that their pension fund assets exceed their vested liabilities. Moreover, the aggregate value of pension assets of the firm in our sample exceed the aggregate value of vested pension liabilities. Some analyses using the broader measure of total unfunded accrued pension liabilities (UAPL) will also be reported. For this variable, 62% of the firms in our basic sample reported a negative value.[5]

Those firms with negative unfunded liabilities have accumulated more in pension assets than the present value of the pension benefits they have promised to their employees. If these benefit promises establish an upper limit on the extent to which the pensions depress private saving,[6] the "superfunded" pensions are potential net contributors to national saving. The extent to which superfunded pensions do increase national saving depends on the response of shareholders. To the extent that share prices ignore the value of these excess reserves, the extra corporate pension fund accumulations will not be offset by reduced shareholder saving. Our analysis will generally treat underfunded and superfunded pension liabilities symmetrically by using a single variable to represent the net liability of firms. In section 7.4, however, we will examine this symmetry assumption explicitly.

The first section of the chapter discusses the data that we use and the basic specification of the corporate valuation equations that are estimated in this chapter. In section 7.2 we present the basic estimates of the effect on firms' market values of the net unfunded pension liabilities that the firms report. The third section discusses the importance of the alternative interest rate assumptions used in calculating the present value of liabilities and presents alternative estimates based on the use of a common interest rate for all firms.

The analysis in sections 7.2 and 7.3 estimates linear relations between the market value of the firm and the net unfunded pension liabilities. Section 7.4 considers two generalizations of this basic specification: separate effects of pension assets and of liabilities, and different effects of positive and negative unfunded liabilities. The fifth section provides some evidence on why firms choose different interest rate assumptions for valuing pension liabilities and, more generally, why firms have different unfunded pension liabilities. There is a brief concluding section that summarizes the fundings, comments on the implication for national saving, and indicates some possible directions for future research.

7.1 The Specification and Data

The framework for our analysis is a valuation model that relates the market value of the firm per dollar of its physical capital to several basic determinants of market value including the firm's unfunded pension liability. The basic specification is thus the same as that used in Feldstein and Seligman (1981) and therefore builds on earlier studies of market valuation by Modigliani and Miller (1958), Gordon (1962), Oldfield (1977), Tobin and Brainard (1977), and others.

Under certain strict conditions, the market value (V) of a firm's equity and debt will be equal to the replacement value of its underlying physical assets (A). More generally, however, the marginal and average values of physical assets will not be the same,[7] and even the marginal value of an additional amount of physical capital will differ from one if there are distortionary taxes[8] or if the firm's capital stock is not in equilibrium. Differences among firms in the observed valuation ratio, $q = V/A$ will reflect perceived differences in the firms' abilities to provide above-average earnings and in the riskiness of their earnings and asset value.

The potential earning ability of a firm depends on such things as market position, patents, know-how, etc. The specification used in the present study represents future earnings by three variables: (1) the current ratio of earnings to physical assets, E/A, where E includes interest payments as well as equity profits;[9] (2) the growth of earnings over the past decade, GROW;[10] and (3) expenditure on research and development as a fraction of the value of the firm's physical assets, RD/A.

The capital asset pricing model implies that the risk of investment in a firm's equity should be measured by the beta coefficient measure of the sensitivity of the firm's share price to the value of the total market portfolio. The beta value for a firm depends on how broadly the "total market portfolio" is defined (equities only; all financial assets; all investment assets including land, gold, etc.) and on the frequency of the observations used for calculating the beta coefficient (daily, monthly, annual, etc.). The present study employs the widely available beta values based on monthly observations and an equity market portfolio that is calculated by Merrill, Lynch, Pierce, Fenner, and Smith.

A second measure of risk included in the current study is the ratio of the net debt to total capital, $DEBT/A$.[11] A higher debt ratio increases the risk of bankruptcy and limits the firm's ability to undertake potentially profitable investment activities.[12]

Because unfunded vested pension liabilities are a form of corporate debt,[13] they should in principle be included with other debts in measuring the market value of the firm (V) and in calculating the net DEBT variable. If the pension liability of the firm were accurately measured,[14] the unfunded vested liability could be added directly to the market value of conventional debt or, equivalently, could be included on the right-hand side of the equation (divided by the replacement value of physical assets) where the expected value of its coefficient would be minus one. More generally, however, the coefficient of the observed unfunded vested pension liability variable, $UVPL/A$, reflects the errors in the measurement of unfunded pension liabilities and the stock market's ability to perceive and reflect the existing liabilities.

The specification of the market valuation equation is thus

$$(1) \qquad \frac{V}{A} = \alpha_0 + \alpha_1 \frac{E}{A} + \alpha_2 \, GROW + \alpha_3 \frac{RD}{A}$$

$$+ \alpha_4 BETA + \alpha_5 \frac{DEBT}{A} + \alpha_6 \frac{UVPL}{A} + \varepsilon,$$

where ε represents a random error. The values of α_1, α_2, and α_3 are expected to be positive, and the values of α_4 and α_6 are expected to be negative. The sign of α_5 (the coefficient of the debt variable) is uncertain. In a strict Modigliani-Miller world, α_5 would be zero. More generally, the increased risks of bankruptcy and the adverse effect of debt on investment opportunities would imply that α_5 is negative. However, if the tax factors discussed by Auerbach (1979) and King (1977) make the value of V/A less than one for equity while the value of V/A for debt is equal to one, firms with higher ratios of debt to physical assets will have higher values of V/A and α_5 may be positive.

As we noted in our introduction, our analysis will examine both the unfunded vested pension obligations and the broader measure of the total unfunded accrued liabilities $(UAPL/A)$.

The specification of equation (1) assumes that the valuation ratio (q) is the same for debt and for equity. If, because of tax or risk factors, a dollar of retained earnings is not worth the same amount as a dollar of capital financed by debt, it would be more appropriate to analyze the effect of pension liabilities on the equity value of the firm (VE). This alternative equity value equation may be written

$$(2) \qquad \frac{VE}{AE} = \beta_0 + \beta_1 \frac{EE}{AE} + \beta_2\, GROWE + \beta_3 \frac{RD}{AE}$$

$$+ \beta_4\, BETA + \beta_5 \frac{DEBT}{AE} + \beta_6 \frac{UVPL}{AE} + \varepsilon,$$

where AE is the "equity value" of the physical assets (i.e., the replacement value of the physical assets minus the value of the net debt and of the preferred shares), EE is the equity earnings of the firm, and $GROWE$ is the 10-year growth of equity earnings. For this purpose, EE is defined as profits after tax plus the equity owners' real gain or loss on net financial assets (i.e., the product of the inflation rate and the firm's net financial debt).

Our analysis is based on data for a sample of large manufacturing firms for 1979. The construction of most of the variables uses the data in the Standard and Poor's Compustat file. Three factors limit the size of the available sample. First, since comparable information on earnings for the decade from 1970 through 1979 must be available, firms that were engaged in significant merger activity had to be eliminated. Second, the interest rate assumed in the pension liability calculation was only available for 1979 for some firms. Third, the information required for inflation adjustment (described below) was not available for all firms. These data requirements and the elimination of a few statistical outliers reduced the sample to 132 firms.

Economists have long recognized that accounting data for assets and earnings can be very misleading in a period of inflation like the 1970s. Beginning with 1976, firms were required to provided information on the replacement value of the firm's capital stock and on the effect of inflation on the value of accounting depreciation and inventory costs. With this information and an estimate of the inflation gain on net financial liabilities, it is possible to estimate an inflation-adjusted measure of accounting profits. This was the procedure found in the earlier Feldstein-Seligman analysis for 1976 and 1977.

Despite the accounting requirement to provide inflation-adjusted information and the widespread recognition of the distortions created by inflation, most financial analysts have continued to focus exclusively on the traditional accounting measures of assets and income. One important indication of this tendency to disregard the inflation-adjusted data is that by 1979 Standard and Poor's no longer included the inflation-adjusted accounts in its Compustat file.

Because we are concerned with market valuation and the perception of the financial community, we have done our analysis with the conventional accounting data as well as with data adjusted for inflation. Because the inflation-adjusted data are not available in the Compustat file, we have approximated the inflation correction for 1979 by using data for 1980 collected from individual annual reports by Daniel Smith and Lawrence Summers and then deflated to the 1979 level. One of the principal accounting distortions caused by inflation is the misstatement of inventory costs for firms that use first-in-first-out (FIFO) inventory accounting. As a further check on our results, we also present estimates only for those firms that used last-in-first-out (LIFO) as the primary method of inventory evaluation.

We are aware of the difficulty of making valid inferences about the effect of unfunded pension liabilities on the basis of equations like (1) and (2). Any omitted variables will bias the estimated coefficient. If, for example, large unfunded vested liabilities are characteristic of financially weak companies, the estimates of β_b and α_b would reflect this weakness and be biased away from -1. Moreover, firms can to some extent influence the size of their reported liabilities by the interest rate assumption that they choose.

A finding that the coefficient of the pension liability variable is substantially different from -1 must be treated with substantial caution since the difference may reflect statistical bias rather than a failure of the financial market to appraise the extent of a firm's pension obligations. In contrast, a finding that the pension liability variable has a coefficient of approximately -1 would be reassuring support for the view that the financial market correctly assesses pension liabilities since finding the appropriate answer by chance alone, although possible, would be very unlikely.

7.2   Effects of Unfunded Pension Liabilities

In this section we present the basic estimates of the effects on the value of the firm of the net pension liabilities as reported by the firms. The next section discusses the importance of the interest rate assumption used in valuing pension liabilities and their present parameter estimates based on alternative revaluated pension liabilities. The estimates in Section 7.4 examine several general specifications of the relation between pension liabilities and the firm's market value.

Equation (1.1) of table 7.1 reports the estimated coefficients corresponding to the specification of equation (1) in the previous section of this

Table 7.1   Reported Pension Liabilities and the Market Value of the Firm

| | | Total Market Value of Debt and Equity | | | | | |
		Eq. $(1.1)^{ac}$	Eq. $(1.2)^{ac}$	Eq. $(1.3)^{ad}$	Eq. $(1.4)^{ad}$	Eq. $(1.5)^{bc}$	Eq. $(1.6)^{bc}$
Unfunded vested liability	UVPL/A	−1.43 (0.82)	—	−1.72 (0.83)	—	−1.70 (0.60)	—
Unfunded accrued liability	UAPL/A	—	−1.42 (0.65)	—	−1.43 (0.65)	—	−1.59 (0.48)
Earnings	E/A	2.06 (0.38)	2.09 (0.38)	1.30 (0.34)	1.31 (0.34)	4.98 (0.41)	5.05 (0.40)
Growth	GROW	0.15 (0.22)	0.17 (0.22)	0.28 (0.22)	0.28 (0.22)	0.33 (0.16)	0.34 (0.16)
Research	RD/A	8.13 (1.02)	8.25 (1.00)	4.31 (1.36)	4.66 (1.35)	5.22 (0.88)	5.33 (0.87)
Beta coefficient	BETA	−0.17 (0.08)	−0.17 (0.08)	0.05 (0.09)	0.05 (0.09)	−0.19 (0.08)	−0.18 (0.08)
Leverage	DEBT/A	0.20 (0.17)	0.20 (0.17)	0.26 (0.19)	0.25 (0.18)	0.34 (0.14)	0.34 (0.14)
Constant	C	0.67 (0.10)	0.68 (0.10)	0.46 (0.11)	0.47 (0.11)	0.41 (0.13)	0.43 (0.13)
Sample size	N	132	132	85	85	132	132
$\bar{R}^2$		0.51	0.51	0.28	0.28	0.68	0.68
SSR		13.35	13.18	5.34	5.30	16.05	15.72

Note: See text for definitions. Standard errors are shown in parentheses. Pension liabilities are reported amounts.
[a]Inflation adjusted.

paper. The sample contains all 132 firms and uses inflation-adjusted accounting measures of income and assets. The mean of the dependent variable, the ratio of the firm's market value to the current value of its physical assets, is 0.87.

Before discussing the coefficient of the pension variable, it is useful to comment on the coefficients of the other variables. An increase in the firm's capital income (i.e., the debt and equity earnings, E) per dollar of physical assets increases the market value of those assets. An extra dollar of current earnings adds approximately two dollars to the market value of the firm. The coefficient of $GROW$ suggests that a higher rate of past increase of earnings may lead to a higher market value but the coefficient

	Market Value of Corporate Equity					
	Eq. $(1.7)^{ac}$	Eq. $(1.8)^{ac}$	Eq. $(1.9)^{ad}$	Eq. $(1.10)^{ad}$	Eq. $(1.11)^{bc}$	Eq. $(1.12)^{bc}$
UVPL/AE	−1.48 (0.84)	—	−1.73 (0.80)	—	−0.67 (0.69)	—
UAPL/AE	—	−1.45 (0.66)	—	−1.41 (0.60)	—	−0.76 (0.51)
EE/AE	2.14 (0.43)	2.16 (0.42)	1.35 (0.37)	1.34 (0.37)	3.98 (0.38)	3.96 (0.38)
GROWE	0.15 (0.25)	0.18 (0.25)	0.24 (0.25)	0.26 (0.25)	0.30 (0.19)	0.33 (0.19)
RD/AE	7.44 (0.95)	7.54 (0.93)	3.59 (1.26)	3.97 (1.25)	4.45 (0.95)	4.32 (0.94)
BETA	−0.30 (0.11)	−0.29 (0.10)	−0.02 (0.11)	−0.01 (0.11)	−0.42 (0.16)	−0.40 (0.16)
DEBT/AE	0.00 (0.10)	0.02 (0.10)	0.12 (0.09)	0.13 (0.09)	−0.06 (0.06)	−0.05 (0.06)
C	0.83 (0.13)	0.84 (0.13)	0.50 (0.13)	0.51 (0.13)	1.13 (0.20)	1.13 (0.20)
N	132	132	85	85	132	132
$\bar{R}^2$	0.44	0.45	0.23	0.24	0.75	0.76
SSR	23.43	23.12	8.41	8.34	54.61	54.07

[b]Not inflation adjusted.
[c]Inventory method = all.
[d]Inventory method = last in first out.

is smaller than its standard error.[15] Companies that spend more on research and development have significantly greater market value, a relationship that should be interpreted with care since it presumably reflects the market's valuation of the general character of companies that spend more on research rather than a direct effect of research spending on the firm's market value. All three of these effects are similar to the estimates for 1976 and 1977 reported in Feldstein and Seligman (1981).

A greater riskiness of the firm, as measured by its beta coefficient, depresses the firm. This is consistent with the theoretical implications of the capital asset pricing model, although contrary to the insignificant effect found for 1976 and 1977. The weak positive effect of leverage on the firm's total value is also contrary to the earlier Feldstein-Seligman finding. One possible explanation of this difference is that the sharp increase in inflation (the consumer price index rose 4.8% and 6.8% in 1976 and 1977, but 13.3% in 1979) might have raised the equity value of the firms with greater net debt (Summers 1982).

The coefficient of the unfunded vested liability variable ($UVPL/A$) is -1.43 with a standard error of 0.82. The effect is thus clearly significantly negative and not significantly different from minus one. By coincidence, this coefficient is almost identical to the 1977 value of -1.44 (standard error 0.47) reported by Feldstein and Seligman (1981). The estimate is consistent with the view that the financial market accepts the conventional measure of the net unfunded vested pension liability and reduces the market value of the firm by an equal amount.[16]

Broadening the definition of unfunded liabilities from vested liabilities to accrued liabilities (eq. [1.2]) leaves all of the parameter estimates essentially unchanged. The coefficient of $UAPL/A$, is -1.42 with a standard error of 0.65. The sum of squared residuals (SSR = 13.18) is slightly smaller than the corresponding SSR for the vested pension liability, suggesting that the financial market may give more weight to the broader means of pension liabilities.

One purpose of the inflation adjustment is to correct the understatement of production costs for firms that do not use the LIFO method of inventory accounting. By 1979, the inflation adjustment had become extremely important; for all nonfinancial corporations as a whole, the inflation adjustment was more than 60% of real after-tax profits. As a further check, we therefore estimated the basic equation for the subset of 85 firms that used LIFO as the primary method of inventory accounting. The results, presented in equations (1.3) and (1.4), are essentially the same as for the entire sample.

Although our emphasis is on the estimates using inflation-adjusted data for earnings and assets, we recognize that the financial community continues to rely primarily on conventional accounting data. We have therefore reestimated the basic equations using the conventional accounting figures; the results are shown in equations (1.5) and (1.6).[17] The estimates of the unfunded pension liability variables are essentially unchanged; they are slightly larger than with the inflation-adjusted data, but the difference is less than one standard error. Earnings, earnings growth, and debt appear to have a larger effect on the value of the corporation, and the level of research and development spending has a smaller effect. The unfunded accrued liabilities continue to have slightly greater explanatory power than the unfunded vested liabilities.

The second set of six equations in table 7.1 are based on the equity value of the firm and used the specification of equation (2) in section 7.1.[18]

The coefficients of the four equations estimated with inflation-adjusted data (eq. [1.7]–[1.10]) are essentially identical to the corresponding coefficients based on the market value of debt and equity (eq. [1.1]–[1.4]). This similarity of results with the two specifications was also found for 1976 and 1977 by Feldstein and Seligman (1981). When the conventional accounting data are used without adjustment for inflation (eq. [1.11], [1.12]), the coefficients of the unfunded pension liability variables are reduced substantially to approximately −0.7 and are about equal in size to their standard errors. On the basis of these two coefficients alone, one could not reject the hypothesis that the true parameter is either zero or minus one. Although we regard the instability of the coefficients estimated with conventional accounting data as evidence against relying on such data without inflation adjustment, we recognize that these estimates can also be interpreted as raising some doubt about the conclusion that the coefficient of the pension variable is significantly negative. We shall therefore continue to present estimates in the later sections of the chapter based on the conventional accounting data as well as on the inflation-adjusted data.

7.3   Alternative Interest Rate Assumptions

It has been customary for pension actuaries to assume a low rate of interest in calculating the present value of pension liabilities. Thus the average interest rate assumed by the 132 firms in our sample was only 7.3%, far less than the 12.1% rate on Baa bonds that prevailed at the end of 1979 or the 10.7% average Baa rate for the year 1979 as a whole.[19] Using a low discount rate increases the present value of vested pension benefits and therefore of the unfunded pension liability.

In considering the effect of the interest rate assumption, it is important to distinguish between vested pension liabilities and the total future pension benefits that a firm expects to pay to its current employees and on the basis of which it may legally determine its funding contributions. In estimating the total future pension benefits, the firm must project the employees' future wage growth (as well as the probabilities of death and of employment separation). The typical pension benefit formula relates an individual's retirement benefits to his wage during a year or a few years immediately before retirement. The present value at any time in an employee's career of the benefits that he will be paid during his first year of retirement depends on the difference between the discount rate and the projected rate of growth of wages. Since pension actuaries have generally assumed a low rate of wage growth, the use of a low discount rate may not produce as substantial a bias in their estimates of total future pension liabilities as it might at first appear. The value of benefits to be paid after retirement, however, depends only on the discount rate, implying that the present value of total future pension benefits is typically overstated.

Vested pension benefits depend only on an employee's previous experience with the firm. Although that experience will entitle the employee to greater future benefits if he stays with the firm,[20] the future annual value of his benefit is fixed if he leaves the firm immediately. Thus, in calculating the present value of vested benefits, the likely future growth of wages is irrelevant. The assumptions of an artificially low interest rate unambiguously raises the value of vested pension liabilities.[21] The same upward bias occurs in the calculations of the present value of unvested benefits based on past service and therefore on the total accrued pension liability.

The 132 companies in our sample assumed interest rates that ranged from 5% to 10.5%. For all but 13 companies, the rate was between 6% and 9%. The assumed interest rates thus differ significantly from each other and from the actual rate of return available on pension fund assets. Since the firms reported pension assets and vested liabilities that are approximately equal in value,[22] a change in the interest rate could have a significant effect on the estimate of unfunded liabilities and therefore potentially on the estimated regression coefficient of this variable in the market value equation.

The effect that changes in the interest rate assumption can have on the present value of vested pension benefits depends on the current distribution of vested benefits among employees and retirees of different ages. Table 7.2 shows the actuarial present value of a dollar a year from age 65 until death evaluated at ages between 45 and 70 for three different interest rates.[23] The closer an employee is to retirement, the nearer in time are his benefits and the less sensitive is their present value to the interest rate assumption. For example, increasing the discount rate from 6% to 8% reduces the value of the pension benefit by 14% at age 65 but 21% at age 60.

Unfortunately, data are not available for each firm on the distribution of vested pension benefits by employee and retiree age. Although the actual distribution will differ among firms, it is clear that most of the "weight" of the typical vested pension distribution is among retirees and older employees in the years just before retirement. This concentration reflects three things. First and most important, the benefits of retirees and older workers are closer in time and therefore subject to less mortality risk and less interest rate discounting. Table 7.2 shows that the present actuarial value of a given benefit is reduced to half or less between the ages of 65 and 55. Moreover, the actuarial present value of a one-dollar annual benefit at age 70 is worth more than the prospect at age 60 of a one dollar benefit from age 65. Second, older workers and retirees have

Table 7.2   **Actuarial Present Value of One Dollar**
                   Annual Pension from Age 65

Age	Interest Rate		
	.06	.08	0.10
70	6.5	5.9	4.3
65	9.0	7.9	6.5
60	6.0	4.9	3.6
55	4.3	3.2	2.2
45	2.2	1.3	0.8

generally accumulated more years of service with a firm and vested benefits are generally proportional to the number and years of service after an initial period. Finally older workers generally have higher earnings and vested benefits are also proportional to earnings.[24]

Bulow (1979) reports that professional actuaries often assume as a rule of thumb that the age distribution of vested benefits is such that the overall present value of vested benefits is inversely proportional to the rate of interest. It is clear from table 7.2 that the actual relation differs by age and that the inverse proportionality rule holds at about age 55 for a comparison of 6 and 8 percent interest rates and at about age 65 for a comparison of 8% and 10% interest rates. Our analysis in this paper uses the inverse proportionality assumption because data for developing a better weighting are not available. While we believe that the resulting estimates of vested pension liabilities are an improvement over using the reported values with varying interest rate assumptions, we caution that the adjustment procedure is only an approximation. It would clearly be desirable to obtain information on the age distribution of vested benefits for all companies in the sample or even for a smaller sample of companies that might be used to develop weights to apply to figures like those of table 7.2.

We have made two different types of interest rate adjustments in recalculating pension benefits. First, we standardized all pension liabilities to the Baa bond rate of 12.1% prevailing at the end of 1979. Since no firm used an interest rate even remotely as high as this, it seems unlikely that the financial market implicitly used such a high rate in evaluating the unfunded pension liabilities. This is confirmed by the estimates presented below that show using such a high discount rate reduces the explanatory power of the market valuation equation and causes the coefficient of the pension liability variables to be small and insignificant.

The second adjustment standardizes all pension liabilities to a discount rate of 7.2%, the average rate used by the 132 firms in the sample. This has the effect of eliminating the relative overstatements and understatements of pension liabilities that result from the variety of interest rate assumptions while changing very little the estimated liability for firms that use a rate close to the average for the group. It is equivalent to assuming that financial markets adjust the stated pension liabilities for deviations from common practice rather than for deviations from a Baa rate.

Table 7.3 summarizes the effect of different interest rate assumptions on the estimated impact of pension liabilities on the market value of the firm. The estimates are based on the specifications presented in table 7.1 and therefore in equations (1) and (2) of section 7.1. For each equation, table 7.3 presents only the estimated pension liability coefficient and the sum of squared residuals for the corresponding equation.

Consider first the effect of the unfunded vested liability on the total market value of the firm. Using inflation-adjusted data and the reported value of the unfunded vested liability implies a regression coefficient of −1.43 with a standard error of 0.82. This figure was presented in equation (1.1) of table 7.1 and is repeated in the first row of table 7.3 corresponding to the "actual" interest rate.

The present value of vested benefits discounted at the Baa rate is approximated by multiplying each firm's reported liability by the ratio of its actual interest rate to the 1979 year-end Baa rate of 12.1%. With this adjustment, almost all firms had negative unfunded vested liabilities. Pension assets exceed the recalculated vested liabilities by amounts that averaged 8.7% of the replacement value of the firm's physical assets. With these adjusted unfunded vested liabilities, the estimated regression coefficient is only −0.31 with a standard deviation of 0.43. The corresponding sum of squared residuals (13.65) is greater than the sum of squared residuals with the actual interest rate (13.35), however, implying that the Baa rate is a less likely specification of the market-valuations model.

By contrast, adjusting the vested pension liabilities to the common average interest rate of 7.2% provides a substantially better explanation of the data (the sum of squared residuals is only 12.89) and implies a regression coefficient of −0.90 with a standard error of 0.33. This evidence is consistent with the view that the financial markets disregard the differences caused by interest assumptions and evaluate pension liabilities in terms of a common average discount rate. Although we have not done a search over different possible interest rates to find a maximum likelihood estimate of this parameter, it is clear that the assumed average rate of 7.2 is substantially more likely than either the Baa rate or the variety of rates actually used by the individual companies. The regression coefficient of −0.90 with a standard error of 0.33 strongly supports the view that unfunded vested pension obligations, when correctly valued, depress the value of the firm by approximately one dollar for every dollar

Table 7.3   **Estimated Effect of Liabilities with Alternative Interest Assumptions**

Interest Rate	Total Market Value of Debt and Equity				Market Value of Equity			
	Vested Liability		Accrued Liability		Vested Liability		Accrued Liability	
	Coefficient	SSR	Coefficient	SSR	Coefficient	SSR	Coefficient	SSR
Inflation Adjusted								
Actual	−1.43 (0.82)	13.35	−1.42 (0.65)	13.18	−1.48 (0.84)	23.43	−1.45 (0.66)	23.12
Baa	−0.31 (0.43)	13.62	−0.48 (0.43)	13.53	−0.39 (0.37)	23.81	−0.56 (0.37)	23.60
Average	−0.90 (0.33)	12.89	−0.89 (0.29)	12.73	−0.92 (0.29)	22.27	−0.88 (0.26)	22.02
Not Inflation Adjusted								
Actual	−1.70 (0.60)	16.05	−1.59 (0.48)	15.72	−0.67 (0.69)	54.61	−0.76 (0.51)	54.07
Baa	0.04 (0.35)	17.09	−0.14 (0.34)	17.07	−0.65 (0.29)	52.87	−0.79 (0.28)	51.81
Average	−0.64 (0.25)	16.26	−0.65 (0.23)	16.04	−0.85 (0.20)	47.88	−0.73 (0.17)	47.99

Note: The coefficient values are the estimated coefficients of the pension liability variable in the specification of equation (1) or (2). Standard errors are shown in parentheses. SSR is sum of squared residuals.

of unfunded obligation or, equivalently, raise the market value of the firm by one dollar for every dollar of pension assets in excess of the vested pension liability.

The results for the total accrued liabilities are very similar. The constant average interest rate has the best explanatory power (with a sum of squared residuals of 12.73) and a coefficient of -0.89. Comparing the sums of squared residuals for total accrued liabilities and vested liabilities suggests that the accrued liability provides a slightly better explanation of the market value of the firm. But the choice between vested and accrued liabilities does not influence the conclusion that the common average interest rate is best and that the effect of net pension liabilities on the market value of the firm is approximately dollar for dollar.

Changing the specification from the total market value of the firm to the market value of equity also has virtually no effect on the estimated coefficients of the unfunded pension liability variables. The specification with the lowest sum of squared residuals again corresponds to the unfunded accrued liability evaluated with the common average rate of return.

When the conventional accounting data are used without inflation adjustment, the estimated coefficients are less stable. For the total market value of the firm, the evidence indicates that the best specification uses the actual interest rate and unfunded accrued liabilities. The coefficient of the pension liability variable is -1.59 with a standard error of 0.48. The Baa rate has a substantially higher residual sum of squares. With the common average interest rate, the coefficient is -0.05 with a standard error of 0.23.

Finally, for the market value of the corporate equity, the best specification corresponds to the common average interest rate. The coefficient of the unfunded vested pension liability is -0.85 with a standard error of 0.20 and therefore quite similar to the estimate with the inflation-adjusted variables. Because the unfunded pension liabilities evaluated at a common average interest rate generally have a better explanatory power than the corresponding reported pension liabilities, we have reestimated the specifications of table 7.1 with these more appropriately measured pension variables. The results are presented in table 7.4. The coefficients of the pension variables estimated for our entire sample of firms have already been discussed in conjunction with table 7.3. For the sample of firms that use LIFO inventory accounting, the unfunded pension liabilities are between -1.54 and -2.03. The coefficients of the other variables are quite similar to their values in table 7.1.

Although we have included five variables that can influence the market value of the firm, it is of course still possible that the unfunded pension liability is correlated with some other omitted variable and that the apparent effort of the unfunded pension liability is really only a reflection of this omitted variable. In particular, it might be argued that "strong" companies fully fund or overfund their accumulated liabilities while "weaker" companies have large unfunded liabilities. To the extent that this is true and that corporate strength and weakness are not reflected in the other variables, the negative coefficient of the unfunded liability will reflect the corporation's generally weak financial position. Although it is clearly impossible to rule out completely such an "omitted variable" argument, we have tried to test for the importance of such an effect by reestimating the inflation-adjusted equations of table 7.4 with the company's bond rating as an additional variable. The bond rating represents an expert judgment about the long-term financial strength of the company. To incorporate this variable, we use the Moody's bond rating for the longest maturity bond issued in 1979 and scale this rating from a 9 for an Aaa rated bond to 4 for a B rated bond.

For the equations determining the total market value of debt and equity, the coefficient of this variable was small (0.04) and barely larger than its standard error. Including it in the equation actually raised the absolute value of the coefficient of the pension liability variable. For the equation determining the market value of corporate equity, the coefficient of the bond rating variable is slightly larger (about 0.09) and about twice its standard error. Including this variable reduces the coefficient of the unfunded pension liability variable by approximately 0.05. Thus including a general measure of the financial strength of the company does not alter the estimated effect of unfunded pensions.[25]

7.4   Additional Specification

The estimates presented in the previous sections assume that there is a linear relation between the market value of the firm and its unfunded vested pension liabilities. This specification implies that a one-dollar increase in the firm's pension liability has the same effect on the firm's value as a one-dollar decrease in the value of the firm's pension assets. The linear specification also implies that the market responds in the same way to unfunded liabilities that are positive as it does to unfunded liabilities that are negative. The present section presents estimates that relax these constraints.

7.4.1   Separating Assets and Liabilities

The equations in table 7.5 include the value of pension assets per dollar of the firms' physical assets (PA/A or PA/AE) as well as the unfunded pension liability variables. All of the equations are based on inflation-adjusted data and separate estimates are presented using the reported pension liabilities and liabilities adjusted to a common average discount rate.

Table 7.4   Adjusted Pension Liabilities and the Market Value of the Firm

| | | Total Market Value of Debt and Equity | | | | | |
		Eq. (4.1)[ac]	Eq. (4.2)[ac]	Eq. (4.3)[ad]	Eq. (4.4)[ad]	Eq. (4.5)[bc]	Eq. (4.6)[bd]
Unfunded vested liability	UVPL/A	−0.90 (0.33)	—	−1.80 (0.60)	—	−0.64 (0.25)	—
Unfunded accrued liability	UAPL/A	—	−0.89 (0.29)	—	−1.54 (0.50)	—	−0.65 (0.23)
Earnings	E/A	1.97 (0.38)	1.98 (0.37)	1.25 (0.33)	1.28 (0.33)	4.88 (0.41)	4.90 (0.41)
Growth	GROW	0.06 (0.21)	0.06 (0.21)	0.33 (0.21)	0.33 (0.21)	0.24 (0.16)	0.24 (0.16)
Research	RD/A	7.75 (1.02)	7.75 (1.01)	3.96 (1.33)	4.36 (1.31)	5.35 (0.89)	5.36 (0.88)
Beta coefficient	BETA	−0.20 (0.08)	−0.20 (0.08)	0.06 (0.09)	0.07 (0.09)	−0.23 (0.08)	−0.22 (0.08)
Leverage	DEBT/AE	0.22 (0.17)	0.22 (0.17)	0.29 (0.18)	0.29 (0.18)	0.37 (0.15)	0.38 (0.15)
Constant	C	0.66 (0.10)	0.67 (0.10)	0.45 (0.10)	0.46 (0.10)	0.42 (0.13)	0.42 (0.13)
Sample size	N	132	132	85	85	132	132
$\bar{R}^2$		0.52	0.53	0.32	0.32	0.67	0.68
SSR		12.89	12.73	5.05	5.03	16.26	16.04

Note: See text for definitions. Standard errors are shown in parentheses. Pension liabilities adjusted to a common average interest.
[a]Inflation adjusted.

The coefficients in equation (5.1) are representative of all of the equations for total market value of debt and equity in this table. The estimated parameter values for the nonpension variables are very similar to the corresponding figures in equation (1.1) of table 7.1, which had the same specification without the separate pension assets variable. The coefficient of unfunded vested pension liabilities is now slightly lower (−1.14 with a standard error of 0.82), while the coefficient of the pension assets variable is −0.55 with a standard error of 0.28.

Including the pension asset variable is equivalent to estimating separate coefficients for vested pension liabilities and pension assets. The coefficient of UVPL/A measures the effect of increases in vested pension liabilities (−$1.14 of market value per dollar of vested pension liability),

	Market Value of Corporate Equity					
	Eq. $(4.7)^{ac}$	Eq. $(4.8)^{ac}$	Eq. $(4.9)^{ad}$	Eq. $(4.10)^{ad}$	Eq. $(4.11)^{bd}$	Eq. $(4.12)^{bd}$
UVPL/AE	−0.92 (0.29)	—	−2.03 (0.54)	—	−0.85 (0.20)	—
UAPL/AE	—	−0.88 (0.26)	—	−1.61 (0.44)	—	−0.73 (0.17)
EE/AE	2.21 (0.41)	2.21 (0.41)	1.30 (0.36)	1.30 (0.36)	4.07 (0.36)	4.02 (0.36)
GROWE	0.03 (0.24)	0.05 (0.23)	0.35 (0.24)	0.36 (0.24)	0.28 (0.18)	0.29 (0.18)
RD/AE	6.88 (0.95)	6.90 (0.94)	3.04 (1.21)	3.54 (1.20)	3.75 (0.87)	3.75 (0.87)
BETA	−0.31 (0.10)	−0.31 (0.10)	0.02 (0.11)	0.03 (0.11)	−0.39 (0.14)	−0.38 (0.15)
DEBT/AE	−0.03 (0.09)	−0.02 (0.09)	0.14 (0.08)	0.14 (0.08)	−0.05 (0.05)	−0.04 (0.05)
C	0.81 (0.13)	0.82 (0.13)	0.48 (0.13)	0.49 (0.13)	1.02 (0.19)	1.04 (0.19)
N	132	132	85	85	132	132
$\bar{R}^2$	0.47	0.47	0.31	0.31	0.78	0.78
SSR	22.27	22.02	7.58	7.60	47.88	47.99

[b]Not inflation adjusted.
[c]Inventory method = all.
[d]Inventory method = last in first out.

while the difference between the coefficients of PA/A and of UVPL/A measures the effect of increases in pension assets (i.e., −0.55 + 1.14 = \$0.59 of market value per dollar of pension assets). This coefficient of pension assets has a larger standard error (0.91), implying that when pension assets and pension liabilities are included as separate variables neither can be estimated with any precision.[26]

Using the liability variables adjusted to a common average interest rate (eq. [5.3] and [5.4]) permits much more precise parameter estimates. The implied coefficient of vested pension liabilities is −0.91 with a standard error of 0.32, while the implied coefficient of pension assets is 0.29 with a standard error of 0.42. This implies that liabilities have a substantial negative effect on the market value of the firm that is not significantly

Table 7.5   Adjusted Pension Liabilities and Assets on the Market Value of the Firm

		Total Market Value of Debt and Equity					Market Value of Corporate Equity			
		Eq. (5.1)[a]	Eq. (5.2)[a]	Eq. (5.3)[b]	Eq. (5.4)[b]		Eq. (5.5)[a]	Eq. (5.6)[a]	Eq. (5.7)[b]	Eq. (5.8)[b]
Unfunded vested liabilities	$UVPL/A$	-1.14 (0.82)	—	-0.91 (0.32)	—	$UVPL/AE$	-1.26 (0.85)	—	-0.91 (0.29)	—
Unfunded Accrued liabilities	$UAPL/A$	—	-1.02 (0.70)	—	-0.83 (0.29)	$UAPL/AE$	—	-1.18 (0.73)	—	-0.83 (0.26)
Pension Assets	PA/A	-0.55 (0.28)	-0.46 (0.29)	-0.62 (0.27)	-0.54 (0.27)	PA/AE	-0.32 (0.22)	-0.20 (0.24)	-0.36 (0.20)	-0.28 (0.21)
Earnings	E/A	2.16 (0.38)	2.16 (0.38)	2.09 (0.37)	2.09 (0.37)	EE/AE	2.14 (0.42)	2.16 (0.42)	2.22 (0.41)	2.21 (0.41)
Growth	$GROW$	0.19 (0.22)	0.19 (0.22)	0.12 (0.21)	0.12 (0.21)	$GROWE$	0.21 (0.25)	0.20 (0.25)	0.11 (0.23)	0.11 (0.24)

Research	RD/A	8.46	8.53	8.02	8.04	RD/AE	7.66	7.70	7.08	7.10
		(1.02)	(1.01)	(1.01)	(1.00)		(0.96)	(0.95)	(0.95)	(0.95)
Beta coefficient	BETA	−0.17	−0.17	−0.19	−0.19	BETA	−0.30	−0.29	−0.30	−0.30
		(0.08)	(0.08)	(0.07)	(0.07)		(0.10)	(0.10)	(0.10)	(0.10)
Leverage	DEBT/A	0.21	0.20	0.24	0.24	DEBT/AE	0.06	0.05	0.04	0.03
		(0.17)	(0.17)	(0.16)	(0.16)		(0.10)	(0.10)	(0.10)	(0.10)
Constant	C	0.72	0.73	0.73	0.72	C	0.87	0.87	0.86	0.86
		(0.10)	(0.10)	(0.10)	(0.10)		(0.13)	(0.13)	(0.13)	(0.13)
Sample size	N	132	132	132	132	N	132	132	132	132
$\bar{R}^2$		0.52	0.52	0.54	0.54	$\bar{R}^2$	0.45	0.45	0.47	0.47
SSR		12.94	12.92	12.35	12.33	SSR	23.05	22.98	21.74	21.70

Note: See text for definitions. Standard errors are shown in parentheses. All amounts are inflation adjusted.

[a] Actual interest rate.

[b] Average interest rate.

different from minus one, while assets have a much smaller effect that may not differ from zero. One possible reason for this asymmetry is that the financial market may regard large pension assets as an indication that the firm projects large pension liabilities that will have to be paid on the basis of future employment service.[27]

The estimates based on the market value of corporate equity imply that pension assets have a greater effect that is not significantly different from the effect of pension liabilities. In equation (5.5), for example, the implied effect of pension assets is $0.94 of market value per dollar of pension assets. With the more precisely estimated coefficients corresponding to a common average discount rate, the implied coefficient of pension liabilities is -0.91 (with a standard error of 0.29), while the implied coefficient of pension assets is 0.55 with a standard error of 0.36. The difference between those two coefficients is marginally significant; the corresponding t-statistic is 1.8 and therefore significant at the 7% level.

Taken at face value, the coefficients in table 7.5 generally imply that each dollar increase in a firm's pension liabilities reduces the firm's market value by about one dollar while each dollar increase in pension assets increases in value by less than one dollar. If this is correct, it provides at least a short-run reason for firms not to fully fund or overfund their pensions. It also implies that, to the extent that firms make pension promises that reduce the savings of employees, the market perceives the extra liability and therefore has the information to adjust other personal saving. At the same time, the lower coefficient of the pension assets variable implies that the market does not accurately reflect the extent of asset accumulation in the pension fund. The net effect of this is that an increase in a funded vested liability reduces the market value of the firm and induces additional saving.

7.4.2   Positive and Negative Net Liabilities

A different but related issue is raised by the fact that pension assets exceed liabilities for the majority of the firms in our sample. Does the market respond differently to "unfunded" pension liabilities that are positive and to the unfunded liabilities that are negative and therefore represent an additional net asset of the firm? To answer this question, we have divided each unfunded pension liability variable into two variables—for example, *PUVPL/A* is *UVPL/A* if this is a positive amount (implying that liabilities exceed assets) and *NUVPL/A* if *UVPL/A* is a negative amount (implying that assets exceed liabilities.)

Table 7.6 presents the estimated coefficients of the positive and negative pension liability variables. These coefficients are based on the same basic specification used in tables 7.1 and 7.4. The pension liabilities are

Table 7.6   **Effects of Positive and Negative Net Pension Liabilities on the Market Value of the Firm**

	Coefficient of Liability Variables If Net Liability Is:		t-Statistics for Equality of Coefficients (Probability)	Sum of Squared Residuals
	Positive	Negative		
Total market value of debt and equity				
Net vested liability	−2.25	−0.52	1.55	12.64
	(0.93)	(0.40)	(0.12)	
Net accrued liability	−1.87	−0.45	1.59	12.48
	(0.69)	(0.40)	(0.11)	
Market value of corporate equity				
Net vested liability	−2.54	−0.51	1.96	21.60
	(0.88)	(0.36)	(0.05)	
Net accrued liability	−1.89	−0.45	1.77	21.47
	(0.63)	(0.35)	(0.08)	

Note: Coefficients are from specifications like eq. (1) and (2) in the text but with unfunded pension liability split into positive and negative variable firms; see text for full description. All equations are based on inflation adjusted data and on pension liabilities adjusted to a common average discount rate.

adjusted to a common average discount rate and all of the data are adjusted for inflation.

All four parameter estimates show a much larger negative coefficient for the firms with actual unfunded liabilities (the "positive" liability coefficients) than for the firms in which assets exceed liabilities. In each case, the pension coefficient for the firms in which assets exceed liabilities is approximately -0.5 with a standard error of about 0.4. These coefficients are therefore not significantly different from either zero or minus one. In contrast, the pension coefficient for the firms in which liabilities exceed assets is approximately minus two with a standard error of about 0.8. These coefficients are all significantly different from zero and again not significantly different from minus one.

An explicit test of the equality of the two pension coefficients in each equation indicates that equality cannot be rejected at the 10% probability level in the equations relating to the total market value of the firm but can be rejected at the 5% and 8% probability levels in the equation for the market value of corporate equity.

How should these estimates be interpreted? One possible interpretation is that, because of the large standard errors, there is no need to distinguish between the two types of firms or to revise the conclusion that an extra dollar of unfunded vested pension liability reduces the market value of the firm by approximately one dollar. An alternative "statistical" explanation is that the equation is misspecified and omits additional variables that are observed by participants in the financial markets and are correlated with the size of pension liabilities. Thus, although the financial market may correctly reduce or increase a company's market value by one dollar for each dollar of positive or negative unfunded vested pension liability, our estimated coefficient instead reflects the impact of the additional omitted variables.

It is, however, also possible that the observed difference between the "positive" and "negative" coefficients are more than statistical artifact and do reflect the way that the financial market responds differently to these two types of firms. Since a firm that fails to fund fully its vested or past service liability incurs a higher corporate tax than would otherwise be necessary, a firm's failure to fund these liabilities may be an indication to the financial market that the firm is in a financially weak position or is not well managed. This could account for coefficients of the unfunded liability variables that are absolutely greater than one. This argument would, however, suggest a symmetrically favorable effect on a firm's market value if its pension liabilities are substantially overfunded and therefore an equally large negative coefficient for firms with negative unfunded liabilities. One reason why this is not observed is that, as we noted earlier in this section, the financial market may regard large pension assets as an indication that the firm has correspondingly large future pension benefits that are not yet vested or based on past service but that can be reasonably anticipated for the future. We can think of no way to test this two-part explanation.

7.5   Why Firms Choose Different Interest Assumptions

As we noted in section 7.3, the choice of the discount rate has a very powerful effect on the value of vested and other accrued pension liabilities. Because these benefits are based only on employees' past service, future wage rates and turnover rates are irrelevant. As a rough approximation, the value of unfunded pension liabilities varies in inverse proportion to the assumed interest rate.

The tax law provides a strong reason for companies to assume a low interest rate. By increasing the value of its pension liability, the firm can justify accumulating more pension assets. For any given stream of anticipated benefits, the accumulation of more pension assets is equivalent to reducing the real cost of those pensions. The reduced cost reflects the fact that the earnings in the pension fund are untaxed while earnings on assets held by the corporation are taxed and the interest rate that the corporation pays on its own debt is deductible from taxable income.

If the tax benefits of early funding were the only influence on the choice of an interest rate assumption, firms would choose the lowest permissible interest rate. But a low interest rate assumption also has its disadvantages. Firms may wish to avoid making the large annual funding payments that would result from a low interest assumption and may not wish to report that they have large unfunded pension liabilities. To the extent that this is true, they will prefer a higher interest assumption.

A large unfunded liability requires a firm to increase the annual contribution to its pension fund. This directly reduces the firm's reported earnings. A firm may fear that this in turn will have an adverse effect on the market price of the firm's stock because portfolio investors do not correctly perceive the reason for the lower reported earnings. Moreover, a firm that has limited access to credit or that faces a rising marginal cost of funds may prefer to postpone funding. To the extent that a firm can fund as much as it wants at a moderate or high interest rate, it will have no incentive to use a lower interest rate.

A large unfunded liability may also be regarded by corporate management as undesirable in itself. It would not be unreasonable for them to fear that such a liability would depress the equity value of the firm and increase its cost of debt. If financial investors are unable to take the firm's choice of interest rate into account in interpreting its reputed liability, the firm may be able to raise its value by selecting a high interest rate that causes pension liabilities to be understated.

Firms that have large vested pension liabilities when calculated at some standard rate will have more incentive to reduce their apparent liability by selecting a high interest rate. Even more likely, firms that have large unfunded liabilities (when valued at a standard interest rate) will have an incentive to choose a high interest rate and virtually nothing to gain by choosing a low rate. Conversely, firms in which pension assets exceed liability (when valued at a standard rate) will have no reason to disguise the size of their promised liability and every reason to increase the size of that liability in order to increase the rate of tax-deductible funding.

The evidence that we have examined indicates that firms do systematically choose their interest rate assumption in the way that this analysis suggests. Table 7.7 presents estimates of the way in which the choice of interest rate is influenced by the firm's pension liability (adjusted to the common average discount rate to permit comparability) and by other variables that measure the firm's financial condition.

Equation (7.1) shows that firms with large vested pension liabilities tend to choose high interest rate assumptions. The assumed interest rate is related even more strongly to the firm's unfunded vested pension liability, a fact shown in equation (7.2). Firms with higher ratios of net debt to assets may be more reluctant to increase the size of their pension fund and therefore may prefer a higher assumed interest rate. The coefficient of $DEBT/A$ in equation (3) is positive but just barely larger than its standard error.

Equations (7.4) and (7.5) indicate that the choice of the interest rate assumption can also be explained by reference to the total accrued pension liabilities, although that variable has somewhat weaker explanatory power than the vested liability. Equations (7.6) and (7.7) indicate that firms with better bond ratings choose higher interest rates.[28] Again the coefficient of this variable is only slightly larger than its standard error and may be due to chance. If it is not due to chance, the positive relation between bond rating and the choice of interest assumptions suggests that the causation is actually from the interest rate assumption to the bond rating. Thus, a firm with a given "true" value of $UVPL/A$ that chooses a high interest rate assumption will appear to have a smaller pension liability. This in turn makes the firm appear financially sound if the rating agency does not take its interest rate assumption into account.

The last three equations are based on data that have not been adjusted for inflation. Those results are quite similar to the corresponding equations with inflation-adjusted data.

It is clear from the estimates presented in table 7.7 that firms do engage in strategic attempts to reduce their reported unfunded vested pension liabilities when the benefits from doing so may outweigh the tax advantages of early funding.

Table 7.7 Factors Affecting the Interest Rate Assumed in Calculating Reported Pension Liabilities

Equation	Inflation Adjusted	VPL/A	UVPL/A	UAPL/A	Debt/A	Bond Rating	Constant	N	$\bar{R}^2$	SSR
(7.1)	Yes	1.88 (0.70)					6.95 (0.14)	132	0.05	128.32
(7.2)	Yes		11.58 (1.73)				7.20 (0.08)	132	0.25	100.61
(7.3)	Yes		10.99 (1.81)		0.48 (0.44)		7.10 (0.12)	132	0.25	99.70
(7.4)	Yes			8.88 (1.54)			7.07 (0.08)	132	0.20	107.80
(7.5)	Yes			8.26 (1.58)	0.69 (0.45)		6.97 (0.12)	132	0.21	105.87
(7.6)	Yes		10.63 (1.99)			0.09 (0.07)	6.62 (0.12)	98	0.22	100.69
(7.7)	Yes		10.56 (2.06)		0.28 (0.68)	0.11 (0.09)	6.41 (0.74)	98	0.21	75.34
(7.8)	Yes		7.66 (1.09)				7.20 (0.08)	132	0.27	98.04
(7.9)	No		7.13 (1.14)		0.46 (0.32)		7.06 (0.12)	132	0.28	96.49
(7.10)	No		6.89 (1.26)		0.41 (0.52)	0.13 (0.09)	6.21 (0.74)	98	0.23	73.03

Note: The dependent variable in all equations in the interest rate chosen by the firm for calculating the pension liability that it reports. The pension liability variables are all based on the common average rate.

7.6 Conclusion

The purpose of the current study has been to assess the extent to which the market value of firms reflects accurately their unfunded pension obligations. Although there are substantial problems in measuring pension liabilities and in specifying an appropriate framework for estimating their effect on market values, the results presented in this chapter can be said to be generally consistent with the view that the market value of firms reflects a conventional measure of unfunded pension obligations or net pension assets.

The value of vested pension liabilities depends critically on the interest rate that firms use to discount future benefit obligations. The 132 large manufacturing firms in the sample used a wide range of interest rates from 5.0% to 10.5% in evaluating their 1979 pension liabilities. The choice of interest rate appears to reflect the deliberate policy by which firms with substantial benefit obligations relative to existing pension assets try to reduce the reputed present value of their obligation. Similarly, firms in which pension assets are large relative to benefit obligations tend to choose low interest rate assumptions in order to increase the tax advantages of early funding.

The financial market appears to "see through" this manipulation of pension liabilities and sets market values that are related more closely to a pension obligation evaluated at a common standard interest rate than to the pension obligations as reported by the firms. Although an appropriate interest rate for evaluating pension obligations would be the long-term interest rate prevailing in 1979, our evidence indicates that market values of firms are related much more closely to pension liabilities evaluated at the average rate used by all of the firms in our sample (7.2%) than to the pension liabilities implied by the Baa rate (12.1%).

The majority of firms in the sample have pension assets that exceed the value of pension liabilities. There is some evidence in our estimates that the market gives more weight to pension liabilities than to pension assets and responds more to variations in the excess of liabilities over assets than to the excess of assets over liabilities. Although we offer some tentative explanations of these asymmetries, we are aware that they might also be an indication of a misspecification of the basic equations.

More research with additional data could help to resolve some of the remaining problems. Using cross-section data on a panel of firms for several years would permit eliminating firm-specific effects that may bias the estimated effect of the pension liabilities. With data for several years, it might also be possible to modify the measurement of earnings to include information on pension contributions and the changes in vested pension liabilities. It would certainly be very useful to obtain data on the age distribution of vested benefit obligations in order to improve the adjustment of total vested obligations to a common rate of interest.

If the two basic findings of this study—that the market appears to see through the "pension veil" and that the market value of the firm reflects pension obligations evaluated at an interest rate that is far below the market rate—are correct, they have important implications for the relation of pensions to national saving. First, pension liabilities are evaluated at an interest rate that is too low; the present value of those liabilities is overstated. Thus, share prices are depressed by larger pension obligations and shareholders have an increased incentive to save. Second, if pension assets are correctly perceived by the financial market, the extent of pension funding will not influence aggregate private saving. Moreover, to the extent that the evidence of Section 7.4 implies that the market gives too little value to pension assets, an increase in pension assets will not reduce other private saving by an offsetting amount. The overstatement of pension liabilities and the possible understatement of pension assets thus suggests that the expanding size of the private pension system may increase total saving by companies and their shareholders.[29]

Notes

1. These interest rates are reported by firms in their annual reports and were tabulated in Kotlikoff and Smith (1983).

2. The same problem also affects the share prices studies of Oldfield (1977) and Gersovitz (1980), as well as any other study that uses the reported values of pension liabilities.

3. In the extreme case in which employees reduce direct personal saving by one dollar for every dollar of present value of promised pension benefits, the introduction of the pension would have no effect on total saving.

4. In the special case referred to in note 3, the provision of a private pension could actually reduce national saving.

5. When the pension liabilities are reevaluated using the market interest rate instead of the lower values assumed by the companies in their calculations, significantly higher fractions of the companies have assets that exceed their liabilities. Using the Baa bond rate prevailing at the end of the sample year suggests that virtually all firms in the sample had pension assets in excess of both vested and past service liabilities.

6. This need not be true if employees reduce their own saving to offset the benefits that they anticipate on the basis of their expected future employment experience and not just the benefit rights that they have already accumulated.

7. Hayashi (1982) shows the conditions under which the marginal and average value of capital are equal.

8. King (1977), Auerbach (1979), and Feldstein and Green (1979) discuss the effect of taxes on the market value of marginal additions to the capital stock.

9. It would in principle be desirable to adjust E by adding to it the difference between the firm's pension contribution and the increase in vested benefits during the year. Such an adjustment would be unlikely to have a substantial effect since completely omitting E or $GROW$ or both does not change the implied effect of $UVPL/A$.

10. This variable is defined in the same way as it was in Feldstein and Seligman (1981): the difference between average earnings in the most recent 5 years and average earnings in the previous 5 years divided by the 1979 value of physical assets in the final years of this 10-year period.

11. Net debt is defined as total financial liabilities minus financial assets. Short-term assets and liabilities are included at book value, but long-term liabilities are revalued by assuming that they have a remaining maturity of 10 years and pay a 9% coupon rate but are valued to have the 1979 year-end yield to maturity of about 12%. For many firms in our sample net debt is actually negative; financial assets including cash and accounts receivable exceed financial liabilities.

12. See Myers (1977) and Gordon and Malkiel (1981).

13. If the unfunded liability is negative, it actually represents a financial asset or "negative debt."

14. See section 1 of Feldstein and Seligman (1981) for a discussion of the problems of pension liability measurement and the inadequacies of the reported estimates. Note in particular that unfunded liabilities are tax deductible when funded or paid. Similarly, until liabilities are paid, the relevant interest rate is a net of tax rate.

15. The measures of earnings and earnings growth should be adjusted by adding the pension expenses and subtracting the increase in accrued pension liability. This correction is not possible with the data available for a single year. It is reassuring therefore that the estimated effect of unfunded vested pension liabilities is not affected by completely omitting both E and $GROW$ from the equation.

16. There are so many problems of measurement that we are reluctant to give a stronger interpretation. Nevertheless, while coefficients not significantly different from minus one could occur by chance in the current and previous study, we regard that as unlikely.

17. The mean of the dependent variable is 1.30, substantially higher than the inflation-adjusted value.

18. The dependent variable is VE/AE where VE is the market value of the firm's stock and AE is the difference between the value of property, plant, equipment, and inventories and the firm's net debt. The mean of this variable is 0.82 when the data are adjusted for inflation and 1.54 when they are not.

19. Despite the tax advantage of investing pension funds exclusively in debt instruments (Black 1980a; Tepper 1981), most pensions invest in both debt and equity and, considering the greater risk of equity as a method of funding nominal liabilities, expect to earn an even higher nominal return on equity. It might, however, be argued that the appropriate rate for discounting future liabilities is a risk-free rate, with any extra return going to shareholders as compensation for assuming the portfolio risk while guaranteeing the benefits. But even a 10-year United States Treasury bond had a 1979 year-end yield of 10.4%.

20. A typical defined-benefit pension plan makes retirement benefits proportional to the product of the final year's (or years') earnings and the number of years of employment with the firm.

21. The low interest rate assumption is advantageous to the firm because it permits the firm to make greater tax-deductible pension contributions. We return to this in section 7.5.

22. The mean absolute value of unfunded vested pension liabilities as a percentage of pension assets was only 6.56%; for total accrued pension liabilities, the corresponding figure was 7.02%.

23. The actuarial present value was calculated using the 1978 age-specific death rates for white males that are presented in the 1980 *Statistical Abstract of the United States*.

24. This may be offset to the extent that retirees had lower nominal earnings before retirement than employees currently have.

25. Jeremy Bulow has told us that he has sought to establish a relation between unfunded pension liabilities and the rate of return on equity over the previous decade (as a measure of the "quality" of the firm) but found none.

26. It is, however, possible to say that the difference between the coefficients of the liability and asset variables is statistically significant.

27. Recall that a firm can accumulate pension assets only to the extent that it can satisfy the Internal Revenue Service that these assets are a reasonable provision against future

pension liabilities. Note also that this explanation assumes that the value of such liabilities will not be offset by lower wages in the future. Stewart Myers has pointed out to us that, when separate coefficients are estimated for pension assets and liabilities, it is not possible to distinguish among different assumed constant discount rates. The superiority of a common rate over varying individual assumptions remains.

28. Recall that the bond rating variable scores Moody's Aaa bonds as 9 and decreases the score linearly with lower bond ratings.

29. Any conclusion about the overall effect of pensions on saving depends also on the response of employees to promised pension benefits. It is of course possible that employees may substitute promised pension benefits for direct saving. If the interest rate that they would anticipate on their own direct saving is less than the interest rate earned by the pension fund, total saving could decline. Alternatively, the higher potential yield on pension saving might induce employees to increase planned retirement consumption by enough to raise the level of current saving despite the higher interest rate. The problem is closely related to the discussion in Feldstein (1978*b*).

Comment   Stewart C. Myers

Professors Feldstein and Mørck have written a worthwhile extension of the previous Feldstein-Seligman paper (1981) on pension funding and share prices. The previous paper's chief result stands: that investors see through over- or underfunding of firms' pension liabilities. I am comfortable with this result because it is consistent with the widely held view that capital markets are information efficient. However, as one person's truth is another's econometric difficulty, I have tried to cast a critical eye on the paper.

Feldstein and Mørck's tests require a valuation model fitted to a cross section of firms. Cross-sectional tests have fallen out of favor in financial research. However, in this case the alternative time-series test would require observing the stock market's reaction to *changes* in a firm's pension funding policy. Because these changes are usually not discrete, easily identified events, like a merger or earnings announcement, time-series tests seem impractical.

Of course, Feldstein and Mørck do not need a completely satisfactory valuation model. They just need to control for profitability, risk, growth, and other factors that affect value, especially variables that might be correlated with pension funding policy. Here the refinements and elaborations could go on forever.[1] However, they have tested enough combinations and definitions of control variables to quiet all but one of my doubts.

I still worry about a "weak firm effect." If highly profitable firms overfund, or poor performers underfund, the causality of Feldstein and

Stewart C. Myers is professor of finance at the Sloan School of Management, Massachusetts Institute of Technology, and a research associate of the National Bureau of Economic Research.

Mørck's equations is reversed. For example, poor performance would cause low stock prices *and* underfunded pensions.

Casual observation suggests that weak firms underfund. Moreover, there are at least three a priori reasons to expect them to do so: (1) The tax advantages of funding are typically less for poorly performing firms, which are more likely to have tax loss carryforwards or to face a low marginal tax rate. (2) Debt covenants are typically written in terms of accounting earnings. A firm under financial pressure may try to loosen the covenants by cutting back pension funding. (3) Managers manage earnings by choice of accounting technique. They can smooth earnings through pension funding decisions. (Feldstein and Mørck find that firms also manage their reported pension liabilities by choice of the rate used to discount vested future benefits.)

Feldstein and Mørck of course recognize the weak firm effect and introduce the firm's bond rating as proxy for it. The book earnings, risk, and growth variables should also help. However, if the weak firm effect is important, it will be difficult to find any manageable set of variables that will control for it in a single-equation, cross-sectional model. Thus, a still more elaborate version of the Feldstein-Mørck chapter would probably not settle the issue. We really need a careful study of the pension funding decision, as distinct from its effects.

Section 7.3 of the chapter explores the effects of adjusting for arbitrary differences in firms' actuarial interest rate assumptions. The results seem to indicate that investors see through these differences and evaluate pension liabilities at a common rate. We learn very little about *what* common rate is used, however.

This point deserves further explanation. The adjustment to a common rate affects only vested pension liabilities (*VPL*). Pension assets are reported at market value. Suppose unfunded vested liabilities (*UVPL*) are calculated at a common Baa rate (12.1%). The calculation is

$$UVPL(\text{Baa}) = VPL\left(\frac{\text{actuarial rate}}{12.1}\right) - PA,$$

where *PA* indicates pension assets.

Using the *average* actuarial rate (7.2%),

$$UVPL(\text{average}) = VPL\left(\frac{\text{actuarial rate}}{7.2}\right) - PA$$

$$= VPL(\text{Baa})\left(\frac{12.1}{7.2}\right) - PA.$$

Thus, the only effect of substituting the average for the Baa rate is to multiply *VPL*(Baa) by a constant. The better fit and more sensible coefficients obtained using the average rather than the Baa rate must therefore reflect a greater relative weight on pension liabilities versus assets. This suggests entering assets and liabilities as separate variables. It does not suggest that investors disregard current interest rates in assessing a firm's pension liabilities.

Feldstein and Mørck do examine pension assets and liabilities separately in section 7.4 of their chapter. The results seem to confirm that the market deducts more from market value for pension liabilities than it adds for assets. If the difference is real, it poses a puzzle: If investors value pension liabilities correctly, which requires a difficult adjustment for differences in actuarial interest rates, why can they not value assets, which require no adjustment?

The work of Black (1980b) and Tepper (1981) suggests a possible explanation. They showed that tax-paying, value-maximizing firms ought to invest their pension fund in taxable bonds, offset by borrowing on the corporate account. Investing any significant fraction in stocks as most firms do, appears suboptimal. Could the low weight given to pension assets reflect a penalty for inferior portfolio strategies?

I would summarize my reactions to Feldstein and Mørck's chapter as follows. Like most good research, it settles some questions and opens up new ones. It confirms that investors recognize unfunded pension liabilities. In fact, it is by far the most thorough and intelligent study of this issue. The most important open question is not whether investors take pension assets and liabilities into account, but how they do so. The different coefficients for pension assets and liabilities suggest the market may value them on assumptions different than Feldstein and Mørck's.

The only issue that might undercut the chapter's main qualitative conclusions is the "weak firm effect"—the possibility that low market value leads to pension underfunding, not vice versa. This possibility will be hard to address without a better understanding of the pension funding decision, not just the capital markets' reaction to it.

Note

1. For example, common-stock betas should not be used to explain the valuation of the firm as a whole. We know that financial leverage affects stock betas.

References

Auerbach, A. 1979. Share valuation and corporate equity policy. *Journal of Public Economics* 11: 291–305.

Black, F. 1980a. The tax advantages of pension fund investments in bonds. NBER Working Paper no. 533.

———. 1980b. The tax consequences of long-run pension policy. *Financial Analysts Journal* (July/August), pp. 21–28.

Bulow, J. 1979. Analysis of pension funding under ERISA. NBER Working Paper no. 402.

———. 1982. The effect of inflation on the private pension system. In *Inflation: Its causes and effects*. ed. R. Hall. Chicago, Illinois: University of Chicago Press.

Feldstein, M. 1978a. Inflation and the stock market. *American Economic Review* 70: 839–47.

———. 1978b. The rate of return, taxation, and personal saving. *Economic Journal* 88:482–87.

Feldstein, M., and Green, J. 1983. Why do companies pay dividends? *American Economic Review* 73:17–30.

Feldstein, M., and Seligman, S. 1981. Pension funding, share prices and national saving. *Journal of Finance* 36: 801–24.

Gersovitz, M. 1980. Economic consequences of unfunded vested pension benefits. NBER Working Paper no. 480.

Gordon, M. 1962. *The investment, financing and valuation of the corporation*. Homewood, Ill.: Irwin.

Gordon, R., and Malkiel, B. 1981. Corporate financial structure. In *How taxes affect economic behavior*, ed. J. Pechman. Washington, D.C.: Brookings Institution.

Hayashi, F. 1982. Tobin's average and marginal q: A neoclassical interpretation. *Econometrica* 50:213–24.

King, M. 1977. *Public policy and the corporation*. London: Chapman & Hall.

Kotlikoff, L., and Smith, D. eds. 1983. *Pensions and the American economy*. Chicago: University of Chicago Press. Forthcoming.

Modigliani, F., and Miller, M. 1958. The cost of capital, corporation finance, and the theory of investment. *American Economic Review* 48:261–97.

Myers, S. C. 1977. Determinants of corporate borrowing. *Journal of Financial Economics* 5:147–75.

Oldfield, G. S. 1977. Financial aspects of the private pension system. *Journal of Money, Credit and Banking* 9:48–43.

Summers, L. 1982. The non-adjustment of nominal interest rates: A study of the Fisher effect. National Bureau of Economic Research Working Paper no. 836.

Tepper, I. 1981. Taxation and corporate pension policy. *Journal of Finance* 36: 1–14.

Tobin, J., and Brainard, W. 1977. Asset markets and the cost of capital. In *Economic progress, private values, and public policy: Essays in honor of William Fellner*, ed. R. Nelson and B. Balassa. Amsterdam: North-Holland.

8   Should Private Pensions Be Indexed?

Martin Feldstein

In recent years, rapid and unexpected increases in the price level have significantly eroded the value of retirees' private pension benefits. An employee who retired in 1970 with a pension equal to 50% of the average manufacturing wage received a monthly check for $289. The 113% increase in the level of consumer prices in the subsequent decade reduced the real value of that pension benefit by 53% to only 24% of the average 1970 manufacturing wage. Although some firms have voluntarily increased retirees' benefits, these adjustments have almost always been far less than the rise in the price level.

Because retirees obviously care about their *real* incomes, it is a puzzle that, after more than a decade of rapid inflation, private pensions are still fixed in nominal terms. Why have employers and employees until now not negotiated pension benefits that are indexed or partly indexed to the price level? Alternatively, why have employee pensions not taken the form of variable annuities based on floating rate instruments whose nominal yield varies in the short run with the rate of inflation (Bodie 1980a, 1980b)?[1] Does current behavior represent a mistake by employees and unions that makes it appropriate in some sense to modify the laws governing pensions to require such indexing?

The present chapter shows that the existing arrangement with purely nominal private pensions may in fact be optimal in the presence of the indexed system of social security retirement pensions. Of course, since an individual who relies on a nominal pension is in effect making a risky investment, there will be unexpected losses and gains. The recent losses

Martin Feldstein is professor of economics, Harvard University, and past president of the National Bureau of Economic Research.

I am grateful to participants in the NBER study of public and private pensions for helpful comments on an earlier version of this chapter.

by retirees should be seen as just such an unfortunate ex post outcome and not as an indication that private pensions either are incompatible with inflation or should be indexed. Because protection against inflation risk can be obtained only at the cost of accepting a lower expected rate of return,[2] the potential retiree will generally choose to be less than fully protected against inflation (i.e., will choose a partially indexed pension). Moreover, social security retirement benefits provide a fully indexed pension that replaces a substantial fraction of previous peak earnings for most current retirees.[3] The combination of social security and a private pension thus provides a total pension arrangement that is substantially indexed even if the private pension is fixed in nominal terms. For most employees, the extent of indexing in the combined pension may be such that no indexing of the private pension would be desired.[4]

The analysis in this chapter makes these ideas more precise and proves specific conclusions. Although the models employed are clearly a simplification of reality, I believe that they capture the essential features of the problem. The first section of the chapter analyzes an economy without social security in which all retirement consumption is financed by a private pension. In section 8.2, social security is introduced and the analysis examines the optimal mix of social security and private pensions as well as the optimal indexing of private pensions. The third section extends this analysis to a social security program with uncertain benefits.[5] There is then a brief concluding section.

8.1   Optimal Pension Indexing without Social Security

The simplest framework within which to analyze the problem of pension indexing is a two-period two-asset model. Employees work in the first period and contribute an amount C to a retirement pension. In the second period of their life, employees are retired and then receive a pension with real (but generally uncertain) value P.

In a defined-contribution type of pension plan, employees invest their pension contributions in a portfolio of bonds and corporate stock. When they retire they receive an annuity based on the value of these assets. Since the value of bonds and their interest payments are fixed in nominal terms, the real rate of return of the bond portion varies inversely with changes in both the price level and the rate of inflation. Although the real value of corporate stock should be unaffected by changes in the price level, changes in the expected rate of inflation do cause changes in real share values (see, e.g., Hendershott and Hu 1979; Feldstein 1980a, 1980b; Summers 1981a). Thus the real value of a defined-contribution pension invested in any combination of bonds and stocks is uncertain.

In the more common defined-benefit type of pension, the employer invests the contributions and promises the employee benefits that depend on the employee's final year's earnings and that then remain fixed in nominal terms.[6] In the simplest interpretation of the defined-benefit plan, the retired employee has a fixed nominal annuity that is analogous to a bond. Because the firm can invest the pension funds in a mix of bonds that exactly matches the benefit obligation, the firm provides this bond yield to the retiree. Although firms may in fact invest pension assets in a mix of stocks and bonds, the equity owners of the firm receive the excess return (if any) generated in this way in exchange for accepting the extra risk of a nonhedged investment.

More generally, however, the employee in a defined-benefit plan may receive benefits that depend on the performance of the pension fund. This is true not only because a low enough value of fund assets can reduce benefits below the promised level but also because successful pension performance can lead to increases in the promised level of benefits and ad hoc "voluntary" increases in benefits to retirees.[7] In what follows, I do not distinguish between defined-benefit and defined-contribution plans.

Although virtually all private pensions are unindexed, this is not necessary. Zvi Bodie (1980a, 1980b) has recently shown that assets invested in a sequence of 3-month Treasury bills provide a very good inflation hedge.[8] Thus, individuals in a defined-contribution plan can achieve an essentially risk-free real return by investing in bills, and an employer who manages a defined-benefit plan can offer an essentially indexed pension without additional risk to shareholders by investing in such bills.

I shall denote the real return on bills as the random variable r_b with mean μ_b and variance σ_{bb}^2. If this type of investment provides a perfect index asset, there is no correlation between r_b and the inflation rate. In some of the analysis that follows, I shall make the stronger assumption that r_b is a constant ($\sigma_{bb}^2 = 0$). Bodie's empirical analysis showed that the return on the minimum real variance portfolio has averaged approximately zero (i.e., $\mu_b = 0$). and the annual standard deviation was approximately one percentage point ($\sigma_{bb} = 0.01$). In the important special case of $\mu_b = \sigma_{bb}^2 = 0$, "bills" are a perfect real store of value and investment in bills provides an indexed pension.

Similarly, I shall denote the real yield on the completely unindexed pension by the random variable r_u with mean μ_u and variance σ_{uu}^2. This yield can be interpreted as the yield that is implicit in setting the level of the nominal annuity of a strict defined-benefit plan, or as the ex post yield on the mix of debt and equity in a defined-contribution plan, or as the ex post yield on a performance-related defined-benefit plan.

The real value of the employee's pension in retirement is given by

$$(1) \qquad P = U(1 + r_u) + (C - U)(1 + r_b),$$

where C is the pension contribution, U is the amount of the contribution that purchases an unindexed pension (of either the defined-contribution or the defined-benefit type), and $C - U$ is the "indexed" portion represented by an investment in bills. The employee's problem in designing a pension is thus similar to a portfolio allocation problem—that is, selecting the value of U that maximizes the employee's expected utility of retirement consumption $E[V(P)]$ subject to the constraint implied by equation (1).[9] I shall assume throughout the analysis that short-sales of either asset are not permitted; thus, $C \geqslant U \geqslant 0$.

If the returns (r_u and r_b) are normally distributed (or if the individual's utility function can be approximated by a quadratic function), the individual's preferences can be represented graphically by a set of indifference curves in terms of the mean and standard deviation of the portfolio's terminal value (Tobin 1958). Figure 8.1 combines these indifference curves with the opportunity locus in the important case in which investment in "bills" provides a fully indexed pension with zero mean return.

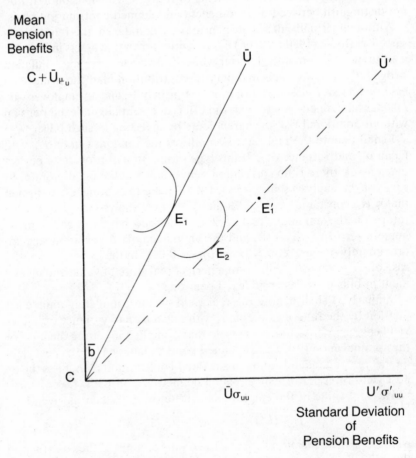

Fig. 8.1   Optimal pension indexing when bills are riskless.

Consider first the line connecting the origin with point $\bar{U}$. The origin represents a pension fund invested exclusively in bills (and is therefore marked with the letter $\bar{b}$). Because there is no uncertainty about the real return on these assets, the standard deviation of the pension benefit is zero. The pension benefit is therefore C, the initial contribution. Point $\bar{U}$ represents the pension that results when the pension is completely unindexed. Since the standard deviation of the return per dollar contributed to the unindexed pension is σ_{uu}, the standard deviation of the pension benefit is $\bar{U}\sigma_{uu}$. Equation (1) implies that, for any U, the expected pension benefit is $E(P) = C - U + U(1 + \mu_u) = C + U\mu_u$. The expected benefit associated with the completely unindexed pension is thus $C + \bar{U}\mu_u$. Any point on the straight line between the origin and $\bar{U}$ represents a feasible pension allocation.

The indifference curve tangent to the $\bar{b}\bar{U}$ line at E represents preferences that lead to a partially indexed pension; any move toward more complete indexing causes a reduction in expected pension benefits that outweighs the reduction in risk.

Different preferences would lead to different degrees of pension indexing. A reduction in risk aversion implies flatter indifference curves (i.e., more nearly parallel to the horizontal axis) and can imply no tangency along the $\bar{b}\bar{U}$ line. In this case, the optimal pension will correspond to point $\bar{U}$ with no indexing at all.[10] Increases in risk aversion shifts the optimum to a more fully indexed pension but, except for the case of "infinitely" risk-averse individuals, the optimum will not involve a fully indexed pension.[11] Thus the optimal pension will not be fully indexed and may be either partially indexed or not indexed at all.

To make these ideas more precise, consider an individual whose preferences can be represented by a constant absolute risk-aversion utility function, $V(P) = -(1/\alpha)e^{-\alpha P}$ with risk-aversion parameter $\alpha > 0$ (Arrow 1971). Since the amount of the pension contribution that is unindexed is U, the value of the pension is the random amount $P = C + r_u U$. Thus,

$$(2) \qquad E[V(P)] = E\left[-\frac{1}{\alpha}e^{-\alpha P}\right]$$

$$= E\left[-\frac{1}{\alpha}e^{-\alpha(C + r_u U)}\right]$$

and, if the return r_u is normally distributed,

$$(3) \qquad E[V(P)] = -\frac{1}{\alpha}e^{-\alpha C - \alpha U \mu_u + \frac{1}{2}\alpha^2 U^2 \sigma^2_{uu}}.$$

Maximizing $E[V(P)]$ with respect to U implies the optimal unindexed share of the pension is

$$(4) \qquad U^* = \frac{\mu_u}{\alpha \sigma^2_{uu}}.$$

For any finite value of the risk-aversion parameter, $U^* > 0$ and the pension is less than completely indexed. Moreover, if the risk aversion and the variance are low enough relative to the expected return, the entire pension fund will be unindexed ($U^* > C$).[12]

Returning to figure 8.1, we can consider the effect of an increase in inflation uncertainty on the optimal extent of pension indexing. An increase in inflation uncertainty (on the assumption that bills permit complete indexing) is equivalent to an increase in the variance of the unindexed pension and therefore a shift in locus of feasible pensions from $\bar{b}\bar{U}$ to $\bar{b}\bar{U}'$. At every point along $\bar{b}\bar{U}'$ the trade-off between risk and return is less favorable; a greater increase in real risk must be accepted for each increase in expected real return. Moreover, at the degree of indexing that was optimal with the lower level of inflation uncertainty (i.e., at point E' on $\bar{b}\bar{U}'$ that corresponds to point E on $\bar{b}\bar{U}$), the individual has the same expected return but more risk. It seems likely, therefore, that with more initial risk and a less favorable risk-return trade-off the individual would choose to index the pension more completely. This is shown in figure 8.1, where the new optimum at E_2 lies closer than E' to the complete indexing point. In the constant absolute risk-aversion case of equation (4) it is also clear that an increase in σ_{uu}^2 causes U^* to fall and the optimal degree of indexing to rise.[13]

This shift in the degree of pension indexing shows two of the adverse consequences associated with an increase in inflation uncertainty. First, in order to reduce the added risk, individuals shift their pensions to a more completely indexed form with lower expected yield. Second, even with a greater degree of indexing, the individual may have a greater risk (as shown in fig. 8.1). The lower indifference curve at E_2 reflects both of these adverse consequences.

The analysis based on figure 8.1 and equation (2) assumed the possibility of a perfectly indexed pension that provides a perfect store of value but no real return.[14] More generally, a pension based on a variable annuity invested in money market instruments ("bills") would provide a random return with mean μ_b, variance σ_{bb}^2, and covariance σ_{Ub}^2 with the return on an unindexed pension fund. With r_b uncertain, it follows from equation (1) that the variance of the pension value is $(C - U)^2\sigma_{bb}^2 + U^2\sigma_{uu}^2 + 2U(C - U)\sigma_{ub}^2$. The minimum variance does not correspond to a pension invested only in bills but to one in which the unindexed fraction is

$$(5) \qquad \frac{\hat{U}}{C} = \frac{\sigma_{bb}^2 - \sigma_{ub}^2}{\sigma_{bb}^2 + \sigma_{uu}^2 - 2\sigma_{ub}^2}.$$

The real returns on an unindexed pension and on bills may be correlated either positively or negatively. If the correlation is negative (e.g., because a higher real short-term interest rate is associated with a higher nominal long rate and therefore with a fall in bond prices or in the real value of a fixed nominal annuity) $\sigma_{ub}^2 < 0$ and $\hat{U}$ is between zero and C, implying that the minimum variance pension is only partially indexed. This case is shown by the $\bar{b}\bar{U}$ curve in figure 8.2; the point marked $\hat{U}$ indicates the minimum variance mix.

Even if the correlation between the real yields on bills and on an unindexed pension is positive, the minimum variance pension is only partly indexed if $\sigma_{ub}^2 < \sigma_{bb}^2$ (i.e., if the regression coefficient of the return on the unindexed pension on the return on bills is less than one). When this is not true (i.e., when $\sigma_{ub}^2 > \sigma_{bb}^2$), the minimum variance pension is invested in bills only.[15] If $\sigma_{ub}^2 = \sigma_{bb}$, the investment opportunity locus looks like bU' in figure 8.2 with the minimum variance at point $\bar{b}$. If, however, $\sigma_{ub}^2 > \sigma_{bb}^2$, the investment opportunity locus looks like $\bar{b}\bar{U}''$ in

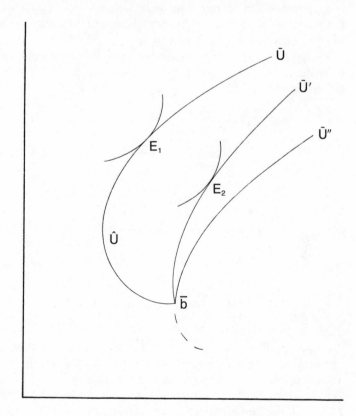

Mean
Pension
Benefits

Standard Deviation
of
Pension Benefits

Fig. 8.2   Optimal pension indexing when bills are risky.

figure 8.2 with an unconstrained minimum variance point that corresponds to a short position in the unindexed pension.

As the indifference curves in figure 8.2 indicate, whenever $\sigma_{bb}^2 > \sigma_{ub}^2$ the optimum pension will never be invested completely in the security that provides the greatest indexing. This is obvious when the minimum variance real return requires only partial indexing ($\sigma_{ub}^2 < \sigma_{bb}^2$); only the portion of the $b\bar{U}$ locus between $\hat{U}$ and $\bar{U}$ is efficient since a more completely indexed pension would have both a lower expected return and greater variance. But even when the unconstructed minimum variance pension is invested in bills only ($\sigma_{ub}^2 = \sigma_{bb}^2$), the optimum pension is at least partly unindexed because at point $\bar{b}$ a small increase in yield can be obtained with essentially no increase in risk.[16] Only in the case where the bills-only pension represents a constrained minimum variance ($\sigma_{ub}^2 > \sigma_{bb}^2$) might an indifference curve be tangent to the opportunity locus at $\bar{b}$. Of course, in all three cases individuals with low enough risk aversion will prefer to have no indexing at all.

These ideas can again be made more precise by considering the special case of a constant absolute risk-aversion utility function. It follows from equations (1) and (2) that

$$(6) \qquad E[V(P)] = E\left[-\frac{1}{\alpha} e^{-\alpha P}\right]$$

$$= E\left[-\frac{1}{\alpha} e^{-\alpha[(C-U)(1+r_b) + U(1+r_u)]}\right]$$

$$= -\frac{1}{\alpha} \exp\left\{-\alpha[(C-U)(1+\mu_b) + U(1+\mu_u)]\right.$$

$$\left. +\frac{1}{2}\alpha^2[(C-U)^2\sigma_{bb}^2 + U^2\sigma_{uu}^2 + 2U(C-U)\sigma_{ub}^2]\right\}.$$

Maximizing $E[V(P)]$ with respect to U implies

$$(7) \qquad U^* = \frac{\mu_u - \mu_b + \alpha C[\sigma_{bb}^2 - \sigma_{ub}^2]}{\alpha[\sigma_{UU}^2 + \sigma_{bb}^2 - 2\sigma_{Ub}^2]}.$$

Since the value of U that minimizes the real variance is $\hat{U} = C(\sigma_{bb}^2 - \sigma_{ub}^2)/(\sigma_{uu}^2 + \sigma_{bb}^2 - 2\sigma_{ub}^2)$, it is clear from equation (7) that the optimal pension will always have fewer bills (and therefore greater variance) than the minimum variance investment. When variations in the real yields on bills and the unindexed pension are negatively correlated ($\sigma_{ub}^2 < 0$), the minimum variance $\hat{U} > 0$ and therefore $U^* > 0$. Moreover, for a sufficiently low degree of risk aversion, $U^* \geq A$ and the pension is completely unindexed. Similarly, if $\sigma_{bb}^2 = \sigma_{ub}^2$, $\hat{U} = 0$ but $U^* > 0$ and, for low enough α, $U^* \geq C$. Thus, even when the unconstrained minimum variance pension requires investing in bills only, the optimal pension will be partly unindexed and may be completely unindexed. Only when

$\sigma_{bb}^2 < \sigma_{ub}^2$ by enough to offset the yield differential $(\mu_u - \mu_b)$ will the pension be invested exclusively in bills but, in that case also, the bills-only portfolio does not achieve the minimum variance.

The results of this section can be summarized briefly. Even when a perfectly indexed pension can be obtained by investing pension funds in money market instruments, individuals will always prefer a less than completely indexed pension. When such bills are a risky asset, the minimum variance pension may be achieved by investing in bills only or by a partly indexed pension, depending on the regression coefficient between the unindexed pension yield and the bill yield. However, individuals will always prefer a pension that has more real risk than the minimum variance pension. In both cases, the individual who has a sufficiently low degree of risk aversion will want a pension that is invested exclusively in the higher-yielding asset and that makes no attempt to reduce the risk of inflation.

8.2   Pension Indexing with Riskless Social Security

As Paul Samuelson (1958) has shown, a pay-as-you-go social security pension pays a real return on tax "contributions" equal to the real growth rate of labor income. This is easily shown in the context of the present two-period model. Assume that there are N_1 workers in the current generation (denoted by the subscript 1) and that each worker earns a real wage of w_1. If the social security program imposes a tax at rate t, the total contribution of these workers is $T_1 = tw_1N_1$. These funds are immediately paid out as benefits to the current retirees (i.e., the previous generation of workers). The next generation of N_2 workers will earn w_2N_2 and pay a total tax of $T_2 = tw_2N_2$ if the tax rate remains unchanged. These tax revenues will then be paid out as social security benefits to the current employees, $B_1 = tw_2N_2$.

The relation between the taxes paid by the current generation of workers (T_1) and the benefits that they subsequently receive (B_1) is thus:

$$(1) \qquad \frac{B_1}{T_1} = \frac{tw_2N_2}{tw_1N_1} = (1 + \gamma)(1 + n)$$
$$= (1 + g),$$

where γ is the growth rate of real wages per employee, n is the growth rate of the labor force, and g is the growth rate of total labor income. Thus, even though social security contributions are not invested, participants earn a real return on their contributions in a growing economy. In the United States economy during the past 30 years, total employee compensation has grown at an average annual rate of about 3%.[17]

The important feature about the social security program in the present context is that its pay-as-you-go character makes it automatically indexed. The real tax revenue available to pay benefits may vary with productivity and with changes in population growth and labor force participation, but it does not depend on the price level. As a result, the United States and other countries with pay-as-you-go social security pensions promise benefits that are fully indexed to inflation.[18] In this chapter, I shall take the pay-as-you-go (i.e., unfunded) character of social security as given[19] and ask how the existence of such social security benefits influence the optimal indexing of private pensions. To begin, I shall assume that there is no uncertainty about the rate of growth of earnings (g) and therefore that social security can provide an indexed pension with a fixed rate of return, g. I shall examine the optimal mix of social security and a private pension in this case and then the effect of an arbitrarily fixed amount of social security on the optimal indexing of the private pension. The fourth section extends the analysis to the more general situation in which uncertainty about real growth of earnings implies uncertainty about the real return on social security.

The simplest case to consider is the one in which bills provide a perfect store of value with no uncertainty and a zero real return. Social security with expected return g and no uncertainty then clearly dominates any investment in bills. The individual prefers a combination of social security and a completely unindexed private pension, with the preferred combination reflecting the individual's risk aversion, the expected returns on an unindexed pension and on social security, and the variance of the real yield on the unindexed pension. It is worth emphasizing that in this important case the optimal private pension is completely unindexed. Private pensions may be indexed only because of departures from the assumptions of this case: uncertain returns on bills or on social security or a suboptimal amount of social security.

This case is illustrated in figure 8.3. Point $\bar{U}$ corresponds to a private pension invested only in bonds and no social security. Point $\bar{b}$ corresponds to a fully indexed private pension invested only in bills and no social security. Point $\bar{S}$ corresponds to social security only, with no private pension. It is clear that point $\bar{S}$ dominates point $\bar{b}$ and that, while any point in the triangle connecting points $\bar{b}$, $\bar{S}$, and $\bar{U}$ is feasible, only points on the $\bar{S}\bar{U}$ line are efficient. The indifference curve is drawn so that the optimal pension (at E_1) is one-half social security and one-half an unindexed private pension.

For an individual with a constant absolute risk-aversion utility function, the optimal amount of the unindexed private pension is

$$(2) \qquad U^* = \frac{\mu_u - \mu_s}{\alpha \sigma_{uu}^2},$$

where μ_s is the yield on social security tax contributions. The optimal amount to be contributed to social security is then $C - U^*$.[20]

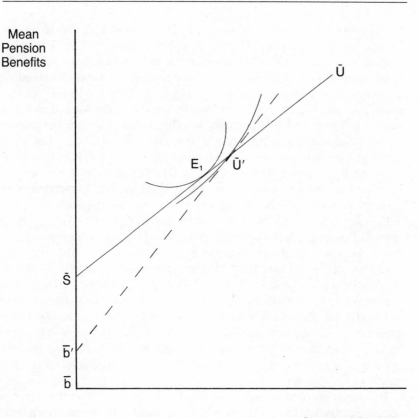

Fig. 8.3   Optimal pension indexing with social security and riskless bills.

Before leaving this case, it is interesting to note the effect of inflation uncertainty on the optimal amount of social security. With constant absolute risk aversion, the effect is unambiguous. An increase in inflation uncertainty implies a higher value of σ_{uu}^2 and therefore depresses U^* in equation (2). More inflation uncertainty implies greater reliance on un-funded social security and less on the funded private pension. Note that this is true even though a completely indexed private pension could be achieved by investing the pension assets in bills. With a more general utility function the effect of an increase in inflation uncertainty is formally ambiguous but is likely to increase reliance on social security. When inflation uncertainty increases, the tradeoff between risk and return becomes less favorable to bonds while the amount of uncertainty at the initial level of social security becomes greater. With greater initial levels of risk and a lower cost of reducing risk, the individual is likely to want to reduce risk by increasing reliance on social security.[21]

Until now, the analysis has assumed that the amount of social security is set optimally. If the size of the social security pension is instead set exogenously at a level that is less than optimal, individuals may want to index partially their private pension. In figure 8.3, the kinked line connecting points $\bar{b}'$ and $\bar{U}'$ represents the efficient frontier when the amount of the social security contribution is constrained to equal one-third of C. If the private pension (i.e., the amount C-S) is completely indexed, the value of the pension will be $C(1 + \mu_s/3)$. This is shown as point $\bar{b}'$, one-third of the way between $\bar{b}$ and $\bar{S}$. If the private pension is completely unindexed, the expected value of the pension is $(C - S)(1 + \mu_u) + S(1 + \mu_s)$ and its standard deviation is $(C - S)\sigma_{uu}$. This is shown as point $\bar{U}'$. If the indifference curve is tangent to the line segment $\bar{b}'\bar{U}'$, the optimal private pension is partially indexed. But since the segment $\bar{b}'\bar{U}'$ is steeper than $\bar{S}\bar{U}$, the indifference curve need not be tangent between $\bar{b}'$ and $\bar{U}'$. In figure 8.3, the relevant indifference curve touches the line at the kink point $\bar{U}'$ where the private portfolio is not indexed at all. Although it may seem surprising that a reduction in the indexed social security pension does not always induce an increased indexation of the private pension, this merely reflects the fact that the private fully indexed pension has a lower yield than the social security pension.

If there is no riskless private asset, the analysis of the optimal mix of social security and the private pension assets and of the impact of changes in the exogenously set level of social security is more complex. In figure 8.4, the $\bar{b}\bar{U}$ curve represents the purely private pension with different combinations of bills and unindexed pensions. If the value of a pure social security pension corresponds to point $\bar{S}_1$, any point on any line between $\bar{S}_1$ and the $\bar{b}\bar{U}$ locus is feasible. However, only the points on $\bar{S}_1\bar{U}$ are efficient; all other feasible points have lower means for the same variance. But if the value of a pure social security pension corresponds to point $\bar{S}_2$, the line connecting $\bar{S}_2$ and $\bar{U}$ (not drawn) is inefficient. The efficient set of feasible pensions correspond to combinations of social security and a partly indexed pension (if the optimum occurs on the straight segment $\bar{S}_2X$) or to a partly indexed pension with no social security if the optimum lies on the segment $X\bar{U}$ of the private pension curve. In either case, the private pension will not be invested only in bills and will in fact contain less in bills than the minimum variance pension fund. Of course, with low risk aversion the indifference curves may not be tangent at any feasible point, implying that the optimum is a completely unindexed private pension.

Constraining the amount of social security to be less than the optimal amount has the same general effect when bills are risky as it does when they provide a perfect index asset. The optimal pensions may involve increased indexing or, if the individual is not very risk averse, no change in the original degree of indexing. In particular, even with the amount of social security reduced, a completely unindexed pension may be optimal. This is illustrated in figure 8.4.

In the case in which the value of the pure social security pension would be $\bar{S}_1$, the optimum pension (at E_1) consists of an equal mix of social security and the completely unindexed pension invested in bonds. Now constrain the amount of social security to be one-third of the total pension contribution: $S = C/3$. This implies that if the private pension is completely unindexed, the total expected pension value is $S(1 + \mu_s) + U(1 + \mu_u) = (1 + \mu_s/3 + 2\mu_u/3)C$ and the corresponding standard deviation is $2C\sigma_{uu}/3$; this combination is shown at point $\bar{U}'$.

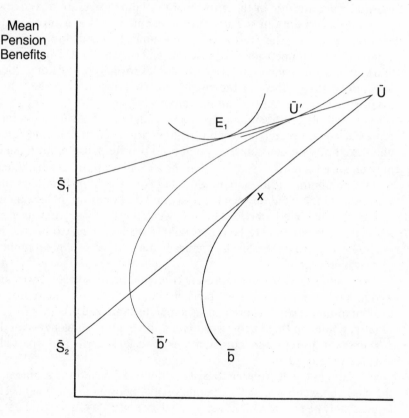

Fig. 8.4   Optimal pension indexing with social security and risky bills.

Similarly, if the private part of the pension is completely indexed, the mean and standard deviation of the total pension value is shown at point $\bar{b}'$. The new opportunity locus is constructed in this way for all points between $\bar{b}'$ and $\bar{U}'$. The new optimum private pensions could involve partial indexing (i.e., correspond to some point on the $\bar{b}'\bar{U}'$ locus), but since the slope of the new locus is steeper than the slope of the $\bar{S}\bar{U}$ line, the optimum may occur at a corner solution at point $\bar{U}'$ as shown in figure 8.4.

8.3   Optimal Indexing with Uncertain Social Security

Although unexpected changes in the price level do not alter the real value of a social security pension, unexpected changes in the growth of the real wage rate or in the growth of the labor force are a source of potential uncertainty in social security benefits that was ignored in the previous section.[22] The present section assumes that social security provides an uncertain pension. Because the general case in which both bills and bonds are also uncertain assets is complex to analyze and not particularly informative, I focus on the case in which bills provide a perfect index asset with zero real return and no variance.

One example of this situation is shown in figure 8.5. As usual, point $\bar{b}$ represents a completely indexed private pension, point $\bar{U}$ a completely unindexed private pension, and point $\bar{S}$ no private pension but reliance only on social security. The shape of the $\bar{S}\bar{U}$ curve, particularly the fact that the minimum variance point does not correspond to $\bar{S}$, implies that variations in the yield on social security and on bonds are independent, negatively correlated, or correlated in a weak positive way.[23] Because this restriction seems to me to be rather mild, I shall not deal explicitly with the alternative case; the results are easily derived by a simple modification of figure 8.5.

Points along the $\bar{S}\bar{U}$ curve represent combinations of social security and a completely unindexed private pension. Points on the $\bar{b}\bar{U}$ line represent combinations of social security and a completely indexed private pension. Finally, points on the line between $\bar{b}$ and the point of tangency with the $\bar{U}\bar{S}$ curve (at X) represent combinations of social security and a partially indexed private plan.

Since the efficient frontier consists of the line bX and the segment of the curve between X and U, several possible pension arrangements can immediately be excluded as never optimal for any utility function. First, it is never optimal to rely exclusively on either social security (point $\bar{S}$) or on a completely indexed private pension (point $\bar{b}$). Further, it is never optimal to use a combination of just social security and a fully indexed private pension (points on line $\bar{b}\bar{S}$) since a higher mean can be obtained with the same variance by using a less than fully indexed private pension.

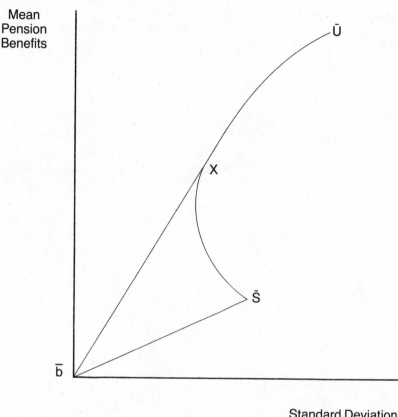

Fig. 8.5   Optimal pension indexing with uncertain social security.

An individual with sufficiently low risk aversion will prefer to have only a private pension and one that is not indexed at all. For such an individual, there will be no tangency on the $\bar{b}X\bar{U}$ locus but the highest feasible indifference curve will touch point $\bar{U}$. With more risk aversion, a tangency will occur along the $X\bar{U}$ curve where the individual has a combination of social security and a completely unindexed private pension. Only with sufficiently great risk aversion will the indifference curve tangency occur along the $\bar{b}\bar{X}$ line where the individual combines social security with a partially indexed private pension.

Figure 8.6 presents a modified form of figure 8.5 in which no ray from the origin (i.e., from point $\bar{b}$) is tangent to the curve generated by combinations of social security and the unindexed private pension. Economically, this occurs when the yield on an unindexed pension is suf-

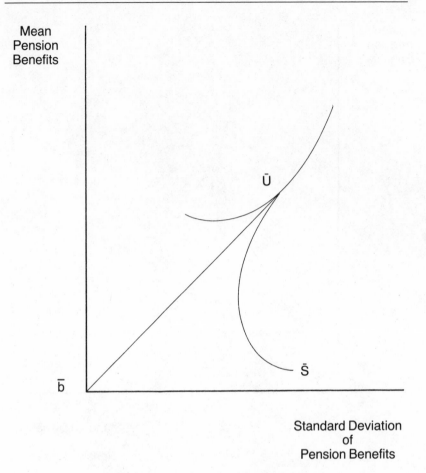

Fig. 8.6   Optimal pension indexing with uncertain social security.

ficiently high relative to its risk. In this case, the efficient set is just the straight line $\bar{b}\bar{U}$. It is never optimal in this case to have any social security, and the optimal private pension is either unindexed (as shown by the highest feasible indifference curve touching the $\bar{b}\bar{U}$ line at $\bar{U}$) or, for a more risk-averse individual, by a partly indexed private pension (with the indifference curve tangent on the $\bar{b}\bar{U}$ line).

8.4   Conclusion

The analysis in this chapter was motivated by an apparent puzzle: despite substantial uncertainty about future inflation rates, private pensions are almost universally unindexed. Moreover, although a variable annuity invested in short-term money market instruments provides a good inflation hedge, almost all private pensions provide a fixed annuity.

The results of the analysis indicate that the existence of unindexed pensions and fixed annuities is not at all surprising. Even without social security, it may be optimal to have a completely unindexed private pension and it is generally not optimal to have a completely indexed pension.

The availability of an optimal (or greater than optimal) amount of social security generally reduces the desired degree of indexing and, under a variety of conditions, makes it optimal to have no indexing at all in the private pension.

Because unexpected changes in the price level do not alter the value of social security pensions, the existence of inflation uncertainty makes a social security pension optimal when it would not otherwise be and an increase in inflation uncertainty is likely to increase the optimal reliance on social security. But despite these conclusions, the analysis shows that including some social security in an overall pension program is necessarily optimal only when both money market instruments and social security have rates of return that are known with certainty. When the real yield on money market instruments is uncertain, the optimal pension arrangement may be a partially indexed private pension even though social security is risk free and has a return that is higher than the expected rate on the money market instruments. Similarly, when social security is risky, the optimal arrangement may be to exclude social security and to use a partially indexed private pension. In all cases, an individual who has a low enough degree of risk aversion will prefer no social security and a completely unindexed private pension.

Notes

1. The key issue is the employee's risk of uncertain inflation. It would not really be indexing if, instead of a constant nominal annual benefit, the benefit rises at a rate that is fixed at the time of retirement. Although the increase in benefits might be related to the expected rate of inflation, the employee would continue to bear the entire risk of unexpected changes in inflation. I shall reserve the term "indexing" for mechanisms that reduce the uncertainty of real benefits by linking benefits either to the price level or to the yield on short-term money market instruments.

2. Pesando (1981) discusses a very different sense in which it is expensive to maintain the real value of pension benefits: keeping the same initial pension benefit and then raising benefits in proportion to the price level clearly increases the expected value of benefits in all subsequent years. My emphasis is on reducing the variance around any expected real stream of benefits. A lower real variance requires investing in assets with a lower expected return and thus increases the cost (i.e., the initial value of assets) required to provide any expected stream of real benefits.

3. An employee who has had median earnings for all of his working life now retires at age 65 with a social security pension that replaces more than 40% of his peak pretax earnings. If he is married and his wife does not claim benefits on the basis of her own income, his benefit will be increased to more than 60% of his peak pretax earnings. Because these benefits are not subject to income or payroll tax, they replace more than 75% of after-tax earnings. Since

social security is indexed by the consumer price index, it is probably overindexed with respect to a true variable-weight measure of retirees' cost of living.

4. For employees with very high earnings, social security benefits are low relative to private pension benefits and the degree of overall indexing of the combined pension is therefore correspondingly low. Although such employees may prefer to have some indexing of their pension benefits, the legal rules for tax deductible ("qualified") pensions presumably prevents "discriminating" among different classes of employees. Moreover, high-income employees tend to have additional portfolio assets and liabilities with which to achieve the overall desired degree of indexing (although generally with less favorable tax treatment). For some lower wage employees the opposite is true; the combined pension provides too much indexing. I return to these below.

5. All of the analysis ignores other forms of individual wealth. The vast majority of retirees depend almost completely on the combination of social security and other pension income. Additional assets generally consist of only an owner-occupied home and a small amount of liquid precautionary balances.

6. The nature of the obligation and of the investment is actually more complicated in practice. Technically the employer is obligated to provide only for the "vested" benefits that are based on existing service. But to prevent a rapid increase in pension costs as employees approach retirement, employers often anticipate future expected pension obligations. Some firms, however, do not fund even their vested obligations fully but substitute an implicit corporate promise. See Feldstein (1981).

7. See Bulow (1981), Miller and Scholes (1981), and Pesando (1981) on the beneficial interest of employees in the pension fund.

8. More specifically, Bodie (1980a, 1980b) showed that to minimize the variance of the real return on assets, i.e., to come as close as possible to a risk-free price-indexed investment, the assets should be invested in Treasury bills because their nominal yield varies directly with inflation. Although the close correlation of the nominal yield on bills and inflation has characterized the past 2 decades, the same relation did not hold in earlier years (Mishkin 1981; Summers 1981a, 1981b); in Bodie's defense, however, it may reasonably be argued that the Federal Reserve policy in the decade before 1953 makes this period irrelevant and that the next decade was one of such price stability that nothing can reasonably be inferred about the relation between inflation and short-term interest rates. Bodie shows also that the historical variance may be slightly reduced by including commodity futures as well. Bodie's optimum assumes that short sales by pensions are not permitted.

9. In principle, the employee decides the size of the pension contribution and the form of investment simultaneously. The present analysis takes the size of contribution as given.

10. If pensions could sell bills short and invest in bonds, the true optimum would be on the extension of line $\bar{b}\bar{U}$ with greater yield and greater risk.

11. Intuitively, an individual who has assumed no risk will always be willing to accept a small amount of risk in order to raise the mean return.

12. Note that a result like (4) can be obtained with constant proportional risk aversion in continuous time models; see Bodie (1979).

13. It is of course possible that an increase in inflation uncertainty could reduce the degree of indexing, that is, that the indifference curve would be tangent to $\bar{b}\bar{U}'$ at a point between E' and $\bar{U}'$. This would imply that risk aversion decreased as risk increased for given yield, surely an unlikely preference.

14. Because a perfect index asset does not exist, such a perfect index pension would have to be a real liability of the corporation and its shareholders. Shareholders would have to be compensated for accepting such risk, and the return to employees might therefore be negative. The analysis based on figure 8.1 and equation (2) can be interpreted as an approximation to either the opportunity that shareholders offer to employees or the opportunity made available by the market.

15. If the constraint that prohibits short positions were relaxed, the minimum variance pension might involve a negative amount of the unindexed pension. Bodie's calculation that the minimum variance portfolio contains only bills is actually a constrained minimum with the short sale of bonds prohibited. Bodie's calculation also assumes $\mu_b = 0$.

16. At $U = 0$, $d\sigma/d\mu = 0$. To see this, note that the variance of the pension is $\sigma^2 = [(C - U)^2\sigma_{bb}^2 + U^2\sigma_{uu}^2 + 2U(C - U)\sigma_{ub}^2]$ and therefore $d\sigma^2/dU = 2[-(C - U)\sigma_{bb}^2 + U\sigma_{uu}^2 + (C - 2U)\sigma_{ub}^2]$. When $\sigma_{ub}^2 = \sigma_{bb}^2$, $d\sigma^2/dU = 0$ at $U = 0$. Since $d\mu/dU = (\mu_u - \mu_b) > 0$, $d\sigma/d\mu = 0$.

17. The rate of return on social security contributions during this period was substantially greater because the tax rate (t) was increased substantially (from 0.020 in 1950 to 0.133 in 1981). Social security taxes are also levied only on a portion of payroll income and not on the entire employee compensation.

18. Before 1972, the United States social security system was not formally indexed. The law was changed occasionally to adjust the benefits of retirees, but real benefits fluctuated around a generally constant ratio of benefits to real wages. However, it was only in the late 1960s that inflation began to appear as a serious and persistent problem for retirees.

19. The alternative would be to accumulate a social security fund and use its earnings to pay benefits. The working generation could guarantee the real value of benefits to retirees, varying the tax rate to obtain the necessary funds.

20. I continue to assume that the total amount of retirement savings is fixed and divided between social security and the private pension.

21. This substitution of a low-yield unfunded social security pension for real capital formation in a funded private pension is another of the adverse consequences of increased inflation uncertainty. Someone who was trying to develop a positive theory of the growth of social security benefits might note that optimal behavior required a rise in relative benefits as inflation and inflation uncertainty increased and that this is indeed what has happened in recent years. A worker with median earnings who retired at age 65 received benefits equal to about one-third of peak earnings until 1972. A change in the benefit formula then caused the ratio to rise rapidly to more than 50% (in 1980) with an implied steady-state value of more than 40%. A more historically minded student of social security might explain the unprecedented rise by the electoral politics of 1972 and the unintended effects of inappropriate indexing formulas.

22. I say "potential" uncertainty because the social security program may guarantee real benefits and allow the tax rate on employees to vary. The present United States legislative debate about the choice between raising taxes and reducing benefits is testing whether the "uncertainty" is "potential" or "actual."

23. The formal condition is that the regression of the unindexed pension yield on the social security yield be less than one.

References

Arrow, K. 1971. *Essays in the theory of risk bearing.* Chicago: Markham.

Bodie, Z. 1979. Inflation risk and capital market equilibrium. NBER Working Paper no. 373.

———. 1980a. An innovation for stable real retirement income. *Journal of Portfolio Management* 7, no. 1 (Fall): 5–13.

———. 1980b. Purchasing-power annuities: Financial innovation for stable real retirement income in an inflationary environment. NBER Working Paper no. 442.

————. 1981. Investment strategy in an inflationary environment. In *The changing roles of debt and equity in financing U.S. capital formation*, ed. B.M. Friedman. Chicago: University of Chicago Press.

Bulow, J. 1981. Tax aspects of corporate pension funding. Paper given at the NBER Conference on Private and Public Pensions, July 13–14, Martha's Vineyard, Mass.

Feldstein, M. 1980a. Inflation and the stock market. *American Economic Review* 70: 839–47.

————. 1980b. Inflation, tax rules and the stock market. *Journal of Monetary Economics* 6: 309–31.

————. 1981. Private pensions as corporate debt. In *The changing roles of debt and equity financing U.S. capital formation*, ed. B. M. Friedman. Chicago: University of Chicago Press.

Hendershott, P., and Hu, S. C. 1979. Inflation and the benefits of owner-occupied housing. NBER Working Paper no. 383.

Miller, M. H., and Scholes, M. 1981. Pension funding and corporate valuation. University of Chicago (Xeroxed).

Mishkin, F. S. 1981. Monetary policy and short-term interest rates: An efficient markets-rational expectations approach. NBER Working Paper no. 693.

Pesando, J. E. 1981. Employee valuation of pension claims and the impact of indexing initiatives. NBER Working Paper no. 767.

Samuelson, P. A. 1958. An exact consumption-loan model of interest with or without the social contrivance of money. *Journal of Political Economy* 66: 467–82.

Summers, L. 1981a. Inflation, the stock market, and owner occupied housing. *American Economic Review* 71: 429–34.

————. 1981b. The non-adjustment of nominal interest rates: A study of the Fisher effect. NBER Working Paper no. 836.

Tobin, J. E. 1958. Liquidity preference as behavior toward risk. *Review of Economic Studies* 23: 65–86.

9 Observations on the Indexation of Old Age Pensions

Lawrence H. Summers

A major issue in the design of both public and private pension plans involves the indexation of benefits to price-level changes. A major purported virtue of current public pensions in the United States is that they provide an asset with a fixed real return. This is regarded as important because of the absence of an indexed bond market. It is frequently alleged that the failure to provide indexed benefits is a major weakness of standard private pension arrangements. These views have influenced the recommendations of groups such as the President's Commission on Pension Policy (1980) and the Advisory Council on Social Security (1979). Both these groups, without detailed argument, strongly endorsed the indexation of social security benefits.

Serious consideration of issues regarding indexation requires the careful specification of an alternative to indexing. It is clearly naive to suppose that social security benefit levels would never be adjusted in the absence of indexation or that real benefits would never be adjusted in the presence of indexing. It also requires recognition of three fundamental principles of modern finance. First, as the Modigliani-Miller theorem demonstrates, repackaging risk does not make it go away. Provisions which insure pension recipients against some risks impose these same risks on the bearers of pension liabilities. Second, risk associated with an asset cannot be measured in isolation but depends on the covariance of its return with other economic events. Third, the consumers' objective is to reduce total risk, not to insulate themselves completely from any one source of uncertainty. While these principles are widely recognized, they have not informed many previous analyses of pension policy.

This chapter examines some positive and normative aspects of the inflation indexation of public and private pensions. A major conclusion of

Lawrence H. Summers is professor of economics, Harvard University, and research associate, National Bureau of Economic Research.

the analysis is that alternative indexing arrangements may have far less impact on actual patterns of risk bearing than is usually thought to be the case. Insofar as inflation indexing has real effects, there is no presumption that they are beneficial. In particular, the precommitment aspects of public indexing may be quite undesirable. There are sound reasons to believe that voluntarily agreed on, nonindexed private pensions may be efficient. Nonindexed pensions may result in an efficient allocation of risks given the other assets and liabilities of pension issuers and beneficiaries. In this case, indexation would impede the efficient allocation of risks.

Discussions of indexation in most contexts invariably focus only on inflation indexation. The reasons for this narrow focus are not clear. Consumers' objective is to minimize uncertainty about their well-being, not just to be free from inflation risk. It is certainly possible to imagine indexing public or private benefit levels to variables other than price indices. In this chapter I develop an intertemporal cost-of-living index (ICOLI) which is superior to conventional price indices as a way of evaluating the changes in real well-being, associated with changes in wealth. The use of this measure has significant implications for the indexation of pensions and for the question of what assets should be held in pension portfolios.

The plan of the chapter is as follows. The first section analyzes the inflation indexation of public old age pensions. Under standard assumptions of either complete legislative discretion or perfect capital markets, there will be no real effects arising from the indexation of social security benefits. If enough imperfections are introduced for indexation to have real effects, there is no presumption that they will be desirable. I argue that, in the context of public pensions, indexation should be thought of primarily as a kind of "no real benefit cut" precommitment. Such a precommitment can have the perverse effect of holding down the size of the program.

The second section examines issues connected with the indexation of private pensions. Because of the noncoercive nature of private pensions, there are important differences from public pensions. Again, however, it is demonstrated that if capital markets are perfect, indexation of benefits will have no real effects. Once imperfections of a kind which permit indexing to have real effects are introduced, it is exceedingly unlikely that full indexing will be optimal. Indeed, some crude empirical calculations suggest that fixing nominal benefit levels may result in efficient risk sharing.

The third section of the chapter extends the analysis by considering the possibility of indexing pensions benefits to variables other than the rate of inflation. There appear to be other sources of aggregate uncertainty which are more important than inflation. A major source of uncertainty comes from fluctuations in the real rate of return which change the price of future consumption and so raise the sustainable standard of living. The merits of indexing benefits to a price index which includes the price of future consumption are assessed. The practicality of this proposal is examined briefly.

The fourth and final section of the chapter summarizes the results and examines their policy implications. A brief discussion of Robert Merton's proposal that social security benefits be indexed to aggregate consumption concludes the chapter.

9.1   Indexing Public Pensions

This section considers the effects of indexing the benefits in public pensions to the price level. Consideration of the possibility of indexing to an alternative aggregate magnitude is deferred to the third section. The analysis here focuses on the effects of changing the size of the program in response to changes in the price level. The issue of indexing in the design of benefit formulas is not considered.[1]

Since 1972, the social security program has in some sense been indexed to the price level.[2] The indexation scheme first enacted was conceptually flawed and led benefits to rise much more rapidly than prices. The error was repaired in new legislation in 1977, which has been gradually phased in. At present, benefits for current recipients are indexed on an annual basis. In July of each year, benefits are increased by the annual rate of CPI inflation over the preceding 12 months. Several advisory groups, including most recently the President's Commission on Pension Policy (1981), have recommended that the frequency of benefit adjustments be increased.

Arguments in favor of indexing the level of public pension benefits do not appear to be very well developed. The argument seems to be that indexing benefit levels provides insurance for beneficiaries against the effects of inflation. Little attention is given to the possibility that this insurance can be provided through private financial transactions. Frequently the consequences of alternative indexing arrangements for the risk characteristics of tax liabilities are not considered. Without considering these facets of the problem, it is impossible to evaluate the merits of indexing public pension benefits.

For clarity it is useful to consider the necessary conditions for indexing benefits to have any real effects at all. This is most easily done recognizing the following pair of "Indexing Irrelevance Propositions" for public pensions.

Proposition 1: If benefits can be adjusted continuously to desired real levels, indexing arrangements will have no real effects on any economic variables.

Proposition 2: If capital markets are perfect, and if private indexed bonds and nominal bonds exist, indexing arrangements will have no real effects, even if benefits can be adjusted only periodically.

The first proposition is obvious once stated. Regardless of indexing arrangements, real benefits will be set at their desired level at each instant. The form of indexing arrangement will affect whether benefit *changes* are or are not necessary, and their magnitudes, but will have no impact on real benefit levels. A similar argument suggests that in a competitive spot labor market, indexing in wage contracts will have no real consequences. This proposition establishes that for indexation to have real effects, benefits can only be adjusted periodically or that some types of legislated benefit adjustments (i.e., real benefit cuts) are not permitted. These possibilities are considered below.

The second proposition is equivalent to the Modigliani-Miller theorems for indexed bonds proved by Liviatan and Levhari (1977). It can be demonstrated as follows. Assume that a consumer has wealth W_0 which he allocates to consumption and various portfolio assets in order to maximize

$$(1) \qquad EU(C, W_T) \text{ s.t. } W_T = \Sigma(1 + r_i)A_i + B,$$

where C is consumption, W_T is terminal wealth, r_i is the real return on asset i, A_i is investment in asset i, and B represents real social security benefits, which may be uncertain. Suppose, for concreteness, that asset 1 is the riskless indexed bond and asset 2 is an otherwise riskless nominal bond. Then, when benefits are indexed, in order for them to have the same real value, the condition $B_{\text{nom}} = B_{\text{real}}(1 + r_2)/(1 + r_1)$ must hold.[3] Now, supposing that this condition does hold, consider any feasible allocation (C, A) when social security is not indexed. The same terminal wealth distribution can be obtained if social security is indexed by taking $\overset{*}{A}_1 = \hat{A}_1 - B_{\text{real}}/(1 + r)$, $\overset{*}{A}_2 = \hat{A}_2 + B_{\text{real}}/(1 + r)$ and making no other portfolio changes. A similar argument can be used to show that switching from indexed to nonindexed benefits does not change the feasible set. It follows that indexing has no real effects under the stated conditions. The argument could be extended to consider taxpayers' behavior and show that indexing has no general equilibrium effects.

This proposition is clearly not literally applicable to the real world since indexed bonds do not exist. However, it is an open question whether or not portfolios of assets with near constant real returns can be formed. If so the irrelevance proposition here will continue to hold. Even in the absence of indexed bonds, or the capacity to manufacture them from existing assets, individuals can undo the effects of nonindexation by borrowing to purchase real durable assets. Thus it seems likely that, at least to the extent that individuals have access to the capital markets, they can negate many of the effects of indexing arrangements.

The preceding discussion demonstrates that capital market imperfections in conjunction with rigidities in adjusting benefit levels are a necessary condition for indexation to have real effects. We now consider the case where individuals have no access to indexed bonds or any close substitute and where benefits are subject to infrequent adjustment.

9.1.1   Indexation as Insurance

If a program can be legislatively modified only infrequently, indexation of benefits will provide insurance against unexpected developments between legislative adjustments. The importance of this insurance depends on the amount of unexpected variation in the price level which takes place between legislative adjustments. Table 9.1 reproduces a chronology of legislative changes in social security benefit formulas. It is clear from the table that benefit adjustments are very common, occurring on average every 4 years. It is useful to get an idea of how far out of line benefits can be over intervals of this length. The likely error in forecasts of the average price level over various horizons can easily be estimated. Forecasts based on estimates of expected inflation were generated by applying an ARMA (1,1) process to annual rates of CPI inflation for 1947–75. The root mean square forecast error rises from 1.1% with a 1-year horizon to 4.2% with a 5-year horizon. These numbers do not suggest that indexation mitigates an otherwise important source of uncertainty and may seem surprisingly small. Suppose, however, that one misestimated the annual inflation rate over a 5-year period by 3%. The average error in estimates of the price level would only be 7.5%.

For two reasons, even these figures overstate the importance of any real uncertainties generated by the nonindexation of benefits. First, the timing of benefit readjustments is endogenous. When the price-level innovation is large, adjustment of benefits can be accelerated. This means that large undesired changes in real benefit levels are unlikely. Second, and more important, benefit adjustments can take account of losses or gains suffered during the preceding period. For simplicity, assume that the target level of real benefits is a constant $\bar{b}$. Now assume that benefits are adjusted each period. Then suppose that in each period benefits are set to satisfy the expression

(2) $$E(B_t) = \bar{B} + (1 + r)[B_{t-1} - E(B_{t-1})].$$

It follows that

(3) $$\sum_1^T \frac{B_t}{(1 + r)^t} = \sum_1^T \frac{\bar{B}}{(1 + r)^t} \frac{(B_T - \bar{B})}{(1 + r)^T}.$$

That is, the uncertainty in the present value of benefits received by an individual (the second term in [3]) is much smaller than the uncertainty associated with benefits in any given year.

Assuming that individuals have a capacity to borrow and lend at the

Table 9.1

Act

1977   Modified to distribute total creditable wages in years 1937–50 over 1–14 years, with 4–14 increment years assumed. Table in the Act (as deemed effective for December 1978) relating PIB's to PIA's frozen for workers who attain age 62, become disabled, or die after 1978. Cost-of-living adjustments applicable in year worker attained age 62 and after, or if earlier, year worker became disabled or died applied to December 1978 PIA's. *Effective for June 1979*, increase of 9.9% in *current* benefit levels. *Effective for June 1980*, increase of 14.3% in *current* benefit levels. *Effective for June 1981*, increase of 11.2% in *current* benefit levels.

[Formula applies to AMW computed for period after 1950]

1950   50% of first $100 plus 15% of next $200. *Effective for April 1952*.

1952   55% of first $100 plus 15% of next $200. *Effective for September 1952*, increase of 12½%, but not less that $5 in *current* benefit levels.

1954   55% of first $110 plus 20% of next $240. *Effective for September 1954*, increase of at least $5 (*current* benefit levels increased by approximately 13%).

[Underlying formula appearing (or deemed to appear) in table in the Act]

1958   58.85% of first $110 plus 21.40% of next $290. *Effective for January 1959*, increase of the greater of 7% or $3 in benefit level.

1965   62.97% of first $110 plus 22.90% of next $290 plus 21.40% of next $150. *Effective for January 1965*, increase of the greater of 7% or $4 in benefit level.

1967   71.16% of first $110 plus 25.88% of next $290 plus 24.18% of next $150 plus 28.43% of next $100. *Effective for February 1968*, increase of at least 13% in benefit level.

1969   81.83% of first $110 plus 29.76% of next $290 plus 27.81% of next $150 plus 32.69% of next $100. *Effective for January 1970*, increase of at least 15% in benefit level.

1971   90.01% of first $110 plus 32.74% of next $290 plus 30.59% of next $150 plus 35.96% of next $100 plus 20% of next $100. *Effective for January 1971*, increase of 10% in benefit level.

1972a   108.01% of first $110 plus 39.29% of next $290 plus 36.71% of next $150 plus 43.15% of next $100 plus 24% of next $100 plus 20% of next $250. *Effective for September 1972*, increase of 20% in benefit level. (Provision for future automatic "cost-of-living" increases.)

1973a   114.38% of first $110 plus 41.61% of next $290 plus 38.88% of next $150 plus 45.70% of next $100 plus 25.42% of next $100 plus 21.18% of next $250 plus 20% of next 50. *Effective for June 1974 through December 1974 but never applicable*. Increase of 5.9% in benefit level eliminated by 1973b legislation.

1973b   119.89% of first $110 plus 43.61% of next $290 plus 40.75% of next $150 plus 47.90% of next $100 plus 26.64% of next $100 plus 22.20% of next $250 plus 20% of next $100. Increase of 11% in 1972a benefit levels, *effective in 2 steps: 7%, for March–May 1974; 4% additional, for June 1974*. (Beginning June 1975, subject to automatic "cost-of-living" increase, under modification of 1972 provision.) Plus 20% of next $75, *effective for January 1975*.

129.48% of first $110 plus 47.10% of next $290 plus 44.01% of next $150 plus 51.73% of next $100 plus 28.77% of next $100 plus 23.98% of next $250 plus 21.60% of next $175. *Effective for June 1975*, increase of 8% in benefit level. Plus 20% of next $100, *effective for January 1976*.

Act

137.77% of first $110 plus 50.10% of next $290 plus 46.82% of next $150 plus 55.05% of next $100 plus 30.61% of next $100 plus 25.51% of next $250 plus 22.98% of next $175 plus 21.28% of next $100. *Effective for June 1976*, increase of 6.4% in benefit level. Plus 20% of next $100, *effective for January 1977*.

145.90% of first $110 plus 53.06% of next $290 plus 49.58% of next $150 plus 58.30% of next $100 plus 32.42% of next $100 plus 27.02% of next $250 plus 24.34% of next $175 plus 22.54% of next $100 plus 21.18% of next $100. *Effective for June 1977*, increase of 5.9% in benefit level. Plus 20% of next $100, *effective for January 1978*.

155.38% of first $110 plus 56.51% of next $290 plus 52.81% of next $150 plus 62.09% of next $100 plus 34.53% of next $100 plus 28.78% of next $250 plus 25.92% of next $175 plus 24.01% of next $100 plus 22.56% of next $100 plus 21.30% of next $100. *Effective for June 1978*, increase of 6.5% in benefit level.

1977   For workers who attain age 62, become disabled, or die before 1979: formula same as preceding formula plus 20% of next $435, *effective for January 1979*.

170.76% of first $110 plus 62.01% of next $290 plus 58.04% of next $150 plus 68.24% of next $100 plus 37.95% of next $100 plus 31.63% of next $250 plus 28.49% of next $175 plus 26.39% of next $100 plus 24.79% of next $100 plus 23.41% of next $100 plus 21.98% of next $435. *Effective for June 1979*, increase of 9.9% in benefit level. Plus 20% of next $250, *effective for January 1980*.

195.18% of first $110 plus 70.98% of next $290 plus 66.34% of next $150 plus 78.00% of next $100 plus 43.38% of next $100 plus 36.15% of next $250 plus 32.56% of next $175 plus 30.16% of next $100 plus 28.33% of next $100 plus 26.76% of next $100 plus 25.12% of next $435 plus 22.86% of next $250. *Effective for June 1980*, increase of 14.3% in benefit level. Plus 20% of next $315, *effective for January 1981*.

217.04% of first $110 plus 78.93% of next $290 plus 73.77% of next $150 plus 86.74% of next $100 plus 48.24% of next $100 plus 40.20% of next $250 plus 36.21% of next $175 plus 33.54% of next $100 plus 31.50% of next $100 plus 29.76 of next $100 plus 27.93% of next $435 plus 25.42% of next $250 plus 22.24% of next $315. *Effective for June 1981*, increase of 11.2% in benefit level.

[Formula applies to AIME]

1977   For workers who attain age 62, become disabled, or die in 1979: 90% of first $180 plus 32% of next $905 plus 15% of excess over $1,085. *Effective for January 1979*. (Provision for future automatic increases in bend points, $180 and $1,085, and for future automatic "cost-of-living" increases after eligibility for benefits.) *Effective for June 1979*, increase of 9.9% in benefit level. *Effective for June 1980*, increase of 14.3% in benefit level. *Effective for June 1981*, increase of 11.2% in benefit level.

For workers attaining age 62 in 1979–83 and applying for old-age retirement benefits of dying in or after

Source: Social Security Bulletin, Annual Statistical Suppement, 1980.

interest rate r, in equation (2), the reduction in lifetime risk due to indexing is clearly negligible. Some data on the financial position of the elderly are presented below. They show that most possess at least a small amount of liquid assets. That is all that would be necessary to buffer any fluctuations in real income due to unexpected changes in the price level. Even for individuals with no access to the capital market, there is some margin for intertemporal substitution in the timing of the purchases of durable goods. It thus seems unlikely that the length of the adjustment period constitutes any significant argument for indexation. The data in table 9.2 certainly suggest that there has been no reduction in the variance in real benefit levels in the post-1972 period when social security was indexed. Admittedly this evidence is difficult to interpret, because there has been an upward drift in benefit levels.

9.1.2   Indexation as Precommitment

None of the preceding discussion suggests any large effect of a policy of indexed benefits. Yet the issue seems to be viewed passionately by many interest groups. One plausible explanation of how indexation can have important effects comes from viewing it as a form of precommitment. The government is committed because of political constraints to maintain the level of benefits, however they are denominated. If benefits are indexed, they cannot be cut in real terms. If not indexed, they cannot be cut in nominal terms. This distinction is frequently cited in discussions of tax bracket indexing as well as social security indexing. It may be the result of any political process in which it is difficult to enact legislation because more than a majority is required, or because it is hard to build a consensus among diverse constituencies. In this situation, it is possible to reduce real benefit levels through inflation erosion and inaction but not through actual legislation. Thus the main effect of indexation may be precommitment to a minimum fixed real benefit level.

At first it may seem as if such a policy should be favored by advocates of a larger social security system. Indexation does prevent reductions in real benefit levels through inflation. On reflection, however, the situation is more complex. The optimum level of real benefits legislated will in general be lower if a constraint is imposed precluding future benefit reductions. The nature of the ambiguity can be highlighted in the context of a highly stylized model.

Suppose that optimum level of benefits in period t is given by X_s where X_s is distributed uniformly on the unit interval and is serially uncorrelated. Assume also that the regret associated with setting a benefit level B_s in period t is given by

$$(4) \qquad R(\mathbf{B}, X) = X - B \qquad \text{if } B \le X$$
$$= a(B - X) \text{ if } b \ge X.$$

Table 9.2   **Ratios of Primary Benefit for Man Retiring at Age 65 at Beginning of Various Years to Earnings in Year before Retirement (%)**

Year	Low-Earnings Individual	Average-Earnings Individual	Maximum-Earnings Individual
1953	53.5	30.7	28.3
1954	51.9	29.3	28.3
1955	54.8	34.3	32.8
1956	53.8	33.5	29.6
1957	52.3	32.5	31.0
1958	50.8	31.9	31.0
1959	52.7	33.5	33.1
1960	51.8	32.8	29.8
1961	49.6	31.7	30.0
1962	48.8	31.3	30.2
1963	46.8	30.3	30.5
1964	46.4	29.8	30.8
1965	48.9	31.5	32.9
1966	48.1	31.3	33.2
1967	52.1	34.2	27.9
1968	49.7	32.4	28.4
1969	47.1	30.8	24.7
1970	52.2	34.3	29.2
1971	51.5	34.3	29.2
1972	52.3	34.9	33.2
1973	58.4	39.4	35.5
1974	56.3	38.3	30.5
1975	59.7	40.7	28.8
1976	60.6	42.4	31.0
1977	61.8	43.6	32.4
1978	62.1	44.4	33.4
1979	62.1	45.3	34.1
1980	64.2	47.1	29.9

Source: Robert J. Myers, "Summary of the Provisions of the Old-Age, Survivors, and Disability Insurance System, the Hospital Insurance System, and the Supplemental Medical Insurance System" (unpublished manuscript, Temple University, June 1980).

Note: Earnings record for average-earnings individual is the annualized average wage for *all* workers in the first quarter of the particular years. Earnings record for low-earnings individual is $3,200 for 1974; for other years, it is the same ratio to the earnings of the average-earnings individual as prevailed in 1974 (namely, 39.8%). Ratios for the average-earnings individual are lower than for the maximum-earnings one in 1963–66 result because the maximum taxable earnings base remained unchanged in 1959–65. Thus the average earner had almost the same "final" earnings as the maximum earner but had significantly lower "career" earnings.

Let policymakers design the social security scheme to minimize the present value of future regrets. That is, they choose a sequence of values B_s in each period to minimize

$$(5) \qquad L = E \sum_{t}^{\infty} R(B_s - X)\beta^{(s-t)}.$$

In the case where there is no precommitment problem, the optimal strategy is clearly to set $B_s = X_s$ in each period and have zero regret. Note that when this strategy is followed, the mean level of benefits is $\overline{X} = 0.5$.

Now consider the optimal strategy when benefits can never be cut. It is immediately obvious that it will never be desirable to set $B_s > X_s$. However, it may be desirable to set $B_s < X_s$. This may be seen as follows. Let $L(\mathbf{B})$ be the expected regret if the optimal strategy is pursued, given that benefits are constrained to be greater than $\mathbf{B}$ in all remaining periods. It follows immediately that if $X_s \leq \mathbf{B}_s$, then the optimal strategy is to set $B_s = X_s$ or to satisfy the first-order condition,

$$(6) \qquad 1 - \beta\left(\frac{dL}{d\mathbf{B}}\right)_{\mathbf{B}=B_s} = 0,$$

if the value of B_s satisfying this first-order condition is less than X_s. The first-order condition (6) states that the marginal gain from increasing benefits in the current period must equal the marginal cost from imposing tighter constraints in future periods. The first-order condition (6) does not provide a basis for computing the optimum level of B_t, since the form of the function $L(\mathbf{B})$ is unknown.

However, it is possible to characterize the stochastic steady state when the optimal strategy is pursued. This may be done as follows. The optimum feasible strategy at time s is given by some function $B_s = f(\mathbf{B}_s, X_s)$, which is clearly monotone increasing in X_s. The maximum attainable value of X_s will be given by $f(\mathbf{B}_t, 1)$, which as shown below does not depend on $\mathbf{B}$. It is clear that ultimately the value of $\mathbf{B}_t$ must approach this limit. The steady state may then be characterized by solving for $f(\mathbf{B}, 1)$.

Equation (6) reveals that the optimum choice of B^* does not depend on $\mathbf{B}$. It can be solved easily in this case. Suppose $f(\mathbf{B}, 1) = B^*$. Then in all future periods $B = B^*$. If $X < B^*$, the "no-cut constraint" ensures this equality. If $X > B^t$, the equality is ensured by the monotonicity of the function $f(\mathbf{B}, X)$. This means that it is easy to evaluate $f(B^*)$. It is given by

$$(7) \qquad E \sum_{0}^{\infty} \beta^t R(B^*) = E \frac{[R(B^*)]}{1 - \beta}.$$

Differentiating (7) and using (6) yields the first-order condition

$$(8) \qquad 1 - \frac{\beta}{1 - \beta} [B^*(1 + a) - a] = 0.$$

It follows that B^* is given by

$$(9) \qquad B^* = \frac{1 - \beta}{\beta(1 + a)} + \frac{a}{1 + a}.$$

Several inferences can be drawn from equation (9). Note first that the steady-state level of benefits B^* can be greater or less than the expected benefit level when full discretion is maintained. By choosing appropriate parameter values in (9), any level of B may be found to be optimal. As the value of the discount factor β increases, the level of benefit declines. This is because when the future counts more highly the cost of constraining one's policy choices is more severe. As one would expect, increases in the value of a also reduce the steady-state value of B.

The stylized model here illustrates an obvious principle that cutting off one's options is undesirable, and a more subtle one that imposing a "no-cut" constraint on a program may reduce its expected funding level. Obviously, the model would accommodate a number of extensions. But it seems unlikely that these qualitative results would be upset by introducing factors such as an upward drift in the expected desired level of funding X_s or allowing it to be serially correlated.

It is difficult to assess the relevance of the effects stressed here. Certainly the current policy debate on social security makes it plausible that the program would be cut in real terms, if this were possible without legislative action. This suggests the importance of the precommitment aspect of indexation stressed here. The failure of Congress to rescind double indexing's effects strongly supports the importance of precommitment effects. Whether or not no-cut commitments have the restraining effects on spending suggested here is more problematic.

9.2   Inflation Indexation and Private Pensions

There are at least two important indexation issues in connection with defined-benefit private pensions. First there is the question of indexing benefits for persons who are already retired. At the present time, most private pensions in the United States provide beneficiaries with level nominal annuities. While adjustments are sometimes made for the effects of inflation, these are rare and relatively small. A second issue is in the calculation of benefits. At present, in most plans, workers' vested benefits are a fraction which depends on years of service and their current salaries. Actual benefits received from a firm depend on a worker's final year salary at that firm. These two aspects of pension indexation are considered separately below.

9.2.1   Indexed Retirement Benefits

It is widely believed that private pensions should offer indexed retirement benefits. For example, the President's Commission on Pension

Policy (1980) "encourages private and state and local pension plans to provide some form of inflation protection for retirees." The failure of private pensions to offer indexed options is a puzzle. Feldstein (1981) suggests that the development of indexed pensions would not have been desirable because workers already had a substantial degree of inflation protection from social security. His analysis assumes that the capital market compensates individuals for bearing inflation risk. The basis for this supposition is not at all clear. Both the issuers and holders of nominal instruments bear risk from inflation uncertainty. There is no obvious reason why the holders rather than issuers of nominal instruments should be compensated for bearing this risk. Indeed, the fact that mean realized returns on bonds and bills have been essentially zero over the last 50 years tends to suggest that the capital market does not compensate individuals for bearing inflation risk.

At the outset, it is useful to consider as a benchmark the special case of a perfect capital market, in the presence of a safe real asset, and unchanging opportunity sets for investors. In this case all individuals in equilibrium will hold some combination of the safe asset and the market portfolio. There is no optimal degree of pension indexing; any form of pension asset is as good as any other. If a firm issues safe real pensions, it will find that its shareholders hedge by purchasing the safe asset. Its pension beneficiaries draw down their holdings of the safe asset and switch their portfolios toward more risky assets. The form of the pension benefit is a matter of irrelevance. This theorem can clearly be proven under much more general assumptions, similar to those that have been used to provide proofs of the generalized Modigliani-Miller theorems. In order to find any effects of alternative indexing arrangements, it is necessary to introduce some capital market imperfections.

The natural imperfection to introduce is a restriction on short sales. This has at least two potentially important effects. First, it may be impossible for individuals to undo the effects of their pension plan. In general, this would require drawing down or selling short their assets held by their pension funds. This consideration, taken by itself, would tend to suggest that efficient private pension arrangements would make benefit levels contingent on the returns on widely traded assets. Second, in general it will be impossible for all individuals to hold the market portfolio. Because of moral hazards, individuals are likely to be locked into holding much more of their wealth in the form of their own homes and human capital than would be included in fully diversified portfolios. This suggests that they would prefer their pension assets to have returns that are negatively correlated with the returns on assets that they are locked into holding.

Hurd and Shoven (this volume) assess the vulnerability of the portfolio of assets held by the elderly to the effects of inflation. They conclude that even when nominal pensions are included, the aged are for the most part well hedged against unexpected inflation. It is likely that their results understate the extent to which the aged are protected from inflation. A very sizable fraction of the wealth of the aged is represented by the gross value of their homes. Both economic theory and empirical evidence (Poterba 1981; Summers 1981a) suggest that owner-occupied housing prices should rise much more than point for point with unexpected inflation. This inference is supported by the recent sharp decline in real house prices.

These factors suggest that nominal pension liabilities may in fact reduce the real uncertainties associated with the wealth position of the aged. Of course, efficient pension arrangement cannot be discussed without also considering the risks borne by corporate shareholders. This aspect of the problem is considered below, after a discussion of the role of indexation in vesting provisions.

9.2.2   Indexed Vesting Provisions

Bulow (1982) has made the important observation that in a competitive labor market a worker's marginal product in each period should equal the sum of his wage and his accrual of vested pension benefits. More generally, his argument suggests that some set of market forces determine an optimal time path for compensation. This optimal compensation path will in general be independent of what pension arrangements are made. If pension benefits are vested in nominal terms, they represent a nominal asset to workers and nominal liability to firms. If the rate of inflation rises, the value of the worker's already accrued pension asset declines. There is no reason why this should be associated with higher subsequent compensation any more than one would expect workers' compensation to be increased just because other parts of their portfolio performed badly.

The common argument that pensions are effectively indexed during the accrual phase, because benefits are tied to final year salaries, is wrong, as Bulow (1982) points out. It ignores the fact that wages and pension accruals are determined jointly. Market forces determine a path of total compensation not a path of wages. If inflation increases and pension rules remain static, so that the rate of growth of pension accruals increases, the rate of wage growth will decline.

Thus, under current institutional arrangements pension wealth is a nominal asset for all workers, not just those who have already retired. At current high rates of interest, the value of the asset is likely to be small for most young workers. As just emphasized, we should not expect the nonindexation of vested benefits to have any effect on the path of compensation. Hence there is no reason to expect that indexing pensions would have any effects on patterns of labor turnover or allocative efficiency. Again by the same arguments made above, in a perfect capital market indexation would have no real effects.

Table 9.3 presents some evidence on the balance sheets of different age

Table 9.3   Composition of Wealth by Age Group, December 31, 1962
(Percentage Distribution of Dollar Aggregates)

	Age of Head (Years)			
Form of Wealth	35–44	45–54	55–64	65 and Over
Net home	31	33	25	22
Automobile	5	4	2	1
Business	23	23	20	12
Liquid assets	10	11	13	16
Investment assets	22	26	38	47
Miscellaneous assets	9	3	2	1
Total	100	100	100	100

Source: Dorothy S. Projector and Gertrude S. Weiss, *1966 Survey of Financial Characteristics of Consumers* (Washington, D.C.: Board of Governors of the Federal Reserve System, August 1966).

groups. The data suggest that the younger part of the population is likely to be even better hedged against inflation than the aged. This inference is strengthened by the observation that the "net home" item in table 9.3 is likely to involve much more offsetting gross home value and mortgage debt for younger households. This implies that the provision of nominal pensions is unlikely to impose serious risks on young workers.

9.2.3   Risk Bearing by Firms

The question which remains to be examined is the impact of alternative pension indexing arrangements on the risks borne by the ultimate owners of pension liabilities. The proximate owners are corporation. The ultimate owners are mainly corporate shareowners, but also other corporate creditors, and taxpayers through the Pension Benefit Guaranty Corporation. Given capital market imperfections, it is reasonable to expect that corporate shareowners will be less well hedged against inflation than will pension beneficiaries. Data in Blume, Crockett, and Friend (1974) confirm that ownership of corporate stock is concentrated among the very affluent. Hurd and Shoven (this volume) report that inflation vulnerability increases with affluence. This inference is strongly confirmed by the data in table 9.4 on the composition of wealth by income class. The share of liquid assets and investment assets (mainly stocks and bonds) rises sharply with income.

The same point may be made more directly. Despite the fact that pension liabilities are nominal, corporate equity returns are systematically negatively related to unexpected inflation. In Summers (1981b) I show that this is quite consistent with rationality on the part of investors. A 1% increase in the permanent rate of expected inflation is estimated to

Table 9.4 **Composition of Wealth for Different Income Classes**
(Mean Amount of Equity in Specified Assets for All Units in Group)

	Total Wealth	Own Home	Auto-mobile	Business, Profession (Farm and Nonfarm)	Portfolio of Liquid and Investment Assets				Miscel-laneous Assets
					All	Liquid Assets	Invest-ment Assets		
All units	20,982	5,653	644	3,881	9,688	2,675	7,013		1,116
1962 income									
0–2,999	7,609	3,204	154	1,454	2,732	1,455	1,277		65
3,000–4,999	10,025	3,390	399	1,261	4,867	1,707	3,160		109
5,000–7,499	13,207	4,495	629	2,286	4,588	1,872	2,715		1,210
7,500–9,999	19,131	7,075	858	2,279	8,610	2,675	5,934		310
10,000–14,999	28,021	9,566	1,364	4,387	12,424	4,448	7,975		379
15,000–24,999	62,966	15,053	2,041	10,229	32,082	8,824	23,258		3,560
25,000–49,999	291,317	32,528	2,835	61,986	141,733	20,404	121,329		52,237
50,000–99,999	653,223	38,298	2,292	277,383	316,988	37,298	279,691		18,263
100,000 and over	1,698,021	88,248	4,282	286,732	1,224,004	59,382	1,164,622		94,755

Source: Dorothy S. and Gertrude S. Weiss, *Survey of Financial Characteristics of Consumers*, 1966.

reduce the present value of real cash flows to shareholders by 3.46% due to tax effects. This calculation does not take any account of pension obligations. Since in most cases pension plans are overfunded, taking account of pension assets and liabilities would increase the estimated negative effect of inflation. If firms offered indexed pensions, the negative effect would be increased still further.

The discussion in this section suggests that the failure of the private market to develop inflation-indexed pensions is not surprising. In a perfect capital market, indexation arrangements would have no real effects. If capital markets are imperfect, one would expect arrangements to evolve which lead to the sharing of otherwise undiversifiable risks. The holders of pension assets appear to be positioned so that they gain from unexpected inflation. The corporations which issue pension liabilities appear, because of a nonindexed tax system, to be in the position of nominal creditors. This means that efficient risk sharing calls for the issuance of nominal pension liabilities. It is interesting to note that similar considerations can explain why indexed bonds have not been issued.

9.3   Indexing to Other Aggregates

Almost all practically oriented discussions of indexation focus on indexing benefits to the general price level. The motivation for this choice is rarely clearly specified. The implicit argument for price-level indexation seems to be that this provides full insurance because real benefit levels are guaranteed. To state this argument is to realize its limitations. Presumably, we care about the real standard of living of pension and social security beneficiaries, rather than their benefit levels from the programs. Only for individuals wholly supported by a given nonadjustable program is there a potential argument for inflation indexation of benefit levels. The discussion in the preceding section made the point that insuring program benefit levels may actually increase the risk borne by beneficiaries if benefits would otherwise have covaried negatively with the assets in beneficiaries' portfolios.

This raises the more general point that if the goal is to provide insurance to beneficiaries, it will in general be desirable to link changes in benefits to changes in the opportunity set faced by consumers. Benefits should be varied so as to play the role of the hedge portfolios in Merton's (1973) intertemporal capital asset pricing model. Of course, the qualifications suggested in preceding sections about whether indexing can have any real effects apply equally in this context. Similarly, the cost of any insurance is that the insured risks are foisted onto the holders of pension liabilities.

These points may be illustrated in a more formal way. Consider the problem of the representative aged consumer. For simplicity, I assume that the horizon is known with certainty and that future prices are known with certainty, so that there exists a safe real asset. The consumer's problem is to

(10) $$\max \int_t^T U(C_s) e^{-\delta(s-t)} ds \text{ s.t. } A_t + \int_t^T B_s e^{-i(s-t)} ds$$

$$= \int_t^T P_s C_s e^{-i(s-t)} ds,$$

where A represents assets, B represents benefits, and i is the nominal interest rate. This problem gives rise to an indirect utility function of the form

(11) $$U = V(A_t, i, \mathbf{P}_t, \ldots, \mathbf{P}_T, \mathbf{B}_t, \ldots, \mathbf{B}_T).$$

It is not difficult to verify that the indirect utility function (11) is homogeneous of degree 0 in A and the vectors $\mathbf{P}$ and $\mathbf{B}$. If for simplicity it is assumed that the rate of inflation is constant, (11) can be rewritten as

(12) $$U = H\left(\frac{A_t}{\mathbf{P}_t}, i_t - \Pi, b_t, \ldots, b_T\right),$$

where π is the rate of inflation and the lower-case values of $\mathbf{B}$ represent real benefit levels. It is immediately apparent from (12) that changes in the rate of inflation will not affect the attainable level of utility only if, first, they do not affect real benefit levels, $\mathbf{B}_t$; second, they leave the real interest rate, $i_t - \pi_t$, unaffected; and, third, they have no effect on real wealth. Conventional indexing schemes are directed at ensuring that the first of these conditions is met. In the preceding section I considered the implications of the fact that the third condition is unlikely to be satisfied. The analysis here, however, suggests that, if it is to ensure beneficiaries' standard of living, indexing must take account of all changes in real wealth and in the real interest rate.

The effect of changes in the real interest rate is of particular interest. Conventional price indexes try to measure the change from period to period in the cost of attaining some level of utility. Normally this is done by finding the change in the purchase price of a fixed bundle of goods. The logic of this procedure is not clear once one recognizes that consumers "spend" most of their income on future consumption. If the price of a washing machine goes down, a consumer is usually thought better off. Has he not also gained if the price in terms of today's dollars of the bundle he plans to buy next period goes down? This suggests that in evaluating the welfare of the aged some sort of intertemporal price index should be employed.

There is another way of looking at the problem which leads to a similar conclusion. Consider an individual who desires a constant real consumption stream and holds all his wealth in the form of an indexed real annuity. Such an individual is exposed to no real risk because his annuity payments exactly match his consumption stream. However, if real interest rates fluctuate, the market value of such a real annuity will vary. The asset will appear risky when risk is measurable in the standard way. This paradox is easily resolved. When real interest rates rise, the value of the annuity declines and so does the price of future consumption. The value of the annuity measured relative to a proper intertemporal cost-of-living index (as described below) remains constant. The same analysis could be applied to the situation of an individual who owns his home, which fluctuates in value as the real interest rate changes.

Pollak (1975) shows how the standard theory of cost-of-living indexes can be extended to the intertemporal case. My goal here is more modest. In an effort to illustrate the potential importance of changes in the real interest rate, I calculate alternative estimates of a Laspyres intertemporal cost-of-living index. The assumed market basket is a constant stream of real consumption over a 10-year period. The purchase price of such a real annuity is given by

$$(13) \qquad P_A = \frac{P_t(1 - e^{-r_t T})}{r_t},$$

where r_t is the real interest rate at time t and T is the annuity horizon. The change in the intertemporal cost-of-living index is given by

$$(14) \qquad \%\Delta\, P_A = \%\Delta\, P_t + \%\Delta \frac{(1 - e^{-r_t T})}{r_t}.$$

The first term in (14) corresponds to the ordinary inflation rate. The second corresponds to the change in the price of future consumption.

The major problem in estimating the intertemporal price index given in (13) is measuring the long-term real interest rate. In the empirical work reported below, the actual ex post rates of inflation were used in calculating the long-term real interest rate. For periods after 1981, when actual inflation data were unavailable, expected inflation as measured in the Livingston survey was used. These data are described in Carlson (1977). Obviously, the use of such a perfect foresight inflation measure is somewhat problematic. Preliminary investigations using the econometric measures of expected inflation developed in Summers (1981a) reached qualitatively similar conclusions.

Estimates of the percentage change in the intertemporal cost-of-living index are shown in table 9.5 along with the rate of CPI inflation. It is clear that movements in real interest rates are an important element affecting the intertemporal index. In the 3 years when CPI inflation was greatest, 1974, 1978, and 1979, the intertemporal index showed only very small increases. This was because the sharp increases in real interest rates reduced the price of future consumption. Increasing real interest rates contributed -7.1% in 1974, -4.7% in 1978, and -6.7% in 1979 to the

Table 9.5   **Alternative Cost-of-Living Indexes**

	% ΔCPI	% ΔP_A
1953	0.637	−0.151
1954	−0.501	1.424
1955	0.359	0.357
1956	2.862	1.977
1957	3.019	1.076
1958	1.771	3.672
1959	1.508	0.110
1960	1.478	3.628
1961	0.671	3.034
1962	1.215	1.982
1963	1.661	5.215
1964	1.216	5.645
1965	1.935	4.318
1966	3.348	1.759
1967	3.041	3.768
1968	4.718	4.172
1969	6.103	5.383
1970	5.482	6.114
1971	3.365	10.112
1972	3.423	6.433
1973	8.775	2.656
1974	12.200	5.105
1975	7.013	5.399
1976	4.822	7.604
1977	6.769	8.255
1978	9.032	4.278
1979	13.319	6.638

Note: Calculations described in text. Yearly values were calculated on a December–December basis.

intertemporal inflation rate. Overall, the correlation between the rate of inflation as measured using the standard CPI and as measured using the intertemporal index was only .45. These crude calculations indicate the importance of aggregate factors other than the price level which may affect consumers' well-being.

It is important to be clear about the legitimate uses of an intertemporal price index like the one developed here. The index provides a correct basis for assessing the change in welfare for a given change in prices and interest rates for an individual who has no future income streams. Even here there is a small problem unless individuals are infinite lived, since the length of their horizon is changing. The more serious issue involves future incomes. It would be appropriate to compare the present value of future incomes to the price index developed here. It should be clear that in such a calculation the effects of a change in the interest rate on the present value of future streams and on the price of future consumption would work in opposite directions. The adjustments under consideration will be important only when the duration of the individual's future consumption and income streams differ significantly. The data in Hurd and Shoven (this volume) suggest that only about half of the wealth of the "young aged" is in the form of future streams of income. This suggests that the price index considered here is likely to be very relevant to assessing their well-being.

Once one contemplates the possibility of indexing benefits to a price index of this general type, other possibilities suggest themselves. Why not also index benefits to changes in real wealth which also change the opportunity set, or to developments which affect future income? Efforts to integrate private pensions and social security represent one small step in this direction. Such indexing schemes involve the same issues of discretion and capital market behavior. It does seem clear, however, that there is no strong logic which supports indexation of benefits to the current price level as against other alternatives.

A second implication of these results is that in making portfolio choices the aged should be concerned about real returns relative to an intertemporal price index like that considered here. Assets should be more highly valued if their returns are positively correlated with the price of future consumption. I plan to address this issue in more detail in future research.

9.4   Conclusions

The analysis in this chapter supports three principal conclusions. First, indexation of both public and private pensions is likely to have only minor effects on real economic behavior. The presence of provisions for discretionary adjustment and the workings of capital markets suggest that indexation provisions will be largely neutralized by other offsetting adjustments.

Second, the effects of increased indexation may well be perverse. The precommitment aspect of public indexing means that the ultimate effect of indexing provisions may be to reduce the size of public pensions. The nonindexation of private pensions probably represents efficient risk sharing. It appears that pension beneficiaries are much better hedged against inflation risks than are the bearers of pension liabilities.

Third, if insurance is the motivation for indexation provisions, there is no reason why such provisions should be confined to inflation. Only under very restrictive assumptions will inflation indexing provide full insurance. In particular, an important source of exogenous uncertainty facing the aged involves the price of future consumption. Changes in an estimated intertemporal cost-of-living index diverge significantly from those in the conventional CPI.

In his contribution to this volume, Robert Merton advocates a novel solution to some of the problems discussed here. He proposes that social security benefits be indexed to the level of aggregate consumption. He argues that, in addition to providing inflation protection, such a plan would offer a form of "standard of living" insurance. In general, the level of consumption is likely to be a proxy for the opportunity set facing consumers. This notion is justified formally in Merton (1973) and Breeden (1979).

Merton's proposed social security plan is self-financing and requires only very infrequent adjustment. The self-financing character of the plan reduces substantially the precommitment problems stressed here. Merton's indexing scheme provides for both increases and decreases in benefit levels, so the "no-cut" constraint is unlikely to bind. It also implicitly makes benefit levels depend on both the level of wealth and real rates of return.

There are, however, a number of types of shocks which are likely to affect real consumption but not optimal benefit levels. These include changes in the taste for leisure, changes in demographic composition of the population, changes in life expectancy, and changes in the distribution of income. The importance of these shocks relative to others causing fluctuations in aggregate consumption is an empirical question. If they are significant, it may be preferable to design indexes based on estimated changes in the opportunity set of the representative aged consumer. The intertemporal cost-of-living index presented here represents a start in this direction.

Notes

1. Indexing in the design of the benefit formula may well cause greater horizontal equity.
2. Though the discussion here focuses on social security, it is clearly applicable to other public pensions such as those for veterans and federal employees.
3. This condition is necessary. In order to talk meaningfully about the effects of indexation it must be assumed that benefit packages have equal value in all cases.

Comment   John Bossons

The debate about whether indexed pensions could add significantly to the welfare of individuals is difficult to resolve. With respect to the indexing of private pension benefits, the obvious question for an economist to ask is, "If their potential benefits are considerable, why do they not already exist?" The obvious answer pointing to innovation costs and externalities is not really an answer; it is necessary to show both that such costs are substantial and that they outweigh potential benefits to the private innovator. The fact that the creation of an entire set of new financial markets would be required to permit intermediation by financial institutions implies a potential for externalities which can leave a substantial gap between social benefits and the benefits which can accrue to private innovators. Nevertheless, the possible existence of such externalities merely points out a way to rationalize the nonexistence of indexed financial instruments.

Summers argues that such rationalizations are irrelevant because the potential benefits are in fact small for the entire set of individuals participating in private pension plans. While I disagree with his conclusion, he correctly emphasizes the necessity of differentiating between mere redistributions of risk and contracting innovations which reduce nondiversifiable risks for participants in both sides of a financial market. His argument rests on three empirical propositions:

1. Indexation is "merely" a repackaging of risk.
2. Capital markets are sufficiently perfect and complete that most individuals can undo whatever portfolio decisions are made by pension plans, so that generalizations of the Modigliani-Miller theorem can be invoked.
3. The composition of nonpension wealth for pensioners and shareholders is such that nominal pensions are if anything negatively correlated in real terms with the return on nonpension wealth for both pensioners and shareholders.

The last empirical point is in turn based on several empirical "facts": (a) the results reported by Hurd and Shoven, in their chapter in this volume, on the "relatively high" extent to which elderly persons are protected from inflation; (b) an observed positive correlation with inflation of real returns on assets into which market constraints (transactions costs) are likely to "lock in" individuals; and (c) an observed negative correlation with inflation of real returns on shares. Given these empirical "facts" and a focus on single-period portfolio optimization, it is no surprise that indexed private pensions do not exist; the same arguments may be used to rationalize the fact that corporations do not issue indexed bonds. In

John Bossons is professor of economics at the Institute for Policy Analysis, University of Toronto.

either case, if Summers's arguments were correct, there could be some small social benefit (at least for some market participants) in establishing markets in indexed financial instruments, but these benefits would be unlikely to outweigh the costs of creating the markets.

I do not agree with this conclusion, and want to emphasize the importance of several factors which Summers ignores in this chapter. Both the empirical "facts" and their implications need to be examined more carefully. As with many second-best questions in policy analysis, one's conclusions depend critically on what constraints are taken as given.

The first point I want to make is that the observed correlations of real returns with inflation may be largely due to the distortions introduced by the lack of indexation in the tax system. The magnitude of these distortions is well known, in part due to work by Feldstein and Summers.[1] Assuming a positive correlation of expected and actual inflation rates, these distortions introduce negative correlation with inflation for real after-tax income to shareholders and positive correlation with inflation for the real after-tax return on owner-occupied housing. If the tax system were completely indexed, these tax sources of correlation between real returns and inflation would disappear. It is of course possible to argue, as Summers does, that the observed failure of the private market to develop indexed pensions and/or to issue indexed bonds may be the result of observable correlations between asset returns and inflation. However, to the extent that these are the result of nonneutralities in the tax system, the "efficiency" of nonindexed pensions in the current context is only a second-best form of efficiency. The observed private nonissuance of indexed bonds may be one of the important social costs of the failure to correct the definition of taxable income for errors introduced by inflation. While it may be second best to stay with nonindexed private pensions given a nonindexed tax system, I would rather interpret this conclusion as yet another argument for tax indexation.

My second point is that an ability of the average retired individual to invest in a portfolio that is relatively well hedged against inflation does not imply that there are no potential social benefits from the introduction of indexed pensions. Hurd and Shoven's results imply that there is no pressing inflation-induced redistribution away from the elderly in the aggregate which might "require" indexed pensions (or new government transfer programs) to offset such a redistribution. But to conclude that this implies no potential social benefits from indexed pensions misses the point. Here I want to argue two propositions. First (and less important), I would argue that the portfolio reallocations reported in the Hurd-Shoven chapter (in particular, from stocks and long-term bonds to liquid assets) reflect the results of a welfare-reducing change in investment opportunities resulting from the nonexistence of a market in indexed long-term bonds. Second, the most important missing market is a market in indexed annuities. As Summers emphasizes, it is relatively easy for individuals to modify their asset and debt portfolios in order to "undo" pension portfolio decisions. It is much more difficult for individuals to combine an optimal portfolio with differing desires for bequests.

The most important potential social gain from the introduction of indexed bonds and pensions is that they make possible the development of a private market in indexed annuities. The nonexistence of such a market requires households to save more than they otherwise would, in order to insure against the risk of living longer than expected. While the extent of the aggregate welfare loss resulting from this market failure may be reduced by the offsetting effects on personal savings of tax distortions that reduce the return on savings, it is still true that the distributional effects of the market failure may be substantial. Even taking into account offsetting tax distortions that at least partly neutralize impacts on aggregate saving, the nonexistence of a market in indexed annuities may have a substantial welfare cost.

With incomplete capital markets, the "benchmark" case of a perfect capital market with a safe real asset has little relevance for the policy questions that are at issue. It is of course obvious that in such a benchmark case there is no social benefit from any degree of pension indexing. The problem with putting much stress on this benchmark is that no safe real asset exists. Moreover, the essence of the lifetime planning problem is its multiperiod nature, with an uncertain planning horizon. Analyzing this problem using one-period portfolio models ignores the importance of the insurance components of the capital markets.

Having said this, I must return to the obvious question cited at the beginning of my comment. If the benefits from indexed annuities are potentially significant, why haven't they been created by the market? One possible answer is that markets in indexed bonds over a spectrum of maturities need to be created in order for insurance companies to be able to offer indexed annuities efficiently; the innovation costs in simultaneously establishing an entire set of markets are obviously nontrivial. An alternative answer is that, on the margin, the market is innovating in -this respect by starting to offer variable annuities. However, even this innovation is costly, in part because of the number of dimensions along which market demand seems to be differentiated. These dimensions (tilt, combination with put and call options reflected in floors and ceilings, etc.) are partly discussed in Bodie and Pesando's contribution to this volume. I will not pursue them here, other than to note that this multidimensionality makes market research and annuity design harder and hence raises innovation costs.

To summarize, I am arguing that to call indexation merely a *repackaging* of risk is to miss the real potential benefit of indexation. Repackaging is an appropriate way of characterizing the question of the effects of introducing indexed pensions in the absence of the creation of a market for indexed bonds. However, if indexed bonds are introduced along with indexed pensions, the situation is changed in two respects. First, a safe real long-term asset would be provided for investors (such as pension funds) whose preferred habitat is long term. No such asset now exists.[2] Second, the ability to obtain indexed annuities would permit households to insure against the risk of living longer than expected. These two institutional changes would entirely change the attainable risk-return trade-offs faced by households and their private intermediaries.

Up to this point, I have focused my comments on Summers's conclusions regarding the indexation of private pensions, both because of the importance of the problem and because the issues raised lie behind other questions dealt with in his chapter. I turn now to the questions of the index to be used and of the indexing of public pensions.

The choice of index is an important issue, though of secondary importance relative to whether *any* private indexed annuities are offered. It is worth noting that three quite different bases for indexing have been suggested by the various contributors to this volume: (1) a general consumer price index (the conventional alternative); (2) a price index for domestic product (i.e., a consumer price index corrected to exclude the effects of changes in the terms of trade); and (3) an index of per capita consumption (the Merton proposal). The first two are more similar to each other than either is to the third.

Summers makes a number of interesting points in supporting the Merton proposal. I want simply to note that there are a number of sources of changes in per capita consumption, some of which would clearly result in redistribution across generations. For example, a change of taste with respect to leisure/labor choice in the existing working generation would cause redistribution between that generation and the elderly. It is not clear that it is efficient to combine these changes with other changes in average consumption against which this indexation would insure. I agree with Merton's comment that the question is empirical, in that taste changes of the younger generation *may* be an empirically unimportant component of the variance in aggregate consumption. But it is important to recognize that this is an issue, and that within the political process the choice of index may introduce moral hazard considerations.

A final comment on this issue is that one factor which will affect the cost of creating markets for indexed bonds and annuities is the ease with which new contracts can be understood by potential buyers. Index-linked contracts are relatively easily understood by market participants if the index is the familiar consumer price index; they will for some time be less easily understood (and so harder to introduce) if the index is per capita aggregate consumption. Even if a per capita consumption index were preferable ignoring transitional costs, this benefit could be more than offset by higher innovation costs.

The issues Summers raises concerning the indexation of public pensions are very different, and basically are concerned with the effect of indexing on the politics of determining real benefit levels. As such, the relevant questions involve models of the political process.

I do not agree with Summers's position, but want to note that there are two ways of looking at this, depending on one's relative weighting of advantages and disadvantages as well as on the extent to which a public pension scheme is funded. The advantage of defining benefits (and contributions) in real terms is that a political decision to change these terms is clearly identified as a real change and not confused by being mixed up with the inflation-induced real changes that would occur in an unindexed public pension scheme in the absence of political decisions. This has two effects. It enhances political accountability, through helping to clarify public understanding of the issues. It may reduce the uncertainty of future real benefits and contributions, although this is arguable. These issues are the same as the arguments for indexing tax rates. The disadvantage is the point made by Summers: namely, that there is inevitably a ratchet effect on benefits (and contributions) that is more binding in an indexed scheme. There seems to be widespread evidence of demand for ratcheted indexing. This is reflected in the design of private contracts discussed by Bodie and Pesando as well as in the design of public plans.

The weights I give to these offsetting factors may be conditioned by my nationality. Canada's public pensions are funded to a greater degree than is social security in the United States; in this case, revealed social preference has traditionally given more weight to certainty. In the case of a nonfunded scheme, the size of the future transfers is uncertain whether public pensions are indexed or not.

In conclusion, I want to stress the interaction between the provision of indexed private pensions and the political demand for publicly administered pensions. One of the relevant indicators of the demand for indexed pensions is the extent to which political pressures for the expansion of public pensions are increased during inflationary periods. Such expansion has occurred in the United States (even if accidentally, through superindexation), and political pressure for such expansion has built up Canada. One of the major potential efficiency losses from the nonindexation of private pensions may occur from a consequent expansion in unfunded public pensions (with consequent potential effects on aggregate private savings) or in funded public pensions (with a consequent shift in control over investments from the private sector to the state). In this connection, the public's perception of the issues may well underrate the extent to which indexation of pensions may be achieved in the private sector through the creation of new markets for indexed bonds and annuities. Efficiency gains from private pension indexation may include the prevention of inefficient political responses to public perceptions; these gains are no less important if the public perceptions are wrong.

Note

1. See, for example, chapters 8 and 9 in Feldstein (1983).
2. The closest existing asset is a portfolio of Treasury bills; see Fischer's chapter in this volume. Treasury bills are an inefficient substitute for a safe real long-term asset for two reasons. First, the ex ante variance of real returns on bills is nonzero. Second, the expected return on bills is held down by their liquidity; in effect, long-term investors are forced to pay for an inefficient degree of liquidity in their portfolios.

References

Advisory Council on Social Security. 1980. *Report of the 1979 Advisory Council on Social Security*. 96th Cong., 1st sess., January 2.

Blume, M.; Crockett, J.; and Friend, I. 1974. Stock ownership in the United States: Characteristics and trends. *Survey of Current Business* 54, no. 11 (November): 16–40.

Bodie, Z. 1981. Investment strategy in an inflationary environment. NBER Working Paper no. 442.

Breeden, D. 1979. An intertemporal asset pricing model with stochastic consumption and investment opportunities. *Journal of Financial Economics* 7, no. 3 (September):265–96.

Bulow, J. 1982. Analysis of pension funding under ERISA. *Quarterly Journal of Economics* 97, no. 3 (August):435–52.

Carlson, J. A. 1977. A study of price forecasts. *Annals of Economic and Social Measurement* 6, no. 1 (Winter):27–56.

Feldstein, M. 1981. Should private pensions be indexed? NBER Working Paper no. 787.

———. 1983. *Inflation, tax rules, and capital formation*. Chicago: University of Chicago Press.

Hurd, M. D., and Shoven, J. B. 1983. The economic status of the elderly. Chapter 13 in this volume.

Liviatan, N., and Levhari, D. 1977. Risk and the theory of indexed bonds. *American Economic Review* 67, no. 3 (June):366–75.

Merton, R. C. 1973. An intertemporal capital asset pricing model. *Econometrica* 41, no. 5 (September):867–87.

———. 1983. A proposal for a public pension plan. Chapter 10 in this volume.

Mullineaux, D. 1978. On testing for rationality: Another look at the Livingston price expectations data. *Journal of Political Economy* 86, no. 2 (April):329–36.

Pesando, J. 1975. A note on the rationality of the Livingston price expectations. *Journal of Political Economy* 83, no. 4 (August):849–58.

Pollak, R. A. 1975. The intertemporal cost of living index. *Annals of Economic and Social Measurement* 4, no. 1 (Winter):179–95.

Poterba, J. 1981. Inflation, income taxes and owner-occupied housing. NBER Working Paper no. 553.

President's Commission on Pension Policy. 1980. *An interim report.* Washington, D.C.: Government Printing Office.

Sims, C. 1980. Macroeconomics and reality. *Econometrica* 48, no. 1 (January):1–48.

Summers, L. H. 1981a. Inflation, the stock market and owner-occupied housing. *American Economic Review* 71, no. 2 (May):429–34.

———. 1981b. Inflation and the valuation of corporate equities. NBER Working Paper no. 824.

10   On Consumption Indexed Public Pension Plans

Robert C. Merton

10.1   Introduction

Most economists using a standard life-cycle analysis would probably agree that the primary objective of a pension system is to provide a standard of living in retirement comparable to that enjoyed during the working years. Nevertheless, there is considerable disagreement on how that objective can best be achieved. Broadly, the disagreements are on the appropriate roles for private pension plans and a public pension plan in the pension system and on whether or not the pension system should also be used for redistribution or transfers. The most elegant approach to the problem would undoubtedly be to solve for the optimal overall pension system with a simultaneous determination of the optimal forms for both public and private parts. However, the analysis here is more limited in its scope because its focus is principally on the public part of the system and because it examines only one of the many possible functions that such a system might serve in any real-world implementation. That is, the sole intent of the system is assumed to be the retirement objective and not, for example, also to redistribute wealth. This chapter should thus be viewed as only a prologue to a more complete functional analysis of the overall pension system, including the important issue of the degree of integration between private and public pension plans.

Robert C. Merton is professor of finance at the Sloan School of Management, Massachusetts Institute of Technology, and research associate of the National Bureau of Economic Research.

Aid from the National Bureau of Economic Research and the National Science Foundation is gratefully acknowledged. My thanks to F. Black, S. Fischer, D. Holland, L. Summers, and L. Thurow for many helpful discussions and to L. Summers for providing me with the data for table 10.1. Any opinions expressed are mine and are not necessarily those of my helpful colleagues, NBER, or NSF.

259

Analysis of the public part of the system is a natural starting place because, whatever form the overall pension system takes, it will surely include a significant public pension plan component. As I shall discuss, there are a number of theoretical arguments to support such a component as part of an optimal system. Moreover, as a practical matter independent of any theoretical welfare arguments that economists might provide to the contrary, the public pension system in the United States, after almost half a century of operating experience, is not going to be eliminated, especially when a significant fraction of the population is not covered by any private pension plan. The current problems with social security do, however, present the possibility for major changes in the structure of the public pension system. It would therefore seem to be somewhat difficult to analyze the optimal design of private pension plans and the associated issue of integration until the structure of the public system is more firmly established.

In theory, the characteristic differences between a public and a private pension system are that participation in a public system is mandatory and that the public system cannot be "custom tailored" to meet the specific preferences of each individual participant. Such a clear distinction is valid if the private system were solely laissez-faire individual saving. However, as the private system has evolved, the operational significance of this distinction, at least at the level of analysis presented here, is less clear. Participation in most existing private pension plans is virtually mandatory. In a typical defined-contribution plan, individual choice of amounts contributed and where the funds are invested is quite limited, and in defined-benefit plans there is typically no choice at all. Therefore, the analysis presented here in the context of a public system is readily adaptable to an organized private pension system.

The arguments for a public pension system with mandatory participation fall into two basic categories: externalities and private market failure. An important example of the former is the utility externality that other people's welfare is one of the arguments of individual utility functions. That is, people care about others and, among other things, will not let them starve in retirement. From this, we get a classical example of the free-rider problem, which cannot be solved by the private markets but can be solved by an appropriately designed mandatory public pension system. A second example is the possibility of economies of scale in information costs. Virtually everyone faces the decision of how much to save for retirement and where to invest those savings during the working years. The marginal cost of obtaining the education and gathering the necessary data to make informed decisions, as well as the time spent implementing these decisions, will vary substantially across individuals as a function of their prior education and their wealth. (Presumably, a professor of finance by virtue of his training would have a lower marginal cost than a professor of physics.) The cost of buying the service of informed decisions will be lower (as a percentage of wealth) for those who are wealthy than for those of modest means. While such costs could be reduced by pooling, this solution almost assumes away the problem because pooling requires adequate information and opportunity to form a cohesive group.

If, therefore, a pension plan were designed which reasonably approximated the plan which most individuals would choose if they were informed, then by making participation in the plan mandatory the resources used in individual education and data gathering would be saved and the maximum benefits of pooling to reduce operating costs could be achieved. The benefits of such mandatory participation must, of course, be compared to the cost in terms of loss in individual freedom of choice. As already noted, existing private pension plans permit little choice. Although this data point favors the hypothesis that the benefits outweigh the costs, it is hardly a sufficient basis for a policy decision.

The second basic category of arguments for a public pension plan is that the efficiency of risk bearing can be improved. That is, the government can provide diversification possibilities which are not available in the private markets and thereby issue financial instruments, which the private sector cannot. One example would be intergenerational risk sharing, which cannot be covered by private markets (see Fischer 1982). Another would be to use either taxes and transfers (see Merton 1981) or taxes and the issue of securities within the pension system to provide diversification of some of the risks of assets which are not tradable (as is the case for much of human capital).

With these general reasons for a public pension plan as background, I shall summarize briefly the consumption indexed plan to be studied before turning to a formal analysis in the context of a simple intertemporal equilibrium model in section 10.2. In section 10.3, I discuss the merits and feasibility of such plans.

The plan is a mandatory fully funded savings plan of the defined-contribution type wherein required contributions by each member of the plan are a fixed proportion of that member's consumption. As with current private defined-contribution plans, each member has an individual account which is credited with his contributions (less any deduction for operating expenses of the plan).

Contributions and earnings in each member's account are invested in aggregate per capita consumption indexed life annuities, defined to be an instrument that pays a constant fraction of aggregate per capita consumption to its holder (the member) each period, such payments beginning at a prespecified date (the date at which the member begins to receive his benefits) and continuing until the member dies. If the member dies before the commencement date, the annuity is worthless. Benefits, therefore, are in the form of a life annuity indexed to aggregate per capita consumption.

The commencement date for benefits is at a specified age (e.g., age 60), whether or not the recipient has retired. This provision is to avoid possibly undesirable distortions of the decision to retire. However, provision could be made for delaying the receipt of benefits to a later age. Contributions are mandatory from some statutory beginning age (e.g., age 21) until the commencement date.

One way to administer such a plan would be to create a public corporation which would be responsible for issuing the indexed life annuities to plan members where these annuities would constitute its senior liabilities. The United States government would be the residual liability or equity holder of the corporation and would have unlimited liability. The assets of the corporation would come from member contributions and be invested in the broadest available portfolio of marketable securities.

The number of units of life annuities issued to an account is on a "mark-to-market" basis at the time each contribution is received. That is, the value of a unit of a life annuity issued is determined by current market prices and mortality tables. To make this possible, it would be necessary for the government to issue aggregate per capita consumption indexed bonds of various maturities.

To prevent attempts to circumvent mandatory participation in the plan, retirement benefits are assumed to be neither assignable nor attachable. For similar reasons, integration of private pension plans with the public plan are permitted, but only to the extent that the combined benefits received by the individual are no less than he would have received from the public plan alone.

10.2   A Simple Intertemporal Equilibrium Model

In this section, a continuous-time consumption choice model of the type presented by Merton (1971, 1973) is used to analyze the system of mandatory saving and consumption linked retirement benefits.

Consider an economy where all people have the same lifetime utility of consumption which is given for a person born at time t_0 by

$$(1) \qquad E_{t_0} \left\{ \int_{t_0}^{t_0 + \tilde{t}} \frac{[c(s; s - t_0)]^{\gamma}}{\gamma} e^{-\rho(s - t_0)} \, ds \right\}, \gamma < 1,$$

where $c(t; \tau)$ is consumption at time t of a person of age τ and E_t is the conditional expectation operator conditional on knowing all relevant information available at time t. Each person has an uncertain lifetime where $\tilde{t}$ denotes the random variable age of death, and the probability that the person will die between τ and $\tau + d\tau$, conditional on being alive at age τ, is given by $\lambda(\tau)d\tau$ where $\dot{\lambda}(\tau) > 0$. Each individual acts so as to maximize (1) subject to his initial wealth w_0.

If the event of death is independent of other economic variables, then, along the lines of the proof of Theorem VI in Merton (1971, p. 400), we can rewrite (1) as

$$(2) \qquad E_{t_0}\left\{\int_{t_0}^{\infty} f(s - t_0; 0)e^{-\rho(s - t_0)}\frac{[c(s; s - t_0)]^{\gamma}}{\gamma}ds\right\},$$

where $f(\tau;\tau')$ is the probability that the person will be alive at age τ conditional on being alive at age τ'. By the definition of $\lambda(\tau)$, f satisfies

$$(3) \qquad f(\tau;\tau') = \exp\left[-\int_{\tau'}^{\tau}\lambda(s)ds\right].$$

By assumption, individuals have no bequest function. Hence it will be optimal for each person to enter into a life annuity contract wherein his wealth goes to the issuer if he dies and he receives a payment if he lives. One such arrangement would be a series of short-term contracts wherein at age τ the individual agrees to bequeath his wealth, $w(t; \tau)$, to the issuer if he dies between τ and $\tau + d\tau$ and the issuer agrees to pay him a dividend $D \cdot dt$ if he lives. If there are enough people in the economy to diversify away completely the risk of individual deaths, and if the contracts (like futures contracts) require no side payments between issuer and purchaser, then the competitive equilibrium dividend will be $\lambda(\tau)w(t;\tau)dt$.

In addition to the annuity contract, the person will choose an optimal portfolio allocation of his wealth. As shown, for example, in Merton (1971), the fractions of his optimal portfolio allocated to the available investments are independent of his wealth or age because his utility function is of the isoelastic form. Therefore, all investors in the economy will hold identical portfolios (except for scale). Hence, without loss of generality, I assume that all people invest in a single security. The rate of return on this security, dM/M, is assumed to follow an Itô process given by

$$(4) \qquad \frac{dM}{M} = \alpha dt + \sigma dz,$$

where the instantaneous expected rate of return α and the instantaneous variance of the return σ^2 are constants over time. It follows from (4) that the return on this security is lognormally distributed. Moreover, as a necessary condition for equilibrium, this security must be a market portfolio (i.e., a portfolio which contains all available investments and holds them in proportion to their market values).

The accumulation equation for the wealth of a person of age τ at time t can therefore be written as

(5a) $\qquad dw(t;\ \tau) = \{[\lambda(\tau) + \alpha]w(t;\tau) - c(t;\tau)\}dt + \sigma w(t;\tau)dz$

if he does not die between t and $t + dt$ and as

(5b) $\qquad\qquad\qquad dw(t;\tau) = - w(t;\tau)$

if he dies between t and $t + dt$.

Along the lines of the derivation in Merton (1971, p. 390), the optimal consumption demand for a person of age τ at time t can be written as

(6a) $\qquad\qquad\qquad c(t;\tau) = a(\tau)w(t;\tau),$

where $a(\tau)$ is a solution to the differential equation

(6b) $\qquad\qquad 0 = \dfrac{\dot{a}(\tau)}{a(\tau)} - a(\tau) + \lambda(\tau) + \mu$

with $\mu \equiv (\rho - \gamma\alpha)/(1 - \gamma) + \gamma\sigma^2/2$. By inspection, optimal consumption is a function of both wealth and age, and the marginal propensity to consume (out of wealth) will be an increasing function of age if $\dot{\lambda}(\tau) \geq 0$. Similarly, the distribution of a person's wealth who is alive at time $t + s$, given his wealth at time t, will depend, not only on his wealth at time t and the return experience on his portfolio between t and $t + s$, but also on his age at time t.

Using Itô's lemma, we have from (6) that

(7) $\qquad\qquad \dfrac{dc(t;\tau)}{c(t;\tau)} = \dfrac{dw(t;\tau)}{w(t;\tau)} + \dfrac{\dot{a}(\tau)}{a(\tau)}\ dt.$

Conditional on the person not dying between t and dt, we have by substitution from (5) and (6) that (7) can be rewritten as

(8) $\qquad\qquad\qquad \dfrac{dc(t;\tau)}{c(t;\tau)} = (\alpha - \mu)dt + \sigma dz,$

and, of course, if he dies then $dc(t;\tau)/c(t;\tau) = - 1$. By inspection of (8), the dynamic path of a person's optimal lifetime consumption follows a Markov process independent of either his wealth or his age (except for the "stopping point"). That is, given his consumption at time t, $c(t;\tau)$, his consumption (if alive) at time $t + s$ has a lognormal distribution which can be represented by

(9) $\qquad\qquad c(t + s;\tau + s) = c(t;\tau)\exp[(\alpha - \mu)s + \sigma\sqrt{s}\,\epsilon],$

where ϵ is a standard normal random variable. Thus, unlike the percentage change in wealth, which is age dependent, the percentage change in consumption is the same for all people alive. It follows, therefore, that

(10)
$$\frac{c(t+s;\tau+s)}{c(t;\tau)} = \frac{c(t+s;\tau'+s)}{c(t;\tau')}$$

for all people alive at time $t + s$ and $\tau,\tau' \geq 0$.

Armed with (8) and (10), we can now proceed to derive the dynamic properties of aggregate per capita consumption, $C(t)$. If $L(t;\tau)$ denotes the number of people of age τ in the economy at time t, then the total population size, $L(t)$, equals $\int_0^\infty L(t;\tau)d\tau$. Therefore, aggregate per capita consumption is equal to

(11)
$$C(t) = \int\limits_0^\infty L(t;\tau)c(t;\tau)d\tau/L(t).$$

If the birthrate at time t is given by $b(t)$, then the change in aggregate per capita consumption is given by

(12)
$$dC(t) = \int\limits_0^\infty L(t;\tau)dc(t;\tau)d\tau/L(t) - H(t)C(t)dt,$$

where $H(t) \equiv \{b(t)[C(t) - c(t;0)] - \int_0^\infty \lambda(\tau)L(t;\tau)[C(t) - c(t;\tau)]\,d\tau/L(t)\}/C(t)$.

The properties of $H(t)$ are, of course, dependent on demographic assumptions. However, they also depend on the distribution of consumption per capita. If, for example, the distribution of per capita consumption were uniform—that is, $c(t;\tau) = C(t)$, for all τ—then $H(t) = 0$, independent of demographics. In a stable population $[b(t) = \int_0^\infty \lambda(\tau)L(t;\tau)d\tau/L(t)]$, $H(t) = -\int_0^\infty \lambda(\tau)L(t;\tau)[c(t;0) - c(t;\tau)]\,d\tau/[L(t)C(t)]$, and the sign of H will depend primarily on the distribution of per capita consumption between the very young and the very old, where the marginal death rate, $\lambda(\tau)$, is largest. If that distribution is approximately equal—$c(t;0) \approx c(t;\tau)$ for large τ—and the population is growing, then the sign of $H(t)$ will equal the sign of $[C(t) - c(t;0)]$, the difference between the general population per capita consumption and per capita consumption of the very young.

Even without taking into account the interaction between population growth and economic conditions, the analysis of stochastic demographic models is formidable. And, while the death rate (at least in the short run) may be exogenous, the birthrate is surely affected by economic conditions. Therefore, although explicit consideration of the process for $H(t)$ is important for many issues in this paper, no such analysis will be undertaken here. Instead, I simply postulate that $H(t) = 0$.[1]

If $H(t) = 0$, then we have by substitution from (8) that (12) can be rewritten as

$$(13) \qquad dC(t) = \left\{ \left[\int_0^T L(t;\tau)c(t;\tau)d\tau \right] \Big/ L(t) \right\} [(\alpha - \mu)dt + \sigma dz]$$

$$= (\alpha - \mu)C(t)dt + \sigma C(t)dz.$$

A comparison of (8) with (13) shows that, except for scale, each person's optimal consumption follows a stochastic process identical to the one for aggregate per capita consumption. That is, conditional on being alive at time $t + dt$, $dc(t;\tau)/c(t;\tau) = dC(t)/C(t)$, independent of the person's age τ. Therefore, we have for person j that his consumption (if he is alive) at time t can be written as

$$(14) \qquad c_j(t) = \beta_j C(t),$$

where $\beta_j \equiv c(t_j;0)/C(t_j)$ and t_j is his birthdate.

Consider now a mandatory savings and retirement plan where, beginning at age T_0, each person must contribute at rate δ times his consumption until, at age T_1, the person begins to receive his life annuity retirement benefits. During the accumulation period of length $\tau_a \equiv T_1 - T_0$, each person's contribution is invested in a per capita aggregate consumption linked life annuity contract matched to his age at the time of the contribution.

Let $A(t,\tau;T_1)$ denote the equilibrium price at time t of a life annuity contract which begins its payments at age T_1 and the purchaser is currently age τ. The promised stream of payments is equal to $C(s)$ per unit of time from time $s = t + T_1 - \tau$ until the purchaser dies. Let $P(t;\tau)$ denote the equilibrium price at time t of a consumption linked pure discount bond of maturity τ which pays \$$C(t + \tau)$ at time $t + \tau$. If, as I have assumed, individual death risk can be diversified away, then the competitive equilibrium price for A can be written as

$$(15) \qquad A(t,\tau;T_1) = \int_0^\infty f(s + T_1;\tau)P(t;s + T_1 - \tau)ds$$

where, as previously defined, $f(\tau;\tau')$ is the probability of being alive at age τ conditional on being alive at age τ'.

For the economy of this section, an explicit formula for the $P(t;\tau)$ can be derived by competitive arbitrage. From (13), $C(t + \tau) = C(t)$ exp $[(\alpha - \mu + 1/2\sigma^2)\tau + \sigma \int_t^{t+\tau} dz(s)]$. Therefore, the realized return on the discount bond between t and $t + \tau$ is $C(t + \tau)/P(t;\tau) = C(t)e^{-\mu\tau}/P(t;\tau)$ exp $[(\alpha - 1/2\sigma^2)\tau + \sigma \int_t^{t+\tau} dz(s)]$. However, from (4), the return per dollar from investing in the market portfolio between t and $t + \tau$ is exp $[(\alpha - 1/2\sigma^2)\tau + \sigma \int_t^{t+\tau} dz(s)]$. Therefore, to avoid arbitrage, $P(t;\tau)$ must satisfy

$$(16) \qquad P(t;\tau) = C(t)e^{-\mu\tau}.$$

It follows from (16) that the instantaneous rate of return on the bond, $dP/P = \alpha dt + \sigma dz$, is the same as on the market. Substituting for P from (16), we can rewrite (15) as

$$(17) \qquad A(t,\tau;T_1) = C(t)e^{-\mu(T_1-\tau)} \int_0^\infty e^{-\mu s} f(s + T_1;\tau)ds.$$

Moreover, it is straightforward to show that, for $\tau < T_1$,

$$(18) \qquad \frac{dA}{A} = [\alpha + \lambda(\tau)]dt + \sigma dz$$

if the owner of the contract is alive at $t + dt$ and $dA/A = -1$ if the owner dies between t and $t + dt$.

Let $V(t;\tau)$ denote the value of the accumulated retirement account for a person of age τ at time t. Under this retirement plan, with accumulations in units of a consumption-linked life annuity, the value can be expressed as

$$(19) \qquad V(t;\tau) = N(\tau)A(t,\tau;T_1),$$

where $N(\tau)$ equals the number of units accumulated at age τ. By Itô's lemma, $dV = N(\tau)dA + \dot{N}(\tau)Adt$ if the person lives to time $t + dt$ and $dV = -V$ if he dies between t and $t + dt$. Under the mandatory saving plan, $\dot{N}(\tau)A(t,\tau;T_1) = \delta c(t;\tau)$ and $N(T_0) = 0$. From (14), $c(t;\tau) = \beta C(t)$, and if the retirement plan is designed to provide fraction $\eta (0 < \eta \le 1)$ of the person's optimal retirement period consumption, then δ should be chosen so that at retirement the number of units accumulated, $N(T_1)$, equals $\eta\beta$.

If the retirement plan is fully funded and actuarially fair, then at age T_0 the present value of the person's future contributions should be equal to the present value of the annuity payments to be received during retirement. Under the terms of the mandatory saving plan, the person will contribute at the rate $\delta c(t;\tau) = \delta\beta C(t)$ (as long as he is alive) until he reaches T_1. Therefore, at age T_0, the present value of his future contributions, $F(t;T_0)$, is given by

$$(20) \qquad F(t;T_0) = \int_0^{T_1-T_0} f(s + T_0; T_0)[\delta\beta P(t;s)]ds$$

$$= \delta\beta \int_0^{\tau_a} f(s + T_0; T_0)P(t;s)ds.$$

If the plan is to provide $N(T_1) = \eta\beta$ units in retirement, then the present value of these retirement benefits at age T_0 is $\eta\beta A(t; T_0; T_1)$. Therefore, δ

must be chosen such that $F(t; T_0) = \eta\beta A(t, T_0; T_1)$, and from (15) and (20) we have that

(21)
$$\delta = \frac{\eta \int_0^\infty f(s + T_1; T_0)P(t; s + \tau_a)ds}{\int_0^{\tau_a} f(s + T_0; T_0)P(t; s)ds}.$$

Substituting for P from (16), we can rewrite (21) as

(22)
$$\delta = \frac{\eta e^{-\mu\tau_a} \int_0^\infty f(s + T_1; T_0)e^{-\mu s}ds}{\int_0^{\tau_a} f(s + T_0; T_0)e^{-\mu s}ds}.$$

By inspection of (22), the required contribution fraction does not depend on endowments or the individual contributor's age. It does, of course, depend on the statutory retirement age, T_1; the accumulation period, τ_a; and the target fraction of retirement period consumption provided by the plan, η. Therefore, δ can be kept constant over time and still meet the objectives of the plan. The only changes required would be in response to large cumulative changes in the mortality tables, f or μ, and these would probably be infrequent. Moreover, because the plan is fully funded and accumulations earn a fair market return, such changes in f or μ as might occur will cause no significant distortions even if δ were not adjusted over time.

To provide a crude estimate of the magnitude of δ, I assume (1) that the accumulation period $\tau_a = 45$ years; (2) that during the accumulation period the mortality rate is a constant, λ, equal to .0138 per year; and (3) that during the retirement period the mortality rate is a constant, λ, equal to .0666 per year and in no event will anyone live longer than 30 years after retirement. The average rate of growth of aggregate per capita real consumption from 1947 to 1981 is approximately 2% per year. If the expected real rate of return on all wealth in the economy, α, is taken to be 4%, then from (13) we derive an estimate for μ of 2%. Substituting these numbers into (22), we have that

(23)
$$\delta = .10\eta.$$

That is, to provide for all of retirement consumption ($\eta = 1$) would require about 10% contribution rate. While such a rate may seem large (requiring contributions of the order of $200 billion in 1981), 10% is a common contribution rate (on income) in many existing private defined-contribution plans, and the current maximum contribution rate for Keogh plans is 15%. To provide further perspective, I would also note that the combined employee-employer contributions to social security in the fourth quarter of 1981 were at an annual rate of $245 billion. It is, of course, unlikely that a public pension plan would be expected to provide for all retirement consumption, and therefore the necessary contribution rate would be considerably less than 10%.

10.3 On the Merits and Feasibility of a Consumption Indexed Public Plan

While the analysis in the previous section demonstrates a consumption indexed public retirement plan, it is presented within the context of a model where such plans are redundant. That is, with perfect markets for both assets and annuities, no utility externalities, and rational and informed people, there is no need for such public intervention. From this base, however, imperfections can be introduced to provide at least a qualitative analysis of the benefits of the plan for comparison with alternative plans if, and when, such intervention were deemed appropriate.

For example, a significant feature of this plan is that contributions be invested in aggregate consumption linked life annuities. If important assets within the economy, such as human capital and real estate, are either nontradable or not available in divisible lots, then even a broad-based portfolio of tradable assets will not provide a fully efficient diversified portfolio. However, an individual's consumption is likely to be strongly correlated with his wealth (or permanent income) whether that wealth is tradable or not, and therefore a security whose return is perfectly correlated with aggregate per capita consumption is likely to represent a better diversified holding than a portfolio containing only marketable securities. Moreover, even when all securities are traded, Breeden (1979) has shown that all efficient portfolios will be perfectly correlated with aggregate consumption.

If there are systematic differences among large segments of the population as to the types of nontradable assets they hold, then it is possible to improve diversification efficiency still further. For example, the young in the economy may be forced to hold too large a fraction of their wealth in human capital because it is not tradable while the old hold too small a fraction in human capital because they cannot buy it. As I have shown elsewhere (1981), risk bearing can be improved by a system that taxes wages and pays wage linked retirement benefits. However, as that analysis amply demonstrates, such further diversification gains are earned at the expense of having a pay-as-you-go retirement system with a risk of significant distortions from the associated taxes and transfers.

Diamond (1977) has suggested that one reason for a social security system is the absence in the private markets of "real" or "indexed" investments by which people of normal means can accumulate savings for retirement. However, "real" fixed-income bonds would only protect such savers against the uncertainties of inflation. They would not protect the saver against the risk of real increases in the standard of living. As shown in table 10.1, real per capita consumption in the United States has increased at an average rate of 1.96% per year from 1947 to 1981.

Table 10.1   **Levels and Growth Rates of U.S. Aggregate Real Consumption and Over-Age-16 Population, 1947–81**

Year	Aggregate Consumption (Billions/1972 $)		Population (Millions)		Per Capita Consumption (Thousands/1972 $)	
	Level	% Change	Level	% Change	Level	% Change
1947	305.8	—	103.4	—	2.957	—
1948	312.2	2.1	104.5	1.1	2.987	1.0
1949	319.3	2.3	105.6	1.0	3.023	1.2
1950	337.3	5.6	106.6	1.0	3.163	4.6
1951	341.6	1.3	107.7	1.0	3.171	0.3
1952	350.1	2.5	108.8	1.0	3.217	1.5
1953	363.4	3.8	110.6	1.6	3.286	2.1
1954	370.0	1.8	111.7	1.0	3.313	0.8
1955	394.1	6.5	112.7	1.0	3.496	5.5
1956	405.4	2.9	113.8	1.0	3.562	1.9
1957	413.8	2.1	115.1	1.1	3.596	1.0
1958	418.0	1.0	116.4	1.1	3.592	−0.1
1959	440.4	5.4	117.9	1.3	3.736	4.0
1960	452.0	2.6	119.8	1.6	3.774	1.0
1961	461.4	2.1	121.3	1.3	3.802	0.7
1962	482.0	4.5	123.0	1.3	3.919	3.1
1963	500.5	3.8	125.2	1.8	3.999	2.0
1964	528.0	5.5	127.2	1.7	4.150	3.8
1965	557.5	5.6	129.2	1.6	4.314	3.9
1966	585.7	5.1	131.2	1.5	4.465	3.5
1967	602.7	2.9	133.3	1.6	4.521	1.3
1968	634.4	5.3	135.6	1.7	4.680	3.5
1969	657.9	3.7	137.8	1.7	4.773	2.0
1970	672.1	2.2	140.2	1.7	4.794	0.5
1971	696.8	3.7	142.6	1.7	4.887	1.9
1972	737.1	5.8	145.8	2.2	5.056	3.5
1973	768.5	4.3	148.2	1.7	5.183	2.5
1974	763.6	−0.6	150.8	1.7	5.063	−2.3
1975	780.2	2.2	153.4	1.7	5.084	0.4
1976	823.7	5.6	156.0	1.7	5.279	3.8
1977	863.9	4.9	158.6	1.6	5.448	3.2
1978	904.8	4.7	161.1	1.6	5.618	3.1
1979	930.9	2.9	163.6	1.6	5.689	1.3
1980	935.1	0.5	166.2	1.6	5.625	−1.1
1981	958.9	2.5	168.6	1.4	5.688	1.1
Average growth rate		3.44%		1.45%		1.96%
Standard deviation		1.75%		0.32%		1.68%

Source: Consumption data are taken from U.S. Department of Commerce, Bureau of Economic Analysis, *National income and product accounts of the United States*, table 1.2. Noninstitutional population 16 and over data are from U.S. Department of Labor, Bureau of Labor Statistics.

Moreover, the annual standard deviation of that growth rate is 1.68%. Hence, if a person's sense of economic well-being depends not only on the absolute level of his consumption but also on its level relative to those around him, then the risk in utility terms of a price level linked investment can be considerable, especially over a long accumulation period. A consumption linked investment protects against both inflation and real changes in the standard of living. It has the further practical advantage of avoiding the index problem because it is not necessary to distinguish between nominal and real changes.

In another context, Fischer (1982) argues that the government should issue bonds linked to wage income. While it is likely that such bonds would be a superior to price level linked bonds for most saving plans, at least in theory, they may not be as efficient as consumption linked bonds. One reason is that changes in wage income capture the returns to only one segment (albeit an important one) of national wealth, while consumption changes depend on all segments. A second reason is that wage income is more likely to have a significant transient component than is consumption since, by the life-cycle hypothesis, consumption depends on permanent income or wealth. How important the difference would be between wage income and consumption linked bonds is, of course, an empirical matter, and one that warrants further study.

There are relatively limited opportunities in existing private markets to accumulate savings in life annuities, and none where those savings are invested in consumption linked investments. In the absence of such instruments, the individual may be forced to save too much relative to his bequest motive. By investing contributions in life annuities, the proposed plan permits a person to accumulate adequate amounts for retirement with smaller contributions. The additional available funds from this reduced contribution rate can be used either for more current consumption or to purchase life insurance or other saving instruments to meet bequest motives. This feature is especially important in a *mandatory* saving plan because, for the *same* target level of retirement benefits, it reduces the welfare loss of the plan to those in poor health or those who have no bequest motive.

A second significant feature of the plan is that retirement benefits are linked to aggregate per capita consumption. The arguments in favor of consumption linked benefits are essentially the same as those given for consumption linked accumulations. So, for example, while a number of people, including Diamond (1977), have argued for real or price indexed fixed annuities for retirement benefits, per capita consumption linked benefits are likely to dominate such annuities because they protect the retiree against both uncertainties in the inflation rate and changes in the standard of living.

The success of a consumption indexed plan (whether public or private) depends critically on the existence of per capita aggregate consumption linked bonds. In their absence, administrators of the plan would be required to estimate the fair market value of such bonds in order to determine how many units to credit to each account during the accumulation period and to determine how much to pay in benefits during retirement. I need hardly mention the extreme difficulties associated with making these appraisals, especially when such instruments have never traded. Moreover, for a public plan, there would likely be times when strong political pressure would be brought to bear on the administrators to "adjust" their appraisals. Even if such pressure were in fact resisted, the mere prospect of a potential conflict of interest could taint the entire system.

In theory, the private sector could create a market for per capita aggregate consumption linked bonds and provide consumption linked life annuities through financial intermediaries. Indeed, some might argue that the fact that such instruments have not been created is strong evidence in favor of the hypothesis that there is no need for them. However, if this hypothesis is correct, then close surrogates for these instruments must already exist in the market, since—as suggested, for example, by Breeden's (1979) analysis—there is a strong theoretical foundation for the belief that an aggregate consumption linked security would be widely demanded. I know of no such combination of available securities.

There is, of course, the alternative hypothesis that the nonexistence of such instruments is an example of private market "failure." That is, even though there would be a demand for these instruments, there is insufficient incentive for investment bankers, for example, to undertake the costs of educating both purchasers and issuers, especially when the latter have no assets that are naturally matched to this type of liability. Similarly, in the absence of a "thick" market for consumption linked bonds, financial intermediaries probably would be reluctant to issue such annuity liabilities because there is no asset which can be purchased to hedge these liabilities. Of course, some intermediaries might be induced to take some limited amount of risk without being hedged, but this limited amount would surely be inadequate for the scale required for pension plans. On the other hand, it appears that the government is a "natural" intermediary to issue consumption linked bonds because it has the power to tax expenditures. That is, the government could institute a consumption tax proportional to the number of consumption linked bonds outstanding and the revenues from the tax would exactly match the required liability payments. Moreover, there appears to be no significant social cost to the government's issuing consumption linked bonds, and there may be social benefits from the government's financing the deficit in this form.[2] While the principal reason for discussing the creation of such bonds here is their essential role in pension plans, I believe that, independent of pension plans, consumption linked bonds would be an ideal investment instrument for private saving generally. If this belief is correct, and if the government did issue such bonds, then it is likely that private financial intermediaries would introduce consumption linked annuities and corporations would issue consumption linked liabilities. The existence of such private sector financial instruments would serve to make consumption indexed pension plans more efficient by providing better pricing information for the plans' annuities and a broader base of securities in which to invest the plans' assets.

Even if the private sector could efficiently provide consumption linked bonds and life annuities, as I noted in my introduction, private pension plans alone cannot handle either information cost or utility externalities. While it is difficult to measure how other people's welfare enters into an individual's utility function, I believe that it is likely to do so in a relative fashion. That is, we are less inclined to worry about or make transfers to those who have a relatively high standard of living. Among those with the same current standard of living, we are more sympathetic toward those who have fallen on "hard times" and experienced a decline from their past standard. If this assessment is correct, then a public plan along the lines discussed here appears to efficiently handle this utility externality for people in retirement. By requiring individuals to make contributions proportional to their consumption during their working years and investing these contributions in per capita consumption linked life annuities, the plan ensures an accumulated amount sufficient to support a retirement consumption path for individuals at a level (relative to aggregate per capita consumption) similar to that which they enjoyed during the working phase of their life. Linking benefits to per capita aggregate consumption provides for a continuation of their standard of living throughout the retirement years. Thus, a plan with these features meets the objective of ensuring an appropriate relative standard of living in retirement for everyone and it also handles the free-rider problem.

These features do not, of course, solve the redistribution problem for those whose relative standard of living is too low during their working years. However, a reasonable argument can be made that it is more efficient to make the necessary transfers by other, more direct means at the time when they are needed (during the working years) instead of attempting to do so indirectly by redistributing future benefits within the retirement plan. There are other good economic arguments for keeping the transfer system and the retirement system separate, but that is not the focus of this paper. I would note, however, that the plan analyzed here would automatically handle much of the redistribution problem for people in their retirement years if a proper transfer system were devised for people during their working years. Transfers received and consumed during the working years will increase future retirement benefits proportionately because the required contributions to the plan are proportional to consumption. Transfers in the form of a total or partial credit for the individual's required contribution to his retirement account would work in a similar fashion, provided that the cost of this transfer is not borne by the retirement plan itself.

Having reviewed the merits of a consumption indexed pension plan, I now turn to the issue of its feasibility. Although the idea of investing accumulations in consumption linked life annuities is new, the basic structure of the plan is simple and is essentially the same as a standard defined contribution pension plan. It is therefore a relatively easy plan to explain and understand. Its format also has the attraction of stability in the sense that neither its basic structure nor the parameters of the structure (such as the contribution rate or the period of accumulation) would require much change over time, even in the face of significant variations in economic conditions. It does, however, require that an appropriate measure for aggregate per capita consumption be chosen.[3] To select the proper measure would require further study to determine how consumer durable purchases should be treated and whether or not to include items such as leisure time which are not normally included in measures of consumption. There is also the issue of what population measure to use. While investigation of these issues is beyond the scope of this chapter, their resolution is not an insurmountable problem. With this measurement problem solved, there does not appear to be any major difficulty with the government's issuing consumption linked bonds and using their prices to determine the value of consumption linked life annuities.

The main feasibility problems with a public plan as described here are likely to be associated with the method of collecting the required contributions and the maintenance of the individual accumulation accounts. Though I have not investigated in detail the amount of computation and record keeping required in the current social security system, it appears likely that the amount required for individual account maintenance would not be significantly larger for a consumption linked plan. However, the collection in such a plan would probably be more difficult than for current social security because the base is consumption rather than income. As outlined, the plan requires that the amount of each contribution be indentifiable in the same way that individual federal income tax payments are identified. Therefore, the method of collection necessary for its implementation would probably be like that of the income tax, with consumption determined as the residual from a cash flow analysis. The feasibility of such a collection system is currently a topic of considerable discussion among economists, principally in the context of the feasibility of an individual expenditure tax (see Aaron and Boskin 1980; Pechman 1980). Although I will not undertake a serious analysis of feasibility here,

I would note that there is an important difference between an expenditure tax and the mandatory contribution part of a fully funded retirement plan. Because it is a defined-contribution plan and accumulations earn a competitive rate, cheating is less of a problem to the extent that people treat contributions as saving and not as a tax. Indeed, the rich, high-income, and well-informed people who might be thought to have the greatest incentive and opportunity to cheat on a tax are probably the most likely to view such contributions as saving, since these are the people who now voluntarily enter into deferred compensation and Keogh plans. In general, those who cheat on contributions are primarily cheating themselves. However, one slight modification which might make the collection part of the plan more effective would be to have withholding of the required contribution based on income, as is currently the practice for social security, and then to have refunds or additional contributions based on the computation of consumption made in conjunction with the filing of federal income tax returns.

A more radical modification of the plan described here was suggested to me by Lester Thurow. The collections for the plan would be done at the aggregate level by a value-added tax. The aggregate amount collected would then be distributed as contributions to individual accumulation accounts in proportion to the amount of income reported on the individual's federal tax return. The administrative benefits of this modification depend on the relative costs of collection for a value-added tax versus a residual cash flow computation on the income tax return. It does have the attractive feature that those who cheat by underreporting income on their federal tax will lose some of their retirement benefits (which they presumably paid for through the value-added tax). The principal disadvantage of this modification is that the aggregate contributions will now be treated as a consumption tax, which can distort the labor leisure decision. However, the credit to individual retirement accounts based on income will act as a subsidy to wage income, which may offset this distortion at least in part.[4] This modification would become considerably more attractive if the government chooses to use a value-added tax to finance general government expenditures.

In summary, although the method of collecting contributions poses the principal feasibility problem for such a public plan, a number of different methods would seem to serve as close substitutes provided that it remains essentially a defined-contribution plan which earns a fair rate of return on accumulations and pays benefits indexed to consumption.

If a policy decision were made to adopt a public pension plan with a basic structure like the one analyzed here, there would still be the further critical policy decision of what fraction of retirement period consumption should be the target for the plan. Presumably, those who are most concerned about the plan's success in dealing with information cost and utility externalities would advocate a high fraction and those who are most concerned about preserving individual choice would advocate a low fraction. The correct policy decision will surely depend on the amount of other retirement saving that people are likely to make, especially in housing and private pension plans. The resolution of this policy issue, therefore, requires an analysis of the overall pension system. Since that was the note on which I began, it seems an appropriate place for me to end.

Notes

1. On the matter of the assumed stability of $H(t)$, I note that because $c(t; 0)$ depends strongly on the initial endowments of the very young, $c(t; 0)/C(t)$ is likely to be larger when the value of human capital relative to other factors of wealth is larger. It also seems reasonable that the birthrate will be higher when the relative economic value of children is high. However, if $c(t; 0)/C(t) < 1$, then comparative statistics reveal that these two effects work in opposite directions on $H(t)$ in a stabilizing fashion.

2. Fischer (1982) discusses a number of social benefits from the government's issuing wage income linked bonds, including possible intergenerational risk sharing that private markets cannot provide. Many of the same benefits would come from consumption linked bonds, and indeed, if a consumption tax is less distorting than a wage tax, then the consumption linked bonds may be superior.

3. It is, of course, not true that every model of lifetime consumption choice will lead to an efficient allocation of retirement consumption which depends only on aggregate per capita consumption. For example, Breeden's (1979) important theorems on this matter will not apply if utility of consumption is state dependent.

4. As I have shown elsewhere (Merton 1981), the distortion of the labor-leisure decision of a consumption tax can be offset by linking future retirement benefits to current wage income.

Comment   Paul A. Samuelson

Not long ago social security was judged to be the most valuable legacy of the New Deal. Now social security is supposed to be in crisis, and people are worried whether they will receive in the end the retirement benefits promised to them. But what does the crisis consist of? Is it the case that taxpayers have reached some ceiling on their ability to finance the scheduled out-payments? No. Many nations tax themselves much more than we do. And, properly measured, America's affluence is still the greatest of any country on earth.

The crisis consists merely in the unresolved debate on how rapidly payroll tax rates should be raised and on whether or not general revenue

Paul A. Samuelson is Institute Professor, Massachusetts Institute of Technology.

sources should be utilized to cover part of social security expenditures. At the deeper philosophical and class-struggle level, the debate is over how redistributive between affluent and poor the public retirement program should be. As a result of recent inflation and certain inadvertent technicalities of indexing, during the 1970s older Americans were given a step-up in their share of the total social pie. Since this result was never explicitly deliberated and decided on by the electorate, now that the size of the social pie has ceased to grow and in view of the present conservative resurgence it is natural that there are second thoughts about the generosity of the social security program.

What is happening in the realm of social security is of course much the same political struggle that is going on in general fiscal policy.[1] Deficits of over $100 billion are in no sense consequences of ceilings on taxable capacity. Conservatives whose central goal is to reduce the weight of government expenditure in the gross national product are not irrational to believe that the ploy of starving the government for tax revenue will in the end force liberal acquiescence in cutting down on transfer and public goods expenditure. The ploy is not irrational, but it is a form of Russian roulette. Contriving or countenancing crises is a tactic that must run the risk that you will go over the abyss before you force the opposition's capitulation short of the brink itself.

Robert Merton's valuable mechanism of a consumption indexed public pension plan sidesteps most of these controversial aspects. Although he abjures consideration of redistributive social security for the most part, his mechanism could adapt to it. He takes for granted full actuarial funding, something which would have to be taken for granted by any voluntary private pension insurance scheme but which has to be argued out in any social contract with respect to mandatory social insurance. In an epoch when most social contracts are hardly worth the paper they are written on, full funding has the virtue that reneging on promises is least likely to be politically feasible.

To obviate argument with those whose major preoccupation is with the Pareto optimality that perfect markets might achieve, Merton bases his case for a public system on "market failure." In particular, he has in mind the many reasons why there are not perfect Arrow-contingent markets for each person's human capital. If you are not able to spread the risks to which your earning power is intrinsically subject onto existing human capital markets, then even the zealots who concentrate on Pareto optimality concede that laissez-faire will lead to deadweight loss that might be ameliorated by various mandatory public schemes.

Avoiding the esoteric Itô-Wiener calculus of instantaneous probabilities, we can understand Merton's results by contemplating a minimally simple model. Each of us works in two periods of life, youth and prime ages, and lives in retirement in a third period. In our first youthful working period we all earn much the same zero-variance wage. As a result of what each of us is then and of what we each do by way of training, there is a stochastic spread of our prime period's earnings. But it is not possible to actuarially borrow on our different human capitals, for a variety of reasons having to do with market imperfections and incompletenesses. (As one example there is the familiar problem of moral hazard: if an insurance company had lent on my brilliant prospects when I was a Harvard Junior Fellow, I might later have refused to write my successful textbook out of the knowledge that the insurance company would be cashing in on the harvest of my efforts; therefore, so the argument goes, I had too little to spend when young and was unable to lay off some of the risks of not writing a best-seller by investing some of my capitalized prospects in a broad index of common stocks, bonds, and real property.)

Aside from the interpersonal stochastic variations in relative earning power, this simplest model will presumably want to postulate that society's aggregates of consumption and capital formation are subject to stochastic variation both in totals and in sectoral parts. As the quasi rents of capital goods fluctuate stochastically, the capitalized values of the securities denoting their ownership will likewise fluctuate, with only some of the dispersions being capable of being diversified away. The resulting overlapping-generations three-period model might be called a Samuelson-Diamond-Merton, or S-D-M, model in consequence of the series of papers (Samuelson 1958, 1967, 1968, 1975a, 1975b, 1976, 1979; Diamond 1965, 1977; Merton 1971, 1975, 1981, 1982).

Some questions suggest themselves.

1. Why does an S-D-M model lead to consumption indexed pension insurance contracts? We must read Merton's lines closely to understand why.

2. Robert Merton makes skillful use of constant relative risk aversion utilities on the part of the people in his system. Maximizing functionals that are sums of independent period utilities, each of which are the same power of the period's consumption, is known to lead to nice linear simplifications. Suppose life utility $= U(c_1) + (1 + R)^{-1} U(C_2) + (1 + R)^{-2} U(C_3)$, where $U(C)$ is log C or C^γ with $1 > \gamma = 0$. Then optimal consumption and wealth decisions at each stage of life are known to involve simple proportionalities. With instantaneous Wiener probabilities, the constancy of relative risk aversion can be dispensed with.

How robust is this simplifying paradigm? I ask not to record doubt but to applaud Merton's statement that his chapter is "only a prologue to a more complete functional analysis of the overall pension system."

* * *

Rather than linger on the analytical complexities of Robert Merton's schemata, I can best use this limited space to reproduce my original conference reactions to his proposal. Then, finally, I can usefully elaborate on two of the points made there: the reservations that must be made to the notion that real people have consistent life-long intertemporal preferences, in terms of which they deliberate ex ante, on which they decide in midstream, and on which they look back with agreement; and the lack of optimality content of the laissez-faire solution even when no market failure is present.

Spontaneous Reactions

Robert Merton's excellent public pension plan, though he never knew it, is the answer to an ancient prayer of mine. In public lectures, I used to complain that two out of the three features that I wanted in a retirement pension were just not available.

1. Not knowing just when I should die, I wanted an *annuity for life*. This, my friendly Prudential agent had long been glad to sell me. (But still I had the impression that, at least until recently, because of moral hazard and lack of popularity, the actuarial loadings and terms of annuity contracts were not all that feasible for the ordinary person outside the field of education.)

2. Not knowing what the future price level would do, I wanted a *real* annuity for life. This was just not available; however, in 1952, when TIAA set up CREF and when we were all still under the innocent illusion that a portfolio of common stocks provided a good hedge against inflation, it looked as if it was possible to begin to meet this second requirement.

3. Noticing that the average real level of consumption was rising in the modern mixed economies, and realizing that my unhappiness increases when I see myself moving down the scale of real income and consumption relative to the people of all ages I live with, my final unreasonable demand was for an annuity that would leave me for life at the same *percentile* level of the working age population's real living as I had become accustomed to.

There was no way I could get these three wishes. And indeed, I suspected that if somebody invented that better mousetrap and beat a path to my door, I would not be able to afford the cost of that mousetrap and would have to scale down my hankerings.

At this point, I did what we all do when we have an itch that we're not able to scratch out of our own resources. I thought of the government. It knows we are all going to die, and when on the average that will happen. So it can reduce variance to zero in working out actuarial annuity terms by merely operating on a pay-as-you-go basis. (So help me, it was Aaron Director, in my first University of Chicago elementary economics course in 1932, who said: "Everyone is going to die; be born; quit work at an average age lower than the average age of death. Why have insurance companies that have to hire salesmen and keep records on each client when the government can simply and cheaply provide for everyone by law and mandatory taxes what we all are going to need?" I have forgotten many things Director taught me, but not those words of pre-Beveridge wisdom.) I do not know whether government can control inflation. But it can tax the nominal fruits of inflation. So it can offer us a *real annuity*.

At this point, the embryo of my 1958 pure consumption model of overlapping generation was kicking in the womb. Government, I realized, has a tax hold on the fruits of Hicks-neutral technical change and every other kind of technical change. So when I am old, it can tap the enriched harvests produced by my contemporary juniors and let me share in what science and technology have brought to the system even without my having stinted myself in my prime years out of prudential forethought for the future.

By this time I was shameless. With the numerosity of my own six children, future taxpayers all, before my eyes, I realized that government could build into the real annuity account that was implicitly accruing on my behalf the *biological interest rate* equal to the steady-state rate of population growth.

One more goody you may think might have occurred to me. Adam and Eve, the very first generation born into an already going concern, Eden, had an opportunity no later generation could enjoy. Adam and Eve could bite into the apple. Doing this enjoyable thing had to be made a sin so that such an irreversible act wouldn't again occur. You may think I am referring to the possibility that my generation, not being able to take it with us, proposed to use it up (*it* being the capital stock built up since the industrial revolution) in our single retirement years. I have nothing so crass and simple in mind as eating up the apple or the milling lathes. What I have in mind is *something for nothing*!

The first generation of social security requirements can get a free ride in an overlapping generation system with a positive Harrod natural rate of growth of population and of neutral technical change. That (almost!) free ride is often the political factor that sells the idea of social security to the democracy. So it happened in FDR's America and in Scandinavia in the late 1950s.

However, there is only one free ride. And along with the free ride of the initial generation, who reap what they never had to pay anything for—namely, social security—there exists the one final gouging of the terminal generation. Particularly when the population growth rate has turned negative and when younger workers begin to ask, "What have our parents done for us lately?" the voters may disavow the promised benefits that everyone had been able to count on.

By now you will realize that Merton deduced by a stochastic optimal-control maximum that I was right to want my three-pronged pension. And his analysis shows that, on a fully funded basis, much of this could be provided for ourselves in each generation by US INCORPORATED—the government—or, in the absence of externalities, moral hazard, and market failure for informational and transaction-cost reasons, a perfect competitive market of like situated persons can recreate for each of them what omniscient benevolent government can create for all of them.

Lingering Questions

Because Merton has put down a concrete plan, we can use it to bring out major issues that a post-1982 social security system must face. Here are a few nonsystematic questions that his plan made me think about.

1. Our tax system keeps track of our respective incomes, not our consumptions. If not impossible, it would still, I suspect, be difficult for us to go over to a consumption tax system—particularly if it is to be graduated. *After* we have seen an *expenditure* tax system, Merton's consumption tax for pension purposes will be just one more aspect of it (and, as he points out, a part that is more self-enforcing than the rest). But I have to wonder whether, before we have such a general system, it will be administratively feasible for so limited an objective. I hope he or someone will work out how much distortion there will be if surrogates (such as income) are used for his consumption targets.

2. As an academic exercise, one can and should separate social security from "redistribution." However, it is a central feature of the welfare state that democracies want to perform much of their redistributions by means of their life-cycle taxes and benefits. The equality that matters is lifetime equality. Social security, properly, tempts egalitarians to use it.

3. There is the further point that redistribution between generations (overlapping and disjoint) is the very essence of any social security discussion. Samuelson-Diamond-Merton models do *not* deduce as theorems that the laissez-faire solution is the optimal one. Although Merton's exposition puts stress on the case of fully funded public pension schemes, the reader must not think that there is something right about fully funded public pension systems. The bargain that full-funding overlapping generation models arrive at between me and my posterity or forebears is only one such bargain, albeit one which is likely to be politically honored. (I elaborate on the nonoptimality of full funding and laissez-faire later.)

4. Having lived in the world before and after social security, I believe that *myopia* is an essential ingredient present in the private and voting behavior equations of the people we are talking about. Much that a steady-state public system accomplishes could have been contrived privately. But it wasn't. And the voters are at least partially aware of their own imperfections. Models that ignore this miss an important point of the problem.

Merit Want Aspects of Social Insurance

In the following amplifications of my Amelia Island oral remarks, I begin with the central feature of the New Deal social security genesis, of which Robert Merton and all the speakers at this National Bureau conference have taken little notice. Democracies introduce upon themselves social security precisely because the voters realize that they are prone to act in too myopic a way in their private spontaneous capacities as consumers and savers.

Americans in the century before 1937 were the richest people on earth. But still it was the case that most people died broke and lived their declining years as charges on their children and on the meager resources of private and public philanthropy. Of course, people had the capability to consume less in their working years and consume more at the older ages. But in fact the extent to which the majority did so was judged by that majority to be deficient.

We have here a clear case of what Richard Musgrave (1959) calls "merit wants." Democracies vote universal conscription in time of war even though (and precisely because) any one person may not volunteer in a regimen where it cannot be assured that others will volunteer. Democracies regulate availability of therapeutic and other drugs, distrusting the revealed preferences and indifference curves of their own citizenry. And often this is not a matter of some ruling elite or bureaucracy telling the consumer herd what is or is not good for them; but, rather, it is a case where most of us do not wish to entrust to our day-to-day impulses the supply-and-demand deployment of these economic items.

The road to Hell is admittedly paved with good intentions. Likewise the descent to tyranny is festooned with rationalizations for merit-want interferences with personal economic liberties. So always the burden of proof has to be against the overruling of each of our indifference curve preferences. Only when the case is made in a strong way are merit wants to be promulgated in the good society.

Where life-cycle rationality is concerned, a prima facie case for merit wants has always been recognized. Precisely where judgments are concerned about the future, particularly the far future, each of us realizes that we do not possess consistent ex ante and ex post preferences. We are prone to sow wild oats we later come to regret. Faced with the fact that most cigarette smokers acquired as teen-agers the dishygienic habit they wish they could get rid of, only a crackpot libertarian could regard as ethically optimal all behavior patterns that arise under voluntarism.

Maurice Allais (1943), Robert Strotz (1956), A. C. Pigou (1944), Oskar Lange (1936-37), and a host of philosophers have elucidated the problem of human myopia where the passage of time is concerned. Even sociobiology, which recognizes that our genetic propensities to react with respect to intertemporal trade-offs were evolved during eons when the caveman's opportunity sets and life expectancies were very different from what they are in modern economic life, militates against the notion that there is something sacrosanct in the representative person's indifference curves between different time-of-life consumptions.

I must emphasize that the point to which I am calling attention is something deeper than the "externalities" point, according to which we introduce compulsion to make sure you save for your old age—because otherwise you would be tempted to save too little under the correct knowledge that the rest of us will be so uncomfortable at the sight of your poverty that we shall be effectively blackmailed into supporting you. Even if there were no such sympathy or envy, if each of us was prone before the 1937 birth of social security to consume more in our working years than on reflection we conceive to be ("ethically") desirable, we could rationally mandate on ourselves a social security system. And even if it were fully funded, there is no realism to the notion that people will in fact undo rates of positive saving by acts of private borrowing or of equivalently reducing the tax-enforced reduction in consumption during the working years. It is precisely because of the existence of myopia—or discrepancy between what one thinks about ex ante and what one's judgments are ex post—that the general run of the citizenry escape realization that they have the power to undo privately what they have voted governmentally on themselves.

It will be no refutation of the fundamental logical and factual point I am making if now, almost half a century after the New Deal debates about social security began, the de facto existence of a social security and widespread corporate pension system should have reduced substantially the irrational element of myopia in the citizenry's overt preference structure. Use develops a muscle. Once each of us lives in an environment where virtually all of us engage in explicit life-cycle savings—voluntary and mandatory—our consciousness is raised. Like the forms into which cement for a cathedral is poured, which have done their duty even though they can later be dispensed with, the social security system must be credited with contributing toward the restructuring of American minds in the direction of much more explicit rationality in making life-cycle consumption saving decisions.

How Unfull Should Funding Be?

There is much reason to believe that the 1937 inception of social security would never have been politically achievable if there had to be an insistence on full funding of the new social insurance scheme. The electorate persuaded itself to create social security only because the first beneficiaries, those with all or part of their working years already behind them at the system's inception in 1937, could be given benefits *their* in-payments never earned at a perceived burden that could appear to be light for many years ahead.

Most legislators and journalists never understood the real financing of social security. But one who did understand it—for example, Marion Crawford Samuelson, whose job as a research assistant on Seymour Harris's project at Harvard was to study the economics of social security—could rationally favor the underfunding of the system on the well-founded grounds that any engineered increments of public thriftiness would in the Great Depression days of mass unemployment and near-zero marginal rates of interest merely have increased the unemployment rates in the 1937–41 prewar period. When markets do not clear in the fashion presupposed by naive neoclassicism or supersophisticated modern rational expectationism, an increase in thriftiness can in fact reduce achieved capital formation and ex post total saving. If Franklin Roosevelt's right hand had taxed to make the social security system fully funded, in all probability his left hand would have been forced by the resulting increment of unemployment to engage in offsetting deficit spending so as to abort the purpose of full funding. During World War II itself, private consumption was indeed restrained by rationing and enforced unavailability of durable goods, but the exigencies of war did not allow increments of capital formation to occur in the interests of later generations of retirees.

Once the postwar achievement of conditions near to full employment had been achieved, undoubtedly an increase in social security tax rates could have been used to increase the total of United States capital. Easier Federal Reserve monetary policy would then be implied to offset any deflationary effects of the fiscal surpluses. However, if it were deemed good public policy to promote capital formation—whether to prepare for a surge of retirees later or for whatever reason—quite without regard to the social security accounts there remained the opportunity for the government to engineer a *general* budgetary surplus: an increase in public saving, other things being equal, could by means of accommodating monetary ease contrive a lower ratio of consumption to capital formation at full employment levels.[2]

Democratic Resolution of Thrift Decisions

So far I have been taking for granted that our unfunded social security system does not conduce to the optimum mix of United States capital formation and current consuming. But, as I have already stated, economic theory does not conclude that the social optimum is achieved by full funding. On the contrary, even if intralifetime myopia or market imperfections were ignorable, and people were all alike, it would still not be the case that the good society would want to entrust to laissez-faire saving decisions or—what is then the same thing—to full-funded social security the task of determining how much capital formation there is to be in the steady state and in the transient approach to it.

To appreciate that there is nothing optimal about laissez-faire saving decisions, consider the recent discovery of oil in North Sea Norwegian waters. None of the political parties is content to leave it up to the current generation of Norwegian savers to determine how fast this exhaustible resource should be used up in the interests of Norwegians now alive as against the interests of Norwegians still to come. Both conservatives and social democrats would reject the shibboleth proposed by Milton Friedman for disposition of Alaskan windfall oil assets, namely, that each present-day Alaskan be given sellable securities that signify each person's pro rata shares. If Alaskan Eskimos and Caucasians wish to go on a glorious binge, then Friedman would argue that this should be allowed to happen. Or, if they wish to bequeath some of their windfall to later generations, then in whatever degree they choose to do so, that is ipso facto the correct outcome. Nothing in economic science or in the calculus of freedom for the individuals who will exist in the stream of history sanctifies such a solution—except the shibboleth that laissez-faire is right whatever are its consequences.

I am not suggesting that some Plato ought to dictate to the Norwegian people how successive generations shall relatively fare, doing so through decisions being made about social security rates and oil exploitation rates. My point is that the Norwegian electorate have the right to second guess by legislation what they believe will occur if they leave the decision to laissez-faire Walrasianism.

My concluding section draws on the analytical studies of steady-state equilibria in overlapping-generation models. Such Modigliani-Turgot models—or, what is the same thing, Samuelson-Diamond-Merton models—generate equilibria which have no necessary proximity to golden rule states.[3] They provide no economic justification for the present fad glorifying full funding of social security, leaving that proposal only with the defense that full funding is the only mode of operation which can be terminated or expanded without losses or profits.

Paradoxes of Exponential Growth

1. The faster a population's (permanent) exponential growth rate, the more workers there will be to support each older retiree (Samuelson 1958). However, the greater the population growth, the more will be the subtractions from per capita production that must be withheld from consumption in order to keep capital widening in step with labor-supply growth (Diamond 1965; Samuelson 1975a, 1976). The two-part golden rule requires that, in a population growing forever at the percentage rate of 100 R per year, the lifetime utility of each generation's representative

person will be at its maximum only if capital's net product equals the biological interest rate of R and if people's intralifetime consumption decisions are made taking into account that same R opportunity cost of successive periods' consumptions (Samuelson 1968). Warning: All technical change is ignored here; production is considered to obey a one-sector neoclassical production function à la Solow (1956); bequest motivations are ruled out. Meade-Lerner total utility considerations, which are not addressed here, also do not sanctify laissez faire's full funding.

2. Laissez-faire life-cycle saving and fully funded social security will lead, under certain rather artificial but often invoked conditions, to precisely the one and the same equilibrium—as private industries cease to save privately exactly the amount that the mandatory public social security system saves on their behalf (Samuelson 1975b, theorem 2).

3. The resulting equilibrium will, in general, deviate forever from the two-step golden rule optimum (Samuelson 1975b, p. 540). However, by appropriately gauged nonfunded social security, society can be swung into the two-step golden rule configuration (Samuelson 1975a, theorem 1).

4. In the singular case where the rate of population growth is the most golden of all rates—in the sense of yielding maximum lifetime utility forever of the representative person of each generation—fully funded social security (which is the same as no *social* security at all!) would by the Serendipity Theorem achieve the two-step golden rule (Samuelson 1976b, fig. 1b).

5. There are some realistic reasons why the most golden population growth rate might involve negative growth rates (Deardorff 1976; Samuelson 1976). To the degree that this is so, the present era of incipient population decline may perhaps be near the optimum. And then, redistribution and myopia aside, the case may be stronger today for fuller funding than it was when the social security system was adopted in 1937.

6. To the degree that the present income tax system leads to too little capital formation (and to deadweight loss), more than full funding of Merton's social security might be desirable. People are forced to pay in more than they will ever perceive themselves to be getting back in their old age. As the public debt is reduced by the overall government surplus, the Federal Reserve's optimal interest rate policy is one low enough to keep employment full with a high ratio of investment to income.

* * *

Finally, I should call attention to the writings of Meade (1956), Dasgupta (1969), and Gigliotti (1983a, 1983b). These are in the ancient Sidgwick-Edgeworth utilitarian tradition that wishes to maximize the product of population and per capita lifetime utility, a view emphasized by A. P. Lerner (1957) and Asimakopulos (1967) in discussion of Samuelson (1958, 1959). The "most golden state" by this utilitarian criterion is not realized by laissez faire's full funding—as the Norwegian oil case well shows.

Notes

1. The fact that the intrinsic rate of population growth has dropped since 1960 is the only genuine new factor that creates a problem for the U.S. social security program. All things considered, steady population decline probably expands society's capacity to afford generous retirement benefits to its elderly. (A partial offset to the implied fall in the ratio of workers to retirees is the drop in the ratio of dependent minors to workers. The decline in the net reproduction rate is itself in good part a consequence of the increased propensity of women to be in the *taxable* labor market, which is another favorable offset. Finally, a declining population requires less *widening* of capital, thereby releasing more for the consumption of each person of any age. See Samuelson [1975a, 1976] for discussion of these crosscurrents.) But even if the population decline is on balance a favorable factor, it admittedly exacerbates the element of deadweight loss involved in financing those benefits by high taxes on the working ages.

2. I have always found it odd that a Martin Feldstein, who registered concern that social security displaces private saving by being unfunded and thereby undermining capital formation, should at the same time play down in policy discussions the Tobin-Samuelson proposals for fiscal surpluses–cum–central bank ease. Feldstein's legitimate concern over the wedge between before-tax and after-tax returns for capital by no legitimate syllogism of logic can serve to rationalize that inconsistency. The fact that chocolate is good does not negate the fact that honey is good.

3. Such equilibria are admittedly Pareto intertemporally optimal. But so too are an infinity of other contrived equilibria. And there is no reason to infer that one Pareto-optimal point is ethically better than all non-Pareto-optimum points.

References

Aaron, H. J., and Boskin, M. J., eds. 1980. *The economics of taxation.* Studies in Government Finance. Washington, D.C.: Brookings Institution.

Allais, M. A. 1943. A la recherche d'une discipline économique. Vol. 1. Paris: Private circulation.

Asimakopulos, A. 1967. The biological interest rate and the social utility function. *American Economic Review* 57 (March): 185–89.

Breeden, D. T. 1979. An intertemporal asset pricing model with stochastic consumption and investment opportunities. *Journal of Financial Economics* 7 (September): 265–96.

Dasgupta, P. A. 1969. On the concept of optimum population. *Review of Economic Studies* 36 (February): 295–318.

Deardorff, A. 1976. The optimum growth rate for population: Comment. *International Economic Review* 17 (June): 510–15.

Diamond, P. A. 1965. National debt in a neoclassical growth model. *American Economic Review* 32 (December): 289–98.

———. 1977. A framework for social security analysis. *Journal of Public Economics* 8: 275–98.

Fischer, S. 1982. Welfare aspects of government issue of indexed bonds. Hoover Institution, January (unpublished paper).

Gigliotti, G. A. 1983*a*. Total utility, overlapping generations, and optimal population. *Review of Economic Studies*, in press.

———. 1983*b*. Total utility, overlapping generations, and optimal social security. Submitted to *Journal of Economic Theory*.

Lange, O. 1936. On the economic theory of socialism, pts. 1–2. *Review of Economic Studies* 4 (October-February): 53–71, 123–42.

Lerner, A. P. 1957. Consumption-loan interest and money. *Journal of Political Economy* 67 (October): 437–41.

Meade, J. E. 1965. *Trade and welfare.* Oxford: Oxford University Press.

Merton, R. C. 1971. Optimum consumption and portfolio rules in a continuous-time model. *Journal of Economic Theory* 3 (October): 373–413.

———. 1973. An intertemporal capital asset pricing model. *Econometrica* 41 (September): 867–87.

———. 1975. An asymptotic theory of growth under uncertainty. *Review of Economic Studies* 42 (July): 375–93.

———. 1981. On the role of social security as a means for efficient risk-bearing in an economy where human capital is not tradable. Chapter 12, this volume.

———. 1982. On consumption indexed public pension plans. Chapter 10, this volume.

Musgrave, R. A. 1959. *The theory of public finance.* New York: McGraw-Hill.

Pechman, J. A., ed. 1980. *What should be taxed: Income or expenditure?* Studies of Government Finance. Washington, D.C.: Brookings Institution.

Pigou, A. C. 1944. *Socialism versus capitalism.* London: Macmillan.

Samuelson, P. A. 1958. An exact consumption-loan model of interest with or without the social contrivance of money. *Journal of Political Economy* 66 (December): 467–82. Reprinted in *Collected scientific papers of Paul A. Samuelson.* Vol. 2. Cambridge: MIT Press, 1966.

———. 1959. Reply [to Abba P. Lerner, Consumption-loan interest and money]. *Journal of Political Economy* 41, pt. 1 (May): 183–84. Reprinted in *Collected Scientific Papers of Paul A. Samuelson.* Vol. 1. Cambridge: MIT Press, 1966.

———. 1967. A turnpike refutation of the golden rule in a welfare-maximizing many-year plan. In *Essays on the theory of optimal economic growth*, ed. K. Shell. Cambridge: MIT Press, 1966. Reprinted in

Collected Scientific Papers of Paul A. Samuelson. Vol. 3. Cambridge: MIT Press, 1972.

———. 1968. The two-part golden rule deduced as the asymptotic turnpike of catenary motions. *Western Economic Journal* 6 (March): 85–89. Reprinted in *Collected Scientific Papers of Paul A. Samuelson.* Vol. 3 Cambridge: MIT Press, 1972.

———. 1975*a*. The optimum growth rate for population. *International Economic Review* 16 (October): 531–38. Reprinted in *Collected scientific papers of Paul A. Samuelson.* Vol. 4. Cambridge: MIT Press, 1977.

———. 1975*b*. Optimum social security in a life-cycle growth model. *International Economic Review* 16 (October): 539–44. Reprinted in *Collected scientific papers of Paul A. Samuelson.* Vol. 4. Cambridge: MIT Press, 1977.

———. 1976. The optimum growth rate for population: Agreement and evaluations. *International Economic Review* 17 (June): 516–25. Reprinted in *Collected scientific papers of Paul A. Samuelson.* Vol. 4. Cambridge: MIT Press, 1977.

———. 1979. Land and the rate of interest. In *Theory for economic efficiency: Essays in honor of Abba P. Lerner*, ed. H. I. Greenfield, A. M. Levenson, W. Hamovitch, and E. Rotwein. Cambridge: MIT Press.

Solow, R. M. 1956. A contribution to the theory of economic growth. *Quarterly Journal of Economics* 70 (February): 65–94.

Strotz, R. 1956. Myopia and inconsistency in dynamic utility maximization. *Review of Economic Studies* 23: 165–80.

11 Retirement Annuity Design in an Inflationary Climate

Zvi Bodie and James E. Pesando

A pensioner who receives his benefit in the form of a nominal annuity has claim to a stream of payments whose nominal value is certain. The *real* value of this claim, however, will be highly uncertain if there exists substantial uncertainty regarding the future level of prices. Because this appears to be the case, and because pensioners are presumably concerned with the real value of their retirement incomes, the challenge of designing an annuity in an inflationary climate merits increased attention. We believe that at least some individuals may find alternatives to the nominal level-payment annuity better suited to their needs or preferences in an environment of substantial inflation uncertainty.[1] If individuals are to make rational choices, they must first understand the risk return and other characteristics of alternative annuity designs. Our primary objective in this chapter is to clarify these issues.

The first task is to examine the streams of real benefits that are likely to be provided by variable annuities (VAs). Although equity-based VAs appear to have fallen into some disfavor, perhaps because of the inherent volatility of common stocks, recent work by Bodie (1980, 1982) suggests that VAs tied to bills or short-term bonds may produce income streams that are quite stable in real terms. Therefore we examine VAs backed by bills, long-term bonds, common stocks, and a mixed portfolio and compare the results with those for a graduated payment, nominal annuity.

Our second task is to examine more recent annuity designs in which floors or floors-plus-ceilings have been added to the standard VA. The

Zvi Bodie is associate professor of finance and economics at the School of Management, Boston University, and a research associate of the National Bureau of Economic Research. James E. Pesando is professor of economics at the University of Toronto and a research associate of the National Bureau of Economic Research.
The authors are indebted to Franco Modigliani for several helpful discussions.

Rockefeller Foundation plan, for example, provides cost-of-living adjustments which equal the average prime interest rate for the year less 3% (Heaton 1977). Once granted, these adjustments are never reduced and thus the annuitant—in effect—has a VA subject to a nominal floor.[2] Annuities provided by the Teachers Insurance and Annuity Association (TIAA) also have a guaranteed nominal floor.[3] In recent years, large firms in both Canada and the United States have frequently made ad hoc cost-of-living adjustments to the pensions of retired workers. In Canada, these adjustments have often been financed from pension fund earnings in excess of the plan's valuation rate (Pesando 1981).[4] Once granted, these adjustments are permanent. Moreover, there appears to be a ceiling on these adjustments in that the real value of the initial benefit is never increased even if "excess" fund earnings might so permit. The second part of the chapter thus examines a variable annuity subject to a nominal floor (VAF) and a variable annuity subject to a nominal floor and a real ceiling (VAFC). The former is suggested by the Rockefeller plan, and both may be viewed as an attempt to formalize the apparent practice of many firms in granting cost-of-living adjustments to retired plan members.

The chapter is organized as follows. The performance of a nominal, level-payment annuity is first contrasted with that of a hypothetical purchasing power annuity for the period 1971–80. The latter is formally equivalent to a VA backed by an index bond yielding a certain real return of 0%. Theoretical distributions of the real payments from VAs tied to alternative asset bases are then presented and serve to illustrate the nature of the trade-off between risk and expected real returns. These payments are also contrasted with those provided by a graduated-payment, nominal annuity. The properties of VAFs are then explored, and simulations are conducted to contrast their performance with VAs backed by identical asset portfolios. The same exercise is then repeated for VAFCs. To place the alternative annuity designs in a final perspective, a historical simulation is conducted for the period 1971–80. The final section is a summary and conclusion.

11.1 The Level-Payment, Nominal Annuity

The nominal and real values of the benefits provided by a nominal, level-payment annuity during the period 1971–80 are illustrated in table 11.1. The annuity is purchased at the beginning of 1971 for the sum of $100,000, the annuity is sold at a (nominal) interest rate of 7.5%, and the benefits are payable with certainty for 10 years.[5] The real value of the annual, nominal payment declines by more than 50% during the decade. Further, it is likely that a substantial portion of this decline was unanticipated. If the anticipated rate of inflation embodied in the nominal rate of

Table 11.1   Illustration of Traditional, Level-Payment Annuity and Purchasing Power Annuity for Period 1971–80

| Year | Inflation Rate (CPI) | Traditional Annuity[a] | | Purchasing Power Annuity[b] | | | |
| | | | | No Tilting ($RV=0$) | | Tilting ($RV=5$) | |
		Nominal Value	Real Value	Nominal Value	Real Value	Nominal Value	Real Value
1971	3.3	14,568	14,095	10,336	10,000	12,748	12,334
1972	7.4	14,568	13,630	10,688	10,000	12,555	11,746
1973	8.8	14,568	12,527	11,629	10,000	13,009	11,187
1974	12.2	14,568	11,165	13,047	10,000	13,901	10,654
1975	7.0	14,568	10,434	13,962	10,000	14,167	10,147
1976	4.8	14,568	9,955	14,634	10,000	14,142	9,664
1977	6.8	14,568	9,324	15,624	10,000	14,380	9,204
1978	9.0	14,568	8,551	17,035	10,000	14,932	8,765
1979	13.3	14,568	7,547	19,303	10,000	16,114	8,343
1980	12.4	14,568	6,714	21,698	10,000	17,251	7,951

[a] Assumes that the nominal interest rate is 7.5%, initial capital is $100,000, annuity is payable with certainty for 10 years, and annuity payments are made at the end of the year.

[b] Assumes a real interest rate of zero. If π is the inflation rate in period t, then the nominal annuity payment $B_t = B_{t-1} * (1+\pi_t)/(1+RV)$ where RV is the interest rate used to determine the base annuity payment (B_0); B_0 equals $RV * A/[1 - (1+RV)^{-T}]$ where A is the initial capital; and T is the number of years the annuity is payable. For $RV=0$, B_0 equals A/T.

interest was 5% then the annuitant would have expected the real value of his benefit to decline at about 5% per year.[6] Deviations around this rate of decline would then have been unanticipated.

For illustrative purposes, the performance of a PPA for the period 1971–80 is also shown in table 11.1. This annuity is fully linked to the consumer price index and is sold at a certain real return of 0%. Earlier work by Bodie (1980) indicates that the minimum-variance portfolio (in the absence of short selling) consists of one-month Treasury bills hedged with commodity futures and that the expected real return on this portfolio would not exceed 0%. We assume for simplicity that a portfolio could be constructed which would provide a certain real return of 0%. The PPA is analytically equivalent to a VA tied to an index bond which provides this certain real return.

Although the stream of real payments provided by the PPA is certain, there is no requirement that this stream of payments be constant. If RV is the annuity valuation rate used to determine the base value of the annuity payment, and if r is the certain real return on the portfolio, then the real value of the annuity payments will change with certainty at an annual rate equal to $(1 + r)/(1 + RV) - 1$. (See Appendix for details.) With $r = 0$ and $RV = 5$, the real benefit declines with certainty at 4.76% per year, as shown in table 11.1. When r and RV are equal, there is no tilt to the projected stream of real annuity payments. If the real return is uncertain, the previous expression depicts the expected degree of tilting in the real payments stream. If pensioners wish to design a stream of pension payments which is expected to decline in real terms, perhaps due to liquidity constraints or estate motives, this is readily accomplished with vehicles other than the nominal, level-payment annuity. The downward tilt in the real benefit provided by a nominal, level-payment annuity is, of course, equal to the expected rate of inflation.

11.2   Variable Annuities with Alternative Asset Bases

The limitations of fixed-dollar annuities in an inflationary climate prompted life insurance companies in the 1950s to offer equity-based VAs. As emphasized by Bodie (1980), however, an equity-based VA exposes the annuitant to substantial investment risk even if it is assumed that the real return on equities is unaffected by unanticipated changes in the rate of inflation.[7] The purpose of this section is to explore the real income streams provided by VAs with alternative asset bases.

Theoretical distributions are presented in table 11.2 for the real benefits provided by VAs backed by one-month Treasury bills, long-term United States government bonds, common stocks, and a mixed portfolio. (The mechanics of a variable annuity are detailed in the Appendix.) The mixed portfolio is the minimum variance portfolio with the same ex-

Table 11.2 Variable Annuities with Alternative Asset Bases: Theoretical Distributions

Portfolio	Expected Real Return[a] (%)	Standard Deviation (%)	Annuity Valuation Rate (%)	Base Annuity Payment[b] ($)	Annuity Payment In Year 5			Annuity Payment in Year 10			Annuity Payment in Year 15		
					Median	Mean	S.D.	Median	Mean	S.D.	Median	Mean	S.D.
Bills	0	1.52	0	6,667	6,667	6,670	227	6,667	6,674	321	6,667	6,678	393
Bills (serial correlation)[c]	0	1.04	0	6,667	6,667	6,677	361	6,667	6,701	679	6,667	6,731	933
Bonds	2.956	7.64	3	8,377	8,377	8,500	1,463	8,377	8,625	2,115	8,377	8,752	2,647
Stocks	7.232	18.61	7.5	11,329	11,329	12,354	5,372	11,329	13,471	8,666	11,329	14,689	12,974
Mixed portfolio[d]	2.956	6.08	3	8,377	8,377	8,455	1,155	8,377	8,533	1,656	8,377	8,613	2,056
Graduated payment[e] nominal annuity (graduation rate=8%)	2.956	—	3	8,377	8,377	8,445	1,080	8,377	8,723	2,531	8,377	9,219	4,236

[a]Mean of the logarithm of the real annual wealth relative. Annuity valuation rate in column 4 is the equivalent annual rate.

[b]Initial capital is $100,000, annual payments are made with certainty for 15 years and are reported in constant dollars.

[c]Based on the following autoregression for the annual real return on bills: $r_t = .76r_{t-1} + e_t$, with $\sigma_e = 1.04\%$ per year and $r_0 = 0$.

[d]Mixed portfolio, consisting of bonds (52%), bills (29%), and stocks (19%), minimizes the variance of the annual real return for the given mean.

[e]Uncertainty regarding the real annuity payments stems solely from uncertainty regarding the price level, which is assumed to be log normally distributed. The continuously compounded rate of inflation (π) follows the following autoregressive process: $\pi_t = .77 + .9\pi_{t-1} + U_t$ with $\sigma_U = 2.00\%$ per year and $\pi_0 = 7.7\%$. The steady-state inflation rate of 7.7% is equivalent to the annual graduation rate of 8%. The graduated-payment nominal annuity assumes an expected real return equal to that of bonds (i.e., 2.956%).

pected return as the long-term bond portfolio.[8] The VAs are purchased for $100,000 and benefits are paid with certainty for 15 years. The real returns on bills, bonds, and stocks are assumed to be lognormally distributed with means of zero, 2.956%, and 7.232%, respectively, and standard deviations of 1.52%, 7.64%, and 18.61%. The means are the continuous time equivalents of annual returns of 0%, 3%, and 7.5%. These parameters, together with the covariances necessary to construct the mixed portfolio, are based on historical data for the period 1953–80.[9] The valuation rates used to determine the base level of the annuity payments are the annual equivalents of the continuously compounded real rates of return. Examination of the historical data indicates that real bill returns, but not those on stocks and bonds, are serially correlated.[10] For this reason, the theoretical distribution of real benefit payments is also calculated for a bills-based VA on the assumption that real bill returns are serially correlated.

The assumption that real returns are lognormally distributed implies that annuity payments are lognormally distributed also. Since the valuation rates used to calculate the base values of the benefits are the annual equivalents of the expected real returns on the portfolios, *median* benefit payments show no tendency to rise or to fall over time.[11] Because these payments are lognormally distributed, they exhibit positive skewness and thus the *mean* payments rise steadily over time. The distribution of real benefits provided by a graduated-payment, nominal annuity is also included in table 11.2. For this annuity, all of the uncertainty regarding the real value of the benefit payments stems from price-level uncertainty. Thus, an additional set of assumptions is required. The price level is assumed to be lognormally distributed, and the continuously compounded rate of inflation is assumed to follow the first-order autoregressive process which characterizes the period 1953–80.[12] The degree of graduation is set equal to 8%, which is the (annual) steady-state rate of inflation implied by the autoregression.[13] The purpose of including the graduated, nominal annuity is to emphasize the fact that while its nominal payments are devoid of risk, its real payments are not.

The distributions of real benefit payments reported in table 11.2 mirror the risk-return characteristics of the underlying portfolios. The stream of real benefits provided by the bills-based VA is smaller and more stable than the stream provided by the bonds-based VA, and so on. Recognition of the serial correlation in bill returns produces a riskier stream of benefit payments, especially as the time horizon increases. Even when this serial correlation is acknowledged, however, bills remain the cornerstone of any VA which is intended to limit uncertainty regarding the real value of benefit payments. The importance of diversification is seen in the comparison of the bonds-based VA, with the VA tied to the mixed portfolio with the same expected return. Although the median benefits are identical, the standard deviation of the real benefit payment in the fifteenth year is 22% smaller for the VA tied to the mixed portfolio.

Note, finally, the real benefit stream provided by the graduated-payment, nominal annuity. We assume that the implicit expected real return is 3% (at an annual rate) and is thus equal to the expected real return on long-term government bonds.[14] This assumption is equivalent to assuming that life companies can hedge graduated-payment, nominal annuities by holding an appropriate sequence of long-term bonds and that competitive pressures ensure that this is the implicit real yield at which these annuities are sold. Because of the 3% return assumption, the median benefits are identical to those for the VAs tied to the government bond and mixed portfolios. The standard deviation of the benefits provided by the nominal annuity is less than those for either of the VAs in year 5 but significantly exceeds them by year number 10.

The significant increase in the riskiness of real benefits provided by the nominal annuity as the annuitant ages merits emphasis. *This is a direct reflection of the substantial serial correlation in the inflation rate.* These results, especially as the annuitant ages, illustrate how inappropriate it is to argue that VAs are inferior to nominal annuities because they transfer all of the investment risk to the annuitant. The results also highlight the importance of acknowledging the serial correlation in inflation rates in attempting any assessment of the risk of the real benefits provided by nominal annuities.

11.3   Variable Annuities with Nominal Floors

As noted, the Rockefeller Foundation Plan provides retiring employees with a variable annuity subject to a nominal floor, or VAF. Sun Life Insurance Company of Canada has recently introduced a VAF, tied to Treasury bills, in which excess earnings above 3% are also used to provide permanent benefit enrichments. The nominal floor in each of these cases is equivalent to the plan sponsor's guaranteeing that the fund will earn a nominal rate of at least 3%. If the fund earns less than 3% in a given period, the plan sponsor fully absorbs the loss. (The mechanics of a VAF and the contrast to a standard VA are detailed in the Appendix.)

The pension plans provided by most large firms in the United States (and Canada) are defined-benefit plans. In them the employee typically receives a benefit equal to a given fraction of his average or final earnings for each year of service. Although the promised benefits are nominal, firms—especially in Canada—have typically granted ad hoc cost-of-living adjustments to the pensions of retired employees. Once made, these adjustments tend to be permanent. Thus the nominal value of the pension benefit is never reduced even if the fund performs poorly. This is, of course, what happens explicitly under the Rockefeller Foundation Plan, which functions as an ordinary defined-benefit plan during the preretirement period.

If the source of these adjustments is pension fund earnings in excess of the plan's valuation rate, and if there is no ceiling on the size of the benefit increases, then the plan member effectively owns a VA with a guaranteed nominal floor, or a VAF. Equivalently, he is provided with a traditional VA plus a put option on the nominal investment earnings of the pension assets with a striking price equal to the plan's valuation rate. *The plan's valuation rate becomes the equivalent of the valuation rate used to set the base payment in a standard VA.* If the nominal return on the pension fund is less than this valuation rate, then the nominal benefit is unchanged and the shortfall is absorbed fully by the plan sponsor.

Let A represent the initial amount in the fund, RV the valuation rate, and $\sigma(\tilde{R})$ the measure of the risk of the nominal return that is relevant to option pricing. The value (A_{VAF}) of the VAF is

(1) $$A_{VAF} = A + \text{put } [A, RV, \sigma(\tilde{R})].$$

For a given A, the value of the put option is an increasing function of both RV and $\sigma(\tilde{R})$. If the fund is invested exclusively in the risk-free nominal asset and thus earns the certain nominal return R_f, the value of the put option is zero as long as $RV \leq R_f$. On the other hand, the value of the put option *is* likely to be large if the nominal return on the pension assets is very uncertain, even if RV is well below the expected nominal return on these assets. If the objective of the plan sponsor were to minimize the value of the put option, he would wish to set a low RV and choose an asset base which would effectively make the VAF into a standard VA. If the sole objective of the employee were to maximize the value of the put option, he would—of course—prefer that the funds be invested in the riskiest asset, or common stocks. As the employee presumably cannot sell his VAF, he might nonetheless prefer that the fund not be invested in risky assets if he wishes the real retirement income provided by the VAF to be stable. This point is examined below.

Simulation results (1,000 trials) are presented in table 11.3 for VAFs tied both to bills and to the mixed portfolio described previously. The interest in bills reflects the fact that they represent the cornerstone of any low-risk stream of real annuity payments. Still-active workers may have enough flexibility to vary their consumption-saving and work-leisure decisions; thus they can assume considerable investment risk. This is less likely to be the case for retired workers. The interest in the mixed portfolio stems from the desire to monitor—in effect—the value of the put option when the uncertainty in the return on pension assets is increased. Because the value of this option depends on the nominal return on the pension fund, simulations are performed for both a low-inflation (3%) and a high-inflation (9%) scenario. The nominal return is equal to

Table 11.3   Variable Annuities with Guaranteed Nominal Floors

Portfolio	Expected Real Return[a] (%)	Standard Deviation (%)	Inflation Rate (%)	Annuity Valuation Rate (%)	Base Annuity Payment[b] ($)	Annuity Payment In Year 5			Annuity Payment in Year 10			Annuity Payment in Year 15		
						Median	Mean	S.D.	Median	Mean	S.D.	Median	Mean	S.D.
Bills	0	1.52	3	3	8,377	7,424 (7,219)	7,447 (7,223)	150 (245)	6,604 (6,203)	6,619 (6,222)	188 (302)	5,867 (5,357)	5,888 (5,375)	204 (313)
Bills	0	1.52	9	3	8,377	7,221 (7,221)	7,334 (7,224)	248 (248)	6,219 (6,219)	6,229 (6,229)	312 (312)	5,365 (5,365)	5,373 (5,373)	322 (322)
Mixed[c]	2.956	6.08	3	3	8,377	8,851 (8,366)	8,943 (8,448)	928 (1,180)	9,369 (8,459)	9,616 (8,595)	1,434 (1,687)	10,020 (8,512)	10,326 (8,724)	1,976 (2,139)
Mixed[c]	2.956	6.08	9	3	8,377	8,473 (8,407)	8,564 (8,489)	1,120 (1,176)	8,633 (8,461)	8,738 (8,577)	1,589 (1,655)	8,684 (8,406)	8,918 (8,671)	1,974 (2,047)
Mixed[c]	2.956	6.08	3	8	11,683	10,787 (9,192)	10,948 (9,289)	747 (1,225)	10,103 (7,326)	10,276 (7,446)	997 (1,407)	9,483 (5,773)	9,629 (5,922)	1,129 (1,339)
Mixed[c]	2.956	6.08	9	8	11,683	9,586 (9,226)	9,701 (9,276)	1,035 (1,263)	7,960 (7,219)	8,070 (7,380)	1,190 (1,390)	6,549 (5,708)	6,706 (5,879)	1,299 (1,370)

Note: Results in parentheses are those for a variable annuity without the nominal floor.

[a]Mean of the logarithm of the real annual wealth relative. The nominal return is the sum of the simulated real return plus the continuous time equivalent of the annual inflation rate noted in the table.

[b]Initial capital is $100,000, annual payments are made with certainty for 15 years, payments are in constant dollars.

[c]Same as in table 11.2.

the sum of the stochastic real return and the continuous time equivalent of these two inflation rates. Both low (3%) and high (8%) valuation rates are included in the simulations for the VAF tied to the mixed portfolio.

When the inflation rate is 3%, the expected real return of zero on the bills portfolio implies an expected nominal return of 3%. Because the valuation rate is also 3%, the floor frequently binds and thus the put option is frequently exercised. The result is that benefits have a higher median *and* a lower standard deviation than do those provided by the corresponding VA. When the inflation rate rises to 9%, the floor never binds and the result is identical to that for the VA. This result occurs because the combination of the high (expected) nominal return relative to the valuation rate and the low standard deviation of bill returns ensures that the realized nominal return always exceeds the valuation rate. Note also that the expected real return of zero together with the valuation rate of 3% causes the stream of real benefits to be tilted downward. This is most easily seen for the VA, but it occurs for the VAF as well.

When the inflation rate rises from 3% to 9%, the put option is occasionally exercised for the mixed portfolio. This is a direct result of its more uncertain return. When the valuation rate (again, the interest rate used to set the base payment) is raised for a standard VA, the sole effect is to tilt the real payments stream downward relative to what it would otherwise have been. When the valuation rate is raised for a VAF, it has the additional effect of raising the value of the put option. When the valuation rate is raised to 8%, which is typical of the rates now used to value defined-benefit plans in the United States, the striking price of the option rises accordingly. The result is a dramatic rise in the value of the put option in the low-inflation scenario. With an expected nominal return of $3 + 3 = 6\%$, the nominal return typically falls short of the valuation rate. By the fifteenth year, the median real benefit is 65% greater than that provided by the corresponding VA. In the high-inflation scenario, the effective value of the put option falls sharply as realized nominal returns fall short of the valuation rate with much lower frequency.

It is interesting to note that proponents of the Rockefeller Foundation Plan, which functions like a VAF, emphasize the importance of investing the pension fund reserve for retired employees exclusively in short-term commercial paper. If the nominal interest rate on short-term securities remains high relative to the plan's valuation rate of 3%, the value of the put option which distinguishes the VAF from a traditional VA will be very small. In effect, the Rockefeller Foundation Plan will have been transformed from a defined-benefit plan in the preretirement period to a defined-contribution plan at the date of retirement, with the plan's valuation rate of 3% used to capitalize the nominal benefits due at the date of the employee's retirement. If inflation were to recede and thus short-term interest rates to fall, the value of the put option would increase. Thus the annuitants stand to gain and the plan stands to lose from a reduction in the rate of inflation.

It is also interesting to note the continued emphasis in policy discussions in Canada on investing pension fund reserves held for retired employees exclusively in short-term securities if excess earnings are to be used to provide cost-of-living protection. Since the VAF is virtually identical to a VA when the value of the put option is small, the use of ad hoc adjustments may simply reflect the metamorphosis of defined-benefit into defined-contribution plans as the market response to increased inflation uncertainty (Pesando 1982). Because most large firms had already introduced defined-benefit plans, the use of VAFs—rendered virtually identical to VAs by the combination of low valuation rates and investments concentrated in short-term securities—may be the most convenient way to effect the metamorphosis.[15]

11.4   Variable Annuities with Nominal Floors and (Cumulative) Real Ceilings

In the preceding section, it was assumed that firms which provide ad hoc cost-of-living adjustments could be regarded as providing their employees with VAFs. Although this may well be true for some firms, the reality may also be more complicated. Firms which make ad hoc cost-of-living adjustments may impose a ceiling on such increases and may also bank underwriting losses (when the nominal floor binds) as a first claim on future excess earnings. In citing options for pension reform in Canada, the Task Force (1979) considered an excess interest scheme which contained a cumulative real ceiling. The real value of any enriched pension could not exceed its initial level, and any excess earnings above the amount necessary to preserve fully the real value of the pension would be banked against future investment shortfalls. In addition, any underwriting losses incurred by the plan sponsor by virtue of the guaranteed nominal floor would be banked, would accumulate at a market rate of interest, and would represent a prior claim on future excess earnings. Only after any accumulated losses borne by the plan sponsor were repaid would excess earnings be used to enrich pensions in pay. Significantly, this illustrative scheme was chosen for study after the federal government solicited input from both firms and members of the employee benefits industry.

The most important feature of a VAFC relative to a VAF is its banking provisions. (This is perhaps most easily seen by considering the case in which there is a real floor equal to the initial benefit. In this case, the annuity would be constant in real terms and the banking provisions would mirror the underwriting experience of a plan sponsor who provided a fully indexed pension and held assets other than index bonds in the pension fund.) Nonetheless, it is useful to consider the options inherent in a VAFC without reference to the banking provisions. By virtue of the ceiling on the real value of the pension benefit, the worker has—in effect—sold a call option on investment earnings in excess of those sufficient to provide full cost-of-living protection. Because the nominal return on the plan's assets is the real return plus the inflation rate, this is equivalent to the worker's having sold a call option on real investment earnings in excess of the valuation rate. Let A_{VAFC} represent the value of the variable annuity subject to both a floor and a ceiling; let $\sigma(\tilde{r})$ be the measure of risk of the real return that is relevant to option pricing, and let A_{VAF} and A be as defined in (1). Then

$$(2) \qquad A_{VAFC} = A + \text{put } [A, RV, \sigma(\tilde{R})] - \text{call } [A, RV, \sigma(\tilde{r})]$$
$$= A_{VAF} - \text{call } [A, RV, \sigma(\tilde{r})].$$

Unlike a VAF, whose value to the beneficiary is at least as great as that of a standard VA, the value of a VAFC may be greater or less than that of the corresponding VA, depending on the relative values of the put and the call. For a given A, the value of the call option is a decreasing function of the plan's valuation rate and an increasing function of the risk of the real return on the plan's assets. The value of the call option will be zero if the pension fund is invested exclusively in a risk-free real asset and if the risk-free real rate of return $r_f \leq RV$. As noted by Bodie (1980), there is no risk-free real asset. A pension fund invested exclusively in bills will, however, earn a real return which is quite stable and which has an expected value of (approximately) zero. The value of this call option will thus be close to zero if (1) the fund holds only bills or their equivalent and (2) the valuation rate is above, say, 3%.[16] In this case, the value of the VAFC will equal that of the VAF. If, in addition, the anticipated rate of inflation is sufficiently high that the nominal bill yield significantly exceeds RV, then the value of the put option contained in both the VAF and the VAFC will equal zero and thus both will be equal in value to the corresponding VA.

Consider first (table 11.4) the distribution of real benefits under a VAFC tied to a bills portfolio when the inflation rate is low. Because the projected stream of real annuity payments is tilted downward (since the expected real return of zero is less then the valuation rate), the ceiling binds rarely and only in the initial years of the annuity payout. Median benefits fall short of those provided by a VAF, primarily due to the banking provisions, but exceed those of a VA. In the high-inflation scenario, the VAFC provides benefits which simply reproduce those of a VA. This result, which was anticipated in the discussion of (2), may be empirically relevant. If so, this might explain the apparent lack of attention that is sometimes accorded to this issue. The Rockefeller Foundation plan, for example, makes no reference as to whether or not a ceiling exists

Table 11.4   Variable Annuities with Guaranteed Nominal Floors and Cumulative Real Ceilings

Portfolio	Expected Real Return[a] (%)	Standard Deviation (%)	Inflation Rate (%)	Annuity Valuation Rate (%)	Base Annuity Payment[b] ($)	Annuity Payment In Year 5			Annuity Payment in Year 10			Annuity Payment in Year 15		
						Median	Mean	S.D.	Median	Mean	S.D.	Median	Mean	S.D.
Bills	0	1.52	3	3	8,377	7,314 (7,219)	7,360 (7,223)	151 (245)	6,348 (6,203)	6,403 (6,222)	185 (302)	5,482 (5,357)	5,543 (5,375)	187 (313)
Bills	0	1.52	9	3	8,377	7,221 (7,221)	7,224 (7,224)	248 (248)	6,219 (6,219)	6,229 (6,229)	312 (312)	5,365 (5,365)	5,373 (5,373)	322 (322)
Mixed[c]	2.956	6.08	3	3	8,377	8,377 (8,366)	8,080 (8,448)	393 (1,180)	8,377 (8,459)	7,900 (8,595)	690 (1,687)	8,377 (8,512)	7,725 (8,724)	973 (2,139)
Mixed[c]	2.956	6.08	9	3	8,377	8,377 (8,400)	7,995 (8,489)	585 (1,176)	8,377 (8,461)	7,865 (8,577)	796 (1,655)	8,377 (8,406)	7,806 (8,671)	971 (2,049)
Mixed[c]	2.956	6.08	3	8	11,683	10,106 (9,182)	10,399 (9,289)	462 (1,226)	8,769 (7,366)	9,063 (7,446)	585 (1,407)	7,564 (5,773)	7,834 (5,922)	561 (1,339)
Mixed[c]	2.956	6.08	9	8	11,683	9,257 (9,226)	9,372 (9,276)	1,129 (1,263)	7,263 (7,219)	7,428 (7,380)	1,420 (1,390)	5,574 (5,708)	5,746 (5,879)	1,470 (1,370)

Note: Figures in parentheses are those for a variable annuity without the floor and ceiling.

[a]Mean of the logarithm of the real annual wealth relative. The nominal return is the sum of the simulated real return plus the continuous time equivalent of the annual inflation rate noted in the table.

[b]Initial capital is $100,000, annual payments are made with certainty for 15 years, payments are in constant dollars.

[c]Same as in table 11.2.

on the cost-of-living increases. Because the valuation rate of 3% exceeds the expected real return on a portfolio of short-term commercial paper (or its surrogate, the prime rate), the question of whether or not there is a ceiling may simply not be empirically relevant.

For the mixed portfolio with a valuation rate of 3%, there is no tilt to the projected stream of real benefits provided by the corresponding VA. For the VAFC, unlike the VAF, the benefit payments are similar in both the low- and the high-inflation scenarios. This is, of course, due to the banking provisions. For both scenarios, the ceiling binds frequently (i.e., the call option is exercised), as evidenced by the fact that median benefits remain at the ceiling in all years. Although we do not attempt to evaluate them explicitly, it would appear that the value of the sponsor's call option exceeds the value of the annuitant's put in these two cases. Note that the median and mean benefits are lower than those of the corresponding VA in all years. Furthermore, in contrast to both the VA and the VAF, the mean benefit for the VAFC is well below its own median, reflecting the reverse skewness induced by the truncation of the upper tail of the distribution. The dramatic decline in the standard deviation relative to both the VA and the VAF is also a result of this truncation and therefore reflects, not a reduction in risk from the annuitant's perspective, but the loss of upside potential. Further evidence that in these two cases the value of the VAFC is considerably less than that of the corresponding VA is provided by table 11.5, which shows the distribution of the real accumulation in the "bank" at the end of year 15. When this number turns out to be positive at the end of a simulation run, it means that the years of "excess" earnings from the portfolio were more than enough to compensate for the years of shortfall.

Raising the valuation rate, as noted in the discussion of (2), reduces the value of the call option. When the valuation rate is set at 8%, median benefits do exceed those provided by the VA for all years in the low-inflation scenario, although they remain less than those provided by the VAF. When inflation is high, and thus the permitted real erosion in the value of benefits is also high, the stream of payments provided by the VAFC and the VA are quite similar. The ceiling frequently binds, but the excess funds so banked are then used to enrich nominal benefits in subsequent years.

To sum up, three empirical results merit emphasis. First, if the pension fund is invested exclusively in bills, the VAFC will provide benefits similar to those provided by a standard VA if (1) the inflation rate is high relative to the plan's valuation rate and (2) the valuation rate is, say, 3% or more and thus significantly exceeds the expected real return on bills. In this case, the value of each of the put and the call options is approximately equal to zero. Second, when the expected real return on the plan's assets is equal to the valuation rate, the real benefits provided by a VAFC are

Table 11.5   Amount in "Bank" at End of Year 15 for VAFCs in Table 11.4

Portfolio	Expected Real Return (%)	Standard Deviation (%)	Inflation Rate (%)	RV (%)	Amount in Bank ($)				
					Median	Mean	Minimum	Maximum	Standard Deviation
Bills	0	1.52	3	3	−1,800	−2,209	−9,421	0	1,787
Bills	0	1.52	9	3	0	0	0	0	0
Mixed	2.956	6.08	3	3	2,591	10,024	−23,458	122,557	16,933
Mixed	2.956	6.08	9	3	3,381	10,898	1,408	127,940	15,459
Mixed	2.956	6.08	3	8	−23,836	−24,112	−61,225	17,841	12,835
Mixed	2.956	6.08	9	8	−63	−770	−13,194	2,988	1,649

likely to be far more stable than those provided by either a VAF or the traditional VA. This result, in essence, reflects the procedure for banking the gains or losses experienced by the plan sponsor. Third, by choosing appropriate combinations of RV and asset allocations, it would appear possible to cancel the values of the put and the call (without setting each equal to zero) and to create a number of VAFCs all having a value equal to A. But the sponsor and annuitant would have to agree on the port-folio's composition, and there would have to be some mechanism for monitoring adherence to it.

As noted, our interest in the VAFC is motivated by the possibility that it may formalize the behavior of at least some firms which make ad hoc cost-of-living adjustments. If so, and if the stream of real payments is smoothed relative to those obtainable from, say, a bills-based VA, then firms must be compensated for their underwriting the attendant invest-ment risk. In principle, this should be reflected in compensating wage differentials. Because the VAFC does not alter the efficient frontier, it will be the basic risk-return trade-offs available in the capital market which dictate the size of these compensating wage differentials.

11.5 Alternative Annuity Designs: Historical Simulations for the Period 1971–80

Historical simulations of the nominal and real benefits provided by VAs, VAFs, and VAFCs for the period 1971–80 are presented in table 11.6 parts A–D. As in table 11.1, the initial capital in 1971 is $100,000 and the payments are made with certainty for 10 years. Of course, VAFs and VAFCs must be underwritten by the plan sponsor (or life insurance company) and their cost may exceed or fall short of the initial capital.[17] Two valuation rates, 0% and 5%, are used in the simulations. The former is the expected real return on the minimum variance portfolio (i.e., bills) while the latter is typical of the rates actually used in the early 1970s to value defined-benefit plans.

Consider first the bill results. When the valuation rate is zero, the real benefit provided by the VA declines from $10,100 in 1971 to $8,794 in 1980—that is, by 13%. This erosion is only modest in view of the substan-tial unanticipated inflation that appears to have occurred in the 1970s. Because the floor never binds, the VAF produces benefits identical to those produced by the VA. Because the ceiling binds in 1971 and 1972, thus causing excess earnings to be banked for future use, the real benefits provided by the VAFC diverge from those provided by the VA and VAF. With a valuation rate of 5%, the floor binds twice (1971 and 1972) so that the final benefit provided by the VAF exceeds that provided by the VA. Because of the banking feature, which requires that the plan sponsor be compensated for prior underwriting losses, the stream of benefits provided by the VAFC differs from that provided by the VA.

The sharpest contrast among the alternative annuity designs occurs with the riskiest asset base, which is common stocks. Consider only the results when the valuation rate equals 5%. Although this rate is less than the expected real rate of return on common stocks, the real benefits provided by the VA, in fact, decline sharply. This result simply reflects the poor performance of the stock market during the decade. The value of the nominal floor (i.e., the put option) is high as evidenced by the fact that the real benefit provided by the VAF in 1980 is almost twice that provided by the VA. The tendency for the VAFC to stabilize the real stream of benefit payments is readily apparent. In 1973 and 1974, for example, annuitants are partially insulated from the precipitous declines in the stock market. When the stock market recovers in 1975, however, real benefits continue to decline as excess fund earnings are first used to repay the plan sponsors for the net underwriting losses they incurred in the previous years.

The final comparison is between the bond portfolio and the mixed portfolio with the identical expected return. Because of the very adverse performance of the bond market, the real benefit by 1980 is much higher for the VA when it is tied to the mixed portfolio. This ex post result is consistent with the greater ex ante risk of the bond portfolio. The comparisons of the results for the VAs, VAFs, and VAFCs are quite straightforward, and only the continuing tendency for real benefits to be stabilized under the VAFC merits note.

11.6 Summary and Conclusion

Nominal annuities, whether level payment or graduated, expose the annuitant to substantial uncertainty about the real value of his retirement income. This is because he is uncertain of the future level of prices and hence of the future rate of inflation. Standard VAs backed by Treasury bills or their equivalent provide much more stable real retirement incomes, even when consideration is given to the serial correlation in real bill returns. VAs backed by common stocks, long-term government bonds, and a mixed portfolio illustrate the risk-return trade-offs inherent in the alternative portfolios. These should be of interest to plan sponsors who may wish, without increasing their own costs, to provide increased annuity choices to plan members.[18]

The cost of a VAF, which is a VA with a nominal floor, is not known with certainty on the date the annuity is purchased and must be underwritten by a plan sponsor or life company. The plan provided by the Rockefeller Foundation functions, in effect, like a VAF. If the objective

Table 11.6   **Alternative Annuity Designs**

Year	Infla-tion Rate (%)[a]	Nominal Return	Variable Annuity[b] RV=0 Nominal	RV=0 Real	RV=5 Nominal	RV=5 Real	Variable Annuity with Nominal Floor RV=0 Nominal	RV=0 Real	RV=5 Nominal	RV=5 Real	Variable Annuity with Nominal Floor, Real Ceiling RV=0 Nominal	RV=0 Real	RV=5 Nominal	RV=5 Real
A. Simulations for a bills-only portfolio, 1971–80														
1971	3.36	4.39	10,439	10,100	12,876	12,457	10,439	10,100	12,950	12,529	10,336	10,000	12,950	12,529
1972	3.41	3.84	10,840	10,142	12,733	11,913	10,840	10,142	12,950	12,116	10,688	10,000	12,950	12,116
1973	8.80	6.93	11,591	9,967	12,968	11,151	11,591	9,967	13,189	11,341	11,626	9,997	12,950	11,136
1974	12.20	8.00	12,518	9,594	13,337	10,222	12,518	9,594	13,565	10,396	12,556	9,623	13,284	10,181
1975	7.01	5.80	13,245	9,486	13,439	9,625	13,244	9,486	13,669	9,790	13,284	9,514	13,385	9,586
1976	4.81	5.08	13,917	9,510	13,449	9,190	13,917	9,510	13,679	9,347	13,959	9,539	13,396	9,154
1977	6.77	5.12	14,629	9,363	13,465	8,618	14,629	9,363	13,695	8,765	14,673	9,391	13,411	8,583
1978	9.03	7.03	15,657	9,191	13,726	8,057	15,657	9,191	13,959	8,194	15,705	9,219	13,670	8,024
1979	13.31	10.38	17,284	8,954	14,429	7,475	17,284	8,954	14,675	7,602	17,335	8,980	14,371	7,445
1980	12.41	10.40	19,082	8,794	15,170	6,991	19,082	8,794	15,429	7,111	19,138	8,820	15,110	6,964
B. Simulations for a stocks-only portfolio, 1971–80														
1971	3.36	14.31	11,431	11,059	14,098	13,640	11,431	11,059	14,099	13,641	10,336	10,000	13,386	12,950
1972	3.41	18.98	13,601	12,725	15,976	14,947	13,601	12,725	15,976	14,947	10,688	10,000	13,842	12,950
1973	8.80	−14.66	11,607	9,981	12,985	11,166	13,601	11,696	15,976	13,738	11,629	10,000	13,842	11,903
1974	12.20	−26.48	8,533	6,540	9,092	6,968	13,601	10,424	15,976	12,244	11,629	8,913	13,842	10,609
1975	7.01	37.20	11,708	8,385	11,879	8,508	18,660	13,364	20,875	14,951	11,629	8,329	13,842	9,914
1976	4.81	23.84	14,499	9,908	14,012	9,575	23,109	15,791	24,621	16,824	14,359	9,812	13,842	9,459
1977	6.77	−7.18	13,458	8,613	12,386	7,927	23,109	14,790	24,621	15,758	14,359	9,188	13,842	8,859
1978	9.03	6.39	14,318	8,405	12,550	7,367	24,585	14,431	24,947	14,644	14,359	8,429	13,842	8,125
1979	13.31	18.44	16,958	8,785	14,157	7,334	29,119	15,085	28,140	14,578	16,039	8,309	13,842	7,171
1980	12.41	32.01	22,386	10,317	17,797	8,202	38,440	17,715	35,378	16,304	21,173	9,578	13,842	6,379

C. Simulations for a U.S.-bonds-only portfolio, 1971–80

Year		RV												
1971	3.36	13.23	11,322	10,954	13,966	13,512	11,323	10,955	13,966	13,512	10,336	10,000	13,386	12,950
1972	3.41	5.68	11,966	11,195	14,056	13,151	11,966	11,195	14,056	13,151	10,688	10,000	13,842	12,950
1973	8.80	−1.11	11,834	10,176	13,239	11,384	11,966	10,290	14,056	12,087	11,629	10,000	13,842	11,903
1974	12.20	4.35	12,348	9,464	13,156	10,083	12,487	9,570	14,056	10,773	12,721	9,750	13,842	10,609
1975	7.01	9.19	13,484	9,657	13,680	9,798	13,634	9,765	14,617	10,469	13,890	9,948	13,842	9,914
1976	4.81	16.75	15,742	10,757	15,212	10,395	15,918	10,877	16,253	11,106	14,634	10,000	15,041	10,278
1977	6.77	−0.67	15,636	10,007	14,391	9,210	15,918	10,188	16,253	10,402	15,625	10,000	15,041	9,626
1978	9.03	1.03	15,797	9,273	13,847	8,128	16,082	9,440	16,253	9,541	16,965	9,959	15,041	8,829
1979	13.31	−1.22	15,605	8,084	13,026	6,748	16,082	8,331	16,253	8,420	16,965	8,789	15,041	7,792
1980	12.41	−4.45	14,911	6,872	11,854	5,463	16,082	7,412	16,253	7,490	16,965	7,818	15,041	6,932

D. Simulations for a U.S. mixed portfolio,ᶜ 1971–80

Year		RV												
1971	3.36	10.89	11,089	10,729	13,678	13,233	11,089	10,729	13,677	13,232	10,336	10,000	13,386	12,950
1972	3.41	7.70	11,943	11,174	14,030	13,126	11,943	11,174	14,029	13,125	10,688	10,000	13,842	12,950
1973	8.80	−1.40	11,777	10,127	13,175	11,329	11,943	10,270	14,029	12,064	11,629	10,000	13,842	11,903
1974	12.20	−0.52	11,716	8,979	12,483	9,567	11,943	9,153	14,029	10,752	12,027	9,218	13,842	10,609
1975	7.01	13.59	13,308	9,531	13,503	9,671	13,567	9,717	15,177	10,870	13,661	9,784	13,842	9,914
1976	4.81	14.75	15,271	10,435	14,758	10,085	15,568	10,638	16,587	11,334	14,634	10,000	14,234	9,727
1977	6.77	−0.25	15,233	9,749	14,020	8,973	15,568	9,964	16,587	10,616	15,625	10,000	14,234	9,110
1978	9.03	3.79	15,809	9,280	13,857	8,134	16,157	9,484	16,587	9,737	16,592	9,740	14,234	8,355
1979	13.31	5.89	16,742	8,673	13,975	7,240	17,109	8,863	16,727	8,665	17,570	9,102	14,234	7,374
1980	12.41	6.82	17,882	8,241	14,217	6,552	18,276	8,423	17,017	7,842	18,768	8,649	14,234	6,560

ᵃBased on the consumer price index. Inflation and security return data are from Ibbotson and Sinquefeld, *Stocks, Bonds, Bills and Inflation* (Financial Analysts Research Foundation, 1977), updated by the authors.

ᵇThe initial capital is $100,000; the annuity is payable with certainty for 10 years; annuity payments are made at the end of the year; *RV* is the interest rate used to determine the initial level of the projected stream of annuity payments.

ᶜMixed portfolio consists of bonds (52%), bills (29%), and stocks (19%).

is to provide a stable stream of real benefits, then a VAF must also be linked to a bills portfolio. When nominal interest rates are high and the valuation rate is low, this VAF will produce results virtually identical to those of a bills-based VA. This is the case for the Rockefeller Foundation Plan. In effect, the Rockefeller Foundation Plan functions as a defined-benefit plan in the preretirement period and becomes a defined-contribution plan at the date of the employee's retirement. This metamorphosis of defined-benefit plans into defined-contribution plans appears to have occurred extensively in Canada and may represent a market response to increased inflation uncertainty.

Because the ad hoc adjustments made by firms are never (to our knowledge) more than those necessary to offset fully the impact of inflation, it is likely that the behavior of many firms is more complicated than that suggested by the VAF. We therefore analyze a VA subject to a nominal floor and a real ceiling, in which underwriting losses and gains by the plan sponsor are banked from one period to the next. Under stylized conditions which might well be met in practice, a VAFC tied to bills would closely replicate the benefits provided by a bills-based VA. More generally, due to the interaction of the floor and ceiling with the banking provisions, it is possible for a VAFC to provide substantially more stable real benefits than a VA tied to the same asset base. Because the risk-return trade-offs available in the capital market have not changed, sponsoring firms in these cases would presumably extract compensating wage differentials from their employees *if* mean benefits were unaffected. As noted in the text, however, mean benefits will be reduced if the implicit call option (pertaining to the real ceiling) proves to be more valuable than the implicit put option (pertaining to the nominal floor).

Appendix: Description of Alternative Annuity Designs

Notation

R_t = nominal rate of return earned on the fund in year t.

RV = interest rate used to determine the base value of the annuity payment; also called the annuity valuation rate or valuation rate.

r_t = real rate of return earned on the fund in year t.

B_t = nominal benefit payment received at the end of year t.

B_0 = base value of the benefit, i.e., the value of B_1 if $R_1 = RV$.

b_t = real benefit received at the end of year t.

A_t = nominal value of the amount left in the fund at the end of year t after B_t is paid out.

P_t = Consumer price level at the end of year t with P_0 set equal to one.
T = Number of years the annuity lasts.

Terms of the Annuities

For all annuities the base value of the annuity payment is determined by

$$B_0 = \begin{cases} A_0/T & \text{if } RV = 0, \\ A_0 RV \left[1 - (1 + RV)^{-T}\right]^{-1} & \text{if } RV > 0. \end{cases}$$

We assume that benefit payments start at the *end* of the first year, so B_0 is not actually paid out but rather serves as the base value for computing the first year's benefit, B_1.

For the *standard variable annuity* the nominal benefit is

$$B_t = B_{t-1}\frac{(1 + R_t)}{(1 + RV)}$$

and the real benefit is

$$b_t = b_{t-1}\frac{(1 + r_t)}{(1 + RV)}$$

or

$$b_t = B_t/P_t.$$

For a *nominal annuity* R_t is nonstochastic, so

$$B_t = B_{t-1}\frac{(1 + R)}{(1 + RV)}$$

and the rate of graduation in the nominal benefit payments is

$$\frac{(1 + R)}{(1 + RV)} - 1.$$

Note that if $RV = R$, we have the conventional level-payment nominal annuity.

For a *purchasing power annuity*, r_t is nonstochastic, so

$$b_t = b_{t-1}\frac{(1 + r)}{(1 + RV)}$$

and the rate of graduation in the real benefit stream is

$$\frac{(1 + r)}{(1 + RV)} - 1.$$

For the *VAF*, the variable annuity with a nominal floor, the nominal benefit is given by

$$B_t = \begin{cases} B_{t-1}\dfrac{(1 + R_t)}{(1 + RV)} & \text{if } R_t > RV, \\[2mm] B_{t-1} & \text{if } R_t \le RV, \end{cases}$$

and the real benefit by

$$b_t = B_t/P_t.$$

The *VAFC*, the variable annuity with a nominal floor and real ceiling, is complicated. The benefit calculation follows an iterative procedure that can be seen by a simple flowchart (fig. 11.A.1).

To create an algebraic flowchart, we need some additional notation:

K_t = amount of money in the "bank"; $K_0 = 0$.
X_t = amount of money available to increase the benefit stream.

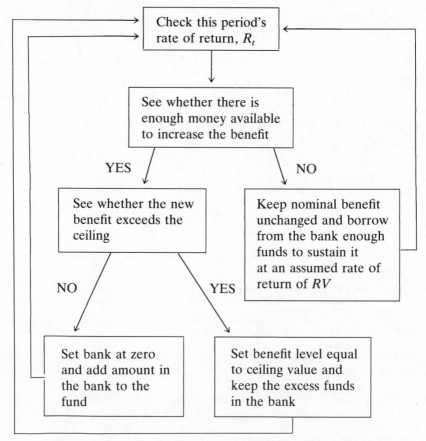

Fig. 11.A.1   Flowchart showing the iterative procedure for calculating benefit stream for a VAFC.

F_t = present value of a \$1 annuity due for $T - t + 1$ years at an interest rate of RV.

$\hat{B}_t$ = benefit which would be payable in the absence of the real ceiling. The benefit calculation follows the following iterative procedure (fig. 11.A.2).

In the unnumbered table below we demonstrate how the procedure works for the VAFC based on the stocks only portfolio reported in table

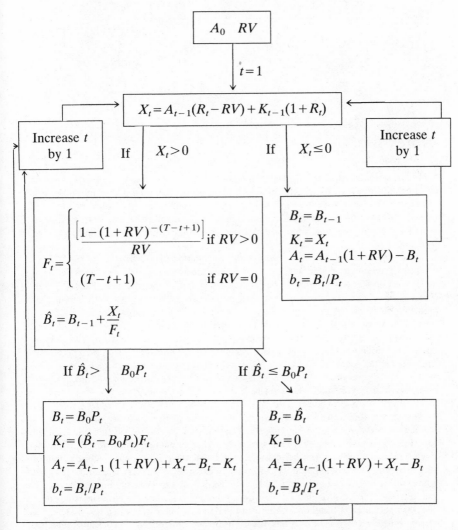

Fig. 11.A.2   Algebraic flowchart showing the iterative procedure for calculating benefit stream for a VAFC.

11.5. In this example, $A_0 = \$100,000$ and $RV = .05$. We present the calculation for the first three years only.

	t	R_t	P_t	X_t	F_t	$\hat{B}_t$
	0	.05	1.0000	...	...	...
1971	1	.1431	1.0336	9,310	8.1078	14,099
1972	2	.1898	1.0688	20,180	7.4632	16,090
1973	3	−.1466	1.1629	−3,274	6.7864	...

	$B_0 P_t$	B_t	K_t	A_t	b_t
	...	12,950	0	100,000	12,950
1971	13,386	13,386	5,781	95,142	12,950
1972	13,842	13,842	16,774	89,464	12,950
1973	...	13,842	−3,274	80,095	11,903

Notes

1. For simplicity, the discussion proceeds as if the retiring plan member's sole source of wealth is his claim to a private pension. If he has other sources of wealth, then the risk-return characteristics of his pension benefit must be analyzed in the context of his total portfolio. See M. Feldstein and L. Summers's chapters in this volume for a discussion of the extent to which households may be able to diversify away the inflation risk implicit in nominal pension benefits.

2. A separate provision in the Rockefeller Foundation Plan provides that the cost-of-living adjustment equal at least 4% if the inflation rate as measured by the consumer price index exceeds 4%. Otherwise, however, the floor is that cited in the text (Heaton 1980). There is no reference to a ceiling on the size of the cost-of-living adjustments. Subsequent discussion of the Rockefeller plan ignores the separate floor provision.

3. TIAA, which manages one of the largest pension plans in the United States, offers its members two annuity designs that resemble VAs containing a nominal floor. The older of these, the traditional TIAA annuity, has a guaranteed minimum nominal floor. This floor is embodied in the guaranteed return of 3%. Unlike the Rockefeller plan (which is characteristic of the hybrid annuities examined at length in the text), this nominal floor does not ratchet upward over time. The asset base in the TIAA annuity consists of a portfolio dominated by long-term bonds, mortgages, and other fixed-interest loans. TIAA pays to its beneficiaries a variable benefit which has been smoothed relative to what it would be under a standard VA design by ignoring unrealized capital gains and losses on these dollar-fixed investments. One consequence of this smoothing is that the guaranteed rate cited previously is far less likely to bind. Another consequence is that there can be cross-subsidization of different generations of annuitants. Currently, for example, TIAA is paying a total nominal rate of return of 11% to new retirees, while the risk-free nominal rate of return in the capital markets is well in excess of that. The interest rate used to determine the initial benefit (called the Assumed Interest Rate, or AIR) is also equal to 11%, so the expected nominal benefit stream is level. Recently, TIAA has offered its members an alternative design (called the Graded Benefit Payment Method), which differs in two respects from the older one. First, the expected nominal benefit stream has been given an upward tilt by using an AIR of 4% to

determine the initial benefit level. Second, the guaranteed nominal floor ratchets upward whenever the interest rate declared in each period actually exceeds 4%. Earnings above 4% are credited at the end of the year and—in effect—are used to purchase an additional TIAA annuity with its own guarantees and dividends. (The interest rate used in calculating the increase in the nominal floor is the guaranteed rate of 3%.) It is worth noting that TIAA has been shortening the average maturity of its portfolio in recent years. If this process were to continue, the TIAA graded-payment annuity would come to look more like the Rockefeller plan annuity.

4. Ontario's Select Committee on Pensions (1981) has recommended that the use of excess investment earnings to provide inflation protection be mandated by law. No reference is made to floors and/or ceilings in the proposed scheme, which the analysis in this chapter shows to be of crucial importance.

5. For the purposes at hand, there is no advantage in explicitly incorporating mortality factors into the analysis. Mortality is thus ignored in all of the illustrations presented in this chapter.

6. More precisely, each year's real benefit would be equal to the previous year's benefit divided by 1.05.

7. In fact, real equity returns appear to be negatively correlated with unanticipated inflation, as noted by Bodie (1976) and Pesando and Rea (1977).

8. The mixed portfolio consists of 52% bonds, 29% bills, and 19% stocks. We do not refer to this as an efficient portfolio for two reasons. First, our portfolio proportions are derived from a single-period variance-minimization procedure which ignores the serial correlation in bill returns. Second, the efficiency of an annuity for a particular household can only be determined if we know all of the household's other assets and liabilities.

9. As noted by Bodie (1982), the mean realized real return on bonds is negative during this period. The mean real return on bonds was set equal to an annual rate of 3%, whose continuous time equivalent is 2.956%, while the other parameters were based on the observed means, variances, and covariances.

10. First-order autoregressions were performed for the logarithms of the real annual wealth relatives of bills, bonds, and stocks. The results are as follows:

Bills: $r_t = -.044 + .768\, r_{t-1}$, $R^2 = .559$, SEE $= 1.04$ (% per year);
   (.205)   (.136)

Bonds: $r_t = -1.619 + .261\, r_{t-1}$, $R^2 = .056$, SEE $= 7.64$;
   (1.493)   (.207)

Stocks: $r_t = 5.847 - .021\, r_{t-1}$, $R^2 = .0004$, SEE $= 19.28$.
   (3.849)   (.201)

Standard errors are in parentheses.

11. The real benefit in year t is given by $b_t = B_0 \, \Pi_{i=1}^{t}[e^{\tilde{r}_i}/(1+RV)]$, where B_0 is the initial projected annuity payment, $\tilde{r}_i$ is the realization of the stochastic logarithmic real return in year i, and RV is the annuity valuation rate. Since b_t is the product of lognormal variates, it is also lognormally distributed: $\log(b_t) = \log(B_0) + \Sigma_{i=1}^{t}\, \tilde{r}_i - t \log(1+RV)$. Because we have chosen RV such that $E(r_i) = \log(1+RV)$, the median value of b_t equals B_0 for all t. By contrast, the mean value of $b_t = B_0 e^{\frac{1}{2}\sigma_t^2}$ where σ_t^2 equals the variance of $\Sigma_{i=1}^{t}\, \tilde{r}_i$. If there is no serial correlation in the $\tilde{r}_i$ series, $\sigma_t^2 = t\sigma^2$ where σ^2 is the variance of r_i in a single year.

Rea (1981) also discusses the design of a variable annuity which produces a payments stream which is expected to remain constant in real terms.

12. The first-order annual autoregression, based on the consumer price index, is

$\pi_t = .794 + .902\, \pi_{t-1}$, $R^2 = .750$, SEE $= 2.003$ (% per year),
   (.597) (.117)

where $\pi_t = \log(P_t/P_{t-1})$ and P_t is the price level at time t.

13. Assume π_t follows the first-order autoregressive process, $\pi_t = \alpha + \rho\pi_{t-1} + \epsilon_t$, where ϵ_t is distributed $N(0, \sigma)$. Then $\pi^* = \alpha/(1 - \rho)$ is the steady-state rate of inflation. Note that $\log(P_t) = \log(P_0) + \Sigma_{i=1}^{t}\tilde{\pi}_t$ where $\tilde{\pi}_t$ is the realization of the inflation process. Let $P_0 = 1$ and let $\pi_0 = \pi^*$. Then median of $\log(P_t) = t\pi^*$; median of $P_t = e^{t\pi^*}$; and variance of

$$\log(P_t) = \sigma_t^2 = \frac{\sigma^2}{(1-\rho)^2}\left\{t - \rho\frac{(1-\rho^t)}{(1-\rho)}\left[2 - \rho\frac{1-\rho^t}{(1+\rho)}\right]\right\}.$$

If B_t is the known nominal benefit in period t, then the real benefit $b_t = B_t/P_t$. Thus $\log(b_t) = \log(B_t) - \log(P_t)$. Let $B_t = B_0e^{gt}$, where g is the rate of graduation, and let $\mu_t = (g - \pi^*)t$. Median $b_t = B_t \div$ median $P_t = B_0e^{\mu_t}$. Since B_t is graduated so as to increase at the anticipated inflation rate, $\mu_t = 0$ and median $b_t = B_0$. Since B_t is nonstochastic, variance of $\log(b_t)$ = variance of $\log(P_t) = \sigma_t^2$. Mean $b_t = B_0e^{\frac{1}{2}\sigma_t^2}$ and the variance of $b_t = B_0^2e^{\sigma_t^2}(e^{\sigma_t^2} - 1)$.

14. The continuously compounded nominal interest rate (R) is thus equivalent to an annual rate of 11%, since the (annual) steady-state rate of inflation built into the illustration is 8%.

15. *If* there were no nominal floor on the pension benefits, any decision to channel pension fund reserves exclusively into bills or their equivalent would have an unambiguous interpretation. Workers, who presumably cannot diversify away the inflation risk inherent in nominal pension benefits, are sufficiently risk averse that they will pay the price (i.e., a low expected real return on their pension wealth) of stabilizing their real retirement incomes.

16. Remember that the standard deviation of the continuously compounded real bill return is only 1.52% per annum, so that the expected real return of zero is about two standard deviations less than 3%.

17. The plan sponsor could underwrite VAFs or VAFCs on either a pay-as-you-go or a fully funded basis. This issue is not explored in this chapter.

18. If the sponsor provides a defined-benefit plan, the lump sum necessary to purchase the requisite annuity could be made available to the employee, who could then choose his preferred VA. If the promised pension is purely nominal (and the firm has no tradition of providing ad hoc adjustments), then discounting the promised payments by the risk-free nominal rate R (as well as by mortality) would identify the lump sum to be offered to the employee.

Comment   Franco Modigliani

Among all the institutions in the financial sphere of the economy, probably none is more seriously affected by inflation than private pensions. This impact does not merely reflect the redistribution from creditors to debtors that is generally supposed to accompany inflation. Indeed, redistribution need not occur at all to the extent that inflation is fully anticipated and is accompanied by an offsetting rise in nominal rates. But the pension contract, just like the fully amortized mortgage, stands to be drastically distorted by inflation even if it is largely or fully anticipated, because both contracts were designed in nominal terms for a world of stable prices.

Franco Modigliani is Institute Professor, Massachusetts Institute of Technology.

The typical defined-benefit pension plan was designed to provide the pensioner with a level fixed *real* payment, equal to some fraction of his pay in the neighborhood of his retirement date, reflecting the number of years of service. In the absence of inflation, that intended goal is achieved by awarding to the annuitant a fixed nominal pension, at the appropriate level, for the rest of his life.

But in the presence of inflation this arrangement turns out to produce results which are quite different and less favorable from the point of view of the beneficiary than the intended ones, in three distinct ways: (1) though the stream of benefits starts at the intended level, its purchasing power will thereafter be reduced by the rise in the price level caused by inflation—the higher the inflation over the retirement period, the smaller the aggregate real value of benefits received by the pensioner; (2) the existence of inflation means that the real income stream from the pension received by the annuitant continuously decreases in time, and the beneficiary gets poorer at a rate which is faster the larger the rate of inflation, whether inflation is anticipated or not; and (3) if, as is usually the case, there is uncertainty about the future path of inflation, then the path of real benefits is not only lowered and tilted down, but also becomes uncertain.

Consequence 1 seems to have largely escaped notice, in part perhaps because it would not be expected to arise for a defined-contribution plan. As for the remaining two, it is sometimes suggested that a rational and prudent beneficiary could readily avoid them by saving a portion of his annuity in the early part of his retirement and thus accumulating reserves to be used to support consumption above the annuity in the later part of his life. But this suggestion clearly has very little merit. Given the uncertainty about the future inflation, it would be difficult for the pensioner to make adequate reserves for the future. Furthermore, even if he did know the future inflation, he would still not know the time of his death and therefore the appropriate amount of reserves to make. To put it another way, any reserves he might accumulate would not benefit from the insurance against the risk of life which is an essential feature of a life annuity.

These three problems, particularly problems 2 and 3, could be effectively and easily handled if there existed in the market "indexed" instruments which offered the lender a constant "real rate" over the life of the loan, e.g., by paying a fixed rate on a principal whose nominal value was periodically revalued so as to maintain a constant purchasing power, or, equivalently, by promising a floating nominal rate equal to a constant (the real rate) plus the rate of inflation. Such instruments would enable the pension fund, by investing in them in appropriate amounts and maturities, to provide the annuitant with an indexed nominal annuity which would guarantee a constant real level of benefits based on the fixed real rate promised by the indexed instrument.

Of course that real rate would, presumably, be lower than the going nominal rate for corresponding maturities, to an extent reflecting anticipated inflation over the life of the instruments. This means that to provide a benefit rate at the same initial level as without inflation would require an accumulation higher than that needed at present on the basis of inflation-swollen nominal rates—though presumably no higher than would have been called for in the absence of inflation.

This simple solution is, unfortunately, not available at present since indexed bonds, or similar indexed instruments, cannot be purchased in the market, nor are they likely to be readily available in the foreseeable future. The chapter by Bodie and Pesando makes a valuable contribution by describing and testing a number of alternative arrangements which, even in the absence of indexed assets, could ensure the annuitant an outcome similar to that which would have occurred with stable prices—a constant level payment in real terms through his life. Ideally the result should be achieved with no, or little, change in the magnitude and nature of the risk borne by the provider of the annuity.

Bodie and Pesando focus on a number of solutions, most of which are variants of one basic design—a design which also provided the basis for proposed solutions to the mortgage problem, as set out in the M.I.T. study, "New Mortgage Designs for Stable Housing in an Inflationary Environment."

Focusing for simplicity of exposition on the case in which the annuitant receives an annuity certain of, say, t years, as the authors themselves do, this basic design can be summarized as follows. First, the nominal annuity is recomputed at regular prearranged intervals, say yearly, by applying to the annuitant's endowment remaining at the beginning of the period, the standard annuity formula, for a number of years equal to the remaining life of the annuity, and using a fixed, agreed interest rate (which the authors call the valuation rate, RV). Second, the endowment remaining to the annuitant at any point is invested in some stated instrument, for example, T-bills or long-term bonds or corporate equities, and so on. Third, the endowment remaining at the beginning of any period is computed by taking the endowment of the previous period, crediting to the annuitant the return from the investment in the chosen asset, and subtracting the annuity paid in that period. In the case of a *life* annuity, the procedure would be essentially the same except that in the first step one would rely on the life annuity formula with an interest rate RV.

It is clear that under this plan the annuity actually received by the beneficiary in nominal terms (or, for that matter, in real terms) will vary from period to period—hence the name of "variable annuity," or VA. But it can be shown that the real path of the annuity, over the life of the contract, satisfies one basic recursive relation. This relation, which can be deduced from a formula presented in the appendix to the chapter, can be stated as follows: the real annuity (at the end) of year t is equal to that of the year $t-1$ multiplied by the factor $(1 + i_t - p_t)/(1 + RV)$, where i_t is the nominal rate of return on the chosen investment and p_t is the rate of inflation in year t.

To see the implications of this type of arrangement, suppose first there existed some instrument whose nominal return could be counted on to be always equal to a constant plus the rate of inflation—or equivalently, whose real return was a constant. It is apparent that, by choosing that instrument as the investment vehicle and by choosing for RV the constant real rate, one would be able to guarantee the beneficiary an annuity which would remain constant in real terms at the initial level throughout the duration of the contract—that is, in effect, a fully indexed pension.

Suppose next the endowment were invested in an instrument whose real return in each period was uncertain but which fluctuated around a known expected value. If RV is set equal to this expected return, the result is a variable annuity, which, in real terms, would tend to fluctuate around the initial level, with a variability around that value depending both on the variability and the serial correlation of the real return on the instrument. If, on the other hand, RV was chosen to *exceed* the expected real return, then the annual payment could be expected to fluctuate around a path declining at a rate equal to the difference between RV and the expected real return. Conversely, the choice of RV *below* the expected real return would lead to a path of expected payments rising in time.

Thus, by relying on different possible assets as the investment vehicle and by appropriate choice of RV, one can construct a whole family of variable annuities differing from each other in terms of the expected real average outcome, in terms of the variability of possible outcomes around that level, and in terms of tilt of the real payment path. From finance theory and empirical evidence, one would generally expect that instruments offering a higher expected return, and thus promising a higher expected average level, would also be characterized by greater variability of the outcome path and also greater uncertainty of the average outcome over finite periods. These inferences are supported by the results reported by Bodie and Pesando for a variety of alternative investment vehicles.

It is widely supposed that very short-term loans of high quality, such as short-term Treasury bills, tend to yield fairly stable real returns, year after year, more stable than any other standard instrument. This view receives striking confirmation in Bodie and Pesando's tests. The results reported in table 11.2 suggest that a VA based on the one-month Treasury bill could be expected to provide a remarkably stable annual real payment. Relying on the parameters of the observed distribution of returns in the period 1953–80, the authors find that the standard deviation of the annual payment is but 5% of the mean after 5 years and remains below 15% even after 15 years. Equally impressive are the results of table 11.5, which reports the annual payments that would actually have been realized for the 10-year period from 1971 to 1980. Even in this troubled period the largest deviation from the starting level is just about 10%.

Unfortunately this highly desirable stability obtained with the Treasury bill as the investment vehicle is acquired at the cost of an extremely low real return which, for the period 1953–80, is actually estimated at zero. For the more recent period 1971–80 the real return is even negative in most years and on the average for the period as a whole, and as a result the real annuity drifts down, even though RV is taken as zero.

The authors have tested several other investment vehicles and notably bonds, stocks and a mixed portfolio consisting of bonds, stocks, and bills designed to minimize variance for the given mean. Relying on the 1953–80 experience, these other instruments imply considerably higher initial and expected average annual payments, but at a cost of an impressively larger variability of outcomes. In the case of common stock for instance, the expected annual payment is 70% larger than in the case of Treasury bills, but the standard deviation goes up by 15 times! Even with the minimum risk portfolio, the level of expected return goes up by but a quarter, while the standard deviation increases by a factor of 200%–300%.

As shown in table 11.5, the relative attractiveness of these alternative instruments would have been even lower during the seventies, because the average return was in all cases substantially below the historical performance, used in table 11.2. Indeed, the average return was lower than that of T-bills, the only exception being stocks, where the difference was not very large. Thus, in addition to the great variability of annual returns exhibited by these types of VAs, the annuitant would have suffered from a markedly declining overall trend if RV had been chosen at a level around the historical return of each asset. In the case of common stock, for instance, it can be seen from the simulation of table 11.5 that even using an RV of 5%, somewhat below the historical average of 7%, the annual payment tends to fall by around 40% of its initial level by the end of the period. Incidentally, the results of this particular simulation—a VA backed by common stocks with an RV equal to 5%—is of particular interest since it provides a good approximation to the outcome of the only type of VA that was actually in existence during the seventies. This was the VA backed by the portfolio of CREF, for which a value of RV of 4% was used—quite close to the 5% assumed in the table. It is apparent that the experience with this instrument was hardly a satisfactory one and that arrangements of this type should not be forced on annuitants without also giving them the option of a less risky alternative such as that consisting of the T-bill-backed VA.

Bodie and Pesando have also explored a few other possible plans which, however, do not strike me as promising. The first is the so-called graduated payment plan in which the *nominal* annuity increases through time at some prearranged rate, intended to match the inflation rate. I have serious objection to graduation for pensions, as I do for mortgages. A graduated annuity is still a nominal contract, which cannot be counted on to eliminate much of the risk of the real outcome when inflation is highly variable. Table 11.2 shows that the graduated payment produces a standard deviation of real outcomes roughly twice as large as that produced by a T-bill-backed VA, even though it is assumed that the graduation exactly coincides with the rate of inflation over the period of the contract. In practice it would be impossible to match the two closely, especially in the case of long contracts. Thus, while the graduation may somewhat reduce the tilt associated with a conventional pension, it might also conceivably increase it if inflation turned out to be sufficiently smaller than the graduation rate.

Finally, Bodie and Pesando have considered the possibility of reducing some of the risk that is borne by the annuitant under a variable annuity by giving him a guarantee that his nominal annuity will never decline, along the lines of the so-called Rockefeller plan. But, as the authors recognize, this guarantee would be nonoperational for the kind of T-bill-backed VA which strikes me as the most feasible arrangement. At least if RV is taken as zero, as would seem appropriate, there is no possibility of the nominal annuity received by the beneficiary ever declining, except if the bill rate itself were negative, which presumably is impossible. Even if RV was taken as 3%, as seems to be the case in the Rockefeller plan, the probability of the nominal rate falling short of 3% seems remote in a period of high inflation. If, on the other hand, inflation should become even lower or somewhat negative, then it is very questionable whether there should be a clause guaranteeing the annuitant against a decline in the nominal payments.

Another possibility considered in this chapter is that of a ceiling on the real level of the annuity with the returns earned by the endowment of the annuitant and not paid to him, returned to the pension fund as a compensation for the risk it is taking in guaranteeing a floor. I have already indicated why I do not regard a floor as a very interesting modification, and there seems to be no justification left for a ceiling either.

As the authors explicitly recognize, the several alternatives explored in this chapter by no means exhaust all possible designs, but I share their view that those examined are by and large the most promising. There is, nonetheless, one more class that deserves brief mention, namely, the class of arrangements that gives the annuitant an option to switch from one instrument to another or from one type of plan to another in the course of his retirement. This could involve switching not only between stock-backed and bill-backed VAs but also between either of these instruments and short-term fixed graduation. For instance, the annuitant could elect to invest in, say, a 3-year nominal instrument choosing simultaneously a lower value for RV with the difference reflecting the expected inflation over the next 3 years. This instrument produces, for the initial 3 years, a sure nominal stream with a fixed graduation at a rate equal to the difference between the nominal rate and RV, and hence related to expected inflation. At the end of 3 years, the annuitant would have an opportunity of choosing another intermediate-term graduation consistent with inflation expected then, but he could also switch to some other form of contract.

Quite generally, I see merits in giving the annuitant as large a choice of instruments and as wide an opportunity to switch between them as is consistent with administrative costs and with his ability to acquire a full understanding of alternatives open to him.

Let me conclude by congratulating Bodie and Pesando for having provided us with an extremely useful analysis which, one may hope, will contribute to significantly advancing the case for a pension design consistent with an inflationary environment.

References

Bodie, Z. 1976. Common stocks as a hedge against inflation. *Journal of Finance* 31 (May): 459–70.

———. 1980. An innovation for stable real retirement income. *Journal of Portfolio Management* 7 (Fall): 5–13.

———. 1982. Investment strategy in an inflationary environment. In *The changing roles of debt and equity in financing U.S. capital formation*, ed. Benjamin M. Friedman. Chicago: University of Chicago Press.

Heaton, H. 1977. Inflation protection for retired employees. *Harvard Business Review* (September/October), pp. 3–4.

———. 1980. Indexing pension payments to inflation without material increases in expected plan costs: The Rockefeller Foundation Plan. Statement to the President's Commission on Pension Policy, Washington, D.C., January 11.

Modigliani, F., and Lessard, D., eds. 1975. *New mortgage designs for stable housing in an inflationary environment*. Federal Reserve Bank of Boston Conference Series, no. 14. Boston: Federal Reserve Bank of Boston.

Ontario Select Committee on Pensions. 1981. *First report*. Toronto: Government of Ontario.

Pesando, J. E. 1981. Employee valuation of pension claims and the impact of indexing initiatives. NBER Working Paper no. 767.

————. 1982. Investment risk, bankruptcy risk and pension reform in Canada. *Journal of Finance* 37 (June): 741–49.

Pesando, J. E., and Rea, S. A., Jr. 1977. *Public and private pensions in Canada: An economic analysis.* Toronto: University of Toronto Press (for the Ontario Economic Council).

Rea, S. A., Jr. 1981. Consumption stabilizing annuities with uncertain inflation. *Journal of Risk and Insurance* 47, no. 4 (December): 596–609.

Task Force on Retirement Income Policy. 1979. *The retirement income system in Canada: Problems and alternative policies for reform.* Ottawa: Government Printer.

12   On the Role of Social Security as a Means for Efficient Risk Sharing in an Economy Where Human Capital Is Not Tradable

Robert C. Merton

12.1   Introduction

In "A Framework for Social Security Analysis," Diamond (1977) describes a number of possible reasons why one should have a program similar to the present social security program. One reason given is market failure, and he goes on to analyze three such failures—the absence of a riskless real investment security, the absence of real annuities, and the problems in insuring the risk associated with varying length of working life. In this chapter, I examine another form of market failure—namely, the nonmarketability of human capital—and show that, under certain conditions, a tax and transfer system not unlike the current social security system can reduce or eliminate the economic inefficiencies that result from such a failure.

Under the standard perfect market assumption used in the analysis of the optimal lifetime consumption–portfolio selection problem, an individual will, in general, prefer to use the private markets to design his own saving-retirement plan where benefits received are a function of the amounts he contributes and the investment experience from the portfolio allocation of these contributions. However, if there are assets of material significance which are not tradable, then this result need not obtain. Because an individual's opportunities to sell his future wage income are

Robert C. Merton is professor of finance at the Sloan School of Management, Massachusetts Institute of Technology, and a research associate of the National Bureau of Economic Research.

Aid from the National Bureau of Economic Research and the National Science Foundation is gratefully acknowledged. An earlier version of this paper was presented at the NBER Conference on Private and Public Pensions, Palo Alto, California, in January 1981, and I thank the participants for their comments. My thanks also to F. Black and P. Diamond for many helpful discussions. Any opinions expressed are mine and are not necessarily those of NBER, NSF, or, for that matter, F. Black or P. Diamond.

generally quite limited, a natural candidate for such a nontradable asset is human capital. As Diamond (1977) noted in his article, there are many possible types of market failures, and any such failure can affect individual welfare and behavior. However, the nontradability of human capital is an especially important market failure because human capital represents a significant fraction of national wealth, and because it is the major part of virtually everyone's initial endowment, its nontradability will affect all people in the economy. Indeed, even under the assumption of perfect certainty, significant welfare losses can occur from its nontradability, and these losses become still larger if this unrealistic assumption is relaxed.

It is well known that a major negative effect on individual welfare caused by the nontradability of human capital is that individuals cannot achieve their optimal life-cycle consumption program because early in life, when most of their wealth is in the form of human capital, they cannot consume as much as they would otherwise choose. This "forced-saving" distortion of the optimal program will obtain in both certainty and uncertainty models, although in certainty models it must be assumed that borrowing (against future wage income) is restricted. Otherwise human capital is tradable, because borrowing is a perfect substitute for sale. However, if future wage income is uncertain, then borrowing is not a perfect substitute for sale, and therefore the availability of credit will not eliminate the welfare loss from this market failure.

In addition to the distortion in the quantity of savings, the nontradability of human capital causes futher welfare losses in an uncertainty model because investors cannot achieve an optimal portfolio allocation of their savings. This nonoptimality manifests itself in two ways. First, investors, especially the young, may be forced to bear more risk in their portfolios than they would choose in the absence of this market failure. Second, for any given level of risk, the portfolios held by investors will be inefficient. That is, in virtually every model of portfolio selection with perfect markets, an investor's optimal behavior is to invest part of his wealth (the risk part) in a well-diversified portfolio of all available risky assets and to invest the balance of his wealth in the riskless asset where the fractional allocation between the two is used to adjust the total risk level of his portfolio.[1] However, if human capital is not tradable, then neither young nor old investors will be able to hold all available assets. Therefore, unless human and physical capital returns are perfectly positively correlated, the risk part of the investors' portfolios will be inefficiently diversified.

The focus of this chapter is on the elimination of this inefficiency in risk sharing, although in the particular model used in the analysis, the derived system of taxes and transfers also eliminates the distortions of savings. The framework for the analysis is an intertemporal general equilibrium model of an economy with overlapping generations where people live for three periods: childhood, work, and retirement.[2] Everyone is assumed to have the same utility function for lifetime consumption, which is of a very specific form. With the exception of the nontradability of human capital, all markets are assumed to be perfect and competitive. There is a single good, and there are two factors of production: homogeneous capital and labor. The stochastic production function is Cobb-Douglas. There is uncertainty about total output, factor shares, and the rate of population growth, and everyone agrees on the joint probability distributions for these random variables. Because labor is homogeneous, the wage rate is the same for all workers. Therefore, the model incorporates only the systematic, or aggregate, risk of human capital and not its individual-specific risks.[3]

The analysis proceeds as follows: In section 12.2, the model is developed and the intertemporal general equilibrium path for the economy when human capital is tradable is derived as a benchmark for an efficient allocation. In section 12.3, under the assumption that labor is supplied inelastically, I derive a system of taxes and transfers which cause the economy when human capital is not tradable to replicate the efficient equilibrium path of section 12.2. This optimal system has constant proportional taxes on both wages and consumption, transfers to retirees equal to the contemporaneous revenues collected from the wage tax, and transfers to children equal to the contemporaneous revenues from the consumption tax. In section 12.4, the assumption of inelastically supplied labor is dropped, and the optimal system of the previous section is shown to distort the labor-leisure choice. However, it is further shown that if an eligibility requirement for retirement benefits (similar in spirit to the one currently used in the social security program) is imposed, then this distortion can be reduced and, under certain conditions, completely eliminated. In section 12.5, a brief summary of the analysis and its connection with some of the issues surrounding the current social security program are discussed.

Although the model used is relatively simple and highly aggregated, the formal derivation of the optimal tax and transfer system is long and somewhat complicated. Hence, before proceeding to the formal derivation, I briefly digress to provide an overview of how the derived system of taxes and transfers serves to correct the inefficiencies caused by the nontradability of human capital.

In general, the nontradability of human capital will cause a portfolio imbalance for younger people in the direction of forcing them to hold too much human capital relative to their holdings of physical capital. An extreme example would be a newborn person whose entire initial endowment is human capital. For older people, the imbalance goes in the opposite direction with too little human capital held relative to their holdings of physical capital. Again, an extreme example would be a retired person who has no human capital.

To restore the proper portfolio balance for both young and old, it follows that the tax and transfer system should take away some of the human capital from the young and give it to the old, and take away some of the physical capital from the old and give it to the young. A wage tax, the proceeds of which are paid to current retirees, accomplishes the first part. That is, the tax takes some human capital away from the young, and, because the retirement benefits are a function of contemporaneous wage earnings, these benefits give older people an investment in human capital. A consumption tax, the proceeds of which are paid to current children, accomplishes the second part. Although the consumption tax takes away from all ages in the population, it takes proportionally more away from older people who as part of a standard life-cycle program will be currently consuming a larger fraction of their wealth. The transfers to children permit them to finance both current consumption and investment in physical capital. By choosing the proper tax rates, this package of taxes and transfers can correct the inefficiencies caused by the nontradability of human capital.

Of course, if human capital were tradable, there would be no need for such a tax and transfer system because the exchanges between young and old would take place directly in the private markets with the young selling claims on their future wage income to the old.

12.2 Equilibrium When Human Capital Is Tradable

12.2.1 Model Assumptions and Individual Optimal Behavior

In this section, an intertemporal general equilibrium model of an economy is developed under the assumption that financial markets are perfect. That is, we make the following assumptions:

ASSUMPTION 1: All assets (including human capital) are tradable.

ASSUMPTION 2: There are no transactions costs, taxes, or problems with indivisibilities of assets.

ASSUMPTION 3: There are enough investors with comparable wealth levels so that each investor believes that he can buy and sell as much of an asset as he wants at the market price.

ASSUMPTION 4: The capital market is always in equilibrium.

ASSUMPTION 5: There exists an exchange market for borrowing and lending at the same rate of interest.

ASSUMPTION 6: Shortsales of all assets, with full use of the proceeds, are allowed.

The aggregate production technology for the economy is described by the Cobb-Douglas-type production function

(1) $$Q(t) = A(t)[I(t-1)]^{\theta(t)}[L(t)]^{1-\theta(t)},$$

where $Q(t)$ is aggregate output produced at time t of the single good which can be used either as a capital good or for consumption; $I(t-1)$ is the amount of capital which must be put in place at time $(t-1)$ in order to be used in production at time t; $L(t)$ is the aggregate amount of labor used in production at time t and is chosen at that date; $A(t)$ is a positive random variable assumed to be independent of the level of investment $I(t-1)$; and $\theta(t)$ is a random variable with range $0 \leq \theta(t) \leq 1$. It is further assumed that the $\{\theta(t)\}, t = 1, 2, \ldots$, are independent and identically distributed with $E_{t-k}[\theta(t)] = \alpha$, for $k = 1, 2, \ldots$, where E_{t-k} is the conditional expectation operator, conditional on knowing all relevant information available as of date $t-k$.

Firms are assumed to be perfect competitors, and they make all production decisions so as to maximize the market value of the firm. When firms' managers make their investment decisions at time $t-1$, $I(t-1)$, they do not know either $A(t)$ or $\theta(t)$. However, when they choose the amount of labor to employ at time t, both $A(t)$ and $\theta(t)$ are known. Hence, the demand for labor at time t is determined by the solution to max $[Q(t) - \omega(t)L(t)]$, which from (1) leads to the first-order condition

(2) $$0 = [1 - \theta(t)]A(t)[I(t-1)]^{\theta(t)}[L(t)]^{-\theta(t)} - \omega(t),$$

where $\omega(t)$ is the wage rate at time t. By multiplying (2) by $L(t)$, we can rewrite (2) to express the aggregate demand for labor, $L^d(t)$, as

(3) $$L^d(t) = [1 - \theta(t)]Q(t)/\omega(t).$$

By inspection of (3), labor's share of output at time t will be $[1 - \theta(t)]$, and therefore the aggregate net revenues of firms available for distribution to shareholders at time t will be equal to $\theta(t)Q(t)$. By the standard accounting identity, aggregate dividends paid (net of new financings), $D(t)$, must satisfy

(4) $$D(t) = \theta(t)Q(t) - I(t),$$

where $I(t)$ is the amount of physical investment chosen by managers at time t in preparation for production at time $t+1$.

Because, at time t, $\theta(t+1)$ is a random variable, both current stockholders and those who will be workers at time $t+1$ face uncertainty not only about aggregate output at time $t+1$ but also about the distribution of that output between the two factors of production. However, if all factors are tradable, it will be shown that this latter uncertainty can be eliminated in the sense that it has no effect on consumer-investor welfare. That is, through efficient risk sharing, factor-share risk can be diversified away.

At each point in time t, there are three securities traded in the financial markets. The first kind is shares of stock in the firms, which represent ownership of physical capital. The random variable return per dollar on these shares between t and $t + 1$ is denoted by $Z_1(t + 1)$. Second is a human capital security which pays $\$\omega(t + 1)$ per share to its owner at time $t + 1$ with no further payments thereafter, where $\omega(t + 1)$ is the wage rate at time $t + 1$. The random variable return per dollar on this security is denoted by $Z_2(t + 1)$. Third is a riskless security which pays one dollar at time $t + 1$ and whose return per dollar between t and $t + 1$ is denoted by $R(t)$.

Each person in the economy lives for three periods. At age 0, his initial endowment is equal to the market value of his human capital. In this childhood period, the individual chooses how much to consume and then allocates his savings in a portfolio decision. He finances these choices by selling part of his endowment in the private market. In the next, work period of his life, he chooses how much to consume of goods and leisure and then allocates his savings in a portfolio decision. In the last, retirement period, he consumes all his wealth because there is no bequest motive.

It is assumed that all people at birth have the same lifetime utility-of-consumption function which at time t is denoted by $U_0(t)$ given by

$$(5) \qquad U_0(t) = \log[c_0(t)] + E_t\{\Gamma \log[\ell(t + 1)] \\ + \log[c_1(t + 1)] + \log[c_2(t + 2)]\},$$

where $c_k(t)$ is the consumption of a person of age k at time t, $k = 0, 1, 2$; $\ell(t + 1)$ is the fraction of the person's work period spent in leisure, $0 \le \ell(t + 1) \le 1$; and Γ is a nonnegative constant.

From assumption (5), it follows that each person of age 1 at time t will have a lifetime utility-of-consumption function, $U_1(t)$, given by

$$(6) \qquad U_1(t) = \Gamma \log[\ell(t)] + \log[c_1(t)] + E_t\{\log[c_2(t + 1)]\}$$

and for each person of age 2 at time t, the lifetime utility-of-consumption function, $U_2(t)$, is given by

$$(7) \qquad U_2(t) = \log[c_2(t)].$$

The solution of the individual's optimal lifetime consumption program is derived in the appendix using the technique of stochastic dynamic programming. Because all assets are tradable, the problem can be formally expressed in the standard form used by Samuelson (1969) and Hakansson (1970) where all income derives from investment in securities. That is, if $w_k(t)$ denotes the wealth of a person of age k at time t, then the dynamic accumulation equation for wealth can be written as

$$(8) \qquad w_{k+1}(t + 1) = s_k(t)\{x_{1k}(t)[Z_1(t + 1) - R(t)] \\ + x_{2k}(t)[Z_2(t + 1) - R(t)] + R(t)\},$$

where $s_k(t)$ is saving by an age k person, $x_{1k}(t)$ is the fraction of his savings which is allocated to shares of firms, $x_{2k}(t)$ is the fraction allocated to the human capital security, and $[1 - x_{1k}(t) - x_{2k}(t)]$ is the fraction allocated to the riskless security.

To use this standard form of the accumulation equation, we adopt the convention of including as part of an investor's wealth the gross value of his human capital, which is defined as the current market price for the wage income he would earn if he were to work 100% of the time during the work period of his life. If we assume no bequests, each person's initial endowment is just his human capital. Therefore, if we include the gross value of each person's human capital in his wealth, it follows that the value of each person's initial endowment at time t will satisfy

(9) $$w_0(t) = p(t),$$

where $p(t)$ denotes the equilibrium price at time t of one share of the human capital security.

It also follows from this convention that each person must buy back the amount of leisure time which he chooses to consume during the work period of his life. Hence, individual saving for age 0 and age 1 people is defined by

(10a) $$s_0(t) \equiv w_0(t) - c_0(t)$$

and

(10b) $$s_1(t) \equiv w_1(t) - c_1(t) - \omega(t)\ell(t),$$

where saving by age 1 people includes a deduction from wealth for *both* consumption of goods and leisure with the price per unit of leisure time equal to the wage rate, $\omega(t)$. The convention of including the gross value of human capital is adopted for analytical convenience only, and the same equilibrium quantities and prices will obtain in the alternative formulation which uses the net (of leisure spent) value of human capital with no separate deduction for leisure.

Because of the no-bequest assumption, the optimal consumption rule for an age 2 person is simply $c_2^*(t) = w_2(t)$. From the analysis in the appendix, the optimal consumption and saving rules for an age 0 person can be written as

(11a) $$c_0^*(t) = \frac{w_0(t)}{3 + \Gamma}$$

and

(11b) $$s_0^*(t) = \left(\frac{2 + \Gamma}{3 + \Gamma}\right) w_0(t).$$

The corresponding behavior rules for an age 1 person can be written as

(12a)
$$c_1^*(t) = \frac{w_1(t)}{2 + \Gamma},$$

(12b)
$$\ell^*(t) = \frac{\Gamma w_1(t)}{(2 + \Gamma)\omega(t)},$$

and

(12c)
$$s_1^*(t) = \frac{w_1(t)}{2 + \Gamma}.$$

As shown in the appendix, age 0 investors and age 1 investors will have the same fractional allocations in their optimal portfolios. That is, $x_{j0}^*(t) = x_{j1}^*(t) = x_j^*(t)$, $j = 1, 2$. Exhibiting the well-known properties of the log utility function, these optimal portfolio weights, $[x_1^*(t), x_2^*(t)]$, do not depend on the level of the investor's wealth and are given by the solution to the equation set

(13)
$$0 = E_t \left[\frac{Z_j(t + 1) - R(t)}{Z^*(t + 1)} \right], j = 1, 2,$$

where $Z^*(t + 1) \equiv x_1^*(t)[Z_1(t + 1) - R(t)] + x_2^*(t)[Z_2(t + 1) - R(t)] + R(t)$ is the return per dollar on the optimal portfolio which is common to both age groups.

Equations (11)–(13) completely describe individual optimal consumption, saving, and portfolio selection behavior at each age and point in time. To determine the corresponding aggregate behavior necessary to derive the intertemporal equilibrium prices and quantities, I now turn to the assumed demographics for the economy.

Let $N_0(t)$ denote the number of children born in the economy at time t. Although $N_0(t)$ is known at time t, I assume it to be a random variable relative to times earlier than t. I further assume that the stochastic process describing the evolution of $N_0(t)$ is exogenous and independent of the level of economic activity.[4] Because each person lives for three periods, it follows that the number of age 1 people in the economy at time t, $N_1(t)$, is given by

(14)
$$N_1(t) = N_0(t - 1)$$

and the number of age 2 people in the economy at time t, $N_2(t)$, is given by

(15)
$$N_2(t) = N_1(t - 1)$$
$$= N_0(t - 2).$$

Hence, at time t, the size of the work force for the economy at time $t + 1$ will be known with certainty, and at that time the number of retirees in the economy at times $t + 1$ and $t + 2$ will also be known with certainty. If $N(t)$ denotes the total population at time t, then $N(t) = N_0(t) + N_1(t) + N_2(t)$, and the dynamics for $N(t)$ can be written as

(16) $$N(t+1) = N(t) - N_0(t-2) + N_0(t+1).$$

If $W_k(t) \equiv N_k(t)w_k(t)$ denotes the aggregate wealth of all age k people in the economy at time t, $k = 0,1,2$, then from (11) and (12), the corresponding aggregate consumption and savings for each age group can be written as

(17a) $$C_0(t) \equiv \frac{W_0(t)}{3+\Gamma},$$

(17b) $$S_0(t) \equiv \left(\frac{2+\Gamma}{3+\Gamma}\right) W_0(t),$$

(17c) $$C_1(t) \equiv \frac{W_1(t)}{2+\Gamma},$$

(17d) $$\mathscr{L}(t) \equiv \frac{\Gamma W_1(t)}{(2+\Gamma)\omega(t)},$$

(17e) $$S_1(t) \equiv \frac{W_1(t)}{2+\Gamma},$$

and

(17f) $$C_2(t) = W_2(t).$$

From the aggregation across all age groups in (17), national wealth, $W(t)$, aggregate consumption, $C(t)$, and aggregate saving, $S(t)$, for the economy can be written as

(18a) $$W(t) = W_0(t) + W_1(t) + W_2(t),$$

(18b) $$C(t) = \frac{(2+\Gamma)W_0(t) + (3+\Gamma)W_1(t) + (6+5\Gamma+\Gamma^2)W_2(t)}{6+5\Gamma+\Gamma^2},$$

and

(18c) $$S(t) = \frac{(4+4\Gamma+\Gamma^2)W_0(t) + (3+\Gamma)W_1(t)}{6+5\Gamma+\Gamma^2}.$$

12.2.2 Equilibrium in the Financial Markets

Because firms are competitive and, from assumption (1), the production technology exhibits constant returns to scale, the equilibrium ex-dividend aggregate market value of firms' shares, denoted by $V(t)$, must satisfy

(19) $$V(t) = I(t),$$

where $I(t)$ is aggregate amount of physical investment made at time t. From (19), (3), and (4), it follows that the aggregate value of firms' shares at time t, prior to paying dividends or issuing new shares, will be equal to the net revenues available for distribution to shareholders, $\theta(t)Q(t)$.

Hence, the equilibrium return per dollar on firms' shares between t and $t + 1$ can be written as

$$(20) \qquad Z_1(t + 1) = \theta(t + 1)Q(t + 1)/V(t)$$
$$= \theta(t + 1)Q(t + 1)/I(t).$$

Because there are $N_0(t)$ people of age 0, the equilibrium market value of gross human capital at time t is $N_0(t)p(t)$, and this is the aggregate amount of the second security, the human capital security, which must be held in investors' portfolios. Because these securities are a claim on gross human capital, the aggregate dollar return on them at time t will be equal to total wages paid at time t plus the dollar amount of leisure time purchased at time t, $\mathscr{L}(t)\omega(t)$. It follows that the equilibrium return per dollar on the second security between t and $t + 1$ is given by

$$(21) \quad Z_2(t + 1) = \{[1 - \theta(t + 1)]Q(t + 1) + \mathscr{L}(t + 1)\omega(t + 1)\}/N_0(t)p(t).$$

As the appendix shows, all investors will allocate their savings in the same relative proportions across the available securities, and hence it follows immediately that in equilibrium this common optimal portfolio must be the *market portfolio* (i.e., the portfolio which holds all securities in proportion to their market values).[5] If $\delta_1(t)$ denotes the fraction of the market portfolio held in the shares of firms and $\delta_2(t)$ denotes the fraction held in human capital, then $[1 - \delta_1(t) - \delta_2(t)]$ is the fraction held in the riskless security. Because there is no net supply of the riskless security, it follows that $\delta_1(t) = 1 - \delta_2(t)$, and financial market equilibrium requires that

$$(22a) \qquad x_1^*(t) = \delta_1(t) \equiv \frac{V(t)}{V(t) + N_0(t)p(t)}$$

and

$$(22b) \qquad x_2^*(t) = \delta_2(t) \equiv \frac{N_0(t)p(t)}{V(t) + N_0(t)p(t)}.$$

The total dollar return to the market at time t is equal to $\theta(t)Q(t) + [1 - \theta(t)]Q(t) + \mathscr{L}(t)\omega(t) = Q(t) + \mathscr{L}(t)\omega(t)$. Therefore, the equilibrium return per dollar on the market portfolio between t and $t + 1$, $Z_M(t + 1)$, is given by

$$(23) \quad Z_M(t + 1) = [Q(t + 1) + \mathscr{L}(t + 1)\omega(t + 1)]/[V(t) + N_0(t)p(t)].$$

Because in equilibrium $Z^*(t) = Z_M(t)$, it follows from a straightforward manipulation of (13) that, in equilibrium,

$$(24) \qquad E_t[Z_1(t + 1)/Z_M(t + 1)] = 1.$$

From (8), (9), (14), (17b), and (17d), it can be shown that

$\mathcal{L}(t)\omega(t) = \Gamma N_0(t-1)p(t-1)Z_M(t)/(3+\Gamma)$, and therefore (23) can be rewritten as

(25) $Z_M(t+1) = Q(t+1)/[V(t) + \left(\dfrac{3}{3+\Gamma}\right)N_0(t)p(t)]$.

Substituting for $Z_1(t+1)$ from (20) and for $Z_M(t+1)$ from (25) into (24), we have, as a condition for equilibrium, that

(26) $E_t[\theta(t+1)] = \dfrac{(3+\Gamma)V(t)}{[(3+\Gamma)V(t) + 3N_0(t)p(t)]}$.

But, by assumption (1) $E_t[\theta(t+1)] \equiv \alpha$, a constant for all t, and hence, from (26), the equilibrium market value of human capital must satisfy

(27) $N_0(t)p(t) = \left[\dfrac{(1-\alpha)(3+\Gamma)}{3\alpha}\right]V(t)$.

Substituting from (27) into (22) we have that the equilibrium portfolio weights in the market portfolio are constants over time and are given by

(28a) $\delta_1 = \dfrac{3\alpha}{3+(1-\alpha)\Gamma}$

and

(28b) $\delta_2 = \dfrac{(3+\Gamma)(1-\alpha)}{3+(1-\alpha)\Gamma}$.

We can now summarize the derived conditions for equilibrium in the financial market. From (19) and (27) the equilibrium values of firms and human capital can be written as

(29a) $V(t) = I(t)$

and

(29b) $N_0(t)p(t) = \left[\dfrac{(1-\alpha)(3+\Gamma)}{3\alpha}\right]I(t)$.

From (29) and the condition that aggregate financial saving must be equal to the market value of all securities, we have that

(30) $S(t) = \left[\dfrac{3+(1-\alpha)\Gamma}{3\alpha}\right]I(t)$.

From (25), (27), and (29a), the equilibrium return on the market portfolio between $t-1$ and t can be written as

(31) $Z_M(t) = \dfrac{\alpha Q(t)}{I(t-1)}$.

From (20), (21), (29), and (31), the returns on shares of firms and human capital between $t - 1$ and t can be written as

(32a)
$$Z_1(t) = \frac{\theta(t)Q(t)}{I(t-1)}$$

$$= \left[\frac{\theta(t)}{\alpha}\right] Z_M(t)$$

and

(32b)
$$Z_2(t) = \left[\frac{(1-\alpha)\Gamma + 3[1-\theta(t)]}{(1-\alpha)\Gamma + 3[1-\alpha]}\right] \frac{\alpha Q(t)}{I(t-1)}$$

$$= \left[\frac{(1-\alpha)\Gamma + 3[1-\theta(t)]}{(1-\alpha)\Gamma + 3[1-\alpha]}\right] Z_M(t).$$

Finally, to determine the equilibrium return on the riskless security, we have from (13), (24), and (31) that

(33)
$$R(t) = 1/E_t[1/Z_M(t+1)]$$

$$= \frac{\alpha}{I(t)} /E_t[1/Q(t+1)].$$

Of course, equilibrium conditions (29)–(33) are not the proper reduced-form equations for these equilibrium prices, returns, and quantities because they contain endogenous variables on their right-hand side. To drive the proper reduced-form equations in terms of the exogenous and predetermined variables of the economy as well as the equilibrium quantities of physical investment, consumption, and output, it is necessary to examine the "real" sector of the economy.

12.2.3 Equilibrium in the Goods and Labor Markets

A necessary condition for equilibrium in the market for physical output is that

(34)
$$Q(t) = C(t) + I(t).$$

From (9), (17a), and (29b), we have that aggregate consumption by age 0 people at time t can be written as

(35)
$$C_0(t) = \frac{(1-\alpha)}{3\alpha} I(t).$$

Because $S_1(t) = S(t) - S_0(t) = S(t) - W_0(t) + C_0(t)$, it follows from (9), (29b), (30), and (35) that aggregate saving by age 1 people at time t can be written as

(36)
$$S_1(t) = \left(\frac{1+2\alpha}{3\alpha}\right) I(t),$$

and therefore, from (17c) and (17e), aggregate consumption by age 1 people must satisfy

(37) $$C_1(t) = \left(\frac{1 + 2\alpha}{3\alpha}\right) I(t).$$

From the equilibrium condition that $Z^*(t) = Z_M(t)$ and the accumulation equation (8), we know that aggregate consumption by age 2 people at time t can be written as

(38) $$C_2(t) = S_1(t - 1)Z_M(t)$$
$$= S_1(t - 1)\alpha Q(t)/I(t - 1) \text{ from (31),}$$
$$= \left(\frac{1 + 2\alpha}{3}\right) Q(t) \text{ from (36).}$$

Therefore, substituting for $C(t)$ from (35), (37), and (38) into (34) and rearranging terms, we have that in equilibrium

(39) $$I(t) = \left[\frac{\alpha(1 - \alpha)}{2\alpha + 1}\right] Q(t).$$

The supply of labor at time t, $L^s(t)$, is equal to $N_1(t) - \mathcal{L}(t)$. From (17c), (17d), (37) and (39), we can rewrite this expression as

(40) $$L^s(t) = N_1(t) - \frac{(1 - \alpha)Q(t)}{3\omega(t)}.$$

For the labor market to be in equilibrium, $L^s(t) = L^d(t)$, and therefore, from (4) and (40), the equilibrium wage rate can be written as

(41) $$\omega(t) = \left[1 - \theta(t) + \frac{(1 - \alpha)\Gamma}{3}\right] Q(t)/N_1(t).$$

Substituting for $\omega(t)$ in (40) from (41), the equilibrium aggregate quantity of labor, $L(t)$, can be written as

(42) $$L(t) = \frac{3N_1(t)[1 - \theta(t)]}{3[1 - \theta(t)] + (1 - \alpha)\Gamma}.$$

Substituting for $L(t)$ in assumption (1) from (42), we have that the equilibrium quantity of output at time t is given by

(43) $$Q(t) = A(t)[I(t - 1)]^{\theta(t)} \left\{\frac{3N_1(t)[1 - \theta(t)]}{3[1 - \theta(t)] + (1 - \alpha)\Gamma}\right\}^{1 - \theta(t)}.$$

This completes the analysis of the intertemporal general equilibrium model of the economy with perfect markets. By substituting for $Q(t)$ from (43) into each of the previously derived equilibrium conditions, the complete set of reduced-form equations for equilibrium prices, quantities, and returns can be written in terms of the exogenous variables $A(t), \theta(t), N_0(t), N_1(t)$, and $N_2(t)$ and the predetermined variable $I(t-1)$. For convenience and ease of reference, these equations for the equilibrium prices, quantities, and returns are presented in tables 12.1, 12.2, and 12.3.

12.3   A System of Taxes and Transfers Which Replicates the Perfect-Market Equilibrium Path When Human Capital Is Not Tradable and Labor Is Inelastically Supplied

In this section, I assume that human capital is not tradable and derive a system of taxes and transfers which cause the economy to replicate the perfect-market equilibrium consumption and saving patterns derived in section 12.2. This system serves two functions: first, by providing transfers to people in the childhood period for consumption, it corrects the savings distortion caused by the nontradability of human capital.[6] This transfer is financed by a proportional consumption tax where the tax rate

Table 12.1	Equilibrium Prices and Quantities in the Real Sector

Aggregate Output

$$Q(t) = A(t)[I(t-1)]^{\theta(t)} \left\{ \frac{3N_1(t)[1-\theta(t)]}{3[1-\theta(t)]+(1-\alpha)\Gamma} \right\}^{1-\theta(t)}$$

Capital Investment

$$I(t) = \left[\frac{\alpha(1-\alpha)}{2\alpha+1} \right] Q(t)$$

Aggregate Consumption

$$C(t) = \left(\frac{1+\alpha+\alpha^2}{2\alpha+1} \right) Q(t)$$

Aggregate Labor Time

$$L(t) = \frac{3[1-\theta(t)]N_1(t)}{3[1-\theta(t)]+(1-\alpha)\Gamma}$$

Aggregate Leisure Time for Workers

$$\mathcal{L}(t) = \frac{(1-\alpha)\Gamma N_1(t)}{3[1-\theta(t)]+(1-\alpha)\Gamma}$$

Wage Rate

$$\omega(t) = \left[\frac{3[1-\theta(t)]+(1-\alpha)\Gamma}{3N_1(t)} \right] Q(t)$$

Table 12.2   Equilibrium Values, Portfolio Allocations, and Returns in the Financial Sector

Aggregate values and returns

National wealth

$$W(t) = \frac{[3(2+\alpha^2) + \Gamma(2-\alpha-\alpha^2)]}{3(2\alpha+1)} Q(t)$$

Aggregate saving

$$S(t) = \frac{[3 + \Gamma(1-\alpha)](1-\alpha)}{3(2\alpha+1)} Q(t)$$

Return per dollar
between t and $t+1$
on market portfolio

$$Z_M(t+1) = \left[\frac{(2\alpha+1)}{(1-\alpha)}\right] \frac{Q(t+1)}{Q(t)}$$

Components of the market portfolio

	Fraction of Market Portfolio, δ_j	Return per Dollar between t and $t+1$, $Z_j(t+1)$
Firms ($j=1$)	$\dfrac{3\alpha}{3+(1-\alpha)\Gamma}$	$\left[\dfrac{\theta(t+1)}{\alpha}\right] Z_M(t+1)$
Human capital ($j=2$)	$\dfrac{(3+\Gamma)(1-\alpha)}{3+(1-\alpha)\Gamma}$	$\left[\dfrac{3[1-\theta(t+1)] + \Gamma(1-\alpha)}{(3+\Gamma)(1-\alpha)}\right] Z_M(t+1)$

Table 12.3   Distribution of Wealth, Consumption, and Saving among Age Groups

	Fraction of National Wealth	Fraction of Aggregate Consumption	Fraction of Aggregate Saving
Childhood (age 0)	$\dfrac{(3+\Gamma)(1-\alpha)^2}{3(2+\alpha^2)+\Gamma(2-\alpha-\alpha^2)}$	$\dfrac{(1-2\alpha+\alpha^2)}{3(1+\alpha+\alpha^2)}$	$\dfrac{(2+\Gamma)(1-\alpha)}{3+\Gamma(1-\alpha)}$
Work (age 1)	$\dfrac{(2+\Gamma)(1+\alpha-2\alpha^2)}{3(2+\alpha^2)+\Gamma(2-\alpha-\alpha^2)}$	$\dfrac{(1+\alpha-2\alpha^2)}{3(1+\alpha+\alpha^2)}$	$\dfrac{2\alpha+1}{3+\Gamma(1-\alpha)}$
Retirement (age 2)	$\dfrac{4\alpha^2+4\alpha+1}{3(2+\alpha^2)+\Gamma(2-\alpha-\alpha^2)}$	$\dfrac{4\alpha^2+4\alpha+1}{3(1+\alpha+\alpha^2)}$	0

τ_c is a constant over time. Second, it provides more efficient risk sharing in the economy by eliminating the unnecessary, or diversifiable, factor-share risk which would otherwise be borne by all age groups in the economy. We eliminate the risk by making transfers to current retirees financed by a proportional tax on wages of current workers where the tax rate τ_ω is a constant over time. This pay-as-you-go tax and transfer system is similar to the retirement component of the present social security system.[7]

To highlight both the benefits and sources of possible distortions to the economy from the system, the appropriate tax rates and transfers to replicate the perfect market equilibrium path of section 12.2 are derived first under the assumption that labor is supplied inelastically. That is, there is no demand for leisure time, and this is accomplished in the model by setting Γ equal to zero in workers' utility functions. In the next section, the effects of introducing demand for leisure into this system are examined. To determine optimal taxes and transfers, the individual lifetime consumption-saving problem is solved taking into account taxes, transfers, and the nontradability of human capital. For notational simplicity, I use the same variable symbols that were used in section 12.2, adding prime signs where necessary to distinguish them from their perfect-market counterparts.

The analysis begins with the examination of the behavior of those who are in the work period of their lives at time t. Let μ_1 denote the fraction of capital investment, $I'(t-1)$, owned through the purchase of shares of firms by age 0 people at time $t-1$. The ownership of this capital is possible as the result of saving out of transfers received in childhood. Because all direct saving can be invested in shares of firms only, aggregate saving by age 1 people at time t can be written as

(44) $S_1'(t) = (1 - \tau_\omega)[1 - \theta(t)]Q'(t) + \mu_1\theta(t)Q'(t) - (1 + \tau_c)C_1'(t)$.

It follows, therefore, that aggregate retirement-period consumption at time $t + 1$ must satisfy

(45)
$$C_2'(t + 1) = \frac{1}{1 + \tau_c}\left\{S_1'(t)\left[\frac{\theta(t + 1)Q'(t + 1)}{I'(t)}\right]\right.$$
$$\left. + \tau_\omega[1 - \theta(t + 1)]Q'(t + 1)\right\},$$

where the second term in the brackets is the retirement transfer payment which is equal to the total taxes on wages collected.

Under the assumption that $\Gamma = 0$, each age 1 person will choose current consumption, $c_1'(t)$, so as to maximize $\log [c_1'(t)] + E_t\{\log [c_2'(t + 1)]\}$ subject to his budget constraint. From (44) and (45), the first-order condition for this maximization can be written in terms of age group aggregates as

$$
(46) \qquad \frac{1}{C_1'(t)} = E_t \left[\frac{\theta(t+1)Q'(t+1)/I'(t)}{C_2'(t+1)} \right],
$$

where it is understood that C_1' and C_2' in (46) are the optimal consumption decisions.

If taxes and transfers are to be chosen so as to replicate the equilibrium in section 12.2, then, as a necessary condition, $I'(t) = I(t)$ and $C_k'(t) = C_k(t)$, $k = 0,1,2$. Therefore, it follows from tables 12.1 and 12.3 that

$$
(47) \qquad I'(t) = \left[\frac{\alpha(1-\alpha)}{2\alpha+1} \right] Q'(t),
$$

$$
(48) \qquad C_1'(t) = \frac{(1-\alpha)}{3} Q'(t),
$$

and

$$
(49) \qquad C_2'(t+1) = \frac{(2\alpha+1)}{3} Q'(t+1).
$$

Substituting these necessary conditions for $C_2'(t+1)$ and $I'(t)$ into (44) and rearranging terms, we have that μ_1, τ_ω, and τ_c must be chosen so as to satisfy

$$
(50) \qquad 0 = [\mu_1 - (1-\tau_\omega)] \left[\frac{2\alpha+1}{\alpha(1+\alpha)} \right] \theta(t)\theta(t+1)
$$

$$
+ \left\{ \frac{2\alpha+1}{\alpha(1-\alpha)} \left[(1-\tau_\omega) - \frac{(1-\tau_c)(1-\alpha)}{3} \right] - \tau_\omega \right\} \theta(t)
$$

$$
+ \left[\tau_\omega - \frac{(1-\tau_c)(2\alpha+1)}{3} \right].
$$

Because τ_ω, τ_c, and μ_1 are assumed to be constants, (50) will be satisfied for all $\theta(t)$ and $\theta(t+1)$ only if

$$
(51a) \qquad \mu_1 = 1 - \tau_\omega,
$$

$$
(51b) \qquad \tau_\omega = \frac{2\alpha+1}{\alpha(1-\alpha)} \left[(1-\tau_\omega) \frac{(1+\tau_c)(1-\alpha)}{3} \right],
$$

and

$$
(51c) \qquad \tau_\omega = \frac{2\alpha+1}{3}(1+\tau_c).
$$

Solving the system of equations (51), we have that as a necessary condition for a replication of the perfect-market economy, τ_ω, τ_c, and μ_1 must be chosen as follows:

(52a)
$$\mu_1 = \frac{(1 - \alpha^2)}{2 + 2\alpha - \alpha^2},$$

(52b)
$$\tau_\omega = \frac{2\alpha + 1}{2 + 2\alpha - \alpha^2},$$

and

(52c)
$$\tau_c = \frac{(1 - \alpha)^2}{2 + 2\alpha - \alpha^2}.$$

A further necessary condition for replication is that the substitution of these values of μ_1, τ_ω, and τ_c into (46) will lead to an optimal consumption choice $C_1'(t)$ that satisfies condition (48). The reader may verify that $C_1'(t) = (1 - \alpha)Q'(t)/3$ does indeed satisfy (46) when μ_1, τ_ω, and τ_c take on the values given in (52).

Of course, unlike the tax rates, τ_ω and τ_c, the fraction of capital investment held by age 0 people, μ_1, is not under direct government control. However, it can be controlled indirectly by choosing the appropriate amount of transfers made by the government to children. To determine this optimal level of transfers, we analyze the optimal consumption-saving decisions made by people who are in the childhood period of their lives at time t.

If $T_0(t)$ denotes aggregate transfers to age 0 people at time t, then aggregate saving by this age group can be written as

(53)
$$S_0'(t) = T_0(t) - (1 - \tau_c)C_0'(t).$$

To satisfy the necessary conditions for replication, $S_0'(t) = \mu_1 I'(t)$ and, from table 12.3, $C_0'(t) = [(1 - \alpha)^2/3(2\alpha + 1)]Q'(t)$. Substituting for $I'(t)$ from (47), for μ_1 from (52a), and for τ_c from (52c), we have from (53) that these necessary conditions will be satisfied if

(54)
$$T_0(t) = \frac{(1 - \alpha)^2[\alpha(1 + \alpha) + 1]}{(2\alpha + 1)(2 + 2\alpha - \alpha^2)} Q'(t).$$

With taxes and transfers that satisfy (52) and (54), we have that $C_k'(t)/Q'(t) = C_k(t)/Q'(t)$ in the perfect-market equilibrium, $k = 0, 1, 2$. Therefore, $C'(t)/Q'(t) = C(t)/Q(t)$, which implies that $I'(t)/Q'(t) = I(t)/Q(t)$. By assumption, $\Gamma = 0$ and therefore the equilibrium quantities of labor will be equal, that is, $L'(t) = L(t) = N_1(t)$, the number of age 1 people in the economy. It follows that equilibrium aggregate output will be the same, that is, $Q'(t) = Q(t)$.

Hence, to ensure that this tax and transfer system will replicate the perfect-market economy, all that remains to be shown is that the government budget constraint is satisfied. Because transfer payments to retirees always equal wage taxes collected, these two cancel. Multiplying aggregate consumption given in table 12.1 by the consumption tax rate from (52c), we have that consumption tax revenues can be written as

$$(55) \qquad \tau_c C(t) = \left[\frac{(1-\alpha)^2}{(2+2\alpha-\alpha^2)} \right] \left[\frac{1+\alpha+\alpha^2}{2\alpha+1} \right] Q(t)$$
$$= T_0(t),$$

from (54). Since consumption tax revenues just equal transfers to childhood-period people, the government budget constraint is satisfied, and the prescribed system of taxes and transfers will cause the economy with no trading in human capital to replicate the intertemporal equilibrium path for the economy when human capital is tradable.

12.4   A System of Taxes and Transfers Which Replicates the Perfect-Market Equilibrium Path When Human Capital Is Not Tradable and Labor Is Elastically Supplied

In the analysis of the previous section, a tax and transfer system was derived which caused the economy to replicate the perfect-market equilibrium path derived in section 12.2. This system eliminates completely the inefficiencies caused by the market failure of no trading in human capital, but it was derived for the special case where labor is inelastically supplied. In this section, we reinstate the labor-leisure choice and examine the effects of the system derived in section 12.3 on the equilibrium path of the economy when labor is not supplied inelastically.

As in section 12.3, we begin by examining the optimal behavior of those who are in their work period at time t. At time t, each age 1 person will choose current consumption and leisure time so as to maximize $\{\Gamma \log [\ell'(t)] + \log [c_1'(t)] + E_t \log [c_2' (t + 1)]\} \equiv \{\Gamma \log [\mathcal{L}'(t)] + \log [C_1'(t)] + E_t \log [C_2'(t + 1)] - (2 + \Gamma) \log [N_1(t)]\}$ where aggregate saving by age 1 people at time t can be written as

$$(56) \quad S_1'(t) = (1 - \tau_\omega)\omega'(t)[1 - \mathcal{L}'(t)] + \mu\theta(t)Q'(t) - (1 + \tau_c)C_1'(t)$$

and $C_2'(t + 1)$ is given by (45). Differentiating with respect to each of the choice variables, $[\ell'(t), c_1'(t)]$, we have that the first-order conditions for a maximum, written in terms of aggregates, must satisfy

$$(57a) \qquad \frac{1}{C_1'(t)} = E_t \left[\frac{\theta(t+1)Q'(t+1)/I'(t)}{C_2'(t+1)} \right],$$

which is identical to (46) in section 12.3, and

$$(57b) \qquad \frac{\Gamma}{\mathcal{L}'(t)} = E_t \left[\frac{(1 - \tau_\omega)\omega'(t)\theta(t+1)Q'(t+1)/I'(t)}{(1 + \tau_c)C_2'(t+1)} \right].$$

Combining (57a) and (57b), we have that

$$(58) \qquad \mathcal{L}'(t) = \frac{(1 + \tau_c)}{(1 - \tau_\omega)} \frac{\Gamma C_1'(t)}{\omega'(t)}.$$

It is straightforward to show that all other first-order conditions for age 0 and age 2 people will be identical to those deduced in section 12.3. Therefore, for the tax and transfer system given in (52) and (54), the optimal consumption and saving behavior per unit of current aggregate output, $Q'(t)$, will be the same here as in the inelastic labor supply case of section 12.3. However, in the perfect-market equilibrium of section 12.2, the optimal aggregate amount of leisure time for workers satisfied the condition that

$$(59) \qquad \mathcal{L}(t) = \frac{\Gamma C_1(t)}{\omega(t)}.$$

A comparison of (59) with (58) shows that both the consumption and wage taxes will cause a distortion of the labor-leisure decision in the direction of demanding more leisure than in the perfect-market case for the same wage rate and consumption.

As in sections 12.2 and 12.3, optimal aggregate work period consumption is given by $C_1'(t) = (1 - \alpha)Q'(t)/3$, and from (58) and (3), it follows that the wage rate which equilibrates the labor market is given by

$$(60) \qquad \omega'(t) = \left\{ 3[1 - \theta(t)] + \frac{(1 - \alpha)\Gamma(1 + \tau_c)}{1 - \tau_\omega} \right\} Q'(t)/3N_1(t).$$

A comparison of (60) with the perfect-market equilibrium wage rate given in table 12.1 will show that when the labor supply is elastic (i.e., $\Gamma \neq 0$), the wage rate expressed as a fraction of current output will be higher with this system of taxes and transfers than in the perfect-market case. However, the equilibrium quantity of labor will be smaller. That is, from (58) and (60), the equilibrium quantity of labor can be written as

$$(61) \qquad L'(t) = \frac{3N_1(t)[1 - \theta(t)]}{3[1 - \theta(t)] + [(1 + \tau_c)/(1 - \tau_\omega)]\Gamma(1 - \alpha)},$$

and from table 12.1 and (61), the ratio of the equilibrium quantity of labor in this section to the quantity in the perfect-market case is given by

$$(62) \qquad L'(t)/L(t) = \frac{3[1 - \theta(t)] + (1 - \alpha)\Gamma}{3[1 - \theta(t)] + (1 + \tau_c)(1 - \alpha)\Gamma/(1 - \tau_\omega)} < 1.$$

For the same quantity of capital investment at time $(t - 1)$, $I(t - 1)$, the ratio of aggregate output at time t in the two cases is given by

$$(63) \qquad Q'(t)/Q(t) = [L'(t)/L(t)]^{1 - \theta(t)},$$

and therefore, from (62), equilibrium aggregate output will be lower with this system of taxes and transfers than in the perfect-market case.

Although the magnitude of the reduction in output caused by the distortion of the labor-leisure decision will, of course, depend on the magnitude of Γ, α, and $\theta(t)$, the effect can be substantial. For example, given the same quantity of capital investment at time $(t - 1)$, if $\Gamma = 1$ (i.e., leisure time has the same utility weight as consumption), $\alpha = .25$, and $\theta(t) = \alpha$, the ratio of $Q'(t)/Q(t)$ will be approximately 0.72, which corresponds to a 28% reduction in output. Moreover, because $I'(t)/Q'(t) = I(t)/Q(t)$, $I'(t) < I(t)$, and therefore the reduction in output will become larger through time.

The distorting effects exhibited here of the wage and consumption taxes on the labor-leisure decision are well known and have been discussed at length in the public finance literature.[8] To my knowledge, no general method for eliminating these distortions has been derived. However, for the problem examined here, it is possible to reduce the magnitude of the distortion without affecting the basic functional purposes of the taxes by adding eligibility requirements for retirement benefits to the system of taxes and transfers. Indeed, for the specific model analyzed here, it is possible to eliminate the distortion entirely by such an addition.

Suppose that, in addition to (52) and (54), the system of taxes and transfers is augmented with a schedule of individual retirement benefits which depend in a progressive way on the relative amount contributed by the individual. For example, let the schedule announced at time t for the individual's retirement benefit at time $t + 1$, $b(t + 1)$, be given by

$$(64) \quad b(t + 1) = \max \{\lambda(t),\ 1 + \gamma(t)[\chi(t) - 1]\}B(t + 1)/N_2(t + 1),$$

where $B(t + 1)$ is the aggregate amount of retirement benefits paid at time $t + 1$, $N_2(t + 1)$ is the number of retirees at time $t + 1$, $\chi(t) \equiv \tau_\omega[1 - \ell(t)]\omega'(t)/\{\tau_\omega[1 - \theta(t)]Q'(t)/N_1(t)\}$ is the ratio of the individual worker's contribution to the average contribution of all workers at time t, and $\lambda(t) \geq 0$ and $\gamma(t) > 0$ are policy variables to be chosen. By inspection of (64), we see that the minimum individual retirement benefit paid, $b_{\min}(t + 1)$, is given by $\lambda(t)[B(t + 1)/N_2(t + 1)]$, and that for the schedule to be feasible, $\lambda(t) \leq 1$.

All those retirees whose contributions relative to the average were less than $\chi_{\min}(t) \equiv 1 - [1 - \lambda(t)]/\gamma(t)$ will receive the same minimum retirement payment independent of the specific amount contributed. Provided that $\lambda(t) < 1$, at least some of the retirees will have contributed more than $\chi_{\min}(t)$, and for them the amount of retirement benefits received will be an increasing function of their relative contributions.

Because in the model studied here all work-period people are identical, it follows that in equilibrium $\chi(t) = 1$, and all retirees will receive the same individual retirement benefits which are given by $b(t + 1) = B(t + 1)/N_2(t + 1) = B(t + 1)/N_1(t)$. Therefore, provided that we choose

$\lambda(t) < 1$, in equilibrium $\chi(t) > \chi_{\min}(t)$ for all workers. Hence, when a worker determines his optimal quantity of leisure time, he will take into account not only the loss of after-tax wages but also the loss of retirement benefits in evaluating the marginal cost of consuming leisure time. Because the magnitude of the marginal loss of benefits depends on the policy variable $\gamma(t)$, the strategy here is to find that value of $\gamma(t)$ which will eliminate the distorting effects of the wage and consumption taxes on the labor-leisure decision.

In the relevant region where $\chi(t) > \chi_{\min}(t)$, aggregate consumption by retirement age people at time $t + 1$ can be written as

$$
(65) \quad C_2'(t + 1) = \Big[[(1 - \tau_\omega)\omega'(t)[N_1(t) - \mathscr{L}'(t)] + \mu\theta(t)Q'(t)
$$
$$
- (1 + \tau_c)C_1'(t)]\frac{\theta(t + 1)Q'(t + 1)}{I'(t)}
$$
$$
+ \Big[1 + \gamma(t)\Big(\frac{\tau_\omega\omega'(t)[N_1(t) - \mathscr{L}'(t)]}{[1 - \theta(t)]Q'(t)\tau_\omega} - 1\Big)\Big]
$$
$$
\tau_\omega[1 - \theta(t + 1)]Q'(t + 1)\Big]/(1 + \tau_c).
$$

For age 1 people at time t, the first-order condition with respect to current consumption will be the same as in (57a). However, the first-order condition with respect to leisure corresponding to (57b) is now given by

$$
(66) \quad \frac{\Gamma}{\mathscr{L}'(t)} =
$$
$$
E_t\left\{\frac{\begin{array}{c}(1 - \tau_\omega)\omega'(t)\theta(t + 1)Q'(t + 1)/I'(t)\\ + \gamma(t)\omega'(t)\tau_\omega[1 - \theta(t + 1)]Q'(t + 1)/[1 - \theta(t)]Q'(t)\end{array}}{(1 + \tau_c)C_2'(t + 1)}\right\}.
$$

Combining (66) with (57a), we have that

$$
(67) \quad \frac{\Gamma}{\mathscr{L}'(t)} = \frac{(1 - \tau_\omega)\omega'(t)}{(1 + \tau_c)C_1'(t)} + \frac{\gamma(t)\omega'(t)\tau_\omega}{[1 - \theta(t)]Q'(t)(1 + \tau_c)}
$$
$$
E_t\left\{\frac{[1 - \theta(t + 1)]Q'(t + 1)}{C_2'(t + 1)}\right\}.
$$

Note that this relation between $\mathscr{L}'(t)$ and $C_1'(t)$ differs from the one given in (58) because of the extra cost of leisure time caused by the loss of retirement benefits. As already noted, in equilibrium, $C_1'(t)/Q'(t)$ $= C_1(t)/Q(t) = (1 - \alpha)/3$; $I'(t)/Q'(t) = I(t)/Q(t) = \alpha(1 - \alpha)/(2\alpha + 1)$; and $\chi(t) = 1$. Substituting these equilibrium conditions along with the tax parameter values given in (52) into (65), we have that in equilibrium, aggregate retirement-period consumption at $t + 1$ can be written as

(68) $$C_2'(t+1) = \frac{\tau_\omega}{1+\tau_c}Q'(t+1).$$

Substituting for $C_2'(t+1)$ from (68) into (67) and noting that $E_t[1 - \theta(t+1)] = 1 - \alpha$, (67) can be rewritten as

(69) $$\frac{\Gamma}{\mathcal{L}'(t)} = \frac{\omega'(t)}{C_1'(t)}\left[\frac{(1-\tau_\omega)}{1+\tau_c} + \frac{\gamma(t)(1-\alpha)^2}{3[1-\theta(t)]}\right].$$

If the policy variable $\gamma(t)$ is chosen such that the term in brackets in (69) is equal to one, then $\mathcal{L}'(t) = \Gamma C_1'(t)/\omega'(t)$, and, by comparison with (59), the distortion of the labor-leisure decision by the wage and consumption taxes will be eliminated. Therefore, the optimal value for $\gamma(t)$ is given by

(70) $$\gamma(t) = \left[\frac{3(\tau_\omega + \tau_c)}{(1-\alpha)^2(1-\tau_c)}\right][1 - \theta(t)]$$

$$= \left[\frac{2+\alpha^2}{(1-\alpha)^2}\right][1 - \theta(t)].$$

A system of taxes and transfers has been derived which causes the economy when human capital is not tradable to replicate the equilibrium path of the corresponding perfect-market economy when human capital is tradable. As summarized in table 12.4, none of the tax or transfer parameters in this optimal system depends on the utility parameter Γ, which determines the individual trade-off between labor and leisure time. Hence, essentially the same system will be optimal in the more general case when Γ is permitted to differ across individuals. However, while in the case examined here any value of $\lambda(t)$ less than one is permissible, care must be taken to choose $\lambda(t)$ not to be too large in the more general case. Otherwise, the labor-leisure choice for some individuals may be distorted. While a sufficient condition to ensure no such distortion would be to choose $\lambda(t) = 0$, there may be other reasons in a more general model why a positive minimum retirement benefit which is independent of individual wage tax contributions would be appropriate.

Finally, it should be pointed out that for the wage tax–retirement benefit part of the system to work, it cannot be a voluntary system. That is, for most values of $\theta(t)$, the present value of aggregate retirement benefits to current workers will be less than the aggregate wages taxes paid by these workers. Because the economy with this system will replicate the perfect-market equilibrium path, it is straightforward to show that the equilibrium shadow value at time t of aggregate retirement benefits to be paid at time $t+1$ will be equal to $(1-\alpha)^2Q(t)/(2+2\alpha-\alpha^2)$. If $\eta(t)$ denotes the ratio of the shadow value of these aggregate benefits to aggregate current wage tax contributions, then $\eta(t)$ can be written as

(71) $$\eta(t) = (1-\alpha)^2/\{(2\alpha+1)[1-\theta(t)]\}.$$

Table 12.4   **An Optimal System of Taxes and Transfers to Correct the Market Failure of No Trading in Human Capital**

Taxes

A tax on wages with a constant proportional tax rate given by

$$\tau_\omega = \frac{2\alpha + 1}{2 + 2\alpha - \alpha^2}.$$

A tax on consumption with a constant proportional tax rate given by

$$\tau_c = \frac{(1 - \alpha)^2}{2 + 2\alpha - \alpha^2}.$$

Transfers

Aggregate transfers to children equal to the total revenues collected by the consumption tax

$$T_0(t) = \left[\frac{(1 - \alpha)^2(1 + \alpha + \alpha^2)}{(2\alpha + 1)(2 + 2\alpha - \alpha^2)}\right]Q(t)$$

and individual transfers to each child given by

$$T_0(t)/N_0(t).$$

Aggregate transfers to retirees equal to the total revenues collected by the wage tax

$$B(t) = \left[\frac{(2\alpha + 1)}{(2 + 2\alpha - \alpha^2)}\right][1 - \theta(t)]Q(t)$$

with individual transfers to each retiree given by

$$b(t) = \max\left\{\lambda(t - 1), 1 + \frac{(2 + \alpha^2)}{(1 - \alpha)^2}[1 - \theta(t - 1)][\chi(t - 1) - 1]\right\}\frac{B(t)}{N_2(t)},$$

where $\chi(t - 1)$ is the dollar wage taxes paid by the individual at time $t - 1$ divided by the average dollar wage taxes paid by all workers at time $t - 1$, and $\lambda(t - 1) < 1$.

By inspection of (71), $\eta(t) < 1$ whenever $\theta(t) < \alpha(4 - \alpha)/(2\alpha + 1)$. Therefore, unless $\theta(t)$ is approximately two to four times larger than its expected value, α, $\eta(t) < 1$ and workers would not, at the margin, voluntarily stay in the system.

12.5   Summary, Conclusions, and Extensions

In the model analyzed here, optimal individual life-cycle behavior in perfect markets calls for saving to be invested in the market portfolio. That is, investors would prefer to hold portfolio allocations of physical and human capital which are in proportion to their respective market values. By investing in this way, investors can eliminate factor-share risk. However, when human capital is not tradable, younger members of the economy will have too much of their savings invested in human capital while older members will have too little. Therefore, each will be exposed to factor-share risk. A constrained Pareto-optimal system of taxes and transfers was derived which corrects this portfolio imbalance and provides to all age groups more efficient risk positions by, in effect, causing their savings to be invested in the market portfolio.

Echoing Samuelson's (1975) comment about his own model of optimal social security, obviously the severe idealizations of the model presented here will have to be qualified before applying the results. The degree of real-world success this system may have in overcoming the efficiency losses from such a market failure will certainly depend on the reasons for the failure, and because such a failure is simply postulated to exist without any explanation for its cause, the analysis presented here does not deal with this issue. Both the magnitude of the efficiency loss and the detailed specification of the optimal system to correct it are, of course, sensitive to the specific general equilibrium model used to analyze the problem. For example, without the assumption of homothetic and logarithmic utility, all individual investors' optimal portfolios would not have been identical, and it is therefore unlikely that the simple system of taxes and transfers derived here would have eliminated all the inefficiencies caused by this market failure.[9] Hence, the analysis should be viewed in terms of the qualitative insights it provides for dealing with the inefficiencies caused by this market failure rather than as a quantitative prescription for policy.

With this purpose in mind, I chose to make two further extreme assumptions to both highlight the effect of this market failure and place the heaviest burden on the system derived to correct it. First, I assumed that the market failure was total, that is, that individuals could neither sell their human capital nor borrow against it in any amount. Second, I assumed that there was no intergenerational utility dependence, that is, that parents made no bequests to children and children had no concern for their parents' welfare. Since certain forms of interpersonal cooperation that are not legally binding can serve as substitutes for either markets or government intervention if there is positive interpersonal utility dependence among the participants,[10] this assumption rules out the possibility of such alternative forms being used to offset the effects of the market failure. While both some amount of marketability of human capital and the existence of intergenerational cooperating family units will tend to soften the impact of this market failure on economic efficiency, and thereby reduce the need for corrective government intervention, further research (possibly along the lines of Barro [1974]) is needed to determine whether or not they would be adequate to eliminate the need for such intervention altogether.

As I noted in the introduction, this model can be used to analyze some of the issues surrounding the present social security system. The wage tax and retirement benefit component of the optimal system derived here bears certain similarities to the funding and retirement benefit part of the present social security system. In both systems, current wages are taxed to pay current retirement benefits. Moreover, the schedule for determining individual retirement benefits in the social security system[11] is similar to the one presented in equation (64) for the system derived here. As was shown in (71) for the optimal system, and as is alleged by some for the present social security system, the present value of retirement benefits for current workers will generally be less than the wage tax contributions made by current workers. Hence, both pay-as-you-go systems require compulsory participation.

Of course, there are also differences between the structures of the two systems. The optimal system derived here requires that aggregate benefits always be equal to current aggregate tax revenues. Under the present social security system, benefits and tax rates are determined separately by law and, with the exception of the financial solvency constraint, the existing law does not require that current benefits be equal to current tax revenues. Because the wage tax rate is constant over time, aggregate benefits in the optimal system will change in a fashion perfectly correlated with changes in aggregate wage income. Therefore, individual benefits in the optimal system are, de facto, indexed to aggregate wage income divided by the number of retirees.[12] In contrast, under present law, individual social security benefits are indexed to the Consumer Price Index.

By construction, the optimal system can never become insolvent in the sense that revenues raised, both currently and in the future, will never be insufficient to pay promised benefits, both currently and in the future. In contrast, the present social security system can become insolvent if promised *future* benefits and tax rates are defined to be equal to the *current* schedule of benefits and tax rates. However, since Congress can and has changed existing law with respect to both benefits and tax rates, the only strictly vested benefits in the system are the current ones, and even these are limited by current tax revenues if the available trust funds should become exhausted. Although in principle Congress could keep the schedule of benefits fixed and correct any deficits or surpluses in the system by changing tax rates, normal congressional behavior appears to be to make changes in both benefits and tax rates.[13] Therefore, aggregate social security benefits are likely to be strongly correlated with aggregate wage income, especially in the intermediate to long run. Hence, as long as such benefits are funded solely by a wage tax, the pattern of retirement benefits from social security may be a reasonable approximation to the pattern of retirement benefits generated by the optimal system derived here.

These derived similarities between the two systems may cast some light on the widely discussed issue of whether social security should be a pay-as-you-go or fully funded system.[14] These derived similarities suggest that a latent function served, at least in part, by the present pay-as-you-go social security system is that of the optimal system derived here, namely, to improve the efficiency of risk bearing in the economy when human capital is not tradable. Indeed, the returns from a fully funded system which invests its contributions in traded securities cannot possibly replicate the returns from investing in a nontraded asset except in the singular case where a traded security exists whose returns are perfectly correlated with those of the nontraded asset. Hence, any system which attempts to replicate the returns from such a nontraded asset must at least appear to be a pay-as-you-go system. When there are significant nontraded assets in the economy, the creation of such a system will cause changes in equilibrium consumption, private saving, and portfolio allocation behavior, although the direction of these changes is, in general, ambiguous. However, as demonstrated in the model analyzed here, the effect of introducing such a system can be to increase economic efficiency whichever direction these changes take.

This analysis does not imply that the present social security system is optimal. Even if it exactly replicated the optimal system derived here, the present social security system would only be optimal if the economic objectives of the system were the same as those of the optimal system. The optimal system presented here is not designed to be the sole, or even the major, source of retirement benefits. Rather it is designed to complement private saving by providing only benefits which (by hypothesis) cannot be purchased in the private market. If the system were to be a general substitute for private saving for retirement (as at least some have suggested is the purpose of social security), then the benefits should also be linked to the returns on physical capital, and these benefits should be funded by additional taxes with such revenues invested in physical capital. That is, the optimal system for this purpose would be partially funded.

As I noted in the introduction, the absence of riskless real annuities was one of the three market failures explicitly discussed by Diamond (1977) as possible reasons for social security. Although Diamond (1977, p. 277) claims that "someone reaching retirement age with a capital sum might reasonably want to purchase a real annuity," only in very singular cases would a person at retirement optimally choose a lifetime annuity whose payments are riskless (even in real terms). As was true for the optimal consumption and portfolio decisions during the accumulation period of their lives, people will generally prefer to bear some amount of risk with respect to their retirement payments in return for a higher level of expected returns. In the model analyzed here, the optimal choice for retirees would be a life annuity whose payments depended on the returns on the market portfolio, and these are certainly not riskless. Thus, the result derived here, that benefits received by retirees are uncertain, should not be viewed as somehow suboptimal.

To reinforce this point at a somewhat more applied level of analysis, note that for a 15-year expected life and a 12% nominal interest rate an actuarially fair, nominally fixed annuity would generate an annual nominal cash flow equal to about 15% of the initial capital sum. For a 4% real interest rate (a number which at times has been suggested to be the long-run average real rate of growth in the economy), an annuity, fixed in real terms, would generate a first-year cash flow of about 9% of the initial capital sum. However, such an annuity would not be actuarially fair because to earn that average or expected real rate of 4%, the provider of the annuity would have to bear the aggregate risks of the economy, which are not diversifiable and certainly not zero. A more appropriate indicator of the proper rate to be applied to a real riskless annuity would be the historical average real return from rolling over short-term Treasury bills which, on a pretax basis, is approximately zero. Hence, an actuarially fair riskless real annuity would generate a first-year cash flow of about 6.7% of the initial capital sum. Therefore, to provide a rather modest first-year retirement income of $13,300, the capital accumulation would have to be $200,000, a considerable sum.

Because it is assumed that the durations of each person's work and retirement periods are exogenous and known with certainty, the model in its present form cannot be used to analyze the other problems of market failures discussed in Diamond (1977) where these durations are uncertain. However, the model can be extended along the lines of the Sheshinski and Weiss (1981) analysis of failure in the annuities market, to take into account durations which are exogenously stochastic. Moreover, because the present model does include a labor-leisure choice in the work period, it should be straightforward to adapt the model to the case where the length of the work period is endogenous, that is, where workers can voluntarily choose early retirement.

As a closing note, the analysis presented here indicates that the nontradability of human capital will, in general, make the solution of distortion problems caused by taxes more difficult. For example, if a proportional consumption tax were proposed to raise revenues for general government expenditures, then, by inspection of (58) and (59), it appears that a wage subsidy (i.e., a negative tax) of $\tau_\omega = -\tau$ would eliminate the distortion of the labor-leisure choice. However, such a negative wage tax will only make worse the problems of efficient risk bearing when human capital cannot be traded because the young will now find themselves forced to hold an even larger proportion of their savings in human capital.

Appendix: Optimal Consumption and Portfolio Decisions

Using the method of stochastic dynamic program, the individual optimal consumption and portfolio rules given in the text are derived.

Define the derived or indirect utility function for a person of age k at time t by

(A1) $$J_k[w_k(t),t] \equiv \max\{U_k(t)\}, k = 0, 1, 2$$

where $w_k(t)$ is the wealth of the person at age k and U_k is the lifetime utility of consumption function defined in assumption (5), (6), and (7). In the usual fashion of dynamic programming, the optimal solution is derived by working backward. From (7), it follows immediately that optimal consumption at retirement, $c_2^*(t)$, is simply given by

(A2) $$c_2^*(t) = w_2(t),$$

and therefore, from (A1),

(A3) $$J_2[w_2(t),t] = \log[w_2(t)].$$

At age 1, the derived utility of wealth function is given by

(A4) $$J_1[w_1(t),t] = \max\{\Gamma\log[\ell(t)] + \log[c_1(t)] + E_t\{J_2[w_2(t+1),t+1]\}\}.$$

From (8) and (10b), we have that

(A5) $$w_2(t+1) = [w_1(t) - c_1(t) - \omega(t)\ell(t)]\{x_{11}(t)[Z_1(t+1) - R(t)] + x_{21}(t)[Z_2(t+1) - R(t)] + R(t)\}.$$

Substituting for J_2 from (A3) and for $w_2(t+1)$ from (A5) into (A4), and maximizing with respect to the choice variables $\{c_1(t), \ell(t), x_{11}(t), x_{21}(t)\}$, we have the following first-order conditions:

(A6) $$c_1^*(t) = [w_1(t) - \omega(t)\ell^*(t)]/2,$$

(A7) $$\ell^*(t) = \Gamma[w_1(t) - c_1^*(t)]/(1 + \Gamma)\omega(t),$$

and

(A8) $$0 = E_t\left\{\frac{Z_j(t+1) - R(t)}{x_{11}^*(t)[Z_1(t+1) - R(t)] + x_{21}^*(t)[Z_1(t+1) - R(t)] + R(t)}\right\}, j = 1,2.$$

From (A6) and (A7), it follows that

(A9) $$c_1^*(t) = \frac{w_1(t)}{2 + \Gamma},$$

(A10)
$$\ell^*(t) = \frac{\Gamma w_1(t)}{(2 + \Gamma)\omega(t)},$$

and

(A11)
$$s_1^*(t) = \frac{w_1(t)}{2 + \Gamma}.$$

These optimal rules are reported in (12) in the text.

Substituting for these optimal rules in (A4), we have that

$$J_1[w_1(t), t] = (2 + \Gamma)\log[w_1(t)] - \Gamma\log[\omega(t)]$$
$$+ \Gamma\log\Gamma - (2 + \Gamma)\log\Gamma + E_t\{\log[Z_*^1(t + 1)]\},$$

where $Z_*^1(t + 1)$ is the return per dollar on the optimal portfolio which satisfies (A8).

At age 0, the derived utility of wealth function is given by

(A13) $J_0[w_0(t), t] = \max\left(\log[c_0(t)] + E_t\{J_1[w_1(t + 1), t + 1]\}\right),$

where, from (8) and (10a) in the text, we have that

(A14) $w_1(t + 1) = [w_0(t) - c_0(t)]\{x_{10}(t)[Z_1(t + 1) - R(t)]$
$$+ x_{20}(t)[Z_2(t + 1) - R(t)] + R(t)\}.$$

Substituting for J_1 from (A12) and $w_1(t + 1)$ from (A14) into (A13), and maximizing with respect to the choice variables $\{c_0(t), x_{10}(t), x_{20}(t)\}$, we have the following first-order conditions:

(A15)
$$c_0^*(t) = \frac{w_0(t)}{3 + \Gamma},$$

(A16) $0 = E_t\left\{\dfrac{Z_j(t + 1) - R(t)}{\substack{x_{10}^*(t)[Z_1(t + 1) - R(t)] \\ + x_{20}^*(t)[Z_2(t + 1) - R(t)] + R(t)}}\right\}, j = 1, 2,$

and from (10a) and (A15), it follows that

(A17)
$$s_0^*(t) = \left(\frac{2 + \Gamma}{3 + \Gamma}\right)w_0(t).$$

These optimal age 0 consumption and saving rules are reported in (11).

By inspection of (A8) and (A16), the fractional allocations in the optimal portfolios of age 0 and age 1 people are identical. Hence, all investors will optimally hold the same relative proportions of securities, and these common optimal portfolio weights are given in the text by (13).

Notes

1. While this characterization of optimal portfolio choice is usually identified with the mean-variance model of portfolio selection, such broad diversification is, indeed, a property of most optimal strategies for risk averters. See Merton (1982), sections III and IV, and especially proposition 4.2.

2. For another overlapping-generations model with the same three-period life, see the appendix to Sheshinski and Weiss (1981). As will be apparent later in my analysis, in the absence of bequests three is the minimum number of periods required in order for trading in human capital (i.e., future wage income) to take place.

3. Of course, this does not imply that such cross-sectional risks among workers are believed to be unimportant.

4. It is, of course, reasonable to expect that population growth will be influenced by the level of aggregate economic activity. For further discussion and a simple model which incorporates such population dependencies, see Merton (1969). However, unlike in the social insurance models of Green (1977) and Smith (1981), demographic uncertainties play no essential role in this analysis.

5. This result is most closely associated with the equilibrium conditions in a mean-variance portfolio model with homogeneous beliefs. However, as seen here, it does hold in other cases, including every model with a representative man. As noted in Merton (1982, sec. IV), "Indeed, if there were one best investment strategy, and if this 'best' strategy were widely known, then whatever the original statement of the strategy, it must lead to simply this imperative: 'hold the market portfolio.'"

6. Indeed, under the extreme assumptions of no borrowing against or sale of human capital and no bequests, children, and therefore society, could not survive without such correction.

7. The terms "pay as you go" and "fully funded" have been used in a variety of ways in the literature. I use them as they are defined in Sheshinski and Weiss (1981, p. 189): a system is "fully funded" if contributions to the system are invested at the market rate of interest and a system is "pay as you go" if taxes on the currently working population are used to finance benefits to the retired population. For a brief description of the present social security system, see Diamond (1977).

8. See Atkinson and Stiglitz (1980) for a general discussion of the consumption and wage taxes and their distortion of the labor-leisure choice.

9. However, a similar system will work to eliminate the inefficiencies in the somewhat more general case where lifetime utility is given by

$$U_0(t) = \log[c_0(t) + a_0] + E_t\{\Gamma\log[\ell(t+1) + b] + \log[c_1(t+1) + a_1] + \log[c_2(t+2) + a_2]\}.$$

Note: $U_0(t)$ is not homothetic. For further discussion of the properties of this utility function, see Rubinstein (1976).

10. See Kotlikoff and Spivak (1981) for an example of such substitution. Kurz (1981) provides some empirical evidence which rejects this extreme no-bequest life-cycle assumption of behavior.

11. For the formula used in the present social security system to determine individual benefits, see Diamond (1977), p. 276, Eq. (1) and n. 8.

12. As mentioned in note 4 above, demographics do not significantly affect the analysis of inefficiencies in this model. Indeed, for a given level of aggregate output, the population size or its age distribution has no effect on aggregate consumption and saving or their distributions among age groups. However, since these aggregates, including aggregate retirement benefits, have this property, per capita consumption and therefore individual welfare are significantly affected. It should be noted that these effects on individual welfare

caused by demographics are identical in both the perfect market and optimal tax and transfer economies.

13. Diamond (1977, p.277) reports that "Congressional attitude appears to be that it is appropriate to increase benefits whenever the system can finance such an increase over the following 75 years . . . ." Since 1977, there have been increases in payroll taxes voted by Congress, and at the current time serious consideration is being given to the reduction of benefits in response to the belief that revenues will not be adequate to fund future benefits at the current levels.

14. See Barro (1974, 1976), Feldstein (1974, 1976), Samuelson (1975), Buchanan (1976), and Sheshinski and Weiss (1981) for discussion on this issue. Unlike the others, but like the model developed here, Samuelson (1975) assumes no bequests.

References

Atkinson, A. B., and Stiglitz, J. E. 1980. *Lectures on public economics*. New York: McGraw-Hill.

Barro, R. J. 1974. Are government bonds net wealth? *Journal of Political Economy* 82 (December): 1095–1117.

———. 1976. Reply to Buchanan and Feldstein. *Journal of Political Economy* 84 (April): 343–50.

Buchanan, J. M. 1976. Barro on the Richardian equivalence theorem. *Journal of Public Economics* 84 (April): 337–42.

Diamond, P. A. 1977. A framework for social security analysis. *Journal of Public Economics* 83 (April): 275–98.

Feldstein, M. S. 1974. Social security, induced retirement, and aggregate capital accumulation. *Journal of Political Economy* 82 (October): 905–26.

———. 1976. Perceived wealth in bonds and social security: A comment. *Journal of Political Economy* 84 (April): 331–36.

Green, J. R. 1977. Mitigating demographic risk through social insurance. Harvard University, November (unpublished paper).

Hakansson, N. H. 1970. Optimal investment and consumption strategies under risk for a class of utility functions. *Econometrica* 38 (September): 587–607.

Kotlikoff, L. J., and Spivak, A. 1981. The family as an incomplete annuities market. *Journal of Political Economy* 89 (April): 372–91.

Kurz, M. 1981. The life-cycle hypothesis and the effects of social security and private pensions on family savings. Technical Report no. 335. Institute for Mathematical Studies in Social Sciences, Stanford University, May.

Merton, R. C. 1969. A golden golden-rule for welfare-maximization in an economy with a varying population growth rate. *Western Economic Journal* 4 (December): 307–18.

———. 1982. On the microeconomic theory of investment under uncertainty. In *Handbook of mathematical economics*, ed. K. J. Arrow and M. D. Intriligator. Vol. 2. Amsterdam: North-Holland.

Rubinstein, M. 1976. The strong case for the generalized logarithmic utility model as the premier model of financial markets. *Journal of Finance* 31 (May): 551–72.

Samuelson, P. A. 1969. Lifetime portfolio selection by dynamic stochastic programming. *Review of Economics and Statistics* 51 (August): 239–49.

———. 1975. Optimum social security in a life-cycle growth model. *International Economic Review* 16 (October): 538–44.

Sheshinski, E., and Weiss, Y. 1981. Uncertainty and optimal social security systems. *Quarterly Journal of Economics* 96 (May): 189–206.

Smith, A. 1981. Intergenerational transfers as social insurance. London School of Economics, January (unpublished paper).

13 The Economic Status of the Elderly

Michael D. Hurd and John B. Shoven

Introduction

This chapter seeks to present a picture of the economic status of the elderly. We examine the change in their cost of living relative to that of the rest of the population; the size, composition, and distribution of their income; and, correspondingly, the size, composition, and distribution of their wealth. We develop and calculate a measure of their vulnerability to one-time unexpected changes in the price level and to an unexpected increase in the long-run rate of inflation (and interest rates). In order to assess the economic welfare of the elderly, we use a variety of data sources, but most of our analysis comes from the Social Security Administration's *Retirement History Survey*. We use the 1969, 1971, 1973, and 1975 surveys from that longitudinal data file.

We seek to determine how the elderly have been faring economically for a number of reasons. First, they are usually considered to be the segment of the population most vulnerable to inflation. The image of an elderly household struggling to get by on a fixed pension or meager interest income from a modest savings account is an enduring one. The past 15 years have seen a marked and, presumably, unexpected increase in the rate of inflation. So, how have they coped? Second, the size and number of governmental programs to assist the aged have increased. At the federal level, social security, Supplemental Security Income (SSI),

Michael D. Hurd is professor of economics, State University of New York, Stony Brook, and is a research associate of the National Bureau of Economic Research and a fellow at the Hoover Institution. John B. Shoven is professor of economics, Stanford University, and is a research associate of the National Bureau of Economic Research.

We admit that if we divide Peter Menell's research assistant stipend by his long hours, we violated the federal minimum wage law. His work was exceptional. We also greatly benefited from the efforts of Phil Farrell and Paul Chen. Reluctantly, we take the blame for the shortcomings.

and medicare have all grown rapidly. How significantly have these programs affected the incomes and wealth of the elderly? Third, it is well known that the labor force participation of the elderly has been falling secularly. Has this meant lower incomes? Finally, some of the assets in which elderly invest for retirement, particularly common stocks, have performed very poorly. How much has this hurt their position?

We want to emphasize that we evaluate the economic welfare of the elderly only in the narrowest sense. A major determinant of the happiness of the elderly is their health, which we do not take into account. Further, we do not evaluate the increased leisure which accompanies their reduced labor force participation. Nor can we assess a number of other factors determining their well-being, such as life expectancy, changing living arrangements and housing, and decreasing intergenerational contact. Without these considerations we do not present our results as a complete assessment of the welfare of the elderly, but we do believe that our data give a good appraisal of how the financial position of the elderly has changed in the past decade or so.

13.1   Cost of Living

In order to assess the incomes and wealth of the elderly, all of which are available only in nominal terms, we must examine what has happened to their cost of living. First we attempt to answer whether their cost of living has changed relative to that of the rest of the population. The possibility of a difference arises because of the elderly's particular expenditure patterns and because of the fact that relative prices have changed. To address this question, a researcher usually compares the Department of Labor's consumer price index (CPI), which uses the expenditure weights of the entire population, with a Laspeyres index which uses the expenditure weights of the elderly. Virtually all researchers who have done this (see, for example, Bridges and Packard 1981) have reached the same conclusion: while expenditure weights vary by age, prices have changed in such a way that over reasonably long time periods the price index of the elderly has risen the same amount as the CPI. Recent results of Boskin and Hurd (1982) are shown in table 13.1. They divide expenditure into 17 categories and calculate cost of living indices for five age groups. The measures are set at 100 in 1967. The first result which is apparent in Table 13.1 is that there is essentially no variation in the index across age groups for the years shown.[1] Thus, the percentage increase in the cost of living since 1967 has been the same for each age group despite significantly different expenditure patterns and sharp changes in relative prices. A second finding, of equal importance for this paper, is shown in table 13.1. For all age groups, the Boskin and Hurd cost-of-living indices have grown more slowly than the official CPI. While their figures show that the cost of

Table 13.1   Cost-of-Living Indices in 1980 by Age (1967 = 100)

Year	Age (Years)					CPI
	< 60	60–64	65–69	70–74	75+	
1967	100.0	100.0	100.0	100.0	100.0	100.0
1968	103.6	103.6	103.5	103.5	103.5	104.2
1969	108.0	108.0	107.9	107.9	108.0	109.8
1974	142.1	142.9	142.9	143.2	144.5	147.7
1975	153.9	154.9	154.8	155.2	156.5	161.2
1980	227.0	229.2	228.4	229.3	230.4	246.8

Sources: First five columns, Boskin and Hurd (1982); last column, *Economic Report of the President* (1982), table B-52.

living was roughly 128% higher in 1980 than 1967, the CPI indicates that the increase was 147%. The reason for this is that the official index weights housing far more than the estimates of Boskin and Hurd, which use a rental value measure of housing expenditure similar to that to be adopted by the U.S. Department of Labor in 1983. The overstatement of inflation by the CPI is important for the elderly, as social security benefits are tied to this measure during the payout period.

13.2   Incomes of the Elderly Population

Given that the cost of living of various age groups has risen proportionately, we can compare real income growth of the elderly with that of the total population by comparing the growth of nominal incomes. Table 13.2 shows per household and per capita income data for both the

Table 13.2   Income of the Elderly and the Entire Population

	1970	1973	1976	1978
Elderly				
1. Personal income ($ billions)	81.84	112.06	160.55	199.53
2. Real income per household ($)	5,692	6,258	6,363	6,718
3. Real income per capita ($)	3,503	3,947	4,104	4,250
Entire population				
4. Personal income ($ billions)	801.	1,052.	1,381.	1,708.
5. Real income per household ($)	10,863	11,581	11,116	11,497
6. Real income per capita ($)	3,362	3,767	3,752	3,997
Income ratios				
7. Per household	.52	.54	.57	.58
8. Per capita	1.04	1.05	1.09	1.06

Source: Statistical Abstract of the U.S., various years.

Note: Conversion from nominal to real incomes used Bureau of Labor Statistics' CPI (1967 = 100).

elderly (head of household age 65 or over) and the entire population. Row 1 in that table shows a series on personal incomes (before tax incomes) of the elderly. It includes, besides the usual sources of income, imputed returns from owner-occupied housing and the income value of medicare and medicaid.[2] Rows 2 and 3 show that real income per household and per capita grew continuously over the period 1970–78, although more than half of the growth occurred between 1970 and 1973. The conversion from nominal to the real incomes of this table used the Bureau of Labor Statistics' CPI. If the CPI overstated the rate of inflation, as we mentioned in section 13.1, then the growth in real income is actually higher than shown. This would be true for the entire population as well, of course. Rows 5 and 6 show real income per household and per capita for the entire population. The percentage growth is substantially higher in the per capita series because of the sharp decline in the number of persons per household in the below-65 group.

Row 7 of table 13.2 displays the ratio of average elderly household personal income to average household personal income for the entire population. We see that elderly households, which are much smaller than nonelderly households in size, had on average 52% as much personal income as the average household in the entire population in 1970. By 1978 the relative household personal income of the elderly had risen to 58%. This change in the relative position of a large subpopulation over such a short time interval is remarkable. Another measure of the relative position of the elderly is shown in row 8 of table 13.2, where the ratios of per capita personal incomes are reported.[3] The elderly have higher per capita incomes than the nonelderly, and they gained on the rest of the population in the first 8 years of the 1970s. The gain in the per capita figures is more modest than in the per household figures because of the decline in the number of persons per household in the nonaged group.

The results of table 13.2 are even stronger when one considers that during this period labor force participation declined among the elderly but increased sharply among the nonelderly. For example, the participation rate of males 65 and over declined from 25.8% in 1970 to 19.7% in 1978; the participation rate of elderly females declined from 9.2% to 7.8%; yet the participation rate of the entire population rose from 60.3% to 62.7%. Despite this, the elderly gained on the nonelderly in terms of relative income. This relative income shift was partly due to the slow growth in real wages. Real before-tax wages grew by only 4.85% for the entire period 1970 to 1978.

In table 13.3 we examine how the poorer households and individuals among the elderly have done relative to an arbitrary real income standard, the official poverty level. It shows a very substantial decrease in the fraction of elderly with incomes less than this standard.[4] This is particularly striking for elderly families, 27% of whom were below the poverty level in 1959. By 1978 only 7.6% of such families had incomes below the poverty level. The incidence of poverty is much higher for unrelated elderly individuals, primarily women, but here, too, significant progress is shown.

Table 13.4 augments the income data of the previous two tables by providing a time series of income composition of the elderly. The figures

Table 13.3   **Persons 65 Years and Over Below the Poverty Level**

	Total (%)	Total Number Below (1,000)	Families (%)	Families Number Below (1,000)	Unrelated Individuals (%)	Unrelated Individuals Number Below (1,000)
1978	14.0	3,233	7.6	1,180	27.0	2,053
1976	15.0	3,313	7.9	1,185	30.3	2,129
1974	15.7	3,308	8.5	1,243	31.8	2,065
1972	18.6	3,738	10.4	1,444	37.1	2,295
1970	24.5	4,709	14.7	1,975	47.1	2,735
1968	25.0	4,632	15.4	2,048	48.8	2,584
1959	35.2	5,481	26.9	3,187	61.9	2,294

Source: Bureau of the Census, *P-60 Series*, various years.

Table 13.4   **Shares of Aggregate Income of Aged Units 65 and Older: Percentage Distribution from Particular Sources of Income**

Source	1963[a]	1967[b]	1976[c]	1978[d]
Retirement pensions	35	39	44	41
Social security	27	29	32	30
Railroad retirement	<1	<1	1	1
Government employee pensions	5	6	5	5
Private pensions or annuities	3	4	6	5
Veteran's benefits	4	3	<1	<1
Earnings	29	25	18	18
Income from assets	14	13	14	15
Income from housing assets	8	8	7	7
Medicaid/medicare	2	7	13	16
Public assistance	5	3	2	2
Other	4	3	2	2
Mean income[e]	$3,504	$4,306	$ 8,708	$10,291
Mean housing services[f]	$ 306	$ 392	$ 736	$ 957
Mean medicaid/medicare[g]	$ 69	$ 330	$ 1,405	$ 1,879
Mean total income	$3,879	$5,028	$10,849	$13,127

Sources: [a]Epstein (1964).
    [b]U.S. Department of HEW, SSA Report No. 45 75-11802.
    [c]U.S. Department of HEW, SSA Publication No. 13-11865.
    [d]*Income of the Population 55 and Over, 1978*, SSA Staff Paper No. 41.
    [e]U.S. Bureau of the Census, *P-60 Series*, various years.
    [f]U.S. Bureau of the Census, *Annual Housing Survey: 1973–1979*.
    [g]*Statistical Abstract of the U.S.*, various years.

show the percentage of total income derived from particular sources. The table shows that social security pensions and private pensions have both become more important income sources. However, the more dramatic shifts involve medicare/medicaid and labor earnings. Labor earnings accounted for 29% of all income of the elderly in 1963 but only 18% in 1976 and 1978. This fall of more than 50% in relative importance and a total of 11 percentage points is more than matched by the growth in medicare/medicaid.[5] Public assistance and veteran's benefits have declined in relative importance. This is probably because they have been displaced by the more generous pensions and medicare benefits.

13.4 Income of the Retirement History Survey Population

The remainder of this chapter uses the Social Security Administration's Retirement History Survey (RHS) as the primary data source. It contained 8,244 households whose ages ranged from 58 to 63 in 1969, whom we could track to 1975, and whose records were complete enough to be usable. We report on their economic status in 1969 and 1975, but we used the intervening 1971 and 1973 surveys to impute values which were missing in either 1969 or 1975. It should be noted that the remainder of our results are not necessarily accurate for the entire elderly population, but rather for a group which was 58–63 in 1969 and 64–69 in 1975.

Table 13.5 divides the RHS sample into six vintages by age of head of household in January 1969. It then shows the mean real income in 1968 dollars of each vintage in 1968 and 1974. The results are presented for couples, singles, and total households. For couples and households, one observes a noticeable decline in income with age in both 1968 and 1974. However, the real incomes in 1974 are higher than one would project

Table 13.5	Mean Real Income (1968 $), by Age and Family Status of RHS Sample					
Age in 1969/ Age in 1975	58/64	59/65	60/66	61/67	62/68	63/69
Couples						
1968	10,764	10,128	10,041	10,204	10,116	8,934
1974	9,853	9,517	8,871	9,276	9,112	8,832
Singles						
1968	4,558	4,245	4,270	4,304	4,178	4,198
1974	4,214	4,796	4,552	4,761	4,503	4,599
Households						
1968	8,868	8,336	8,077	8,172	7,976	7,239
1974	7,757	7,781	7,154	7,396	7,148	6,978

Note: Age is age of family head in 1969 and 1975.

simply from the income-age profile in the 1968 cross section. For couples, we roughly estimate that there is an upward shift in the income-age relationships of at least $1,000, or about 10%. This can be seen in figure 13.1. One would imagine that incomes would continue to drop at age 64, reflecting increased retirement; instead, income is substantially higher among couples whose heads were 64 in 1974.[6] The upward shift is less for households. The figures for singles are clouded by compositional changes—there are more singles in 1974 than in 1968, particularly widows. These new entrants into the single category bring with them assets and corresponding income from the previous couples category.

Two other observations should be noted here: (1) among couples and households real income is lower in 1974 than in 1968 for all age groups. This is a normal pattern with aging, and it is due to the sharp increase in the fraction of the RHS population retired. The drop in the real income of each vintage is not an indication that consumption or welfare of each vintage decreased. (2) In this table and in subsequent ones, we have

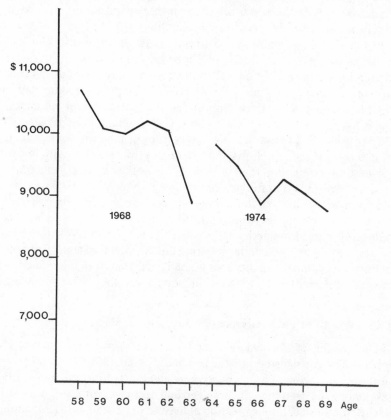

Fig. 13.1   Real income of couples.

used the Boskin-Hurd cost-of-living deflator (of table 13.1) rather than the official CPI.

Table 13.6 shows the distribution of real income in 1968 and 1974 by family type. Several points can be made about them. First, the median real incomes are substantially less than the mean incomes. For example, for households in 1968, the median income was $6,658 whereas the mean was $8,136. The most striking fact about these distributions, however, is the increase in the incomes of those in the lower tail of the distribution. Most dramatically, single women in the lowest 5% of the income distribution had incomes less than $208 in 1968.[7] This figure was raised more than sixfold to $1,327 in 1974. The largest single contributor to this increase was the eligibility for medicare at age 65, although social security receipt was also a major factor. The lower tail of the other income distributions also was raised substantially from 1968 to 1974, while the real income of those in the upper tail of the distribution was lowered (with the exception of the single-women category, which again particularly reflects the compositional changes previously discussed). The reduction of the real incomes of those in the upper tail of the income distribution is primarily a result of decreased labor force participation.

Table 13.7 gives additional information about the distribution of income in the RHS sample. It displays the Gini coefficient of income inequality for both 1968 and 1974. The Gini coefficient has been constructed so that a measure of zero reflects complete equality and one complete inequality. This commonly used measure has been estimated at .4746 for family income for the entire U.S. population in 1966 (Okner 1975). Table 13.7 shows that inequality is lower than this for our sample of elderly. Further, it shows that inequality was substantially lower in 1974 for this population than in 1968. We hypothesize that the increase in inequality observed in the population aged 62 and 63 in 1969 relative to the younger members of the sample is due to the fact that some of the 62- and 63-year-olds have retired, while others have not. Inequality is sharply reduced for this vintage by 1974 when the vast majority of them have retired. In general, we cannot separate out the effects of aging from those of time on income inequality, but we believe that most of the reduction in inequality from 1968 to 1974 in our population does reflect its aging.

13.5   Wealth of the Retirement History Survey Population

Our results of the last two sections have shown that the elderly's income has grown faster than the rest of the population, that the composition of their income has changed, and suggest that income inequality is less among the aged than the nonaged and decreases with age. A measure of the elderly's economic position at least as important as their income is their wealth. In this section, we calculate nonhuman capital balance

Table 13.6   **Income Distribution (1968 $) of Retirement History Survey Population, Ages 58–63 in 1969**

Percentile Points	Households		Couples		Single Males		Single Females	
	1968	1974	1968	1974	1968	1974	1968	1974
5	840	1,840	1,840	3,007	484	1,673	208	1,327
10	1,455	2,413	3,050	3,783	919	2,217	676	1,775
25	3,492	3,538	5,400	5,351	2,180	3,003	1,484	2,560
50	6,658	5,681	8,551	7,504	4,844	4,302	3,198	3,525
75	10,600	8,775	12,201	10,665	7,820	6,231	5,250	5,160
90	15,310	13,073	17,626	15,566	11,030	8,111	7,840	7,763
95	20,160	17,007	23,232	21,188	14,000	11,955	9,786	9,608
Mean	8,136	7,219	10,072	9,276	5,731	5,237	3,870	4,302
N	7,947	8,074	5,785	4,585	603	795	2,059	2,694

Source: Retirement History Survey.

Table 13.7   Gini Coefficients of Income Inequality
                  for RHS Sample by Age and Family Status

Age in 1969	58 and 59	60 and 61	62 and 63
Couples			
1968	.357	.368	.380
1974	.349	.332	.340
Singles			
1968	.447	.432	.462
1974	.372	.311	.311
Households			
1968	.415	.427	.440
1974	.400	.366	.373

Note: Gini coefficient is defined as 2A in the chart below.

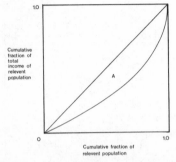

sheets of the Retirement History Survey population. Information on means and the distribution of wealth will be presented. Our wealth calculation includes the capitalized value of all cash flows except labor income. That is, the entries under pensions and annuities, SSI, welfare and other transfers, medicare, social security, and transfers from relatives are all capitalizations of current or anticipated flows using a real discount rate of 4% and the correct life expectancy for each unit.

Table 13.8 gives mean assets over households reporting positive values and the percent reporting positive values.[8] This permits us to separate the change in mean value into a change in "participation" and a change in mean value of those participating. The table indicates a decrease in the fraction of the sample owning homes from 68.3% to 64.8%. The average house appreciated 62% in nominal terms or about 9.3% real. Among participants, farm values only increased at about the inflation rate, even though farmland generally increased at a much faster rate. This probably was due to a higher rate of retirement among wealthy farmers. Both farm and business ownership decreased substantially. The people in the sample were paying off home mortgages (only 15.3% had them in 1975, vs. 22.8% in 1969) and farm mortgages. The participation in United States bonds is down sharply and the participation in the stock market is down slightly. There is an increase in both the real balance and the

Table 13.8   Mean Wealth and Income over Households
                    Having Positive Values, RHS Sample

	1969		1975	
	% Having Positive Values	Mean ($)	% Having Positive Values	Mean ($)
Wealth				
House, market value	68.3	18,411	64.8	28,880
House, mortgage	22.8	6,743	15.3	8,495
Farm, market value	10.6	36,515	6.9	52,269
Farm, mortgage	2.9	13,287	0.6	27,114
Business, market value	8.3	48,301	4.2	62,506
Other property, market value	17.2	22,352	14.8	31,209
U.S. bonds	24.0	3,088	17.8	4,147
Stocks/bonds/shares	19.0	24,593	18.4	25,406
Loan assets	9.2	8,697	9.9	15,489
Checking accounts	56.6	1,072	61.5	1,224
Savings accounts	53.0	6,735	58.1	12,122
Income				
Government pensions	7.4	3,063	10.5	4,730
Private pensions	16.9	2,291	22.5	2,438

participation in savings accounts. As one would expect, there is an increase in the fraction of the RHS population receiving or anticipating receiving pensions. This is partly due to vesting and partly due to the lack of accurate information before retirement about pension rights.

As far as inflation vulnerability is concerned, it is difficult to see any shift away from vulnerable assets between 1969 and 1975, even though inflation had increased substantially.

In table 13.9 we present average asset and liability holdings in 1969 over our entire sample and over a number of subsamples.[9] Mean wealth in 1969 was a rather modest $71,302. We view the distribution of wealth, however, to be the most striking information in the table. The mean wealth of the poorest 10% of the population was $15,324, or only 21% of the average for the whole sample. Over 86% of their wealth is in the form of social security and medicare. On average, all other assets sum to only $2,123 for this group. In contrast, social security and medicare amount to 43% of the wealth of the whole population and only 15% of the wealth of those in the upper 10% of the wealth distribution.

Those in the wealthiest 10% of the RHS sample in 1969 had on average 3.3 times as much wealth as the entire RHS population. The value of their corporate stocks and bonds was almost eight times as great as for the sample population, and their business wealth was over eight times as great as for the average of the whole sample. Their shares of farm wealth, United States bonds, other property, and loan assets was also higher than their share of total wealth. Proportionately, they had less of their wealth

Table 13.9   Balance Sheet of the RHS Sample, 1969, Mean Values

	All	Nonfarm	10% Wealth Tail	90% Wealth Tail	Couples	Singles	Singles Males	Singles Females
1. Net house	11,343	10,346	635	24,710	13,528	6,996	5,470	7,449
2. Net farm	3,574	...	109	31,079	4,789	1,115	3,201	496
3. Net business	3,580	3,385	17	31,149	5,028	671	1,111	538
4. Net other property	4,179	3,984	175	23,840	5,323	1,878	2,064	1,816
5. U.S. bonds	807	822	32	3,673	897	627	995	515
6. Corporate stocks and bonds	5,247	5,050	36	41,806	6,839	2,046	2,635	1,866
7. Loan assets	841	674	22	5,548	1,018	486	642	438
8. Bank accounts	4,775	4,584	371	18,509	5,274	3,770	4,039	3,680
9. Nonproperty debts	(388)	(317)	(162)	(1,571)	(499)	(166)	(360)	(108)
10. Pensions and annuities	6,645	7,033	269	22,956	7,670	4,585	6,574	3,974
11. SSI	...	...	...	...	...	...	...	...
12. Welfare and other transfers	338	345	619	716	333	348	350	346
13. Medicare	7,086	7,021	5,061	8,010	8,225	4,797	3,828	5,088
14. Social security	23,275	23,598	8,140	28,516	27,067	15,654	12,530	16,560
15. Transfers from relatives	...	...	...	...	...	...	...	...
16. Total wealth	71,302	66,423	15,324	238,942	85,474	42,811	43,078	42,657
17. N	8,164	7,201	813	816	5,452	2,712	622	2,090

in houses, SSI, welfare, social security, and medicare. Bank accounts and pensions form roughly the same proportion of the portfolio of the wealthy as of the average portfolio for the RHS sample.

Singles were substantially poorer than couples, with their wealth barely half that of couples. Single women have roughly the same wealth as single men, although the composition varies somewhat. On average, single women have smaller financial assets but a more valuable claim on social security and medicare. This latter fact is primarily due to their longer life expectancies. If their longer life expectancy is taken into account, their financial position may be worse than that of single men in that they have to use about the same wealth to finance a longer expected retirement. Farmers were much wealthier than the rest of our sample: their mean wealth was $108,083.

Table 13.10 contains the balance sheets for the same subpopulations of the RHS sample as table 13.9, but the figures are for 1975. Mean wealth for the whole sample has risen to $107,243 in current dollars. The mean wealth of those below the tenth and above the ninetieth percentile points are $25,682 and $321,455, respectively. By examining row 17, we can see the compositional changes. The number of couples is down by 759, while the number of single women is up by 652 and the number of single men by 187. The mean wealth of the single women now exceeds that of single men.

The relative amounts in tables 13.9 and 13.10 can best be assessed by referring to table 13.11, which reports the percentage change in real mean values of the various balance sheet entries. It shows a 16.7% average real gain in house value between 1969 and 1975, a 34% decrease in average farm value, and a 52% decrease in real business value. The real value of stocks and bonds was down more than 20% for the entire RHS population, and about 26% for those in the top 10% of the wealth distribution. This is at least partly due to decreased participation. Substantially more real wealth was held in the form of bank accounts in 1975, perhaps because of the effective deregulation of interest rate ceilings during this period. Pensions and annuities were up 22% for the whole population.

The overall gain in real wealth was 4.8%. Apparently, the wealth distribution became somewhat more equal in that the mean wealth of the poorest 10% increased 16.8% while that of the richest 10% fell 6.2%. The poor performance of the stock market may account for much of this decline.

Table 13.12 gives a more complete picture of the wealth distributions in 1969 and 1975. The first point to make is to contrast these distributions with the income distributions of table 13.6. The wealth distributions changed far less between 1969 and 1975. This is because the 1969 wealth figures include the capitalized value of assets (such as social security and

Table 13.10 Balance Sheet of the RHS Sample, 1975, Mean Values

	All	Nonfarm	10% Wealth Tail	90% Wealth Tail	Couples	Singles	Singles	
							Males	Females
1. Net house	19,000	17,085	1,147	56,013	24,629	11,562	10,664	11,828
2. Net farm	3,366	(54)	10	25,942	4,828	1,434	2,353	1,163
3. Net business	2,479	2,456	(118)	20,846	3,992	480	644	430
4. Net other property	5,934	5,514	254	34,042	8,297	2,811	2,940	2,774
5. U.S. bonds	894	885	37	3,243	1,077	653	859	592
6. Corporate stocks and bonds	5,683	5,542	38	42,383	7,898	2,755	3,378	2,572
7. Loan assets	1,620	1,476	48	9,517	2,236	807	930	770
8. Bank accounts	9,185	8,816	671	33,186	11,153	6,583	6,972	6,468
9. Nonproperty debts	(520)	(488)	(469)	(1,661)	(716)	(263)	(337)	(242)
10. Pensions and annuities	11,618	11,798	624	36,943	14,404	7,935	10,032	7,315
11. SSI	710	754	2,393	144	423	1,089	736	1,193
12. Welfare and other transfers	708	727	632	718	710	709	1,082	596
13. Medicare	10,954	10,858	7,728	12,923	13,527	7,553	6,725	7,797
14. Social security	35,152	35,117	12,499	45,411	44,148	23,262	18,803	24,578
15. Transfers from relatives	461	421	186	1,806	433	497	121	608
16. Total wealth	107,243	100,905	25,682	321,455	137,033	67,865	65,903	68,444
17. N	8,244	7,676	815	824	4,693	3,551	809	2,742

Table 13.11 Percentage Real Change in Mean Value of Balance Sheet Entries between 1969 and 1975 for RHS Sample

	All	Nonfarm	10% Wealth Tail	90% Wealth Tail	Couples	Singles	Singles Males	Singles Females
1. Net house	+16.7	+15.1	+25.9	+58.0	+26.9	+15.2	+35.9	+10.7
2. Net farm	−34.4	⋯	−93.6	−41.8	−29.7	−0.1	−48.8	−63.4
3. Net business	−51.7	−49.4	⋯	−53.4	−44.7	−50.1	−59.6	−44.3
4. Net other property	−1.0	−3.6	−2.4	−0.6	+8.6	+4.3	−0.7	+6.4
5. U.S. bonds	−22.8	−25.0	−19.4	−38.4	−16.3	−27.4	−39.8	−19.9
6. Corporate stocks and bonds	−24.5	−23.5	−26.4	−29.3	−19.5	−6.2	−10.7	−3.9
7. Loan assets	+34.2	+52.6	+52.0	+19.6	+53.1	+15.7	+0.9	+22.5
8. Bank accounts	+34.0	+34.0	+26.0	+24.8	+47.4	+21.7	+20.3	+22.5
9. Nonproperty debts	(−6.6)	(+7.3)	(+101.7)	(−26.4)	(−0.0)	(+10.4)	(−34.8)	(+56.1)
10. Pensions and annuities	+21.8	+16.9	+61.7	+12.8	+30.9	+20.6	+6.3	+28.3
11. SSI	⋯	⋯	⋯	⋯	⋯	⋯	⋯	⋯
12. Welfare and other transfers	+46.0	+46.8	−29.6	−30.7	+48.6	+42.0	+115.4	+20.0
13. Medicare	+7.7	+7.8	+6.4	+12.5	+14.6	+9.7	+22.4	+6.8
14. Social security	+5.2	+3.7	+7.0	+11.0	+13.7	+3.6	+4.6	+3.4
15. Transfers from relatives	⋯	⋯	⋯	⋯	⋯	⋯	⋯	⋯
16. Total wealth	+4.8	+5.9	+16.8	−6.2	+11.7	+10.5	+6.6	+11.8

Table 13.12   Wealth Distribution of RHS Sample

Percentile Points	All Households	Nonfarm	Couples	Singles	Single Males	Single Females
			1969			
N	8,164	7,201	5,452	2,712	622	2,090
5%	16,415	15,824	27,658	10,833	10,298	11,323
10%	21,990	21,356	33,926	14,877	13,237	15,688
25%	35,070	33,681	46,027	21,708	18,847	22,544
50%	54,224	52,166	63,612	33,499	29,317	34,145
75%	79,430	76,262	89,737	52,315	52,594	52,019
90%	118,298	109,706	135,111	76,883	80,933	76,099
95%	161,817	145,283	190,298	102,978	105,767	102,592
Mean	71,302	66,423	85,474	42,811	43,328	42,657
			1975 (1969 $)			
N	8,244	7,676	4,693	3,551	809	2,742
5%	19,049	18,772	34,220	14,643	13,068	15,667
10%	23,701	23,267	40,602	18,371	15,688	19,386
25%	36,247	34,942	55,292	25,002	22,029	26,114
50%	59,142	57,074	76,310	36,419	33,475	37,146
75%	89,008	85,788	106,563	56,817	54,249	57,166
90%	131,778	122,097	154,835	86,191	87,393	85,302
95%	174,318	155,769	212,852	112,041	113,249	111,681
Mean	74,734	70,317	95,498	47,293	45,925	47,696

medicare) which generated no current income in 1969. Further, the income distributions were affected by labor income and retirement, whereas the wealth distributions exclude human wealth. Table 13.12 confirms that the wealth of couples was around twice that of singles throughout the distribution. Table 13.11 showed that the mean real wealth of the wealthiest ten percent of the sample fell by 6.2% while table 13.12 shows the ninety-fifth percentile point rising by 8.7%. The reconciliation is that the very richest households in the sample did quite poorly. In fact, the real wealth of the wealthiest household declined by 50%. Table 13.12 also confirms that single women were as well off as single men

Table 13.13   Percentage Growth Rates in Wealth from 1969 to 1975

	All	Position in Wealth Distribution			
		5%–25%	25%–50%	50%–75%	75%–100%
Mean wealth growth	65.3	83.5	71.3	64.4	46.7
Median wealth growth	54.8	62.3	60.7	56.9	39.6

Note: Prices grew by 43.5%.

whether the measure is the mean, the median, or the wealth distribution itself.

Table 13.13 shows mean and median growth rates in nominal wealth for different quartiles of the wealth distribution. As measured by either the mean or median, the top quartile in the wealth distribution had lower growth rates than the rest of the sample. Our overall assessment is that wealth inequality declined modestly for this population between 1969 and 1975.

The final table concerning the wealth of the RHS population is table 13.14. It shows wealth and real wealth appreciation by age and marital status. To avoid the compositional problems encountered in previous tables, we have included in this table only those whose marital status was unchanged from 1969 to 1975. The implications of table 13.14 are most easily seen by examining figures 13.2 and 13.3 in which median and mean real wealth by age may be found. We observe two important results in

Table 13.14   **Median Wealth by Age and Marital Status in 1969 (Holding Household Composition Constant)**

	Age in 1969/Age in 1975 (Years)					
	58/64	59/65	60/66	61/67	62/68	63/69
All						
N	1,258	1,118	1,128	1,088	1,201	1,002
Wealth in 1969	52,907	52,892	54,685	56,375	56,394	54,938
Wealth in 1975	92,526	92,093	91,995	87,383	85,849	82,275
% real change	21.8	21.3	17.2	8.0	6.1	4.4
Couples						
N	865	769	729	687	735	611
Wealth in 1969	62,895	60,830	64,291	66,857	69,624	67,711
Wealth in 1975	111,154	109,740	112,395	109,726	111,221	103,351
% real change	23.2	25.7	21.8	14.4	11.3	6.4
Singles						
N	393	349	399	401	466	391
Wealth in 1969	31,686	29,949	34,829	35,098	33,428	38,154
Wealth in 1975	49,923	49,268	51,532	50,739	47,187	53,697
% real change	9.8	14.6	3.1	0.7	−1.6	−1.9
Single males						
N	80	66	88	84	107	72
Wealth in 1969	27,503	27,880	29,714	28,470	27,978	30,174
Wealth in 1975	47,890	47,538	53,804	44,498	42,142	56,267
% real change	21.3	18.8	26.2	8.9	5.0	29.9
Single females						
N	313	283	311	317	359	319
Wealth in 1969	32,205	30,347	35,358	36,228	34,513	38,692
Wealth in 1975	50,324	51,090	51,514	52,005	47,899	53,260
% real change	8.9	17.3	1.5	0	−3.3	−4.1

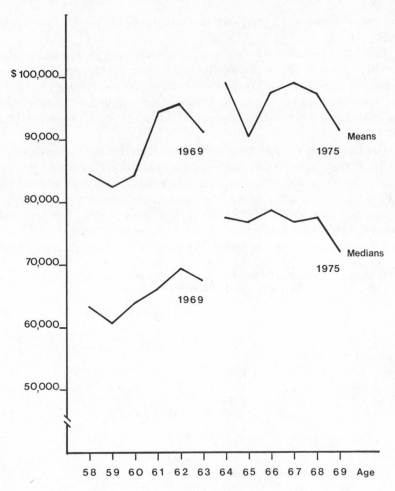

Fig. 13.2   Real wealth of couples by age.

figures 13.2 and 13.3. As measured by the medians, the wealth of couples and of the entire sample was about $10,000 higher in 1975 than in 1969, taking into account the aging of the sample. We base this observation on the shape of the wealth by age profile in 1969 and 1975: it appears to have shifted up by about $10,000. The second observation is that although most cohorts had an increase in real wealth over the period, the youngest cohorts had the largest increases and the oldest cohorts had the smallest. This may be seen more easily in figure 13.4, where we display the growth in real wealth by cohort. It is clear that the rate of wealth accumulation falls with initial age. We take this to be fully consistent with a life-cycle model of consumption in which there were unanticipated capital gains in some assets. These results indicate that even though the cross-section

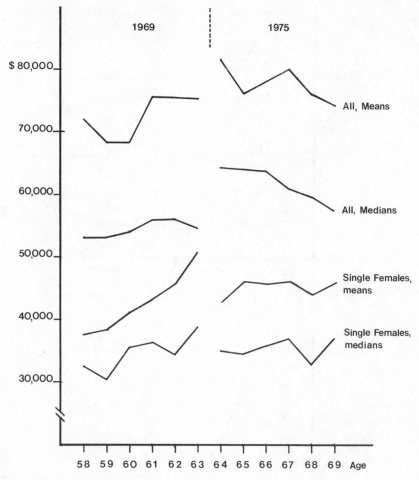

Fig. 13.3   Real wealth of single women and all by age.

wealth profile may not drop with age, the individuals in the cohort are
consuming according to life-cycle theory.

13.6   Income and Wealth

Income is often taken to be an indicator of economic well-being; for
example, poverty levels are defined by income. Most economists, however, would probably say that wealth is a better indicator as it is a better
measure of permanent economic position. In this section, we study the
stability of the income and wealth distributions over time and the correlation between income and wealth.

The first column in table 13.15 gives the probability that a household

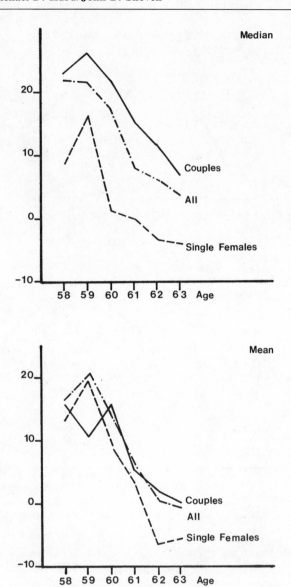

Fig. 13.4   Percentage change in real wealth by age in 1969.

will be in a specified part of the income distribution in 1975, given that the household was in that part of the distribution in 1969. The entries are, therefore, one minus the transition probabilities. For example, if a household was in the lower 5% income tail in 1969, the probability is .197 that it was in the lower 5% income tail in 1975. We see that the income stability of the lower tail is fairly weak, at least much weaker than the stability of the upper tail. Undoubtedly the reason is that the income at the upper tail

Table 13.15   Conditional Probabilities in the Income and Wealth
Distributions for the RHS Sample

	Income	Wealth
Lower 5%	.197	.554
Lower 10%	.368	.616
Lower 25%	.599	.745
Lower 50%	.746	.822
Upper 25%	.639	.719
Upper 10%	.547	.630
Upper 5%	.518	.610

Note: Numbers shown are the probabilities of being in the specified tail of the 1975 distribution given that household was in that tail in 1969.

partly reflects wealth, which tends to be more stable than earnings. This result confirms the notion that there is considerable mobility in the income distribution and that it is generally not accurate to say that poverty as measured by income is a permanent state.

The second column of table 13.15 gives the corresponding conditional probabilities in wealth. It is evident that there is much more stability in the wealth distribution than in the income distribution. This calculation ignores an important and stable form of wealth, human capital. If that were included, the distribution would surely be even more stable. Even though the entire distribution of wealth moved up between 1969 and 1975, as reported in earlier tables, the lower wealth tail remained low. That fact and the stability of the lower wealth tail indicate that the same households that were poor in wealth in 1969 were poor in 1975.

The usefulness of income as an indicator of economic well-being can also be examined by studying the correlation between income and wealth. Tables 13.16 and 13.17 give the cross-tabulations of income quartiles by wealth quartiles in 1969 and 1975. In each cell two numbers are given: the upper is the absolute frequency of the cell; the lower is the percent of the row and column. Thus, 14.5% of the sample is in both the lower income and lower wealth quartiles, and 57.9% of those in the lowest income quartile are also in the lowest wealth quartile. We see that there is substantial but by no means exclusive concentration along the diagonals: in 1969 49.2% of the observations were in the same income and wealth quartiles. Although low income is a very good predictor of wealth, it is not completely accurate; for example, 15.7% of those in the lowest income quartile were in the upper half of the wealth distribution; about 26% of those in the lower half of the income distribution were in the upper half of the wealth distribution.

The 1975 data show a higher correlation between income and wealth: about 56% of the observations were in the same income and wealth quartiles. Income is a stronger indicator of wealth: 7.8% of those in the

Table 13.16   Cross-Tabulation of Income Quartiles by Wealth Quartiles, 1969, RHS Sample

Income Quartiles	Wealth Quartiles			
	0%–25%	25%–50%	50%–75%	75%–100%
0%–25%				
Table %	14.5	6.6	2.8	1.2
Row and column %	57.9	26.4	11.1	4.6
25%–50%				
Table %	5.8	10.1	5.6	3.5
Row and column %	23.4	40.3	22.4	14.0
50%–75%				
Table %	1.6	7.3	10.0	6.2
Row and column %	6.5	29.2	39.9	24.5
75%–100%				
Table %	.4	2.5	7.5	14.6
Row and column %	1.6	10.0	30.0	57.4

Table 13.17   Cross-Tabulation of Income Quartiles by Wealth Quartiles, 1975, RHS Sample

Income Quartiles	Wealth Quartiles			
	0%–25%	25%–50%	50%–75%	75%–100%
0%–25%				
Table %	17.5	5.6	1.3	.7
Row and column %	69.9	22.3	5.2	2.6
25%–50%				
Table %	5.5	11.5	6.1	1.9
Row and column %	22.0	46.2	24.5	7.4
50%–75%				
Table %	1.5	6.0	11.0	6.5
Row and column %	5.8	24.0	44.1	26.1
75%–100%				
Table %	.6	1.9	6.6	16.0
Row and column %	2.3	7.5	26.3	63.9

lowest income quartile were in the upper half of the wealth distribution. The most important reasons for the increased correlation are that before retirement an important component of income comes from an unmeasured component of wealth, human capital, and that several important measured components of wealth, social security and medicare, do not yet yield an income flow before retirement.

13.7   The Effects of Inflation on the Elderly

We next investigate the vulnerability of the elderly to unanticipated changes in the price level and the inflation rate. As we mentioned in the introduction, it is commonly held that the elderly are particularly vulnerable to inflation. To investigate the accuracy of this impression, we develop and calculate three different vulnerability measures. The first two reflect the vulnerability to a *price level* shock where interest rates, the rate of inflation, etc., all remain unaffected. The third measure calculates vulnerability to an inflation rate shock where the long-run expected rate of inflation and nominal interest rates are revised upward. For all measures we classify assets and liabilities into three categories: those which offer a real or indexed return and are therefore protected from unanticipated price changes or inflation changes, those whose real values are reduced by inflation, and those whose real values increase with inflation. The classification is shown in table 13.18.

Our first measure of vulnerability (V_1) measures the percentage loss in real wealth per percent unanticipated increase in the price level. It is simply defined as nominal assets less nominal liabilities (the sum of category 2 entries in table 13.18 less those in category 3) divided by total net worth. The idea is that the real value of nominal assets and liabilities decline point for point with unanticipated jumps in the price level. A V_1

Table 13.18

(1) *Protected from price level shocks and inflation*
Social security
Medicare/medicaid
Transfer payment benefits
Houses[a]
Other physical assets
Common stocks

	Price Sensitivity to Inflation Change	
	1969	1975
(2) *Vulnerable to price changes and inflation (financial assets)*		
U.S. bonds	3.5	2.4
Corporate bonds	8.0	6.1
Private pensions	9.4	5.0
Loan assets	1.0	1.0
Bank accounts	1.0	1.0
(3) *Gain from price changes and inflation (financial liabilities)*		
Mortgage liabilities	6.4	6.1
Other debts	2.5	2.5

[a]There is a theoretical reason for thinking that houses are overindexed: the value of houses will rise faster than inflation due to their tax treatment. Thus, our vulnerability measures may overstate true vulnerability.

value of zero would mean that the household is completely protected against price level jumps, whereas an index of one would indicate that the household's real wealth declines 1% for each 1% rise in the price level. Our second measure, V_2, differs only in that it treats common stocks as nominal assets and is therefore in category 2. Theoretically, stocks represent a claim to the income flows of real capital and unanticipated increases in the price level should increase their real value to the extent the company is leveraged. That is, the stockholders should gain at the expense of the bondholders. The performance of the United States stock market in the past 17 years is such that one would not want to carry this argument too far, and hence the calculation of V_2.

The third measure, V_3, differs in that it attempts to measure the sensitivity of the elderly's wealth position to an unexpected increase in the inflation rate and the long-term nominal interest rates. We assume a strict point-for-point Fisher effect. The difference between this vulnerability and V_1 and V_2 is that for V_3 the maturity of assets is important. For example, a 1% price level increase would depress the real value of a consol by 1%. However, a 1% increase in inflation which drove interest rates from 7% to 8% would immediately reduce the value of a consol by 12.5%. We attempt to calculate in V_3 the immediate fall in real wealth as a fraction of total wealth for a one point increase in inflation. The weights in table 13.18 give the sensitivity of the value of various balance sheet entries to a rise of 1% in nominal interest rates. In general, the items are less vulnerable to an interest rate increase in 1975 because of shorter durations. For example, the maturity of average government bonds was reduced from 50 months to 32, and of average outstanding corporate bonds from 12 years to 10.

The medians of our vulnerability measures are shown in table 13.19. For all households in the RHS sample in 1969, the median of the V_1 measure is .05. This means that a 10% unexpected increase in the price level would reduce the real wealth by one-half of 1%. Vulnerability does not seem to depend greatly on marital status, but is slightly lower for single women than for single men. We noted earlier that single women hold a somewhat higher fraction of their wealth in social security and medicaid and less in financial assets. The poorest 10% of the sample have essentially zero net financial assets and hence are unaffected by price changes. However, those in the top 10% of the wealth distribution are more vulnerable than average; the median value of V_1 over the group was .19 in 1969. Vulnerability was up somewhat in 1975 over 1969 due primarily to the large increase in bank accounts and private pensions.

V_2, which adds common stocks to the list of vulnerable financial assets, is somewhat higher than V_1, but the median is still very modest. In 1975, for instance, the median V_2 stood at .12 for the whole RHS population. At that point, a household is 88% indexed from price level shocks. Even V_3, the wealth sensitivity to long-run inflation increases, is not too great as

Table 13.19   Measures of Vulnerability for Subpopulations of RHS Sample

		All House- holds	Couples	Singles	Single Males	Single Females	Wealth Tails Lower 10%	Wealth Tails Upper 10%
A. Medians								
V_1	1969	.05	.05	.05	.07	.04	0	.19
	1975	.10	.12	.08	.13	.07	0	.26
V_2	1969	.06	.06	.06	.08	.05	0	.35
	1975	.12	.13	.09	.14	.08	0	.37
V_3	1969	.06	.06	.06	.08	.05	0	.44
	1975	.15	.20	.10	.17	.08	0	.62
B. 90%								
V_1	1969	.39	.37	.45	.55	.41	.13	.53
	1975	.44	.42	.46	.56	.44	.16	.59
V_2	1969	.45	.43	.51	.62	.46	.21	.72
	1975	.48	.47	.51	.60	.48	.18	.69
V_3	1969	2.81	2.71	3.08	4.17	2.68	.16	3.70
	1975	1.63	1.54	1.75	2.12	1.63	.21	2.16

Note: V_1 and V_2 measure the percentage decrease in the real value of net worth per percent unexpected increase in the price level. They are defined as net nominal financial assets divided by total net worth. V_2 includes common stocks as a nominal asset while V_1 treats stocks as real assets. V_3 calculates the percent decrease in the real value of net worth for a 1% unanticipated change in long-run inflation reflected in a 1% rise in long-run interest rates. Common stocks are treated as real assets.

measured by the median figure. Here, as in all cases, those in the upper wealth tail are more vulnerable. The overall impression from the median is that the wealth positions of most of the sample are not substantially harmed by increases in the price level or in the inflation rate. Certainly these results indicate much less inflation vulnerability than the common impression.

The lower portion of table 13.19 gives the percentile point defining the upper 10% of the vulnerability distribution. It indicates that there is a wide distribution of vulnerability, particularly vulnerability to long-run inflation. While the median figure for V_3 in 1969 for the entire population was .06, those in the upper 10% of the vulnerability tail had a V_3 of greater than 2.81%. That is, for each extra point of inflation, they immediately lost at least 2.8% in wealth. The 90% points indicate that not only is median vulnerability among the wealthy high, but there are substantial numbers with quite high vulnerability. For example, the ninetieth percentile point among the wealthy in 1969 was 3.70. Correspondingly, almost no poor had substantial vulnerability.

Although median vulnerability increased only slightly from 1969 to 1975, the upper part of the distribution decreased substantially. This is shown in figure 13.5 in which some of the data of table 13.19 have been graphed. The incidence of high vulnerability has decreased. For example, the fraction of the sample having greater V_3 than V_2 decreased from 15% in 1969 to 6% in 1975.

Tables 13.20 and 13.21 give the distribution of V_1 and V_3, respectively, by age cohort for 1969 and 1975. They show a consistent, although weak, age effect in that the older cohorts have higher levels of vulnerability. More informative, however, may be that both tables indicate that more than 25% of the RHS sample would actually gain from a price level hike or an increase in inflation. Some of the data from tables 13.20 and 13.21 appear in figures 13.6 and 13.7. It appears that, at least at the median, there was a slight upward shift in the distribution of V_1 between 1969 and 1975. This is not conclusive, of course, as the difference could be due to a shift in the distribution at about age 63 or 64, rather than a secular shift. The distribution of V_3 by age shows some tendency to increase with age; however, the most important feature of figure 13.7 is the downward shift in the 90% point.

We have calculated vulnerability indices by classifying assets according to our view of their vulnerability to inflation. If the indices are useful predictors of real wealth changes of the elderly, we should find that households with small values of the indices in 1969 had greater growth in real wealth than households with large values of the indices. To test the predictive power of the indices, we regressed the percentage change in wealth between 1969 and 1975 on a constant, wealth in 1969, and vulnerability in 1969 (V_1). This regression was calculated for the entire sample and by age and by wealth quartile. Similar regressions were calculated with V_3 on the right-hand side instead of V_1. There were a total of 24 estimated coefficients on the vulnerability indices. All had a negative sign; the smallest t-statistic was 4.5 in absolute value. Thus, larger values of the vulnerability index were associated with smaller gains in real wealth between 1969 and 1975. The estimated coefficients indicated the differences associated with changes in the indices were not trivial. A typical result is that a change of either V_1 or V_3 by two standard deviations is associated with a change in wealth growth of about 25%. Average wealth growth over the period was 63%. Thus, typical variation in vulnerability observed in the data is associated with changes in wealth growth which are substantial compared with mean growth.

13.8 Conclusion

All of our calculations indicate that on average the elderly have done well economically over the last decade. The aggregate data taken from official sources show that incomes of the elderly have increased faster than incomes of the rest of the population even though the labor force

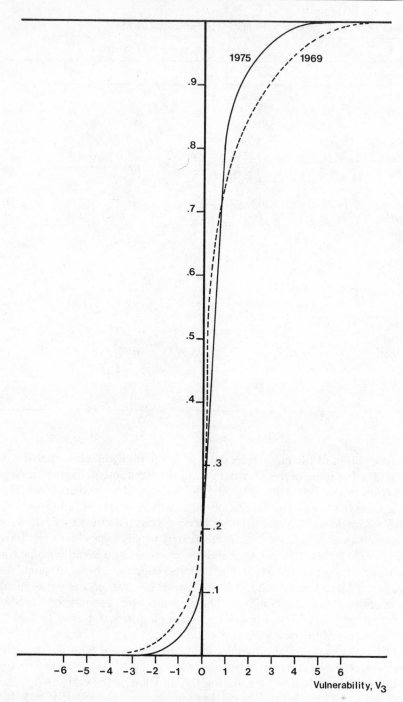

Fig. 13.5   Distribution of inflation vulnerability, V_3.

Table 13.20   **Price Vulnerability (V_1) Distribution by Age**

Percentile Points	Age in 1969/Age in 1975 (Years)					
	58/64	59/65	60/66	61/67	62/68	63/69
5%						
1969	− .24	− .21	− .20	− .18	− .14	− .16
1975	− .13	− .11	− .09	− .06	− .05	− .06
10%						
1969	− .14	− .12	− .11	− .08	− .06	− .07
1975	− .05	− .03	− .02	− .01	0	− .01
25%						
1969	− .02	− .01	− .01	0	0	0
1975	0	0	.01	.01	.01	.01
50%						
1969	.03	.04	.04	.06	.06	.06
1975	.07	.10	.12	.13	.13	.12
75%						
1969	.19	.20	.21	.21	.23	.24
1975	.23	.26	.29	.30	.31	.31
90%						
1969	.37	.37	.38	.40	.42	.42
1975	.41	.44	.45	.44	.47	.47
95%						
1969	.50	.49	.49	.51	.53	.53
1975	.52	.56	.57	.56	.57	.58

participation of the elderly declined in this period while the opposite is true for the nonelderly. Our data from the Retirement History Survey support this finding, although some caution should be used in extrapolating from our sample to the rest of the elderly population. However, the RHS data do show possibly larger income gains than the aggregate data show. This appears as a shift in the income profile by age between 1969 and 1975. Similarly, there appeared to be a shift in the wealth profile for the most important part of the sample—couples. Thus, although no cohort gained in real wealth, it seems that taking into account the aging of the sample, wealth was higher. These results offer support for the life-cycle hypothesis of consumption: wealth gain between 1969 and 1975 decreased systematically by age in 1969.

Our results on inflation vulnerability are consistent with the gains in wealth of the elderly. The popular conception is that the elderly are vulnerable to inflation; yet, during the inflation of the early 1970s, the elderly gained in wealth. Our vulnerability indices are consistent with this gain. Even though the elderly on average appear to have maintained their

Table 13.21   Inflation Vulnerability (V_3) Distribution by Age

Percentile Points	Age in 1969/Age in 1975 (Years)					
	58/64	59/65	60/66	61/67	62/68	63/69
5%						
1969	−1.36	−1.36	−1.25	−1.08	−.92	−1.04
1975	−.78	−.63	−.64	−.43	−.35	−.36
10%						
1969	−.88	−.75	−.72	−.50	−.42	−.47
1975	−.40	−.22	−.14	−.09	−.04	−.05
25%						
1969	−.12	−.07	−.04	−.02	−.01	−.01
1975	0	0	0	0	0	0
50%						
1969	.04	.05	.06	.06	.08	.07
1975	.08	.15	.21	.24	.23	.19
75%						
1969	.63	.68	.78	.91	.90	.95
1975	.52	.72	.93	.96	.93	.90
90%						
1969	2.53	2.54	2.87	2.79	3.10	3.11
1975	1.43	1.63	1.75	1.69	1.74	1.75
95%						
1969	3.66	3.87	4.02	3.96	4.19	4.04
1975	1.98	2.19	2.31	2.21	2.31	2.30

income and wealth positions, our results indicate that there is a wide distribution of income, wealth, and inflation vulnerability. In the latter especially, a substantial part of the elderly population is inflation protected, yet some individuals are quite vulnerable. The situation is made more tolerable, however, because the highly inflation-vulnerable individuals are concentrated among the wealthy, who are better able to afford the inflation risk.

We may speculate that the inflation of the latter part of the decade has not overly harmed the elderly because in 1975 the elderly typically were not vulnerable as measured by our index, and that index seemed to have good predictive power of the effects of inflation during the early part of the decade. That this is the correct view rather than the popular view that the elderly have suffered during the inflation period is supported by a recent poll.[10] According to this poll, 68% of the people less than 65 years old think that finances are a very serious problem for most people over 65; but only 17% of the people over 65 think finances are a serious problem for the elderly.

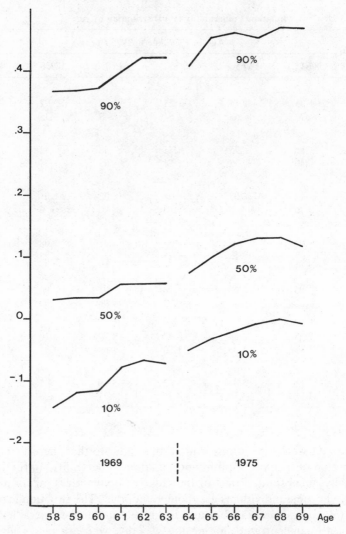

Fig. 13.6   Percentage points of price vulnerability by age.

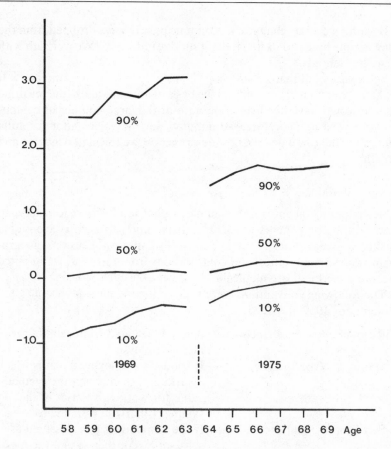

Fig. 13.7   Percentage points of inflation vulnerability by age.

Appendix

Description of the Data

The Retirement History Survey (RHS) is a national longitudinal survey of 11,153 households whose heads were 58–63 years old in 1969. The surviving households were interviewed every 2 years through 1979. Detailed data on financial characteristics, work behavior, and health were obtained. The file is especially useful for this study because the RHS data were matched to social security earnings records which give contributions to social security throughout the working life through 1974. Therefore, it is possible to calculate exactly the social security benefits a worker would receive were he to retire.

Because we study changes in economic position, we dropped from the 1969 sample households that did not survive until 1975. We were left with 8,244 households.

For a variety of reasons, missing values occurred on the data tape.[11] If we had eliminated households on the basis of missing values, the resulting sample would have been small because of the large number of components of wealth. Therefore, we imputed missing values after carefully examining the raw data. We now describe how we calculated income and wealth.

Income Variables

In computing income for the sample in 1969 and 1975, we took a broad view of the components of income. In addition to such conventional income sources as social security, wage, rent, interest, pensions, government transfers, annuities, and contributions from relatives, we imputed income from medicare/medicaid and owner-occupied housing.

The following conventions were used to impute missing income components for 1969 and 1975.

Respondent's Wage Income — delete household from sample for income analysis.[12]

Spouse's Wage Income — If spouse's employment status was "working," then assign the median value for working spouses in the sample, otherwise assign zero.

Self-Employment Income — If the respondent was classified as self-employed, then assign the median value for self-employed respondents with valid responses; otherwise assign zero.

Respondent Rental Income — Assign median rental income for respondents with positive values.

Spouse Rental Income — Assign zero.

Interest Income 1969 — Assign .056 x [U.S. Bonds] + .04 x [Savings Accounts] + .06 x [Stocks + Bonds + Shares] + .06 x [Loan Assets].

Interest Income 1975 — Assign .078 x [U.S. Bonds] + .05 x [Savings Accounts] + .10 x [Stocks + Bonds + Shares] + .10 x [Loan Assets].

Other Variables 1969 — Assign zero.

Other Variables 1975 — If the response was coded that the household had the income source, then assign the median value for all households with the income source and valid replies; otherwise assign zero.

Housing services for owner-occupants were valued at 3% of the gross housing value for 1969 and 1975.

Medicare/medicaid values for the 1975 income data are computed as follows.[13] All households without social security income are assigned medicare values of zero. For those households receiving social security, male members are assigned the average medicare value for men their age receiving medicare in 1975. Female members are assigned the average medicare value for females their age receiving medicare in 1975. All households are assigned the average medicaid value for households 65 and over in 1975.

Wealth Variables

The total wealth of each household was computed from the individual wealth components, some of which were stock variables (e.g., house value) and some of which were capitalized flow variables (e.g., present discounted value of a stream of pension benefits). The first step was to obtain a valid value for each component of each household's wealth.

The general strategy for imputing missing values was to retain the individual component of each record. The hierarchy for imputations had three levels. At the first level, we used all valid observations. Then, if an item was missing for 1975 (1969), its value was imputed if possible from the previous (next) wave of the RHS by multiplying the available value by the growth rate in the median value of such assets or income for all nonmissing respondents between the previous (next) wave of the RHS and 1975 (1969). Imputations used the most recent wave of the RHS that had a valid value, but could go as far back (forward) as 1969 (1973). If a datum could not be imputed by reference to a similar question in another year for the same respondent, the third level of the imputation hierarchy was to set the datum equal to the median of all nonmissing replies for other respondents in that year.

Flow variables were capitalized into stock variables using a 3% discount rate. The horizons over which different variables were capitalized were:

Pensions	— Until expected death date of respondent.
AFDC Benefits	— For three years.
All Other Flow Variables[14]	— Until the maximum expected death date of respondent or spouse.

All capitalizations were compounded annually.

Medicare/medicaid wealth was computed using the mean 1975 (1969) benefits for elderly persons. This was capitalized at a 3% discount rate for both respondent and spouse with the expected date of death. Then the present value of the flow received before age 65 was subtracted off where the individual was not yet age 65.

Expected social security wealth is computed using the Social Security Administration Earnings Record (through 1974). The algorithm to compute 1975 (1969) social security wealth is based on the social security law in effect on January 1, 1975 (1969). The social security primary insurance amount (PIA) is calculated for each person based on his or her earnings record, assuming the individual retires as soon as possible (age 62 or as soon as sufficient quarters of covered employment are accumulated after age 62 for those not yet eligible by age 62). It is assumed that for married couples, the male's potential PIA is always greater than or equal to the female's PIA, so that the male's social security wealth is always based on his own PIA computed from his own earnings record. The female's social security wealth is taken as the maximum of her own PIA or her spouse or widow's benefit based on her husband's PIA. She is allowed to switch from her own benefit to her spouse or widow's benefit over time, but not from spouse's benefit to her own benefit.

Single men and women have a social security wealth based on their own PIA only. Widows at the time of the initial survey (1969) are treated as never married (no possible widow benefit calculated) because the SSA Earnings Record match file does not contain any information on their deceased spouse. For surviving widows of original 1969 male respondents, however, there is information on the deceased spouse. These widows are allowed to draw a widow's benefit if it is greater than the benefit based on their own PIA. In computing the potential widow's benefit for surviving spouses, the deceased husband is treated as if he had retired at the earliest possible age according to the rules normally applied to living male respondents, unless that age would be a year later than 1975, in which case he is treated as if he had retired at age 65.

If a respondent does not have sufficient covered quarters of employment by 1975 (1969) to be eligible for social security benefits on retirement, then his current work status and his expectation about receipt of social security benefits in the future are taken into account to estimate whether he ever will be eligible for benefits and at what date. These estimates are used to calculate social security wealth.

Average life expectancies for men and women are used to determine the length of the stream of income. The streams are capitalized at a 3% discount rate.

If a spouse of a respondent does not have sufficient quarters of covered employment by 1975 (1969) to be separately eligible for social security retirement benefits, then it is assumed that he or she will never accumulate sufficient quarters to be eligible. A male spouse then ends up with zero social security wealth, and a female spouse with a social security wealth based only on their potential spouse and widow benefits.

Notes

1. We choose 1968, 1969, 1974, and 1975 as much of the income and wealth data in later tables refer to those years.
2. The major exclusion is income in kind such as food stamps and subsidized housing.
3. Because we have no measures of scale effects in household size, we cannot say which is the better measure of economic position.
4. If we were to include the increase in subsidized housing and food stamps, the decrease would be even greater.
5. We have assumed that the elderly value these government programs at their insurance value. It is possible that this exaggerates their worth if the elderly would not have bought this coverage themselves. This type of valuation problem always exists for transfers that are in kind rather than cash transfers.
6. Income at age 63 is actually income of the year preceding when the head was 63. Thus the sharp drop at 63 reflects retirements at 62.
7. Of course these very low incomes do not necessarily show permanent economic status. We examine this issue further below when we study income transition and wealth.
8. Units reporting ownership of the asset but not its value are excluded from this table. Thus, participation is slightly higher than indicated here.
9. We estimated missing values. A description of our method may be found in the appendix to this chapter.
10. New York *Times*, November 19, 1981.
11. For example, respondent did not know the value of an income source, respondent did not answer the question, the response was miscoded.
12. These households, which accounted for less than 5% of the sample, were deleted because no other variables were good proxies for the major component of income.
13. It is assumed that medicare/medicaid was zero in 1969 based on the age of the survey respondents.
14. Supplementary security income, other public assistance, income from private insurance and annuities, benefits from private welfare agencies, income from relatives, income from other sources.

Comment   Daniel Feenberg

Michael Hurd and John Shoven address a number of questions related to the financial well-being of the elderly in the United States and come to relatively reassuring conclusions. Certainly they find nothing to substantiate widely held views that the elderly are an immiserized class. Here follows a brief recapitulation of their findings.

Daniel Feenberg is a research associate of the National Bureau of Economic Research.

From 1970 to 1978 the ratio of per capita income of the elderly to that of the general population has risen from 1.04 to 1.06 while per household income has risen from .52 to .58 times that of the general population. This increase in income came in spite of a decrease in labor force participation from 25.8% to 19.7% (males) and 9.2% to 7.8% (females) over the same period. In the general population, participation rates actually rose slightly, from 60.3 to 62.7. There has been a dramatic decrease in the fraction of elderly below the poverty line. For unrelated individuals the incidence of poverty has gone from 61.9% in 1959 to 27.0% in 1978, while for families the incidence is reduced from 26.9% to 7.6%.

Hurd and Shoven discuss the appropriateness of using the CPI to deflate the incomes of the elderly in the light of their quite different expenditure patterns. Their conclusion, that the CPI overstates inflation about equally for the elderly and nonelderly alike, is consistent with other studies.

The Retirement History Survey provides Hurd and Shoven with a rich source of data on the amount and form of wealth holdings for a sample of the population age 58–63 in 1969, and on the same group of individuals 6 years later. Hurd and Shoven adopt a comprehensive definition of wealth that includes the present value of medicare/medicaid, welfare, SSI, and social security in addition to the liquid assets and housing which constitute the more traditional definition. On the liability side, only current debts are included, however. In particular, expected tax liabilities are excluded.

The balance sheets constructed from these data provide much of interest. We learn that the average wealth among 64–69-year-olds in 1975 was $107,243, but that the lowest 10% of the distribution averaged only $25,682. Since that figure includes the present value of means-tested welfare programs, and since almost one-third is the form of expected medicare/medicaid benefits, it is clear that at least a minority of the elderly are in severe financial difficulty. Especially among this group the valuation of medical benefits at cost to the government may be an exaggeration of their value.

A related issue not addressed here is whether the observed wealth is sufficient to maintain consumption throughout an individual's retirement. Kotlikoff and Summers (1981) conclude (from the same data) that assets are sufficient to allow most retirees to consume at a level comparable to their average preretirement level, but not at their immediate preretirement rate. The balance sheets also provide some valuable information about the effectiveness of social welfare programs in relieving poverty, where poverty is defined on a longer time frame than the usual annual basis. We can see that 34% of SSI goes to the lowest 10% of the wealth distribution but 2% goes to the highest 10% of the wealth distribution. "Welfare and other transfers" are equally distributed at all levels of wealth. Although the minimum social security benefit is not broken out, this would be an ideal setting in which to examine its effectiveness.

The material on the effect of inflation on the real wealth of the elderly is clearly the centerpiece of the chapter. From the individual balance sheets and some plausible assumptions about the effect of inflation on the market values of particular asset types, a distribution of inflation vulnerability can be inferred. In 1975 the calculated median reduction in wealth associated with a permanent one point increase in the expected rate of inflation is only 0.2%. The ninetieth percentile of vulnerability experiences a loss of only 1.5% of total wealth per point of expected inflation, while about 24% of households gain from inflation.

These are remarkable figures. While it is to be expected that averaged over all individuals the effects of inflation will wash out (one person's nominal asset is another's nominal debt), the individuals in the sample are of an age which requires net assets to finance retirement. The data show, however, that these assets are mostly in the form of housing and government transfers, which are assumed to be real assets. Further, the average duration of financial assets (chiefly bank accounts) is short, so that changes in the expected rate of inflation (as opposed to changes in the price level) have a limited effect.

A number of technical objections may be made to this result. Houses are probably a better than real asset while corporate stock is probably worse than nominal. Interest rates do not change point for point with inflation. Real tax liabilities depend on the rate of inflation, but taxes are ignored throughout the chapter. Financial assets may be subject to substantial underreporting,[1] while the value of government transfers is generally imputed by Hurd and Shoven and therefore not subject to respondents' possibly faulty memories. While the practical significance of these biases is problematic, they are probably not of sufficient size to much affect the result. Even so, it should not be thought the elderly, or at least some among them, have not been hurt by inflation. A small thought-experiment may make the distinction clear.

Imagine an economist called to the White House in 1932. He is asked to investigate complaints of hardship caused by the fall in the stock market. He might well conclude that reports of stock market vulnerability are grossly exaggerated and that even the wealthy are well protected from changes in the price of stocks. He might also add that they are much better protected in 1932 than they had been only 3 years previously.

Inflation vulnerability, like stock market vulnerability, is a self-limiting disease. As nominal assets and liabilities depreciate in real value, the measure of vulnerability tends toward zero. Table 13.21 shows the tremendous reduction in the variance of vulnerability to changes in the rate of inflation that took place between 1969 and 1975. At both the 10% and 90% points of the vulnerability distribution, sensitivity is reduced by about one-half for all age groups. That the median vulnerability about doubles is of less significance, because the median vulnerability is so close to zero. From the data given it is not possible to determine the cause of this shift. It may be the result of passive acceptance of shifts in the real value of the components of the portfolio. It might, however, be the result of a deliberate and costly effort to reduce inflation risk.

Readers interested in further study of the issues raised in this chapter may wish to consult Clark, Kreps, and Spengler (1978) for a general survey of work on the economics of aging.

Note

1. It seems likely that the Retirement History Survey substantially understates property income and wealth. Evidence for this is readily available from the income data contained in the Statistics of Income annual. For 1975, dividend, interest, and pension income of $44 billion is reported by taxpayers claiming the age exemption. Given 20.2 million elderly (only about one-half of whom file tax returns), this implies property income of $2,200 per capita. This seems quite large relative to the reported financial assets in table 13.10. A more detailed examination could be done if property income figures were reported. Nevertheless, underreporting is likely to be a problem mostly among the very wealthy. Medians may not be much affected.

References

Boskin, M., and Hurd, M. 1982. Are inflation rates different for the elderly? National Bureau of Economic Research Working Paper no. 943.

Bridges, B., and Packard, M. 1981. Prices and income changes for the elderly. *Social Security Bulletin*, January, pp. 3–15.

Clark, R.; Kreps, J.; and Spengler, J. 1978. Economics and the aging: A survey. *Journal of Economic Literature* 16 (September): 919–62.

Economic Report of the President. 1982. Washington, D.C.: Government Printing Office.

Epstein, L. A. 1964. Income of the aged in 1962: First findings of the 1963 survey of the elderly. *Social Security Bulletin* (March), pp. 3–24.

Internal Revenue Service. 1978. *Statistics of income—1975, individual income tax returns.* Washington, D.C.

Kotlikoff, L. J., and Summers, L. 1981. The adequacy of savings. NBER Working Paper no. 627.

New York Times. 1981. Poll detects "myths" about problems of aged. November 19.

Okner, B. A. 1975. Individual taxes and the distribution of income. In *The personal distribution of income and wealth,* ed. J. Smith. New York: National Bureau of Economic Research.

United States. Various years. *Statistical abstract.*

United States Bureau of the Census. *Annual housing survey. Part C. Financial characteristics of the housing inventory, 1973–1979.* Washington, D.C.: Government Printing Office.

———. Various years. *P-60 series.* Washington, D.C.: Government Printing Office.

United States Department of Health, Education, and Welfare, Social Security Administration. 1975. *Demographic and economic characteristics of the aged: 1968 social security survey.* SSA Research Report no. 45 75-11802. Washington, D.C.: Government Printing Office.

United States Department of Health and Human Services, Social Security Administration. 1979a. *Income of the population aged 55 and over: 1976.* SSA Publication no. 13-11865. Washington, D.C.: Government Printing Office.

———. 1979b. *Longitudinal retirement history survey 1969, 1971, 1973, 1975.* Data tape and supporting documents available from SSA.

———. 1981. *Income of the population 55 and Over, 1978.* SSA Staff Paper no. 41. Washington, D.C.: Office of Research and Statistics.

United States Department of Labor, Bureau of Labor Statistics. 1981. Consumer price index. *Monthly Labor Review*, August, p. 89.

14 Portfolio Composition and Pension Wealth: An Econometric Study

Louis-David L. Dicks-Mireaux and Mervyn A. King

14.1 Introduction

Much empirical research has been devoted to examining the effects of social security and private pension wealth on household savings. In contrast there has been very little study of the consequences of pension wealth for the *composition* of household portfolios. Given that the two types of pension wealth are not perfect substitutes for other assets, it is likely that they would affect optimum portfolio choices among other assets. This microeconomic impact has macroeconomic implications. Because the financial structure of the private sector's net worth is an important determinant of both real decisions (corporate investment, for example) and financial variables (such as interest rates and their term structure), any effect of pension wealth on the portfolio composition of households' nonpension wealth will have macroeconomic consequences. In this chapter we estimate the portfolio effect of pension wealth using individual data for 10,118 Canadian households. Throughout the chapter we regard pension wealth as an exogenous variable beyond the control of an individual household. Although this is clearly true of social security wealth, it is possible to alter private pension wealth by choosing an occupation which offers more or less attractive retirement compensation. We shall ignore this possible source of endogeneity.

Louis-David L. Dicks-Mireaux is affiliated with Harvard University and with the National Bureau of Economic Research. Mervyn A. King is Esmée Fairbairn Professor of Investment, the University of Birmingham, and a research associate of the National Bureau of Economic Research.

This study was funded by NSF grant SES 7914209. The views expressed here are those of the authors and should be attributed neither to the NSF nor to the NBER. The authors are grateful to David Reitman for help with the computation of the pension wealth series and to Alan Auerbach, John Bossons, James Pesando, and other participants at the Amelia Island conference for helpful comments.

To model asset demands satisfactorily, our specification must allow for the empirical observation that most households do not own all of the assets which we are able to distinguish. For each of the 12 assets in our study there is a significant number of households with zero holdings, and only two households own all 12 assets. We construct below a model of the probability of owning a particular combination of assets. In the estimation of individual asset demand equations, the failure of households to hold complete portfolios leads to two problems. First, the demand for an asset depends on the particular combination of other assets in the portfolio. Second, estimates of demand equations which use data only for those households with positive holdings will be subject to sample selection bias. We discuss, and attempt to resolve, these econometric difficulties in section 14.3.

Because our sample consists of a single cross section of households, we cannot examine the effects on portfolio behavior of variables which are uniform across households. These are variables which, although they may vary over time, are identical for all households at the date of interview. The most important of such variables are the relative prices of different assets, including the inflation rate.[1] One exception is that part of the price which reflects households' marginal tax rates. The data on net worth are, however, both comprehensive and of good quality, and we are able to compute estimates of both social security and private pension wealth. There is also substantial variance of pension wealth among the population, which allows us to identify the effects of pension wealth on the dependent variables. The sample and the construction of estimates of tax rates, pension wealth, and permanent income for each household in the sample are described in sections 14.2 and 14.4. In section 14.3 we discuss alternative approaches to modeling the mixed discrete-continuous portfolio choice problem facing households and explain our preferred method. Estimates of the model are contained in section 14.5, and simulations of the effects of changing the levels of both social security and private pension wealth on portfolio composition are presented in section 14.6. This section also contains estimates of the effect of the two types of pension wealth on total household savings.

14.2 The Sample

The data used in this study refer to 12,734 Canadian families in 1977 and come from the Statistics Canada micro-data tape, Income (1976), Assets and Debts (1977) of Economic Families and Unattached Individuals, which contains data collected as a supplement to the 1977 Survey of Consumer Finances.[2] Unless otherwise stated, all tables are derived from this tape and money figures are expressed in Canadian dollars. The survey covers a stratified random sample of the noninstitutional population and provides a particularly rich source of information on household ownership of assets and liabilities, incomes, and other individual and household characteristics. A family or household will be defined here as a group sharing a common dwelling and related by blood or marriage. The data refer to market values in May 1977 and the income data to the calendar year 1976. For the econometric analysis 2,616 households were excluded. These included 139 "special family units," primarily those with high incomes, for whom data on age and other characteristics were not recorded on the tape to protect their identity. Because our main interest is in estimating equations in which the dependent variables are relative shares of assets in household portfolios, neither this omission nor the stratification of the sample leads us to suspect sample selection bias. In addition, of the total value of assets and debts held by the complete sample (computed using population weights), these "special family units" only held 7.3% and 2.4%, respectively. The sample was further reduced to 10,118 households by deleting households headed by a woman, for reasons explained below in the construction of permanent income.

The data on net worth are given for 15 categories of assets and liabilities. These were aggregated into 12 classes for the portfolio composition analysis by defining equity in owner-occupied housing to be net of any mortgage liability and equity in own businesses to be net of loans specifically for this purpose, and by aggregating two forms of consumer debt into a single category of personal debt. The 12 assets are: cash, deposits, bonds, stocks and shares, registered home ownership savings plans (RHOSP), registered retirement savings plans (RRSP), other nonliquid financial assets (ONLFA), passenger cars, equity in owner-occupied housing, equity in other real estate, equity in a business or farm, and personal debt. Market values of assets are recorded (for cars and equity in real estate and own businesses these are the respondents' own estimates) except for bonds, which are given at face value. In all the tables, and in the presentation of the empirical results presented, debt is measured as a positive variable. The survey data exclude social security and pension wealth (which we discuss below), consumer durables other than cars, equity in life insurance, and other assets such as the expected value of future inheritances and support from relatives and children. The percentage composition of wealth by asset is given in table 14.1. Column 1 gives the share of assets in the total wealth of the sample of 12,734 households using population weights. These weights were not used in calculating the shares in columns 2 and 3. In the second column are the shares of assets in the total wealth of the sample used for our empirical work. The third column shows the average of the asset shares of individual households in the same sample as column 2. This is in contrast to columns 1 and 2, which are the asset shares of the aggregate portfolios of

Table 14.1   Percentage Composition of Wealth by Asset, 1977 (Shares Are Defined with Respect to Total Assets)

Assets	Canada[a] (1)	Sample[b] (2)	Average of Individual Household Asset Shares[b] (3)
Total deposits	11.0	9.4	16.0
Total bonds	3.3	2.6	2.7
Cash	0.2	0.2	1.6
Stocks and shares	1.9	1.3	0.7
RHOSP	0.2	0.2	0.6
RRSP	1.8	1.8	1.5
Other nonliquid financial assets	4.2	2.1	1.1
Passenger cars	4.8	4.8	16.6
Home equity	41.6	38.3	44.0
Real estate equity	9.4	9.8	5.9
Business equity	21.6	29.5	9.3
Personal debt	4.8	5.3	56.0
Mean total assets ($)	48,600	58,474	58,474
Mean net worth ($)	40,391	55,357	55,357
Mean social security wealth ($)[c]	na	72,799	72,799
Mean private pension wealth ($)[c]	na	26,940	26,940
Mean permanent income ($)[c]	na	22,598	22,598

[a]Calculated over all 12,734 households using population weights.
[b]Calculated over sample of 9,788 households, with *no* weights applied.
[c]Authors' estimates.

their respective samples. In effect, the shares in the second column are a weighted estimate of those in column 3, where the weights are individual household wealth.

As the focus of this study is portfolio composition, any variation across assets in the accuracy of the data will be critical. Detailed evaluations of the data can be found in Statistics Canada (1979) and Oja (1981), and the ensuing discussion draws heavily on these sources. To assess the quality of the data involves a comparison with outside estimates of the wealth components, and these in turn are unlikely to be free of all error. If we ignore this, then discrepancies between the two may be attributed to sampling error, incomplete response rates, and underreporting in the survey data. As we employ the data in unweighted form and do not address issues of wealth distribution or of the level of national wealth, the first source of error is not of concern to us. The overall response rate was 79.7%, and where imputations of items of wealth were made, they were generally no greater than 10% in magnitude. Oja (1981) concludes that neither of these sources of error in the data is a major concern.

This suggests that underreporting is the main source of error. Davies (1979), in a study of a similar survey in 1970, concluded that the major source of underreporting is nonreporting of assets at the household level. This may affect both the probit and share demand parameter estimates. However, compared to previous surveys some improvements were introduced in the 1977 survey. Real assets, which account for about 80% of nonpension wealth, appear to be accurately recorded in the 1977 survey. The grossed-up value of each of the financial assets and debt varies from 20–30% to 90–100% of outside estimates. It should be noted, however, that these figures refer to a comparison of aggregate values of wealth items and therefore include all three sources of error.

14.3   An Econometric Model

In our data set we are able to distinguish between 12 assets (to be precise, 11 assets and one category of debt). Most models of portfolio behavior predict that, in the absence of restrictions, individuals would choose to hold nonzero quantities of all assets. Table 14.2 shows the distribution of households by the number of assets held and illustrates that such a prediction is only accurate for two households in our sample. To ignore this feature of household behavior would be not only to produce biased estimates of the parameters of the demand functions for assets but also to ignore a misspecification in that the demand for an asset depends on the set of other assets held by an investor. It is clear, therefore, that the principal econometric difficulty we face is to estimate

Table 14.2   **Distribution of Household Portfolios by Number of Assets Held, 1977**

Number of Assets Held	Frequency	%
0	81	0.8
1	213	2.1
2	547	5.4
3	1,166	11.5
4	2,071	20.5
5	2,532	25.0
6	1,842	18.2
7	988	9.8
8	433	4.3
9	174	1.7
10	55	0.5
11	14	0.1
12	2	0.0
Total	10,118	100

jointly the decisions of how many and which assets to hold and the quantity of each asset which is held conditional on its ownership. This raises a number of interesting econometric issues (discussed more fully in King [1982]) which have been ignored in previous studies. In one of the few published econometric studies of portfolio composition, Feldstein (1976) simply excluded households that did not have positive holdings of any assets.

The theoretical considerations which suggest that individuals may hold incomplete portfolios are of two kinds. First, there are partial equilibrium factors such as transactions costs, which may be interpreted in a broad sense to include the costs of monitoring and managing a portfolio. Economies of scale may imply that it is optimal to select a portfolio with only a limited number of assets. Second, there are general equilibrium effects. Auerbach and King (1982) show that in a world of distortionary taxes, no equilibrium can exist without constraints on individual portfolios. Constraints on short sales are the most obvious example, and these lead to an equilibrium in which investors have specialized portfolios. The asset (or assets) in which an investor specializes is determined by his marginal tax rate. Auerbach and King (1982) model explicitly the case of three assets: corporate equity, corporate bonds, and municipal bonds. But similar considerations apply to a world with many assets. Complete specialization in a single asset (the most favored for tax purposes) results only if it is possible to achieve the constrained optimal allocation of consumption over states of the world by owning only the assets in question. If, as will be the case in practice, this is impossible, the particular combination of assets owned by an individual will reflect the trade-off between considerations of tax savings and aversion to risk.

In principle, therefore, we need to construct a joint discrete and continuous choice model. We cannot simply estimate an asset demand system using observations of those with positive holdings for two reasons. First, not all households own each asset, and to omit the sample of nonholders would lead to sample selection bias. This problem is familiar. The second difficulty is less familiar and more serious. The proportion of an individual's wealth which is invested in a particular asset depends on the combination of assets in the portfolio. Suppose, for example, that an individual holds only one other asset in addition to asset j. Then the proportion of his wealth invested in asset j will clearly differ from that which he would invest if he owned all 12 assets given values for observable characteristics. The discrete and continuous aspects of the problem are obviously inseparable.

Suppose that households maximize expected utility as a function of the 12 asset holdings subject to both a budget constraint and a set of short sales constraints on each of the assets. The resulting set of first-order conditions may be inverted to give asset demand functions only if we know which constraints are binding, that is, if we know which combination of assets the household owns. The first-order conditions do not tell us this. It is for this reason that a multivariate tobit specification, although a seemingly natural way to model the problem, is an inappropriate specification. The multivariate tobit model (see Amemiya 1974; Lee 1981) embodies the essential feature of a tobit model that a single index for each asset determines both the discrete and continuous outcomes. But this is not the correct representation of the behavior of an optimizing investor subject to short sales constraints (this is demonstrated formally and discussed further in King [1982]). The solution to the investor's optimization problem is twofold: that combination of assets is chosen which leads to the highest level of expected utility, and, given this optimal combination, the corresponding set of first-order conditions may be inverted to determine asset demands. The discrete choice amounts to selecting from a very large number of mutually exclusive alternatives. In fact, with J assets the number of distinct combinations of assets is equal to 2^J.[3] For 12 assets this means we have 4,096 mutually exclusive alternatives. Optimal asset demands are given by a switching regressions model in which the demand system depends on the particular combination of assets owned. Again the number of regimes is equal to the number of possible combinations.

To estimate individual equations for the probability of owning each of these 2^J alternatives would almost certainly involve more parameters than we have observations, even with a sample of 10,118 households. Moreover, with the same number of regimes we cannot estimate distinct demand equations for each regime. The only feasible approach is to compute the implied probabilities of all mutually exclusive combinations containing the asset in question. Suppose that alternative i is chosen if the following linear index is positive, if

$$(1) \qquad X\beta_i + u_i > 0, \qquad i = 1, \ldots 2^J,$$

where X is a $(1 \times N)$ row vector of N observable characteristics and β_i is an $(N \times 1)$ column vector of associated parameters.

The u_i are assumed to be identically and independently distributed, with a distribution function denoted by F. Let d_i denote a vector of dummy variables with the ith element equal to unity if the investor owns combination i and all other elements equal to zero. The probability of holding asset j may then be written as

$$(2) \qquad p(j) = \sum_{i \in s} \int_{-\infty}^{X\beta d_i} dF; \ S \mid \text{all } i \text{ containing } j,$$

where β is an $(N \times I)$ matrix of parameters.

The determinants of the probability of owning asset j can be represented as interaction terms between observable characteristics and dummy variables for the combinations of other assets owned by the individual. Again this involves an excessively large number of parameters. To reduce the number of parameters to a feasible magnitude, we must assume some independence between combinations. If we assume that the effects of observable characteristics on the probability of choosing asset j are independent of the particular combination, then the probability is a function of characteristics and dummy variables with no interaction terms. This still implies a very large number of parameters, because there are as many dummy variables as there are combinations of assets containing asset j. (The precise number is 2^{J-1}, which in our case is 2,048.)[4] But if we are prepared to assume independence over observable characteristics, we might as well assume independence over unobservable characteristics. This assumption implies that the probability of choosing asset j is a function of observable characteristics and independent of the other assets owned (an alternative derivation of this specification is given in King [1982]). There are no cross-equation constraints because the probabilities of owning each asset do not sum to unity. Hence we shall estimate independent probit equations for each asset in turn.

The continuous choice open to a household is its demand for assets given the combination of assets which forms its optimal portfolio. The functional form of the demand for a given asset depends on the other assets owned, and there is a discrete jump in the demand function as the combination of assets owned changes. If households face short-selling constraints, these jumps embody the "spill-over" effects of the constraints on asset demands. As the dependent variable we take the logistic transformation of the proportion of wealth invested in each asset. We use this transformation to justify our assumptions about parameter restrictions below and to reduce heteroscedasticity. The demand function for asset j is:

$$(3) \qquad \ln\left(\frac{p_j}{1-p_j}\right) = C_{ij} + Z\theta_{ij} + u_j, \qquad \begin{aligned} j &= 1, \ldots, J \\ i &= 1, \ldots, 2^{J-1}, \end{aligned}$$

where p_j is the proportion of wealth invested in asset j, C_{ij} is the constant term, and Z is a vector of observable characteristics. All parameters, as written, are indexed by the combination of assets in the portfolio denoted by i which runs from $i = 1, \ldots, 2^J$. In this general form there are again too many parameters. We shall consider a simple case of the shift effect of different assets combinations in which $\theta_{ij} = \theta_j$ for all i and

$$(4) \qquad\qquad C_{ij} = \sum_{k=1}^{J-1} C_{kj} d_{ki}$$

for all i,j.

In other words, the constant term for a particular combination is equal to the sum of fixed coefficients for each asset contained in the combination (where d_{ki} is unity if combination i contains asset K, and zero otherwise). These assumptions imply that the effect of adding an additional asset, or of a change in one of the exogenous variables, on the demand for an asset is independent of the other variables or assets owned, except insofar as it affects the value of p, the proportion of the portfolio invested in the asset. The absence of interaction terms is rendered more plausible by the logistic specification of the dependent variable. With these assumptions the explanatory variables in (3) are the vector Z and the 11 dummy variables corresponding to all assets other than j. The equations we shall estimate are

$$(5) \qquad \ln\left(\frac{p_j}{1 - p_j}\right) = \sum_{k \neq j} C_{kj} d_{ki} + Z\theta_j + u_j, \qquad j = 1, \ldots, J.$$

We shall be particularly interested in those variables relating to social security and private pension wealth. Because of the logistic transformation, the system of J equations given by (5) does not satisfy the aggregation condition that

$$(6) \qquad \sum_{j=1}^{J} p_j = 1.$$

We judged it better to sacrifice the imposition of the adding-up constraint to obtain the benefits described above. Although we report below the results of estimating equation (5) for all 12 assets, when simulating the model to examine the effects of change in pension wealth or portfolio composition we shall drop one of the equations. This is described further in section 14.6.

Equations (5) were estimated using observations for those with positive holdings of the asset in the dependent variable. To correct for sample selection bias we included the inverse of Mills's ratio from the estimated probit equations as an additional regressor (Heckman 1979). For a discussion of the assumption of the joint normality of u_j and the error term in the probit equation, see King (1982). This procedure does not give consistent standard errors, but we computed a consistent estimate of the covariance matrix using the results of Greene (1981). These adjustments deal with those people who do not own the asset in question. Less significant is the issue of how to deal with those households which report that they own only one asset. It would be possible to deal with this by including an additional inverse Mills's ratio in the regression using a bivariate probit analysis, but there are strong reasons for supposing that in these cases the data are misrecorded, and so we have chosen to omit the observations with portfolios consisting only of one asset. In any event, the numbers involved are very small. For five assets the number of such cases is zero and in three further cases it is three or less. For deposits it is 69, for cash 141, for passenger cars 63, and for home ownership 50.

14.4 The Construction of Data

In this section we explain how we computed estimates of pension wealth and tax rates. The method employed to construct estimates of permanent income for each individual in the sample is described in the appendix and is a summary of that given in King and Dicks-Mireaux (1982).

The most important component of wealth for which we do not have direct observations is the value of the right to future private pensions and old age social security payments. Social security wealth is defined as that accruing from the public retirement income system. It comes from five sources: Old Age Security (OAS), the Guaranteed Income Supplement (GIS), the Spouses' Allowance (SPA), and the Canada and Quebec Pension Plans (CQPP). The OAS provides flat-rate benefits which are taxable, and were equal to $1,634.34 in 1976 to those aged 65 and over. Eligibility for GIS is based on receipt of OAS, and those who have no income other than OAS receive the maximum benefit of $1,146.30 and $2,035.80 (in 1976), for single and two-pensioner families, respectively. The SPA is payable to a pensioner's spouse, provided he or she is 60–64 years old and would, except for age, qualify for OAS and the GIS at the two-pensioner family rate. Both these benefits are reduced, at different rates, if income is received from sources other than OAS. These benefits have been fully indexed to increases in the consumer price index (CPI) since 1972 and are all financed from general tax revenue.

The Canada and Quebec pension plans, which are virtually identical with automatic transferability of benefit credits, were established in 1965 and cover almost the entire labor force. Both plans are contributory and earnings related. Contributions are paid by individuals aged 18–70 years and not receiving plan benefits, at a rate of 3.6% shared equally by employers and employees and paid in full by the self-employed, on earnings between a lower and upper bound. Both plans provide three types of benefits: retirement pensions, survivors' benefits, and disability benefits.

Since 1976 the eligible age for receipt of retirement benefits has been 65. The benefit level is calculated as 25% of adjusted career average earnings (ACAE), multiplied by the average value of the yearly maximum pensionable earnings (YMPE) in the final 3 working years. The ACAE is the mean value of the ratio (with a maximum value of one) of earnings to YMPE in the best 85% of earning years. The intent of the system appears to be to index the YMPE to the average wage and salary index, although in practice it has on occasion failed to achieve this. Benefit payments are indexed to the CPI. Survivors' benefits include death benefits, surviving spouses' pensions, disabled widowers' pensions, and orphans' benefits. The surviving spouses' pensions (the one of most concern to us) are 60% of that which would have been paid to the deceased contributor if the spouse is 65 years or older, plus a flat-rate component if aged 45–65. For those less than 45 years old, the pension level is determined by age, the number of dependent children, and disability.

The plan is a recent one and transitional arrangements were used to introduce it, which created further variation in the value of pension rights across individuals. Persons aged 55 and less in 1966 were to be eligible for full pensions at age 65; in effect, the closer an individual was to age 55 in 1966 the greater the "bonus" or net benefit received. Those who were 56 or more years old would contribute for less than 10 years and receive a prorated pension.

For each individual in the sample we constructed an estimate of the present value of social security wealth, using estimated age-earnings profiles (for the CQPP component), and the relevant survival probabilities.[5] For the present value calculation the nominal discount rate was chosen to be equal to the rate of change of the wage and salary index. In other words, for the pension plans, the real discount factor for the years up to the age of retirement is one. The rate of inflation was assumed to be 5%, so that for the postretirement years the real discount rate is 2.5%, which is the growth rate of productivity (or the difference in the growth rates of the wage and salary and consumer price indexes). For wives allowance was made for nonparticipation in the labor force at various stages of the life cycle by adjusting the level of the age-earnings profile in a fashion identical to that used in estimating permanent income. In addition to the retirement pension, only the surviving spouse's pension, for those over 45, was included in the calculation. In computing the flat-rate components of social security wealth, we assumed that everyone of at least 65 years of age receives OAS. We made no allowance for SPA because the age-earnings profile implicitly assumes that spouses effectively work until they are 65. Current and future eligibility for the GIS was determined using the appropriate needs test.

In estimating the present value of private pension wealth, actual receipts were used for retirees, and an expected pension was imputed for those in pension plans who were below retirement age (assumed to be 65). The imputation was based on a regression for pension receipts of retirees in terms of permanent income, age, and occupation. To allow for sample selection bias the inverse Mills's ratio, computed from a probit model of positive pension receipts for retirees, was included as an explanatory variable. To convert these benefit levels into a present value it is necessary to make some assumption about current and future pre- and postretirement indexation. Indexation provisions vary widely across pension plans, and any assumption (although we do take notice of what evidence is available) applied uniformly across households will be only an approximation.[6] The heterogeneity of the pension plans across occupations will be captured to some extent in the imputation of pension receipts. We assume that prior to retirement, benefits are effectively indexed to the rate of growth of wages and salaries. Postretirement we assume the level of indexation is 60% of the CPI, which, given the rate of inflation of 5%, yields a real discount rate for postretirement years of 4.5%. With the information available, it was difficult to incorporate survivors' pensions. The procedure used assumes that any living spouse will be entitled to one-half of the household's pension income, regardless of whether he or she is widowed.

A more detailed description of the Canadian retirement income system and of the construction of the wealth estimates is presented in Dicks-Mireaux (1981).[7] Mean values of wealth in these various forms in the sample of 10,118 households were the following: for net worth recorded in the survey, $53,611; social security wealth, $72,455; and for the 4,381 households with private pension wealth, $60,587.

In this final section we briefly examine how personal saving is treated for tax purposes and describe how the marginal tax rate was computed for each household. Both are done with respect to the 1976 tax law, to which the recorded income data relate. The first $1,000 of interest and dividend income, as of 1974 and 1975, respectively (with capital gains included in 1977), are tax exempt. Unlike the United States, Canada has no exemption for state and local bond interest income. Since 1972 realized capital gains have been taxed with a 50% exclusion provision and no distinction between short- and long-run gains. Associated outlays and expenses may be excluded, but there is no adjustment for inflation when calculating taxable gains.[8]

The Canadian Registered Home Ownership Savings Plan (RHOSP) originated in 1974. It permits tax deductions for contributions of up to $1,000 per year, with a lifetime maximum total of $10,000 excluding interest earned and accumulated in the plan, for up to 20 years. Withdrawn funds are not taxed insofar as they are used to acquire an owner-occupied home. In addition, when this wealth is transformed into a house its imputed income is untaxed. Canada differs from the United States in that mortgage interest and local property taxes are *not* deductible.

The tax treatment of private pension plans, since 1972, is like that of an expenditure tax. Contributions are exempt, and receipts less $1,000 for those over 65 are taxed. All federal pension receipts are taxed, unlike United States social security. Registered Retirement Savings Plans (RRSP) were introduced in 1957 and are available to everyone.[9] Their tax treatment is the same as that for private pension plans except that there is a maximum deduction on contributions: ($3,500), $5,500 or 20% of earned income, whichever is less, if (were) not covered by a private pension plan. Furthermore, interest on money borrowed by an individual to pay premiums into his own RRSP is also tax deductible. It is worth noting that contribution limits were very low at first and were raised substantially in 1971 and 1976.

In Canada husbands and wives are assessed separately for tax purposes. For the econometric analysis of household portfolio composition, the relevant marginal tax rate was taken to be that of the male household head. In married households some account should be made for wives purchasing or holding assets. One would expect, however, that in general, rational cooperative behavior would allocate the legal pattern of ownership and purchases so that tax savings were maximized, which would equalize the marginal tax rates faced by husbands and wives.[10] In this case the husband's tax rate is indeed appropriate for our purposes.

The calculated marginal tax rate is potentially endogenous with respect to portfolio composition. Only total earnings and total income of the husband are recorded in the survey, and therefore taxable income had to be estimated. This was done as follows.[11] Total income was calculated as net employment income plus unearned income. Of the deductions which can be applied to this to derive net total income, allowance was made for those relating to Canada and Quebec and employer-sponsored pension plan contributions, unemployment insurance premiums, and registered home ownership plans. In addition to the basic exemption, those related to age, marriage, and wholly dependent children were applied to net income to give taxable income. In the absence of any information on expenditures and the different kinds of unearned income, it was not possible to take into account any other exemptions or deductions. The tax rate was then computed and incorporates the provincial tax laws which consist of a tax rate applied to the basic federal tax payable.[12] Table 14.3 shows the mean values of the constructed variables and asset shares, for each subsample with positive holdings of each asset.

14.5 Empirical Results

In this section the empirical estimates of the discrete and continuous choice models of asset demands are presented. Table 14.4 shows the maximum likelihood estimates of the probit model for positive holdings of each asset.[13] A priori, it is not clear what effect on the probability of holding each asset one should expect of the three components of wealth. For example, both social security and private pension wealth may be thought of as real illiquid assets; though less so, in both respects, for the latter. Consequently, one might expect their presence to reduce the likelihood of holding assets with similar characteristics. On the other hand, some illiquid assets may not be perceived by households to be part of retirement saving—for example, cars—while liquid financial assets such as bonds may be. As shown by the coefficients on the three wealth-

Table 14.3 Wealth, Portfolio, Income, and Tax Characteristics for Subsamples with Positive Holdings of Each Asset (All Figures Are Calculated as Means of Individual Observations for Which $p_j \neq 1$)

Variable[a]	Total Sample	De-posits (1)	Bonds (2)	Cash (3)	Stocks and Shares (4)	RHOSP (5)	RRSP (6)	ONLFA (7)	Cars (8)	Home Equity (9)	Real Estate Equity (10)	Business Equity (11)	Debt (12)
Share of asset in total assets (p_j), %	...	17.7	10.1	1.8	7.8	12.0	9.0	14.0	19.4	60.8	30.1	48.1	157.3
SSW/W	1.3	14.4	2.2	15.7	2.2	1.0	8.5	2.5	6.6	2.6	2.0	0.5	6.1
PPW/W	0.5	3.4	2.1	3.3	0.9	3.3	9.4	0.3	2.8	0.9	0.8	0.1	3.5
W/Y	2.4	2.9	3.7	2.8	5.0	2.2	4.5	6.0	2.8	3.6	4.8	7.1	2.2
SSW/Y	3.2	3.5	3.4	3.6	3.2	2.8	3.2	3.6	3.6	3.8	3.7	4.1	3.5
PPW/Y	1.2	1.0	1.3	1.0	1.5	1.6	1.4	1.0	1.0	1.0	1.1	0.5	1.1
Permanent income (Y), $'s	22,598	21,367	22,683	21,084	24,734	27,785	25,087	21,437	21,860	20,776	21,669	20,446	22,849
Marginal tax rate of household head	30.3	31.1	33.9	30.7	37.6	36.3	38.4	33.6	31.9	31.1	34.0	31.0	32.4
No. of observations for which $p_j > 0$ and $p_j \neq 1$	9,788	8,789	2,592	8,676	895	447	1,630	751	8,295	6,960	1,906	1,876	6,327
No. of observations for which $p_j \equiv 1$	330	69	3	141	0	0	0	0	63	50	0	2	3

[a]W = net worth; SSW = social security wealth; PPW = private pension wealth.

to-permanent-income ratios, all three types of wealth do have significant effects on the choice of which asset to hold. The effect of the level of wealth differs between its three components. Except in the case of debt, the probability of holding each asset rises with the ratio of nonpension wealth W to permanent income. Private pension wealth has a significant positive influence on holdings for all assets except business equity and ONLFA, and is particularly strong for deposits, bonds, cars, and home equity. This form of wealth does not appear to be very different from nonpension wealth. In contrast, however, we observe that social security wealth has significant negative effects on positive holdings of deposits, bonds, home equity, and to a lesser extent stocks and shares. Both private pension and social security wealth have similar positive effects on the discrete choice to own an RRSP, the former being statistically more significant.

Clearly, as we argued earlier, the marginal tax rate has a significant influence on the discrete choice to hold particular assets, for example a positive one on stocks and shares and RRSPs.[14] Because of our inability to observe whether individuals have or have not exhausted the tax deductions or exemptions associated with a particular asset, the exact interpretation is not quite as clear-cut. In general, permanent income Y has a significant positive effect. The negative influence on home equity (in comparison to that on RHOSPs) is, perhaps, surprising. However, the positive effect on holding an RHOSP may be largely related to the tax savings it offers via income averaging, regardless of whether or not it is ultimately used to purchase a home. Also, unlike the United States, the tax advantage of home ownership versus renting is limited to the nontaxation of imputed income from the former. Its insignificance in the cash equation attests to the transactions role of cash. Low household earnings, which may reflect transitory shocks or the position on the age-earnings profile, in contrast tend to have a negative influence. Either asset holdings have been run down or, simply, little or no saving is possible. The apparently contradictory positive effect on holdings of bonds, stocks and shares, and other nonliquid financial assets may reflect that households with these assets may receive most of their total income from them.

Of the remaining explanatory variables, low age has a negative effect except on business equity (youthful entrepreneurship) and debt. Education when significant has a positive influence; its insignificant role in cash and home equity is understandable, but with regard to business equity it is perhaps surprising. Marriage has mixed effects: a strong role in owning a home, and a negative role in holding an RHOSP or RRSP.

Estimates of relative asset share demand equations are given in table 14.5, at the end of which is a detailed description of the explanatory variables used. These equations model the continuous choice of how much to hold of each asset given the choice of which assets are held.

Table 14.4   **Probit Model for Positive Asset Holdings**
(Standard Errors in Parentheses)

Explanatory Variable[a]	Assets				
	Deposits (1)	Bonds (2)	Cash (3)	Stocks and Shares (4)	RHOSP (5)
Constant	-2.531 (0.909)	-2.300 (0.807)	0.012 (0.860)	-6.897 (1.148)	-12.691 (1.801)
Marginal tax rate	0.783 (0.180)	1.066 (0.159)	0.622 (0.170)	1.607 (0.228)	-0.345 (0.307)
Ln Y	0.372 (0.095)	0.127 (0.084)	0.095 (0.090)	0.511 (0.119)	1.100 (0.181)
W/Y	0.104 (0.008)	0.021 (0.003)	0.017 (0.004)	0.031 (0.003)	0.004 (0.004)
SSW/Y	-0.095 (0.016)	-0.064 (0.015)	-0.017 (0.015)	-0.033 (0.023)	0.121 (0.042)
PPW/Y	0.097 (0.018)	0.090 (0.011)	0.052 (0.015)	0.042 (0.014)	0.032 (0.016)
Married	0.069 (0.080)	0.274 (0.073)	0.108 (0.076)	-0.058 (0.102)	-0.572 (0.141)
Education: secondary or above	0.297 (0.048)	0.241 (0.034)	-0.004 (0.041)	0.304 (0.044)	0.293 (0.052)
Age < 40	-0.350 (0.046)	-0.457 (0.037)	-0.164 (0.042)	-0.502 (0.049)	0.083 (0.064)
Household earnings < \$6,000	-0.273 (0.054)	0.490 (0.048)	-0.181 (0.052)	0.154 (0.068)	-0.743 (0.130)
Nos. above limit	8,789	2,592	8,676	895	447
Nos. below limit	1,260	7,523	1,301	9,223	9,671
$\chi^2(9)$	1,064.6	814.0	219.2	713.9	382.7
The probability P of positive asset holdings evaluated at the sample means	0.912	0.241	0.876	0.068	0.027
The change in P for:					
25% increase in $\dfrac{SSW}{Y}$	-0.015	-0.018	-0.003	-0.004	0.008
25% increase in $\dfrac{PPW}{Y}$	0.004	0.007	0.003	0.001	0.004

			Assets			
RRSP (6)	ONLFA (7)	Cars (8)	Home Equity (9)	Real Estate Equity (10)	Business Equity (11)	Debt . (12)
− 10.200	− 5.112	− 3.401	6.091	− 1.483	− 11.129	− 7.494
(1.109)	(1.076)	(0.809)	(0.833)	(0.869)	(0.984)	(0.768)
2.060	1.093	1.384	1.240	1.540	− 0.273	0.450
(0.212)	(0.214)	(0.161)	(0.168)	(0.171)	(0.183)	(0.145)
0.875	0.335	0.346	− 0.754	− 0.028	0.925	0.726
(0.114)	(0.112)	(0.085)	(0.087)	(0.091)	(0.101)	(0.080)
0.039	0.036	0.029	0.220	0.044	0.198	− 0.014
(0.003)	(0.030)	(0.004)	(0.009)	(0.003)	(0.006)	(0.002)
0.037	0.022	0.036	− 0.035	− 0.002	0.216	0.147
(0.023)	(0.020)	(0.014)	(0.016)	(0.016)	(0.019)	(0.014)
0.036	− 0.027	0.107	0.120.	0.002	− 0.189	0.030
(0.012)	(0.016)	(0.016)	(0.013)	(0.012)	(0.015)	(0.012)
− 0.358	− 0.189	0.469	1.524	0.398	− 0.258	− 0.200
(0.094)	(0.096)	(0.070)	(0.076)	(0.082)	(0.091)	(0.067)
0.243	0.137	0.118	− 0.031	0.147	− 0.003	0.052
(0.038)	(0.047)	(0.042)	(0.037)	(0.037)	(0.041)	(0.034)
− 0.552	− 0.263	− 0.067	− 0.182	− 0.302	0.396	0.522
(0.044)	(0.050)	(0.042)	(0.039)	(0.039)	(0.044)	(0.034)
− 0.337)	0.202	− 0.433	− 0.161	− 0.026	− 0.349	− 0.507
(0.065)	(0.063)	(0.048)	(0.052)	(0.051)	(0.056)	(0.043)
1,630	751	8,295	6,960	1,906	1,876	6,327
8,488	9,367	1,760	3,108	8,212	8,240	3,788
1,426.8	319.8	1,496.5	3,231.0	724.2	2,544.9	1,654.2
0.119	0.066	0.859	0.770	0.172	0.153	0.635
0.006	0.002	0.007	− 0.010	− 0.003	0.051	0.049
0.002	− 0.001	0.006	0.008	0.002	− 0.010	0.003

[a]Dummy variables take the value unity when the description applies to the household, zero otherwise. Individual variables refer to the head of a household.

Table 14.5   Asset Demand Equations (Standard Errors in Parentheses)
Dependent Variable ln $(p_j/1 - p_j)$

Explanatory Variable	Assets				
	Deposits (1)	Bonds (2)	Cash (3)	Stocks and Shares (4)	RHOSP (5)
Marginal tax rate	1.268 (0.223)	1.181 (0.443)	1.596 (0.710)	2.839 (0.872)	−0.214 (0.701)
Ln Y	−0.008 (0.018)	−0.141 (0.065)	−0.541 (0.085)	−0.044 (0.109)	−0.150 (0.071)
W/Y	−0.024 (0.004)	−0.019 (0.007)	−0.051 (0.009)	−0.015 (0.008)	−0.113 (0.017)
SSW/Y	0.006 (0.024)	−0.057 (0.047)	−0.003 (0.052)	−0.026 (0.092)	0.052 (0.088)
PPW/Y	0.013 (0.016)	0.002 (0.032)	0.090 (0.044)	0.023 (0.039)	−0.005 (0.031)
SSW/W	0.00007 (0.00007)	−0.001 (0.001)	0.0003 (0.0001)	0.003 (0.004)	0.002 (0.001)
PPW/W	−0.00005 (0.00013)	0.001 (0.001)	−0.003 (0.002)	0.001 (0.006)	−0.002 (0.001)
No. of persons with life insurance	0.102 (0.020)	−0.023 (0.032)	0.029 (0.040)	−0.094 (0.060)	−0.046 (0.050)
Farm family dummy	−0.097 (0.102)	−0.410 (0.177)	0.294 (0.201)	−1.152 (0.305)	0.278 (0.375)
Married dummy	−0.070 (0.074)	0.109 (0.173)	0.538 (0.231)	−0.263 (0.281)	0.171 (0.190)
Self-employed dummy	0.187 (0.084)	0.408 (0.146)	−0.007 (0.165)	0.114 (0.225)	0.101 (0.271)
Unemployed or not in labor force dummy	−0.006 (0.062)	0.295 (0.112)	0.178 (0.121)	0.246 (0.235)	0.018 (0.166)
No. of children < 18 years	−0.113 (0.018)	−0.084 (0.032)	−0.018 (0.034)	0.022 (0.059)	−0.083 (0.050)
No. of children aged 18–24 in full-time schooling	0.111 (0.062)	−0.054 (0.093)	0.162 (0.120)	0.007 (0.160)	0.030 (0.154)
D1	— (—)	−0.318 (0.173)	−0.136 (0.134)	−0.775 (0.380)	0.071 (0.315)
D2	−0.031 (0.042)	— (—)	−0.157 (0.084)	−0.224 (0.122)	−0.053 (0.094)
D3	0.165 (0.061)	−0.155 (0.100)	— (—)	−0.546 (0.213)	−0.030 (0.175)
D4	−0.017 (0.064)	0.014 (0.084)	−0.106 (0.126)	— (—)	−0.228 (0.129)

				Assets		
RRSP (6)	ONLFA (7)	Cars (8)	Home Equity (9)	Real Estate Equity (10)	Busi- ness Equity (11)	Debt (12)
0.753 (0.534)	0.595 (1.119)	0.881 (0.256)	−0.512 (0.197)	−0.870 (0.501)	−1.268 (0.471)	0.008 (0.337)
−0.171 (0.058)	−0.008 (0.166)	0.100 (0.025)	0.123 (0.029)	0.139 (0.081)	0.453 (0.060)	0.009 (0.029)
−0.025 (0.005)	−0.012 (0.012)	−0.041 (0.004)	−0.028 (0.004)	0.009 (0.006)	0.005 (0.006)	−0.093 (0.006)
−0.155 (0.054)	−0.005 (0.088)	0.122 (0.018)	−0.009 (0.017)	−0.031 (0.034)	−0.006 (0.043)	0.142 (0.028)
0.026 (0.021)	−0.025 (0.065)	0.008 (0.015)	0.018 (0.014)	−0.018 (0.024)	0.127 (0.046)	−0.003 (0.020)
−0.0004 (0.0018)	−0.001 (0.001)	0.0004 (0.0001)	−0.0002 (0.0004)	−0.001 (0.003)	−0.002 (0.002)	0.0009 (0.0001)
0.0002 (0.0016)	0.004 (0.011)	−0.0003 (0.0001)	−0.003 (0.002)	−0.002 (0.006)	0.003 (0.005)	−0.0001 (0.0002)
−0.091 (0.032)	−0.108 (0.093)	0.049 (0.017)	−0.022 (0.017)	−0.026 (0.032)	0.012 (0.051)	0.041 (0.027)
−0.600 (0.155)	−1.165 (0.398)	−0.506 (0.087)	−1.305 (0.081)	−0.098 (0.169)	0.955 (0.127)	0.245 (0.146)
−0.061 (0.146)	−0.098 (0.339)	−0.088 (0.109)	0.204 (0.097)	−0.349 (0.187)	−0.189 (0.213)	−0.080 (0.116)
0.188 (0.121)	0.034 (0.312)	−0.053 (0.073)	−0.197 (0.069)	−0.093 (0.110)	0.078 (0.110)	0.069 (0.114)
0.015 (0.125)	0.503 (0.285)	−0.022 (0.054)	−0.009 (0.055)	−0.145 (0.115)	−0.059 (0.217)	−0.015 (0.084)
−0.043 (0.029)	−0.148 (0.088)	0.025 (0.015)	0.032 (0.015)	0.001 (0.029)	0.026 (0.040)	0.094 (0.022)
0.080 (0.082)	0.178 (0.266)	0.099 (0.052)	0.011 (0.050)	0.030 (0.086)	−0.246 (0.147)	0.207 (0.080)
−0.130 (0.207)	0.240 (0.577)	−0.691 (0.058)	−0.934 (0.058)	0.019 (0.146)	−0.119 (0.170)	−0.291 (0.082)
−0.155 (0.063)	−0.025 (0.191)	−0.217 (0.036)	−0.209 (0.037)	−0.263 (0.069)	−0.387 (0.112)	−0.357 (0.059)
−0.146 (0.119)	0.237 (0.322)	0.160 (0.051)	0.058 (0.051)	−0.309 (0.106)	−0.060 (0.152)	−0.097 (0.079)
0.035 (0.073)	−0.314 (0.226)	−0.170 (0.055)	−0.084 (0.054)	−0.158 (0.091)	−0.376 (0.147)	−0.061 (0.087)

Table 14.5 (continued)

Explanatory Variable	Assets				
	Deposits (1)	Bonds (2)	Cash (3)	Stocks and Shares (4)	RHOSP (5)
D5	−0.040 (0.086)	0.019 (0.122)	−0.305 (0.170)	0.072 (0.207)	— (—)
D6	0.121 (0.051)	0.058 (0.073)	−0.145 (0.101)	0.290 (0.128)	−0.187 (0.107)
D7	−0.116 (0.067)	0.048 (0.098)	−0.168 (0.133)	−0.173 (0.155)	−0.007 (0.183)
D8	−0.909 (0.056)	−0.491 (0.109)	−0.538 (0.108)	−0.296 (0.219)	−0.476 (0.169)
D9	−2.002 (0.047)	−1.632 (0.082)	−1.585 (0.091)	−1.303 (0.179)	−1.118 (0.109)
D10	−0.398 (0.047)	−0.174 (0.073)	−0.262 (0.092)	−0.158 (0.131)	−0.465 (0.126)
D11	−0.751 (0.066)	−0.736 (0.107)	−0.378 (0.128)	−0.339 (0.172)	−0.661 (0.179)
D12	−0.713 (0.041)	−0.339 (0.070)	0.056 (0.082)	−0.018 (0.139)	0.065 (0.102)
V1	−0.002 (0.011)	0.015 (0.022)	−0.066 (0.022)	−0.066 (0.054)	0.015 (0.024)
V2	0.013 (0.009)	0.006 (0.016)	0.010 (0.018)	0.008 (0.029)	−0.058 (0.022)
V3	0.023 (0.009)	0.010 (0.016)	0.010 (0.019)	0.039 (0.028)	−0.011 (0.027)
V4	0.008 (0.011)	−0.003 (0.044)	−0.024 (0.020)	−0.024 (0.029)	0.016 (0.030)
V5	0.086 (0.029)	0.152 (0.003)	0.022 (0.057)	0.187 (0.089)	0.025 (0.128)
V6	−0.003 (0.002)	−0.008 (0.265)	−0.002 (0.004)	−0.010 (0.007)	0.002 (0.012)
V7	0.055 (0.168)	0.234 (0.173)	0.143 (0.340)	0.112 (0.592)	−0.447 (1.335)
Inverse of Mills's ratio	−0.180 (0.168)	0.138 (0.260)	3.386 (1.166)	−0.065 (0.312)	0.073 (0.213)
SE of equation	1.674	1.504	2.722	1.700	0.915
Degrees of freedom	8,756	2,559	8,643	862	414
Mean p_j	0.087	0.042	0.003	0.027	0.065

				Real Estate	Business	
			Home	Estate	ness	
RRSP	ONLFA	Cars	Equity	Equity	Equity	Debt
(6)	(7)	(8)	(9)	(10)	(11)	(12)
−0.072	0.152	−0.614	−0.381	−0.196	−0.116	−0.505
(0.106)	(0.419)	(0.074)	(0.101)	(0.150)	(0.250)	(0.115)
—	0.020	−0.196	−0.247	−0.159	−0.474	−0.317
(—)	(0.209)	(0.044)	(0.044)	(0.077)	(0.122)	(0.071)
−0.155	—	−0.280	−0.365	−0.100	−0.206	−0.114
(0.087)	(—)	(0.059)	(0.059)	(0.096)	(0.144)	(0.095)
−0.364	−0.248	—	−0.791	−0.184	−0.546	0.122
(0.119)	(0.274)	(—)	(0.052)	(0.099)	(0.135)	(0.080)
−1.046	−1.124	−2.219	—	−1.490	−1.093	−1.605
(0.088)	(0.242)	(0.041)	(—)	(0.093)	(0.150)	(0.062)
−0.164	−0.145	−0.429	−1.018	—	−0.880	−0.324
(0.068)	(0.196)	(0.040)	(0.039)	(—)	(0.106)	(0.066)
−0.295	−0.225	−0.696	−1.499	−0.739	—	−0.148
(0.091)	(0.257)	(0.057)	(0.056)	(0.087)	(—)	(0.087)
0.073	−0.024	0.475	0.132	−0.146	0.212	—
(0.067)	(0.197)	(0.036)	(0.036)	(0.069)	(0.103)	(—)
0.029	0.028	−0.095	0.094	0.031	−0.079	−0.078
(0.028)	(0.060)	(0.010)	(0.014)	(0.029)	(0.036)	(0.014)
0.021	0.044	−0.038	0.016	0.013	0.035	−0.074
(0.015)	(0.046)	(0.007)	(0.008)	(0.016)	(0.021)	(0.012)
0.007	−0.084	−0.002	0.009	0.004	−0.001	−0.040
(0.014)	(0.045)	(0.008)	(0.008)	(0.015)	(0.021)	(0.012)
0.034	0.074	−0.022	0.009	−0.017	−0.048	−0.038
(0.015)	(0.046)	(0.009)	(0.009)	(0.016)	(0.025)	(0.015)
0.051	−0.174	−0.040	−0.051	−0.024	−0.038	−0.110
(0.052)	(0.125)	(0.026)	(0.024)	(0.047)	(0.077)	(0.053)
−0.011	0.011	0.002	0.001	0.0005	0.006	0.006
(0.005)	(0.010)	(0.002)	(0.002)	(0.004)	(0.006)	(0.004)
0.890	−0.556	−0.192	−0.122	0.229	−0.864	−0.194
(0.596)	(0.777)	(0.167)	(0.142)	(0.297)	(0.676)	(0.461)
0.138	−0.974	0.452	0.327	−0.040	−1.075	0.560
(0.162)	(0.555)	(0.174)	(0.093)	(0.254)	(0.103)	(0.189)
1.187	2.120	1.374	1.297	1.326	1.782	1.884
1,597	718	8,262	6,927	1,873	1,843	6,294
0.050	0.056	0.104	0.644	0.241	0.456	0.085

Footnotes on the following page.

The explanatory variables in the vector Z of equation (5) relating to wealth on which we focus are the ratios of the three components of wealth to permanent income and the ratio of the two forms of pension wealth to net worth (nonpension wealth). The first set of variables captures the scale effects of wealth on asset demands, the second set the composition effect of wealth on portfolio behavior. Nonpension wealth has a significant depressing scale effect on the relative shares of all assets, apart from real estate and business equity. In contrast, the estimated coefficients on private pension and social security wealth are rarely significant and are of different size and sign. Statistically significant point estimates occur for RRSPs, cars, and debt for SSW and cash and business equity for PPW. The compositional influence of pension wealth is also very small, with significant coefficients found only for SSW/W in the demand for cars and debt. At a first glance it would appear that for the continuous choice decision the portfolio composition effects of pension wealth are small, and this is borne out in the simulations in section 14.5. This finding may in part be a result of the level of aggregation of assets. If we had chosen to group assets into a smaller number of categories, some of the significant discrete choice effects would instead have shown up in the continuous choice model estimates.

The dummy variables D1–D12 take the value unity when assets 1–12 are held, zero otherwise. These capture the effect of the particular portfolio combination the household holds on the relative share demand for each asset. The significant role of these asset ownership dummies (and also the number of persons with life insurance, which is a form of dummy for this type of wealth) evidently justifies their inclusion in the estimated equations. In most cases, the gross effect of the ownership of other assets

---

Footnotes for Table 14.5

Index of Explanatory Variables

D1–D12 are dummy variables which take the value unity if the household has positive holdings of assets 1–12, where the numeric index corresponds to the equation column numbers.

Dummy variables take the value unity when the description applies to the household, zero otherwise. Individual variables refer to the head of a household. A farm family is one which any member receives more than 50% of his income fom self-employment in farming. The labor force status dummies relate to the week in which the survey was undertaken.

V1–V7, a piecewise function of age, (A). Define the following dummies for household i: $b_{1i} = 1$ if $A_i < 30$, zero otherwise; $b_{2i} = 1$ if $30 < A_i < 40$, zero otherwise; $b_{3i} = 1$ if $40 < A_i < 50$, zero otherwise; $b_{4i} = 1$ if $50 < A_i < 60$, zero otherwise; $b_{5i} = 1$ if $60 < A_i < 75$, zero otherwise; $b_{6i} = 1$ if $75 < A_i$, zero otherwise.

Then V1–V7 correspond to: $V1_i = b_{1i}(A_i - 15) + 15 \Sigma_{j=2}^{6} b_{ji}$; $V2_i = b_{2i}(A_i - 30) + 10 \Sigma_{j=3}^{6} b_{ji}$; $V3_i = b_{3i}(A_i - 40) + 10 \Sigma_{j=4}^{6} b_{ji}$; $V4_i = b_{4i}(A_i - 50) + 10) \Sigma_{j=5}^{6} b_{ji}$; $V5_i = b_{5i}(A_i - 60) + 15 b_{6i}$; $V6_i = b_{5i}(A_i - 60) + 225 b_{6i}$; $V7_i = b_{6i}$, which is a linear piecewise function of age with a quadratic form between the ages of 60 and 75.

is to reduce the relative share held in a particular asset, and most of the positive dummy coefficients are insignificant. An exception to this is the increase in demand for deposits contingent on ownership of cash or an RRSP, or life insurance. Although it is difficult to summarize these results, some features are worth noting. Home equity (D9), primarily because of its large share in homeowner household portfolios, has a very strong negative effect on the demand for all other assets. In contrast to ownership of nonfinancial assets, the holding of financial assets appears to have an insignificant effect on the relative shares of financial assets held (except for stocks and shares). The demand for other nonliquid financial assets is virtually unaffected by other asset ownership, presumably because of its residual nature.

Relative share demand has a negative income elasticity for financial assets and a positive elasticity for nonfinancial assets. Households with lower permanent income are less willing or unable to tie up their wealth in what in effect are less liquid assets. More so than in the discrete choice model, the interpretation of the role of the tax rate is hampered by the nonlinearities embodied in the exemption and deduction rules. The parameter estimates are accordingly mixed; given the initial deductions the positive effect on deposits, bonds, and stocks and shares is understandable, but the insignificant influence on RHOSPs and RRSPs which have potentially large tax breaks is surprising. The insignificant effect on home and real estate equity may be attributed to the absence of mortgage interest deductibility for tax purposes. The imputed income from home ownership is untaxed.

The remaining explanatory variables are intended to cover socioeconomic characteristics of the household which might affect asset demands, transitorily or otherwise, such as labor force or marital status and the number of dependent children. To capture any life-cycle features of these demands we include a piecewise function of the household head's age, using variables V1–V7 which allow us in a linear regression to incorporate a nonlinear function of age (these variables are discussed further in King and Dicks-Mireaux [1982]). Neither marriage or the number of children aged 18–24 in full-time schooling appear to influence portfolio composition significantly. In the former case, notable exceptions are the understandable positive influence on cash holdings and home equity and the less obvious negative one on real estate equity. In the latter case, this may reflect the relatively complete government funding of university education. In contrast young children have reduced the demand for financial assets, with no significant effects on nonfinancial assets other than to increase the demand for home equity. Neither labor force dummies (in contrast to low household earnings in discrete choice behavior) influence portfolio composition. Up to the age bracket 60–75 years the age terms V1–V7 suggest, in general, a cumulative rise in relative asset share demands. For both cars and debt the opposite is true. The terms V5 and V6 imply that between the age of 60 and 75 the age effect on the demand for financial assets reaches a maximum, while for other assets it continues to rise. This possibly reflects a greater initial role, in providing for retirement income, of decumulating financial assets.

The inverse of Mills's ratio clearly indicates that in its absence sample selection bias will occur in estimating equations of the form (5) for nonfinancial assets and cash. The former are available to most households in relatively less divisible units than financial assets, while zero holdings of cash are clearly due to rather special factors.

14.6   The Effect of Pension Wealth on Portfolio Composition

In this section we use the empirical estimates in simulations to examine the effect of changes in pension wealth on household portfolio composition. To do so correctly we must take into account two factors. First, changes in pension wealth may affect asset demands directly, as in the estimated equations, and indirectly, via their effect on the level of nonpension wealth. Second, because individual households hold very different combinations of assets it is important to compute the response for each household and then to aggregate over households to discover the overall effect.

In the simulations we consider separately the effects on portfolio composition of a 25% increase in the ratio of social security and private pension wealth to income. This particular choice of effect to simulate is suggested by the substantial earnings-related elements of both forms of wealth. In these exercises some assumptions had to be made. The effect of these wealth changes on the discrete choice of which assets to hold is excluded, that is, the combination of assets each household owns is taken as given. This was done because within the present model specification we have been unable to devise a computationally simple way of incorporating these effects. The estimates for all 12 demand equations were presented in section 14.5, but to impose the adding-up constraint for asset shares we drop the home equity equation.[15] Note that because the shares p_j are defined with respect to total assets this constraint only applies to the 11 assets and not to debt. Finally, the approach is a partial equilibrium one in that we take no account of how the increase in either type of pension is to be paid for or funded; and we assume the supply elasticity of the assets to be infinite.

We incorporate in the simulations the possible adjustment in the level of nonpension wealth by households in the face of changes in pension wealth. This response is modeled as follows: given an exogenous change in pension wealth an individual may choose to hold less nonpension wealth. Having made this choice, he or she then decides how to allocate this wealth among assets. Formally this offsetting behavior may be interpreted in terms of the coefficients of the wealth terms in the estimated equations. We can write the asset demand equations as

$$(7) \qquad \ln\left(\frac{p_j}{1-p_j}\right) = \alpha_1 \frac{TW}{Y} + \alpha_2 \frac{SSW}{W} + \alpha_3 \frac{PPW}{W}$$

$$+ S\emptyset_j + u_j, \qquad j = 1, \ldots, J,$$

where S is the vector of all nonwealth explanatory variables, $\emptyset$ is its associated parameter vector, and TW is "effective" total wealth. It is defined by

$$(8) \qquad TW = W + \delta_s SSW + \delta_p PPW,$$

where δ_s and δ_p reflect the extent to which social security and private pension wealth, respectively, are regarded as equivalent to nonpension wealth. Equation (7) can, therefore, be written as

$$(9) \qquad \ln\left(\frac{p_j}{1-p_j}\right) = \alpha_1 \frac{W}{Y} + \alpha_1 \delta_s \frac{SSW}{Y} + \alpha_1 \delta_p \frac{PPW}{Y} + \alpha_2 \frac{SSW}{W}$$

$$+ \alpha_3 \frac{PPW}{W} + S\emptyset_j + u_j, \qquad j = 1, \ldots, J.$$

It is clear that, unless pension and nonpension wealth are considered as equivalent (i.e., $\delta_s = \delta_p = 1$), there is no reason to expect the estimated coefficients on the three wealth-to-income ratios to be the same. Indeed, they are not (see table 14.5), and for a given change in pension wealth, if households adjust their holdings of other wealth, they will do so by a value of δ_s or δ_p. In fact the nature of the offset as implied by the individual demand equations differs as between private pension and social security wealth and the estimates differ also across assets. The range of values is in fact quite wide: a $-\$6.2$ to $+\$3.6$ change in W/Y with respect to a one-dollar rise in SSW/Y, and $-\$23.3$ to $+\$2.0$ for PPW/Y. This lack of conformity in the estimated offsets across equations is perhaps understandable in the absence of cross-equation constraints.[16] If we regard the offsets implied by the individual demand equations as appropriate, changes in the ratio of pension wealth to permanent income will only affect asset demands via the composition effects α_2 and α_3. For example, any change in SSW/Y has an effect of $\alpha_1\delta_s\Delta(SSW/Y)$ on asset demand. This is simultaneously matched by a change of $-\delta_s\Delta(SSW/Y)$ in W/Y, resulting in a change in asset demand equivalent to $-\alpha_1\delta_s\Delta(SSW/Y)$. The combined effect is therefore zero. The changes in SSW and W do, however, affect asset demands by changing the value of the ratios SSW/W and PPW/W. If an alternative single value for the offset of δ_0 is imposed on all the equations, the net scale effect on asset share demands becomes $\alpha_1(\delta_s - \delta_0)\Delta(SSW/Y)$.

The effects of pension wealth on portfolio composition are examined for three different assumptions about the response of nonpension wealth to changes in pension wealth. The three assumptions are that the offsets are (a) zero; (b) the weighted average of the offsets implied by the estimated demand equations, the weights being the aggregate shares of each asset in the sample; and (c) an estimate derived from an econometric model of total household savings in nonpension wealth.

The values of the offsets (for a one-dollar increase in pension wealth) used were $0.56 and −$6.03 for the weighted average of the demand equation estimates, and −$0.27 and −$0.23 for the aggregate estimate of social security and private pension wealth, respectively. The zero offset can be interpreted as the short-run behavioral response to a change in pension wealth. Households smooth their adjustment of wealth via changes in savings but reallocate their portfolio immediately. The two nonzero offsets can be thought of as different steady states in which the complete desired adjustment of the level of nonpension wealth has also been made.

Before describing the simulation exercises we turn to the specification of the model of total household savings. The model presented is one which is developed in more detail in King and Dicks-Mireaux (1982). Wealth holdings (excluding pensions) over the life cycle are modeled as a nonlinear function of age (using the piecewise function adopted in the estimation of [5]), household socioeconomic characteristics, and the size of private and social security wealth. To control for differences in permanent income, all the wealth variables are deflated by it. The life-cycle model has been criticized on the grounds that one can observe a large number of households owning amounts of wealth which appear incompatible with the need to finance that part of retirement consumption not financed by pensions or social security. Indeed, in the Canadian sample we found this to be true. Nevertheless, the behavior of the majority of households is consistent with the predictions of the life-cycle model (King and Dicks-Mireaux 1982). Consequently, in estimating the model we exclude households with net worth of less than $2,500. Table 14.6 shows the results of estimating a probit model for holding low net worth. This was used to compute the inverse of Mills's ratio, which was included in the net worth regression, presented in table 14.7, to allow for sample selection bias induced by truncating the dependent variable.

In table 14.6 we see that low educational attainment and household earnings are correlated with small wealth holdings. This suggests an explanation for why such households may not act as predicted by the life-cycle model, namely, that they do not plan for the future or are unable to manage their own financial affairs, or may receive such low earnings that the optimal life-cycle consumption plan implies that retire-

Table 14.6   **Probit Model for Small Wealth Holdings**
              (Standard Errors in Parentheses)

Variable[a]	$W < \$2,500$
Constant	4.209
	(0.752)
Ln Y	-0.475
	(0.080)
Household earnings $< \$6,000$	0.353
	(0.052)
No. of persons unemployed	0.229
	(0.030)
Age < 40	0.884
	(0.052)
Self-employed	-0.067
	(0.117)
Home owner	1.899
	(0.042)
Farm family[b]	-0.406
	(0.202)
Married	0.018
	(0.064)
Education: secondary or above	-0.361
	(0.047)
Nos. below limit	1,839
Nos. above limit	8,279
$\chi^2(9)$	4,116.2

[a]Dummy variables take the value unity when the description applies to the household, zero otherwise. Individual variables refer to the head of a household.
[b]A family in which any member receives more than 50% of his income from self-employment in farming.

ment consumption is less than or equal to the expected value of old age social security payments.

Estimates of the model,

$$(10) \qquad \left(\frac{W}{Y}\right)_i = \alpha_0 + \sum_{j=1}^{7} a_j v_{ji} - \delta_s \left(\frac{SSW}{Y}\right)_i - \delta_p D_1 \left(\frac{PPW}{Y}\right)_i + u_i$$

are shown in table 14.7.

The variables are defined as earlier. In addition, D_1 equals one if household i is eligible for a private pension plan, zero otherwise, and δ_s and δ_p are the implied offsets given by the definition of total wealth in (8).

As the life-cycle model predicts, asset holdings rise (apart from a small dip at ages 50–60) up to the age bracket 60–75 and then fall. The implied offset to nonpension wealth from an additional dollar of social security or private pension wealth is 27 and 23 cents, respectively; the larger effect of

Table 14.7   Net Worth (W) Regression: Truncated Sample $W > \$2,500$
(Standard Errors in Parentheses) Dependent Variable W/Y

Constant	11.825
	(2.764)
V1	0.071
	(0.043)
V2	0.084
	(0.027)
V3	0.177
	(0.028)
V4	−0.002
	(0.032)
V5	0.049
	(0.086)
V6	−0.009
	(0.007)
V7	−0.094
	(0.512)
Farm family dummy	7.376
	(0.257)
No. of persons unemployed	−0.361
	(0.105)
No. of adults in household	0.145
	(0.076)
No. of persons with life insurance	0.115
	(0.064)
Ln Y	−1.013
	(0.256)
SSW/Y	−0.269
	(0.061)
PPW/Y	−0.227
	(0.047)
Inverse of Mills's ratio	−1.379
	(0.175)
S.E. of equation	5.182
R^2	0.182
Degrees of freedom	8,263

the former possibly due to its being indexed. The macroeconomic effects of introducing a public pension plan using a hypothetical but broadly realistic simulation model of the economic-demographic system of Canada in the mid-seventies is examined by Denton and Spencer (1981). Among several experiments they consider the effect of different savings offset assumptions with respect to contributions.

Additional explanatory variables were introduced. A test for homothetic preferences is possible by including permanent income. The sign of the coefficient implies that the higher is permanent income, the lower is the ratio of wealth to permanent income. The elasticity evaluated at the mean value of Y/W is -0.31. Farm families possess greater wealth than is predicted by the simple model which may reflect the importance of land prices to the value of such families' net worth. Unemployment has a depressing effect on wealth, and household size appears to have little significant influence on wealth holding. Measured wealth does not include the value of life insurance policies, and we know only the number of persons in each household covered by life insurance. We might expect that, ceteris paribus, the more members covered the less would be the level of household wealth invested in other assets. But in fact the coefficient on the life insurance variable is positive, suggesting rather that purchase of life assurance is correlated with a greater than average preference to save (resulting perhaps from a higher than average degree of risk aversion).

The simulation exercises are now described. The purpose of the first simulation is to illustrate how the effect of a change in pension wealth differs between two households which differ with regard to the number of assets held. This is done for a 25% increase in SSW/Y using the wealth offset from the aggregate savings model reported above. The two portfolios we consider are the "modal" portfolio, which consists of deposits, cash, cars, home equity, and personal debt, and a "complete" portfolio in which all assets are held. As shown in table 14.2 portfolios of five assets are the most popular, and almost half of these consist of the modal portfolio (1,022 households). In each case the predicted portfolios (columns 1 and 2 in table 14.8) are calculated using the mean characteristics of those holding the modal portfolio. These were permanent income of $24,098, nonpension wealth of $29,286, social security wealth of $77,684, and private pension wealth of $32,311. The household head is 41 years old, and the dummies imply high probabilities of being married and employed but not of being a farm family. The mean number of adults with life insurance and of dependent children above and below 18 years of age is 0.75, 1.59, and 0.07, respectively.

The two predicted portfolios obviously differ, with the proportion of assets held in nonfinancial form being less in the complete portfolio.[17] Columns 3 and 4 of table 14.8 give the changes in asset shares following the increase in SSW/Y. In both cases the effects are small. With more

Table 14.8   Predicted Portfolio of the "Average" Individual with the Modal Portfolio and a Complete Portfolio Following a 25% Increase in SSW/Y

Assets	Initial Portfolio %		Change in Portfolio (Percentage Points)	
	Hold 5 Assets	Hold All Assets	Hold 5 Assets	Hold All Assets
Total deposits	4.51	1.36	0.04	0.01
Total bonds	—	1.99	—	−0.08
Cash	0.13	0.03	0.001	0.00
Liquid financial assets	4.64	3.38	0.04	−0.07
Stocks and shares	—	1.11	—	−0.02
RHOSP	—	0.74	—	0.05
RRSP	—	2.41	—	−0.27
Other nonliquid financial assets	—	3.93	—	−0.01
Nonliquid financial assets	—	8.19	—	−0.25
Total financial assets	4.64	11.57	0.04	−0.32
Passenger cars	8.05	0.65	0.83	0.07
Home equity	87.31	74.77	−0.87	0.48
Real estate equity	—	7.34	—	−0.19
Business equity	—	5.67	—	−0.04
Total nonfinancial assets	95.36	88.43	−0.05	0.32
Personal debt	4.30	0.72	−0.59	0.10

assets being held, the absolute changes in the modal five assets are reduced. In the modal portfolio the shares of financial and nonfinancial assets rise and fall, respectively, while in the complete portfolio the opposite occurs.

In tables 14.9 and 14.10 we have simulated the effect of changes in pension wealth on portfolio composition for a single representative household which holds the mean portfolio of the sample of 9,788 households. Both tables 14.9 and 14.10 indicate that neither change in both types of pension wealth has a large effect absolutely or proportionately on portfolio composition. Comparing the two tables we observe that the effects on portfolio composition of changes in both types of pension wealth are similar for the zero wealth offset assumption. For the nonzero offsets the changes in nonfinancial assets are negative in both tables but larger for changes in private pension wealth. The direction of change in financial asset holdings is different for the two increases in pension wealth. For example, social security in contrast to private pension wealth has a negative effect on the portfolio share of RRSPs held.

The final simulations presented in tables 14.11 and 14.12 show the effect of the two changes in pension wealth on the aggregate portfolio of the sample. The method employed was to calculate the change in the

Table 14.9   **Change in the Mean Portfolio of the Sample for a**
25% Increase in *SSW/Y*, Given for Different Offsets
in Nonpension Wealth with Respect to Social Security Wealth

Assets	Initial Asset Share (%)	Change in Asset Share (Percentage Points) Offset to Wealth		
		Zero	Average of Demand Equation Estimates	Aggregate Estimate
Total deposits	9.44	0.004	−0.004	0.08
Total bonds	2.58	−0.12	−0.03	−0.11
Cash	0.23	0.00	−0.01	0.00
Liquid financial assets	12.25	−0.08	−0.08	−0.03
Stocks and shares	1.27	0.38	0.37	0.38
RHOSP	0.16	0.00	0.00	0.01
RRSP	1.79	−0.18	−0.20	−0.18
Other nonliquid financial assets	2.07	0.19	0.15	0.21
Nonliquid financial assets	5.29	0.19	0.15	0.21
Total financial assets	17.54	0.11	0.07	0.18
Passenger cars	4.86	0.42	0.34	0.46
Home equity	38.28	−0.23	−0.28	−0.30
Real estate equity	9.77	−0.20	−0.16	−0.21
Business equity	29.54	−0.10	−0.04	−0.13
Total nonfinancial assets	82.45	−0.11	−0.07	−0.18
Personal debt	5.33	0.53	0.03	0.63

value of wealth held in each asset for each household and then to compute the new economy-wide portfolio. Since households own different combinations of assets, it would be incorrect to simulate this effect by using a representative household assumed to hold the intitial mean sample portfolio. A comparison of tables 14.9–14.10 and 14.11–14.12 reveals the aggregation biases inherent in doing this. In converting shares to absolute values and in calculating the new level of total assets (net worth plus debt), the relevant offsets to net worth and the change in personal debt as predicted by our equation estimates were used.

The magnitude of the predicted changes in portfolio shares reported in tables 14.11 and 14.12 are small, and consequently we refrain from making strong statements about the differences in these changes as between assets or between the two types of pension wealth increase. The results reported in table 14.12 for the weighted average offset are clearly an exception. The large changes are a result of the high value of the offset to nonpension wealth. For several assets this led to negative predicted asset shares, which makes little sense in our framework.[18] For these

Table 14.10   **Change in the Mean Portfolio of the Sample for a 25% Increase in *PPW/Y*, Given for Different Offsets in Nonpension Wealth with Respect to Private Pension Wealth**

Assets	Initial Asset Share (%)	Change in Asset Share (Percentage Points) Offset to Wealth		
		Zero	Average of Demand Equation Estimates	Aggregate Estimate
Total deposits	9.44	0.03	1.00	0.04
Total bonds	2.58	-0.02	0.06	-0.02
Cash	0.23	0.01	0.03	0.01
Liquid financial assets	12.25	0.02	1.09	0.03
Stocks and shares	1.27	0.41	0.48	0.42
RHOSP	0.16	0.00	0.03	0.00
RRSP	1.79	0.01	0.08	0.01
Other nonliquid financial assets	2.07	-0.01	0.03	-0.01
Nonliquid financial assets	5.29	0.41	0.62	0.42
Total financial assets	17.54	0.43	1.71	0.45
Passenger cars	4.86	0.01	0.33	0.02
Home equity	38.28	-1.11	-2.28	-1.12
Real estate equity	9.77	-0.04	-0.26	-0.05
Business equity	29.54	0.71	0.50	0.70
Total nonfinancial assets	82.45	-0.43	-1.71	-0.45
Personal debt	5.33	0.00	0.81	0.01

reasons we exclude these results from the discussion below. Negative shares were also predicted, when using the aggregate model offset, for cash in both tables. For the zero offset assumption the predicted asset share changes are similar in both tables, and apart from home equity are negative. When the aggregate offset is used almost half of the predicted changes in shares are positive. The signs of these changes are similar for the two increases in pension wealth but larger in absolute size for the increase in social security wealth.

The simulations appear to suggest rather small effects on portfolio composition of changes in pension wealth. However, before jumping to such a conclusion one should take account of the exclusion of the influence of pension wealth on the choice of which assets to hold. The estimates of the discrete choice model of asset demands reported in table 14.4 indicate that such an influence exists. At the bottom of this table the change in the probability, evaluated at the sample means and assuming a zero offset to nonpension wealth, of holding an asset is given for the two increases in pension wealth employed in the simulations. In addition, it is

Table 14.11   **Aggregate Portfolio of the Sample, and Its Change after a 25% Increase in *SSW/Y***

Assets	Initial Asset Share (%)	Change in Asset Share (Percentage Points) Offset to Net Worth		
		Zero	Average of Demand Equation Estimates	Aggregate Estimate
Total deposits	9.44	−0.22	0.94	−0.91
Total bonds	2.58	−0.14	−0.12	−0.11
Cash	0.23	−0.10	−1.41	−0.38
Liquid financial assets	12.25	−0.46	−1.41	−0.38
Stocks and shares	1.27	−0.03	−0.16	0.07
RHOSP	0.16	−0.003	0.09	−0.07
RRSP	1.79	−0.18	−0.26	−0.10
Other nonliquid financial assets	2.07	−0.01	−0.23	0.18
Nonliquid financial assets	5.29	−0.22	−0.56	0.08
Total financial assets	17.54	−0.68	−1.15	−1.32
Passenger cars	4.86	−0.13	3.68	−2.80
Home equity	38.28	0.98	2.28	0.45
Real estate equity	9.77	−0.16	−0.97	0.55
Business equity	29.54	−0.01	−3.84	3.12
Total nonfinancial assets	82.45	0.68	1.15	1.32
Personal debt	5.33	−0.15	4.17	−3.28

clear from table 14.8 that a change in the number and type of assets held will affect the nature of the portfolio composition adjustment.

14.7 Conclusion

The major result of our study is that, whereas there seems to be an identifiable effect of pension wealth on total private saving, the effect on portfolio composition is less significant. Moreover, within the area of portfolio composition the main effect is in terms of the particular number and combination of assets held rather than the amount of any given asset as a proportion of total wealth.

We have also demonstrated the need for, and the difficulties of constructing, a joint discrete and continuous choice model of asset demands. The empirical results suggest that to ignore the joint nature of the decision process would be an incorrect specification of household portfolio behavior.

Table 14.12   **Aggregate Portfolio of the Sample, and its Change after a 25% Increase in *PPW/Y***

| | | Change in Asset Share (Percentage Points) Offset to Net Worth | | |
Assets	Initial Asset Share (%)	Zero	Average of Demand Equation Estimates	Aggregate Estimate
Total deposits	9.44	−0.27	−0.46	−0.55
Total bonds	2.58	−0.05	−1.17	−0.03
Cash	0.23	−0.10	−1.57	−0.26
Liquid finiancial assets	12.25	−0.42	−3.20	−0.84
Stocks and shares	1.27	−0.01	−0.48	0.03
RHOSP	0.16	−0.01	−2.62	−0.07
RRSP	1.79	−0.01	−2.31	0.03
Other nonliquid financial assets	2.07	−0.02	1.75	0.10
Nonliquid financial assets	5.29	−0.05	−3.66	0.09
Total financial assets	17.54	−0.47	−6.86	−0.75
Passenger cars	4.86	−0.61	−14.41	−2.34
Home equity	38.28	1.11	−29.78	0.93
Real estate equity	9.77	−0.08	4.73	0.40
Business equity	29.54	0.05	39.46	2.12
Total nonfinancial assets	82.45	0.47	6.86	0.75
Personal debt	5.33	−0.71	−16.01	−4.75

Appendix: The Construction of Estimates of Individual Permanent Income

The model for permanent income (defined as normal age-adjusted manual earnings) is[19]

(A1) $$\ln Y_i = Z_i\gamma + s_i - c(A_i),$$

where Z_i is a vector of observable characteristics for individual i, γ is the associated parameter vector, and s_i is an unobservable variable measuring characteristics, such as skill or drive, which is constructed such that its mean value is zero and has variance σ_s^2. The term $c(A_i)$ is a cohort effect which reflects that, for given Z, younger generations are better off than their elders because of technical progress and capital accumulation.

Current earnings differ from permanent income because there exists an age-earnings profile over the life cycle, and a transitory component. Earnings in year t are therefore given by

(A2) $$\ln E_{it} = \ln Y_i + h(A_{it} - \bar{A}) + u_{it}.$$

The function h measures the age-earnings profile (assumed constant across the population), and A is a "standard" age with respect to which permanent income is defined. The transitory component of earnings, u_{it}, is assumed to have zero mean and variance σ_u^2, and to be uncorrelated with s_i. Combining (A1) and (A2) gives the earnings equation

(A3) $$\ln E_{it} = Z_i \gamma + g(A_{it}) + s_i + u_{it},$$

where $g(A_{it}) = h(A_{it} - \bar{A}) - c(A_{it})$. The error term $s_i + u_{it}$ has zero mean and variance $\sigma_s^2 + \sigma_u^2$. Estimation of (A3) provides consistent estimates of γ and the function g. By imposing a cohort effect using outside information, both h and c could be identified. The minimum variance estimator of s_i, the unobservable individual-specific effect, is given by

(A4) $$\hat{s} = \alpha(s_i + u_{it}),$$

where

(A5) $$\alpha = \frac{\sigma_s^2}{\sigma_s^2 + \sigma_u^2}.$$

Therefore, given values for σ_u^2 and σ_s^2, $\hat{\gamma}$ and c, permanent income may be constructed for each individual. With observations on earnings for only one year, it is not possible to obtain estimates of σ_s^2 and σ_u^2 as well as γ from (A3). A value of 0.5 for α was therefore assumed. This value was based on the results of studies which used longitudinal data to estimate the relative magnitudes of σ_s^2 and σ_u^2.[20]

The earnings equation (A3) was estimated for male household heads and for wives separately. Female-headed households were deleted from the sample because a substantial fraction of these were headed by elderly women, probably widows, and for them permanent income is determined primarily by the lifetime earnings of the deceased husband, for which no information was available.

Equation (A3) implicitly assumes individuals are in "full-time" employment and does not allow for systematic changes in labor supply resulting from spells of unemployment during part of the year. Hence the equation was estimated for all individuals whose annual earnings were greater than \$2,000. The sample selection bias induced by this truncation of the dependent variable was corrected for using the two-stage procedure proposed by Heckman (1979). Equation (A3) was estimated by OLS, with the inverse of Mills's ratio computed from a probit model of earnings greater or less than \$2,000 included as an additional explanatory variable, to give consistent estimates of γ and the g function. A discussion of the estimates can be found in King and Dicks-Mireaux (1982), and details of them are available on request.

For individuals included in the earnings regressions, permanent income is equal to the age-adjusted structural component of earnings given by observable variables, plus one-half of the residual in the earnings equation. For the excluded 1,873 male household heads, permanent income was predicted by the structural component alone. The same procedure was adopted for wives but with an explicit adjustment (based on educational attainment and the presence of dependent children) for nonparticipation in the labor force at various stages of the life cycle. By this method, the estimate of the permanent income of wives is independent of that of their husbands, and vice versa. In neither the probit nor earnings regressions of husbands or wives do explanatory variables pertaining to the spouse enter. It is not entirely obvious which characteristics of a spouse should affect the labor participation or earnings choice of the other. To the extent that some do, there is the more general problem of how to model this. Does the wife make her decision conditional on that of her husband, or vice versa? We choose to assume that these decisions are made independently.

Household permanent income is the sum of the estimates for husbands and wives. Mean estimated permanent income of men is $15,928 and of wives $7,451.

Notes

1. Strictly speaking, the relevant variables are the expected relative prices and inflation rate, which will in general differ across individuals. This source of variation is allowed for insofar as it can be explained by the observable individual characteristics included in the demand equations.

2. All computations on this data base were carried out by the authors and should not be attributed to Statistics Canada. Further details of the data base may be found in Statistics Canada (1979).

3. This is because

$$\sum_{j=0}^{J} J_{C^j} = \sum_{j=0}^{J} J!/[J!(J-j)!] = 2^J,$$

which includes the combination owning zero assets.

4. In the context of a logistic distribution as applied to the ownership of consumer durables, Amemiya (1975) examines a three-good case and Billowes (1982) presents estimates for a model with six durables. In the latter case the number of dummy variables was too great to allow estimation of the model.

5. The estimated age-earnings profiles are those estimated for the purpose of constructing our measure of permanent income.

6. A brief summary of the evidence on pension plan indexation in Canada, and relevant references, can be found in Dicks-Mireaux (1981).

7. Other sources of information about the retirement income arrangements in Canada are Statistics Canada (1978) and Wolfson (1979).

8. This calculation differs as between three types of asset. For personal use property, such as personal and household effects, cars, boats, or cottages, gains are reported only if the proceeds of sale were more than $1,000. A gain on own homes is not taxed if the house was a principal residence. Listed personal property (works of art, jewelry, and collectors'

items) is similarly treated except that losses may be offset against gains where the original adjusted cost is greater than $1,000. All gains and losses on other capital properties must be reported. If the loss exceeds $1,000, the excess may be used to reduce taxable capital gains and other income in 1975, 1977, and future years. For business, farm, or professional equity and real estate (other than owner-occupied homes), capital cost or depreciation allowances are available. Rates for commonly held assets are 5% and 10% for buildings of brick and wood, respectively, 20% on machinery and equipment, and 30% on vehicles.

9. The American IRA and Keogh plans, before the 1981 change in the tax law, were only available to self-employed persons or those without company-sponsored plans.

10. Certain features of the tax law facilitate this optimizing behavior. Spouses may contribute to each others' RHOSP and RRSP, and unused portions of eligible deductions for interest and dividend income are transferable. This suggests that when deductions are not fully exhausted, and a husband's marginal tax rate is greater than or equal to his wife's, our procedure is appropriate.

11. A more detailed account is available on request from the authors.

12. In the case of Quebec the procedure is different, and allowance was made for this.

13. To compute a consistent estimate of the covariance matrix of the demand equations, we required the same sample to be used in both the probit and second stage of the estimation procedures. Consequently, households for which the asset share equaled unity were excluded from the probit model for that asset.

14. The insignificant negative effect of the tax rate on the probability of owning an RHOSP may partly be a problem of endogeneity, as the RHOSP deduction was incorporated in the calculation of the tax rate.

15. Home equity was chosen because of its large share in household portfolios. Consequently, any proportional errors in forecasting changes in its share due to its residual role will be reduced. Bonds, which are the most susceptible to measurement error in the survey, were not used because of their small share. In any event, as most of the predicted changes were of small magnitude, any errors are also small. Indeed, the difference between the change in the portfolio share of home equity predicted by the estimated equation and that calculated as a residual was typically no larger than ∓ 0.5 percentage points.

16. One may also ask whether, if the offsets were constrained to be similar across equations, the remaining parameter estimates would change significantly.

17. A disturbing factor in this exercise is that without imposing the adding-up constraint on the predicted portfolio of all assets, the share of home equity was only 9.3%. With only five assets the difference between the predicted and imposed share of home equity was only -5.2%.

18. The possibility of predicting negative aggregate portfolio shares of assets arises for the following reason. In predicting the new level of total assets at the level of the individual household, nothing in the model precludes negative holdings. This is more likely the larger the offset employed in the simulation. Consequently, although the predicted asset shares by construction must be positive, when they are multiplied by total household assets to get the value of each asset held negative values can arise. In the simulation performed the aggregate value of net worth and total assets after summing over households was always positive. However, the aggregate value of the decline in holdings of particular assets was in several cases greater than the initial value, and hence the predicted aggregate shares are negative.

19. This definition excludes the annuity value of receipts of gifts and inheritances, on which no data are available in our sample, and also "supernormal" profits (and losses).

20. These studies, which used United States data, were Lillard (1977), Lillard and Willis (1978), and Lillard and Weiss (1979). See King and Dicks-Mireaux (1982) for further discussion of this point.

Comment   Alan J. Auerbach

In this chapter, Dicks-Mireaux and King have made an ambitious attempt to deal with a number of difficult empirical problems. For this, they are to be commended. Not surprisingly, perhaps, the ultimate findings are somewhat inconclusive. Nevertheless, many interesting issues arise along the way.

To estimate the effects of pension wealth on portfolio allocation, Dicks-Mireaux and King estimate both probit equations, to determine whether individuals hold particular assets, and share equations, given that they do. Before doing this, they must calculate many of the key explanatory variables, such as permanent income, pension wealth, social security wealth, and marginal tax rate. In each case, they demonstrate great attention to detail, doing an admirable job in light of the limitations in the raw data. However, many of these limitations are rather severe. It is unlikely that one could improve greatly on the accuracy of the calculations that Dicks-Mireaux and King perform, but it is also unlikely that some of their constructed variables are very accurate. For example, pension wealth of the working population is based on the pensions being received by current retirees with the same characteristics. Given the changes that have occurred over time in the coverage and nature of private pensions (the raison d'etre of this study, after all), this may be a problem. Likewise, the permanent income of women is adjusted for the fact that women in general do not work full-time over their lifetimes. However, the adjustment ignores the possibility of unobservable differences in participation among women with the same observable characteristics but different current participation behavior: two otherwise observationally equivalent women, one who works and one who doesn't, have the same predicted pattern of lifetime labor force participation. Presumably, variables relating to the husband's characteristics might be included here, although this would raise additional questions with which the authors, quite justifiably, prefer not to deal.

The arrival at the estimable equation (5) is preceded by a journey through combinatorics. Section 14.3 of the chapter shows just how difficult a task Dicks-Mireaux and King have undertaken. I would take issue with their ultimate estimation procedure for a couple of reasons. First, it is not clear why the logistic transformation is appropriate. The asset shares are bounded above and below by one and zero, as are probabilities, but the zero bound represents a constraint rather than a natural limit. Since we observe a truncated version of the underlying error distribution (for which the authors correct by inclusion of the inverse

Alan J. Auerbach is affiliated with the University of Pennsylvania and is a research associate of the National Bureau of Economic Research.

Mills's ratio from the relevant probit equation), why should the symmetry of the logistic distribution hold for the observed errors?

Perhaps a more serious problem with equation (5) is the inclusion of dummy variables for other positive asset holdings. To evaluate this procedure, we must know first how the error terms u_j are generated. If they come from allocation mistakes, or from individual-specific differences, one would expect them to be correlated across equations: if I buy more housing, I will buy less of all other assets. This means that the probability of holding other assets, and hence the dummy variables for such assets, may be correlated with the error term in (5). This would lead to inconsistent estimates of the coefficients C_{kj}.

Turning to the empirical findings, I find it somewhat difficult to interpret the separate effects of the different wealth income and wealth composition terms. According to equations (7)–(9), we should think of the coefficients of SSW/Y and PPW/Y as telling us the extent to which these two types of pension wealth are perceived as net household wealth in the sense analyzed by Barro. Meanwhile, the coefficients of SSW/W and PPW/W are intended to indicate the effects of wealth composition. However, this seems like an artificial distinction. For example, social security wealth, being less liquid, may not count fully as "real" wealth, but this would be the same reason for its effect on portfolio shares. Moreover, given the potential errors in calculating permanent income, wealth may be almost as good a measure of permanent income as the value used. As a result, it is not surprising that the implied wealth offsets from the equations are rather unbelievable.

The pension variables do appear to help in explaining whether individuals hold certain assets (table 14.4), but in the asset demand equations neither social security wealth nor pension wealth (divided by income or wealth) has a very significant effect. This is difficult to interpret, as are the coefficients for these wealth variables from specific equations.

Except for those simulations that use the wealth offset inferred from the asset demand equations using (9), the estimated effects of changes in pension wealth or social security wealth on portfolio composition are remarkably small. However, this outcome merely reflects the poor performance of these variables in the asset demand equations.

Perhaps the most valuable contribution of this chapter is its attention to modeling the portfolio behavior of typical investors, who often hold a small number of the assets available. While I have expressed reservations about some of the techniques used in this chapter, further work along these lines should be encouraged.

References

Amemiya, T. 1974. Multivariate regression and simultaneous equation models when the dependent variables are truncated normal. *Econometrica* 42: 999–1012.

——. 1975. Qualitative response models. *Annals of Economic and Social Measurement* 4: 363–72.

Auerbach, A., and King, M. A. 1983. Taxation, portfolio choice and debt-equity ratio: A general equilibrium model. *Quarterly Journal of Economics* 98, November.

Billowes, E. 1983. The ownership of consumer durables in the U.K. Ph.D. diss., University of Birmingham.

Davies, J. B. 1979. On the size distribution of wealth in Canada. *Review of Income and Wealth* (September), pp. 237–59.

Denton, F. T., and Spencer, B. G. 1981. A macro-economic analysis of the effects of a public pension plan. *Canadian Journal of Economics* 14: 609–35.

Dicks-Mireaux, L-D. L. 1981. Canadian retirement wealth: Legislation and construction. Harvard University. Mimeographed.

Feldstein, M. S. 1976. Personal taxation and portfolio composition: An econometric analysis. *Econometrica* 44: 631–50.

Greene, W. H. 1981. Sample selection bias as a specification error: Comment. *Econometrica* 49: 795–99.

Heckman, J. J. 1979. Sample selection bias as a specification error. *Econometrica* 47: 153–62.

King, M. A. 1982. The structure of discrete and continuous choices: Modelling asset demands. Mimeographed. University of Birmingham.

King, M. A., and Dicks-Mireaux, L-D. L. 1982. Asset holdings and the life cycle. *Economic Journal* 92: 247–67.

Lee, L-F. 1981. Simultaneous equations models with discrete and censored variables. In *Structural analysis of discrete data with econometric applications*, ed. C. F. Manski and D. McFadden. Cambridge: MIT Press.

Lillard, L. A. 1977. Inequality: Earnings vs. human wealth. *American Economic Review* 67: 43–55.

Lillard, L. A., and Weiss, Y. 1979. Components in variation in panel earnings data: The Gary income maintenance experiment. *Econometrica* 47: 437–54.

Lillard, L. A., and Willis, R. S. 1978. Dynamic aspects of earnings mobility. *Econometrica* 46: 985–1012.

Oja, G. 1981. The distribution of wealth in Canada. Paper read at the Seventeenth General Conference of the International Association for Research in Income and Wealth, August, Gouvieux, France.

Statistics Canada. 1978. *Social security national programs*. Ottawa.

———. 1979. *Evaluation of data on family assets and debts 1977*. Ottawa.

Wolfson, M. C. 1979. The lifetime impact of the retirement income system: A quantitative analysis. Appendix 5 in *The retirement income system in Canada: Problems and alternative policies for reform*. Report of the Task Force on Retirement Income Policy, vol. 2. Ottawa.

Contributors

Alan Auerbach
Department of Economics
University of Pennsylvania
Philadelphia, Pennsylvania 19104

Fischer Black
Massachusetts Institute of
  Technology
50 Memorial Drive
Cambridge, Massachusetts 02139

Zvi Bodie
School of Management
Boston University
704 Commonwealth Avenue
Boston, Massachusetts 02215

John Bossons
Institute for Policy Analysis
University of Toronto
Toronto, Ontario M5S 1A1
Canada

Jeremy Bulow
Graduate School of Business
Stanford University
Stanford, California 94305

Louis-David L. Dicks-Mireaux
National Bureau of Economic
  Research
1050 Massachusetts Avenue
Cambridge, Massachusetts 02138

Daniel Feenberg
National Bureau of Economic
  Research
1050 Massachusetts Avenue
Cambridge, Massachusetts 02138

Martin Feldstein
Harvard University
Department of Economics
Littauer Center
Cambridge, Massachusetts 02139

Stanley Fischer
Department of Economics
Massachusetts Institute of
  Technology
Cambrige, Massachusetts 02139

Benjamin Friedman
Harvard University
Department of Economics
Littauer Center
Cambridge, Massachusetts 02138

Jerry Green
Department of Economics
Harvard University
Littauer Center
Cambridge, Massachusetts 02138

441

J. Michael Harrison
Graduate School of Business
Stanford University
Stanford, California 94305

Michael Hurd
Department of Economics
SUNY, Stony Brook
Stony Brook, New York 11794

Mervyn King
University of Birmingham
Department of Economics
P.O. Box 363
Birmingham, B15 2TT
England

Edward P. Lazear
Graduate School of Business
University of Chicago
1101 East 58th Street
Chicago, Illinois 60637

Jay Light
School of Business
Harvard University
Soldier's Field Road
Boston, Massachusetts 02136

Peter Menell
Department of Economics
Stanford University
Stanford, California 94305

Robert Merton
Sloan School of Management
Massachusetts Institute of
   Technology
Cambridge, Massachusetts 02139

Franco Modigliani
Department of Economics
Massachusetts Institute of
   Technology
Cambridge, Massachusetts 02139

Randall Mørck
National Bureau of Economic
   Research
1050 Massachusetts Avenue
Cambridge, Massachusetts 02138

Stewart C. Myers
Sloan School of Management
Massachusetts Institute of
   Technology
Cambridge, Massachusetts 02139

James E. Pesando
University of Toronto
Institute for Policy Analysis
150 St. George Street
Toronto, Ontario M5S 1A1
Canada

Paul Samuelson
Department of Economics
Massachusetts Institute of
   Technology
Cambridge, Massachusetts 02139

Myron S. Scholes
Graduate School of Business
1101 East 58th Street
University of Chicago
Chicago, Illinois 60637

William Sharpe
Graduate School of Business
Stanford University
Stanford, California 94305

John B. Shoven
Department of Economics
Fourth Floor, Encina Hall
Stanford University
Stanford, California 94305

Lawrence Summers
Harvard University
Department of Economics
Littauer Center
Cambridge, Massachusetts 02139

Irwin Tepper
386 Highland Street
Newton, Massachusetts 02160

David A. Wise
John F. Kennedy School of
    Government
Harvard University
79 Boylston Street
Cambridge, Massachusetts 02138

Richard Zeckhauser
John F. Kennedy School of
    Government
Harvard University
79 Boylston Street
Cambridge, Massachusetts 02138

Author Index

Subject Index

447